# Chinese Foreign Relations

# Chinese Foreign Relations

*Power and Policy of an
Emerging Global Force*

## Fifth Edition

Robert G. Sutter

ROWMAN & LITTLEFIELD
Lanham • Boulder • New York • London

Published by Rowman & Littlefield
An imprint of The Rowman & Littlefield Publishing Group, Inc.
4501 Forbes Boulevard, Suite 200, Lanham, Maryland 20706
https://rowman.com

6 Tinworth Street, London SE11 5AL, United Kingdom

British Library Cataloguing in Publication Information Available

**Library of Congress Cataloging-in-Publication Data**
Names: Sutter, Robert G., author.
Title: Chinese foreign relations : power and policy of an emerging global force / Robert G. Sutter.
Description: Fifth edition. | Lanham, Maryland : Rowman & Littlefield, 2021. | Series: Asia in world politics | Includes bibliographical references and index.
Identifiers: LCCN 2020030021 (print) | LCCN 2020030022 (ebook) | ISBN 9781538138281 (cloth) | ISBN 9781538138298 (paperback) | ISBN 9781538138304 (epub)
Subjects: LCSH: China—Foreign relations—1976- | China—Politics and government—1976-2002. | China—Politics and government—2002- | World politics—1989-
Classification: LCC DS779.27 .S873 2021 (print) | LCC DS779.27 (ebook) | DDC 327.51—dc23
LC record available at https://lccn.loc.gov/2020030021
LC ebook record available at https://lccn.loc.gov/2020030022

# Contents

# Preface to the Fifth Edition

This edition is substantially different from earlier editions of this volume. Those editions devoted considerable coverage to the pros and cons in an ongoing debate over whether China would continue the moderate approach to foreign affairs that prevailed in the first years of the twenty-first century. That debate has now ended with the ever stronger measures of assertive foreign policy carried out under the direction of Chinese Communist Party leader and state president Xi Jinping (2012–).

This edition thus removes much of the language in the previous editions dealing with the now past debate. It focuses more on the challenges to the international status quo posed by more assertive Chinese foreign policy behavior. In so doing, it differs from existing surveys of recent Chinese foreign relations in offering a comprehensive assessment of newly prominent unconventional Chinese levers of power and influence in foreign affairs that have heretofore been disguised, hidden, denied, or otherwise neglected or unappreciated by foreign specialists. A variety of in-depth government, think tank, and media reports throughout Western countries and those states located along China's rim have featured varied explanations and disclosures about these unconventional levers of power and influence. They provide the sources in support of the comprehensive treatment in this volume. The author judges that without careful treatment of the evidence in these disclosures, an assessment of Chinese foreign relations will be partial and flawed.

# Acknowledgments

The publication of this major revision of this book depended on the expert guidance and sustained support of Susan McEachern, vice president and senior acquisitions editor at Rowman & Littlefield Publishers, and the publisher's effective and efficient production staff.

As noted in the preface to this fifth edition, the author is greatly indebted to the many investigators and specialists in the United States, Europe, and the Asia-Pacific who in the past three years have revealed unconventional Chinese levers of power and influence in foreign affairs that were heretofore disguised, hidden, denied, or otherwise neglected or unappreciated by foreign specialists in assessing Chinese foreign relations. They have underscored with empirical data and specific case studies why this volume is markedly different from previous editions, which devoted considerable attention to ongoing debates on whether China's moderate approach to foreign affairs at the start of the twenty-first century would continue. That debate is now seen as ended as we are compelled to assess the multifaceted power and policy of the emerging global force of China.

# Abbreviations

| | |
|---|---|
| ACFTA | ASEAN-China Free Trade Agreement |
| ADIZ | air defense identification zone |
| AG | Australia Group |
| AIIB | Asian Infrastructure Investment Bank |
| AIT | American Institute in Taiwan |
| APEC | Asia-Pacific Economic Cooperation |
| ARATS | Association for Relations across the Taiwan Strait |
| ARF | ASEAN Regional Forum |
| ASEAN | Association of Southeast Asian Nations |
| ASEM | Asia-Europe Meetings |
| AU | African Union |
| BRI | Belt and Road Initiative |
| BRICS | Brazil, Russia, India, China, South Africa group |
| C4ISR | command, control, communications, computers, intelligence, and strategic reconnaissance |
| CACF | China-Africa Cooperation Forum |
| CASCF | China–Arab States Cooperation Forum |
| CBMs | confidence-building measures |
| CCP | Chinese Communist Party |
| CDM | Clean Development Mechanism |

| CIDCA | China International Development Cooperation Administration |
| CIS | Commonwealth of Independent States |
| CMG | China Media Group |
| CPEC | China-Pakistan Economic Corridor |
| CPTPP | Comprehensive and Progressive Agreement for Trans-Pacific Partnership |
| CWC | Chemical Weapons Convention |
| DPJ | Democratic Party of Japan |
| DPP | Democratic Progressive Party |
| EAEC | East Asian Economic Caucus |
| ECFA | Economic Cooperation Framework Agreement |
| EEU | Eurasian Economic Union |
| EU | European Union |
| FAC | Foreign Affairs Commission |
| FDI | foreign direct investment |
| FIE | foreign-invested enterprise |
| FOCAC | Forum on China-Africa Cooperation |
| FTA | free-trade agreement |
| FY | fiscal year |
| G7 | Group of Seven |
| G20 | Group of Twenty |
| GDP | gross domestic product |
| GEF | Global Environmental Facility |
| ICT | information and communications technology |
| IISS | International Institute for Strategic Studies |
| IMF | International Monetary Fund |
| INF | Intermediate-Range Nuclear Forces |
| IPR | intellectual property rights |
| ISAF | International Security Assistance Force |
| JCC | Joint Cooperation Committee |
| JCPOA | Joint Comprehensive Plan of Action |
| KMT | Kuomintang |

| | |
|---|---|
| LAC | Latin American–Caribbean |
| LDP | Liberal Democratic Party |
| LNG | liquefied natural gas |
| MAC | Mainland Affairs Council |
| MFN | most-favored-nation status |
| MOFA | Ministry of Foreign Affairs |
| MOFTEC | Ministry of Foreign Trade and Economic Cooperation |
| MTCR | Missile Technology Control Regime |
| NGO | nongovernmental organization |
| NMD | national missile defense |
| NPC | National People's Congress |
| NPT | Nonproliferation Treaty |
| NSC | new security concept |
| NSG | Nuclear Suppliers Group |
| OECD | Organisation for Economic Co-operation and Development |
| PA | Palestinian Authority |
| PLA | People's Liberation Army |
| PRC | People's Republic of China |
| RMA | revolution in military affairs |
| ROC | Republic of China |
| ROK | Republic of Korea |
| SARS | severe acute respiratory syndrome |
| SCO | Shanghai Cooperation Organization |
| SEF | Taiwan's Straits Exchange Foundation |
| SETC | State Economic and Trade Commission |
| SOE | state-owned enterprise |
| SOFA | Status of Forces Agreement |
| SRCA | Silk Road Cities Alliance |
| SSC | State Security Commission |
| TAC | Treaty of Amity and Cooperation |
| THAAD | Terminal High Altitude Area Defense |

| | |
|---|---|
| TMD | theater missile defense |
| TPP | Trans-Pacific Partnership |
| UNCLOS | United Nations Convention on the Law of the Sea |
| UNSC | United Nations Security Council |
| WHA | World Health Assembly |
| WHO | World Health Organization |
| WMD | weapons of mass destruction |
| WTO | World Trade Organization |

*Chapter One*

# Continuity and Change in Contemporary Chinese Foreign Policy

This introductory chapter defines the scope of the volume as well as the specific focus of each chapter. It briefly introduces the importance of the acute US rivalry now underway with China, it previews material in the volume assessing debates about China's strategy in foreign affairs, and it details changes in Chinese behavior over time, favoring an approach that views Chinese foreign policy and practice as contingent on often changing interests and circumstances. It summarizes recent discussion of why China has not superseded the United States as Asia's leader, and it does so by assessing newly disclosed unconventional Chinese levers of foreign influence as well as more conventional means.

The fifth edition of this book, which was published in a first edition in 2008, focuses on the course of Chinese foreign relations and the major changes brought about by China's rise in international prominence during the thirty years since the end of the Cold War. As reviewed in chapter 3, China's current importance as the world's second-largest and still strongly growing economy is evidenced in China's status as the top trader with more than 120 countries, the world's largest manufacturer, and the largest holder of foreign exchange reserves. China accounts for more than one-quarter of global economic growth. Chinese advances in a robust state-directed drive to achieve leadership in the high-technology industries of the future, including artificial intelligence (AI), 5G communications networks, the Internet of Things (IoT), nano- and biotechnology, electric vehicles, aviation, and space, are captured in the government-fostered "Made in China 2025" program and other comprehensive efforts seen as challenging and preparing to overtake the US lead in these key areas.

Beijing has been careful to avoid confronting America as it has ascended, but as discussed in chapters 4 and 6, the past decade has witnessed an ever more assertive and expansive Chinese foreign posture, directed by China's quest for wealth and power at the expense of the United States, which is seen in decline. Gone are the days of the first decade of the twenty-first century and earlier when China followed the dictums of senior leader Deng Xiaoping (d. 1997) to avoid the international spotlight and leadership. Strongman leader Xi Jinping, in power since 2012, has promoted a much more prominent role for China in world affairs and has backed it up with substantive programs and initiatives that benefit China at the expense of others, notably the United States and its leading allies and partners.

Against this backdrop came the most important change in US policy toward China in fifty years. The National Security Strategy of the Trump administration (released in late 2017) used harsh language unseen in executive branch discourse since the Nixon administration to emphasize that China posed a greater international danger to the United States than any other country. Senior administration leaders duly noted long-standing US differences with China over such issues as Taiwan, human rights, trade imbalances, and the respective Chinese and US arms buildups aimed at each other in Asia, but they also highlighted new issues reflecting heightened urgency, with some viewing China as an existential threat to the United States.[1] Most important was the judgment that China's headlong economic advance, employing widespread espionage, cyber theft, domestic protectionism, and international mercantilism, has now led China to seek dominance in the high-tech industries that are key to American economic and military power. This judgment held that if the United States did not sustain leadership in these industries, its economy and national defense would become second to and increasingly dominated by China.[2]

At first the administration's overall resolve against China was mixed; senior leaders remained seriously conflicted on economic issues during late 2017 and early 2018, and President Trump remained avowedly unpredictable and avoided using the language of his administration's stated strategy when referring to China.[3]

The 115th Congress rose to the challenge, showing extraordinary activism and bipartisan determination in crafting and approving legislation calling for a new "whole-of-government" American pushback against challenges seen posed by China. Congressional Republicans and Democrats joined senior administration officials in voicing urgent concern with American security and economic competitiveness in the face of an ever more powerful China, which if not countered would become dominant in high technology and national defense. The close collaboration between the administration and both Democrats and Republicans in Congress broke the mold of past practice, where Congress usually served as a brake and obstacle to executive initiatives dealing with China. Despite acute partisanship in Washington, opposing China now represented one of the few areas where both sides of the congressional aisle and the controversial administration agreed.[4] President Trump complemented this effort with a sequence of punitive tariffs against China beginning in mid-2018, with more to come. Vice President Mike Pence and other senior administration leaders weighed in with authoritative statements and policy directives focused on the acute rivalry between the United States and China.

These developments settled one of the points of debate about Chinese foreign policy highlighted in previous editions of this book. That debate centered on whether the accommodation, moderation, and reassurance of the United States seen in Chinese foreign relations since the Cold War, and especially prominent in the first decade of this century, was likely to continue. Indeed, the pattern of authoritarian initiatives to suppress dissent and strengthen domestic controls, along with the dramatic purges of government corruption, saw Xi Jinping stoking Chinese nationalistic ambitions with widely publicized and assertive foreign policy initiatives. Chinese international behavior challenged China's neighbors, the United States, and a variety of established international institutions and norms.[5] Prior to Xi's ascendance, some analysts in China and abroad foresaw a clear road ahead for China. They viewed Chinese leaders as following a moderate strategy that dealt pragmatically with world conditions and conformed to international norms in pursuing Chinese interests focused on development, which required international stability.[6] In contrast, others, including this writer, judged that China's approach to foreign affairs depended on many variables inside China and abroad that could change. Many of these variables were beyond the control of the Chinese leadership. China's leadership also demonstrated sometimes contradictory approaches in dealing with these issues. As a result, this author's assessment was that continued moderation in Chinese foreign relations would be contingent on circumstances that could change. Meanwhile, a number of foreign critics portrayed Chinese leaders as authoritarians determined to hold on to power by following an approach of hiding their intentions of dominance as China builds greater power through ongoing foreign interactions.[7] In the event, those forecasting continued moderation and pragmatic accommodation by China have been proven wrong. Debate continues between those forecasting Chinese foreign policy contingent on circumstances and those seeing a well-crafted Chinese strategy seeking regional dominance and world leadership.

## CONTINUITY AND CHANGE

Chinese officials and sympathetic publicity and propaganda outlets have worked hard over the years to stress continuity in Chinese foreign policy. In several respects, this strongly emphasized image of China as pursuing a consistent strategy is in line with arguments of foreign specialists that China is indeed is on the path of a strategic foreign policy plan. Of course, Chinese authorities consistently deny that China seeks regional and global dominance, whereas specialists abroad often perceive a consistent Chinese strategy toward such dominance and leadership. In contrast, this writer and some others who see China's foreign policy behavior as remaining contingent on circumstances, without a powerful strategy guiding China's rise, find the image of consistency stressed in the Chinese government's foreign policy discourse misleading. In particular, the practice of Chinese foreign relations has continued to be full of often abrupt changes that seem linked to changed circumstances.

China's image building in foreign affairs involves attentive efforts by the Chinese Foreign Ministry, as well as various other government, party, and military organizations that deal with foreign affairs; numerous ostensibly nongovernment organizations with close ties to the Chinese government, party, and military offices; and the massive publicity/propaganda apparatus of the Chinese government. The opinions of these officials, nongovernment representatives, and media outlets provide sources used by international journalists, scholars, and officials in assessing Chinese foreign relations. On the whole, they boost China's international stature while conditioning the people in China to think positively about Chinese foreign relations.

Points of emphasis in Chinese publicity on foreign affairs include the following:

- China's foreign policy is consistent.
- China follows consistent principles in dealing with foreign issues, which assures a moral position in Chinese foreign relations.
- The Chinese government deals effectively with international events and adopts policies and actions in accord with its principles and moral leadership.
- Abiding by principles and seeking moral positions provide the basis for effective Chinese strategies in world affairs.
- Such strategies ensure that China does not make mistakes in foreign affairs, an exceptional position reinforced by the fact that the People's Republic of China is seen to have avoided publicly acknowledging foreign policy mistakes or apologizing for its actions in world affairs. [8]

Many in China and some foreign journalists, officials, and others base their analyses of Chinese foreign relations on the information provided by the above-mentioned Chinese outlets. Their analyses show how China's image-building efforts, which enjoy support from the Chinese people and various constituencies in China, support a leading role for China in Asian and world affairs.

However, the actual behavior of China in dealing with foreign affairs—behavior that can be assessed both from the perspective of China as well as from the perspective of foreign governments and others concerned—shows repeated change driven by changing circumstances at home and abroad.

## Principles versus Interest-Based Foreign Policy

While China's foreign policy actions are usually said to be based on adherence to righteous and moral principles, there are notable weaknesses in China's long-avowed adherence to such principles. More than twenty years ago, Chinese foreign policy expert Samuel Kim labeled China's "peculiar" operational code of conduct "firmness in principle and flexibility in application." The result for Kim and other foreign observers is a gap between principle and practice, with China repeatedly attempting to show, through often convoluted discussion of a sometimes dizzying array of various and often newly created sets of principles governing Chinese foreign relations, that China is an exception to the interest-based policies and practices of great powers. Chinese discourse does not address the net effect of all the different sets of Chinese principles, which, as seen by Kim and others, allows China to be all things to all nations on all salient international issues and thereby provides little in the way of concrete guidance on how and why China behaves the way it does in a particular set of circumstances. [9]

The course of Chinese foreign relations is littered with examples where principles were reinterpreted or put aside in favor of other sets of principles as Chinese interests in a foreign relationship changed. India's Jawaharlal Nehru seemed truly surprised when his efforts to nurture a cooperative relationship with Chinese premier Zhou Enlai under the rubric of the Five Principles of Peaceful Coexistence during the mid-1950s appeared to count for little as China pursued border interests at odds with India's interests. [10] Noncommunist Southeast Asian leaders could be forgiven for their skepticism as they observed China's flawed observance of its principle of noninterference in other states' internal affairs at various times in their checkered relationships with China. For example, Deng Xiaoping reached out to improve relations with noncommunist Southeast Asian neighbors in the mid-1970s as China was constructing a broad front of nations to oppose Soviet-backed Vietnam's pending attack against the Chinese-backed Khmer Rouge government in Cambodia. Deng did so on the understanding that these governments would accept reconciliation with China while Beijing at the same time continued support for the tens of thousands of insurgents China had trained, supplied, and supported in their armed struggles against the very Southeast Asian leaders with whom Deng was seeking to improve relations.[11]

Albania's Enver Hoxa was more vocal than other more important communist leaders in Hanoi and Pyongyang, as well as less prominent communist leaders aligned with Beijing, whose interests were adversely impacted by China's surprise opening to the United States in the early 1970s despite longstanding Chinese commitments to the communist leaders in their struggle against American imperialism. Meanwhile, Pakistan, the only country with which China has been able to sustain a close relationship since the early 1960s, saw China's commitment to an "all-weather" relationship diminish for many years as China in the post–Cold War period backed away from previous support for Pakistan's position in the Kashmir dispute in order to open the way for improved Chinese relations with India. More recently, China has increased support for Pakistan, thus alienating India.[12]

## China's Exceptional Exceptionalism

It is common for states to redefine their foreign policies as their interests change in light of changing circumstances at home and abroad. And when states follow those changed interests and shift stated policies and commitments deemed principled and moral in new directions to the detriment of others, they rarely apologize, and they tend to only grudgingly acknowledge the negative consequences and mistakes.

Leaders of the United States are widely seen as prone to an arrogant sort of exceptionalism in foreign affairs. They are loath to apologize for policy changes or international actions that sometimes grossly harm others or are at odds with American principles. Nonetheless, the American political process, open media, active interest groups, and regularly scheduled elections allow for recognition of foreign policy failings and proposed remedies. In contrast, Chinese exceptionalism in foreign affairs is much more exceptional than that of the United States. One reason is the continuing need for the Chinese Communist Party (CCP)–led governing system to sustain its legitimacy, partly through an image of correct behavior in foreign affairs consistent with Chinese-supported principles.

## Explaining China's Interest-Based Behavior in Foreign Affairs: Change and Uncertainty

Whatever importance one gives to the wide array of principles and moral norms that are said by the Chinese government to govern Chinese foreign relations, the fact is that the private calculus of Chinese leaders in making key foreign and domestic policy decisions remains shrouded in secrecy. It is a crime subject to serious punishment to disclose such matters. Thus the explanation of Chinese foreign policy decisions provided in this volume joins other studies in basing its analysis mainly on patterns of Chinese behavior that can be observed and supported by evidence from Chinese and international sources.[13]

A defining feature of the foreign policy behavior of the People's Republic of China (PRC) is change. As noted above, it seems impossible to explain these changes realistically on the basis of the muddled array of principles used in Chinese foreign relations over the past sixty years. And the changes seem in this writer's view to belie a consistent Chinese foreign policy strategy. The discussion in this book finds greater accuracy in explaining Chinese decisions as heavily interest based. As seen below and as explained in later chapters, Chinese foreign policies have changed markedly and frequently, apparently driven by changing calculations of Chinese interests, which were in turn driven by changing circumstances at home and abroad. Perceiving the reasons for these course changes in Chinese policy is easier in retrospect. At the time, the changes often came as a surprise, adding to China's reputation as a power prone to unpredictable behavior, often resulting in coercion and violence.

Because of the secrecy that has continued to surround Chinese leaders' decision making, it is hard to know with precision why Chinese leaders shifted course in foreign policy at different times over the years. During Mao's rule (1949–1976), the interests seen driving Chinese foreign policy were often perceived as focused on fostering and promoting domestic and international revolution, though Mao also valued domestic development and made several policy initiatives, including the opening to the United States in the late 1960s, to buy time and gain leverage in order to protect China's national security. Deng Xiaoping's leadership (1977–1997) and that of subsequent leaders had a clearer focus on the top priority of sustaining Communist Party rule through effective economic development. Foreign policy was to serve this primary goal.

Nevertheless, the leaders wrestled periodically with conflicts of interests. Thus, for example, questions over how far to go in accommodating the United States in the interests of fostering a strong united front against Soviet expansion were superseded after the Cold War and the collapse of the Soviet Union in 1991. In their place came questions about how to balance Chinese goals to lead the international struggle against US superpower "hegemonism" and seek a multipolar world order versus a more pragmatic pursuit of peace and development beneficial to China and others it interacted with. As the issue of Taiwan's independence rose to prominence with the visit of Taiwan's president to the United States in 1995, Chinese leaders struggled to balance the imperatives to protect China's claim to Taiwan and prevent Taiwan independence with the need to sustain and deepen their advantageous economic and other ties with Taiwan's main protector, the United States. More recently, since 2009, advocates of a more assertive Chinese posture on sensitive territorial and other issues involving the United States and many of China's neighbors have seriously complicated China's ongoing effort to reassure those and other concerned governments that China's rise would be peaceful and not adverse to their interests.

Key periods with intervening changes in Chinese foreign relations can be broken down as follows.[14] Though the focus of this volume examines Chinese foreign policy since the end of the Cold War, earlier changes are noted to reflect the long-standing Chinese foreign practice of substantial and sometimes surprising change:

1949–1953: Amid domestic consolidation and isolation from most non-communist countries, China showed strong support for revolution at home and abroad in opposition to the United States. Against this background, miscalculations resulted in war with the United States in Korea, which both sides sought never to repeat.

1954–1957: Chinese-backed Viet Minh forces defeated French forces in Indochina. China echoed Soviet-backed peaceful coexistence and improved relations with India and other neighbors. China received substantial economic and military assistance from the Soviet Union and its East European partners.

1958–1965: Mass domestic mobilization in the ultimately disastrous Great Leap Forward was accompanied in 1958 by Chinese artillery attacks on islands held by Chiang Kai-shek's forces in the Taiwan Strait. The United States reacted with threats of nuclear war, and the Soviet Union chafed over China's provocative international behavior and irrational economic policies involving large amounts of Soviet assistance. Moscow ended aid in 1960, and Sino-Soviet polemics within the international communist movement led to intensified competition among newly independent developing countries and insurgents resisting colonial rule. Radical Chinese policies in support of various foreign groups and nations generally failed to make many lasting gains. Growing Chinese influence in Indonesia collapsed in 1965 with a bloody purge of communists and pogroms against ethnic Chinese, killing half a million.

1966–1968: Excesses during a violent radical phase of "Red Guard diplomacy" in the early years of the Cultural Revolution saw the collapse of government, including senior levels of the Foreign Ministry. China's relations with all but a handful of states suffered serious setbacks. Chinese mobs assaulted Soviet diplomats and set fire to the British mission, forcing foreign officers to flee the flames into the hands of a mob.

1969–1978: Soviet military pressure and the threat of nuclear attack forced China's opening to other states helpful in China's search for security. The United States, for its own reasons, was seeking reconciliation. Cooperation against Moscow would bind the United States and China together amid an intense leadership struggle in China that did not subside until the death of Mao and the arrest of the Gang of Four in 1976, and the ascendance of Deng Xiaoping to leading power in 1978.

1979–1989: China repeatedly maneuvered for advantage between the United States and the Soviet Union. Most of the time it found improvements with the Soviet Union less beneficial than the advantages of cooperative relations with the United States.

The developments in Chinese foreign relations since 1989 are the focus of this book. As noted below, they reflect four significant shifts in Chinese foreign behavior, but they also show elements of continuity. The latter include the following: After the end of the revolutionary and often highly disruptive leadership of Mao Zedong (d. 1976), the leaders of the CCP-led government have focused on promoting China's economic development while maintaining political and social stability in China. Their efforts have helped support one-party rule in China. Foreign policy serves these objectives by sustaining an international environment that supports economic growth and stability in China. The Soviet Union continued to pose a massive strategic challenge, but with the end of the Cold War and the USSR by 1991, China was free from the US or Soviet superpower threat that had dominated its foreign policy calculations since before the establishment of the People's Republic of China in 1949.

Thereafter, Chinese leaders for many years focused on supporting domestic growth and stability through active and often moderate Chinese diplomacy, designed to reassure neighboring countries and other concerned powers, notably the United States, which remained the dominant world power in Chinese foreign policy calculations. Chinese leaders tried to demonstrate that China's rising economic, military, and political power and influence should not be viewed as a threat but should be seen as an opportunity for greater world development. In the process, Chinese diplomacy gave greater emphasis to engagement with and conformity to the norms of regional and other multilateral organizations as a means to reassure those concerned about the possible negative implications of China's increasing power and influence. [15]

Chinese foreign policy placed acute emphasis on seeking international economic exchange beneficial to China's development. Foreign direct investment, foreign aid, foreign technology, and foreign expertise remained critically important in China's economic growth in the post-Mao period. China became the center of a variety of intra-Asian and other international manufacturing and trading networks. It rose to become the world's largest trading nation and the largest consumer of a variety of key world commodities and raw materials. Today China depends fundamentally on a healthy world economy in which Chinese entrepreneurs promote economic development as an essential foundation for continued rule of the CCP government. At the same time, the world economy depends increasingly on China. The Chinese government exerts ever greater influence in international economic matters as a key manufacturing center for world markets and an increasingly prominent trading nation with a positive balance of trade and large foreign exchange reserves used for increasing foreign investment.[16]

Chinese nationalism and Chinese security priorities are also important determinants in contemporary Chinese foreign policy. The CCP government has placed greater emphasis on promoting patriotism and nationalism among the Chinese people as communism has declined as a source of ideological unity and legitimacy. Nationalism supports the CCP's long-standing priority of preventing Taiwan's moves toward de jure independence and separation from China. The Xi Jinping government has also appealed to Chinese nationalism in advancing Chinese claims, using coercive means short of the direct application of military force, in disputed territories in the East and South China Seas. These territories are seen to have been taken from China by foreign powers when China was weak and vulnerable during the nineteenth and twentieth centuries; restoring them to Chinese rule is widely supported by Chinese elite and public opinion.[17]

Meanwhile, Chinese leaders are in the third decade of often double-digit annual percentage increases in defense spending. They have built advanced military power and voiced determination to take coercive measures if necessary to achieve nationalistic goals, especially regarding Taiwan and other disputed territories, even in the face of opposition by the power of the United States and its allies and associates.[18] More broadly, Chinese leaders seek to build what they call "comprehensive national power"—particularly economic, military, and political power—as China seeks an as yet not clearly defined leading role as a great power in Asian and world affairs.

Reinforcing nationalism and Chinese security priorities is the so-called victim mentality influencing Chinese popular and elite opinion. China's enduring concern with the United States (or in the past the Soviet Union) working with countries near China to establish a strong presence around China's periphery has been reinforced by a strong sense among Chinese elites and in public opinion that China has been the victim of foreign imperialism and dominance for much of the past two centuries and should work assiduously to prevent such dominance in the future. Chinese and foreign specialists acknowledge that citizens and leaders of the People's Republic of

China have long been conditioned through the education system, government-sponsored media coverage, and various other means to think of China as having been victimized by international powers beginning in the early nineteenth century. Emphasis on this historical conditioning was strengthened after the CCP crisis at the time of the Tiananmen demonstrations and the bloody crackdown in 1989 and continues up to the present. Sensing that communism no longer provided adequate ideological support for continued CCP rule, Chinese authorities instituted an education campaign and other measures that encouraged government-supporting patriotism by recalling the more than one hundred years of foreign affronts to Chinese national dignity. On the one hand, this victim mentality has been created and used by Chinese authorities to foster unity and support for the government in the face of foreign challenges. On the other hand, it has become so widespread and deeply rooted in Chinese elite and public opinion that it requires Chinese officials to deal with the United States and other powers, notably Japan, with an often prickly sense of nationalism that impedes collaboration, even in areas of mutual interest.[19]

Regarding major changes in China's approach to foreign affairs, as discussed in detail below, uncertainty and debate over the durability of China's comparatively moderate and accommodating foreign policy grew among foreign specialists and policy makers as the Xi Jinping government adopted more assertive foreign policies and behavior that challenged China's neighbors, the United States, and existing international norms and institutions. This marked the fourth substantial change in Chinese foreign behavior since the end of the Cold War.

The four stages in Chinese foreign policy and practice seen since 1989 and demonstrated in the various chapters of this volume can be summarized as follows:

> 1989–1996: China used generally pragmatic means to climb back to international importance following the imposition of Western isolation toward China after the Tiananmen crackdown in 1989, the decline of China's strategic importance to the West as a result of the end of the Cold War, and Taiwan's international prominence as a new democracy. China remained on the defensive, parrying US-led sanctions, restrictions, and often strident criticism. America loomed not so much as a strategic threat but as an ideological antagonist seeking in various nonmilitary ways to weaken and undermine China's one-party communist rule.

> 1996–2001: In the mid-1990s, China's strong actions involving the use of military force in defense of claims on Taiwan and territories in the South China Sea alarmed and alienated many neighboring countries. In response, Beijing adopted a new set of principles in its "new secur-

ity concept" (NSC), which recalled the Five Principles of Peaceful Coexistence in pledging a policy of reassurance to China's neighbors. Nevertheless, China's moderation was not directed toward the United States. China persisted with steady attacks against perceived US hegemonism and took careful aim against US alliances in the Asia-Pacific. The US bombing of the Chinese embassy in Belgrade prompted mass demonstrations that destroyed US diplomatic properties and a major debate on whether Chinese foreign policy should change its focus on stability and development in order to confront American hegemonism.

2001–2009: Faced with an initially tough American stance against China under the George W. Bush administration, Beijing played down its recent emphasis on confronting US hegemonism and broadened its reassurance efforts to now include the United States. Its objections to US alliances subsided; China did not want to be seen pressing its Asian neighbors to make a choice they didn't want to make between aligning with the United States and aligning with China. US-China relations remained smooth, despite major disagreements over the US invasion of Iraq and China's unfair trade practices, until the first year of the Obama administration.

2009–2020: Beginning in starts and stops in 2009 and becoming a more general trend under the rule of party leader and president Xi Jinping (2012–), there was an upsurge of Chinese opposition to US security and other policies in the Asia-Pacific, more assertive Chinese positions and commentary directed at China's neighbors, and for a time stepped-up Chinese support for North Korea during a period of leadership succession that featured egregious North Korean attacks on South Korea. The solidification of a closer relationship with Russia targeting US and allied weaknesses proceeded rapidly following Russia's invasion of Crimea and the imposition of Western sanctions. Chinese behavior and assertiveness raised serious concerns throughout its eastern and southern flanks. The behavior saw major advances in Chinese control over contested islands in the South China Sea, to which the usually restrained government of President Barack Obama eventually reacted with strong criticism and some concrete measures against Chinese behavior in this matter and in other sensitive trade and human rights issues in Sino-American relations. The Obama policies failed to halt China's advances at America's expense. Against this background came the harsh national strategies of the Trump administration and its actions targeting China as America's top international threat. Beijing reacted firmly but sought to avoid escalating tensions with the United States.

# HOW TO GAUGE CHINA'S FOREIGN ASCENDANCE AMID ACUTE RIVALRY WITH AMERICA

An underlying question addressed in this volume involves how to assess the implications of China's international rise since the end of the Cold War. An ongoing debate in the United States over China's rise has recently stressed the danger of Chinese dominance in high-technology industries deemed essential in determining leadership in international economic and national security. Unfortunately, this writer and apparently many others have been frustrated in seeking a clear view of whether China or the United States is winning in the newly prominent competition to lead in production of technology that will dominate international economic and national security. The field of high-technology industry and production has many ambiguous elements and is subject to constant change, making clear assessment very difficult even for specialists.[20]

Obviously US government policy makers are urged to mobilize intelligence and other sources to achieve as clear an understanding as possible of the "balance of power" between the United States and China in this as well as other more traditional areas such as defense and economic influence. Other concerned observers are urged to do the same within the limits of their access to relevant information. For readers of this book, a useful way to assess the implications of China's international rise discussed in the following chapters and summarized below is to assess which way the overall balance of power between the United States and China is evolving in Asia. Notably the conclusion of the book assesses and compares the strengths and weaknesses of rising China and the United States.

American strategists have long focused on the US-China balance of power in the region as the most important area of Sino-American competition.[21] Many still do so today.[22] The reasons include the following: China has long given top priority to nearby Asia in its foreign policy. The area is also a top priority in recent American foreign policy. If China is attaining leading international control, that development should show up first in nearby Asia. Without control of its surroundings, rising China's leadership elsewhere would remain vulnerable. Thus, measuring how well or poorly China's influence is spreading in the region at the expense of the United States, the long-standing leading power in the region, represents a useful way to gauge the realities of relative power between the two states, showing whether traditional US leadership in Asia is in jeopardy and China's rise to regional and global dominance is imminent.[23]

As discussed in detail in later chapters, Chinese leaders have made strenuous efforts to advance China's power and influence in Asia, which generally comes at the expense of US interests. Salient achievements include China's control of much of the South China Sea and China's strong influence in

Cambodia, Laos, and arguably Myanmar, thereby impeding the Association of Southeast Asian Nations (ASEAN) from taking positions or steps that China opposes. Beijing's Belt and Road Initiative (BRI) has consolidated Chinese influence in Central Asian countries and in important countries in South and East Asia. The Chinese relationship with Russia has moved well beyond its past status as an axis of convenience, becoming instead an axis of the world's leading authoritarian countries seeking largely compatible mutual interests.

Nevertheless, an assessment using conventional metrics of international influence, involving economic, military, political, and cultural elements making up China's overall regional importance, provides some confidence in this writer's judgment that Beijing will not soon become Asia's leader and that the United States remains in a leading position in the region in several important respects.

## Chinese Limitations

Six sets of factors limit and constrain China's rising influence in Asia. As explained in the following chapters and in the conclusion, taken together with China's strengths, these limits and constraints show that China's rise in Asia represents an important development that might presage a power shift in the region from US leadership to Chinese leadership, but such an outcome remains far from certain. The six factors are China's domestic preoccupations, China's strong economic interdependence, China's insecure position in Asia, gaps and shortcomings in China's international economic policies, US leadership in Asia, and Asian "hedging."

Chinese domestic preoccupations include weak leadership legitimacy; pervasive corruption; widespread social turmoil requiring internal security budgets greater than national defense budgets; an aging population; and an unsustainable economic model of overdependence on exports, high resource intensity, and massive environmental damage requiring multifaceted reforms, with no clear plan for implementation among competing interests in China. A salient implication for China's outreach in Asia and the world is that Beijing needs to keep financial and other related resources at home in case of negative domestic developments. China cannot afford a generous international posture. Rather, it follows fairly strictly a "win-win" formula, where China's win set focuses on economic advantage enhancing Chinese wealth and power. Thus, Chinese financial lending and investment in nearby Asia and elsewhere seeks to make a profit and get adequate payback for Chinese commitments of money and resources. The length of time and modes of payback can vary. If money or raw materials are not available, China commonly seeks control of equity or long-term leases of equity, including large tracts of land, ports, railroads, and other key facilities.

Regarding China's interdependence, China's foreign trade remains heavily dependent on foreign investment, which creates webs of production that are frequently controlled by foreign companies. China needs sophisticated components from abroad and depends heavily on export markets in Europe and the United States.

Chinese insecurities in Asia, the third factor, show up in reviewing China's progress in the prolonged effort to expand Chinese influence in Asia. China has been free from superpower containment since the end of the Cold War thirty years ago. Yet the progress it has made in spreading its influence in nearby Asia during these three decades has been mixed. Recent Chinese advances in Southeast Asia and Central Asia, noted earlier, are offset by serious shortcomings and setbacks. Relations with Japan remain very poor. Relations with North Korea were at their lowest point until extraordinary pressure from the Trump government brought about moderation and outreach from North Korea. The mix of Chinese demands for deference and bullying on the one hand and often grandiose promises of economic beneficence on the other has brought positive results, seen in China developing close economic ties with South Korea, Australia, and India. But overall relations with all three countries are worse today than they were in the previous decade, partly as a result of China's use of coercion against the interests of these key powers. For a time, Taiwan's voters seemed intimidated by China's massive military buildup opposite Taiwan, its concurrent clandestine penetration through covert operations to disrupt and influence Taiwan opinion, and Taiwan's extraordinary economic dependence on China. But, fearing dominance, voters reversed course in 2016, choosing a president much less deferential to Beijing. That president's chances of being reelected increased markedly in the lead-up to the January 2020 Taiwan election as voters in Taiwan watched closely the unpredicted mass demonstrations in Hong Kong against Beijing's influence there. The experience strongly reinforced Taiwan voters' determination to maintain vigilance and resolve in the face of escalating pressure from China. Capping this list, the biggest setback in China's advancing influence and control in Asia came in arousing US opposition.

Gaps and shortcomings in China's international economic policies, the fourth factor, are seen in the highly publicized Belt and Road Initiative, which as will be shown in the following chapters has progressed erratically, with both strengths and weaknesses. China's investment and infrastructure development remain far from dominant among the most important developing countries in Asia, as well as most areas of the developing world. China's trade growth—a big draw for foreign relations in the past—stopped in 2015 and 2016, with only modest gains since then. The list of lagging or scrapped major BRI projects, announced earlier with great fanfare, substantially offset China's advances under the plan.

The two final factors, US leadership in Asia and Asian "hedging," are interrelated. Asian governments distrust each other and yet need regional stability for economic growth, their top policy priority, so they long relied on the United States to undertake the costs (estimated at more than $100–150 billion a year) and risks (the lives of US military personnel) of maintaining regional stability. They recognized that no other power was prepared to undertake such costs and risks. The Trump National Security Strategy and various national defense strategies reassured Asian governments on this score. In the main, Asian governments welcome this US commitment. China does not, and it has attempted in various ways to undermine the US military presence in the region.

Facing rising Chinese influence and expanding demands, other Asian governments tend to hedge, seeking to get along with both rising China and the United States and so avoid costly tension and conflict. In this context, US security forces are seen as supporting the status quo. They provide a useful counterweight to check China's ambitions at the expense of its neighbors.

To achieve development, the Asian governments also rely on their export-oriented economies. They recognize that the United States has provided investment, advanced technology, and, most important, an open market for the vast array of manufactured goods exported by the various production chains in Asia. Much of the output of these chains reaches a final stage in China and is exported from there to the United States. Thus, many Asian countries have important stakes in these Chinese exports. This process features a seemingly massive cost for the United States in a trade deficit of around $500 billion a year. President Trump's trade policies put this situation in jeopardy. A protracted closing of US markets would almost certainly seriously upset Asian leaders and possibly undermine Asian support for US leadership in the region. The crisis for Asian leaders would be compounded, as there is no readily available substitute for the US market. China's managed trade routinely runs an overall trade surplus, and other trading partners in Asia and elsewhere are unwilling or unable to bear even a fraction of the cost of such large trade deficits.

## A NEW ELEMENT: CHINA'S UNCONVENTIONAL LEVERS OF POWER AND INFLUENCE

In assessing the course and implications of China's rise in Asia and the world, this edition goes beyond the past practice of examining evidence of conventional Chinese behavior and levers of power and influence in foreign affairs to assess newly prominent unconventional aspects of Chinese influence abroad that heretofore have been disguised, hidden, denied, or otherwise neglected or unappreciated by specialists assessing Chinese foreign relations. This change has been required because the sharp downturn in the American relationship with China in the past three years has been accompanied by an outpouring of evidence of unconventional Chinese practices designed to increase China's power and influence in foreign affairs. As seen in the chapters that follow, the evidence comes from investigations carried out by the US government and the governments of US allies and partners; by progressive, moderate, and conservative think tanks in the United States and in allied and partner countries; and by investigative journalists and scholars from those states.

For an evidence-based analyst like this writer, the wave of new information calls into question the efficacy of assessments based on the conventional determinants used in his and others' past analysis of the limitations of China's rise in Asia. Thus, in contrast with the previous practice of this writer and many others in this field of study, the revised edition of this volume devotes significant attention to assessing the overall importance of this new information.

As discussed in the chapters of this book and evaluated in the conclusion, heading the list of China's unconventional sources of power that are now receiving growing attention by American and other foreign policy makers and specialists is Beijing's mendacity and hypocrisy as it espouses economic globalization while it doubles down in a three-decade-long effort using state-directed development policies to plunder foreign intellectual property rights and undermine international competitors. Beijing does so with hidden and overt economic coercion, egregious state subsidies, and import protection and export promotion using subsidized products to drive out foreign competition in key industries. The massive profits flow into efforts to achieve dominance in major world industries and build military power to secure China's dominance in Asia and world leadership. They allow companies like Huawei to attempt to dominate international communications enterprises, and they support massive state-directed Chinese efforts to lead the high-technology industries that will define economic and eventually military leadership in world affairs. In this calculus, China may remain "hemmed in" by the United States and its allies and partners in major parts of nearby Asia, but it may outflank American power with a breakthrough providing high-technology control.

Shown here are specific examples of unconventional Chinese measures to pressure nearby Asia to follow China's preferences and undermine the interests of the United States and its allies and partners.[24] The following chapters discuss these and similar instances throughout the world, and the appendix at the end of chapter 13 provides a final overview of these practices.

1. Corrupt practices in development projects associated with the Belt and Road Initiative, and earlier involving the military regime in Myanmar, the Gloria Arroyo government in the Philippines, the Najib Razak government in

Malaysia, and arguably today in the Philippines, Laos, and Cambodia, along with several Pacific Island states.

2. Chinese leaders employed corrupt practices, special economic benefits, and other benefits for the Hun Sen regime of Cambodia, notably during Hu Jintao's extraordinary stay in the country in 2012. They won over the Hun Sen government with special deals beneficial to the ruling elite but less so to the broader society in return for Cambodia playing the role of the main obstacle to efforts by the Philippines and Vietnam in ASEAN to challenge Chinese expansionism at their expense in the South China Sea; it later became clear that China was using its leverage with Hun Sen to develop ports and airfields useful for eventual Chinese military operations in the country.

3. Cambodia joined Laos and Myanmar—also strongly influenced by Chinese largesse provided in nontransparent development projects and other means—to shape ASEAN deliberations in ways that avoided friction with China and increasingly emphasized the positives and ignored the negatives of expanding Chinese influence and control in the region and China's creation, occupation, and militarization of islands in territories claimed by Southeast Asian states in the South China Sea.

4. Chinese influence operations involved special benefits for leading officials and others in Australia, New Zealand, and several Pacific Island states, as well as penetration and control of the Chinese diaspora (including student groups), the chambers of commerce, and the media in these countries, along with the media in Singapore and several other countries in the region.

5. The BRI worked in tandem with Huawei's subsidized efforts to expand control of regional communications, which the US government and others viewed as enabling Chinese penetration and manipulation of regional communications and as providing Chinese companies with advantages in the race for leadership in high-technology industries. The installation of such expensive, hard to maintain, and hard to replace systems provided an important source of lasting Chinese influence in recipient countries.

6. Beijing's hidden hard sticks along with the carrots of the BRI were on display in its recent unpublicized coercion of Vietnam, the Philippines, and Malaysia—the Southeast Asian states with holdings and claims in the disputed South China Sea. These included chilling private warnings to the first two that contesting Chinese claims would lead to defeat in war, and harassment of ongoing oil and gas exploitation efforts of Vietnam and Malaysia, notably employing a massive 12,000-ton coast guard warship to harass and intimidate the much smaller vessels used by Vietnam and Malaysia to supply oil and gas ventures and the foreign firms involved in these ventures. Beijing's goal in the latter effort is to halt and expel foreign ventures from the contested South China Sea, making China the only acceptable partner for the other claimants in pursuing development of oil and gas resources.

7. Along these lines, Beijing has positioned itself as key to Myanmar's resolving satisfactorily the long-standing differences it has with the impressive armed forces of the Wa state and other nearby independent forces along the Chinese border that have decades of close collaboration with the Chinese security forces. A more recent source of regional leverage comes from China's ever closer cooperation with Russia, which has a common aim of weakening the American security position and those of its allies along Asia's rim. A vivid demonstration of China-Russia collaboration over Japan and Korea came with a gross intrusion of Russian warplanes into South Korean and Japanese airspace in 2019, which was backed by accompanying Chinese military aircraft. Vladimir Putin's Russia shows strong support for China in the disputed South China Sea through joint exercises in the sea and through criticism of the ruling against China's claim by a UN Law of the Sea (UNCLOS) tribunal in 2016.

While Beijing denies or obscures the above practices, it advocates vague values of "win-win" and "the community of shared future." Despite China's obfuscation, the above practices overall underline a determination of a formidable authoritarian power to remove serious obstacles in its headlong pursuit of interests at the expense of others. The perceived obstacles involve the interests of the United States and its allies and many partners. Those interests include (1) the rule of law; (2) the rights of small nations in contested issues with large nations, including the right to join with other powers in protecting themselves and their interests in the face of dominance; (3) transparent, free, and fair economic dealings in line with governance accountable to the populations concerned; (4) human rights, democracy, and political rights and freedoms, including the rights to dissent and popular empowerment leading to governments accountable to the people; and (5) religious freedom and nondiscrimination against minorities.

There is no easy answer for the United States and the many other concerned powers in countering these kinds of often disguised or hidden applications of unconventional Chinese power. It remains unclear how seriously they impact US and other countries' interests, but the concluding chapter of this book offers a judgment based on the impressive Chinese gains as well as losses coming from these efforts. It is clear that these practices have become more important with China's rise and that they need careful examination in any assessment of the US rivalry with China in Asia and elsewhere in the world. America and its partners can neither rely on avowed Chinese assurance about China's "peaceful" rise nor take comfort that continued US support for state sovereignty, accountable governance, and free and transparent trade and investment places the United States on the side of "the good guys" in world politics, nor that such practices along with free and fair economic competition assure continued primacy of the United States. Unfortunately, the record of Chinese practices shows that Beijing is unbridled in its pursuit of key ambitions, and in Asia as elsewhere in much of the world, there are many self-serving, authoritarian, and corruptible leaders inclined to side more with an enabling China.

In sum, the above conundrum and the analysis that goes with it will preoccupy this writer and other specialists for many years to come. One clear impact of the problem is that it weighs heavily in support of those in the United States, in other Western-aligned countries, and in many of China's neighbors who argue against significant improvement in their relations with China without considering thoroughly the negative implications for them that stem from closer exposure to the guile and mendacity of China's unconventional statecraft. On balance, prevailing trends argue in particular for more acute competition and tension in China-US relations, with serious implications impacting major world areas.

## THE PURPOSE AND SCOPE OF THIS BOOK

This book explains thoroughly the determinants of and significant developments in Chinese foreign relations since the Cold War. Chapter 2 assesses the foreign policy priorities of Chinese leaders and the importance of these priorities relative to Chinese leaders' domestic priorities. It also examines how the changing patterns of Chinese decision making and worldviews are in turn changing Chinese foreign policy and behavior. Chapter 3 assesses the importance of Chinese economic development and economic globalization on Chinese foreign relations. Chapter 4 looks at China's growing role and ambitions concerning international governance, including increasing Chinese involvement in regional and global organizations that deal with world affairs. Chapter 5 is an examination of Chinese national security concerns and their effect on Chinese foreign relations, China's role in international nonproliferation and arms control regimes, and the role of the Chinese military in China's foreign relations. The next seven chapters assess China's relations with key powers and world areas. The last chapter offers conclusions about the likelihood of a power shift in Asia based on conventional metrics of power, along with a balanced assessment of the impact of the many unconventional levers of influence increasingly employed in China's foreign policy.

*Chapter Two*

# Leadership Priorities, Decision Making, and Worldviews

Chinese Communist Party general secretary and president Xi Jinping, in power since 2012, became the most important Chinese foreign policy leader since Mao Zedong. Under his leadership, he consolidated control over CCP central organs related to foreign affairs. His approach to foreign policy, "Xi Jinping Thought on Foreign Affairs," represented the reference point of Chinese foreign policy professionals. Xi began his first term in office (2012–2017) with major emphasis on a more assertive foreign policy in pursuit of the China Dream of National Rejuvenation. His speeches made clear Beijing's intention to rise to leadership in Asia without much reference to how the interests of China's neighbors and other concerned countries would be impacted by China's ambitions.[1]

Reflecting China's greater prominence in world politics under his leadership, Xi began his second term in office in 2017 by putting aside the foreign policy instructions of Deng Xiaoping that had guided China's more cautious and reactive foreign policy making since the end of the Cold War. Deng had instructed that Chinese leaders should focus on developing China's economy and domestic strength, while in foreign affairs China should hide China's strength, take a low-key posture to minimize external attention, bide its time, and never take the lead. Xi espoused a much more proactive "big power diplomacy with Chinese characteristics," a subset of "Xi Jinping Thought on Socialism with Chinese Characteristics for a New Era," which was added to China's national constitution in 2018 along with a provision allowing Xi to stay in power beyond the normal limit of two five-year terms.

The consequences of these changes in foreign policy priorities, decision making, and practice included such manifestations of assertiveness as China's massive island building and related militarization in the disputed South

China Sea and the enormous Belt and Road Initiative (BRI) with a global scope and a purported value of more than $1 trillion of Chinese financing. They also included China's enhanced efforts to gain leadership positions and greater influence in the United Nations and other international organizations it favors. As discussed in the following chapters, apart from more conventional tools of statecraft, Beijing also stepped up efforts on a global scale to manipulate and control the policies and practices of foreign governments and organizations through overt and covert use of China's economic power; "elite capture" in foreign countries involving outright corruption and contractual benefits; overt and covert media influence; control of various countries' communications and security surveillance systems; mobilization of the Chinese diaspora, students, and business interests abroad; and widespread espionage for economic and foreign policy benefit.

To place the above recent shifts in Chinese foreign relations in context, this chapter reviews how and why the Chinese leadership's foreign policy priorities have changed in the past thirty years since the end of the Cold War. It also assesses the related development of Chinese leaders' foreign policy decision making and their world outlook.

## THE EVOLUTION OF CHINESE PRIORITIES AFTER THE COLD WAR

As noted above and discussed in the following chapters, Chinese foreign policy went through two stages of overall development in the post–Cold War decade of the 1990s. In 1989–1996, China used generally pragmatic means to climb back to international importance. It was defensive and sensitive to US-led sanctions and challenges involving Taiwan and sovereignty claims in the South China Sea. In the mid-1990s, China's strong use of military force in defense of claims to Taiwan and territories in the South China Sea alarmed and alienated many neighbors. In response, Beijing endeavored to reassure neighbors that China was not a threat. Nevertheless, China's moderation was not directed to the United States. The US bombing of the Chinese embassy in Belgrade in 1999 prompted mass demonstrations that destroyed US diplomatic properties and a major debate on whether Chinese foreign policy should change its focus on stability and development in order to confront American "hegemonism."

The end of the Cold War saw the collapse of Soviet military power, which markedly improved China's overall security situation. For the first time, the People's Republic of China (PRC) was not facing an immediate foreign threat to its national security. However, the sharp international reaction to China's harsh crackdown on dissent after the June 1989 Tiananmen incident caught Chinese leaders by surprise. They reportedly had expected developed nations to restore stable relations after a few months. They had not counted on the rapid collapse of communism in Eastern Europe, the subsequent march toward self-determination throughout the Soviet republics, and ultimately the end of the Soviet Union in 1991. China's strategic importance as a counterweight to the Soviet Union ended as Beijing faced the most serious challenge to the legitimacy of the Chinese communist government since the Cultural Revolution (1966–1976). Moreover, Taiwan's concurrent moves toward greater democracy and self-determination received growing positive attention in the United States and the West. [2]

Despite US-led sanctions, high-level Chinese visits to Asian capitals and elsewhere in the developing world strengthened China's stature at home and abroad. Chinese leaders also gave high priority to the military and public security forces. Thus began a long series of double-digit annual percentage increases in China's defense budget that persisted for more than two decades, making China Asia's leading military power and a challenger to the United States. [3] With the decline in communist ideology, Beijing played up themes of patriotism and Chinese nationalism to support its one-party rule. US and other criticisms of the authoritarian system in China were portrayed not as attacks against unjust arbitrary rule but as assaults on China's national integrity, recalling "imperialist" pressures on China in the nineteenth and twentieth centuries. [4]

Deng Xiaoping called for faster growth and increased economic reform and interchange with the developed economies of Asia and the West during a tour of southern China in 1992. A subsequent economic boom saw several years of double-digit growth, which then declined a bit to the still rapid pace of 7–8 percent annual growth. Foreign business and government leaders' interest in the China market grew markedly, leading to the end of most Western sanctions against China. [5]

Following Deng Xiaoping's guidelines, the new third generation of leaders headed by president and party leader Jiang Zemin continued the post-Mao policies, emphasizing fostering a better economic life for the people of China in order to justify their continued monopoly of political power. They depended heavily on foreign trade and related foreign investment and assistance for China's economic development. They emphasized the maintenance of a peaceful international environment, especially in nearby Asia, which would facilitate trade, investment, and assistance flows so important to Chinese economic well-being. [6]

The leaders broadened international contacts by increasing efforts to meet the requirements of the United States and others regarding market access, intellectual property rights, and other economic issues in order to become a member of the World Trade Organization (WTO). China's record in meeting these commitments proved mixed, as Beijing maneuvered to gain the advantages of engagement without incurring costs for Chinese state-directed and other practices that the leadership wished to preserve. China was the largest recipient of assistance from the leading international financial institutions, and it accepted concurrent commitments and responsibilities coming from the World Bank, the International Monetary Fund (IMF), and the Asian Development Bank.[7]

Chinese leaders remained sensitive on matters of national sovereignty and international security issues close to home. But they adjusted to world pressure when resistance appeared detrimental to broader Chinese concerns. Examples of this adjustment included Chinese cooperation with the international peace settlement in Cambodia in 1991, willingness to join the 1968 Treaty on the Nonproliferation of Nuclear Weapons and to halt nuclear tests by the end of 1996 under an international agreement, willingness to abide by the terms of the Missile Technology Control Regime, and efforts in 1994 to help the United States reach an agreement with North Korea over the latter's nuclear weapons development program. Beijing also endeavored to meet international expectations on policing drug traffic, curbing terrorism, and some environmental issues.[8]

China took a hard line against outside criticism of its political authoritarianism and poor human rights record. It continued to transfer sensitive military technology or dual-use equipment to Pakistan, Iran, North Korea, and other potential flash points despite criticism from Western countries. And it used rhetorical threats or demonstrations of military force to intimidate those challenging China's sovereignty claims or control over Taiwan, the South China Sea, and Hong Kong.[9]

As a general rule, Chinese leaders tended to approach foreign policy issues pragmatically on a case-by-case basis, calculating the costs and benefits of adherence to international norms or other requirements.[10] But the Chinese calculus was also influenced by rising nationalism among Chinese leaders and the Chinese people more broadly. Viewing the world as a highly competitive, state-centered system, Chinese leaders were generally slow to embrace multilateralism and interdependence, with the notable exception of economic matters promoting China's development. They were inclined to see the world in fairly traditional balance-of-power terms. In the decade after the Cold War, they stressed that the world was becoming more multipolar (that is, a number of competing large nation-states), though in the face of undiminished US dominance and the seeming willingness of the incoming George W. Bush administration to counter Chinese challenges, they came to play down multipolarity, seeking to reassure America.[11]

Chinese suspicions of the prevailing Asian and international order centered on the dominant role played by the United States and its allies and associates. As China's economic and military power grew, official Chinese commentary saw the United States and its allies as unwilling to share power with China and seeking to keep it weak for as long as possible.[12] Chinese leaders recognized that the United States exerted predominant influence in East Asia and the western Pacific, in international financial and political institutions such as the World Bank and the United Nations that were particularly important to Beijing, and regarding issues acutely sensitive to China involving Taiwan and human rights. [13]

Chinese leaders maneuvered carefully and sometimes forcefully to defend and protect key interests challenged by America while accommodating US concerns in other areas. A military face-off with two US aircraft carrier battle groups in the Taiwan area in 1996 and the trashing of US diplomatic properties in China by Chinese demonstrators after the US bombing of the Chinese embassy in Belgrade in 1999 illustrated how far Chinese leaders were prepared to go in fending off perceived American pressure. [14]

Party leader and president Jiang Zemin exerted increasing influence in Chinese policy making during the 1990s. Jiang outmaneuvered sometimes formidable leadership competition, notably from former president Yang Shangkun. He initiated a more flexible position on Taiwan in early 1995 and subsequently led Beijing's harsh response to Taiwan president Lee Teng-hui's unexpected visit to Cornell University later that year. [15]

Deng Xiaoping's death in 1997 saw Jiang assume the actual position of China's paramount leader. His overall standing, of course, was much weaker than that of Deng, whose prestige and leadership credentials traced back more than sixty years. But Jiang was especially active in foreign affairs, leading Chinese efforts to sustain an effective approach toward the United States, adjusting the mix of incentives and sanctions in Chinese policy toward Taiwan, and creating a more coherent and active Chinese policy toward its periphery in Asia. [16] In 1997, Jiang smoothly accomplished the transition of Hong Kong to Chinese rule, the reconfiguration of Chinese leadership and policy at the Fifteenth CCP Congress, and a Sino-US summit—the first since the Tiananmen crackdown. [17]

Jiang and his associates subsequently carried out ambitious multiyear efforts to transform tens of thousands of China's money-losing state-owned enterprises (SOEs) into more efficient businesses. Beijing's major programs to promote economic and administrative efficiency succeeded in protecting China from negative fallout from the 1997–1998 Asian economic crisis and in promoting changes in China's financial systems to protect against vulnerabilities seen elsewhere in Asia. There were few signs of disagreement among senior leaders over the broad policy emphasis on economic reform, though sectors affected by reform often resisted strenuously. China anticipated joining the WTO in 2001 or 2002, which strengthened the need for greater economic efficiency and reform. [18]

The reforms also exacerbated social and economic uncertainties, which reinforced the government's determination to maintain a firm grip on political power and levers of social control. [19] By late 1998, instability caused by economic change and growing political dissent prompted significant suppression of political dissidents by the PRC leadership—a trend that has continued with little interruption up to the present.[20]

Against this background, foreign affairs generally remained an area of less urgent policy priority. Improved relations with the United States and an upswing in China's relations throughout its periphery supported China's intent to minimize disruptions and to assist domestic endeavors at reform. The government remained wary of challenges posed by Taiwan, efforts of Japan and the United States to increase their influence at China's expense, and India's nuclear weapons development. Chinese officials voiced concern over the downturn in US-China relations at the outset of the George W. Bush administration but appeared determined to cooperate with the US-led antiterrorism campaign begun in September 2001.[21]

## TWENTY-FIRST CENTURY FOREIGN POLICY PRIORITIES

The first two decades of this century were marked by two distinct phases in Chinese foreign relations. Faced with many problems and comparatively weak leadership at home and an initially tough American stance against China under the George W. Bush administration, Beijing played down rhetorical emphasis in the 1990s on confronting US hegemonism. It broadened reassurance efforts toward China's neighbors to now include the United States. Chinese and US leaders came to see the wisdom of pragmatic engagement that promoted common ground while dealing with differences through dialogues. This positive trajectory allowed China to advance its power at home and influence abroad in a period of "strategic opportunity," where Deng Xiaoping's instructions for a low profile and nonconfrontational foreign policy seemed appropriate.[22]

Beginning erratically in 2009 and becoming a more general trend under the rule of party leader and president Xi Jinping (2012–), an upsurge of assertive Chinese opposition to and positive initiatives in competition with the policies and interests of the United States and its allies and partners became the central direction of Chinese foreign relations. Beijing now put aside Deng's instructions, seeking ever more power, influence, and leadership in Asia and the world, with an eye toward taking advantage of American and allied weaknesses and undermining the many US interests at odds with those of rising China.[23]

### Political Leaders and Institutions

China's third-generation leadership was under Jiang Zemin, with Mao's being the first generation and Deng's the second. This third generation was followed by the fourth generation, led by president and party leader Hu

Jintao (2002–2012), and the fifth generation, led by Xi Jinping (2012–present). The level of political skills of the fourth generation showed as Hu Jintao and his colleagues handled more or less effectively a number of difficult domestic and foreign policy concerns ranging from sustaining economic growth during the global recession of 2008–2010 to repeated crises caused by North Korea's nuclear weapons development and other provocations.[24] The transfer of power to fifth-generation leaders beginning in 2012 was disrupted by the removal from power in March 2012 of Politburo member Bo Xilai amid a major scandal involving Bo's wife and the murder of a British businessman long associated with Bo and his family, the arrest of Bo's lieutenant after he sought refuge in the US consulate in Chengdu, and Bo's reported ambition to seek a position on the Politburo Standing Committee at the Eighteenth CCP Congress in late 2012.[25]

Against this background of leadership division and instability, Xi Jinping began his rule with an unprecedented anticorruption campaign that continued up to the present, removing and punishing many thousands of officials convicted of sometimes gross corruption and including those in the top ranks of the leadership seen likely to challenge his rule. He followed with a broadranging effort to reestablish Chinese Communist Party control, under his leadership, throughout the government, army, and other administrative bodies. These practices came along with an intense propaganda emphasis on Xi and his paramount leadership, bordering on the personality cult seen under Mao. Overall, Chinese decision making in foreign policy and domestic affairs shifted sharply from the collective leadership pattern seen in the third and fourth generations in the post–Deng Xiaoping period to a level of dominance by one leader not seen since Mao Zedong ruled China.[26]

Composed of technocrats, economists, managers, and other professionals, the fourth-generation leaders were seen as pragmatic, avoiding dramatic changes in existing policies promoting economic development, though the leaders also gave more attention to the disadvantaged and others left behind as a result of sweeping economic changes. They remained strict in enforcing laws and regulations against those who would seek to challenge one-party rule in China.[27]

The institutionalization of China's politics was the result of a proliferation of institutions from the top down. Chinese Communist Party and National People's Congress (NPC) sessions and plenums were regularly scheduled and held, and planning and budgetary cycles were adhered to. The principles of class struggle were replaced by budgets geared to a socialist market economy and political constituencies. Socialist laws continued to be promulgated, although enforcement remained problematic.[28] The authorities endeavored to bring emerging economic and social elites into the Communist Party. Jiang Zemin successfully changed party practices to advance the recruitment of such wealthy and influential people into the party's ranks.[29]

As a political force, the Chinese military demonstrated less influence than during the Mao and Deng periods. The military had less representation than in the past in the high-level CCP Politburo. The leadership, now an urban, educated elite, was civilian based. In the past two decades, only two or three of the twenty-plus members of the Communist Party Central Committee Politburo represented the military; none of the nine- or seven-member elite Standing Committee of the Politburo represented the military. Of course, China's remarkable military buildup showed strong leadership support behind military modernization.[30]

In a significant departure from the collective leadership under Jiang Zemin and Hu Jintao, Xi Jinping dominated decision making across the board and also broke the recent pattern of regularized leadership succession, setting the stage for prolonged personal rule. Personal rivalries of senior leaders remained hidden. In maneuvering to succeed Hu Jintao, two candidates, Xi Jinping and Li Keqiang, each backed by different leadership groups, emerged at the Seventeenth CCP Congress in 2007. Xi and Li were designated China's first- and second-ranking leaders at the Eighteenth Congress in 2012, but Xi since created a large gap of power and prestige between himself and Li as well as other members of the top leadership. Whether Xi's ambitions went beyond his ability to control remained an open question, but the realities of power suggested continued authoritarian rule under his direction for the foreseeable future.[31]

## Economic and Social Trends

At the start of the twenty-first century, economic growth sustained the overall rise in the standard of living that characterized Chinese development over the previous two decades. A relatively young, well-trained labor force with modern technical skills increased in number. The rapidly improving infrastructure of rail, roads, and electronic communications greatly reduced perceived distance and helped link the poorly developed interior to the booming coastal regions.

Chinese development remained heavily dependent on foreign trade, investment, and scientific/technical exchange. The government faced daunting problems—notably ailing SOEs and a flawed banking/financial system. The massive and often wasteful use of energy and other resources and a widespread shortage of uncontaminated water headed the list of major environmental problems that appeared hard to resolve without large production cutbacks or expensive technology. China's foreign-invested manufacturing and infrastructure development seemed at odds with the important goal since the Hu Jintao period of shifting China from dependence on foreign trade to an economy driven by domestic consumption. Chinese household consumption remained low. Government support for social services improved from a low base, but Chinese families continued to rely on personal savings to cover education, health care, and retirement expenses that in other countries were met with government funds. The interest payments on massive domestic savings were held artificially low, providing plenty of funding from banks to SOEs but disadvantaging savers. Thus, people had less money to devote to consumer spending.[32]

The global economic crisis and recession of 2008–2010 saw sharp cutbacks in Western consumption of Chinese and other imports. In 2009 the overall Chinese economy turned sharply downward. Unemployment rose dramatically. The leadership took concrete steps to promote large-scale infrastructure and other domestic development and spending. In 2010 the Chinese economy resumed double-digit growth but faced new uncertainties with continued stagnation in major export markets in Europe and Japan and weak growth in the United States.[33] Stricter requirements for energy efficiency registered substantial progress, though air and water pollution remained major problems.[34]

A long list of proposed economic reforms, many with a market orientation welcomed by China's private sector and free-market economies abroad, were announced under Xi Jinping's leadership in 2013 but were weakly implemented. The current government gave priority to deepening CCP control of levers of power in the economy, promoting international economic outreach under the ambitious Belt and Road Initiative backed by government banks and large companies aligned with the Chinese party-state leadership, and impressive efforts involving research and development in advanced technologies, giving China the edge in leading and controlling these critically important manufacturing sectors going forward. A maturing and more expensive Chinese labor force, the demands of its growing aging population, the saturation of China with modern infrastructure projects reaching the point of diminishing returns, and the major impact of trade and economic disputes with the United States explained the decline in Chinese growth rates. Trade levels were flat in 2015 and 2016, and more recent rates of increase were modest; domestic consumer consumption was hampered by the heavy savings prompted by concerns over education, health care, and retirement expenses.[35]

Leadership differences reflecting diverging policy preferences and bureaucratic and institutional interests influenced the Chinese policy process. One result of China's external outreach was the growing importance of ministries with responsibility in foreign affairs, such as the Ministry of Foreign Affairs (MOFA) and the Ministry of Foreign Trade and Economic Cooperation (MOFTEC). The latter, especially, became more important as Beijing joined the WTO. In 2003, MOFTEC changed its name and became China's Commerce Ministry. For many years, the National Development and Reform Commission of the PRC sustained broad and strong powers dealing with economic policies. Central regulatory bodies such as the State Economic and Trade Commission also became more important for a time.[36]

As leading officials in the central government agreed on a course of action, they often found their plans thwarted by poor implementation further down the bureaucratic chain of command or in the provinces. The decentralization of economic authority that had proven so effective in promoting growth in the post-Mao period meant that the central leaders were often unable to see their priorities implemented.[37] Thus, developed countries had long experience with the weaknesses of the implementation of central Chinese government guidelines on such sensitive economic issues as Chinese infringement of intellectual property rights (IPR). Lax Chinese administrative control hit home in 2008 when it was discovered that the Chinese supply of milk was widely tainted and had caused deaths and widespread illness among babies and small children.[38]

As noted above, Xi Jinping's rule established greater CCP control of the creation and implementation of policies that restricted the freedom of action of localities on economic policies, though the provincial and other local administrations had years of experience in pursuing their ambitions despite central injunctions. Thus, for example, recent scholarship demonstrates how provinces not directly involved with the international outreach of China's BRI were nonetheless able to characterize long-standing local projects, heretofore unable to gain approval for government funding, as part of the massive BRI effort and thus receive the desired government funding for the projects.[39]

Manifestations of social discontent and instability remained a major concern.[40] Chinese government figures available in the past but not in recent years showed that the number and frequency of these demonstrations grew to seventy-four thousand reported in 2004 to one hundred thousand "mass protests" reported annually for several years. The Chinese government's determination to maintain tight social control resulted in a massive crackdown on dissent in Tibet in 2008 and the unprecedented resort to a Maoist mass campaign and thought reform concentration camps for more than one million Uighurs and other residents of Xinjiang beginning in 2017 and lasting up to the present. Chinese authorities rely increasingly on high-technology surveillance of behavior and facial recognition and other personal identification throughout China's cities to track and apprehend potential troublemakers. Internet and other communication vehicles are tightly monitored and controlled. In 2018, Chinese expense for internal security surpassed China's rapidly rising defense budget by 20 percent.[41]

Although certainly worrisome for Chinese leaders concerned with preserving stability and continued CCP rule, these developments seemed to have a way to go before they posed a major or direct threat to the government. Notably, the discontented needed to establish communications across broad areas, groups needed to establish alliances with other disaffected groups, and the alliances needed to put forth leaders prepared to challenge the regime and gain popular support with credible moral claims. Success also required a lax or maladroit regime response. The attentiveness of the government to dissidence and the ruthless crackdown on the Falun Gong beginning in 1999 strongly suggested that Beijing remained keenly alert to the implications of social discontent and was prepared to use its substantial coercive and persuasive powers to keep it from growing to threatening levels. [42] What this overall domestic situation meant for Chinese foreign relations was that Beijing continued to give priority to spending at home in the interests of stability rather than expenditures abroad seeking foreign influence. A bottom line here was that China retained the "win-win" formula governing China's financial support in the BRI and other efforts. A "win" for China in such financing was that Beijing expected to be paid back and make a profit from the foreign endeavors. China was not in a position to make significant expenditures abroad that would not be paid back.

## China's Goals in Foreign Affairs

Regime survival remained the leaders' top priority and continued to drive Chinese leadership preoccupations with the myriad domestic issues noted previously. Against this background, Chinese government policies and practices in international affairs on the whole were at least until recently of somewhat less immediate importance and lower priority. They reflected goals and objectives in world affairs that had existed in China for decades. Chinese leaders appeared to have reached consensus on these objectives, although they frequently did not agree on the means by which to achieve them. [43]

Chinese leaders continued to share certain overarching goals:

- They sought to perpetuate their power and avoid the fate of the Soviet Union and other Eastern European communist regimes.
- They pursued territorial unification and integrity, especially with Taiwan and, to a lesser degree, claims in the East China, South China, and Yellow Seas and claims regarding India.
- They also sought to modernize China's economic, technological, and military capabilities and improve social conditions while maintaining stability.

In addition, China had strategic objectives that reflected its status as a rising power:

- Regional preeminence: Xi Jinping's emphasis on the China Dream and on China undertaking a leadership role in world affairs and the concurrent behavior of China using conventional and unconventional international levers of power to rise at the expense of its neighbors, the United States, and other concerned countries added to the growing judgment among foreign specialists and policy makers that China sought to be the dominant power in Asia.[44] This came despite strong US opposition and repeated Chinese denials that it sought regional hegemony. The Chinese denials were among the relevant pieces of evidence cited by this writer in chapter 1 and by many others of the mendacity prevailing in Chinese official discourse on foreign policy.

• Global influence: The rhetoric and practice of Chinese foreign policy during Xi's rule also made clear stronger Chinese interest in leading global affairs. Here, too, the United States was seen standing in China's way as Beijing worked closely with Vladimir Putin's Russia and other anti-US powers to revise international governance and norms in ways that reduced the influence of the United States and Western-aligned countries. Unlike Putin, Xi Jinping's government sought to sustain many of the economic and other benefits China derived from close economic interchange with Western-aligned developed countries, but it also sought to benefit from weakening US and other resistance from Western-aligned countries to China's authoritarian practices at home and self-serving economic and other practices abroad that violated existing norms.[45]

Under Jiang Zemin and Hu Jintao, China's officials approached the objectives listed here in an international environment where Chinese leaders tended to view China's influence as growing at an impressive rate but far from dominant, and where external and internal factors limited China's freedom of action and possible assertiveness in world affairs. At the start of the twenty-first century, Chinese perceptions of global trends appeared to be in flux and a matter of considerable internal debate. Chinese leaders, as reflected in official comments, believed in the 1990s that the world was becoming multipolar, with the United States as the single superpower but increasingly less able to exert its will as other countries and regions opposed US initiatives. This view changed sharply beginning in the mid- to late 1990s because of the striking disparities between US economic performance and that of other major powers and also because of US leadership in the Balkan crisis, US policy on missile defense, the US war on terrorism, and other issues.[46]

The Chinese then apparently concluded that the world would be unipolar in the near term, with the United States exerting greater influence than Chinese commentators had originally calculated. Chinese leaders often perceived that this influence was not benign regarding China's key interests, notably Taiwan and around China's periphery.[47] Chinese commentary expressed concern about the expansion and strengthening of the US alliance structure and the ability of US-led alliances to intervene regionally and globally.[48]

Developments in the past decade altered Chinese perspectives of China's power and that of the United States. China's quick rebound and America's slow recovery from the global economic crisis and recession of 2008–2010 added to perceptions in China that a multipolar world—with China as a leading power and America in decline—was emerging. The perceptions fed into the ongoing Chinese foreign policy debate, with some officials and other commentators urging China to take more initiatives to enhance and secure its interests, even at the expense of smooth relations with the United States and its allies and associates. Partly in response to the recent Chinese assertiveness, the United States launched the wide-ranging and widely publicized rebalance with the Asia-Pacific, thereby ushering in a new phase of Sino-American competition for influence in Asia. As noted and explained in more detail in following chapters, Xi Jinping's government advanced China's international power and influence in ways that the Obama government failed to counter effectively, paving the way to the Trump government's across-the-board pushback against perceived challenges and dangers posed by Beijing's international advances.[49]

Meanwhile, despite China's turn from traditional Marxist-Leninist-Maoist ideology, components of this tradition continued to influence the thinking of Chinese officials who saw themselves locked in a struggle of values with the West and particularly the United States, which they saw as bent on dividing or "Westernizing" China. Also common was the long-standing Chinese tendency to focus on a primary adversary in world affairs, to exaggerate its threat to China, and to seek domestic and foreign power to offset and counter this threat. Patterns of behavior reflecting this tendency can be seen repeatedly in later chapters examining Chinese leaders' policies and behavior toward the United States and its interests in Asia in the post–Cold War period.

As Chinese leaders became more active in bilateral and multilateral diplomacy, they exerted greater influence in international forums like the United Nations, the WTO, arms control discussions, and other groups that China favored. China also exerted more influence by using conventional and unconventional means to weaken and make more pliable and open to Chinese wishes such international groups as the Association of Southeast Asian Nations (ASEAN) and the European Union (EU) that stood in the way or otherwise complicated China's rise. And Beijing also sought to have its way in newly created or recently prominent international groups where China played a leading role.

# CHANGING PATTERNS IN DECISION MAKING
# AND WORLD OUTLOOK

The foreign policy and behavior of the PRC is determined by leaders who make decisions on the basis of what they think about the issues being decided. The patterns of decision making and the international outlook of Chinese leaders changed in the post–Cold War period:

- China's greater opening to the outside world since the death of Mao and China's remarkable integration with international economic, security, political, and other multilateral organizations accompanied greater transparency and openness in Chinese foreign policy decision making.
- The number of people in and outside the Chinese government involved in Chinese foreign policy decision making grew enormously from the Maoist period. At that time, the government, party, and military bodies supporting foreign policy decisions by the CCP leader were much smaller than today's impressive array of agencies and specialists.
- Those influencing Chinese decision makers today also represented a much broader set of Chinese interests in international affairs, notably in international economics and overall global stability and governance. This trend contrasted with the predominantly security-oriented interests that dominated Chinese leadership concerns over foreign affairs during much of the Cold War. These security-oriented interests were focused on narrower concerns about preserving national sovereignty and security against superpower opposition.
- The outlook of Chinese decision makers on international affairs at times appeared more cosmopolitan and compatible with prevailing international trends and norms, with less emphasis than in the past on the need for China to be on guard and prepared to take assertive and forceful action against dangerous and predatory powers seeking to exploit, oppress, and constrain China. At other times, guarded suspicion seemed more salient. Most recently, Xi Jinping's leadership was much less defensive in the face of many international trends and norms seen at odds with China's determined drive toward international leadership. China's more proactive use of conventional and unconventional levers of power increasingly challenged global norms and groups, particularly those backed by the United States and its allies and partners, which impeded China's assertive ambitions.[50]

This assessment highlights what is known of the prevailing structure and processes in the Chinese government's decision making on foreign policy and the international outlook of Chinese decision makers. It shows that within the Chinese government, the CCP, and the People's Liberation Army

(PLA), the three key administrative groups governing China, the structure and capacity supporting Chinese decision making on foreign policy are more regularized, institutionalized, and extensive than in the past. It also demonstrates the trends of Chinese leaders moving away from past defensiveness toward more accommodation and conformity regarding prevailing international trends and norms, notably in the late 1990s and the first decade of the twenty-first century. Beijing is subsequently seen to shift toward more assertiveness in using its ever-growing conventional and unconventional levers of power to counter norms and organizations supported by the United States and its allies and partners and to manipulate existing institutions and create new institutions to favor China's interests. China's now extensive role in global governance is covered in chapter 4.

Despite the changes involved in Chinese foreign policy decision making, this assessment shows that key decisions, as in the past, were usually made in secrecy. Sometimes, even senior officials involved in the policy process were in the dark about how and why policy changes were made. It also shows enduring suspicion of the United States and Western values and norms, fed by nationalist ambitions of a Chinese government dissatisfied with key elements of the status quo and determined to use growing wealth and power to change perceived adverse circumstances in Asia and the world.

As noted in chapter 1, Xi Jinping's assertiveness in foreign affairs made clear to a growing array of specialists abroad that the expectation that China, as it promised, would continue to rise in benign ways prevalent during the so-called peaceful rise phase of Chinese foreign relations in the first decade of the twenty-first century was incorrect. Indeed, closer examination of unconventional Chinese practices during that decade and later showed Chinese officials and others working as agents for China advancing internationally through covert corrupt practices, elite capture, influence operations, enormous theft of intellectual property for economic and military advances, and overt as well as covert collaboration with Russia, North Korea, Iran, Venezuela, and other states opposed to the United States and its allies and partners. Such practices were those of a revisionist power in key areas of world politics. Adding to China's determination to have its way against the international circumstances and forces seen impeding its headlong drive for leadership in Asia and the world was the extraordinary emphasis in the Chinese worldview of China's righteousness.

Enduring Chinese suspicion of the United States' seeking Beijing's commitment to international norms—seen as favoring the United States and its Western values and constraining China's rise—appeared repeatedly, even during periods when China and the United States were trying to improve relations and when Beijing seemed anxious to accommodate and benefit from closer engagement with Western powers. For instance, Chinese foreign policy repeatedly saw abrupt shifts toward confrontation during international crises involving China. The accidental US bombing of the Chinese embassy in Belgrade in May 1999 prompted a sharp turn toward the negative in China's approach to the United States.[51] The danger of reversal in Chinese policy toward the United States surfaced again in 2001 as a result of the April 1 clash between a Chinese jet fighter and a US reconnaissance aircraft in international airspace near China's southern coast.[52] In contrast with China's accommodating approach toward neighboring countries, labeled China's "good neighbor" policy, mass demonstrations against Japanese diplomatic and business installations in China in 2005 resulted in damage and destruction that went on for several days until curbed by Chinese authorities.[53]

More important, after China reassessed its rising power in comparison with the declining power of the US and Western-aligned states, the scope and intensity of Chinese assertiveness regarding long-standing disputes with neighbors over maritime claims in the East and South China Seas came as unwelcome surprises to nearby countries and to the United States and other powers concerned with the regional order. An impressive buildup of Chinese naval, coast guard, fishing, oil exploration, and dredging forces and equipment allowed repeated assertive actions to advance Chinese control, notably through the rapid creation and militarization of outposts in the disputed South China Sea beginning in 2013. The PLA Navy, maritime surveillance forces, and Chinese foreign policy organizations continued to employ intimidation, coercion, and harassment along with stern verbal warnings against fishing, energy prospecting, maritime surveillance, and military and diplomatic actions by foreigners involving Chinese-claimed territorial and other rights in waters along China's rim. Efforts by Japan, South Korea, and several Southeast Asian nations to support their claimed rights and interests, along with complaints from the United States, Australia, India, and other concerned powers, were dismissed or met with truculent Chinese attacks.[54]

Meanwhile, as China shifted, sometimes abruptly, from an accommodating posture to an assertive posture in dealing with the United States, key neighbors, and others of importance in Chinese foreign policy, suspicions of China harboring revisionist intentions were reinforced by the prevailing secrecy surrounding top-level Chinese foreign policy decision making. To this day, US officials remain in the dark about how senior Chinese leaders deliberated in the weeks following the crises in May 1999 and April 2001.[55] Similar uncertainty pervades reviews of what is known of Chinese decision making during the April 2005 demonstrations against Japan and in the repeated episodes of intimidation and assertiveness against neighbors in recent years. Xi Jinping demonstrated Chinese strength in promoting greater activism in foreign affairs, but assessors struggle to determine who was actually making decisions and what issues and priorities were driving those decisions.[56]

What the previously mentioned episodes show is that even though much more was known than in the past about Chinese foreign policy decision making, especially as it involved economic issues, major political and security issues remained shrouded in secrecy. This was the intent of the Chinese authorities. Those in China who revealed information that was defined by Chinese authorities as coming under a very broad purview of national security were arrested and prosecuted.

Even key Chinese decisions in international economics, such as the considerations that top leaders focused on in making the final decision for China to accept significant compromises in 1999 to reach agreement with the United States in order to join the WTO, were not clearly known. Discussions with US officials about the days leading up to the final agreement in November 1999 showed that Premier Zhu Rongji, backed by senior economic policy leader Wu Yi and other key officials, was instrumental in reaching the final agreement with the US negotiating team. But the motives and arguments in senior Chinese leadership deliberations and those of President Jiang Zemin and other leaders with a role in or influence on the final decision remained unknown.[57]

One of the most important international security issues facing Chinese decision makers involved the international crisis brought about by North Korea's development of nuclear weapons and the concurrent leadership transition. The range of Chinese interests in the crisis, including avoiding war, preserving stability in Korea and northeastern Asia, and preventing the spread of nuclear weapons, appeared clear. Yet Chinese officials and specialists were sometimes frank in acknowledging that they remained in the dark and uncertain about what top Chinese decision makers actually said in conveying Chinese priorities during secret communications with the reclusive North Korean regime.

For example, it was unknown in China and abroad whether Chinese leader Hu Jintao and his colleagues adopted a uniformly accommodating posture to North Korean leader Kim Jong Il during the latter's initially secret ten-day visit to China in January 2006 and his later visits in 2010 and 2011.[58] How much, if any, pressure the Chinese leader was prepared to exert on his North Korean counterpart in order to ensure that the North Korean crisis was managed along lines acceptable to China remained a mystery. In the event, China's leaders publicly supported the ailing Kim's arrangement transferring leadership to his inexperienced son, Kim Jong Un, after Kim's death in December 2011. The younger Kim's repeated provocations saw President Xi Jinping pull back public demonstrations of support, but the scope and content of Chinese efforts to get Pyongyang to change course remained unknown.[59] With the various concurrent summit meetings between North Korea and China and North Korea and the United States beginning after an intense period of crisis in 2017–2018, Chinese leaders were perhaps more transparent about Chinese policy and practice in their frequent interchange with American counterparts.

## KEY DECISION MAKERS IN CHINESE FOREIGN POLICY

There was general agreement among Chinese and foreign specialists regarding the continued decisive role of the "paramount" leader at the top of the hierarchy of government, party, and military actors influencing Chinese foreign policy decision making. Mao Zedong, Deng Xiaoping, Jiang Zemin, and Hu Jintao played that role in the past, and today Xi Jinping holds that position of power. It was generally held that Mao and Deng were strong and decisive in guiding Chinese foreign policy, where Jiang and Hu were seen as much more consultative and cautious in their foreign policy roles.

Xi Jinping moved quickly to establish personal control over foreign policy and national security, as well as key domestic policy areas. He took the leadership positions of the CCP's top-level so-called leading small groups that deliberate over and decide policy dealing with international political, economic, and security matters. He strengthened these deliberative bodies with an eye toward more efficient policy making and implementation, thereby avoiding bureaucratic obstacles and obstruction by special interests. Xi established a new leading small group, the State Security Commission (SSC), which he led. It provided leadership for Chinese national security policies. As the SSC focus centered on internal security, the most important leading group dealing with foreign affairs, the Foreign Affairs Leading Small Group, was upgraded in 2018 to become the Foreign Affairs Commission (FAC) mirroring the SSC, with Xi leading both.[60]

Xi was also more active than previous leaders in using foreign affairs work conferences for deliberations among the wide range of administrative bodies concerned with key issues in foreign affairs. The Central Work Conference on Peripheral Diplomacy held in 2013 was the first ever dealing with China's neighborhood relations. In November 2014, he convened a broader-ranging Foreign Affairs Conference, the first since 2006. According to Suisheng Zhao, a leading expert in Chinese decision making, that meeting marked the end of Deng Xiaoping's cautious foreign policy approach in favor of Xi Jinping's signature "big power diplomacy," with China advancing rapidly in pursuit of the China Dream involving leadership in Asia and an ever more powerful international role. Xi convened another Foreign Affairs Work Conference in 2018 attended by the entire top party leadership, including Politburo members from outside Beijing, that stressed China's global ambitions and the strict requirement of Communist Party control, under the leadership of Xi Jinping, in all foreign policy work.[61]

Control through CCP channels was an important way for Xi and his close advisers to monitor and correct the wide range of organizations involved in foreign policy making and implementation. Those organizations included government, party, and military bodies that dealt with ever more complicated international matters regarding diplomacy, security, economics, culture, education, science, environment, and a host of other important subjects. The Ministry of Foreign Affairs was in charge of diplomacy. It received a boost in its status with the appointment to the Politburo of Yang Jeichi, the first career Foreign Ministry official to reach this rank in more than twenty years. The ministry's leading role in foreign affairs was offset in recent years by the importance of economic relations and the related Chinese Commerce and Finance Ministries and the National Development and Reform Commission, which supervised bilateral and multilateral economic cooperation and exchanges, serving as an official coordination agency for China's Belt and Road Initiative. State development banks, state-owned enterprises, and Huawei and other strongly state-supported ostensibly private firms also played major roles abroad. [62]

Also more active were various foreign influence efforts carried out overtly and covertly by the International Department of the Chinese Communist Party and the Communist Party's largely secret departments dealing with united front work and so-called overseas Chinese affairs. Complementing these efforts was the impressive scope of Chinese espionage for economic, national security, and political benefit carried out by the intelligence units of the Chinese security agencies and the Ministry of Defense. Those clandestine efforts also involved a host of informal agents carrying out operations to gain access to high technology, influence key foreign decision makers, and spread information and misinformation beneficial to China's interests. [63]

More overt influence efforts were carried out by the Confucius Institutes supervised by the Ministry of Education, propaganda carried out by the party's publicity department and the Information Office of the State Council, and the dialogues and other exchanges and joint exercises conducted by the Chinese military.

Xi Jinping's strong decision-making power in foreign affairs was complemented by his activism in traveling abroad and in meetings with foreign leaders in China. In marked contrast with Hu Jintao, Xi sought and appeared to enjoy the limelight in international affairs. Xi had six colleagues in the top-level CCP Politburo Standing Committee. Though second-ranking party leader and premier Li Keqiang was very active in foreign affairs, official Chinese media coverage and international attention clearly gave top priority to Xi. The Chinese president made use of Politburo meetings, the large foreign affairs conferences, and new national security and foreign affairs commissions to set China's foreign policy agenda. [64] He took direct personal responsibility for managing key foreign policy relationships, notably China's contentious relations with the United States, ever closer relations with Russia, and the positives and negatives in China's relations around its periphery in nearby Asia.

## WORLDVIEW OF CHINESE LEADERS

Few foreign specialists had meaningful contacts with senior Chinese leaders to the point of understanding more than the general outlines of their thinking on world affairs and how this affected their leanings in foreign affairs. Thus, the judgments in their assessments remained tentative. Chinese specialists who had close contacts with senior Chinese officials generally said little about this subject. When they did address it, they tended to emphasize that those officials remained more wary of the United States and the US-dominated international order than some others in China who adopted a more moderate and relaxed view of the United States and the international situation. The Chinese specialists also emphasized that senior Chinese leaders showed more sensitivity than others in China to perceived threats or affronts coming from foreign sources.[65]

Assessments of Chinese foreign policy thinking at the start of this century made the case that Chinese foreign policy and behavior were changing markedly in directions more in line with international norms, especially regarding economic and cultural matters and constructive participation in multilateral organizations. These changes in Chinese policy were seen as influenced by a more pluralistic range of Chinese decision makers whose diverse interests were reflected in foreign policy and behavior. They also highlighted a prevailing worldview among this elite that emphasized seeing international affairs in terms of competing states, with China required to maintain its guard against exploitation and oppression as it sought to develop national wealth and power and greater influence in Asian and world affairs. Overall, there was some optimism that the recent trend of increasing Chinese foreign policy conformity with and adherence to international norms, along with continued emphasis on promoting general trends toward world peace and development, were likely to continue.[66]

On assuming the leading CCP position in 2002, Hu Jintao appeared to follow the pattern of generally cautious moves toward moderation in Chinese foreign affairs seen in the latter years of Jiang Zemin. Hu Jintao's leadership featured emphasis on "peaceful development" and supporting a "harmonious" world.[67] Coincident with China's recalibration of its rising power relative to a declining United States after the international financial crisis of 2008–2009 came Chinese assertiveness and truculence in foreign affairs, which focused on the United States and China's neighbors during the later years of Hu's rule. Xi Jinping's priorities subsequently depicted a worldview of ascendant China facing numerous obstructions from a declining America representing the key proponent of international organizations and norms seen at odds with China's growing ambitions for Asian and global leadership.[68]

Roots of recent Chinese assertiveness and toughness lie in the deep and rich soil of the world outlook of Chinese elites and public opinion. A review of the various worldviews propounded by leaders of the PRC since 1949 indicates how difficult it remained for China to fully accept existing international norms and an accommodating posture to the United States, Western countries, and China's neighbors with a large stake in the prevailing regional and international order. As specialists in China have repeatedly emphasized in recent years, China's rising international prominence brought to the fore nationalistic and zero-sum realist foreign policy calculations on the part of a variety of influential foreign policy actors in China that put those Chinese leaders arguing for progressive accommodation to existing international norms in a more defensive and increasingly less influential position. These nationalistic and realist calculations tapped into strongly engrained Chinese views of world affairs that were perpetuated by the communist government's massive propaganda apparatus for the sake of strengthening one-party communist rule.[69]

There is little disagreement among Chinese and foreign specialists that Chinese officials and the rest of the Chinese people have been long conditioned through the education system and government-sponsored media coverage to think of China as having been victimized by international powers since the early nineteenth century. As noted in chapter 1, emphasis on this historical conditioning was strengthened after the CCP crisis at the time of the Tiananmen demonstrations and bloody crackdown in 1989 and has continued to the present. The patriotic education campaign with related media coverage encouraged regime-supporting patriotism in China by recalling the more than one hundred years of foreign affronts to Chinese national dignity. With this focus, foreign complaints about human rights and other abuses in China after the Tiananmen crackdown were depicted as the latest in a long series of foreign efforts to abuse and victimize China. As such, they elicited negative responses from Chinese people directed at foreign governments criticizing China's communist rule.[70]

The emphasis on China's historical victimization by foreign powers, which continued to be strongly stressed by Chinese education, media, and propaganda organs, heavily influenced the world outlook of China's leaders and people.[71] Among lessons for the present were the following:

• The world was viewed darkly. It was full of highly competitive, unscrupulous, and duplicitous governments that were seeking their selfish interests at the expense of China and others.

- To survive and develop, China needed power—military power backed by economic power and political unity. If there was disunity at home, foreign powers would use Chinese differences to exploit China, just as they had in the past.
- China was an aggrieved party. It suffered greatly at foreign hands for almost two centuries. It needed to build its power and influence to protect what it has and to get back what was rightfully China's. This meant restoration of Taiwan to Chinese sovereignty and securing other Chinese territorial claims.
- China did not dominate the world order; other powers did—during the Cold War, the United States and the Soviet Union; after the Cold War, the United States. China needed to work toward an international balance that helped Chinese interests and avoided outside dominance. In this vein, Chinese leaders in recent years emphasized the benefits of a multipolar world order where China would have greater freedom of maneuver and security than in an international order dominated by the United States. [72]

Complementing this historical discourse showing China as the victim of predatory outsiders were other features influencing China's worldview to various degrees:

- The ideological and revolutionary drive of Mao Zedong and his colleagues to foster revolution in China and abroad was largely ended, though as noted above, China's leaders remained determined to preserve Communist Party rule in the face of perceived political challenges and values supported by the West.
- Chinese self-reliance, important in the latter Maoist period, was put aside with China's ever-growing interdependence with the world, especially in economics and trade. Nevertheless, with the exception of North Korea, China scrupulously avoided alliances with or formal dependence on other states as it sought ties with other countries based on the "win-win" formula that has determined Chinese foreign relations recently. Chinese cooperation with others was contingent on a "win" for China that was within the scope of a win set defined narrowly in terms of tangible benefit for the Chinese state.
- Chinese officials have recently fostered an idealized depiction of benevolent Chinese imperial interaction with China's neighbors. The hierarchical order of international relations with China at the center, seen during much of the Ming and Qing dynasties from the fourteenth to nineteenth century was depicted showing Chinese naval expeditions and other foreign interchange that reflected China's purported unwillingness to be expansionist. At the same time, the grandeur of these regimes saw China at the apex of world power—an order with China at the top and others deferring—an

appropriate order for the current age according to some Chinese commentary.[73]

- As discussed in chapter 1, Chinese official discourse and related scholarship tended to play down foreign depictions of Chinese leaders changing foreign policies and even overall alignments as Chinese interests shifted with changing circumstances at home and abroad. Rather, they portrayed Chinese policies and practices as consistent, based on appropriate principles in line with broad moral goals, and aligning China's approach with the "progressive" forces in international affairs.[74]
- As noted in chapter 1, a major implication of such Chinese reasoning was an acute sense of Chinese exceptionalism. Many Chinese truly believed that the PRC always followed morally correct foreign policies in the interest of progressive world forces. They believed China had done nothing wrong in world affairs. Thus, if difficulties arise with neighbors, the United States, or other states over foreign policy concerns, the fault naturally lies with the other party or some other circumstance, but never with China. Such an international outlook was deeply rooted among Chinese elite and public opinion.

The overall result of China's acute sense of grievance against past international victimization on the one hand and the strong sense of righteousness in the foreign policy and practice of the PRC on the other hand supported a Chinese popular and elite worldview of poor self-awareness of Chinese international shortcomings and sharp sensitivity to international pressure. This situation made it very hard to deal with differences, especially with issues of wide interest in China like Taiwan, Japan, the United States, and the widely publicized maritime territorial claims.

One lesson going forward was that although some foreign and Chinese specialists looked on the bright side and saw China conforming more to international norms, more sober views saw such conformity as tactical, mainly adjusting to circumstances. They saw those adjustments shifted in ways that support Beijing's long-standing nationalistic grievances and ambitions but are at odds with international stability. They averred that with the dramatic change in China's perception of its power relative to perceived opponents in the United States and elsewhere, Chinese leaders adopted more forceful efforts, using conventional and unconventional levers of power to carry out revisionist ambitions in the region and more broadly.

## Chapter Three

# China's Role in the World Economy

Today, China's greatest importance in foreign affairs is as the world's second-largest economy. China's modernization and economic advance spread and deepened throughout the vast country and into all corners of the globe. These developments support active diplomacy in multilateral and bilateral relations. They provide large and growing leverage that Chinese leaders use often in conventional ways by winning favor and showing disapproval to countries through giving or taking away advantageous trade, investment, financing, and access to China's state-restricted market, and leverage that the leaders use often in unconventional ways, such as widespread covert bribery and other corrupt practices; elite capture (e.g., providing high-paid employment for standing or recently retired foreign leaders) and related influence operations; and penetration and control of media, communications, surveillance systems, and other key infrastructure for purposes of political manipulation and espionage as well as economic benefit. China's economic progress also provides the basis for the fastest-growing military modernization of any country in the post–Cold War period. Taken together, China's growing economic and military capacity changes the balance-of-power calculus of China's neighbors and other concerned countries, notably the United States. [1]

As China's reforms toward greater influence of free-market enterprise and less state control stalled over the past two decades, the Xi Jinping government emphasized ever greater central direction of the economy, notably through a robust revival of Communist Party control. The success of this Chinese economic development model of stronger state capitalism involved self-serving industrial policies and mercantilist protectionism fostering highly subsidized national champion industries that often absorbed or wiped out international competition through predatory pricing, illicit or forced technology transfers, and selected corporate buyouts backed by Chinese government

45

funds. This Chinese development model posed very serious challenges for the free-market policies of the United States and Western-aligned countries. For its part, the Chinese government viewed the free-market policies of the West as discredited, notably as a result of their failure in creating and dealing with the financial crisis and recession of 2008–2009. Beijing also associated free-market economic policies with the liberal political values of the West, which remained anathema for Xi Jinping and his colleagues determined to preserve China's one-party rule. Beijing came to promote its economic model internationally as a favorable one when compared with the previously dominant free-market systems of the West.[2]

Against this background, prominent American leaders and many others among Western-aligned countries viewed with alarm China's advances in high-technology industries. They depicted Chinese state-directed economic programs such as Made in China 2025 as designed to catch up with and surpass the United States and others among developed Western-aligned countries in the key high-technology industries of the future. As noted in chapter 1 and explained in more detail below, China was indeed advancing rapidly in a robust state-directed drive to achieve leadership in the high-technology industries of the future, including artificial intelligence, 5G communications networks, the Internet of Things, nano- and biotechnology, aviation and space, and electric vehicles. A common assessment was that Made in China 2025 and other comprehensive efforts showed that China was challenging and preparing to overtake the United States' lead in these key areas. The result in America and abroad was heightened urgency, with some viewing China as an existential threat now seeking dominance in the high-technology industries that were key to American economic and military power. In this view, without the United States sustaining leadership in these industries, its economy and national defense would become second to and increasingly dominated by China.[3]

Meanwhile, the success of China's economic practices allowing for the high-technology advances endangering America and the West were viewed as supported by China's ambitious foreign economic policy outreach, notably in the global Belt and Road Initiative (BRI). There was considerable debate about the longer-term viability and effectiveness of this controversial Chinese effort, Xi Jinping's signature foreign policy initiative, but overall it had a negative impact on US policies and those of some other Western-aligned countries. Notably, Chinese practices in the BRI featured the corruption, influence operations, and other hallmarks of Beijing's unconventional levers of influence abroad as well as the often egregious use by the Chinese government of economic leverage and other pressures in support of Chinese companies involved in BRI-related enterprises. And the BRI challenged Western modes of financing development abroad; it won market share for heavily state-supported Chinese companies of key importance in China's high-technology drive; and it provided important leverage for China to manipulate and make more pliant and accommodating of Chinese economic, security, and diplomatic practices and interests of various Western and other governments and multilateral organizations, like the European Union (EU) and the Association of Southeast Asian Nations (ASEAN), which otherwise complicated or opposed China's practices in its headlong drive toward regional and global leadership.[4]

This chapter reviews China's contemporary economic importance in world affairs; assesses the motives, accomplishments, and shortcomings of the Belt and Road Initiative; reviews the impact of recently acute US-China economic frictions; and discusses the economic challenges facing China in the period ahead.

## CHINA'S ECONOMIC IMPORTANCE

China's role in today's world depended fundamentally on the success of the almost forty years of economic reforms and international outreach begun in the post-Mao period by Deng Xiaoping and his successors. China's growing international economic capacity and profile increased its heretofore limited importance to a wide range of countries in the developed and developing world as a trading partner, a recipient and source of investment, and a creditor.[5]

Prior to that time, the People's Republic of China exerted important influence in world affairs in different ways and for different reasons. During the rule of Mao Zedong (d. 1976), China's vast size, strategic location, revolutionary and nationalistic zeal, and broad popular mobilization made it a formidable opponent for both the United States and the Soviet Union and an important determinant in the foreign policy calculations of neighboring Asian countries. China's importance grew as it developed nuclear weapons and the ballistic missiles to deliver them to targets as far away as Washington, DC. Ironically, China's prevailing backwardness in economic development for much of this period made China more difficult for the US and Soviet superpowers to deter and to counter adverse Chinese moves, thereby increasing China's importance in their calculations.[6]

The influence China exerted on the world economy continued to grow, but so did China's dependence on key variables in the world economy that the Chinese leadership did not control. The latter included access to energy and other resources, periodic downturns in international demand for Chinese products, and recently the punitive tariffs, high-technology restrictions, and export controls of the Trump administration in the United States. The latter in particular caused disruption of foreign investment in China and various international production chains centered on China as the final exporter that depended on free access to the US market. On top of this list came the enormous global economic crisis accompanying the COVID-19 global pandemic. The world economy that China contributed to and relied on was in jeopardy in 2020.[7]

In 2013 the Chinese government announced an array of difficult reforms with uncertain prospects, endeavoring to move away from dependence on the United States and other Western-aligned countries and to rely more on domestic consumption to drive China's economic growth. As detailed below, these reforms stalled as the Xi Jinping leadership doubled down on party control of the economy that supported the development of so-called national champion industries in high technology but was insufficient to advance domestic consumption enough to drive forward China's economic independence.[8]

From 1979 to 2014, the average annual growth rate of China's gross domestic product (GDP) was about 10 percent. By 2010, China became the world's second-largest economy, after the United States. In 2011, it became the largest manufacturer, surpassing the United States. In 2012, it became the world's largest trader. By that time, China was also the second-largest destination of foreign investment, the largest holder of foreign exchange reserves, and the largest creditor nation.[9] Several predictions said that China was on track to surpass the United States, the world's largest economy, in the next decade.[10]

Chinese growth rates declined steadily from 12.8 percent in 2012 to 6.7 percent in 2016. The rate of GDP growth was 6.8 percent in 2017, 6.6 percent in 2018, and 6.1 percent in 2019. Amid the global pandemic, China's growth rate declined 6.8 percent in the first quarter of 2020.[11] The International Monetary Fund (IMF) forecasted in 2019 that China's real GDP growth would slow each year over the next six years, falling to 5.5 percent in 2024. The Organisation for Economic Co-operation and Development (OECD) projected that punitive tariffs and trade and investment restrictions between the United States and China could reduce China's real GDP in 2021–2022 by 1.1 percent relative to the OECD's baseline economic projections. Remaining stalled was the wide range of over sixty sets of mainly economic reforms announced by the Chinese leaders in 2013 that were focused on dealing with existing or anticipated economic weaknesses involving the inefficient practices of state-owned enterprises (SOEs) and the state banking system, resource and energy scarcities, massive environmental problems, and China's strong dependence on the health of the global trading economy.[12]

## Foreign Investment and Trade

Active foreign direct investment (FDI) in China continued in recent years, and growing Chinese investment abroad surpassed China's FDI in 2016.[13] Chinese foreign trade growth stopped in 2015, and overall trade was less in 2016 than 2015. Trade levels grew again in 2017 and 2018 but stalled in the face of US punitive tariffs in 2019. Foreign trade declined by 6.4 percent in the first quarter of 2020.[14]

China's trade, which continued to play a major role in China's rapid economic growth, featured strong dependence on foreign investment coming into China and trade relations managed by Chinese officials in ways that provided China with a large trade surplus each year. Foreign-invested enterprises (FIEs) were responsible for a significant portion of China's foreign trade; FIEs accounted for 42 percent of Chinese exports and 44 percent of Chinese imports in 2018. There were reportedly 445,244 FIEs registered in China in 2010, employing 55.2 million workers, or 15.9 percent of the urban workforce.[15]

The large role of FIEs and their often extensive supply-chain networks meant that a large portion of Chinese trade was so-called processing trade, where firms in China obtained raw materials and intermediate inputs from abroad, processed them locally, and exported value-added goods. Estimates of the extent of such processing trade vary. Among higher estimates, two professors from Peking University reported in 2012 that thanks to China's encouragement of close interaction with foreign firms in special export zones and other means, processing trade constituted about half of China's total trade. According to China's Commerce Department in 2019, the total value generated by the exports of China's processing trade in 2018 was $797 billion and accounted for 32 percent of China's total exports that year. The total value of imports reached $470 billion, 22 percent of China's total imports, for a trade surplus of $327 billion.[16] Such processing trade saw China at times add only a small amount to the product, and the finished product often depended on sales to the United States or the EU. The trade of components and semifinished products also resulted in extensive double counting in Chinese trade figures.[17]

Meanwhile, underlining China's heavy interdependence on the international economy, the Singapore ambassador in China told Chinese media in August 2013 that 60 percent of the goods that at that time were exported from China and the ten Southeast Asian states of ASEAN were ultimately manufactures that went to the United States, Europe, and Japan. Only 22 percent of these goods stayed in the China-ASEAN region.[18]

According to the United Nations Conference on Trade and Development (UNCTAD), from 1990 to 2015, global annual FDI flows grew from $205 billion to $1,746 billion (up 752 percent), while the stock of FDI rose from

$2,197 billion to $26,729 billion (up 1,116 percent). China's global FDI inflows grew rapidly after it began to liberalize its trade regime in 1979 and joined the World Trade Organization (WTO) in 2001. They remained relatively constant in 2016–2018—averaging $138 billion a year. [19]

The cumulative level of FDI in China from 1979 to the end of 2010 was more than $1 trillion; about 40 percent of the FDI in China came from Hong Kong, 10 percent from the British Virgin Islands (a well-known tax haven), 8 percent from Japan, and 7 percent from the United States. The largest sector for FDI flows in China in recent years was manufacturing, which often accounted for more than half of total annual FDI in China. [20] FIEs registered in China were a major source of China's productivity gains and accounted for a significant share of China's industrial output. That level was 25.9 percent in 2011. In addition, as noted above, a bit less than half of China's foreign trade was accounted for by foreign-invested firms in China. The largest foreign investors in China (based on FDI stock through 2017) were Hong Kong (52.6 percent of total), the British Virgin Islands (10.6 percent), Japan (6.1 percent), Singapore (4.0 percent), and Germany (3.2 percent). [21]

A notable feature of investment into China was the practice of Chinese investments abroad in order to circumvent domestic government controls by sending the investment funds to an offshore destination and then bringing them back as a foreign investment. [22] These so-called round-trip investments seemed to be specific to China and had an apparently important bearing on how to assess the scope and importance of Chinese investment data. This practice was seen to result in a significant overstatement of both outward and inward FDI in China. Studies estimated that 20 to 30 percent of capital leaving China was "round-tripped" back as foreign investment in the domestic Chinese economy. Much of this round-tripped investment was done through Hong Kong and other so-called tax havens such as the British Virgin Islands. As noted above, such havens remained among the top destinations for Chinese outward FDI. [23]

## Foreign Aid

China's foreign aid remained difficult to assess, given the lack of reliable official data. The Chinese government's first white paper on foreign aid was released in 2011; it provided an overall figure of China's cumulative foreign assistance and data on other trends, but not enough information to determine the cost of Chinese assistance to specific countries or during specific times. The *China Statistical Yearbook, 2003–2006* released an annual aid figure of $970 million, but specialists judged that this did not include loans, a major form of Chinese aid. A former US government foreign aid official, Georgetown University professor Carol Lancaster, judged in 2007 that China's annual aid ranged in value between $1.5 billion and $2 billion. [24] Studies that inventoried various reports of loans, state-sponsored investment, and other official Chinese financing came up with much larger figures, though aid specialists judged that much of these efforts would not qualify as aid and that it was difficult to determine when and whether reported aid and loan pledges were actually ever made and disbursed. Chinese financing at times involved interest-free or concessional loans, but it also involved trade and investment agreements, including arrangements whereby Chinese loans were to be repaid by commodities (e.g., oil) produced as a result of the development financed with China's help.[25]

Chinese aid efforts received an especially high profile in Africa. Some reports emphasized the benefit China received from offering assistance without the conditions that Western donors imposed. China followed a policy of "noninterference" in the internal affairs of governments being pressed by Western donors because of gross abuses of power or corruption. China was also able to expedite assistance without lengthy processes dealing with environmental and social standards, and the public buildings, roads, and infrastructure built with Chinese assistance were often completed expeditiously by Chinese contractors who had a tendency to use Chinese labor and served as prominent reminders of Chinese assistance. Deborah Brautigam, a specialist on foreign aid and Chinese involvement in Africa, estimated that Chinese aid to Africa in the years 2001–2009 amounted to $2.1 billion.[26]

The second Chinese white paper on foreign assistance was issued in 2014; it offered better information focused on the three-year period 2010–2012. In that period, China provided $14.4 billion in aid in the form of grants, interest-free loans, and concessional loans. More than half of that went to Africa, where fifty-one countries received Chinese aid. Thirty Asian nations received around 30 percent of China's foreign aid, and nineteen countries in Latin America and the Caribbean accounted for 8 percent. China's aid to Oceania accounted for 4.2 percent of its aid over the 2010–2012 period. A plurality of China's aid (44 percent) went to economic infrastructure projects, which the white paper defined as transport and communications, broadcasting and telecommunications, and power supply construction. The second-largest spending category was social and public infrastructure (27 percent of the total aid), which included the construction of schools, hospitals, and other civil projects.[27]

From 2010 to 2012, there was a large increase in concessional loans, which accounted for more than half of Chinese aid, and a large decrease in interest-free loans, which accounted for less than 10 percent. Compared with grants or interest-free loans, the use of concessional loans expanded the scope of Chinese foreign aid as it raised funds from the market. It reduced the financial burden on the Chinese government as it only covered the interest difference between concessional and commercial loan rates. The recipient country was required to pay back the debt.[28] Periodic reports showed that some developing countries, such as the poorly administered Kingdom of Tonga in the Pacific Islands, imprudently took on too much Chinese debt and faced strong pressure to pay what they owed.[29]

In 2018, China reorganized its foreign aid decision-making process and created a new agency, the China International Development Cooperation Administration (CIDCA). The new body was headed by a former official of the National Development and Reform Commission, China's top economic policy-making organ. Subordinate officials came from the Ministry of Commerce and the Foreign Ministry. The deliberations of CIDCA remained secret, and the actual amounts of Chinese assistance were hard to discern. Part of the reason for this secrecy had to do with worry about popular backlash in China to giving money abroad when development needs remained at home.[30] A study by the Japanese government in 2019 assessed Chinese foreign economic commitments to discern foreign aid as defined by the OECD. It found that Chinese foreign aid was valued at $4.9 billion in 2014, $6.0 billion in 2015, $5.8 billion in 2016, $6.1 billion in 2017, and $6.4 billion in 2018. Overall the value of Chinese foreign aid was seen as similar to that of Sweden and Turkey.[31]

Meanwhile, China continued to receive considerable foreign aid, and for a time it was difficult to determine whether it was a net contributor or recipient of foreign assistance. The *Economist* in January 2015 reported that "as recently as 2010 it [China] was still a net recipient of foreign assistance."[32] China was the leading recipient of international assistance in the 1980s and the 1990s from international financial institutions. Even as China rose to become the world's second-largest economy, the World Bank annually provided about $1.5 billion in loans to China. The Asian Development Bank provided loans annually worth $1.3 billion. Reports by the OECD showed that at least until recently Japan, Germany, and France provided China with official development assistance. The EU also maintained annual programs of assistance in China. Many EU members other than Germany and France, as well as other developed countries (e.g., Canada, Australia), maintained a variety of assistance programs in China, as did such prominent Western foundations and nongovernmental organizations as the Ford Foundation and the Gates Foundation. China also benefited greatly from international donors' efforts to combat avian flu and to support the Global Fund for AIDS, Tuberculosis, and Malaria.[33]

In April 2010, Chinese media reported that twenty-four UN agencies, such as the UN Development Program, that provide assistance to China had reached an agreement to extend their assistance for another five years. The value of this assistance was not specified. The OECD issued a report later in 2010 that showed that donor countries provided China with an annual amount of aid valued at $2.6 billion a year.[34] The UN Development Program highlighted its continued active role in China in 2019.[35]

In the past two decades, it also became clear that China gained assistance through various climate change and environmental programs. The Clean Development Mechanism (CDM) under the Kyoto Protocol was reported to be an important source of China's clean technology acquisition from foreign countries. The CDM allowed developed countries with a greenhouse gas reduction commitment to invest in emission reduction projects in developing countries as an alternative to more expensive emission reductions in developed countries. As Georgetown University professor Joanna Lewis pointed out in 2008, "the CDM has become a vehicle for China to help stimulate investment in projects that mitigate greenhouse gas emissions and to help cover the incremental cost of higher-efficiency or low-carbon technology."[36] China's National Development and Reform Commission said that China had approved a total of 2,443 CDM projects as of March 2010.[37] An independent study showed that China was among the highest beneficiaries among developing countries regarding CDM projects.[38] An unexplored but presumably important consideration for China's economic modernization was the role these technology transfers from developed countries played in China's rapid ascent up the technology ladder to a position of global leadership in the production of renewable and clean energy equipment.[39]

Regarding foreign assistance, China was the largest recipient of environmental aid from the World Bank. It received 17 percent of the total funding for climate change projects from the Global Environmental Facility (GEF) through the World Bank during 1991–2002. The overall value of the aid was more than $300 million. From 2002 to 2009, the value of GEF funding to China was $122 million. In 2008, a World Bank loan of $200 million funded a large energy-efficiency project in China. In 2010, the Asian Development Bank reportedly approved a loan of $135 million to support building so-called green power plants in China. The UN Development Program was involved in an energy-efficiency project in China. Many foreign governments, including the United States, Canada, Australia, Switzerland, and Norway, supported bilateral cooperation projects in China dealing with climate change.[40]

## GROWING CHINESE FINANCING AND INVESTMENT ABROAD: THE BELT AND ROAD INITIATIVE

The combination of trade surpluses and FDI added to China's foreign exchange reserves, the largest in the world, valued at $3 trillion in 2019. Against this background, China's outbound direct investment has increased rapidly in recent years. According to UNCTAD, from 2007 to 2016, China's FDI outflows rose from $27 billion to $183 billion in 2016, a 578 percent increase (while inflows over this period grew by 60 percent). The reasons for the increased FDI outflows centered on government-supported initiatives to use FDI to gain access to intellectual property rights (IPR), technology, and know-how in order to move Chinese firms up to the top ranks of the value-added chain in manufacturing and services, boost domestic innovation and development of Chinese brands, and help Chinese firms (especially SOEs) to become major global competitors. Other reasons involved China's slowing economy and rising labor costs, prompting greater Chinese overseas FDI in order to expand business opportunities and to relocate less competitive firms from China to low-cost countries. China's nonfinancial FDI in the generally less developed BRI countries remained modest at $15.6 billion in 2018, up 8.9 percent over the previous year. China's FDI outflows declined in 2017 and 2018, reflecting a crackdown by the Chinese government on investment deemed wasteful as well as greater scrutiny by foreign governments of China's efforts to obtain advanced technology firms and other strategic assets. Still, China was the world's second-largest source of FDI outflows (after Japan).[41]

Meanwhile, under the rubric and global scope of the Belt and Road Initiative and related Chinese foreign economic efforts, China solidified its position as the world's largest financer of development projects abroad, surpassing the World Bank. Many of the projects involved in part foreign investment and/or foreign assistance, but most involved financing provided mainly by the leading Chinese government banks, the China Development Bank and the Export-Import Bank of China, loaning overseas.[42]

A major turning point in Chinese financing and investment abroad came with Xi Jinping's much greater emphasis on activism in foreign affairs than the previous Chinese governments. The financing and investment initiatives abroad announced by President Xi, Prime Minister Li Keqiang, and other senior Chinese leaders received enormous publicity from China's massive state-directed propaganda apparatus. The leaders' proposals involved planned expenditures of hundreds of billions of dollars in investments, loans, and other mechanisms to promote development in less developed countries designed to advantage Chinese economic interests and international influence. Among the vehicles for the new loans and investment push were commitments that together amounted to about $200 billion to a Chinese Silk Road Fund; a China-proposed Asian Infrastructure Investment Bank (AIIB); a China-backed New Development Bank established by the five so-called BRICS countries (Brazil, Russia, India, China, and South Africa); and a Chinese-proposed Shanghai Cooperation Organization (SCO) Development Bank involving China, Russia, and the four former Soviet republics in Central Asia that made up the core membership of the SCO.[43] Over time, it became clearer that the main financing of BRI-related projects would be provided by China in bilateral deals with various governments through the China Development Bank and the Export-Import Bank of China.

The new commitments came in the context of Xi Jinping's launch in speeches in Kazakhstan and Indonesia in 2013 of what was known respectively as the Silk Road Economic Belt (encompassing China and the Eurasian countries reached by land to its west) and the Twenty-First Century Maritime Silk Road (encompassing China and the Eurasian, Pacific-, and Indian Ocean–bordering countries reached by sea to China's south and west). The two eventually merged in Chinese official discourse, becoming One Belt and One Road (OBOR), and more recently the Belt and Road Initiative. Official statements on the purpose and scope of the effort varied, though the scope grew to encompass most of the world, even Latin America and the Arctic.[44]

One of the few comprehensive statements defining the effort came coincident with Xi Jinping's keynote address at the March 2015 Boao Forum on Asia annual conference emphasizing China's "common destiny" with neighboring countries. Beijing released on March 28 an action plan suggesting steps to be taken under the rubrics of the Silk Road Economic Belt and the Twenty-First Century Maritime Silk Road initiatives. The plan was created by the National Development and Reform Commission, the Ministry of Foreign Affairs, and the Ministry of Commerce and was endorsed by the State Council. It was as much a vision statement as it was a plan of action. The main substance of the plan was laid out in sections dealing with "framework" and "cooperation priorities" that detailed a very wide range of proposed or possible policies and practices. The details showed that while China was focused on developing infrastructure projects connecting China more closely with its neighbors, Beijing remained open to pursuing a broadly defined range of actions favored by China and neighboring states involving promoting enhanced policy coordination across the ever-broadening geographic scope of the effort, financial integration, trade liberalization, and people-to-people connections.[45]

The new proposals were surprising to close observers of Chinese financing and investment abroad; they came during a period of reassessment of the advantages and disadvantages of China's use of large-scale government lending and other means as part of a broad-gauge "going out" strategy over the previous decade. Similar to the Xi Jinping government's economic initiatives, Chinese leaders in the previous decade also offered and signed numerous agreements reportedly worth many billions of dollars that focused on building infrastructure in order to gain secure Chinese access to oil and other raw materials needed for China's resource-intensive economic growth. The costs of the Chinese loans and investment were often repaid in oil or other commodities. And in that period, Chinese leaders repeatedly called attention to multibillion-dollar funds created by China in support of Chinese investment plans in different parts of the developing world.[46]

The official results of the reassessment of the decade of experience with the "going out" strategy were not announced. Available commentary in official Chinese media and international media showed a mixed record of accomplishment with many shortcomings. For example, specialists who searched beyond the headlines of multibillion-dollar investment plans and loan deals found that in many countries the deals more often than not were not executed as proposed or were not done at all. Large-scale infrastructure agreements worth many billions of dollars involving Nigeria, the Philippines, Myanmar, Sri Lanka, Mexico, and Greece failed to go forward. Adding to this checkered record of accomplishment, major actual and proposed Chinese investments in Libya, Iraq, Sudan, Afghanistan, Syria, and other risky locations collapsed in the face of war and domestic conflict in recent years.

Emblematic of these trends, the deputy dean of the National School of Development at Beijing University observed in the *China Daily* in February 2015 that "over half of China's overseas investments are not profitable."[47] In part to offset the risk of investment in unstable parts of Africa, the Chinese government sometimes saw the wisdom of avoiding bearing alone the risk of Chinese investments in the region by launching in 2014 a $2 billion African Development Fund to be invested through the African Development Bank.[48] Meanwhile, China's hailed $3 billion investment in a large copper mine in Afghanistan and other purported and aborted investments in mining ventures were very common. Against this background, China Mining Association vice chairman Wang Jiahua told the China Mining Congress and Exhibition in Tianjin in November 2013 that about 80 percent of China's overseas mining investments had failed.[49] Reflecting the new Xi Jinping government's emphasis on promoting investment abroad, meetings between the Indonesian president and President Xi Jinping in 2015 featured agreements on tens of billions of dollars in planned investment. However, the Indonesian Investment Coordinating Board reported at this time that China had planned $24.27 billion of investment in Indonesia between 2005 and 2014, but only $1.8 billion, equal to 7 percent, was actually invested. The report showed that Indonesia was a difficult place for foreign investment but added that Japan, another major investor in Indonesia, was three and a half times more likely than China to follow through on its investment plans.[50]

Meanwhile, data and assessments at this time provided by ASEAN, the *Economist*, and the *China–Latin America Economic Bulletin* showed that the Chinese record of actual investment abroad amounted to much less than one expected after reading repeated news stories and commentary over the previous decade of a variety of multibillion-dollar Chinese investment plans similar to those fostered by the Xi Jinping government. The data and assessments showed that China's actual investment in Southeast Asia, Africa, and Latin America amounted to a significant but still modest amount for these areas, ranging from about 10 percent for ASEAN to around 5 percent each for

Africa and Latin America. Even when one took into account underreporting by the Chinese government of investment abroad, China's low percentage of investment after many years of pledges and plans to increase investment was a notable finding.[51]

Up to now, it is probably too early to give a definitive assessment of the impact of Xi Jinping's Belt and Road Initiative and related economic efforts on Chinese relations with developing and developed countries throughout the world. The purpose of the efforts became clearer in the comments of Chinese officials as the various programs unfolded and evolved. Chinese leaders and lower-level officials and commentators revealed the specific benefits China sought. There were economic benefits and strategic benefits.[52]

The perceived economic benefits were as follows:

- China's massive foreign exchange reserves were said to be better employed in infrastructure development and investments abroad in Asia and elsewhere than in US government securities and other such low-paying investments abroad.
- Asia's and other developing areas' massive need for infrastructure meshed well with China's massive overcapacity to build infrastructure after thirty years of rebuilding China. Meshing the two would allow competitive Chinese construction companies to continue productive growth in building Chinese-funded infrastructure in neighboring and other countries.
- Connecting remote western and southern regions of China with neighbors through modern infrastructure in Asia would serve to develop these backward Chinese regions more rapidly and thereby help bridge the wide economic development gap between interior and coastal provinces in China.
- The Chinese-supported infrastructure would allow many Chinese industries with excess capacity or facing higher-wage demands or more stringent environmental restrictions in China to relocate to nearby or more distant countries and continue to prosper and develop.
- The Chinese-funded connection with neighbors and countries farther away would facilitate trade and the increased use of Chinese currency in international transactions.
- Developing trade routes including road, rail, and pipeline connections to China from the Arabian Sea through Pakistan, from the Bay of Bengal through Myanmar, and overland through Central Asian states and Russia was said to reduce China's vulnerability to possible foreign interdiction of seaborne shipments of oil and other needed goods to China. In particular, Chinese strategists worried about such vulnerability of Chinese imports and exports passing through the Indian Ocean and the Strait of Malacca.

The perceived strategic benefits were as follows:

- South China Sea territorial disputes and Chinese intimidation and divisive tactics in dealing with ASEAN and its member states were seen to have led to what some Chinese commentators saw as "negativity" in recent China–Southeast Asian relations. The BRI and other initiatives acted to change the subject in China–Southeast Asian relations in ways that improved Chinese influence and image.
- The Chinese initiatives were seen as an effective way to use China's geographic location and large foreign exchange reserves in crafting policies and practices that offset American efforts to advance US regional influence and standing through the Obama government's rebalance policy and later US strategies in Asia.

While generally emphasizing the positive, the surge of Chinese commentary in the initial years of the new push on Silk Road efforts also contained statements by Chinese officials and commentators showing reservations about the risks involved. (Such comments waned as Xi Jinping became established as a strongman ruler determined to assert Communist Party leadership and discipline throughout official ranks.) There were economic risks and political risks. [53]

The perceived economic risks were as follows:

- Since the more viable investment opportunities in developing countries had already been taken, China would focus often on less secure investment opportunities. Given this reality, some commentators warned against repeating the shortcomings, noted earlier, seen in China's "going out" efforts using Export-Import Bank and China Development Bank funding to seek energy and resources over the previous decade.
- Beijing continued to emphasize that it was a "developing" country with major internal needs. Thus, the "win-win" formula governing Chinese funding abroad usually required assurance that the funding would be paid back in some way. The long-term commitment to infrastructure development in less than secure countries increased the chance for changes and unrest that, as noted above, had destroyed or undercut massive Chinese investments carried out or planned throughout the developing world and even in Europe. Chinese commentary also noted that longer-term investment was more prone to loss due to corruption in such less-than-stable countries. All of the above undercut the likelihood of Chinese outlays being paid back.

The perceived political risks were as follows:

- China's Asian neighbors were seen as wary of coming under China's sway as a result of the closer economic connections called for in the BRI and related plans. Chinese commentators warned Beijing against appearing as Japan did in the late 1980s when Tokyo prompted regional fears as it bought resources and deepened investment using its highly valued currency and other economic advantages.

- China also had a mixed reputation in its support for labor standards, environmental protection, the quality of work, and sustaining large Chinese-built infrastructure projects. Backlash came in African and Latin American countries and was seen in changing attitudes working against China among rulers in Asian countries, including Myanmar, the Philippines, and Sri Lanka.

Many of the above shortcomings received attention in official Chinese commentary during and after the second BRI summit in 2019. As in coverage of the first BRI summit two years earlier, Beijing commentary duly hailed the second BRI summit, featuring participants from more than 150 countries. Following past practice, the 2019 summit served as a forum for political and economic leaders to sell their vision for the initiative's ongoing projects. But this time the Chinese government notably shifted its strongly positive discursive focus since the launch of the Belt and Road Initiative and added room for addressing concerns on such issues as debt encumbrance, corruption, and environmental degradation. Overall, Beijing remained strongly committed to the BRI, with state counselor and foreign minister Wang Yi ending 2019 with a speech lauding the 2019 BRI summit attended by 40 national leaders and 6,000 representatives from 150 countries and 92 international organizations. Bilateral agreements between China and various countries and organizations were the basis for the BRI, and Wang said that 16 countries and international organizations signed such agreements in 2019, bringing the total to 199.[54]

Although Chinese commentary portrayed Chinese objectives as benign, mutually beneficial, and focused on development, as discussed in more detail in subsequent chapters dealing with Chinese relations with individual countries and regional groups, recent in-depth studies and reports by foreign specialists revealed a variety of heretofore ignored or poorly considered Chinese policies and practices. Those policies and practices involved conventional tools of statecraft as well as unconventional ones that China chose to publicly ignore, deny, or otherwise obscure. These tools involved frequent use of corruption, elite capture, and related influence operations to win over leaders to agreements that benefit China and the foreign leaders but not necessarily their countries. These agreements often capitalized on and severely disrupted Western efforts through the Paris Club and other means to assist poor countries with debt management, allowing China to exploit these newly solvent states to take on often unsupportable debt from China.[55]

Beijing applied its economic and other leverage covertly and overtly to win support for its proposed digital Silk Road that secures control of communications in various states by such powerfully state-backed Chinese firms as Huawei and ZTE. Strengthening the latter added to the support these firms supplied for Chinese ambitions to control advanced technologies of the industries of the future. Also, control of data from these countries added to advantages China had in the race for leadership in artificial intelligence. When wedded with China's higher profile in television and news media control in various states, such communications control was seen as of use in PRC efforts to manipulate and influence elite and public opinion in various countries to support China on controversial issues including human rights, demonstrations in Hong Kong, the anti-Muslim crackdown in Xinjiang, and China's expansionism in the South China Sea. Such communications control could also be combined with the widespread sale of Chinese surveillance equipment to many states, providing access to intelligence and other information of concern to Chinese authorities. [56]

Chinese development of ports, airfields, and other infrastructure under the BRI rubric provided the basis for China attaining foreign military access agreements, allowing the deployment of expanding Chinese military power in the South China Sea and the Indian Ocean in particular. Corrupt deals, elite capture, and economic pressure were among the tools China used under the rubric of the BRI to weaken the unity and resolve of international groups, notably the EU and ASEAN, to stand against Chinese policies and practices coming at their expense. Meanwhile, from an American perspective, a clear common implication of China's BRI policies and practices was that they worked against the interests of the United States and many of its allies and partners in the existing international order. China sought to use the BRI to change that order in ways that heightened China's power and weakened that of the United States. [57]

One final motive in Chinese practice under the BRI that received little publicity was unearthed by recent scholarship. It showed that Chinese provincial and lower-level officials used the rubric of the BRI to carry out development projects in their locales that were unable to get government approval until they were rebranded as BRI projects. In many cases these projects had little to do with foreign matters but received their BRI funding nonetheless. An implication of this trend was that China's stated expenditures under the massive initiative included a good deal of such domestic-focused development. [58]

## IMPACT OF US-CHINA "TRADE WAR,"
## HIGH-TECHNOLOGY RIVALRY

The Trump administration's punitive tariffs in reaction to unfair trade practices, massive theft of intellectual property, and other Chinese economic challenges began in 2018 and grew to cover most US imports from China. Beijing reciprocated with tariffs on US imports and other measures that negatively impacted American business with China. Negotiations to ease trade tensions begun in late 2018 moved in fits and starts, leading to a phase one deal in January 2020 that remained to be implemented under very uncertain circumstances notably caused by the COVID-19 pandemic and downward spiral of US-China relations over that and other issues.[59]

The United States accompanied the tariffs with tighter controls on Chinese purchases of US high technology and the companies that make high technology. The government imposed major restrictions on US purchases of equipment and services from China's leading high-technology and communications company Huawei and other such high-technology firms. It led efforts with allies and partners to restrict Chinese purchases of high technology and to restrict the access of Huawei and other such high-technology companies to the markets of allies and partners. A major justification was that Huawei (and other such companies) would comply with Chinese government mandates to secretly share with them sensitive information on foreign countries held by Huawei as a result of its role in the communications infrastructure of those states.[60]

Additional pending US government steps to counter China included export controls that could further hamper Chinese companies' access to high technology from the United States and the many other countries that used US high technology. Efforts to curb widespread Chinese spying and theft to acquire US high technology illegally saw an upsurge in counterespionage efforts targeting China and restrictions on visas for Chinese specialists working in high-technology fields in the United States. In a high-profile case, the United States had Canada arrest the chief financial officer of Huawei, the daughter of the company's founder and leader, in Vancouver for extradition to the United States on charges of illegally subverting sanctions on Iran.[61]

The trade war was only part of the dramatic hardening in American policy toward China during the Trump administration. The US whole-of-government counter to varied Chinese challenges featured a variety of US government efforts targeting adverse Chinese practices over many issues that had long bedeviled the relationship. They involved unfair trade practices, theft of intellectual property, human rights, Taiwan, expansionism in the South China Sea, and the ongoing respective buildups of US and Chinese military forces facing each other along China's rim.

New issues emerged to give a much greater sense of urgency to American efforts to counter Chinese challenges. One was the awareness that China used a variety of covert and unconventional means along with traditional propaganda and lobbying to influence American elite and popular opinion in directions favoring China and to weaken US resolve in countering China. The FBI director was outspoken on the need for a whole-of-society American effort to counter what was seen as nefarious Chinese efforts to beguile American opinion while stealing US industrial and security secrets in seeking to undermine US power and influence perceived as standing in the way of Chinese dominance in Asia and world leadership. The charges were well received in Congress, where conservatives and liberals came together in hearings, letters to the responsible administration leaders, and legislation in calling for a whole-of-government US pushback against China.

An even more important driver in creating a sense of urgency in American efforts to counter China was the shared administration-congressional concern with Chinese efforts to undermine American leadership in the high-technology industries of the future, seeking to overtake the United States and secure a dominant leadership position for China in controlling and directing these fields. The consequences of such dominance were viewed as dire. They not only included America becoming second to and dependent on China economically but American military power, reliant on high technology, becoming second to China and thereby less able to counter China's expansive ambitions for leadership and control in Asia and the world.[62]

As noted earlier in this chapter and in chapter 1, the high-technology fields that received strong attention in the American debate about China included artificial intelligence, 5G communications networks, the Internet of Things, nano- and biotechnology, aviation and space, and electric vehicles. Specialist literature and media investigations assessing whether China or the United States was winning in the race for leadership in such fields often had a hard time supporting judgments on which side was ahead and why. Part of the problem was that important advances in these fields were not yet invented. What did become clear was acute US-China competition to build the next generation of industrial and military power, which was at the heart of the recent US-China rivalry. The so-called Fourth Industrial Revolution saw advanced states headed by the United States and China attempting to exploit emerging high-technology breakthroughs for industrial purposes to promote economic growth and competitiveness.

Each country's defense leaders and organizations were also keenly focused on using high-technology advances for military purposes. Chinese and American military leaders were aware that dual-use high technologies such as artificial intelligence, big-data analytics, robotics, and other advances were often invented and produced in the commercial sector. And they were aware of the rapidity of the emergence and breakthrough of such new technologies. The result in China was a state-directed effort emphasizing a military-civil fusion to absorb advanced technology from the commercial sector and state-directed efforts to purchase companies abroad capable of advancing high-technology defense production.

One key element of this high-technology competition between the United States and China involved technology that has already been invented and developed. It concerned digital network competition. As the ever-growing world need for improved high-speed internet communications advanced, China is often depicted as well ahead of the United States in developing and deploying the next generation of wireless communication, the fifth generation or 5G. China's robust domestic construction of 5G infrastructure was married to plans for the so-called digital Silk Road abroad, encompassing a Chinese effort to export telecommunications equipment and infrastructure, fiber-optic submarine cables, mobile networks, cloud computing systems, electronic commerce, and so-called smart cities. China's strong state-supported and state-directed effort at home and abroad seemed to put US efforts led by competing private companies dealing with issues posed by national and local governments at a disadvantage. China attaining the "first mover" advantage in developing and employing 5G systems also meant that international rules determining how the world regulated the internet would be more heavily influenced by China. Since Chinese party control of key Chinese industries and economic enterprises grew under Xi Jinping, and China's National Intelligence Law was judged to require Chinese companies to cooperate with Chinese government requests for information, the expansion of China's digital communications equipment and infrastructure meant that Chinese digital infrastructure deployed abroad could be used by Chinese authorities for purposes of intelligence, influence operations, and other means advantageous to the state.

American concern over China's 5G development was at the heart of the Trump administration's restrictions targeting Huawei, China's leading company developing and deploying 5G and related technology and infrastructure abroad. The US government worked with considerable success to persuade intelligence officials among US allies of the dangers to security posed by communications equipment provided by Huawei or other Chinese companies. The American effort was less successful in persuading government decision makers in several allied states. These efforts were viewed by some allies and partners as coming late, as Huawei was already involved in their respective communications systems, and purging the Chinese firm would be costly and wasteful. Also, Huawei and related firms provided equipment that Western-aligned competitors, without the strong state support Chinese companies enjoyed, might be unable to provide in an expeditious way. And the Trump government was less than uniform in its opposition to Huawei, notably avoiding blanket restrictions in order to allow rural American communities to proceed with plans to use Huawei telecommunications equipment.[63]

Tempering keen American angst over China's advances in 5G development and deployment were some US specialists who judged that the "first mover" advantage might be exaggerated. Huawei's products were attractive because they were less expensive due to heavy financial support by the Chinese government, but they were viewed as being highly insecure. What was deemed more important by these specialists was that the United States creates secure 5G networks from the start. They advise coordinated and funded US government efforts focused on reliable 5G, along with close cooperation with American allies and partners.[64]

## OUTLOOK: CHALLENGES FACING CHINA'S ECONOMIC LEADERSHIP

The impact of the trade war and related acute rivalry with the United States headed the list of serious economic problems for the Chinese government in the period ahead. The phase one agreement did not deal with many fundamental economic differences. It was quickly overtaken by events with the Trump government hurtling toward the November 2020 election finish line with a platform focused on sharp criticism of Chinese handling of the coronavirus and a host of other US complaints. Economic performance was important for President Trump and his election campaign in 2020, but it was probably even more important for the legitimacy of the Chinese one-party state than it was for the democratically elected US president. Meanwhile, the COVID-19 pandemic placed both world-leading economies in an economic downturn of major proportions.

Among the immediate consequences of the trade war and broader US-China economic competition over the past two years were the following:

- An across-the-board negative impact on China's economy, reducing the growth of Chinese exports to close to zero and depressing exports to the United States in absolute terms.
- Investors at home and abroad slowed investment in China's trade-intensive sectors.
- The trade networks producing manufactured products for export, with China at the center, were shifting away from reliance on China and toward other locales for export to the United States.
- China was stressing more self-reliance and less dependence on the US market, but there was no immediate market available to purchase the output of the existing production chains focused on the United States and its heretofore lucrative market.[65]

Meanwhile, US-led efforts blocked Chinese purchase of and access to high-technology companies in developed countries. They complicated Chinese companies' access to high-technology equipment and curbed Chinese advances in the control of telecommunications in developed countries. US criticisms added to the serious complications facing China's Belt and Road Initiative as heretofore hidden or denied Chinese ambitions for local penetration; influence operations; control of communications, media, and discourse; and military expansion increased broad international wariness of Beijing's intentions.

The above problems came as the growth rate of the Chinese economy continued to gradually decline, as did the workforce. The list of ongoing domestic challenges for the Chinese economy reviewed below involved protracted issues with no easy solution, encumbering Chinese international advances in the years ahead.[66] All the above difficulties were compounded by the impact the coronavirus had on China and its longer-lasting impact on the various countries China relied on for inputs and to purchase Chinese exports.

• *Industrial policy and state-owned enterprises.* China failed to implement the 2013 reforms for a more efficient, more market-oriented economy. It doubled down on industrial policies employing state-owned enterprises and targeted ostensibly private firms to lead state-directed industrial policies at home and abroad. Accounting for about one-third of Chinese industrial production and employing a large part of China's urban workers, SOEs put a heavy strain on China's economy in terms of inefficiency and the need for heavy financial backing by state banks.

• *State-dominated banking sector, excess credit, and growing debt.* China's banking system remained largely dominated by state-owned or state-controlled banks. Banking in China faced several major difficulties because of its financial support of SOEs and its failure to operate more on market-based principles. Results included excessive and wasteful production of unneeded goods and rising debt levels. Relatedly, China's combined household, corporate, and government debt levels rose rapidly over the past decade. Much of the rise in that debt came from the corporate sector, supported by the state banking system. In dollar terms, China's corporate debt rose from $3 trillion in 2006 to $17.8 trillion in 2016 (up $14.8 trillion) and greatly exceeded US corporate debt levels. Such credit growth risked undermining future growth by sharply boosting debt levels, causing overcapacity in many industries, contributing to bubbles (such as in real estate), and reducing productivity by providing preferential treatment to SOEs and other government-supported entities.

• *Rule of law.* The absence of the rule of law in China led to widespread government corruption, financial speculation, and misallocation of investment funds. The Xi Jinping government conducted an unprecedented anticorruption campaign to curb such abuses. The government also reemphasized Communist Party discipline throughout the economic system of China. Nevertheless, it remained commonly held that government "connections," not market forces, were the main determinant of successful firms in China, leading to greater expense and waste in production and other economic enterprises.

- *Growing pollution.* Despite extensive publicity surrounding Xi Jinping as a leader in the fight against climate change and international efforts to create a cleaner environment, the fact remained that the level of pollution in China continued to pose extraordinary problems for Chinese development. The Chinese government often disregarded its own environmental laws in order to promote rapid economic growth. Authoritative foreign reports said that China contributed about 60 percent of the growth in global carbon dioxide ($CO_2$) emissions from 2000 to 2016 and that its emissions would surpass the combined $CO_2$ levels of the United States and EU by 2025. The health costs of China's air pollution in 2015 were said to be $1.4 trillion; as a percentage of GDP, the costs of water pollution and soil degradation were an additional 2.1 percent and 1.1 percent, respectively. Remedial measures were underway, but the problems were enormous. Meanwhile, China became a major global producer and user of clean and renewable energy technology.

- *Aging population.* The number of people aged over sixty was growing fast and could reach 240 million in 2020 and 360 million by 2030. The population share of people aged over sixty could reach 20 percent by 2020 and 27 percent by 2030. With a low birth rate as a result of the long-standing "one child" per family policy and other factors, the working population was declining as the elderly population rose. The Chinese government and the families of the elderly faced challenges trying to meet the costs to the country of expanded spending on health care and elderly services.

Substantial foreign economic challenges facing China in addition to the troubles initiated by the United States include energy security and various environmental and climate change issues treated below.

## Uncertain Energy Security

The need to be on guard to deal with economic vulnerability was very apparent in Chinese leaders' approach to China's fast-growing need for imported raw materials, especially oil. China became the world's largest importer of oil, and it consumed a large share of other international raw materials, including iron ore, copper, aluminum, nickel, and timber. Chinese leaders at times adopted an overtly mercantilist approach to gaining access to oil and gas resources overseas. They showed serious reservations about the international market in these critically important commodities. This led Chinese purchasers of international oil to strive vigorously to diversify sources. In the recent past, China's top suppliers were Saudi Arabia and Iran, but China bought even more oil from a diverse range of suppliers that included Sudan, Russia, and Angola. More recently, Russia had become China's top crude oil supplier, surpassing Saudi Arabia. Meanwhile, government-backed Chinese enterprises sought control of foreign oil fields that were available for purchase and paid a premium for the rights to develop those fields.

China's growing dependence on imported oil and gas, especially Middle East oil, also meant that China depended even more on US forces to secure the sea lines of communication between the Persian Gulf and the Chinese coast. Some Chinese strategists worried that the US Navy might close these channels and try to "strangle" China in the event of conflict over Taiwan or other issues. Despite predictions by some Western commentators and in Chinese government pronouncements about the expanding reach of China's emerging "blue-water" navy, Chinese strategists had few realistic options to counter US power so far from Chinese shores, at least over the next five years. Their longer-term plans were seen to involve a series of ports and other access points useful in securing very exposed lines of shipping from the Persian Gulf to China. The first Chinese military base abroad was begun in Djibouti in 2017. Reports forecast future bases in Pakistan, Cambodia, and elsewhere, while Chinese island building and militarization of outposts in the South China Sea strengthened Chinese control in those shipping lanes.[67]

## Environmental and Climate Change Issues

China for many years remained on the defensive regarding its environmental practices and the consequences on the Chinese and world environment of China's rapid growth. Throughout the 1990s and into the next decade, Chinese leaders worked hard, on the one hand, to avoid being considered an international laggard on environmental practices while, on the other, to avoid environmental obstacles to the rapid development of China's economy. On the positive side, Chinese leaders since the early 1990s took serious steps to deal with worsening environmental conditions in China. Premier Li Peng was particularly instrumental in putting ecology on the political map. Laws were passed on air, water, solid waste, and noise pollution. Enforcement mechanisms were bolstered, and funds for cleanup, inspection, education, and enforcement increased repeatedly in the 1990s.[68] Despite good intentions at the top, Beijing had serious problems, especially compliance and follow-through with funding and implementation of promised programs. Enforcement authority remained weak and fragmented, and penalties were anemic. Local officials tended to judge proposed projects by the number of jobs they created and the revenue they generated rather than by the environmental damage or good they did.[69]

With close to 10 percent annual growth and extensive foreign investment focused on manufacturing, China faced enormous environmental problems at the start of the twenty-first century. Demand for electric power grew rapidly and was met predominantly by coal-fired plants. Automobiles clogged roads in major cities. Air pollution went from bad to worse. Efforts to develop hydropower using dams on China's rivers were controversial, as the projects displaced large numbers of people and had major environmental impacts on people in China and in other countries downstream from the new dams. Serious depletion of water resources in northern China was exacerbated by water pollution, pervasive throughout China.[70]

The Chinese leadership at the time gave more emphasis than its predecessors to the need for sustainable development in China. However, the results more often than not were mixed.[71] As they had done in the past, Chinese officials responsible for environmental protection agreed in 2006 that an investment of 1.5 percent of GDP was required to effectively curb pollution and that an investment of 3 percent of GDP was needed to substantially improve the environment. The Chinese government appeared more serious than in the past about reducing the wasteful use of energy in Chinese production, and significant progress was made in this area during the Eleventh Five-Year Plan (2005–2010) and continued into the next decade. China also continued its stronger emphasis on increasing the importance of renewable energy, notably hydroelectric power, and made gains as a manufacturer and eventually a major user of solar panels and wind turbines.

The nation still lacked a powerful national body that was able to coordinate, monitor, and enforce environmental legislation. The devolution of decision-making authority to local levels often placed environmental stewardship in the hands of officials who were more concerned with economic growth than with the environment. Meanwhile, the capital and will to promote the massive spending necessary to reverse several decades of environmental damage remained enormous.

The international consequences of China's environmental problems were varied and usually negative. Dust storms from eroding land in northern China polluted the atmosphere in Korea and Japan, leading to popular and sometimes official complaints and concerns. Air pollution from China affected locales to the east as far away as the Pacific coast of the United States. Chinese dams on the Mekong River and other Asia rivers originating in Tibet had negative impacts on the livelihood of people in neighboring countries, complicating official relations. Extensive international publicity regarding China's poor environmental record made international opinion less patient with Chinese government explanations that China, as a developing country, should not be held to strict environmental standards. As a result, China's image in world affairs declined.[72]

China avoided the negative international spotlight when the United States refused to agree to the Kyoto Protocol to reduce pollution and other emissions. The US position became the focal point of international criticism, with little attention devoted to China's refusal to agree to binding commitments on greenhouse gas emissions.[73] In response to growing domestic and international pressures for stronger Chinese actions to curb environmental damage, the Chinese government in 2007 and 2008 established senior-level working groups to deal with international pressure that China conform more to growing world efforts to curb the negative effects of climate change. Chinese diplomats and senior officials were in the forefront in bilateral and multilateral meetings in calling attention to China's concerns over climate change. They emphasized that China and other developing countries should not see their growth thwarted by environmental restrictions and that developed countries should bear the initial responsibility for concrete actions to deal with the growing issue. At home, Chinese officials took new measures to curb investment in energy-intensive industries and to improve the poor standard of energy efficiency in Chinese manufacturing.[74]

China was seen in the West as partly responsible for the collapse of the international climate change meeting in Copenhagen in December 2009. Chinese leaders defended their position that Chinese economic development should not be encumbered by binding commitments to reduce greenhouse gases. The energy intensity of Chinese production continued to decline according to goals set by the Chinese government for the Eleventh Five-Year Plan, though China's position as the world's largest emitter of greenhouse gases solidified, with ever larger Chinese emissions. The massive global economic crisis beginning in 2008 distracted attention from broad-gauge international solutions to climate change, reducing the negative spotlight on China's role and responsibility.[75]

China showed strong interest in working with the Obama administration and other developed countries in coming up with international accords that would curb the growth of greenhouse gas emissions without major complications for Chinese economic development. China's stress on greater success in achieving energy efficiency in recent years and its future plans along these lines were nonetheless unlikely to offset projections that China's $CO_2$ emissions in 2035 would be double the amount seen in 2011.[76] Over time, China's stronger interest in domestic energy efficiency and curbing pollution in the country resulted in energy use policies more in line with international climate change ambitions. Notably, Beijing now saw its overall interests better served by putting aside China's past opposition to undertaking domestic economic changes to meet standards proposed at the Copenhagen Climate Change Conference in 2009, and it supported the requirements of the Paris

Climate Change agreement in 2016. With the Trump government decision to withdraw from the Paris agreement, Xi Jinping and Chinese publicists positioned Beijing as the world leader in climate change efforts.[77]

China in 2019 was the top emitter of greenhouse gases, burned more than half of the coal used globally, and was faulted for reemphasizing coal industries at home and exporting coal-fired electricity generation plants abroad under the BRI rubric. Nevertheless, Beijing was also the leading market for solar panels, wind turbines, and electric vehicles, and it manufactured two-thirds of solar cells installed worldwide. China was making significant progress in shifting energy use to renewables and in increasing energy efficiency. China's diplomatic stature in discussions on climate change was high, as the US administration opposed international climate change agreements. China began to develop the world's largest carbon trading scheme, meant to cover 25 percent of global $CO_2$ emissions. China took the side of developing countries in calling on developed countries to do more in line with their greater responsibilities under international climate change agreements. China continued to insist that it was a developing country.[78]

*Chapter Four*

# China, Multilateralism, and International Governance

China's growing involvement with and dependence on the world economy headed the list of reasons explaining China's ever-broadening and deepening involvement with various multilateral organizations. Most notably, scholars and specialists saw remarkable changes and increased Chinese activism in Asian regional multilateral organizations, with China taking a leading role in creating such structures as the China-ASEAN Free Trade Agreement and a regional security body that included Russia and four Central Asian states, known as the Shanghai Cooperation Organization (SCO). The Chinese approach in these endeavors strove to meet the interests of the other participants while ensuring that Chinese interests, including development and stability, were well served. China also participated actively in recent years in loosely structured global groups, notably the G20, involving the world's twenty leading powers, and the BRICS group, involving Brazil, Russia, India, China, and South Africa. China was the driving force in developing the Asian Infrastructure Investment Bank (AIIB) founded in 2016 and having 102 members in late 2019. China's Belt and Road Initiative (BRI) began in 2013 as two separate Chinese initiatives to develop infrastructure and greater connectivity, respectively, with countries connected to China by land and countries connected by sea. Its scope broadened to include most countries. China used the organization to interact with members, notably during summit meetings in China in 2017 and 2019. As noted in chapter 3, the 2019 summit was attended by 40 national leaders and heads of international organizations and more than 6,000 representatives of 150 countries and 92 international organizations.[1]

China's approach to multilateralism changed markedly after China became an active participant in such endeavors on entry into the United Nations in 1971. At one level of analysis, there has been a steady trend since then toward closer Chinese government cooperation with the United Nations and an ever wider range of multilateral organizations and the international norms they supported. The record of Chinese adherence to multilateral guidelines and norms remained mixed, however.[2]

Chinese engagement with international economic organizations was the most active and positive. The reasons seemed obvious: these organizations provided numerous material benefits for China's development, and China's active participation ensured that it played an important role in decisions affecting the world economy on which Chinese development depends. There were some limits on Chinese cooperation with international economic institutions. For example, China did not cooperate closely with international organizations that sought to regulate scarcities in the global oil market. As noted previously, rather than rely fully on the global energy market and international groups that tried to facilitate its smooth operation, China at times pursued an independent approach to ensure that it had the energy it needed for economic growth. China gave little attention to international complaints of rising energy prices and other negative results for the world oil market that resulted, for example, when China purchased foreign oil rights at high prices.[3]

During the first decade of this century, China's more active and positive approach in Asian regional economic, security, and political organizations seemed to reflect a priority of the Chinese government to demonstrate that China's rising power and influence should not be seen by China's neighbors and the region's dominant outside power, the United States, as a danger. China did not want to prompt these states to seek measures to cooperate against the interests of rising Chinese power. China's attentive diplomacy and deference to the interests of its neighbors reassured most of them of Chinese intentions, giving rise to significant improvement in Chinese relations throughout its periphery. The ten Association of Southeast Asian Nations (ASEAN) states, for example, warmly welcomed Chinese engagement, which they saw as generally consistent with the organization's emphasis on managing disputes through protracted consultations and avoiding interference in each other's internal affairs. On the other hand, as seen in later chapters dealing with Taiwan and Japan, the governments there at various times were in the lead among those in Asia who judged that the recent rise of Chinese military power along with China's economic power and positive multilateral diplomacy was inconsistent with China's avowed peaceful intentions toward its neighbors and posed a serious threat to their security and regional stability.

As noted earlier, beginning in 2009 and 2010, China began to show more assertiveness toward its neighbors and the United States regarding regional territorial disputes and other differences. During the transition to the Xi

Jinping government in 2012, Chinese officials and commentary began an approach that persists until now that gave much less emphasis to reassuring neighbors and the United States, with some Chinese officials arguing that China's past accommodating stance had sent "the wrong signal" to neighboring disputants and the United States.[4] China's truculence was accompanied by coercive and intimidating behavior designed to cow its neighbors and other concerned powers, including America. China also manipulated multilateral groups like ASEAN in ways that divided the membership on issues sensitive to China, allowing Chinese interests to prevail at the expense of the unity and effectiveness of the regional group.[5]

Competition between China and the United States for influence among regional countries and for support for the respective preferred regional groups of America and China added to tensions that in the recent past China sought to avoid. The reasoning of Chinese leaders for this significant change of course remains unknown. Many have argued that China's growing economic and military capabilities combined with perceived US weakness and decline during a period of military withdrawal from Iraq and Afghanistan led Chinese decision makers to feel less constrained as Beijing repeatedly applied its newly prominent power to pressure and intimidate weaker neighbors over territorial and various other disputes.[6]

Meanwhile, it was noted earlier that in the case of international regulation of environmental practices, China was reluctant to commit to international norms if they infringed on Chinese efforts to expand economic growth. And the Chinese government's approach to international human rights regimes long focused on engaging in protracted dialogue and cooperation where possible or needed in order to avoid international sanction. China nonetheless consistently avoided significant commitments that impeded its ability to coerce those in China who were seen as challenging the communist administration.[7] China's cooperation with international arms control measures grew steadily over the past two decades, although the Chinese government continued to avoid commitments that impeded Chinese independence in certain areas sensitive to important Chinese interests. Beijing also implemented UN sanctions against North Korea's nuclear weapons development in ways that allowed large-scale smuggling of oil and needed resources, and worked with Russia to preclude sanctions that might result in regime change in Pyongyang.[8]

There were discernible stages in Chinese cooperation with multilateral organizations and international norms. In the 1970s and early 1980s, as China moved slowly toward greater engagement with international and regional multilateral organizations, it kept its involvement with the United Nations at a low level. It joined only a small number of UN agencies. One reason was Maoist suspicion that such international groups were dominated by foreign powers pursuing selfish interests at odds with China's. Another reason was the lack of experience and expertise in the Chinese Foreign Ministry and the overall Chinese government apparatus after the chaos of the Cultural Revolution. Meanwhile, Beijing focused on bilateral relations with the United States and the Soviet Union, endeavoring to position China effectively in the changing and often dangerous Cold War in Asia. Bilateral ties that could be controlled by Chinese elites without outside interference were also the focus of China's dealings with neighboring countries. The multilateral groups that China did join, it joined with little actual cost to its sovereignty and ability to avoid constraints or costly commitments, while the symbolic benefits of membership (prestige, recognition, standing out as a leader for developing world interests, and having a voice in world affairs) were enhanced.[9]

This approach of limited involvement gave way to much greater participation during the late 1980s and the 1990s, a period coinciding with China seeking international outreach to counter isolation imposed by Western powers after the Tiananmen crackdown. China's membership in international organizations nearly doubled between 1984 and 1996 (from twenty-nine to fifty-one), and its membership in international nongovernmental organizations tripled over the same period (from 355 to 1,079). During this period, China also joined all the major intergovernmental organizations within the UN system.[10] China's participation in multilateral arms control treaties was faster than the increase in the number of new treaties themselves: between 1982 and 1996, China's accession to such treaties went from two to twelve.[11]

Having put aside the Maoist practices of the past, Chinese officials gained more experience in international organizations and better perceived the benefits of greater involvement. As China's international stature rose, it appeared necessary to become involved in a wider range of international organizations and activities in order to protect and foster the ever wider range of Chinese foreign policy interests. Indeed, China depended on some of these groups, notably the World Bank, the International Monetary Fund (IMF), and the Asia Development Bank, for important assistance in its economic modernization plans.

As the bipolar Cold War order crumbled, China endeavored to promote a multipolar world where various power centers, including a rising China, would work within the United Nations and other multilateral forums to influence the course of world developments. Greater Chinese involvement in multilateral organizations and groups was also useful in projecting an activist image in Chinese foreign policy following the Tiananmen massacre of 1989, when the United States and other countries were isolating China. At the same time, such involvement reassured neighbors and others concerned with China's rapidly rising economic and military strength that Beijing was prepared to follow the international norms supported by these multilateral groups.

Specialists differed in assessing what this record of greater involvement actually meant for the Chinese government's attitude toward the international norms supported by the multilateral groups. A prevailing view held that Beijing was particularly reluctant to allow such participation to curb its freedom of action regarding key issues of security and sovereignty or to require costly economic or other commitments by China. Its participation involved maneuvering to pursue narrow national interests without great concern for international norms. It meant primarily burnishing China's global image, deflecting international opprobrium, and securing Chinese interests more effectively.[12]

Following the late 1990s, China was more active in its support for and initiation of multilateralism and moved further in adopting cooperative norms, particularly in economic and some security areas. In this period, China actively defended the United Nations and its Security Council as the legitimate locus of international security consultations, intensified its contributions to the ASEAN Regional Forum, joined the WTO, took an active part in the ASEAN Plus Three process, established a China-ASEAN Free Trade Area, promoted multilateral cooperation in the six-member SCO, and worked to ease tensions on the Korean Peninsula through the Chinese-fostered six-party talks. In the current decade, the foreign policy activism of the Xi Jinping government has seen China take significant initiatives like the BRI, the BRICS New Development Bank, the AIIB, and the Free Trade Area of the Asia-Pacific. The moves were in direct competition with initiatives supported by the United States, and they appeared as challenges to US-supported international financial institutions. Apart from these implications for Chinese competition with the United States, the reasons for these more activist stances included the following:

- Chinese leaders became more confident in their progress, economically and diplomatically, since the 1990s and also came to recognize more clearly the benefits—especially in terms of international assistance to deal with its internal problems—of certain multilateral organizations.
- Beijing recognized that its economic and diplomatic success placed it in a more prominent position to operate more actively within regional and world affairs.
- China at the turn of the century seemed compelled by international realities to put aside for a time previous efforts to promote a multipolar world; promoting international multilateralism became a useful fallback position that guarded against US unilateralism contrary to Chinese interests and built international coalitions in favor of a more "democratic" world order that would not be dominated by US leadership.[13]

By this time, the Chinese government appeared to have truly accepted cooperative multilateralism as a means for attaining attractive economic and trading opportunities.[14] A more mixed picture continued to prevail on human rights, environmental, energy, and international security questions, including arms control. While more cooperative in several instances, China remained concerned with defending narrow Chinese sovereign national interests, and it was particularly on guard in the face of possible US-led efforts to constrain Chinese power or compromise Chinese interests.[15] Examples included the following:

- China's strong resistance to US-led efforts to promote greater human rights and democracy through the United Nations and other international bodies
- Chinese reluctance to join international bodies led by developed countries to manage disruptive twists and turns in world energy markets
- Chinese refusal to commit to international environmental regimes that might curb China's economic independence and rapid growth
- China's refusal to join the US-led Proliferation Security Initiative and its reluctance for many years to participate in the US-led Asian regional security dialogue, the Shangri-La Forum
- China's continued weapons development cooperation with key associates, notably Pakistan, despite US and other international criticism that these steps were contrary to arms control commitments made by the Chinese government
- China's use of Asian regional organizations to exclude the United States from the region and to press for the reduction and withdrawal of US forces from around China's periphery in Asia

Greater Chinese activism in international organizations and governance in the post–Cold War period was notably illustrated by the development of China's role in the United Nations and related organizations and the development of China's role in Asian regional organizations. Those developments are reviewed later in this chapter. To protect and foster its ever-growing international economic and other interests in other parts of the world, the Chinese government also became more involved in a variety of organizations in other world regions. Those involvements are treated in later chapters dealing with Chinese relations with different world areas.

## CHINA'S RECENT CHALLENGES TO INTERNATIONAL GOVERNANCE

In the period of China's greater assertiveness in world affairs under strong-man leader Xi Jinping, prominent specialists in China and abroad at first tended to continue to gauge China's approach toward international governance largely on the basis of how well or poorly China conformed to the existing norms of the liberal international order. Beijing was depicted as an important player and stakeholder in many existing governance regimes, seeking to be more active and to contribute more to these organizations. China's reservations about cooperating on issues sensitive to Chinese interests and changes that China sought in some organizations were duly noted, but the overall trend seemed not substantially out of line with the existing order. Thus, foreign assessments went along with Chinese judgments that China's proposed changes in the international order—such as reforming the international system to correct "unjust" arrangements, strengthening the influence of developing countries, expanding the idea of state sovereignty into new areas of state behavior, and buttressing the equality of sovereignty—were adjustments of the existing order, not radical acts of departure or revisionism. Underlining these judgments, China repeatedly reaffirmed its commitment to an open economic system and other long-standing features of the liberal international order while resisting proposed changes regarding issues sensitive to China, such as foreign intervention in other states' internal affairs.

Against this background, Michael Swaine of the Carnegie Endowment for International Peace concluded in 2016 that there was "not much new" in Chinese views of global governance since 2008–2009.[16] The definitive Chinese break at the Nineteenth Chinese Communist Party Congress in 2017 with the low-profile foreign policy advocated by Deng Xiaoping in favor of much greater prominence for China as Asian leader and global power did not initially change assessments of China's approach to global governance. Suisheng Zhao of the University of Denver in 2018 focused on greater Chinese activism in global governance in contrast to the American retreat from past support for the existing world order seen in the Trump administration's pullback from international obligations and involvement in the Trans-Pacific Partnership, the Paris climate change accord, UNESCO, and other world bodies. He advised that Xi Jinping was "taking advantage" of President Trump's retreat from global leadership as the Chinese president vowed to provide China's solutions to global governance. Though foreign media and specialist commentary raised the question of whether Beijing was intent on overhauling the post–World War II order, Professor Zhao judged that China was not ready to step into America's shoes. The judgment was that China embraced the Westphalian principles of state sovereignty and the fundamental norms of the post–World War II order while adapting to the liberal norms of globalization; China was seen as a revisionist stakeholder. It was dissatisfied not with the fundamental rules of the order but with its status in the hierarchy of the order.[17]

Meanwhile, an exhaustive study by the RAND Corporation in 2018 concluded that China on the one hand was ever more supportive of the overall international order while on the other hand it challenged and sought to revise some aspects of the order. Foreshadowing later developments involving direct Chinese attacks against US policies and practices, the RAND study differentiated between Beijing's strong support for what RAND authors called a UN-centric order based on sovereignty and the US-dominated liberal order focused on human rights and US alliance structures. The study saw Beijing as challenging the latter while supporting the former.[18]

Debate over China seeking to change global governance became stronger in 2018 following the publication of Trump administration national strategy documents in late 2017 and early 2018 directly identifying China as a revisionist power posing the greatest danger to American security. The debate prompted Alastair Iain Johnston of Harvard University in 2019 to more systematically assess how revisionist China had become regarding the world order, concluding that "China is not challenging the so-called liberal international order as much as many people think." Like the RAND study, he concluded that China gave strong support to the UN system, and he judged that Beijing provided medium support to existing orders governing international trade and investment and low support to those world systems regarding such political development issues as human rights.[19]

In contrast to the above moderate judgments on China and global governance came a variety of progressive, moderate, and conservative think tank reports and in-depth academic studies over the past three years, often supported by government reports and investigative journalism, that document a wide variety of cases of Chinese practices throughout the world that demonstrate acute challenge to the United States and its allies and partners with an interest in the existing liberal order.[20] They were written by specialists in the United States, Europe, Australia, and other countries around China's periphery that were on the receiving end of the Chinese challenges. They showed Chinese party, government, and military agents working in often disguised and hidden ways that could be and often were denied by Chinese authorities to undermine existing governance policies and practices seen in the way of China fulfilling broadening international ambitions. These efforts were demonstrated to have ever greater support from the Chinese government, allowing for in-depth action across the globe. Overall, the evidence showed that China was not yet ready to call for the overhaul of the international order, but its actions in support of ambitions to change the world order had reached a point where China was actively promoting the China model for international emulation. The findings of these studies are detailed below following a brief review of key aspects of how Chinese officials depicted China and world governance.

## China's Current View of Global Governance

Regarding contemporary Chinese depictions of world governance and China's role, Xi Jinping repeatedly pointed to the changing international balance of power and an array of global challenges as driving the need to reform global governance. As China was seen as ever more powerful and influential, Xi said it needed to make the international order more reasonable and just in order to protect the common interests of China and other developing countries. The Chinese leader duly affirmed the principles of the United Nations Charter and promoted Chinese activism in setting the rules for international involvement in oceans, polar regions, cyberspace, outer space, nuclear security, anticorruption, and climate change. He and his colleagues depicted the Trump administration's practices of "unilateralism" and "protectionism" as the main challenges to the current world order. They argued in favor of the policies and practices seen in the G20 and the East Asia Summit and the China-led Belt and Road Initiative, the China-backed Conference on Interaction and Confidence-Building Measures in Asia (CICA), and the Shanghai Cooperation Organization.[21]

Official Chinese commentary hailed China's leading international role as the largest supplier among UN Security Council members of UN peacekeeping forces; the second-largest contributor to the UN peacekeeping fund and to general UN expenses; and the country with the largest diplomatic network in the world, surpassing the United States for the first time in 2019.[22] Beijing recently parried US government accusations that China sought to change the world order in line with its narrow ambitions with charges that American withdrawal from the 2015 Iran nuclear deal, the Intermediate Nuclear Forces (INF) Treaty, and the UN Human Rights Council undermined the world order, while America's long wars in Southwest Asia and war threats elsewhere were fundamental threats to the international order.[23]

Official Chinese discourse and debate on whether China provided a model for the world to follow has been occasionally active in past years, but the overall result was continuation of China's reluctance to promote its development approach as better than the US-supported liberal order or other approaches. Such diffidence changed against the background of a massive Chinese diplomatic and propaganda effort holding up the BRI and related Chinese economic practices and organizations as favorable to world development. Xi Jinping in 2017 affirmed that China offers a new option for other countries and nations that seek to speed up development and preserve their independence. He backed away from explicitly supporting a China model for export a few weeks later, but more recent Chinese publicity and propaganda organs have been replete with commentary claiming that the world was embracing Xi's vision for development[24] and official reportage citing the view that "China's economic model has been proven to be effective in spurring economic growth and social development . . . and [other countries] should follow the model."[25] Such commentary added to other evidence of various Chinese challenges to the existing global governance model discussed below to demonstrate the extent of Chinese ambitions as an aspiring superpower determined to change a wide range of international norms and regulations seen hampering its ambitions.[26]

## Partnership Diplomacy

An additional dimension of Chinese foreign relations that impacted China's approach to multilateralism and global governance was the long-standing concern to protect China's national sovereignty and avoid multilateral organizations that would entail requirements that would impinge on Chinese sovereignty and freedom of action. And in the past three decades, China emphasized that whatever agreements China makes, it did so applying the "win-win" principle, whereby the agreement would have to represent an overall positive for China's win set, which tended to focus on concrete benefit for China's advancing wealth and power. Against this background, the main activities China undertook, with important international efforts like the BRI or its dealings with the SCO, ASEAN, and others, often focused on bilateral deals or arrangements between China and concerned governments.[27]

As China emphasized bilateral relationships as the most important avenue for China in pursuing changes in global governance and other interests in foreign affairs, Beijing since the end of the Cold War created a multilevel structure with its bilateral relationships that signaled to observers at home and abroad how close and compatible the foreign countries were to China as far as global governance and other issues were concerned. Seen by Chinese experts as an "indispensable component" of the Chinese grand strategy was what was known as China's partnership diplomacy. Beginning in 1993, China established more than one hundred partnerships with foreign governments and several international organizations.[28]

The effort in the 1990s focused on partnerships and links with major powers such as Russia, the United States, Japan, and the EU. Specialists at that time interpreted the effort along with the Chinese government's concurrent emphasis on promoting a "new security concept" in managing world affairs as a way to establish an alternative to the US-based alliance system then dominating international politics after the collapse of the Soviet Union and the end of the Cold War.[29]

As China subsequently rose in power and prominence, Beijing employed the framework of partnerships it was building as a means to offer its strategic reassurance to its counterparts, promising neighbors and other concerned powers long-term and harmonious bilateral relations with mutual economic and other benefits in exchange for more collegial relations with China. The hoped for result was understanding and support for China's interests and aspirations. In the first decade of the twenty-first century, Beijing emphasized China's intent to rise peacefully. Later, under Xi Jinping's leadership, the emphasis focused on creating a "community of common destiny." The policies and practices of creating this community emphasized repeated bilateral consultations through various channels seeking to develop closer ties, greater mutual trust, and an overall environment beneficial to China's advancing power and influence.[30]

On the basis of the degrees of convergence and agreement between China and other countries, Beijing created several labels to distinguish the various grades of partnerships. It created more than twenty of these in China's official lexicon. To newcomers, the categories seemed confusing, but Chinese Foreign Affairs University specialist Shengsong Yue recently clarified the situation and demonstrated how the categories were the result of extensive Chinese official deliberations and reflected clear priorities in Chinese foreign relations.[31]

Thus, the first large category was eighty "strategic partnerships." These were long-term and forward-looking relationships reflecting China's strategic interests. The top-ranking and the closest relationship in this broad category was China's *comprehensive strategic partnership of coordination* with Russia. The next level down of close relationships were the *comprehensive strategic cooperative partnership* and *strategic cooperative partnership* Beijing had with eighteen countries, eleven of which were located around China's periphery, with the seven others located in Africa. These countries were expected to support and work closely with China, moving relations forward in the same direction for mutual benefit.

The next level in order of importance consisted of the *comprehensive strategic partnership*, the *strategic partnership*, and the *strategic cooperative relationship*. There were fifty-two nations and four groups (the EU, ASEAN, the African Union, and the Pacific Islands) in these categories. They ranged from many European countries to some of China's neighbors, countries that were major energy and resource suppliers to China and countries located along China's proposed Silk Road trade, investment, and infrastructure routes. The remaining countries and organizations that were not among the eighty noted above having variations of "strategic partnership" with China were thirty-five having a *comprehensive cooperative partnership*, a *cooperative partnership*, a *friendly cooperative relationship*, or a *traditional friendly relationship* with China.

The importance of partnership diplomacy in Chinese foreign relations was apparent with the large spike in newly created partnerships in 2004 and 2005 (eleven each year) and since the onset of the Xi Jinping government, with a total of forty-four new partnerships and twenty-four upgraded partnerships in its first five years. With the emphasis in the Xi Jinping period on China taking the lead in shaping the international order in line with its desired community of common destiny toward a multilateral and democratic one favoring the majority, China's partnership network expanded vigorously.

Countries signing on to China's Belt and Road Initiative were in the lead in establishing and upgrading strategic partnerships with China.

Of course, the United States remained outside the Chinese strategic partnership network. America and its allies and partners remained committed to an international order seen prevailing after the Cold War that gave priority to their interests and values. China now clearly articulated a view that the US alliance structure was at odds with its ambitions and what Beijing viewed as a preferable international order with greater agency for China and other countries not so closely tied to the United States. China's partnership network was an important element used by China to achieve its goals. Obviously, many allies and partners of the United States also had partnerships with China. Beijing's economic importance topped the list of reasons why. China's economic and other related international importance in competition with the United States added to the significance of China's international partnership network as a tool employed in a gradual process of changing international norms and institutions in ways beneficial to China. The process involved weakening US power and influence at odds with China advancing its own interests.

## BURGEONING ANALYSIS OF CHINESE CHALLENGES TO PREVAILING NORMS: TARGETING AMERICA

As noted above, analysts in the United States and other foreign countries who based their assessments on evidence of Chinese practices as well as on avowed Chinese policies were compelled to adjust their views of Chinese international intentions because of an outpouring of research and analysis over the past three years. This writer is one of those evidence-based analysts who has been compelled to change his analysis in light of the new evidence. That recent research and analysis provided detailed treatment of Chinese practices that severely challenged the existing order heretofore seen as advantageous for and supportive of the United States and its interests.

As seen below, this research and analysis came from various quarters in the United States and abroad. In the United States, some of the think tanks involved had long advocated a tougher policy toward China. The Center for Strategic and Budgetary Assessments, which recently published detailed disclosures of China's hidden and heretofore neglected efforts to influence international politics against America and in favor of China and its authoritarian norms and expansive interests, was arguably in this category of groups critical of China. And the International Republican Institute, with its graphic treatment of often hidden, disguised, or underappreciated Chinese practices undermining existing governance norms, might be seen as following political loyalties in its grim portrayal of Chinese challenges, which is similar to the rhetoric of the current US Republican administration. However, some of the most graphic disclosures of often nefarious and egregious Chinese behavior came from the Center for American Progress, widely viewed as a left-leaning group sharply critical of the Trump administration, and whose founder and current board member John Podesta served in senior positions in the Obama government and directed Hillary Clinton's 2016 election campaign. Concurrently, veteran and other analysts at such politically centrist think tanks as the Council on Foreign Relations, the National Bureau of Asian Research, and the German Marshall Fund weighed in with assessments and disclosures underlining the challenges China poses to the existing order. Meanwhile, the assessments coming from other foreign countries represented a mix of political perspectives that on the whole validated the findings of their American colleagues.

Salient examples of Chinese behavior are listed here and discussed in more detail in relevant sections of this book. In this chapter, they are presented in ways that juxtapose Chinese behavior with China's avowed positions in foreign affairs. The contrast between the two shows duplicity that warrants vigilance and diligence in discerning the actual motives and implications of Chinese foreign behavior.

*China's avowed "noninterference in internal affairs" versus Chinese influence operations and political warfare.* Despite China's decades-long avowal that it does not interfere in other countries' internal affairs, Chinese practices in this broad category interfered in often gross ways in the political, social, and related affairs of targeted countries. They included the following:

- *Mobilization of ethnic Chinese and Chinese students.* These practices involved embassy and consulate officials and other agents recruiting, monitoring, and controlling ethnic Chinese abroad and employing them for purposes in line with Chinese interests. A subset involved efforts to control and influence Chinese students abroad to counter perceived anti-China forces in various countries. The scope of such efforts focused on the many countries with large ethnic Chinese and Chinese student populations. The United States and Australia were notable examples. The efforts became more prominent when developments in the country concerned moved in directions opposed by the Chinese government.
- *Substantial financial and other assistance to key individuals and institutions that were prepared to support China's interests.* This involved large campaign contributions to political parties in some democracies, employment of recently retired or active government or political leaders in paid positions in organizations backed by the Chinese government favoring Chinese interests, and recruitment of local business leaders with high salaries and benefits to work in organizations backed by China to pursue Chinese interests. See examples below involving Italy, Australia, New

Zealand, and Tonga, among many others. Also involved was the use of corrupt practices involving payments and padded contracts to win support for Chinese infrastructure and other projects in line with China's BRI and other efforts. Among the many salient examples here were Cambodia, Malaysia, the Maldives, Ecuador, Kyrgyzstan, and Montenegro. Collectively, these efforts were labeled "elite capture," allowing the Chinese government to use such influential individuals for Chinese purposes.

- *Leveraging trade and investment dependencies to coerce countries to follow China's interests.* Such practices became routine in Chinese statecraft as seen in an illuminating report from the Center for New American Security.[32] A recent episode came when Australia's support for an independent investigation of the origins of the coronavirus in China prompted Chinese cutoff of Australian beef imports.[33] A very costly and ostensibly nongovernment Chinese boycott of South Korean business and tourism came in retaliation to the deployment of the US THAAD antimissile system in South Korea, which Beijing deemed to be against its interests. And Chinese officials warned Germany and other European countries that their large trade interests in China would be seriously impacted if they did not favor the Chinese company Huawei for their telecommunications modernization, despite strenuous opposition from the United States. Meanwhile, Chinese interference increasingly targeted foreign businesses, carrying out or threatening retaliation for the statements or actions deemed offensive to China by the enterprises or their representatives, including large sports groups like the National Basketball Association (NBA).
- Resorting to arrests and detentions of foreigners or dual citizens holding foreign passports in retaliation for actions by foreign governments or in pursuit of foreign-based dissidents. Notable examples included the arrests of Canadians in China on account of Canada's detention of Huawei's chief financial officer for extradition to the United States; reported extralegal abduction and rendition to China of dissidents from Thailand and Hong Kong; and Chinese security agents illegally coming to the United States and other countries to carry out intimidation of anti-China dissidents.
- Chinese interference in foreign elections, involving, among others, Australia, New Zealand, Malaysia, and most recently the United States.[34]
- Large-scale information operations to build support in foreign media, seeking media control in some developing countries (e.g., Kenya) with poor media infrastructures, and establishing greater influence in more developed countries (e.g., Italy).
- Fostering pro-China views in educational institutions such as the Confucius Institutes and the wide-ranging training and educational opportunities provided by the Chinese government and Communist Party.

Recent in-depth analyses have shown the impressive and expanding scope of Chinese overseas united front influence operations carried out by the Chinese Communist Party, its overt International Liaison Department, and various disguised or hidden influence and espionage operations, many under the direction of the United Front Department of the Communist Party, with others directed by the military and China's espionage agencies. These efforts seemed relatively benign in countries closely aligned with China's interests, but they appeared very much focused on interfering in the internal affairs of countries that seem opposed or resistant to Chinese interests.

*"China Committed to Globalization" versus seeking state-directed industrial dominance and other interests.* "China Committed to Globalization" was the *China Daily* headline for Chinese vice premier Han Zheng's message at the Fiftieth World Economic Forum in Davos, Switzerland, in January 2020.[35] In contrast, the reality of Chinese economic practices examined by the Center for American Progress (CAP) and other think tanks showed China's determination to use its economic size and importance to compel acceptance of Chinese practices that eroded existing free-market norms and grossly disadvantaged the United States and many allied and other developed countries.

Examples of egregious Chinese erosion of the economic norms of open and free markets in globalization involved the common practices, highlighted by CAP, of the Chinese government supporting Chinese industrial firms to gain access to US advanced technology through state-backed funding, espionage, required joint ventures, and coerced technology transfers. This step allowed the next steps of developing competing industries in China without permitting US or other foreign competition. These Chinese firms then emerged on the international market with heavily state-subsidized products that wiped out international competition and placed China in the lead of a key new industry.[36]

US industry complaints about such predatory Chinese practices risked losing access to China's market. And even if advanced US industries didn't follow coerced technology transfer demands from China, they still risked cyber theft and human agent espionage. Past authoritative US estimates of the loss of US wealth to Chinese cyber theft and other espionage was several hundreds of billions of dollars annually. By 2015, US businesses were facing a host of new self-serving Chinese market regulations that imposed new barriers that disadvantaged American and other foreign companies. Beijing released the "Made in China 2025" plan, which called for Chinese firms to supplant their foreign competitors in China and in global markets and provided financial and regulatory support to achieve these goals. Beijing also implemented a new cyber security law requiring foreign firms to store data on mainland Chinese servers and hand over proprietary source codes and other trade secrets to pass a national security review process. These requirements exposed US data and intellectual property to misuse and theft. Along these lines, the US trade representative in its report on China in March 2018 laid out a long list of Chinese practices out of line with its WTO commitments at the time of entry in 2001 and at odds with international economic norms, asserting that they represented an "existential threat" to the American economy.[37]

Meanwhile, as in the cases of the above-noted sanctions against South Korea and threats against European businesses, Beijing went well beyond existing economic norms to coerce others to bend to its will on a variety of issues. Adding to this mix were rising Chinese demands that foreign companies, in their activities in their home countries or elsewhere outside China, follow Chinese demands on issues deemed sensitive to the Chinese government. Thus, the Marriott Corporation, other hotel chains, and various airlines in 2018 had to change their treatment of Taiwan to accord with China's view that Taiwan is part of China or risk losing their business in China.[38] That China would be making more demands of this kind under the Xi Jinping government was signaled when the Chinese foreign minister visiting Canada in 2016 scolded a Canadian journalist for asking the Canadian foreign minister about a sensitive human rights issue in China.[39] That retribution very much out of line with economic norms of globalization had become the norm in China's foreign policy became clearer when the coach of the Houston Rockets basketball team voiced support for pro-democracy demonstrators in Hong Kong in 2019. The result was immediate loss of market access to China until the team and the NBA apologized profusely and endeavored to restrict any team member or those attending games in the United States or elsewhere from showing support for the Hong Kong demonstrators.[40]

*"No matter how far China develops, it will never seek hegemony'" versus common Chinese applications of coercion and intimidation to achieve China's advances at others' expense.* The quoted remarks from a Xi Jinping speech[41] in December 2018 are a common refrain, especially when China addresses its neighbors having long experience with past Chinese aggression and coercion and who are fearful that such practices will return as China rises in regional prominence and strength. In these instances of China endeavoring to reassure its neighbors, Beijing often adds that its BRI and other economic ventures are designed to bring China and its neighbors closer together in seeking mutual economic benefit and development. The result reinforces China's efforts to create its desired "community of common destiny."[42]

Unfortunately, the rhetoric and economic interchange was often accompanied by strong applications of force, short of military attack. A recent set of evidence, as noted in chapter 1, was Beijing's hidden hard sticks along with the carrots of the BRI in its unpublicized coercion in 2019 and 2020 of Vietnam, the Philippines, and Malaysia—the Southeast Asian states with holdings and claims in the disputed South China Sea. China's sticks involved chilling private warnings to the first two that contesting Chinese claims would lead to defeat in war, and harassment of the ongoing oil and gas exploitation efforts of Vietnam and Malaysia, notably employing a massive 12,000-ton coast guard warship to harass and intimidate the much smaller vessels used by Vietnam and Malaysia to supply the oil-gas ventures and the foreign firms involved in these ventures. China's goal in the latter effort was to halt and expel foreign ventures from the contested sea, making China the only acceptable partner for the other claimants in pursuing development of the oil and gas resources.[43]

As reviewed in chapter 9, Beijing openly rebuffed international law when it rebuked the International Law of the Sea Tribunal's ruling in July 2016 against China's expansive claims in the South China Sea. It relied on AS-EAN's most China-dependent countries, Cambodia and Laos, to thwart ASEAN statements on the ruling, and it followed with strong coercion that saw none of the ASEAN countries willing to speak in support of or even mention the ruling.

As in the case of using Cambodia and Laos to thwart ASEAN criticism of China, Beijing used diplomatic pressure backed by its strong economic and military power to dissuade ASEAN from policies that China opposed. If practiced by the United States, such action would be viewed by China as "hegemonism." Meanwhile, those Southeast Asian states with increasing security ties with the United States were privately and sometimes publicly warned of adverse consequences. China made it clear that it sought an AS-EAN-China code of conduct regarding the South China Sea that would limit the ability of Southeast Asian nations to call on the US military for support on these matters. If it appeared that Asian hosts of regional meetings were prepared to allow even veiled criticism of China in concluding statements on the results of the meeting, Chinese diplomats put aside diplomatic norms and barged into offices demanding changes in the documents, as happened in Papua New Guinea in 2018 in an episode later labeled "tantrum diplomacy." Such improper behavior was not isolated; it happened with Chinese officials attending the annual Pacific Islands Forum meeting in September 2018.[44] Meanwhile, as seen in chapter 11, Chinese diplomats lobbying in Europe in favor of Huawei in 2019 were resolute in pursuing bullying tactics in seeking their objectives.

In Asia and Europe, China looked to exploit opportunities in ways beyond the pale of normal international governance to drive wedges between the United States and its allies, such as seen in the strong, ostensibly nongovernment retribution against South Korea over the THAAD deployment. And, as reviewed in chapter 11, despite its avowed constructive relationship with the EU, Beijing showed the other side of its Janus-faced policy as it gave top priority in wooing the less advanced Central and Eastern European members of the EU, getting some of the latter to weaken EU efforts sought by leading EU powers to counter offensive Chinese policies.

Taken as a whole, the above evidence supports the judgment of Council of Foreign Relations specialist Elizabeth Economy that China has reached a stage where it is exporting its political and development model as it strives to undermine that of the United States and Western countries. Dr. Economy highlighted various Chinese training programs for foreign practitioners learning the strengths of the Chinese model. The programs came in tandem with Chinese sales of comprehensive surveillance systems that allow Chinese high-technology companies to control the communications of various states while supporting authoritarian leaders abroad with advanced security systems in ways that boosted China's influence and leadership. As discussed below, in dealing with the United Nations, Beijing used its economic importance to the organization and the world to foster UN cooperation with and endorsement of China's BRI and UN support for Chinese definitions and positions on human rights and internet governance. The World Health Organization's strong support of China's handling of the COVID-19 pandemic brought Chinese influence in the United Nations and its various organizations into the middle of the recently acute US-China rivalry. [45]

The above evidence also seemed to validate specialists such as Liza Tobin of the US government who argued that Xi Jinping's promotion of the community of common destiny and what was discerned as the political, security, development, and other elements of the concept showed the wide range of areas where Beijing believed it must restructure global governance to enable China to integrate with the world and attain global leadership. She judged that the implications of Chinese success in such restructuring were grim for the United States and like-minded nations. A global network of partnerships centered on China would replace the US treaty alliances, the international community would regard Beijing's authoritarian governance model as superior to Western electoral democracy, and the world would credit the Communist Party of China for developing a new path to peace, prosperity, and modernity that other countries can follow. [46]

## The United Nations and UN-Related Organizations

After joining the United Nations in 1971, the Chinese government sought to maximize benefits and minimize costs while playing an increasingly prominent role in international governance through the United Nations and related organizations. Chinese economic reforms and international economic outreach saw China in the early 1980s join the World Bank and the IMF. China soon became the largest borrower from the World Bank and worked closely with the IMF in learning techniques and gaining advice important for Chinese economic reforms and development. Combined with loans and assistance from the Asian Development Bank, which China joined in the mid-1980s, and assistance provided by developed countries, China became the largest international recipient of foreign assistance in the 1980s and much of the 1990s. In recent years, China sought a more prominent position in the IMF, consistent with its status as the world's second-largest economy. Frustration with the slow IMF process to grant a more prominent position to China reportedly influenced Beijing to move ahead in 2015 with the AIIB as well as the New Development Bank and a proposed SCO Development Bank.[47]

China relied heavily on its position as a permanent member of the UN Security Council to ensure that its interests were protected regarding the many international issues considered by the council in the post–Cold War period. This was especially important as the United Nations changed its approach to international affairs. During the Cold War, the council tended to emphasize the articles of the UN Charter that supported a state-based system of order. This met with the preferences of the Chinese government, which took positions against allowing interference in its own and other nations' internal affairs. This emphasis gave way to greater concern in the United Nations with individual justice, a developing norm of humanitarian intervention, and a focus on the promotion of democracy—tendencies that often were seen as potentially or actually problematic by Chinese authorities, who remained concerned that such intervention could at some point be directed at China or Chinese interests abroad.[48]

Specific changes seen in UN policies and practices after the Cold War that had important and sometimes negative implications for Chinese interests included the following:

- The veto was rarely used, and resort to its use was likely to be regarded as a breach of a developing informal norm of nonuse.
- There was an increase in the scope and number of peacekeeping operations, many of which cited humanitarian motives as part of the reason for intervention; these should more accurately be described as peace-building operations, to be used predominantly in internal conflicts, with mandates that can include the holding of elections, refugee assistance, human rights protection, and economic reconstruction.
- Secretaries-general, especially Kofi Annan (1997–2006), promoted the idea of humanitarian intervention and the priority of individual sovereignty over state sovereignty. The UN secretary-general gave increased attention to human rights. In 1993, the United Nations appointed a high commissioner for human rights. The UN Security Council also created international criminal tribunals to try those indicted for war crimes.
- UN-related institutions such as the IMF and World Bank became more intrusive and extended their reach into the policy-making realm of domes-

tic societies. The performance criteria on which loans were conditioned increased severalfold after the 1980s, and ideas of good governance were promoted.

• The numbers of nongovernmental organizations vastly increased in the post–Cold War period and received better access to and more information from bodies such as the IMF, the World Bank, the Human Rights Committee, the Committee against Torture, and other UN-related bodies that tended to intervene in states' internal affairs.[49]

China's position as one of the five permanent members of the UN Security Council helped ensure that the United States and other powers could not continue to shun China as a result of the Tiananmen crackdown or for other reasons if they expected Chinese cooperation, or at least acquiescence, with their initiatives before the Security Council. Thus, despite past close Chinese association with the notorious Khmer Rouge in Cambodia, Western powers sought Chinese involvement and assistance in coming up with a 1991 peace plan for Cambodia that was backed by the five permanent members of the UN Security Council. The United States and other Western governments tended to mute their criticism of Chinese human rights and other policies at the time of the international confrontation with Iraq following Baghdad's invasion of Kuwait in August 1990. Seeking UN Security Council endorsement for the use of force against Iraq made Washington and other Western capitals more sensitive to China's possible use of its veto power in the Security Council.

Beijing's general practice in this post–Cold War period was to go along with whatever broad international consensus prevailed on particular issues being considered by the United Nations. Chinese representatives especially wished to avoid choosing sides on sensitive issues dividing the developing countries of what was called the Third World, and they generally kept a low profile on those issues. Beijing also was less inclined than in the past to join the Third World bandwagon against such isolated states as Israel, especially following the normalization of Sino-Israeli diplomatic relations in 1992. Beijing in the 1990s and, to a somewhat lesser degree, in the first decade of the twenty-first century did line up with anti-US forces on issues where the United States was isolated—such as the US effort to use military force against Iraq in 1997–1998 because of its failure to comply with UN mandates. In these cases, Chinese diplomats usually positioned themselves behind other powers and rarely took the lead in attacking the United States. China followed a similar practice in the lead-up to the US-led military attack on Saddam Hussein's regime in 2003, standing in the UN Security Council a step or two behind Russian and French diplomats who led the criticism of the US-led military operation. In the past decade, China came to regret not standing against Western powers seeking military intervention in Libya in

2011, and it subsequently joined with Russia in blocking UN endorsement of such intervention in Syria.[50]

China's general opposition to international sanctions and other such pressure to coerce governments to conform to UN-supported norms remained a feature of Chinese diplomacy up to the present, even though China sometimes bent its resistance in cases where strident opposition would isolate it or hurt other significant Chinese interests. In the case of US- and European-led efforts since 2005 to pressure Iran to halt nuclear programs seen as promoting a nuclear weapons program, China worked closely with Russia to seek compromises and procedures that would avoid imposition of significant sanctions on a country that was an important energy supplier for China and a key Chinese political partner in the Middle East. China also held out against firm US and other pressure in the United Nations for stronger UN-backed sanctions against the egregious human rights violations fostered by the Sudan government's practices in a civil conflict that claimed many thousands of lives and displaced millions. China endeavored to muster support from authoritarian and other governments that would be sufficient to head off binding sanctions that would seriously complicate China's intense interest in oil from the African nation. China also used its influence with considerable success to muster sufficient international support to prevent or moderate proposals for strong UN actions involving international sanctions being imposed on North Korea, Myanmar (Burma), and Zimbabwe for their illegal and repressive policies.[51]

On the other hand, China actively participated in a variety of UN peacekeeping operations designed to support UN-backed administrations against often strong and violent opponents. China did not obstruct international tribunals investigating crimes of former leaders in Serbia and Rwanda. It seemed to oppose an international tribunal to investigate war crimes of the Chinese-backed Khmer Rouge regime in Cambodia, but did so discreetly, supporting the current Cambodian government as it delayed for years the start of the tribunal. As illustrated in the cases of the UN-backed intervention against Iraq for its invasion of Kuwait in 1990 and the US-led military intervention into Iraq in 2003, China opposed the actions with varying degrees of intensity but was reluctant to take a strong stand of opposition that would jeopardize important interests in China's relations with the United States and other powers.[52]

Exceptions to China's low-risk strategy in the United Nations often centered on Taiwan. Chinese foreign policy gave top priority to blocking Taiwan from gaining entry into the United Nations or UN-affiliated organizations. To battle against efforts by Taiwan's diplomatic allies seeking to raise the issue of Taiwan's representation in the United Nations, Beijing in January 1997 used its veto power for the first time in twenty-five years. It did so to block approval for UN peacekeepers in Guatemala until Guatemala agreed to reduce its support for Taiwan's efforts to gain UN entry. In 1999, China repeated the pattern by blocking the continuation of UN peacekeeping operations in Macedonia, which had recently established diplomatic relations with Taiwan.

Chinese authorities were seen to have mishandled the initial months of the SARS epidemic in China in 2002–2003, leading to the spread of the disease to Taiwan and other neighboring areas. Senior Chinese leaders subsequently adopted more effective policies and endeavored to change policy in directions favored by Chinese neighbors. However, they remained uncompromising in the face of Taiwan's efforts to gain entry as an observer to the World Health Organization (WHO), a UN-affiliated body directing the international effort against the epidemic. Beijing continued its tough stance against Taiwanese representation or participation in WHO efforts to deal with the avian flu epidemic that was seriously affecting China and neighboring countries in 2005–2006. The coming to power in 2008 of a moderate Taiwan government intent on improving relations with China eased to some degree Taiwan-China competition involving the United Nations and affiliated organizations.[53] The election of a new Taiwanese government with a firm stand against China's demands in 2016 led Beijing to resume efforts to exclude Taiwan from dealing with the World Health Organization and the World Health Assembly, even though the pandemic COVID-19 in 2020 was seen by the US government and others as warranting Taiwan's participation.[54]

The importance of the United Nations and related organizations in Chinese foreign policy in the post–Cold War period failed to hide China's reluctance in these bodies to undertake costly commitments or substantial risks. China's behavior seemed to reinforce its image in the United States and among Western powers as a "free rider" or at least a "cheap rider" in undertaking costs and commitments for common regional and global goods. China remained strongly wedded to its "win-win" approach in international relations. If China was going to extend effort and resources for a common good, it generally had to be shown that such actions resulted in tangible benefits for China defined in a fairly narrow Chinese win set. For example, China repeatedly publicized its role as the largest participant among the permanent members of the UN Security Council in UN peacekeeping efforts. It rarely pointed out that its contributions until very recently were as noncombatants, and thus generally its personnel were positioned out of harm's way. It avoided highlighting the fact that Chinese participants, like those from Bangladesh and other large contributors of UN peacekeepers, were paid from the UN peacekeeping budget. And China rarely noted the size of its peacekeeping budget contribution, which rose from a very low base and for many years was at the same low level as that of Italy.[55]

Meanwhile, though China strongly supported the United Nations as the ultimate arbiter of international issues, it remained reluctant to see its allotment to the UN budget rise from a remarkably low level, which for many years was about the same as that of Spain. In 2012, the Chinese Institute of International Studies (an institute associated with China's Foreign Ministry) reported that China agreed to a "hefty" increase of its UN dues, from the previous level providing 3.19 percent of the UN budget to a level providing 5.15 percent. The new level was said to "overtake Canada and Italy" and to make China the sixth-largest contributor to the UN budget. Reflecting the kind of rhetoric used by China to minimize costs in the UN and other international bodies, the report emphasized China's status as a "developing country" that should receive "the preferential policy rate intended for 'low per-capita countries.'" Thus, the report stressed that the increase in China's payment to the UN represented "a heavy burden." For comparison purposes, the US dues at that time amounted to 22 percent of the UN budget, and Japan's dues amounted to 10.8 percent.[56] Subsequently, China's funding for UN peacekeeping in the 2013–2015 period rose to a level (6.64 percent of the overall budget) approaching the level of Great Britain; this level was far behind Japan (10.83 percent) and very far behind the United States (28.38 percent).[57]

In 2015, Xi Jinping led a major change in China's approach to the United Nations, UN peacekeeping and funding for peacekeeping, and other UN programs. In his first address to the UN General Assembly and an earlier speech at the UN Sustainable Development Summit in September, Xi made clear China's intention to work with other governments to alleviate global poverty. Generous pledges were made: US$2 billion for an investment fund to help poorer nations meet goals, with the objective to give $12 billion by 2030; debt relief for the least developed and smaller nations; a $1 billion donation over a decade for a UN peace and development fund; eight thousand peacekeepers for the new standby peacekeeping force; and $100 million in military support for the African Union (AU) for peacekeeping missions over the next five years. Making the world a better place for all was the stated aim as Beijing focused on widely publicized support for the United Nations to lay to rest international claims that China was not doing enough to support its great-power status. At that time, China was one of the biggest contributors to international peacekeeping efforts; with a total of 3,079 troops and police deployed, it ranked ninth among 124 countries. It continued to play an important role in antipiracy operations along shipping routes in the Indian Ocean.[58]

China's support for UN peacekeeping and its dues supporting the UN regular budget rose markedly. It became the second-largest funder of UN peacekeeping, providing 15 percent of the budget by 2021. In 2019, China had 2,534 military and police peacekeepers in seven of the fourteen ongoing

UN peacekeeping operations, ranking eleventh among the 122 contributors to UN peacekeeping and the largest contributor of peacekeepers among the five permanent UN Security Council members. Since first dispatching UN peacekeepers in 1990, China has sent about forty thousand peacekeepers to twenty-four UN-commanded peacekeeping operations and special political missions in Africa, the Middle East, Southern Europe, Southeast Asia, and Latin America. Chinese participation in UN peacekeeping began to include combat forces with deployments in South Sudan and Mali starting ten years ago.[59]

China also became the second-largest funder of the UN regular budget, which was substantially less than the UN peacekeeping budget, paying 12 percent of the annual budget in 2019. The United States provided more than 20 percent of payments for both UN budgets, but in the three years of the Trump administration, the United States pared back funding, withdrew from key UN bodies, and failed to make overdue payments.[60] For its part, China used its reliable funding and strong support for UN programs and its world-wide economic clout, notably as a major financier for infrastructure and other development in poorer countries through the Belt and Road Initiative and other efforts, to exert greater influence and control in the United Nations. Meanwhile, widespread corrupt practices associated with Chinese-foreign deals conducted under the rubric of the BRI seemed evident in a scandal in 2015 involving large financial payments to senior UN officials by a Chinese developer seeking to build a UN center in China.[61]

The UN secretary-general fully endorsed China's BRI at the two BRI summits held in China in 2017 and 2019. The BRI and other broad foreign policy goals were endorsed in UN documents and pronouncements. The previous UN emphasis on approaches to human rights and international inter-vention for humanitarian reasons favored by the United States seemed to fade as China had success in using UN deliberations to foster its view of human rights and state sovereignty in support of its interests and those of other authoritarian regimes. Beijing notably succeeded in curbing critical discus-sion of China's mass detention of a million Muslims in a crackdown on dissent in Xinjiang and in obtaining recognition for China's claim that its policies in the area were based on opposing terrorism.[62]

China's effective work within the various UN organizations saw Beijing select Chinese officials to direct four of the fifteen UN specialized agen-cies.[63] No other country had two or more such positions, with France, Great Britain, and the United States each leading one. A face-off of Chinese and US lobbying in support of competing candidates for the UN Food and Agri-culture Administration in October 2019 resulted in an overwhelming victory for the Chinese candidate, reportedly showing how far US influence relative to rising China had declined in the United Nations. The results reinforced China's avowed intent seen in official commentary to use the UN's authority in promoting China's favored multilateralism and to oppose "the unilateralism practiced by some Western powers."[64]

## China and Asian Regional Organizations

The end of the Cold War and the impact of economic globalization led to a much more fluid dynamic among Asian governments and governments like that of the United States that had a strong interest in Asia.[65] One salient development was the growth of a variety of regional multilateral organizations to deal with economic, political, and security matters. Some of these bodies, like the ASEAN Plus Three (ten ASEAN members plus China, Japan, and South Korea) and the SCO (made up of Russia, China, Kazakhstan, Kyrgyzstan, Tajikistan, and Uzbekistan), deliberately excluded non-Asian powers like the United States. Others, like the Asia-Pacific Economic Cooperation, the ASEAN Regional Forum, and the East Asia Summit, included a wide range of countries strongly involved with Asian affairs. China played an active role in all these bodies.

China often took initiatives in working with ASEAN and fostering such regional groups as the SCO and the six-party talks. During the previous decade, its approach seemed accommodating to neighboring powers, with the notable exception of Taiwan and Japan. As noted earlier, this pattern changed with advancing Chinese economic, military, and political capabilities that enabled Beijing to pursue a more assertive and coercive stance in advancing Chinese territorial ambitions and other interests at the expense of neighbors and the United States. Against this background, the Xi Jinping government launched the China-backed Belt and Road Initiative, the Asian Infrastructure Investment Bank, and a range of other regional economic plans well crafted to benefit China's economic advancement and spread Chinese influence at odds with competitors in the United States and Japan.

Although ASEAN members suffered as a result of the Asian economic crisis of 1997–1998, its organization of ten governments provided the basis for many of the Asian regional groupings. Members of ASEAN had been working together since the late 1960s and had established some basic norms that facilitated cooperation. The members were at least outwardly more cooperative and accommodating than the more powerful governments of northeastern Asia—China, Japan, South Korea, and North Korea. The latter remained at odds over serious historical, territorial, and strategic disputes and rivalries, resulting in ASEAN providing the lowest common denominator for many Asian regional organizations.

At the turn of the century, China took the lead among Asian and other powers in establishing new frameworks of cooperation with ASEAN.[66] China's proposal for a China-ASEAN Free Trade Agreement set the pace for other powers to follow with their economic proposals for ASEAN. China became the first major power to sign the ASEAN Treaty of Amity and Cooperation, prompting many other powers to follow suit. China's trade relations with ASEAN grew faster than those of other powers, and it became ASEAN's leading trading partner and a major destination for ASEAN's foreign investment. China supported Malaysia's hosting of an inaugural East Asia Summit in December 2005. Malaysia and China initially favored a grouping based on the ASEAN Plus Three membership but bowed to pressures from Japan, Indonesia, and Singapore that membership be broadened to include India, Australia, New Zealand, and probably Russia, with the door remaining open to possible US participation, which began in 2010.

In more recent years, China was less likely to defer to those in ASEAN disagreeing with China on sensitive territorial and other issues; it was more likely than not to pressure and manipulate ASEAN leaders on such matters. The rivalry between China and the United States grew as Beijing maneuvered in response to the Obama administration's so-called rebalance policy begun in 2011. The US government now gave unprecedented attention to ASEAN and its member states, endeavoring to strengthen their independence and national capacities in line with American interests in fostering an order in Asia where the United States would play a leading role, and dominance by an opposing power, notably China, would be avoided. The American government was reacting to a variety of Chinese acts of assertiveness since the start of the Obama government in 2009, such as pursuing far-reaching territorial claims in the South China Sea and increased pressures on the United States regarding Taiwan, Tibet, economic issues, and other sensitive concerns.[67]

Beijing reacted to the rebalance by upping the ante in its competition with the United States. Part of its efforts involved manipulating ASEAN to ensure that the organization would avoid siding against China and with the United States on South China Sea issues. It did so notably by persuading Cambodia, increasingly dependent on China economically and diplomatically, to squelch criticism in ASEAN of China's expansionism in the South China Sea. The Chinese expansionism resulted in 2013 in Beijing's massive island building in disputed South China Sea features, rapidly creating islands with landing strips and other facilities for military use and giving China power dominance over the vast ocean area. Though Southeast Asian claimants, notably the Philippines and Vietnam, complained and sought US support, ASEAN remained impotent, hampered by Cambodia's pro-China stance and increasingly fearful of harsh Chinese retribution in response to challenges to Beijing's claims and supporting actions.

In northern Asia, the SCO was founded in 2001, based on an organization known as the Shanghai Five, which was established in 1994 with a membership including all present SCO members except Uzbekistan. China was a major financial supporter of the group and provided its headquarters in China. The group developed slowly; it endeavored at first to build mutual trust among members and to ease any concerns about military deployments and border issues. Concern with transnational terrorism was also a priority of the SCO members, which rose with the September 11, 2001, attack on America and the subsequent US-led war against the terrorist-harboring Taliban regime in Afghanistan. For a time, most SCO members cooperated closely with the US-led military effort, but China remained wary of the US military presence along its periphery. In 2005, a pro-democracy uprising in Kyrgyzstan was successful in changing the government, while demonstrations for political change in Uzbekistan were put down harshly by the authoritarian regime. China and Russia backed Uzbekistan's subsequent demands that US forces leave the country, and the SCO in mid-2005 said that Western military forces should set a deadline for departing the region.

China and Russia remained determined that the SCO would not allow US membership, though nearby states were given observer status. Under the auspices of the SCO, China and Russia in August 2005 conducted a major military exercise near the Chinese coast that seemed to have little to do with long-standing SCO concerns with border security and combating terrorism and transnational crime. The large show of force involving long-range Russian bombers and thousands of Chinese troops seemed designed to send a strong signal to the United States, Japan, and Taiwan about Chinese and Russian military preparedness and resolve.[68]

China and Russia became less concerned with the United States as the American-led forces in Afghanistan withdrew and bases for these forces were closed in Central Asia. The two powers appeared to have competing interests in Central Asia, especially as China announced its Silk Road development plans beginning in 2013 that provided the foundation for the massive BRI of later years. Russia had little to counter the ever stronger economic expansion of China into an area of keen strategic importance to Moscow. Nevertheless, Russian president Vladimir Putin and Chinese president Xi Jinping managed such differences effectively as they gave higher priority in cooperating ever more closely with one another in pursuit of interests at the expense of the United States in their respective spheres of influence—China in Asia and Russia in Europe and the Middle East. Facing US-led sanctions in reaction to Russian aggression against Ukraine and the annexation of Crimea, Putin needed and received Xi Jinping's diplomatic and economic support. During the Obama years, the powers converged in taking advantage of perceived weakness in US and other Western responses to Russian and Chinese expansionism in their respective spheres of influence. The Trump government's tough national security strategies saw a pause in their expansionism, but closer cooperation in military and economic relations continued. In this context, the SCO was of lower importance. Beijing seemed displeased with Russian support for India's joining the group in 2017, but that came with China's close ally Pakistan also joining. America was kept away, and the discourse in the SCO continued with criticism of US policies.[69]

China played a key role in the now long moribund six-party talks (including North and South Korea, the United States, China, Japan, and Russia) that began in 2003 and ended in 2009 to deal with North Korea's nuclear weapons development. Although not a formal multilateral organization, the talks held out the potential for development of a regional organization in northeastern Asia, if and when the various issues raised by the North Korean nuclear issue moved toward an acceptable resolution.

As discussed in chapter 8, reacting to the Trump administration's dramatic application of pressure on North Korea to halt nuclear weapons development in 2017 and concurrent US administration pressure on China to more rigorously enforce UN-mandated sanctions against North Korea, China and Russia called for revived six-party talks. Beijing and Moscow subsequently countered the US pressure by advocating a more moderate step-by-step escalation of tensions more in line with North Korean interests. North Korean summitry involving South Korea, China, and the United States in 2018 showed that the four powers were now the key actors in determining Korean stability, overshadowing interest in reviving six-party talks.

*Chapter Five*

# Chinese National Security Policies

## CHINA'S NATIONAL SECURITY CONCERNS AND MILITARY ACTIONS

During the first decade of the twenty-first century, there was an apparent disconnect between China's avowed national development and foreign policies and China's national security policy. As discussed earlier, Chinese officials for many years articulated a relatively clear national development policy and related foreign policy. That Chinese approach was laid out authoritatively in the December 2005 Chinese government document "China's Peaceful Development Road" and was repeated in similar documents for several more years. This approach was consistent with the thrust of Chinese leadership pronouncements since the turn of the century, emphasizing Chinese leaders' determination to pursue a long-lasting foreign policy to reassure neighbors and the United States, avoid trouble abroad, and seek international cooperation and a harmonious world order as China developed and rose peacefully in importance in Asian and world affairs in the twenty-first century.[1] The approach was welcomed in the United States and among China's neighbors, with many observers seeing it as providing a lasting basis of closer mutual cooperation with China. As it turned out, such reassurances faded with the greater assertiveness in China's approach to foreign affairs beginning notably with the US and Western decline seen in the global economic crisis of 2008–2009 and culminating in Xi Jinping's dramatic advances in regional and global leadership, overtaking Deng Xiaoping's longstanding injunction on China keeping a low profile in foreign affairs.

## Military Modernization, Peaceful Development, and the United States

Skeptical Western observers who were concerned that the Chinese foreign policy reassurances of 2005 and later were tactical and could reverse with changing circumstances noted at that time the disconnect between China's national development and foreign policies and China's national security policies. In particular, the December 2005 document and the follow-on documents and statements made little or no reference to military conflict, the role of the rapidly modernizing People's Liberation Army (PLA), and other key national security questions. When asked about this, one senior Chinese Foreign Ministry official said in May 2006 that China's national security policy was less clearly developed than China's national development policy.[2] In fact, however, the broad outlines of Chinese national security policy were and have remained fairly clearly laid out in official Chinese documents and briefings.[3] They—and the remarkable recent advances in China's military modernization in the post–Cold War period—were in the lead among Chinese statements and behavior that called into question just how peaceful and cooperative China's approach to Asia and the world would actually be.

Chinese national security pronouncements and military advances and operations highlighted a broad range of international concerns and obstacles centered heavily on the United States that needed to be overcome in China's quest for national reunification and an international order compatible with Chinese interests. Authoritative Chinese white papers on military modernization and strategy made clear that China's peaceful development strategy was far from uniformly implemented and did not represent the sum and substance of China's international approach. In fact, as we have seen in recent years, China's avowed peaceful development strategy was accompanied by a range of statements and actions showing a significantly more muscular Chinese foreign policy, developing to a high point under Xi Jinping.

During the administration of Xi Jinping's predecessor, Communist Party general secretary and state president Hu Jintao (2002–2012), there were obvious contrasts and contradictions in Chinese official pronouncements and actions dealing with trends in international security. On the one hand, authoritative Chinese foreign policy pronouncements emphasized China's view of an emerging harmonious world order in which China was rising peacefully in national strength and international influence. China often was seen as occupying its most influential position in world affairs in the modern era. In contrast, white papers on national security,[4] public presentations by authoritative Chinese military representatives, and the continuation of an impressive buildup and modernization of the Chinese military forces in those years revealed Chinese leadership's ardent concern about China's security in the prevailing regional and international order. This concern continued despite twenty years of double-digit percentage increases in China's defense budgets and despite the view of many foreign specialists that China was becoming Asia's undisputed leading military power and an increasingly serious concern to American security planners as they sought to preserve stability and US leadership in Asia.[5]

By the early twenty-first century, Chinese military modernization programs had reached the point where they strongly suggested that the objective of the Chinese leadership was to build Asia's most powerful defense force.[6] China's military growth complicated China's relations with the United States and some Asian neighbors, notably Taiwan, Japan, India, Vietnam, and South Korea. Leaders from the United States and some Asian countries were not persuaded by the Chinese leadership's pledges to pursue the road of peace and development. They saw Chinese national security policies and programs as real or potential threats to their security interests.[7]

Chinese national security pronouncements duly acknowledged that with the end of the Cold War, the danger of global war—a staple in Chinese warning statements in the 1970s and 1980s—had ended. However, Chinese national security statements rarely highlighted the fact that Chinese defense policy was being formulated in an environment that was less threatening to China than at any time in the past two hundred years. Typically, in the 2010 white paper on national defense, the international system was represented as stable, but "international strategic competition" was "intensifying," "security threats" were "increasingly" volatile, and world peace was "elusive."[8] The critical Chinese response to the Obama government's emphasis beginning in 2011 on military as well as economic and political reengagement with Asia under the rubric of the US policy of rebalance in the Asia-Pacific region reflected sometimes thinly disguised and sometimes forthright Chinese suspicion of a revival of American efforts to constrain and contain China's spreading influence.[9] The advent of the Trump administration and its 2017 National Security Strategy and 2018 National Defense Strategy viewing China as the top foreign danger to the United States prompted China's National Defense White Paper of July 24, 2019, to focus on the dramatic rise of military and broader strategic competition between the top two world powers.[10]

PLA pronouncements and Western scholarship had long made clear that the United States remained at the center of the national security concerns of Chinese leaders.[11] The 2004 white paper presented a widening military imbalance of grave concern to China caused by US military technological advances and doctrinal changes referred to as the "World Wide Revolution in Military Affairs" (RMA). Authoritative PLA briefings in 2008 presented growing US military power as the most serious complication for China's international interests, China's main security concern in the Asian region, and the key military force behind Chinese security concerns over Taiwan,

Japan, and other neighbors. Explaining China's concerns in the Asia-Pacific region, the 2010 white paper warned that "the United States is reinforcing its regional military alliances, and increasing its involvement in regional security affairs." The 2019 white paper said the United States "has provoked and intensified competition among major countries, significantly increased its defense expenditure, pushed for additional capacity in nuclear, outer space, cyber and missile defense, and undermined global strategic stability."[12]

Chinese statements and the PLA buildup opposite Taiwan underlined Taiwan as the most likely area of US-China military conflict. And the United States and its military allies continued to be seen as the principal sources of potential regional instability in Asia. China responded harshly to indications of closer US-Japanese strategic cooperation over Taiwan, notably a statement supporting a peaceful resolution of the Taiwan issue that was released following the US-Japan Security Consultative Committee meeting in February 2005. The Trump administration's broad-ranging improvements in American government relations with Taiwan, including sales of advanced fighter aircraft, publicized US naval and air force passages through the Taiwan Strait, and White House meetings with high-level Taiwan leaders, prompted repeated warnings of strong Chinese opposition.[13]

PLA and other Chinese officials registered strong determination to protect Chinese territory and territorial claims, including areas having strategic resources such as oil and gas. As Chinese-Japanese and other territorial conflicts involving energy resources in the East and South China Seas grew in scope and intensity, they intruded ever more directly on these PLA priorities. The Chinese Foreign Ministry claimed that US secretary of state Hillary Clinton's intervention in disputes about the South China Sea at the ASEAN Regional Forum meeting in Hanoi in July 2010 represented an "attack on China."[14] The United States was routinely portrayed as the main obstacle in China's pursuit of greater control in the South and East China Seas. Chinese concerns increased over US and allied forces controlling sea lines of communication, which were essential for increasing oil and liquefied natural gas flows to China. The Chinese government appeared uncertain as to how serious was the strategic danger posed by the vulnerability of China's energy flows from the Middle East and Africa through the Malacca Strait and other choke points in Southeast Asia and what should be done about it. Chinese national security officials openly debated these issues.[15] The Chinese government pursued solutions including overland oil and gas pipelines that would bypass the Malacca Strait, and a steady buildup of Chinese naval capabilities, including the development of Chinese aircraft carriers, that would provide more military power to protect Chinese trade, energy flows, and other maritime communications. In 2017, China established its first overseas base for military operations in Djibouti, a strategically located country highly dependent on Chinese loans for infrastructure and development.

Foreign assessments said future Chinese bases were likely in locations along Chinese shipping lanes in other states highly dependent on China, notably Pakistan and Cambodia. [16]

Given the record of US policies and behavior regarding China and Chinese interests, the concern Chinese leaders demonstrated over the strategic intentions of the United States regarding China and its interests in Taiwan, Japan, Asia, and world affairs seemed warranted. The George W. Bush administration worked more closely with Taiwan's government in efforts to support Taiwan's defense against China than any US administration up to that time since the break in official US relations with Taiwan in 1979. It also worked more closely in defense collaboration with Japan, which focused on Taiwan and other possible contingencies regarding China, than at any time since the normalization of US and Japanese relations with China in the 1970s. Policy statements such as the National Security Strategy of the United States of 2002 and the Quadrennial Defense Report of 2006 made clear that the US military was able and willing to take steps to sustain Asian stability in the face of possible adverse consequences of China's rising military strength. Bush administration leaders emphasized US uncertainty over China's longer-term strategic intentions; they affirmed that they were not fully persuaded by Chinese pronouncements on peace and development and remained unsure whether China would be a friend or a foe of the United States. They built up US forces in Asia and collaborated with Japan and other allies and partners, including India, in part to ensure that US interests and Asian stability would be sustained in the face of possible disruptive or negative actions by Chinese military forces.

The Barack Obama administration continued American resolve in the face of China's military buildup as it carried out the most significant US reengagement with the Asia-Pacific region in many years. Speaking to reporters on the way to Beijing in January 2011, Secretary of Defense Robert Gates publicly affirmed US determination to deal effectively with advancing Chinese military capabilities. [17]

Although President Trump was avowedly unpredictable in foreign affairs and sustained what he viewed as a strong personal relationship with President Xi Jinping, US national security and defense strategies and behavior reflected strong resolve to defend US interests and those of key allies and partners, including Taiwan, in the face of increased coercion and pressure by China. Also, top administration officials repeatedly attacked China's Belt and Road Initiative (BRI) as designed in part to build economic dependencies on the part of strategically located but poorly endowed states that could be exploited by China for strategic advantage, including operations of Chinese naval and air forces from those countries' seaports and airports. [18]

In this context, it appeared reasonable for Chinese leaders to carry out the acquisition, development, and advancement of military capabilities specifically designed to defeat US forces, especially if they were to intrude in a confrontation regarding China's avowed top priority: restoring Taiwan to Chinese sovereignty. And as the Chinese leaders devoted ever greater effort to this military buildup, the US advancement of its military deployments and defense cooperation with Taiwan, Japan, Australia, India, and others also seemed logical in order to deter Chinese attack and preserve stability. Of course, the result was an escalating arms race and defense preparations that was very much at odds with the harmonious international environment depicted in Chinese pronouncements and propaganda. [19]

## Growing Military Capacity and Objectives

Overall, Chinese defense acquisition and advancement showed broad ambitions for Chinese military power. While they appeared focused on dealing with US forces in the event of a Taiwan contingency, these forces supported China's remarkably successful use of the coast guard, maritime militia, diplomatic and economic coercion, and massive dredging and construction of military installations on disputed South China Sea islets and reefs, resulting in de facto Chinese control of much of the area. Chinese military capacities ranged widely and could be used by Chinese leaders as deemed appropriate in a variety of circumstances. [20]

Salient Chinese defense acquisitions and modernization efforts included the following:

- Research and development in space and other surveillance systems to provide wide-area intelligence and reconnaissance and the development of antisatellite systems to counter the surveillance and related efforts of potential adversaries. Growing Chinese capacity in using sensors to enhance acoustical awareness in nearby seas potentially degraded the ability of US submarines to deploy in these waters.
- Cruise missile acquisitions and programs that improved the range, speed, and accuracy of Chinese land-, air-, and sea-launched weapons, including submarine-launched missiles that traveled much faster than the speed of sound and targeted sea and land surface forces. Longer-range land-based antiship cruise missiles further challenged the ability of US naval forces to deploy within striking distance of Chinese targets.
- Ballistic missile programs that involved missiles with multiple warheads and that improved the range, survivability (through mobile systems in particular), reliability, accuracy, and response times of tactical, regional, and intercontinental-range weapons to augment or replace current systems.
- Development of ballistic missiles capable of targeting US or other naval combatants.

- Construction and acquisition of advanced conventional-powered submarines with subsurface-launched cruise missiles and guided torpedoes, and nuclear-powered attack and ballistic missile submarines to augment or replace older vessels in service.
- Development and acquisition of more capable naval surface ships armed with advanced antiship, antisubmarine, and air defense weapons.
- China attaining the position as the most active developer of hypersonic variants of the above-noted conventionally and nuclear armed cruise and ballistic missiles. The speed and low-altitude trajectory of such weapons precluded effective defense in most present circumstances.
- Air force advances, including hundreds of modern multirole fighters, advanced air-to-air missiles, airborne early-warning and control system aircraft, aerial refueling capabilities, and unmanned aerial vehicles.
- Air defense systems involving modern surface-to-air missiles covering all of Taiwan and much of the maritime rim of coastal China and air defense fighters. Longer-range Chinese antiaircraft missiles posed a potential threat to such key elements of US maritime defense as AWACS and tanker aircraft.
- Improved power projection for ground forces, including more sea- and airlift capabilities, special operations forces, and amphibious warfare capabilities.
- Research and development of defense information systems and improved command, control, communications, and computer systems.
- Development of cyber warfare capabilities.
- Increased tempo and complexity of exercises in order to make the PLA capable in joint interservice operations involving power projections, including amphibious operations.[21]

The Chinese advances meant that no single Asian power could match China's military power on continental Asia. With the possible exception of Japan, no Asian country was capable of challenging China's naval power and airpower in maritime eastern Asia. Should Beijing choose to deploy naval and air forces to patrol the sea lines of communication in the Indian Ocean, only India would conceivably be capable of countering China's power.[22]

Looking to the future, it is possible to bound the scope of China's military buildup. Available evidence shows that it was focused on nearby Asia. The major possible exceptions included the long-range nuclear weapons systems that targeted outside Asia and Chinese cyber warfare and space warfare capabilities. China used its long-range nuclear weapons to deter the United States and other potential adversaries by demonstrating a retaliatory, second-strike capability against them.[23]

The objectives of the Chinese military buildup seemed focused first on Taiwan, preventing its move toward independence and ensuring that China's sovereignty will be protected and restored. More generally, Chinese forces can be deployed to defeat possible threats or attacks on China, especially China's economically important eastern coastline. Apart from conflict over Taiwan, they were designed to deal with a range of so-called local war possibilities. These could involve territorial disputes with Japan, Southeast Asian countries, or India or instability requiring military intervention in Korea. Meanwhile, the Chinese military played a direct role in Chinese foreign policy; it sought to spread Chinese international influence, build military relationships with neighboring countries and others, and support a regional and international environment that will foster China's rise in power and influence. This role involved continued active diplomacy by Chinese military officials, increasing numbers of military exercises with Asian and other countries, Chinese arms sales to and training of foreign military forces, and more active participation by Chinese national security officials in regional and other multilateral security organizations and agreements. [24]

The Chinese military remained on course to continue a transformation from its past strategic outlook, that of a large continental power requiring large land forces for defense against threats to borders. The end of the threat from the Soviet Union and the improvement of China's relations with India, Vietnam, and others eased this concern. China moved away from a continental orientation requiring large land forces to a combined continental/maritime orientation requiring smaller, more mobile, and more sophisticated forces capable of protecting China's inland and coastal periphery. Unlike the doctrine of protracted land war against an invading enemy prevalent until the latter years of the Cold War, Chinese doctrine continued its more recent emphasis on the need to demonstrate an ability to attack first in order to deter potential adversaries and to carry out first strikes in order to gain the initiative in the battlefield and secure Chinese objectives.

To fulfill these objectives, Chinese forces needed and further developed the ability to respond rapidly, to take and maintain the initiative in the battlefield, to prevent escalation, and to resolve the conflict quickly and on favorable terms. Chinese military options included preemptive attacks and the use of conventional and nuclear forces to deter and coerce adversaries. Chinese forces expanded power-projection capabilities, giving Chinese forces a solid ability to deny critical land and sea access (e.g., the Taiwan Strait) to adversaries and providing options for force projection farther from Chinese borders. [25]

To achieve these objectives, Chinese conventional ground forces evolved, consistent with recent emphasis, toward smaller, more flexible, highly trained, and well-equipped rapid reaction forces with more versatile and well-developed assault, airborne, and amphibious power-projection capabilities. Special operations forces played an important role in these efforts. Navy forces built on recent steps forward, with more advanced surface combatants and submarines having better air defense and better antisubmarine and antiship capabilities. Their improved weaponry of cruise missiles and torpedoes, an improved naval air force, and greater replenishment-at-sea capabilities broadened the scope of their activities and posed greater challenges to potential adversaries. Air forces grew with more versatile and modern fighters; longer-range interceptor/strike aircraft; improved early-warning and air defense; and longer-range transport, lift, and midair refueling capabilities.

The Chinese military in recent years was in the process of implementing a multiyear military reform effort, the most comprehensive in its history, said by some reports to be completed at the end of five years of effort in 2020. The past emphasis on ground forces was further reduced, with enhanced support for naval and air power. These military forces were reorganized with an eye toward being used increasingly in an integrated way consistent with an emphasis on joint operations that involved more sophisticated command, control, communications, computers, intelligence, and strategic reconnaissance (C4ISR); early-warning; and battlefield management systems. Improved airborne and satellite-based systems aided detection, tracking, targeting, and strike capabilities and enhanced operational coordination of the various forces.[26]

Chinese strategic planners built on the advantages that Chinese strategic missile systems provided. Estimates vary, but it appeared that China possessed more than 1,500 short-, medium-, and intermediate-range, solid-fuel, mobile ballistic missiles (with a range under four thousand miles) and short-range cruise missiles with increased accuracy and some with both nuclear and conventional capabilities. China also modernized and introduced a small number of longer-range nuclear missiles capable of hitting the continental United States, and it was developing a viable submarine-launched nuclear missile that would broaden Chinese nuclear weapons options. Chinese nuclear missiles had smaller and more powerful warheads with multiple reentry vehicle capabilities. The development of hypersonic variants of these weapons would compound already formidable defense problems for the United States and other possible opponents. The emphasis on modern surveillance, early-warning, and battle management systems with advanced C4ISR assets seen in Chinese planning regarding conventional forces also applied to nuclear forces.

These advances added to China's existing military abilities. They posed concerns for the United States, Taiwan, Japan, and many other Chinese neighbors; they presented an overall strategic reality of increasing Chinese military power that influenced the strategic outlook of most of China's neighbors. Those abilities included the following:

- The ability to conduct intensive, short-duration air and naval attacks on Taiwan as well as prolonged air, naval, and possibly ground attacks. China's ability to prevail against Taiwan was seen as increasing steadily, especially given lax defense preparedness and political division in Taiwan. Massive US military intervention was viewed as capable of defeating a Chinese invasion, but Chinese area denial capabilities could substantially impede and slow the US intervention.

- Power-projection abilities to dislodge smaller regional powers from nearby disputed land and maritime territories and the ability to conduct air and sea denial operations for two hundred miles along China's coasts.
- Strong abilities to protect Chinese territory from invasion, to conduct ground-based power projection along land borders against smaller regional powers, and to strike civilian and military targets with a large and growing inventory of ballistic missiles and medium-range bombers armed with cruise missiles.
- A limited ability to project force against the territory of militarily capable neighboring states, notably Russia, India, and Japan.
- Continued ability to deter nuclear and other attacks from the United States and Russia by means of modernized and survivable Chinese nuclear missile forces capable of striking at these powers.

As China's military capabilities continued to grow more rapidly than those of any of its neighbors, China solidified its position as Asia's leading military power. As China's global involvement and international interests grew, its military modernization program became more focused on investments and infrastructure to support a range of missions beyond China's periphery. These missions involved power projection, sea-lane security, counterpiracy, peacekeeping, humanitarian assistance/disaster relief, and noncombatant evacuation operations. Overall, the situation clearly posed serious implications and complications in China's foreign policy. The situation made it much harder for Chinese officials to persuade skeptical neighbors, the United States, and other concerned governments that China's rising power and influence would be peaceful and of benefit to all.

Finally, the challenges prompted by China's military advances were increasing because of the acute competition between the United States and China seeking leadership in the high-technology industries of the future economy, which was discussed in chapter 3. In both countries a sense of urgency prevailed in efforts to counter the other. In the United States, a strong shared administration-congressional concern centered on Chinese efforts to undermine American leadership in the high-technology industries of the future, seeking to overtake the United States and secure a dominant leadership position for China in controlling and directing these fields. Each country's defense leaders and organizations were keenly focused on using the high-technology advances for military purposes. Chinese and American military leaders were aware that the diffusion of dual-use high technologies such as artificial intelligence, big-data analytics, robotics, and other advances were often invented and produced in the commercial sector. And they were aware of the rapidity of the emergence and breakthrough of such new technologies. The result in China was a state-directed effort emphasizing military-civil fusion to absorb advanced technology from the commercial sector, and state-directed efforts to purchase companies abroad capable of advancing high-technology defense production. Continued active Chinese industrial espionage and cyber theft added to American antagonism in the intense competition with China.[27]

The outlook for intense Chinese defense challenges and competition with the United States and its allies and partners seems strong. The Xi Jinping government seeks to avoid military conflict with the United States or its allies and partners in pursuing its objectives through various tactics that leave military conflict as a last resort. These tactics are displayed in China's pursuit of its territorial and maritime claims in the East and South China Seas and along the disputed Sino-Indian border. China's continued militarization by placing antiship missiles and long-range surface-to-air missiles on outposts in the South China Sea combined with the use of coast guard forces and economic coercion to force smaller countries to bend to its demands. The Chinese defense white paper of 2019 rebuffed the Trump administration strategies targeting China. Xi Jinping's posture in the US-China trade war did little to change the various serious frictions with the United States over intellectual property rights, industrial espionage, state-directed industrial policies, and other matters critical in the acute US-China competition to lead in the technologies driving future industries and national defense systems. China's developing ballistic missiles were capable of attacking bases as far away as Guam, striking US aircraft carriers, and penetrating US defenses to hit a range of American cities. China's advances in hypersonic variants of such weapons, its advances in sensors and other means to counter US submarines, and its advances in space and cyber warfare all attested to the widespread rivalry and growing tension with the United States.

Adding to the concern prompted by major advances in Chinese military capabilities and China's purported resolve to use these forces if necessary was the view held by many officials in neighboring governments about what their countries had experienced in past dealings with the People's Republic of China (PRC). Though the Chinese government worked hard to distort the historical record in its favor and most Chinese seemed to believe the historical "party line" that China was never aggressive toward its neighbors, the history of the use of force in Chinese foreign policy remained well known among regional officials. The record provided little assurance that China's avowed peaceful development in the twenty-first century would be sustained. The PRC government resorted to the use of force in international affairs more than most governments in the modern period. The reasons were varied and included Chinese determination to deter perceived superpower aggression, defend Chinese territory and territorial claims, recover lost territory, and enhance China's regional and global stature. Studies of Chinese leaders' strategic thinking led to the conclusion that modern Chinese leaders, like those in the past, were more inclined than not to see the use of military force as an effective instrument of statecraft. [28]

Although facing superpower adversaries with much greater military might, Mao Zedong frequently initiated the use of military force to keep the more powerful adversary off balance and to keep the initiative in Chinese hands. Deng Xiaoping was much more focused than Mao on conventional Chinese nation building; he sought to foster a peaceful environment around China's periphery in order to pursue Chinese economic modernization. However, in 1979, Deng also undertook strong military action against Soviet-backed Vietnam, and he continued for several years to confront Soviet power throughout China's periphery despite China's military weakness relative to the Soviet superpower. In the post–Cold War period, Chinese officials judged that the Taiwan president's visit to the United States in 1995 so challenged Chinese interests that it warranted nine months of military tensions in the Taiwan Strait. These tensions included live-fire military exercises, ballistic missile tests near Taiwan ports, and a private warning from a senior Chinese military leader of China's determination to use nuclear weapons to deter US intervention in a Taiwan confrontation. [29]

China's growing stake in the international status quo and its dependence on smooth international economic interchange were seen to argue against Chinese leaders' resorting to military force to achieve international objectives. At the same time, the rapid development of Chinese military capabilities to project power and the change in Chinese doctrine to emphasize striking first to achieve Chinese objectives and advancing maritime control were seen as increasing the likelihood that China would use force to achieve the ambitions and objectives of the Chinese government. Against this background, it was not surprising that an active debate continued over Chinese national security intentions and whether they override the Chinese government's concurrent public emphasis on promoting peace and development in Chinese foreign affairs.

As part of the debate, policy makers in the United States and allied countries were asked to balance their concern over Chinese military advances with an assessment of the many shortcomings seen in China's military modernization. The argument maintained that if deterrence failed in the Taiwan Strait, in the East or South China Seas, or elsewhere, US policy makers and strategic planners would need to understand and exploit the gaps in and limitations of China's military modernization to ensure that the United States and its allies were able to prevent China from using force to achieve its policy objectives. Those limitations involved the following two sets of factors:

1. Regarding leadership and quality of personnel, highlighted limitations include an outdated command structure in transition to a more effective structure, serious gaps in quality of personnel, lagging standards of professionalism, and continued corruption despite a major recent crackdown on such practices.[30]
2. Regarding weaknesses in combat capabilities, noted areas needing substantial improvement include logistical weaknesses, insufficient strategic airlift capabilities, limited numbers of special mission aircraft, and deficiencies in fleet air defense and antisubmarine warfare.[31]

Adding to the list of Chinese vulnerabilities is weak ballistic missile defense, which could become seriously problematic for China were the United States to follow the advice of some American strategists and build conventional ballistic missiles to target China in response to China's large buildup of conventional ballistic missiles targeting US forces and US allies in Asia.[32]

## WEAPONS OF MASS DESTRUCTION: DEVELOPMENT, PROLIFERATION, AND NONPROLIFERATION

The development and deployment of nuclear weapons and ballistic missiles capable of carrying those weapons were critically important to China's national defense. They also continued to play an important role in Chinese foreign policy as a source of international power and influence.[33]

For many years, Chinese authorities followed sometimes avowed and sometimes secret policies involving the transfer of nuclear weapons, ballistic missiles, and related equipment and technology to selected countries for economic, foreign policy, and defense reasons. In the post–Cold War period, the Chinese government changed policies in these areas in important ways. While the pace and scope of Chinese nuclear weapons and ballistic missile development continued steadily to improve and expand Chinese capabilities in these areas, the Chinese government stopped its egregious proliferation policies of the past, supported and joined many leading international arms control regimes, and endeavored to change China's past international image as an outlier to a responsible member of the international arms control community.[34]

The recent record showed Beijing continuing to develop its nuclear forces capable of targeting the United States, Russia, and regional powers, while its stronger short-range and cruise missile development increased its ability to intimidate Taiwan and other neighbors and to warn their US backers. Chinese activities related to the proliferation of weapons of mass destruction (WMD) narrowed and slowed markedly in the post–Cold War period as the PRC joined and adhered to varying degrees to a number of international proliferation regimes. Some Chinese proliferation activities continued to pose challenges for US and others' interests, and they sometimes met with criticism and economic sanctions from the United States. [35]

## China's Development of WMD Capabilities

*Nuclear Forces*

Beijing's multifaceted nuclear forces had been developed since the 1950s and served a variety of missions, including the following:

- Deterring US or Russian nuclear attack
- Deterring any regional threat to China's national security from superpower conventional forces or other powers
- Backing China's efforts to regain lost territory, seek regional prominence, and gain greater global stature

The variety of Chinese nuclear weapons and delivery systems reflected the changing nature of the perceived threat China faced over the past sixty years—first the United States, then both the United States and the Soviet Union, then the Soviet Union, and recently the United States. It also reflected the changing preferences of senior Chinese leaders, especially following Mao's death in 1976. Particularly important were challenges and opportunities posed by Beijing's mixed ability to keep up with technological advances important in the development of nuclear weapons and delivery systems.

China continued to develop a nuclear capability able to target Taiwan and Asia-Pacific states, US forces in the Asia-Pacific region, the United States itself, and Russia. China's development of short-range ballistic and cruise missiles increased its ability to intimidate Taiwan. Both US theater missile defense (TMD) efforts on behalf of Taiwan, Japan, South Korea, and other regional partners and the development of enhanced US national missile defense (NMD) concerned Beijing's leaders at the turn of the twenty-first century. At that time, Chinese officials warned against closer US defense cooperation with Taiwan, including US TMD support for the island, and they registered concern about the effect NMD would have on the global strategic balance. The fact that the United States continued going forward with such programs did not seriously derail US-China relations.

China ostensibly sought an air-, sea-, and land-based triad for its nuclear weapons. Improvements in submarine ballistic missile launches and the successful completion in developing new longer-range bombers foreshadowed bringing the triad to reality, though up to now Beijing had relied on land-based missiles. Backward Chinese aviation and limited submarine capabilities meant that the United States could neutralize most PRC air or naval delivery systems. Thus, Beijing's triad actually focused on three categories of land-based ballistic missiles—long, medium, and short range.

Developing long-range, mobile, solid-fuel ballistic missiles remained a top priority for the Chinese government and substantially strengthened Beijing's deterrent to US or Russian nuclear attack. Beijing's stronger, well-developed, and growing array of shorter-range ballistic missiles, along with current or developing cruise missiles, provided greater opportunity to use force, notably either conventionally armed or nuclear-armed missiles.

Through missile modernization, China was striving to increase the credibility of its deterrent by improving the readiness and survivability of the force. Because of technological shortcomings and economic limitations, China could not afford the technology or inventory needed to counter the United States warhead for warhead. Indeed, foreign specialists sometimes judged that China lacked the will to develop a massive WMD force; they averred that China's concept of limited deterrence both created a sufficient sense of security for China's leaders and helped forge the morale of its war fighters needed to persevere in a WMD environment.[36]

Specialists strongly debated whether Beijing's growing military power, notably its short-range missile capabilities, meant that it was preparing to depart from its past defensive posture, which stressed China's public commitment not to be the first to use nuclear weapons or to engage in offensive military activities using nuclear-capable weapons. Specialists also warned of Chinese use of these missiles, probably armed with conventional warheads, as a means to force Taiwan to come to terms on reunification and to reduce the likelihood of US military intervention in a Taiwan conflict. Others disagreed, stressing among other things that Beijing did not yet have the combination of sufficient technological, intelligence, and other support to carry out such an offensive posture.[37]

## Chemical and Biological Weapons

Much less was known about Chinese capabilities in chemical and biological weapons. Beijing publicly asserted that it adhered to international norms and did not have biological or chemical weapons. Chinese interest in both areas had a long history, dating back to charges that Japan widely used such weapons against Chinese forces in World War II. Such charges were a mainstay in Chinese publicity against most of the nations China had fought in the past seventy years. The modernization of Chinese chemical, biological, and related technologies and industries meant that the PRC had ample ability to produce most known chemical and biological weapons.[38]

## China's WMD Proliferation and Nonproliferation Activities

Beginning in the early 1980s, China's weapons proliferation activities emerged as an issue of growing concern for US and other international policy makers. This trend persisted for more than thirty years. Chinese companies were seen by US officials and other observers to have exported to several countries a variety of goods useful in building nuclear weapons, chemical weapons, and ballistic and cruise missiles.[39] In some cases, China provided critical materials, equipment, and technical assistance to nations that could not otherwise acquire these items for their weapons programs. Most notably, China provided Pakistan with a basic nuclear weapons design and substantial assistance in fabricating weapons-grade nuclear material. Moreover, China provided some countries with production technologies, allowing these nations to build certain missile systems with little external assistance.

China's proliferation behavior improved dramatically in the post–Cold War period and especially since the mid-1990s. The Chinese government gradually agreed to sign a number of key nonproliferation treaties, such as the Nuclear Nonproliferation Treaty (NPT) and the Chemical Weapons Convention (CWC), and developed internal bureaucratic and regulatory structures to carry out these commitments. China still engaged in exports of concern to the George W. Bush administration. This US government repeatedly imposed sanctions on Chinese entities (though not on the Chinese government) for transfers related to ballistic missiles, chemical weapons, and cruise missiles to Pakistan, Iran, and other countries. At that time, senior US intelligence and national security officials highlighted Chinese weapons proliferation to Iran and missile proliferation to Pakistan and reported Chinese missile proliferation to Iran and North Korea. The Barack Obama government imposed sanctions on various occasions on numerous entities in China for weapons proliferation. The Trump administration also sanctioned Chinese firms on such matters, including announced sanctions in August 2017 on several Chinese firms and individuals assisting North Korea's weapons program and sanctions announced in February 2020 on five Chinese firms or individuals for aiding Iran's missile program and one Chinese individual for assisting Pakistan's weapons program.[40]

Nevertheless, since the end of the Cold War, the overall scope of Chinese proliferation activities declined significantly. The geographic distribution of Chinese proliferation-relevant exports narrowed from almost a dozen countries to three: Iran, Pakistan, and North Korea. The character of China's exports similarly narrowed in recent years from a broad range of nuclear materials and equipment (much of it unsafeguarded) and complete missile systems to exports of dual-use nuclear, missile, and chemical technologies. In addition, during much of the 1980s and 1990s, China's nuclear and missile assistance directly contributed to the nuclear and missile programs in other countries; in recent years, such assistance was indirect at best. The frequency of such exports also declined. Chinese leaders were loath to restrict China's own national defense programs; they appeared to weigh carefully the pros and cons of restrictions on Chinese weapons and weapons technology transfers abroad, leading to some ambiguities and loopholes in their commitments that were criticized by the United States and others.[41]

Regarding negotiations and agreements on arms control and disarmament, Chinese officials were active during the Cold War in UN-related and other international bodies dealing with these matters. They repeatedly asserted that the United States and the Soviet Union needed to undertake substantial cuts in their arsenals and programs before powers like China with smaller numbers of nuclear weapons could be expected to agree to restrict their weapons development. China rebuffed international criticism of its transfers of WMD equipment and technology abroad, its large sales of conventional weapons in the 1980s to Iran and Iraq (notably, China sold $5 billion worth of weapons to Iraq in 1983–1988), and its multibillion-dollar sale at that time of several dozen intermediate-range ballistic missiles to Saudi Arabia. China sometimes denied transferring or selling weapons and equipment despite overwhelming evidence to the contrary.[42]

An upsurge in US and international concern with nuclear and other WMD proliferation followed the end of the Cold War and the US-led military attack in response to Iraq's invasion of Kuwait in 1990–1991. This upsurge prompted Chinese leaders to begin to see the wisdom of curbing egregious proliferation activities and joining and conforming to international agreements and norms supported by nations seeking to regulate WMD development and proliferation. China in the 1990s moved to adhere to international agreements on arms control in several areas.

China promised tentatively to abide by the Missile Technology Control Regime (MTCR) in November 1991 and February 1992 and later reaffirmed that commitment in an October 4, 1994, joint statement with the United States. The MTCR, set up in 1987, was not an international agreement and had no legal authority. It remained a set of voluntary guidelines to control the transfer of ballistic and cruise missiles that were capable of delivering at least 500 kilograms (1,100 pounds) of payload at least 300 kilometers (186 miles). Presumably with the MTCR guidelines in mind, on November 21, 2000, Beijing said that it had no intention of assisting any other country in developing ballistic missiles that could be used to deliver nuclear weapons (missiles with payloads of at least 500 kilograms and ranges of at least 300 kilometers), and it promised to issue missile-related export controls "as soon as possible." The PRC published those regulations and a control list (modeled on the MTCR) on August 25, 2002.[43]

China formally acceded to the NPT on March 9, 1992. The NPT did not ban peaceful nuclear projects, and on May 11, 1996, the PRC issued a statement promising to make only safeguarded nuclear transfers. On July 30, 1996, China began a moratorium on nuclear testing and signed the Comprehensive Test Ban Treaty in September 1996, though, like the United States, China has not yet ratified the treaty. The Chinese premier, on September 10, 1997, issued nuclear export control regulations in support of China's pledges on nuclear transfers.

China joined the Zangger Committee, which regulates international nuclear trade, on October 16, 1997. Also in October 1997, China acceded to strong US pressure and promised not to start new nuclear cooperation with Iran. This angered the Tehran government and led to a serious temporary decline in China-Iran relations. On June 6, 1998, the UN Security Council (including China) adopted Resolution 1172, which asked states to prevent exports to India's or Pakistan's nuclear weapons or missile programs (China had been a major supplier to Pakistan in both areas). The PRC issued regulations on dual-use nuclear exports on June 17, 1998. In May 2004, China applied to join the Nuclear Suppliers Group (NSG), which accepted China as a member after the US government decided to support China's entry.[44]

In November 1995, China issued its first public defense white paper, which focused on arms control and disarmament. China formally signed the CWC in January 1993. On April 25, 1997, China deposited its instrument of ratification of the CWC before the convention entered into force on April 29, 1997. From 1993 to 1998, the PRC issued export control regulations on chemicals. In October 2002, the PRC issued regulations for export controls concerning dual-use biological agents and related technology. On December 3, 2003, China issued a white paper on nonproliferation that stated that China's control lists regulating Chinese transfers of possible WMD components were almost the same as those of such arms control groups and regimes as the Zangger Committee, NSG, CWC, the Australia Group (AG) on chemical and biological weapons, and MTCR.

Among some perceived gaps in Chinese adherence to international arms control efforts, China is not yet a member of MTCR or the AG. In June 2004, China expressed willingness to join MTCR. China did not join the ninety-three countries signing the International Code of Conduct against Ballistic Missile Proliferation in The Hague on November 25, 2002. China has not joined the Proliferation Security Initiative announced by President George W. Bush on May 31, 2003. China cooperated with UN-backed efforts against North Korea's missile and nuclear tests in 2006, 2009, 2013, and 2017, though it remained reluctant to impose sanctions or other pressure on Pyongyang. China also cooperated in varying degrees with US-backed efforts to sanction Iran for its reported development of nuclear weapons capabilities. China agreed with the Barack Obama government and other members of the UN Security Council in support of the Joint Comprehensive Plan of Action (JCPOA), signed in 2015, which seeks to curb Iran's suspected development of nuclear weapons. It criticized the Trump administration's withdrawal from the plan.[45]

The Intermediate-Range Nuclear Forces Treaty between the United States and the Soviet Union prohibited cruise and ballistic missiles with range capabilities between 500 and 5,500 kilometers. Citing Russian development of such weapons, the Trump administration withdrew from the agreement in 2019. US officials reportedly sought to use the withdrawal to allow US development of such weapons to counter China, which was not a party to the agreement. China developed a large array of ballistic and cruise missiles of these ranges, giving Beijing a large strategic advantage against American forces in the Asia-Pacific region. China sharply criticized US withdrawal from the agreement and made clear that Beijing would not limit its arms development in US-proposed trilateral US-Russia-China arms agreements.[46]

## CHINA'S APPROACH TO INTERNATIONAL TERRORISM

Other features of Chinese national security policy that significantly impacted China's foreign policy and overall approach to world affairs included Chinese policies and practices related to international terrorism. Chinese leaders broadly supported the US-led war on terrorism that began after September 11, 2001. There were some initial reservations over US policy and actions voiced by Chinese leaders during the lead-up to the war in Afghanistan, which toppled the terrorist-harboring Taliban regime. Chinese leaders registered concern in particular over the US military presence in Central Asia, and they worked in generally subtle ways to support regional efforts opposing long-term US military presence in this area. Chinese leaders opposed the US-led military intervention against Iraq, but they were careful that China's opposition, as voiced in the UN Security Council and other venues, was less salient than that voiced by fellow UN Security Council permanent members. Letting France and Russia take the lead, China avoided serious problems in Chinese efforts to sustain positive ties with the George W. Bush administration.

China avoided close association with the Barack Obama administration's escalation of military force against resurgent Taliban insurgents in Afghanistan. It duly endorsed the May 2, 2011, killing of Osama bin Laden by American special forces as "a positive development in the international struggle against terrorism."[47] After the 2014 announcement of the withdrawal of American and NATO combat troops from Afghanistan, China met with outgoing and incoming Afghan leaders, who urged China to take a leadership role in dealing with the conflict in the country. Repeated high-profile Chinese-Afghan leadership meetings failed to hide China's uncertainty about potentially costly commitments in a very unstable country on the one hand, while on the other hand China increasingly worried about terrorists from Afghanistan entering China and exacerbating already serious Chinese problems in pacifying violent dissent among ethnic Uighurs in the Xinjiang Autonomous Region and elsewhere in China.[48]

Presumably related to the withdrawal of US-led forces from Afghanistan was notable Chinese security involvement and activities with Tajikistan and Afghanistan's Wakhan Corridor. Increased Chinese security presence in both areas was seen to maintain domestic security in Tajikistan and prevent Afghan instability spreading to Tajikistan and China's restive Xinjiang region. The deployment of the People's Armed Police based in Tajikistan, as well as joint operations with Tajik and Afghan forces, remained focused on securing the Afghan border with Tajikistan and China.[49]

Maoist China had a long record of using terrorist techniques to intimidate and resist opponents at home and abroad. Chinese foreign policy was replete with examples of close collaboration with and support for movements and governments that employed terrorist methods in order to achieve ends that the Chinese government supported. The more pragmatic Deng Xiaoping government saw Chinese foreign policy interests better served by preserving regional and international stability conducive to Chinese economic development. As a result, Chinese foreign policy cut back sharply on military, training, and other support for radical groups that engaged in terrorist methods. By 1980, China's long record of support for the Palestine Liberation Organization and some more radical groups that engaged in terrorist activities against Israel had changed. In contrast to its stance in the past, China clearly indicated its opposition to terrorist practices against Israel and supported Israel's right to exist. Eventually, improved China-Israel relations led to formal diplomatic relations between the two states in 1992.[50]

It took Chinese officials a long time to pull back support for governments that harbored terrorists or that engaged in gross terrorist activities at home or abroad. If other important Chinese interests seemed to require good relations with such states, Chinese government policy was to preserve good relations, giving antiterrorism a lower priority. Thus, in the 1980s and into the 1990s, Chinese officials provided strong support for the Khmer Rouge resistance in Cambodia and for governments in Pakistan, Iran, Syria, and Libya that were associated with terrorist activities. China also provided some aid to the Taliban regime in Afghanistan. Even after the September 11, 2001, attack, China continued strong and constructive involvement with terrorist-harboring regimes, such as Sudan, Iran, and Syria.[51]

The Chinese government was anxious to advance relations with the George W. Bush administration and viewed the attacks of September 11, 2001, as an opportunity to improve relations. It voiced sympathy with the United States after the attacks; allowed President Bush to use the Asia-Pacific Economic Cooperation (APEC) leaders meeting in China in October to rally support for antiterrorist action; and began closer cooperation with US antiterrorism, intelligence, and other officials. In December 2001, the US-China Interagency Counterterrorism Working Group was established; it met periodically in the following years. It had representatives from the two countries' law enforcement, intelligence, military, diplomatic, and financial agencies. China joined in efforts against international money laundering and the US Container Security Initiative (designed to screen cargo entering the United States) and allowed an FBI liaison office to open in Beijing in 2002. Also in 2002, Chinese officials welcomed the US government's identification of the East Turkistan Islamic Movement, which targets China's Xinjiang Autonomous Region, as a terrorist group.[52]

The Chinese government worked with Russia and some Central Asian governments to preserve regional stability and curb terrorist activity under the auspices of the Shanghai Five organization begun in 1996 (with China, Russia, Kazakhstan, Kyrgyzstan, and Tajikistan as founding members) and its successor organization, the Shanghai Cooperation Organization (SCO, founded in June 2001 with the addition of Uzbekistan). It showed particular concern over international support for dissident groups in the western Chinese region of Xinjiang that sometimes engaged in terrorist activities. On the one hand, Chinese officials welcomed the US-led war that toppled the Taliban regime in Afghanistan because the latter was seen to support transnational terrorism, including groups in China. On the other hand, the Chinese government worked to use the SCO and China's bilateral relations with Russia and Central Asian states to register opposition to long-term US military presence in Central Asia.[53]

From the outset of the global war on terrorism, the Chinese government stressed that the United Nations should play the leading role. This was in part designed to counter some actions by the United States in the war against Afghanistan and particularly in the period leading to the US-led military invasion of Iraq—both justified in part by the George W. Bush administration as counterterrorism measures. China supported most international conventions against terrorism.

In Asia, China continued multilateral and bilateral antiterrorist activities with SCO members. It also held antiterrorism exercises with Pakistan, India, and other countries. Antiterrorism was a prominent feature of China's burgeoning cooperation with the Association of Southeast Asian Nations (ASEAN). China was a member of APEC's Counterterrorism Task Force, and China featured antiterrorism cooperation in interaction with the European

Union and some European powers. China cooperated with a wide range of governments and international agencies in securing the 2008 Olympic Games in Beijing from terrorist threats. [54]

As acute international antiterrorist efforts waned after a decade of US-led war against terrorism following the September 2001 attack on America, Chinese leaders focused on internal security in the restive Xinjiang Autonomous Region of the People's Republic of China and its large Muslim ethnic Uighur population. Violent actions by anti-regime Uighurs occurred periodically in the region and elsewhere in China. They were linked to the East Turkestan Islamic Movement (ETMI) and related groups opposed to Chinese rule and favoring independence for Xinjiang. ETMI was classified by the US government as a terrorist group. An increase in such domestic anti-regime attacks in 2012–2014 was followed by an unprecedented Chinese government "Strike Hard" campaign. [55] In the last five years, China's crackdown in Xinjiang escalated to include internment camps, forced labor, and daily indoctrination programs for more than a million Uighur and other Muslims in Xinjiang. Beijing also made extensive use of technological advancements to monitor Xinjiang residents. Besides surveillance cameras equipped with facial recognition, the government also collected information such as biometric data, data usage, and location. This sweeping approach was used to combat what China considered to be a serious terrorism threat. The longer-term objective encouraged cultural assimilation and internal migration to areas where Turkic minorities predominated, resulting in marginalizing dissent and cultural opposition to regime norms.

The internment camps and other harsh Chinese measures were sharply criticized in the media and by politicians in the United States and other Western countries, but little concrete action was taken by these states. Beijing's strong relationships with predominantly Islamic countries resulted in little official criticism from these governments. Beijing continued to work constructively with an array of countries, such as Saudi Arabia, whose policies fostered the spread of Salafi ideas that China opposed at home, as well as other countries like Iran, which the United States considered a sponsor of terrorism. Many governments concerned with terrorism or anxious to monitor domestic dissent were attracted to Chinese surveillance methods, equipment, and technical expertise for use in their countries. China's ever-increasing role in the United Nations and other international bodies acted as a brake on international condemnation and raised the chance of Beijing's approach to terrorism becoming a more widely accepted world practice. A variety of international terrorist groups targeted China as a result of the crackdown in Xinjiang, raising the possibility of terrorist danger for the ever-increasing large numbers of Chinese working and traveling abroad, notably in Pakistan, Nigeria, and other countries with significant terrorism problems. [56]

## MILITARY DIPLOMACY, ARMS ACQUISITIONS AND SALES, AND PEACEKEEPING

After the Cold War, Chinese military diplomacy, arms acquisitions and sales, and peacekeeping operations became important features in Chinese foreign policy. Chinese military leaders were among the most active Chinese officials to engage in international relations in this period. The PLA high command broadened and accelerated senior-level international exchanges in an effort to expand China's international influence, to increase opportunities for arms sales and purchases of equipment and technology, to ease concern over China's rising power, and to deepen PLA leaders' international experience. Some of the top PLA leaders took a place among the world's most widely traveled and internationally experienced military leaders. [57]

A centerpiece of PLA efforts was cooperation with Russia, which was for three decades the key supplier of modern military equipment to the Chinese armed forces. Russian arms sales to China averaged $1–$2 billion annually. As discussed in detail in chapter 11, leaders Vladimir Putin and Xi Jinping fostered an ever closer and cooperative relationship, with defense cooperation involving extensive arms sales and large-scale military exercises. [58]

Chinese military leaders endeavored to develop close contacts with the US military, but extensive contacts were cut after the Tiananmen crackdown in 1989. They were resumed by the second term of the Clinton administration, but the defense officials of the George W. Bush administration, backed by strong sentiment in Congress, reversed this trend and allowed only slow and incremental improvement in US military ties with China. Chinese objections to US arms sales to Taiwan led to China-initiated halts in military exchanges. Military exchanges then improved, despite rising US-Chinese differences over China's truculence and assertiveness over territorial disputes in Asia and America's rebalance to Asia in ways seen negatively by China. Most recently, US and Chinese military and defense officers maintained close contacts in order to avoid unwanted confrontation amid strong US-China international competition and tension over such regional hot spots as Taiwan, the South China Sea, and North Korea. [59]

Chinese officials for a time worked hard to end the embargo on military sales to China undertaken by the European powers and Asian and Pacific powers aligned with the United States. They appeared to be having some success in getting the Europeans to end their arms embargo in 2005 until the US government intervened strongly against such action. Although closely aligned with the United States, Israel made use of opportunities for significant sales of advanced military equipment and technology to China. The George W. Bush administration, however, had some success as it strongly pressed Israel to curb such sales to China. [60]

Chinese arms sales abroad were an important source of funds for the PLA and the Chinese government in the 1980s and part of the 1990s. China supplied a wide array of arms to both sides during the Iran-Iraq War of the 1980s. Reforms conducted in the latter 1990s removed the PLA from business ventures at home and abroad. This, plus the fact that Chinese arms were often not competitive with the more sophisticated equipment available from other suppliers, meant that promoting arms sales abroad became a somewhat less salient feature of recent Chinese foreign policy. From 2005 to 2009, China sold approximately $8 billion worth of conventional weapons systems worldwide. China at times surpassed Germany, France, and the United Kingdom to become the third-largest arms exporter (after the United States and Russia). Overall, China accounted for about 5 percent of the world's exports of arms. Between 2008 and 2018, China exported some $15.7 billion worth of conventional weapons across the globe, making it the fifth-largest arms supplier in the world—behind the United States, Russia, Germany, and France.[61]

The bulk of Chinese international military interchange more recently involved visits of PLA leaders abroad and visits of foreign counterparts to China. Other elements included usually small military exercises with various countries, ship visits, and some training of foreign military personnel in China and of PLA officers abroad. A growing feature of Chinese military diplomacy was China's increasing role in UN peacekeeping operations. In 2008, China joined UN-backed efforts to escort merchant ships in the Gulf of Aden and in waters off Somalia because of the danger of piracy.

China sustained an active pace and scope of military exchanges for decades. In 1996 China hosted more than 140 military delegations from more than sixty countries and sent military delegations to forty countries. In November 1997, a PLA deputy chief of staff visited France and Japan, paving the way for higher-level Chinese military visits to both countries. Germany sent its military chief of staff to China for the first time in 1998, and Australia received the Chinese defense minister in 1998. In November 1997, the PLA also welcomed its first high-level officer (a vice chief of staff) from South Korea. In 1997, the total number of attachés accredited by foreign embassies in China reached sixty-three.[62]

By 2000, official Chinese media and other sources revealed that the number of foreign delegations that the PLA was involved with at home and abroad in the 1990s nearly doubled since the previous decade. From 1999 to 2002, the PLA sent over twenty thousand people in more than eight hundred specialized technical delegations overseas to investigate, cooperate in research, and participate in studies.[63]

Building on this momentum, an official Chinese media account of military diplomacy in 2004 highlighted important Chinese security initiatives with regional groups like the ASEAN Regional Forum and the SCO and joint military exercises with Britain, France, Australia, Pakistan, India, and Vietnam. At the end of the decade, China reported that the PLA held forty-four joint military and training exercises, did twenty-eight humanitarian missions abroad, and established defense dialogues with twenty-two states. In the previous two years, it had sent ships to visit more than thirty countries and welcomed ships of more than twenty nations visiting China; defense ministers or chiefs of staff of sixty countries visited China in the two-year period. In 2014 China hosted thirty-one joint exercises and other training programs. China participated for the first time in the Rim of the Pacific annual naval exercise hosted by the United States.

The pace and scope of military interchanges continued to grow. In 2017 the Chinese military conducted fifty-two exercises with foreign forces, with the vast majority held outside China. Exercises were held in East and Southeast Asia, the Indian Ocean including the Red Sea and the Persian Gulf, Africa, the Mediterranean Sea, the Baltic Sea, and the northern Atlantic Ocean. The Chinese military relationship with Russia became much closer with strong arms sales and joint exercises, reaching a high point with the participation of more than three thousand Chinese troops in Russia's September 2018 VOSTOK exercises, the largest military exercise in Russia since the 1980s.[64]

Developing in parallel with expanding Chinese military diplomacy was China's participation in UN-backed international peacekeeping operations.[65] China had negative experience with UN military operations against it during the Korean War, and Chinese leaders for a long time remained wary of international efforts to use the United Nations or other means to intrude in other countries' internal affairs. Thus, China strongly supported Serbia in 1999 in the face of NATO-led military intervention seeking to curb repression and restore peace in Kosovo. As the United Nations supported more intrusive measures to ensure peace in the post–Cold War period, China did not block these efforts and showed increasing signs of joining them.[66] In 1990, China began sending military observers to UN peacekeeping operations. In 1992, China agreed to participate in the most intrusive UN peacekeeping operation up to that time, the UN Transitional Authority in Cambodia. China supported the mission politically and financially, and it sent an engineering battalion to participate. In January 2000, China sent fifteen civilian policemen to the UN Transitional Authority in East Timor, the first time that China sent civilian policemen to UN peacekeeping operations. By 2002, China had sent more than 650 military observers, 800 engineering troops, and 198 civilian policemen to take part in UN peacekeeping operations. In December 2010, 1,955 Chinese personnel were serving in nine UN missions. By that time, China had dispatched 17,390 military personnel to nineteen UN peacekeeping missions; nine persons had died while on duty. Up to that time, China had not sent combat troops to peacekeeping operations. That pattern ended when China in 2014 deployed 170 combat troops as UN peacekeepers in Mali, and in 2015, 700 Chinese combat troops arrived in South Sudan for UN peacekeeping duty.[67]

As Chinese security personnel spread in several locations, their numbers surpassed those of any of the other UN Security Council permanent members. The more narrow national interests of China were served in these deployments in some respects. The UN peacekeeping budget paid for the services of the Chinese troops. The personnel gained valuable experience when they deployed and pursued operations in various foreign locales and in the company of troops from other nations.

As noted in chapter 4, China increased its previous modest commitment to the UN peacekeeping budget. In 2010, its contribution was somewhat less than 4 percent of the overall peacekeeping budget; it rose to more than 6 percent. Xi Jinping's 2015 change in China's approach to the United Nations focused on UN peacekeeping and funding for peacekeeping and other UN programs. China became the second-largest funder of UN peacekeeping, providing 15 percent of the budget by 2021. In 2019, China had 2,534 military and police peacekeepers in seven of the fourteen ongoing UN peacekeeping operations, ranking eleventh among the 122 contributors to UN peacekeeping and the largest contributor of peacekeepers among the five permanent UN Security Council members. Since first dispatching UN peacekeepers in 1990, China has sent about forty thousand peacekeepers to twenty-four UN-commanded peacekeeping operations and special political missions in Africa, the Middle East, Southern Europe, Southeast Asia, and Latin America.[68]

During the 1980s and 1990s, China abstained from UN resolutions that authorized the use of force for peace enforcement. Even when Iraq invaded Kuwait, China refused to vote in support of the US-led military effort to drive Iraq out of Kuwait. However, after the September 11, 2001, attack on the United States, China for the first time voted to endorse an American-led military action against a foreign country. As noted earlier, China opposed the US-led war against Iraq in 2003 but did endorse an intrusive UN Security Council resolution to disarm Iraq. It regretted its failure to block UN support for the NATO military intervention in Libya in 2011, and it joined Russia in blocking UN support for military intervention in Syria's civil war.[69]

## Chapter Six

# Relations with the United States

Chapter 2 shows the central importance of the United States in Chinese foreign policy in the period after the Cold War. Chapter 1 depicts four periods demonstrating an erratic pattern in Chinese-US relations featuring periods of acute tension and acrimony and periods of close engagement and cooperation. During the 1990s and into the first decade of the twenty-first century, the United States appeared to hold the stronger hand in the relationship, with American policy initiatives often offensive to China prompting Chinese reactions. In some instances, such as China's militant behavior during the Taiwan Strait crisis of 1995–1996 and its response to the US bombing of China's embassy in Belgrade in 1999, the Chinese reactions were strong and violent, compelling substantial adjustments in US policy. Later, the United States became embroiled in protracted wars in Iraq and Afghanistan and faced acute economic problems during the global economic crisis and recession beginning in 2008. By contrast, China avoided costly international obligations and sustained strong economic growth during the world recession.

Against this background, China began a new phase in its foreign policy, which is featured prominently in the international activism of current Chinese president Xi Jinping. China took a series of initiatives designed to advance control of disputed territory in the East and South China Seas in coercive ways short of using military force that came at the expense of several neighbors and at the expense of US interests and influence in regional affairs. In 2010, China pressed the US government harder than in the recent past in seeking concessions on Taiwan and Tibet policy. It launched prominent trade and investment mechanisms in Asia and, more broadly, attempted to exclude the United States and compete with US-backed regional and international economic and financial institutions. President Xi Jinping and other top Chinese leaders ignored the complaints of US president Barack Obama

about Chinese practices. The complaints included China bullying its neighbors, engaging in cyber theft of intellectual and other economic property and
other egregious violations of international economic norms, avoiding international responsibilities, and establishing rules and economic arrangements
in Asia and the world at odds with the interests of the United States and other
nations dependent on free trade and economic interchange. Lower-level officers and official Chinese media addressed, rebuked, and dismissed the US
complaints, and the offensive Chinese behavior continued.

Officials and prominent experts in the United States and China at different times in the past argued in favor of some overall framework for the
China-US relationship that would allow the two powers to cooperate more
closely and manage their differences more effectively. Shared opposition to
the Soviet Union provided the foundation of a strategic framework for Sino-
American cooperation initiated by US president Richard Nixon and Chinese
chairman Mao Zedong. That framework lasted for two decades but shattered
completely amid strident American reaction to the Chinese crackdown at
Tiananmen in 1989 and the concurrent demise of the Soviet empire. Subsequent frameworks failed to move forward. Examples included the Clinton
administration's effort to establish a strategic partnership with China that was
abandoned by the incoming Bush administration, the Bush administration's
call on China to become a "responsible stakeholder" in international affairs
that met with an unfavorable response in China, and American calls for the
Obama administration to establish a closer "G2" relationship with China as
the key element in world politics that met with unfavorable responses from
China in particular. Subsequently, a China-backed framework to establish a
"new type of great-power relationship" with the United States seemed failed
amid American suspicions that China was playing a double game in encouraging high-level bilateral discourse while pursuing policies that undermined
American interests.[1]

The main reasons for these failures are the strong Sino-American differences noted in earlier chapters and discussed below. Adding to the negative
mix is the state-fostered Chinese elite and public view of foreign affairs and
particularly their negative view of the United States reviewed in chapter 2.
As shown there, China has a unique sense of self-righteous exceptionalism in
foreign affairs that will not change easily. The United States is also known
for exceptionalism in international affairs. And both countries are big—the
world's most powerful; their approaches to each other will not be easily
changed by smaller powers or other outside forces.

# DEVELOPMENTS DURING THE GEORGE H. W. BUSH AND CLINTON ADMINISTRATIONS

Against this background, post–Cold War US-China relations have followed a tortuous course with many vicissitudes. Though he anticipated shock and disapproval at the Tiananmen crackdown from the United States and the West, Deng Xiaoping failed to foresee the breadth and depth of American disapproval, which would profoundly influence US policy into the twenty-first century. The influence was compounded by the surprising and dramatic collapse of communist regimes in the Soviet bloc and other areas, leading to the demise of the Soviet Union by the early 1990s. These developments undermined the perceived necessity for the United States to cooperate pragmatically with China despite its brutal dictatorship because of a US strategic need for international support against the Soviet Union. Meanwhile, Taiwan's authoritarian government was moving steadily at that time to promote democratic policies and practices, marking a sharp contrast to the harsh political authoritarianism in mainland China and greatly enhancing Taiwan's popularity and support in the United States. [2]

The Chinese government presided over strong economic growth beginning in 1993, and Chinese leaders reflected more confidence as they dealt with American pressures for change. However, they eschewed direct confrontation unless provoked by US, Taiwan, or other actions. The contentious American domestic debate over China policy was not stilled until the September 11, 2001, terrorist attack on America muffled American concerns over China for a while.

President George H. W. Bush (1989–1993) took the lead in dealing with severe problems in US-China relations caused by the Tiananmen crackdown and the decline in American strategic interest in China as a result of the collapse of the Soviet bloc. He resorted to secret diplomacy to maintain constructive communication with senior Chinese leaders, but the latter remained fairly rigid and made few gestures to help Bush justify a continued moderate US stance toward China. Though the Bush administration said all high-level official contact with China would be cut off as a result of the Tiananmen crackdown, President Bush sent his national security adviser and the deputy secretary of state on secret missions to Beijing in July and December 1989. When the missions became known in December 1989, the congressional and media reaction was bitterly critical of the administration's perceived duplicity. [3]

Bush eventually became frustrated with the Chinese leadership's intransigence and took a tough stance on trade and other issues, though he made special efforts to ensure that the United States continued most-favored-nation (MFN) tariff status for China despite opposition by a majority of the US Congress and much of the American media. Reflecting more positive

American views of the Republic of China (ROC) government in Taiwan, the Bush administration upgraded US interchange with the ROC by sending a cabinet-level official to Taipei in 1992, the first such visit since official relations were ended in 1979. He also seemed to abandon the limits on US arms sales set in accord with the August 1982 US communiqué with China by agreeing in 1992 to a sale of 150 advanced F-16 jet fighters to Taiwan worth more than $5 billion.[4]

Presidential candidate Bill Clinton used sharp attacks against President Bush's moderate approach to China to win support in the 1992 election. For candidate Clinton, using China issues to discredit the record of the Republican incumbent proved to be an effective election ploy. Once in office, President Clinton showed little interest in China policy, leaving the responsibility to subordinates.[5]

Assistant Secretary of State for East Asia Affairs Winston Lord negotiated with congressional leaders in 1993 to establish the human rights conditions the Clinton administration required before renewing MFN tariff status for China. However, Chinese government leaders stoked American business pressures to get Clinton to intervene in May 1994 to reverse existing policy and allow for unimpeded US renewal of MFN status for China.

Pro-Taiwan interests in the United States, backed by American public relations firms in the pay of entities and organizations in Taiwan, took advantage of congressional elections in 1994 giving control of Congress to pro-Taiwan Republican leaders. They pushed for allowing a US visit by ROC president Lee Teng-hui. Under heavy domestic political pressure, President Clinton intervened again and allowed Taiwan's president to visit the United States.

China's militant reactions and a resulting military confrontation between the United States and China in the Taiwan Strait (1995–1996) eventually involved two US aircraft carrier battle groups sent to the Taiwan area to deter China. Concurrently, the Clinton administration moved to a much more coherent engagement policy toward China. In moves welcomed by China's leaders, the president held US-China summit meetings in 1997 and 1998. Other progress beneficial to China included US-China agreement on China's entry into the World Trade Organization (WTO) and US agreement to provide permanent normal trade status for China.

As Clinton had sought partisan advantage in attacking George H. W. Bush's moderation toward China, the Republicans in control of Congress returned the favor in strident attacks against Clinton's new moderation toward Beijing. The president's engagement with China also came under attack from organized labor interests within the Democratic Party.[6] The Chinese government was anxious to keep the economic relationship with the United States on an even keel and was disinclined to punish such congressional critics or take substantive action against them. More likely were Chinese invitations to such critical congressional members for all-expenses-paid trips to China in order to persuade them to change their views by seeing actual conditions in China.

President Clinton's more active and positive engagement with China saw such high points as the China-US summits in 1997 and 1998, the Sino-US agreement on China's entry into the WTO in 1999, and passage of US legislation in 2000 granting China permanent normal trade relations status. Low points in the relationship during this time included strong congressional opposition to the president's stance against Taiwan independence in 1998, the May 1999 bombing of the Chinese embassy in Belgrade and Chinese demonstrators trashing US diplomatic properties in China, strident congressional criticism in the so-called Cox Committee report of May 1999 charging administration officials with gross malfeasance in guarding US secrets and weaponry from Chinese spies, and partisan congressional investigations of Clinton administration political fund-raising that highlighted illegal contributions from sources connected to the Chinese regime and the alleged impact they had on the administration's more moderate approach to the PRC.

## TWENTY-FIRST CENTURY DEVELOPMENTS

The initial toughness toward China of the George W. Bush administration began to subside with the September 11, 2001, terrorist attack on America and later developments. There followed several years of generally cooperative relations where the two sides dealt with differences in a burgeoning array of official dialogues and worked together to address such sensitive issues as North Korea's nuclear weapons program and efforts by Taiwan's president to promote greater separation and independence of Taiwan from China. The Taiwan issue declined in importance as Taiwan president Ma Ying-jeou took power in May 2008 and carried out a policy of accommodation and reassurance toward China that was welcomed by both the PRC and US governments.

The Barack Obama government strove in vain to preserve the overall positive momentum in US-China relations seen in the latter Bush years. Relations deteriorated over trade and related economic policies and a range of other issues, notably reaching a low point during the prolonged US presidential primaries and election campaign in 2012, which featured often harsh attacks on China. Toward the end of the rule of Chinese leader Hu Jintao (2002–2012), China became more assertive in support of its interests at odds with the United States, notably claims to disputed territory along its rim, especially in the East and South China Seas. For its part, the Obama government focused on a new approach known as the "pivot" to and later as the "rebalance" in the broad Asia-Pacific region that had military, economic, and diplomatic dimensions at odds with Chinese interests. Amid widely publicized assessments of deep mutual suspicion and mistrust among Sino-American leaders, US-China relations became overtly competitive as both powers sought greater influence and power in Asia. Overall, the developments seriously challenged but did not reverse the continued strong pragmatic interest on both sides to seek cooperation where possible and to avoid conflict and confrontation.[7]

## RELATIONS DURING THE
## GEORGE W. BUSH ADMINISTRATION

George W. Bush became president in 2001 with a policy more critical of China than the policy of his predecessor. The new president was wary of China's strategic intentions and took steps to deter China from using military force against Taiwan. Relations deteriorated when on April 1, 2001, a Chinese jet fighter crashed with a US reconnaissance plane in international waters off the China coast. The jet was destroyed and the pilot killed. The reconnaissance plane was seriously damaged and made an emergency landing in China. Amid intense negotiations and delays, the US crew and eventually the plane returned to the United States.

Subsequently, both governments established a businesslike rapport that emphasized cooperation and played down differences. The course of US-China relations became smoother than at any time since the normalization of relations between the two countries. The terrorist attack on America on September 11, 2001, soon led to US preoccupation with the wars in Afghanistan and Iraq and the broader war on global terrorism; US strategic attention to China as a threat was secondary. Chinese leaders gave priority to managing a difficult leadership transition and sustaining an authoritarian regime amid a vibrant economy and rapid social change. Though a wide range of differences spanning from Taiwan and Tibet to trade and human rights remained, the two powers showed cooperation in dealing with North Korea's nuclear weapons program and the pro-independence maneuvers of Taiwan president Chen Shui-bian.[8]

Both governments prepared for contingencies in case their counterpart turned aggressive or otherwise disrupted the prevailing order in ways adverse to their respective interests. Both powers used growing interdependence, engagement, and dialogues to foster webs of relationships that would tie down or constrain possible policies and actions deemed negative to their interests.[9] On the whole, the Chinese government of President Hu Jintao welcomed and supported the new directions in US China policy. The US approach fit well with the Chinese leadership's broader priorities of strengthening national development and Communist Party legitimacy that were said to require China to use carefully the "strategic opportunity" of prevailing international circumstances seen as generally advantageous to Chinese interests.[10]

As China expanded its military power along with economic and diplomatic relations in Asian and world affairs at a time of US preoccupation with war in Iraq and other foreign policy problems, the Bush administration debated the implications of China's rise in Asian and world affairs.[11] Some US officials judged that China's rise was designed to dominate Asia and in the process to undermine American leadership. A more moderate view came from US officials who judged that China's focus was to improve China's position in Asia in order to sustain regional stability, promote China's development, reassure neighbors, prevent balancing against China, and isolate Taiwan. This school of thought judged that China was not focused on isolating and weakening the United States in Asia, but it held that China's rise was having an indirect and substantial negative impact on US leadership in Asia, largely because of US policies and practices seen in the region as much more controversial and maladroit than Chinese policies and practices.

A third school of thought was identified with US deputy secretary of state Robert Zoellick, who by 2005 publicly articulated a strong argument for greater American cooperation with China. This viewpoint held that the United States should work cooperatively with China in order to encourage the PRC to use its rising influence in "responsible" ways in accord with US interests. It put less emphasis than the other two on competition with China and more emphasis on cooperation. Bush administration policy came to embrace the third point of view. The US administration increasingly emphasized positive engagement and a growing number of dialogues with China, encouraging China to act responsibly and building ever-growing webs of relationships and interdependence. This pattern fit well with Chinese priorities regarding national development in a period of advantageous international conditions while building interdependencies and relationships that constrained possible negative US policies and behaviors.

The Republicans lost control of the US House of Representatives and the US Senate in the 2006 election, and the Bush administration faced greater criticism of its foreign policies, including policies toward China, from congressional Democrats backed by the American media. Congressional critics focused special attention on economic problems, including the large trade deficit with China and a resulting loss of American jobs. Against this backdrop, Treasury Secretary Henry Paulson was appointed to lead a new Strategic Economic Dialogue with Chinese counterparts. They met twice a year in an effort to manage differences and ease tensions, especially over salient trade and related economic problems.

The overall positive stasis in US-China relations that emerged in the latter years of the George W. Bush administration generally met the near-term priorities of the US and Chinese governments. Neither the Chinese leadership nor the US administration sought trouble with the other. Both were preoccupied with other issues. Heading the list of preoccupations for both governments was dealing with the massive negative consequences of the international economic crisis and deep recession begun in 2008. Other preoccupations of the outgoing Bush administration included Iraq, Afghanistan, Pakistan, Iran, broader Middle East issues, North Korea, and other foreign policy problems, which came on top of serious adverse economic developments. China, for its part, faced a major leadership transition in 2012. Differences remained, notably growing trade and economic disputes paired with continued military buildups along China's rim that worsened an ongoing security dilemma between the two powers.

## RELATIONS DURING THE
## BARACK OBAMA ADMINISTRATION

As a presidential candidate in 2008, Barack Obama was unusual in recent US presidential politics in not making a significant issue of his predecessor's China policy. Like President Bush, the new president showed a measured and deliberative course with China involving pursuing constructive contacts, preserving and protecting American interests, and dealing effectively with challenges posed by rising Chinese influence and power.[12]

A major theme in President Obama's initial foreign policy was to seek the cooperation of other world powers, notably China, to deal with salient international concerns such as the global economic crisis and recession, climate change, nuclear weapons proliferation, and terrorism. He and his team made vigorous efforts to build common ground with China on these and related issues. China's leaders offered limited cooperation, disappointing the Obama government.[13]

More worrisome, Chinese actions and statements in 2009 and 2010 directly challenged the policies and practices of the United States:

- Chinese government patrol boats confronted US surveillance ships in the South China Sea.
- China challenged US and South Korean military exercises against North Korea in the Yellow Sea.
- Chinese treatment of US arms sales to Taiwan and President Obama's meeting with the Dalai Lama in 2010 was harsher than in the recent past.
- Chinese officials threatened to stop investing in US government securities and to move away from using the US dollar in international transactions.
- The Chinese government responded very harshly to American government interventions in 2010 urging collective efforts to manage rising tensions in

the South China Sea and affirming the US-Japan security treaty during Sino-Japanese disputes over East China Sea islands. [14]

The Obama government reacted calmly and firmly to what Secretary of State Hillary Clinton called these "tests" of a new assertiveness by China. At that time, the US government also found that prominent Chinese assertiveness and truculence with the United States and neighboring Asian countries over maritime, security, and other issues seriously damaged China's efforts to portray a benign image in Asia. Asian governments became more active in working closely with the United States and in encouraging an active US presence in the Asia-Pacific. Their interest in closer ties with the United States meshed well with the Obama government's broad effort under the rubric of the US rebalance to Asia in order to "reengage" with the countries of the Asia-Pacific, ranging from India to the Pacific Islands. The overall effect was a temporary rise in the position of the United States, with China on the defensive. [15]

Explanations of the beginnings of what would turn out to be a protracted phase-up to the present of greater competition in US-China relations overriding previous cooperation varied. Chinese commentators tended to see the starting point in the rising challenges it faced as the Obama government's rebalance policy was announced in late 2011. Many Chinese commentators saw the policy as encircling and designed to contain and constrain China's rising influence in Asia. [16] For their part, Obama government officials and many other Americans tended to see the new competition posed by greater Chinese assertiveness and challenges to the United States as coming from altered Chinese views of power realities between the two countries and in Asian and world affairs. The US-initiated international financial breakdown and massive recession added to perceived American weaknesses seen in declining American strength, notably because of the draining wars in Iraq and Afghanistan. On the other hand, China emerged from the economic crisis with strong growth, flush with cash, and more confident in its state-directed growth model as opposed to the now deeply discredited American free-market approach. Under these circumstances, Chinese elite and popular opinion looked with increasing disapproval on the cautious and reactive approach of the Hu Jintao government (2002–2012). In foreign affairs, accommodating the United States and regional powers over long-standing Chinese interests involving Chinese security, sovereignty, and other sensitive issues seemed overly passive and misguided. Though Hu's approach was in line with Deng Xiaoping's instruction that China should keep a low profile in foreign affairs and focus on domestic development, opinion in China now favored a more robust and prominent Chinese international approach. The result over the following years was an evolution of greater boldness, activism, and considerable use of coercion, generally short of using military force, in employing

Chinese economic, political, and military power to meet the broad goals in what incoming leader Xi Jinping in 2012 called the "China Dream." The goals involved China unified with disputed territories under its control and with a stature unsurpassed in Asia as a leading world power. [17]

The administration of President Barack Obama had considerable success in implementing the various security, economic, diplomatic, and political elements of what was initially called the pivot to Asia and was soon relabeled the US rebalance policy in Asia. The policy approaches seen in the rebalance policy were considered by Obama government officials from the outset of the administration and were initiated in a series of speeches and announcements in late 2011 and early 2012. The record showed that the main initiatives of the rebalance policy were followed and duly implemented by the Obama government. Incoming president Donald Trump in 2017 ended the rebalance policy amid policy controversy and uncertainty, with potentially negative consequences for US standing in Asia.

The Obama rebalance policy was also criticized in the United States and elsewhere in Asia. It was seen as too weak to deal with the challenges posed by China. And growing American opposition eventually blocked approval of the Trans-Pacific Partnership (TPP), the economic centerpiece of the rebalance policy. As noted above, China's Communist Party leader and president Xi Jinping (2012–) departed from past pragmatic Chinese cooperation with the United States in carrying out often bold and disruptive policies that notably came at the expense of China's neighbors and US interests in the Asia-Pacific region. How to deal with rising China figured prominently in the American rebalance policy from the start. The Obama government adjusted policy to take account of Chinese concerns and to more effectively manage growing Chinese challenges. Critics said that the rebalance framework needed strengthening in order to protect American interests in the face of Chinese and other challenges. Republican presidential candidate Donald Trump promised harsh measures to counter unfair Chinese economic practices, and he strongly opposed the TPP. He had little to say about the security and political aspects of US policy toward China, while his avowed policy toward Asian allies undercut the emphasis on strengthened US-allied cooperation in the rebalance policy.

The evolving and varied elements in the rebalance policy were in line with the interests of most Asia-Pacific governments, though China objected, sometimes strongly. From the outset, the initiatives reinforced long-standing US priorities in Northeast Asia involving China, Japan, and Korea, while they increased the American priority placed on the broad expanse of the Asia-Pacific ranging from India to Japan to New Zealand and the Pacific Islands. The United States adjusted the emphasis in the policy. At first (2011–2012) it focused on strategic initiatives, which were particularly controversial in China. It shifted in late 2012 to greater emphasis on economic and diplomatic initiatives, though security dimensions continued to develop. As China's challenges to US policy grew, the Obama government toughened its public posture toward China and deepened regional involvement to counter adverse Chinese behavior. The initiatives were often extensions of longstanding trends in US policy and practice; they built on and called greater attention to the positive advancements of American interests in the region by the George W. Bush and earlier administrations. [18]

Security aspects of the rebalance included the following:

1. The Obama government avowed high-priority attention to the Asia-Pacific region following US military pullbacks from Iraq and Afghanistan. The Asia-Pacific's economic and strategic importance was said to warrant heightened US policy attention even as America withdrew from Southwest Asia and appeared reluctant to intervene militarily in other world conflicts.
2. The Obama government pledged to sustain close alliance relationships and maintain force levels and military capabilities in the Asia-Pacific region despite substantial cutbacks in overall US defense spending. If needed, funding for the Asia-Pacific security presence was said to come at the expense of other US military priorities.
3. US officials promoted more widely dispersed US forces and basing/deployment arrangements, which indicated the rising importance of Southeast Asia, the Indian Ocean, and the western Pacific in tandem with strong continuing support of long-standing American priorities, notably those in Northeast Asia. The advances involved developing deployment arrangements or supporting and supply arrangements in Australia, the Philippines, Singapore, and India, among others.
4. The dispersal of US forces and a developing US air-sea battle concept [19] were viewed as means to counter growing "area denial" efforts in the Asia-Pacific region, mainly by China.

Economic aspects of the rebalance involved strong emphasis on the US pursuit of free trade and other open economic interchange. President Obama and his economic officers stressed that American jobs depended on freer access to Asia-Pacific markets. Against the backdrop of stalled World Trade Organization talks on international liberalization, the United States devoted extraordinary attention to the multilateral Trans-Pacific Partnership arrangement involving twelve Asian and Pacific countries in order to promote freer market access for American goods and services. The high standards of the TPP regarding such issues as safeguarding intellectual property rights and limiting state intervention in economic policies were seen to pose a challenge to China. Indeed, a successful TPP was deemed likely to prompt China to join, thereby bringing about a change in Chinese neomercantilist policies and practices that grossly disadvantaged American sales to China and competition with China in international markets.

Political and diplomatic aspects of the rebalance were manifest in significantly enhanced and more flexible US activism and engagement both bilaterally and multilaterally in pursuing American interests in regional security and stability, free and open economic exchange, and political relations and values involving the rule of law, human rights, and accountable governance. The Obama government markedly advanced US relations with the Association of Southeast Asian Nations (ASEAN) and with the various regional groups convened by ASEAN. US engagement showed sensitivity to the interests of so-called third parties, notably China's neighbors, when pursuing bilateral US relations with China. The US rebalance demonstrated how the United States adapted to and worked constructively with various regional multilateral groupings, endeavoring overall to build a regional order supported by the rule of law, good governance, and other accepted norms.

While the rebalance enhanced US competition with China, as well as American challenges to China's area denial security strategy and its neomercantilist economic policies and practices, it also strongly emphasized enhanced American engagement with China. Thus, the greater US engagement with Asia seen in the rebalance included greater US engagement with China. Examples of such enhanced engagement were the remarkable in-depth discussions seen in the informal summit between the Chinese and US presidents in California in June 2013 and in their later summit meetings. The greater Sino-American engagement was designed to reassure not only China but also China's neighbors that US efforts to compete for influence and to dissuade China from taking assertive and disruptive policies toward its neighbors were done in ways that did not result in major friction or confrontation with China, which was at odds with the interests of almost all of China's neighbors. In effect, the rebalance involved a delicate "balancing act" of American resolve and reassurance toward China that seemed to work reasonably well until China's coercive expansionist efforts in disputed areas of the East and South China Seas, along with other adverse behavior, prompted a toughening in the Obama government's posture toward China.

The prominence and initial success of the rebalance almost certainly influenced the Chinese leadership's most significant changes in Chinese foreign relations since the death of Deng Xiaoping. Deng had stressed that China should bide its time in foreign affairs and focus on domestic modernization. However, after the 2008 economic crisis and subsequent recession, China's comprehensive national power was rising remarkably as the United States and its allies faced protracted problems at home and abroad. Against this background, Beijing shifted to an assertive foreign policy exacerbating long-standing Chinese differences with the United States and others that was more in line with the China-centered nationalism prevalent in Chinese elite and public opinion. The shift came about with the transition from the comparatively weak and risk-adverse collective leadership of Hu Jintao to the strongman rule carried out by Xi Jinping, who took over leadership of the Communist Party in 2012.[20]

A temporary pause in rising US-Chinese tensions came with the lead-up to the January 18–20, 2011, visit of President Hu Jintao to Washington. The harsh Chinese rhetoric criticizing American policies and practices subsided; the Chinese put aside their objections to high-level military exchanges, and Secretary of Defense Robert Gates reestablished businesslike ties at the top levels of the Chinese military during a visit to Beijing in early January 2011; China used its influence to get North Korea to stop its provocations against South Korea and to seek negotiations over nuclear weapons issues; China avoided undercutting international sanctions to press Iran to give up its nuclear weapons program; China allowed the value of its currency to appreciate in line with US interests; and Chinese officials were more cooperative over climate change issues at an international meeting in Cancun than they were a year earlier.[21] For his part, President Obama made clear during 2011 and 2012 that he would pursue closer engagement with China as part of his administration's overall new emphasis on American rebalance with the Asia-Pacific. Obama administration leaders from the president on down articulated the outlines of a new emphasis on American reengagement with the Asia-Pacific that promised more competition with China for influence in the region while averring strong US interest in greater engagement with China.[22]

Both sides endeavored to manage growing competition and rivalry with continued close engagement and pragmatism. The more than ninety official dialogues dealing with all aspects of the multifaceted relationship remained active.[23] The on-again, off-again pattern of exchanges between the military leaders of both countries—the weakest link in the array of dialogues between the two countries—was on again with improved exchanges in 2012–2015. President Obama and President Xi avowed commitment to manage differences effectively during summit meetings in 2013 and 2014 and looked positively toward their meeting slated for September 2015.

The so-called Taiwan issue—historically the leading cause of friction between the United States and China—remained on a recent trajectory of easing tensions. Taiwan's election in 2012 and the victory of incumbent president Ma validated the continued moderate approach to cross-strait relations, foreshadowing closer engagement along lines welcomed by both Beijing and Washington.[24] Local Taiwan elections in November 2014 nonetheless saw a resurgence of the opposition Democratic Progressive Party (DPP) and a decline of the ruling Nationalist (Kuomintang) Party. The DPP was viewed very suspiciously by Beijing. Once they won the January 2016 Taiwan presidential and legislative elections, cross-strait relations became tenser.[25]

Meanwhile, despite growing Sino-US distrust, there were also episodes demonstrating notable cooperation and seeming trust building between the two powers. One instance was the Sino-American handling of the case of Chen Guangcheng. The prominent Chinese civil rights activist escaped house arrest in April 2012 and fled from his home province to Beijing, where he eventually took refuge in the US embassy. After several days of talks between US officials working with Chen on one side and Chinese officials on the other, a deal was reached to safeguard Chen and his family and to provide Chen with medical treatment. Chen subsequently changed his mind and appealed for American support to go to the United States with his family. Intensive renewed US-Chinese talks concurrent with the annual Security and Economic Dialogue between top American and Chinese department leaders then underway in Beijing resulted in a second deal where Chen and his family were allowed to leave for the United States on May 19, 2012.[26] Earlier that year, the US government showed remarkable restraint beneficial to China as it imposed strict silence on what occurred in the daylong visit of a senior deputy of the ambitious Chongqing municipality leader Bo Xilai who fled to the US consulate in Chengdu in February. The deputy was reportedly seeking refuge and safety from municipality forces; while in the consulate, an official escort to Beijing was arranged to take him to the capital where he provided information leading to the downfall and jailing of Bo Xilai, then challenging Xi Jinping for the top leadership position. Concurrently, the American government remained silent about the extraordinary episode.

Meanwhile, the Obama government after mid-2012 played down the emphasis seen in 2011 and early 2012 on American security and military moves that added directly to the growing security dilemma with China. National Security Adviser Tom Donilon went to extraordinary lengths to emphasize the nonmilitary aspects of the rebalance and to play down US competition with China prior to President Obama's trip to the region in November 2012. Concurrently, the secretary of defense and the secretary of state similarly emphasized the broad and multifaceted reasons for strong and sustained American engagement with Asia and played down competition with China.[27]

Unfortunately, the pragmatic engagement of President Obama with the Chinese leaders ran up against long-standing differences between the two countries. Four categories of Chinese differences with the United States have deep roots, with many going back to ideological and strategic issues of the Maoist period. They are as follows: (1) opposition to US support for Taiwan and involvement with other sensitive sovereignty issues, including Tibet and disputed islands and maritime rights along China's rim; (2) opposition to perceived US efforts to change China's political system; (3) opposition to the United States playing the dominant role along China's periphery in Asia; and (4) opposition to many aspects of US leadership in world affairs.

US differences with China have involved clusters of often-contentious economic, security, political, sovereignty, foreign policy, and other issues. Most have become more important for the United States as China has grown recently to be seen as a "peer competitor" with the United States, with the possibility of overtaking and dominating America. As in the past, areas of friction developed in tandem with a wide range of cooperation between the two governments and societies that had developed notably during the period of pragmatic cooperation over the previous decade. However, the Trump administration, more than any other US government since normalization of relations over forty years ago, signaled a radical course change in US policy toward China, viewing Beijing more as a malign competitor than a promising partner.

## Xi Jinping Challenges America

After taking the leading Communist Party and government positions in late 2012 and early 2013, President Xi repeatedly placed other foreign and domestic priorities above his avowed but increasingly hollow claims to seek a positive relationship with the United States. As noted earlier, Xi's preferred framework for US-China relations, which called for a "new type of great-power relationship" that would respect China's "core interests," was viewed warily by the United States. The framework marked the most recent in the list of proposals noted earlier that have failed to create a structure to bridge differences and create lasting cooperation in the post–Cold War period.

As Xi Jinping began the process of changing Chinese policies with major negative implications for the United States, the caution and low profile of Hu Jintao's leadership were viewed with disfavor. The string of Chinese actions and initiatives were truly impressive in seven different areas.

First, the government orchestrated the largest mass demonstration against a foreign target ever seen in Chinese history (against US ally Japan over disputed islands) in September 2012. It followed with diplomatic, military, and economic pressure against Japan not seen since World War II. Second, China used coercive and intimidating means to extend control of disputed territory at neighbors' expense, notably in rapidly building island military outposts in the disputed South China Sea. Third, ever-expanding advanced Chinese military capabilities were aimed at American forces in the Asia-Pacific region. Fourth, Chinese cooperation with Russia grew steadily closer as each power endeavored to undermine US influence in their respective spheres of influence. Fifth, unfair Chinese restrictions on access to China's market, demands that foreign enterprises share sensitive manufacturing and production data, industrial espionage and cyber theft for economic gain, gross infringements on international property rights, and reluctance to contribute regional and global common goods all advanced as China's economy grew. Sixth, China used its large foreign exchange reserves, massive excess construction capacity, and strong trading advantages to develop international banks and to support often grandiose Chinese plans for Asian and global infrastructure construction, investments, loans, and trade areas that excluded the United States and countered American initiatives and support for existing international economic institutions. Finally, Xi Jinping tightened political control domestically in ways grossly offensive to American representatives seeking political liberalization and better human rights conditions in China.[28]

President Obama proved to be less than effective in dealing with the various challenges posed by Xi Jinping's actions. His administration gave top priority to supporting an overall positive US approach to engagement with China. Differences were usually dealt with in private consultations. Even if they seemed important, they were kept within carefully crafted channels and were not allowed to spill over and impact other elements in the relationship. Thus, the Obama government followed a deliberative and transparent approach to China policy that was predictable and eschewed "linkage," the seeking of US leverage to get China to stop behavior offensive to the United States by linking the offensive Chinese behavior to another policy area where the United States would threaten actions adverse to important Chinese interests. It was easy for China to determine how the US president was likely to act in the face of Chinese challenges; unpredictable uses of power against China seemed unlikely, allowing China to continue its advances at American expense.

Against this background, US dissatisfaction with Chinese behavior at American expense grew. Republican leaders in Congress and the Republican Party platform in the 2016 election were harsh in condemning various Chinese practices. Many China-related issues were prominent in the presidential campaign, although overall they came behind other foreign policy concerns like Islamic extremism and Russia.

Going into the campaign, debates over US policy in the Asia-Pacific focused heavily on perceived US weaknesses in the face of growing challenges from China. Notably, rising China's prominent leader Xi Jinping was viewed as prone to coercive strongman tactics at home and abroad that kept his opponents and competitors off balance and on the defensive. In the Asia-Pacific, Chinese authorities created an environment of increasing tensions that was viewed in China and elsewhere to benefit Xi at the expense of his opponents and competitors, including the United States, heretofore relied on as the region's stabilizer and security guarantor.

As the US election campaign progressed, this broad concern with China remained active, but it was overshadowed by strong debate on two sets of issues: international trade and the proposed Trans-Pacific Partnership accord, and candidate Trump's controversial proposals on burden sharing among allies, nuclear weapons proliferation, and North Korea. Criticism of the TPP received broad bipartisan support and posed increasingly serious obstacles to US government approval of the pact. Trump's controversial proposals were unpopular and were opposed by senior Republicans in Congress along with many others. Mr. Trump avoided bringing them up in the immediate aftermath of the US election.[29]

Though most presidential candidates voiced harsh criticism of Chinese policies and behavior, the mix of strong differences and positive engagement seen in the Obama administration's policy toward China was reflected in the candidates' similarly mixed policy recommendations. The contenders' views were also in line with American public opinion, which, on balance, disapproved of the Chinese government but ranked China lower than in the recent past as an economic threat and viewed China's military as less threatening to US interests than terrorism, nuclear weapons development in North Korea and Iran, various conflicts in the Middle East, climate change, refugee flows, and infectious diseases.[30]

According to Donald Trump, the main problem the United States had with China was that the United States wasn't using its power to influence them. The source of US power over China, according to Trump, was US economic strength. Overall, Trump was not hostile to or confrontational with China, having said, "We desire to live peacefully and in friendship with Russia and China. We have serious differences with these two nations . . . but we are not bound to be adversaries." Trump tended to avoid discussing China as a national security threat. He averred that issues with China could be dealt with through negotiations, using American strengths as leverage.[31]

Officials and specialists in Beijing saw negatives with both the Democratic candidate, Hillary Clinton, and the Republican choice, Donald Trump. Like many Americans, they were frustrated with the downward trend in US-China relations and judged that the trend would worsen at least to some degree if Clinton were elected. Some in Beijing nonetheless voiced confidence that mutual interests and highly integrated US-China government relationships would guard against relations going seriously off track. Chinese derision of Trump earlier in 2016 shifted to seeking advantage, given the candidate's disruption of US alliances along China's rim and emphasis on seeking common ground with China through negotiations. Overall, a common view was that China could "shape" President Trump to behave in line with its interests, as Donald Trump was seen as less ideological and more pragmatic than Hillary Clinton.[32]

President-elect Trump upended these sanguine Chinese views when he accepted a congratulatory phone call from Taiwan's president in December 2016. The call was reportedly facilitated by long-standing Republican Party leaders, reflecting the party's 2016 platform that was remarkably supportive of Taiwan as well as harsh toward China. When China complained, Mr. Trump condemned Beijing's unfair economic policies and its building of military outposts in the disputed South China Sea, and he went on to question why the United States needed to support a position of one China and avoid improved contacts with Taiwan. President Trump eventually was persuaded to endorse—at least in general terms—the American view of the one-China policy. His informal summit meeting with President Xi Jinping in Florida in early April 2017 went well. The two leaders met again on the sidelines of the G20 summit in July and held repeated phone conversations over North Korea and other issues in the lead-up to the US president's visit to Beijing in November. Despite serious differences between the two countries, both leaders seemed to value their personal rapport. President Xi organized a remarkable visit for President Trump in China, prompting President Trump's personal gratitude and appreciation.[33]

After the Florida summit, the Trump government kept strong political pressure on China to use its leverage to halt North Korea's nuclear weapons development. Planned arms sales to Taiwan, freedom-of-navigation exercises in the South China Sea, and other US initiatives that might have complicated America's search for leverage with China in order to stop North Korea's nuclear weapons development were temporarily put on hold. The two sides also reached agreement on a one-hundred-day action plan to further bilateral economic cooperation prior to the first US-China Comprehensive Economic Dialogue set for July.[34]

As President Trump registered dissatisfaction with China's efforts on North Korea in June, the Taiwan arms sales and freedom-of-navigation exercises went forward. And the July economic dialogue reached no agreement on actionable new steps to reduce the US trade deficit with China and ended in obvious failure. News leaks of senior administration meetings showed the president rejecting compromises with China that were supported by senior administration economic officials in favor of unilateral punitive tariffs against adverse Chinese trade practices. The administration avoided harsh economic measures in the lead-up to the president's trip to China in November, but they emerged in 2018.[35]

The Trump government's National Security Strategy of December 2017 and its National Defense Strategy of January 2018 employed harsh words about China not seen in official administration documents since before the Nixon administration. They viewed Beijing as a predatory rival and the top danger to American national security. Added to China's military power and assertive actions in the Asia-Pacific was the danger China posed to the United States as it carried out its plan to be the leading country in various high-technology industries seen as essential for sustaining US international leadership and national security.[36]

In communications with Congress, administration leaders repeatedly highlighted the latter danger, which represented a newly prominent and important issue in 2018 added to long-standing American grievances against

China. US trade representative Robert Lighthizer issued a dire warning against the many covert and overt ways China unfairly took advantage of the United States. He said such practices represented "an existential threat" to the United States. Meanwhile, FBI director Christopher Wray highlighted for Congress another newly prominent issue, China's overt and covert influence operations, including espionage in the United States. He warned repeatedly that America needed a "whole-of-society" effort to counter Beijing's perceived nefarious intentions.[37]

Congressional members of both parties saw the wisdom in the administration's warnings and began to take action, making 2018 the most assertive period of congressional work on China since the tumultuous decade after the Tiananmen crackdown. However, the broader impact on American politics was diluted for several reasons. First, President Trump did not use and appeared ambivalent about the anti-China language seen in the administration's strategy documents. Thus, he repeatedly expressed friendship and respect for President Xi, whose support he continued to seek in dealing with North Korea. Against this background, Mr. Trump disapproved forward US movement with Taiwan as he attempted negotiations with North Korea's Kim Jung Un at a summit in Singapore in June 2018. Second, senior administration officials remained seriously divided on economic issues with China. White House economic adviser Gary Cohn's resignation in March 2018 weakened the moderates. Initial punitive tariffs ensued. Third, public opinion was generally unaware of the China danger—it stuck to its long-standing view of not liking the Chinese government but also seeking to avoid trouble with China.[38] Fourth, the media remained largely unaware of the major shift. They tended to focus on President Trump's antics and his seeking of trade protectionism for his political supporters.[39]

The specific steps Congress used in hardening policy toward China involved the following:

- extensive hearings on the challenges Chinese policies and practices pose for American interests;[40]
- a variety of individual bills on specific issues, some of which were incorporated into such important legislation, requiring congressional approval, as the annual National Defense Authorization bill;[41] and
- letters to the administration signed by bipartisan congressional leaders warning of Chinese actions and urging firm responses.[42]

A bipartisan group of twenty-seven of the most senior senators, headed by Senate majority whip John Cornyn and Senate minority leader Charles Schumer, sent a letter in May to the top American economic negotiators with China, urging a firm line against recent Chinese technology theft and ambitions. Another letter to senior Trump administration officials by a group of twelve senators, including prominent liberal Elizabeth Warren, urged defense against Chinese influence operations in democracies around the world. In August, a letter signed by sixteen senators including long-standing conservative critics of China and some leading liberals stressed opposition to Chinese international lending practices.[43]

Members sometimes grumbled about the adverse impact of the Trump government's punitive tariffs on their constituents, and they sometimes opposed imposing tariffs on allies at the same time tariffs were being imposed on China. Overall, there was much less opposition to the tariffs against China.[44] Congress disapproved of President Trump's decision in May 2018 to ease the harsh sanctions against the prominent Chinese high-technology firm ZTE in response to a personal plea from the Chinese president. In the end, however, Congress proved unwilling to stand against the president's compromise on sanctions on ZTE.[45]

Bills strengthening US support for Taiwan urged the American Defense Department and the US government more broadly to come up with strategies to bolster US-Taiwan military ties, assist Taiwan in countering escalating efforts by Beijing to isolate Taiwan, and promote higher-level contacts between the US and Taiwan governments. A stand-alone bill advocating more and higher-level US official visits to Taiwan, known as the Taiwan Travel Act, passed Congress with unanimous approval and was signed by President Trump in March 2018. Taiwan generally enjoys broad support in Congress, but achieving a unanimous vote on an issue strongly opposed by China indicated how negative a turn Congress was taking in regard to the Chinese government and its concerns.[46]

The Trump government took a variety of relatively small steps to show greater support for Taiwan despite Beijing's opposition. But after his reversal following the phone call with the Taiwan president in December 2016, President Trump reportedly remained wary of more dramatic steps on Taiwan policy that might jeopardize China's cooperation on higher-priority issues, notably North Korea. Trump reportedly was upset that a deputy assistant secretary of state in March 2018 gave a public speech in Taipei attended by the Taiwan president where he hailed ever-strengthening US-Taiwan relations. And the president reportedly reviewed the guest list of US officials attending the inauguration of the new unofficial American embassy in Taipei to assure that no higher-level official that might be offensive to China would be attending. The Taipei office inauguration coincided with President Trump's June 12 summit with the North Korean leader in Singapore, reinforcing his unwillingness to jeopardize Chinese support at that critical time.[47]

The National Defense Authorization Act FY 2019, the most important foreign policy legislation in 2018, underlined hardening toward China.[48] Harsh language accused Beijing of using military modernization, influence operations, espionage, and predatory economic policy to undermine the United States and its interests abroad. In response, the law directed a whole-of-government US strategy targeting Chinese challenges; required the Defense Department to submit a five-year plan to bolster US, allied, and partner strength in the Indo-Pacific region; extended the authority and broadened the scope of the Maritime Security Initiative covering Southeast Asia to include the Indo-Pacific region; required a US strategy to strengthen military ties with India; prohibited China's participation in Rim of the Pacific naval exercises; required a public report on China's military and coercive activities in the South China Sea; broadened the scope of the annual report to Congress on Chinese military and security developments to now include "malign activities," including information and influence operations, as well as predatory economic and lending practices; and limited Defense Department funds for Chinese-language programs at universities that host Confucius Institutes.

The act's provisions on Taiwan reaffirmed various aspects of long-standing American commitments to Taiwan. They sought in particular to enhance US arms sales and higher-level US defense and related personnel exchanges, training, and exercises with Taiwan. The act required a comprehensive Defense Department assessment of Taiwan's military forces and reserve forces within one year, including recommendations for US actions to assist Taiwan and a plan on how the United States would implement the recommendations.

The act contained a separate set of provisions to modernize, strengthen, and broaden the scope of the interagency Committee on Foreign Investment in the United States (CFIUS) to more effectively guard against the risk to US national security seen posed by Chinese and other predatory foreign investment. It also included key reforms in US export controls that would better protect emerging technology and intellectual property from Beijing and other potential adversaries.

Chinese officials responsible for US-China relations were aware that President Trump's approach to foreign affairs was the opposite of President Obama's as far as the former president's well-known features of deliberation, transparency, predictability, avoiding linkage, and restrained use of power were concerned. Nonetheless, they remained confident into early 2018 that whatever differences President Trump had with China could be dealt with readily through negotiations and making what the US president called "deals" that would perhaps involve some economic or other comparatively minor concessions from China. Thus, they were not well prepared for President Trump's decisive use of punitive tariffs against China beginning in 2018.[49]

An administration announcement in June promised steep tariffs on $50 billion of Chinese higher-technology imports seen to have benefited from China's abuse of American and international intellectual property rights. An announcement in July said that planned punitive tariffs of 10 percent would be imposed on $200 billion of Chinese imports. An August 1 announcement increased the rate of those proposed tariffs to 25 percent at the end of the year. As those tariffs were implemented in September, the United States threatened tariffs on an additional $267 billion of Chinese imports if Beijing retaliated, which it promptly did with Chinese punitive tariffs covering most of China's imports of American products. [50]

Throughout the fall, administration officials continued to turn up the rhetorical heat on China. In September, Trump, in the world spotlight at the UN General Assembly, condemned China for influence operations seeking to undermine the Republican Party in US midterm elections. Terry Branstad, former Iowa governor, current US ambassador to China, and "friend" of Xi Jinping (Xi favors Iowa), published a harsh editorial condemning China's influence operations in Iowa. National Security Council senior China official Matthew Pottinger at Chinese embassy National Day celebrations issued a blunt warning of impending US competition. National Security Adviser John Bolton and Secretary of State Michael Pompeo doubled down on criticism of China in prominent media interviews.

Vice President Mike Pence inaugurated a new public phase of the Trump government's toughening against China in a speech in October 2018 explaining to the American people, the media, and international audiences the wide extent of the US policy shift and its purported durability. Citing the administration's National Security Strategy, he detailed key elements in the current wide-ranging Trump administration response to China's many challenges. [51]

Other tough measures against China not seen in past US practice came from various US agencies. Sanctions were imposed on a Chinese company and officials for purchasing weapons from Russia in violation of US sanctions against Russia. Then came the publicized arrest in Belgium during an FBI-engineered sting operation and deportation to the United States of a Chinese security official involved in espionage to steal US military technology. Warning strongly against Beijing's intentions in Latin America, the administration in September condemned China's continued expansion of diplomatic relations at the expense of Taiwan in the region as adverse to US interests and regional stability. It repeatedly attacked China's self-serving and predatory ambitions seen in Xi Jinping's ever-growing Belt and Road Initiative (BRI), now involving Chinese infrastructure building, loans, investments, and port acquisitions throughout most of the world. The United States opposed continued World Bank assistance of about $2 billion in loans annually to China despite its prominent economic status, and it objected to any International Monetary Fund (IMF) bailout for Pakistan that would compensate China for its large-scale "predatory lending" to the country under the rubric of China's BRI. The Trump government was reported in October to seek withdrawal from the Intermediate-Range Nuclear Forces (INF) Treaty controlling intermediate ballistic missiles so that the United States could develop and deploy such missiles to counter the ballistic missile advantage in the Asia-Pacific held by China, not a signatory of the INF treaty.

Entering November, the Justice Department rolled out what was called a "New Initiative" to combat Chinese economic espionage. Standing in for absent President Trump, Vice President Pence repeatedly criticized Chinese economic and military practices, underscoring the administration's hard line for international audiences in remarks at annual multilateral summit meetings in Asia. Reflecting the toughening toward China, the US Navy announced its third deployment in 2018 of warships sailing through the Taiwan Strait. With the opening to China in the 1970s, the United States halted warships patrolling the Taiwan Strait. Reportedly some warship transits occasionally took place since then, but they were rare and were not publicized, presumably in deference to China's sensitivities.[52]

The overall result was a negative atmosphere for the Trump-Xi summit at the G20 meeting in Argentina on December 1. The summit resulted in a temporary halt to escalating US punitive trade tariffs against China, pending agreement involving extensive US demands by March 2019. Indeed, on the same day of the summit came the arrest of the chief financial officer and daughter of the president of China's leading telecommunications firm, Huawei, by Canadian authorities in Vancouver for extradition to the United States. The US charges involved Huawei's involvement in subverting US sanctions against Iran. Beijing reacted strongly, arresting and detaining Canadians in China, but it avoided actions against the United States. More negatives followed with National Security Adviser Bolton's strong attack on China's policies in Africa in a speech on December 13 and with President Trump's signing on December 31 of the Asia Assurance Initiative Act, which provided $1.5 billion in funding for carrying out US programs in Asia and US support for Taiwan and other regional partners along the lines of provisions in the National Defense Authorization Act of August, noted above.

Following their meeting in Argentina resulting in a halt to new trade tariffs, both President Xi and President Trump emphasized the positive in their phone conversation of December 29, with Trump averring that "big progress" is being made in preparation for official talks on economic differences slated for January. The US negotiation team was headed by US trade representative Robert Lighthizer and his subordinates known for their tough approach to China. Congress finished the year with other legislation likely to be revived in the 116th Congress taking aim at Beijing's massive crackdown on dissent among Uighur Muslims in northwestern China and continued repression in Tibet, and it proposed penalties against Chinese high-technology firms that violate US international sanctions.[53]

As trade negotiations dragged on into 2019, administration spokespersons were publicly more restrained in criticizing China. Nevertheless, the whole-of-government pushback against Chinese practices went forward. The Justice

Department publicized for media use and popular information a wide array of convictions of Chinese agents or those working for Chinese authorities engaged in egregious episodes of espionage, intellectual property theft, and influence operations. Department officials featured these episodes in briefings conducted in various locations designed to inform media and people outside Washington, DC, of the extent and impact of these Chinese challenges. Department officials also visited various universities, warning of clandestine Chinese espionage using Chinese students to seek advanced technology and influence operations through Confucius Institutes. For its part, Congress sustained an anti-China drumbeat with legislation, hearings, letters, and other public bipartisan demonstrations to reassure Asia of US support in the face of China, to criticize China-Russia cooperation, to condemn acute suppression in China's Xinjiang, and to spotlight dangers posed by Confucius Institutes.[54]

By this time, mainstream American media were no longer so distracted by President Trump's antics, and they focused on the Chinese challenges to America. Repeated news stories about China's perceived ambitions to overtake America's lead in high-technology industry, placing US military technology leadership in jeopardy, headed the list of issues having a negative impact on American public opinion. A widely respected annual Gallup poll in early February 2019 found a sharp deterioration in American views of China. Twenty-one percent of Americans now considered China the country's greatest enemy, compared to 11 percent at the same time in 2018. The level of American popular disapproval of the Chinese government grew by 20 percent from the previous year.[55]

The strength of American popular opposition to Chinese challenges showed in analyses demonstrating a coming together of groups of disgruntled Americans now more focused on the China danger. Those groups were seen as key elements of President Trump's so-called political base. Trump's unexpected victory pulled together the following: people afraid of being displaced by alien immigrants and perceived pernicious foreign influence; workers concerned about being sold out to China and angry about the complicity of elites in the betrayal; Christians frustrated with obstacles to proclaiming the Gospel, with China as the largest malefactor; and manufacturers worried about having their technology stolen and market access blocked. All four groups now gave the China danger an overall higher importance in American public opinion. Their respective China concerns received forceful articulation by ideologues like Steve Bannon, were echoed in the recent rhetoric of Mike Pence, were pursued in the policies advocated by such close advisers as Peter Navarro and Stephen Miller, and were encouraged by advice from hawkish Washington think tanks and nationalistic commentators on Fox News. Against this background, it was no accident that Politico reported that China was the "global menace" featured above any other international danger at the annual Conservative Political Action Conference that President Trump addressed at length in March 2019.[56]

The growing tensions between the US and Chinese governments resulted in atrophy of the scores of official dialogues used in the past to manage tensions and build positive interchange in Chinese-American relations. The establishment and widespread use of consultative mechanisms, often known as dialogues, was a means to allow for private discussion of US-China differences in ways that did not negatively impact the overall relationship. China favored these dialogues to deal with sensitive issues that if publicized could cause more friction than sought by Beijing, embarrassment over compromises or unpopular commitments made by China, or criticism among Chinese elite and public opinion. American leaders also often favored keeping secret the dialogue discussions with China, notably when the current policy was being criticized by Congress, the media, and public opinion.[57]

President Trump agreed with President Xi at their first meeting at the Mar-a-Lago resort in April 2017 to establish four high-level mechanisms for senior leaders to discuss issues. They are known as the diplomatic and security dialogue, the comprehensive economic dialogue, the social and people-to-people dialogue, and the law enforcement and cyber security dialogue. Other important dialogues took place between the two militaries. While the various dialogues met, they did not achieve much. And rather than shielding differences from public view, US government leaders beginning in 2018 were much more public than past American administrations in registering US concerns over major differences with China, through words and actions that often embarrassed and upset Chinese government counterparts.[58]

Moreover, the wide range of engagement involving a variety of cooperative US-China programs fostered by many US government departments and agencies with Chinese counterparts became subject to review by the Trump government to assess the benefit for American interests. Overall, this engagement atrophied. Unlike in the recent past when American officials tended to avoid confronting Beijing over various disputes in order to preserve and advance such positive programs of engagement with China, the tables had turned, with senior US leaders now giving top priority to countering China's adverse practices and showing diminished concern for negative fallout for any remaining positive interchanges with Beijing.

## RECENT CROSSCURRENTS IN AMERICA'S CHINA DEBATE, 2019–2020

Apart from President Trump and some administration leaders hailing the progress achieved in the "phase one" trade deal announced in January 2020, other evidence that the US government might be moderating its approach to

China included these seven pieces of evidence.[59] First, President Trump remained ambivalent and was usually more positive toward China than any other senior administration official. He rarely used the language of his tough National Security Strategy focused on China as the primary US national security danger. Second, administration leaders tended to be less vocally critical of China concurrent with ups and downs in yearlong US-China trade negotiations. The phase one deal was a cause of public celebration for them. Third, the administration kept postponing the imposition of proposed export controls regarding advanced US computer chips going to Huawei, despite the US government's strong rhetoric against the firm. Fourth, Congress was very critical of China's policies on such sensitive issues as Hong Kong and Xinjiang, but its legislative impact was scattered and notably less significant than in 2018. Fifth, while public opinion in 2020 registered increased disapproval of China than seen in the ratings in 2019, there was little evidence that the US public shared the urgency to counter China's behavior seen in the administration's strategies strongly backed by bipartisan congressional leaders. Sixth, more than one hundred China and foreign policy experts signed a letter disagreeing with administration policy, calling for greater moderation toward China.

Last but not least, Democratic candidates gave little priority to China and were much more moderate than the debate in Washington. Joe Biden averred that the United States was notably more powerful than China and could handle challenges coming from Beijing; latecomer Michael Bloomberg remained quiet on China—presumably to avoid controversy over his extensive business dealings with Xi Jinping and other Chinese leaders. Before declaring his candidacy, Mr. Bloomberg defended Xi Jinping's harsh crackdown on Muslim Uighurs in China. When asked by a reporter, Bernie Sanders said that he did not consider China as an existential threat to the United States. He, like Elizabeth Warren, saw the problem with China in economic terms and as caused by US big business, not China. Warren also focused on big business, not China. Pete Buttigieg did see China's economic rise and quest for high-technology leadership as a real danger, yet his remedy was not to confront China; and he advised that cooperation with China was needed on climate change and other issues. Senator Amy Klobuchar saw utility in well-managed US-allied pressures on China, but of one hundred tasks she said she would do in her first one hundred days as president, only one related to China—steel dumping.

Nevertheless, despite these crosscurrents of relative moderation, sustained hardening seemed to continue to characterize the official American posture toward China.

- The Justice Department and its most famous component, the FBI, in February 2020 publicly revived their high-profile initiative begun in late 2018 highlighting egregious Chinese intellectual property rights (IPR) theft and the danger of mercantilist Chinese support for Huawei and related companies leading to high-technology dominance and US subservience.[60]

- Secretary of State Pompeo continued a steady drumbeat of charges against various Chinese targets. Pompeo also gave unprecedented support for Taiwan against China. Defense Department leaders were less vocal but clearly supportive of the hard line on China.[61]

- Bipartisan congressional support for the above measures continued strong.

- US media was now much more aware of and sometimes echoed the sense of urgency about China seen in the remarks of administration and congressional officials than was the case in 2018.[62]

- As noted in chapters 1 and 4, a large volume of detailed studies by conservative, centrist, and liberal think tanks in the United States, Europe, and Australia and other countries neighboring China, and in-depth journalistic accounts from a similar wide range of reporters, exposed China's heretofore often disguised and hidden use of unconventional levers of power with the overall aim of undermining America. Taken together, these studies reinforced prevailing judgments in Washington that China was not to be trusted as it pursued its systematic efforts to change the world order in ways that benefited China and weakened the United States.[63]

- The key elements of President Trump's political base supported tough measures against China. The president appealed to this audience as he repeatedly labeled the coronavirus impacting America and much of the rest of the world as "the Chinese virus" and rebutted criticism that such labeling was unfair and racist.[64]

## Short-Term Outlook

Despite the difficulty in forecasting American politics after an impeachment trial of an avowedly unpredictable president in an election year dominated by a pandemic with dire consequences for American health and prosperity, China's behavior remained a key determinant of the level of US attention China issues receive going forward. Before the coronavirus crisis, Beijing appeared to favor a low posture, avoiding confrontation. That changed as Chinese and US leaders emphasized self-serving narratives about their respective handling of the coronavirus. Top-level charges and countercharges saw relations decline sharply, with each side blaming the other. As noted above, the Trump administration also saw political advantage in targeting China in the election campaign, claiming that the Democratic candidate, former vice president Joe Biden, had a long record of accommodating Chinese advances at American expense. US public opinion now registered very negative views of the Chinese government. Commentators in the United States and China commonly forecast a type of Cold War between the strident opponents.

## Chapter Seven

# Relations with Taiwan

Along with relations with the United States, Chinese leaders in the post–Cold War period have consistently given high priority to dealing with what they call the "Taiwan issue" in China's foreign relations. As in the case of Chinese relations with the United States, China's relations with Taiwan followed a sometimes tortuous path. China on the one hand interacted with the United States and other foreign countries with an interest in Taiwan following the four stages in Chinese foreign policy and practice seen since 1989 as explained in chapter 1. The record demonstrated an erratic pattern in Chinese-US and other foreign relations, featuring periods of acute tension and acrimony and periods of close engagement and cooperation. On the other hand, because of Taiwan's unique position as what the People's Republic of China (PRC) government sees as the key "domestic" issue in Chinese foreign relations, sharp changes in Taiwan government policies impacting PRC interests in recent decades added to the volatility of the Taiwan issue in Chinese foreign relations. In a broad sense, China's approach has involved three main elements: positive incentives, mainly involving ever-growing economic exchanges, complemented by two types of coercion, seen in the impressive Chinese military buildup focused on Taiwan and in the continued Chinese efforts to isolate Taiwan internationally. Meanwhile, in recent years, Taiwan has been the foremost target of hidden, disguised, and heretofore underappreciated Chinese government operations, which have been featured in recent international government and think tank reports and are duly considered in this revised survey of Chinese foreign relations. Sometimes, Chinese leaders appeared confident that the mix of positive and negative incentives will meet Chinese interests regarding Taiwan. But at other times they appeared frustrated and uncertain about how to prevent Taiwan's moves toward permanent separation from China. [1]

Taiwan's moves toward greater separation grew from 1989 to 2008. This trend seriously challenged China's leaders, who give high priority to preserving Chinese sovereignty and nationalistic ambitions. Beijing's response featured the large-scale buildup of Chinese military forces directed at Taiwan and the United States and others, such as Japan, which might possibly get involved in a military conflict over Taiwan. And it involved periodic assertions by China of its determination to use forceful means to prevent Taiwan's independence. These Chinese actions alarmed leaders from Taiwan, the United States, Japan, and a number of other countries. They also underlined the fact that, however accommodating China's declared foreign strategy might appear, Beijing could change quickly and sharply toward a more confrontational strategy, notably if leaders in Taiwan moved toward permanent separation or independence from China. The volatility of the Taiwan "hot spot" and its unpredictable consequences for China's overall foreign policy were enhanced by the fact that China often seemed unable to control the actions of the leaders in Taiwan, notably President Lee Teng-hui (1988–2000) and President Chen Shui-bian (2000–2008), who repeatedly pursued opportunities to increase Taiwan's independence from China.[2]

Chinese concerns over Taiwan subsided markedly when Taiwan voters in 2008 repudiated the pro-independence initiatives of Lee Teng-hui and Chen Shui-bian and elected President Ma Ying-jeou, who focused on a policy of reassurance and deepening engagement with China. The United States and other concerned powers supported the easing of tensions in the Taiwan Strait. Cross-strait economic, social, and political exchanges grew impressively. Taiwan became ever more dependent on the Chinese economy. Taiwan's military declined relative to China's strong defense buildup. Its diplomatic options were tightly constrained by China.

President Ma was reelected in 2012, but public approval of his government declined substantially. Mass demonstrations in Taipei in March and April 2014 called "the sunflower movement" opposed a proposed cross-strait service trade agreement supported by the Ma government. The protesters and opinion polls demonstrated rising anxiety on the island over Taiwan's growing integration with China. Anti-China sentiment in Taiwan grew with China's firm stance against a popular uprising in Hong Kong beginning in September 2014 demanding direct popular elections. These developments helped Taiwan's opposition Democratic Progressive Party (DPP) to landslide victories in January 2016 presidential and legislative elections, marking a major setback for Beijing.

Incoming president Tsai Ing-wen had a strong mandate to stand firm in defense of Taiwan sovereignty against perceived PRC pressure. President Tsai nonetheless was much more cautious and measured in dealing with cross-strait issues than was the previous DPP president, Chen Shui-bian. However, she refused to endorse the so-called 1992 consensus. That was a vague understanding on the notion of one China said to have been reached by senior Taiwan and PRC envoys in 1992. The consensus was used by the Ma government and Beijing to allow various economic and other agreements governing cross-strait relations to go forward. Beijing's position held that such agreements and interchanges could not be reached without recognition of one China. Beijing followed a "one-China principle," which stated that the PRC is the sole government of China, and Taiwan is part of China. Though the Ma Ying-jeou government disagreed with Beijing's one-China principle, it found the 1992 consensus acceptable as a means to pursue enhanced cross-strait relations. Tsai would not endorse the 1992 consensus because she judged doing so would weaken Taiwan's sovereignty.[3]

The impasse between Beijing and the Tsai government led to steadily increasing PRC pressures against Taiwan, militarily, diplomatically, and economically. Though Tsai's approval rating was low in early 2019, voters in Taiwan reacted strongly against the PRC pressures. And months of mass demonstrations against PRC rule in Hong Kong beginning in mid-2019 increased Taiwan voter antipathy to China, leading to Tsai's strong reelection in January 2020 and setting the stage for continued impasse and rising tensions with Beijing.

A major new element defining China's policy toward Taiwan was the much more positive US government treatment of Taiwan as it faced pressures from Beijing. The Obama government policy avoided significant change in policy toward Taiwan as it continued support for President Ma and his accommodations with China. The remarkable hardening of US policy toward China in the Trump administration saw a series of incremental but nonetheless substantial and often unprecedented steps forward in support of the Taiwan government.[4]

## THE IMPACT OF CHINA-TAIWAN TENSIONS, 1995–2008

The relevant context of the cooperation and easing of tensions over cross-strait relations beginning in 2008 was the tumultuous period dating from Taiwan president Lee Teng-hui's visit to the United States in 1995 to the end of the administration of Taiwan president Chen Shui-bian in 2008. Tensions in cross-strait relations and the perceived danger of conflict in the Taiwan area rose dramatically in the mid-1990s, lasting until the election of Ma Ying-jeou in 2008. In the end, Taiwan voters reacted strongly against the extremes of Taiwan leaders in this period, establishing a momentum for improvement of cross-strait relations. China welcomed this turn of events and supported the momentum.

## Developments during Lee Teng-hui's Presidency

China's post–Cold War search for a stable and peaceful international environment prompted Chinese efforts to smooth over differences and emphasize common ground, especially with China's neighbors and major trading partners. These efforts did not work with Taiwan.[5] The Taiwan government was not prepared to accept the terms of the PRC for establishing improved relations, especially demands that Taipei adhere to a one-China principle as defined by Beijing. And Beijing was not nearly as accommodating with Taiwan as it was with other governments with which it had disputes.[6]

The so-called Taiwan issue rose to unique status as a driving force in Chinese international and security policy priorities in the 1990s.[7] Following the end of martial law in Taiwan in 1987, greater democracy emerged on the island. With it came a rising sentiment in favor of greater separation from the mainland and a more prominent and distinctive role for Taiwan in world affairs. Chinese leaders gradually became seriously concerned about a perceived movement toward political independence, reaching fever pitch after President Lee Teng-hui visited the United States in 1995.[8]

Beijing saw the Clinton administration's reversal of policy—first denying Lee a visa and then granting him one amid broad media and congressional pressure—as a major setback in Chinese foreign policy. China resorted to provocative military exercises designed to intimidate the people of Taiwan and their international supporters prior to important legislative and presidential elections on the island in December 1995 and March 1996, respectively. The military actions cowed Taiwan for a few months until the United States eventually sent two aircraft carrier battle groups to the Taiwan area in 1996.

Beijing intensified efforts to isolate Taiwan internationally,[9] whittling away Taiwan's shrinking band of diplomatic allies.[10] China took advantage of the high-profile US-China summits of 1997 and 1998 to portray a common US-China front. Beijing endeavored to turn to its advantage President Clinton's affirmation in Shanghai on June 29, 1998, of the "three nos"—no support for two Chinas, or one China, one Taiwan; no support for Taiwanese independence; and no support for Taiwanese representation in international organizations where statehood is required.[11]

Lee Teng-hui, chafing under Chinese pressure, announced in an interview in 1999 his view that the China-Taiwan relationship was one between two separate states, what Lee called a "special state-to-state relationship." Seeing this as a bold step toward independence, Beijing suspended formal exchanges through the cross-strait offices and escalated military pressures along the Taiwan Strait.[12]

Chinese officials and senior leaders warned strongly against the DPP candidate, Chen Shui-bian, in the 2000 presidential election. Unfortunately for Beijing, the warnings helped Chen improve his very narrow margin of victory against the runner-up candidate, who was more acceptable to Beijing. Chinese leaders subsequently avoided such tactics for a time, though strongman leader Xi Jinping was more insistent on Taiwan accommodating China's requirements. [13]

## Developments during Chen Shui-bian's Presidency

President Chen Shui-bian entered office in 2000 appearing more moderate on cross-strait relations than was widely anticipated. At first, Chen used formulas designed to eschew independence for Taiwan while not accepting China's demand that he agree to adhere to the one-China principle. China continued to refuse to return to a dialogue with Taiwan's government (which had been suspended following Lee Teng-hui's "state-to-state" comments in 1999). It increased strong efforts to isolate Taipei internationally and reached out to opposition parties as a means to isolate Chen. [14] Concurrently, the China market grew in importance for Taiwan. The PRC accounted for about three-quarters of Taiwan's total foreign investment. Bilateral trade amounted to more than $40 billion in 2003, growing at an annual rate of 30 percent. Hundreds of thousands of Taiwan citizens worked on the mainland. [15]

Chen Shui-bian shifted to a much more assertive stance with pro-independence proposals targeting China in the run-up to the 2004 presidential election. [16] Chinese and US officials viewed the proposals as steps toward independence. [17] Against this background, China passed an Anti-Secession Law in 2005, warning that moves by Taiwan toward greater separation, notably a declaration of independence, would be met with force. [18]

In Taiwan, political forces were divided on cross-strait issues. President Chen Shui-bian, his ruling DPP, and some other politicians represented the so-called pan-green camp—one side of the political spectrum that continued to push for reforms that strengthened Taiwan's status as a country permanently separate from China. On the other side was the so-called pan-blue camp, made up of the formerly ruling Kuomintang (KMT) party and their ally, the People's First Party, which generally was more cautious in taking political steps that might antagonize China. [19]

Seeing the rise of instability and an increased danger of conflict in the Taiwan area, President Bush publicly rebuked Taiwan's president on December 9, 2003. Chinese officials urged US and international pressure to rein in the Taiwan leader. [20]

Chen's narrow reelection victory in March 2004 showed Chinese and other observers how far the Taiwan electorate had moved from the 1990s, when pro-independence was a clear liability among Taiwanese voters. On the other hand, Chen's party did poorly in the island-wide legislative election of December 2004, seen as a public rebuke of the assertive president. For his part, Chinese president Hu Jintao and other Chinese officials showed moderation by muting China's past insistence on reunification under the one country, two systems formula, which was used to govern Hong Kong's return to China and was long rejected by large majorities in Taiwan.[21]

President Chen's administration wound down with a reputation for poor governance, rising corruption scandals, and low approval ratings, but the controversial Taiwan leader renewed the kinds of pro-independence, anti-China initiatives that had caused the flare-up of tensions in his first term in office. The new initiatives concerned Beijing and angered President Bush.[22] The Chen administration's relations with the United States reached a point where US hosting of stopovers for Chen's transits on trips abroad became restrictive and involved locales as far away from Washington as possible.[23]

China duly registered public opposition to Chen's initiatives but placed more emphasis than ever on working in consultation with the Bush administration to deal with Chen's maneuvers. It continued to reinforce the impressive military buildup focused on Taiwan and to deepen Taiwan's economic interdependence with the mainland. Looking beyond the Chen administration, Chinese officials built on increasingly positive connections they developed with the opposition pan-blue leaders and broader segments of Taiwan business elites and other Taiwan opinion leaders.[24]

In the end, the Taiwan voters had had enough of the Chen administration's governance failings and cross-strait maneuvers. The Taiwan legislative elections in January 2008 and the Taiwan presidential election in March 2008 saw landslide victories for KMT candidates, notably presidential candidate Ma Ying-jeou, who pledged to pursue policies of reassurance and moderation in cross-strait relations.[25]

## THE MOMENTUM OF IMPROVING RELATIONS, 2008–2016

President Ma reassured China that his government would not move Taiwan toward independence and stressed closer economic, social, and other contacts across the strait. The cross-strait agenda now focused on building closer and mutually advantageous economic and social ties. The growing Chinese military buildup opposite Taiwan and reaching agreement on Taiwan's desired greater international participation were harder to deal with.[26]

On the whole, the improvements in cross-strait relations were rapid and impressive. The security situation in the Taiwan Strait relaxed. A major economic development was the establishment of a free-trade agreement in 2010 known as the Economic Cooperation Framework Agreement (ECFA), which provided privileged access to Chinese markets and other economic benefits for various important constituencies in Taiwan.[27] There was no significant reduction of China's powerful military presence directly opposite

Taiwan. President Ma was also reluctant to engage in talks with China on a possible peace agreement.

The numerous cross-strait agreements saw burgeoning face-to-face interaction between Taiwan and Chinese authorities after decades without direct dealings. The agreements were between ostensibly unofficial organizations—Taiwan's Straits Exchange Foundation (SEF) and China's Association for Relations across the Taiwan Strait (ARATS). They required officials of the two governments to deal with each other on a host of transportation, food safety, financial regulation, and law enforcement issues. In effect, three channels of communication were now active between the Taiwan and Chinese authorities: the SEF-ARATS exchanges, exchanges between the leaders of the Chinese Communist Party (CCP) and Taiwan's KMT, and widening government-to-government coordination and cooperation on a variety of cross-strait issues.[28]

Meanwhile, the Ma Ying-jeou government achieved a breakthrough in getting China to allow Taiwan to participate in the annual World Health Assembly (WHA) meeting as an observer using the name "Chinese Taipei." Other evidence of progress in China-Taiwan relations over issues regarding Taiwan's participation in international affairs was the diminishment of what had been intense Taiwan-China competition for international recognition.[29]

The Bush administration welcomed the efforts of the Ma government and China's positive response as stabilizing and beneficial for all parties concerned. President Ma worked hard to keep his transit stops in the United States discreet in ways that would not complicate US relations with China. High-level contacts occurred between the US and Taiwan governments in quiet and private ways that avoided upsetting China, and US military consultations with and advice to Taiwan's armed forces continued.[30]

The Bush administration delayed until close to the last minute approval of a large arms sales package for Taiwan. It was worth $6.5 billion. The package in 2008 represented about half of what Taiwan wanted; it did not include sixty-six F-16 fighters that Taiwan had been requesting for years. China strongly criticized the sale and suspended military contacts with the United States for a year.[31]

The incoming Barack Obama government welcomed the new stability in cross-strait ties. Like the outgoing Bush government, the Obama administration relied on President Ma and his team to continue to manage cross-strait ties in positive ways that would not cause the Taiwan hot spot to reemerge.[32] The Obama government followed through with a $6 billion arms package for Taiwan in 2010. The package did not include F-16 fighters; it prompted sometimes strident public complaints along with limited substantive retaliation from China.[33] Later US arms sales included another large arms package worth more than $5 billion in 2011 that proposed significant upgrades in the capabilities of Taiwan's existing F-16 fighters.[34]

Leading into Ma Ying-jeou's second term (2012–2016), cross-strait moderation and growing engagement developed smoothly at first. The overall trend appeared advantageous for China as momentum in the direction of closer China-Taiwan ties continued along with the Ma government's repeated rejection of independence. China's military buildup seemed effective in dissuading Taiwan from disrupting existing trends. In effect, China intimidated Taiwan and thereby prevented moves toward greater separatism and independence. The military balance in the Taiwan Strait changed markedly in China's favor. In the face of China's buildup, the Ma government failed to follow through with earlier promises to sustain a comparatively low level of defense spending at 3 percent of GDP. China's buildup featured annual double-digit increases.[35]

Taiwan became ever more dependent on China economically. Hillary Clinton in June 2014 was the latest in a long list of non-US government notables and specialists warning Taiwan that overdependence on China economically would make the island more vulnerable to unwanted Chinese pressures.[36] Taiwan's total trade with China grew from $31.3 billion in 2000 to $124.4 billion in 2013 (a 297 percent increase). The PRC was Taiwan's largest trading partner, its largest export market, and its second-largest source of imports. According to Taiwan's Mainland Affairs Council (MAC), the share of Taiwan's exports to China rose from 3.2 percent in 1985 to 28.5 percent in 2013 (this increased to 39.7 percent if exports to Hong Kong was included), while the share of its imports from China rose from 0.6 percent to 15.8 percent (16.4 percent if Hong Kong was included). Taiwan enjoyed large annual merchandise trade surpluses with the mainland; it was $39.2 billion in 2013.[37] In 2018, 41 percent of Taiwan's goods exports went to mainland China and Hong Kong.

Taiwan was a major source of foreign direct investment (FDI) flows to the PRC, although the exact level remained unknown. According to the Taiwan Investment Commission, Taiwan's approved FDI flows to China grew from $2.6 billion in 2000 to $13.1 billion in 2011 but declined during the next two years (totaling $8.7 billion in 2013). The stock of Taiwan's approved FDI to China from 1991 to 2013 was $133.7 billion, 80 percent of which was in manufacturing. It was often claimed that the total level of Taiwan FDI in China could be as high as $300 billion. That was partly because Taiwan investors were believed to invest in China through Hong Kong entities in order to avoid scrutiny by Taiwan's government. The Taiwan government estimated that 405,000 citizens—2.4 percent of Taiwan's working population of 17.1 million citizens—were working in the PRC as of 2017; most were involved with the more than seventy thousand Taiwan companies operating there.[38]

The Ma Ying-jeou government endeavored to break out of the Chinese-imposed diplomatic isolation of Taiwan and negotiated with Beijing in achieving some breakthroughs in international recognition and involvement. However, the scope of Taiwan's involvement remained carefully controlled by China, and Taipei seemed unable to do much to change the situation on its own.[39]

As noted at the outset of this chapter, the popularity of President Ma and the ruling Nationalist Party declined markedly in Ma's second term. Anxiety rose in Taiwan over the pace, scope, and direction of Taiwan's closer engagement with ever more dominating China. Against that background, DPP candidates scored a major victory in island-wide elections in November 2014 and did the same in the January 2016 presidential and legislative elections. In sum, political dynamics in Taiwan were changing determinants in the recent cross-strait progress between Taiwan and China and in raising major questions about future trends.[40]

## American Support for Taiwan under Ma Ying-jeou[41]

In response to the dramatic shift in Taiwan's approach to China under President Ma Ying-jeou, the US government played down past emphasis on Taiwan's role in cooperation with the United States in sustaining a favorable military balance in the Taiwan Strait. Rather, it sought to support Ma's new approach of reassurance as an important means for sustaining stability and peace. Despite the shifts toward greater criticism and competition in US-China policy since Ma's ascendance, the Obama government policy toward Taiwan was more durable and consistent. The Obama government sold a large amount of weapons to Taiwan but avoided provoking Chinese ire with the sale of advanced fighter aircraft or submarines requested by Taiwan. China viewed with suspicion the Obama government's rebalance in Asia policy highlighted since 2011. The Obama government was careful to keep Taiwan outside the scope of the rebalance in its initial explanations of the new policy, and later official US references affirming Taiwan's role avoided specifics or actions that risked raising China's ire over the very sensitive Taiwan issue in US-China relations.[42]

American policy makers concerned with Taiwan repeatedly highlighted the very good state of bilateral relations and the calm that prevailed in cross-strait ties, a welcome comparison to the headaches for US policy posed by active nearby hot spots in the East and South China Seas and North Korea. Signs of low US tolerance for Taiwan actions that could disrupt cross-strait ties included US officials warning against the DPP candidate, Tsai Ing-wen, regarding her China policy following US official meetings with the candidate prior to the Taiwan election in 2012. This episode marked a rare American official intervention into a friendly democracy's electoral process.[43]

Specialists and media highlighted declines in US support for Taiwan under the Obama government. The administration strongly disagreed, but it followed policies in the rebalance, in dealing with sales of sensitive weapons, and in reacting to the approach of the DPP presidential candidate, noted above, that underlined declining support for policy initiatives that would support Taiwan but risk upsetting China and come at a possibly significant cost for US relations with China. By contrast, George W. Bush started his administration with a strong rebalancing against perceived Chinese assertiveness in Asia by placing Taiwan at the center of his approach, warning that he would do "whatever it takes" to help Taiwan defend itself against Chinese attack.[44]

Congress at times was the source of strong support for Taiwan and pressure on the administration to do more for Taiwan. But the weak congressional signs of support of Taiwan in the first term of the Obama government were overshadowed by declining interest and opposition to Taiwan's wishes. Few members visited the island, and those who did sometimes came away with views adverse to Taiwan's interests. After visiting Taiwan in August 2010, Senator Arlen Specter came out against irritating China by selling Taiwan the F-16 aircraft sought by President Ma.[45] Likewise, in a public hearing in June 2010, Senate Intelligence Committee chairwoman Dianne Feinstein cast US arms sales to Taiwan as a liability for US foreign policy and pressed Secretary of Defense Robert Gates for options to resolve the impasse between the United States and China over the issue.[46]

The decline in congressional support was also influenced by the fracturing and decline of the Taiwan lobby in Washington. Reflecting the often intense competition in Taiwan politics between the Nationalist or KMT party and the Democratic Progressive Party in recent decades, DPP representatives in Washington and like-minded US interest groups, such as the Formosan Association for Public Affairs on one side and KMT representatives in Washington and supporting interest groups on the other side, repeatedly clashed while lobbying congressional members. Ma Ying-jeou's appointment of the head of the KMT's Washington office, a veteran of these partisan squabbles with the DPP, as his choice to lead the Taiwan government's office in Washington saw the partisan divisions persist. An overall result was confusion on Capitol Hill and a decline in Taiwan's influence there.[47]

Against this background, several respected and prominent former officials and specialists called for an American pullback from continued support for Taiwan roughly consistent with the approach of Senator Feinstein and some others in Congress. Former vice chairman of the Joint Chiefs of Staff William Owens argued in November 2009 that because of the need for friendly ties with rising China, the United States should reassess the Taiwan Relations Act and curb American arms sales to Taiwan. Academic China specialist Bruce Gilley argued in January 2010 that Taiwan's détente with China should seek neutralization along the lines of Finland's position in the Cold War and that such neutralization should be supported by the United

States. International relations scholar Charles Glaser said in March 2011 that the key to avoiding US conflict with China was accommodating Beijing by withdrawing commitments to Taiwan. In January 2011, Joseph Prueher, former ambassador to China and former commander of the US Pacific Command, hosted prominent business leaders and China specialists and produced a report that called for a reevaluation of US arms sales to Taiwan that were seen to create strongly negative implications for US interests. In the largest and most thorough study of issues in US-Chinese relations in many years, Carnegie Endowment for International Peace China specialist Michael Swaine warned in 2011 of the potentially disastrous consequences for the United States of its ongoing commitment to defend Taiwan against rising Chinese power.[48]

Since 2012 and 2013, rising American tensions with China over disputes in the East and South China Seas were accompanied by an increase in congressional, nongovernment specialist, and media attention to Taiwan's role in proposed American plans for dealing with Chinese assertiveness. For its part, the Obama government remained generally mum on Taiwan's role in this regard. While US government representatives eventually came to say that Taiwan was part of the rebalance, they avoided disclosing how this would assist in dealing with Chinese assertiveness. One reason for the Obama government restraint was presumably that such discussion would heighten attention to the Taiwan issue in US-China differences in Asia, causing more serious friction in US-China relations than the Obama government judged warranted under the circumstances. The Obama government, congressional representatives, and specialists were in agreement in complimenting the actions of the Ma Ying-jeou government—a major stakeholder in the contested claims—for generally adhering to peaceful means in dealing with differences and in reaching pragmatic understandings with Japan and the Philippines over fishing rights in disputed territories. They also appreciated Taiwan's criticism of China's abrupt declaration of an air defense identification zone over the disputed East China Sea islands in late 2013.[49]

Pushing against Obama government restraint was an array of congressional representatives, specialists, and commentators arguing in favor of greater US attention to Taiwan in this period of tension with China. Generally, the hardened views against China of these observers crowded out the arguments of only a few years earlier noted above for neutralizing Taiwan, accommodating Chinese demands over Taiwan, and withdrawing US support for the island.

The push against Obama government restraint regarding Taiwan and China was intensified by the now common discourse in congressional deliberations and media commentary that the Obama government was too timid in the face of challenges in such sensitive international areas as Ukraine, Syria, Iraq, Afghanistan, and elsewhere.[50] Few observers supported US combat operations to meet American objectives, and the critics probably recognized that the president's policies were in line with public opinion polls showing war weariness in America. Nonetheless, the critics saw the stakes in competition with China as long term and serious; they argued for stronger American actions that would show negative costs for China's interests if it pursued its so-called salami slicing in nearby disputed territories. They were prepared to risk some of the negative consequences for the United States that would flow from serious disruption of the existing relationship with China.

Against this background, Taiwan was involved in some proposed American actions to counter China as the United States moved from the positive engagement side of the policy spectrum to an approach that balanced against and endeavored to deter Chinese expansionism. Strategists and specialists argued that to effectively deter expanding China required credible American strategies to deal with confrontation with China. Taiwan was often at the center of such proposed strategies and was seen by some as "the cork in the bottle" if the United States needed to shore up radars, defenses, and other anti-China military preparations along the first island chain running from Japan through Taiwan to the Philippines.[51]

Taiwan was also involved in options raised in congressional deliberations and specialist commentaries on what the United States could do in order to raise the cost for China of its continued salami slicing in the nearby seas. According to this view, by raising the costs to China with these Taiwan-related options (as well as other options), the United States could show Beijing that its interests would be better served with a less aggressive approach in the East and South China Seas.[52] The Ma Ying-jeou government reacted very warily to these suggestions, while the Obama government ignored them. They included using the sale of advanced jet fighters to Taiwan as a way to upset the Chinese security calculus along its periphery in ways costly to China, with the implicit understanding that more such disruptions of Chinese plans would come unless it ceased its assertiveness and expansion in the East and South China Seas. Another option was for American officials to speak out more forcefully in support of popular demonstrations such as those led by Taiwan's so-called sunflower movement. US support for the freedom to speak out against feared Chinese dominance shown during the sunflower movement presumably would prove the United States to be more open to a change in Taiwan's existing approach to China.

Meanwhile, another US option regarding Taiwan built on the Obama government's strong recent criticism of China's use of coercion and intimidation of neighbors in disputes in the East and South China Seas. The new US government rhetoric raised the question of why the United States was not showing the same concern with long-standing Chinese military coercion and intimidation of Taiwan. Strong American statements against such intimidation, if backed by substantive support, would seriously complicate China's plans for what Beijing sees as the resolution of the Taiwan issue—a major cost to the Chinese government.

The increased attention to Taiwan related to the hardening US policy toward China was reinforced by other factors increasing the American focus on Taiwan. Thanks in part to stronger efforts by the Taiwan office in Washington and to the particular interest in Taiwan by committee chairs and ranking members in the House and Senate, the number of members of Congress visiting Taiwan and the stature of these members increased.[53] In 2012, a general election year when overseas congressional travel usually declines, there were fifteen representatives who visited Taiwan. In 2013, there were four senators and eighteen representatives who visited Taiwan. In January–August 2014, one senator and fourteen representatives visited Taiwan. Chairman Ron Wyden (D-OR) of the Senate Committee on Finance visited in August, and Chairman Buck McKeon (R-CA) of the House Armed Services Committee led a congressional delegation that same month. Congress continued to pass legislation and urge the US administration in various ways to encourage Taiwan's democratization, to meet Taiwan's self-defense needs, and to assist with Taiwan's bid to participate in regional economic integration and international organizations such as the World Health Assembly and the International Civil Aviation Organization (ICAO).

The convergence in congressional-administration support for Taiwan came with important differences, with congressional representatives pressing the government to strongly reaffirm the so-called six assurances of the Ronald Reagan administration that long governed US support for Taiwan and with congressional requirements for reports and closer monitoring by the administration of Taiwan's defense needs.[54] Meanwhile, the Senate Foreign Relations Committee captured the views of many supporters of Taiwan in Congress and elsewhere who saw Taiwan's future closely tied to its economic connections and role in Asian and world affairs, arguing that Taiwan's joining the US-backed Trans-Pacific Partnership (TPP) international economic agreement was an essential step in securing Taiwan's overall strength and well-being.[55]

Of course, congressional deliberations also reflected perceived shortcomings and criticism of Taiwan's policies and practices. Senator John Cornyn, a strong supporter of US arms sales to Taiwan, expressed public frustration in February 2013 with Taiwan's seemingly halfhearted efforts to persuade the United States to sell advanced fighter jets to Taiwan.[56] A staff member supporting House Armed Services Subcommittee chair Representative Randy Forbes told an audience in Washington in April that year that Taiwan had "slipped off the congressional agenda."[57] A strong supporter of Taiwan, American Enterprise Institute specialist Dan Blumenthal in February 2014 wrote about the prevailing fatalism in American opinion about Taiwan and the perceived weak American commitment to protect the island from Chinese coercion.[58] At that time, international relations scholar John Mearsheimer caused some controversy when he assessed cross-strait trends and advised America to "say goodbye to Taiwan."[59]

## TAIWAN AND THE HARDENING OF RECENT US-CHINA RELATIONS

President Xi Jinping's government remained resolute in pursing pressure tactics to compel the Tsai Ing-wen government to compromise and accept the 1992 consensus and to move toward the one country, two systems formula Beijing used in the reunification of Hong Kong with the PRC. Among other moves, it established diplomatic relations with seven countries that previously recognized Taiwan; pressured host countries to force Taiwan's unofficial representative offices to change their names; forced US and other foreign firms to change how they publicly dealt with Taiwan to conform with Chinese-approved guidelines; blocked Taiwan's participation as an observer at international meetings; stepped up deployments and provocative military operations of the PRC military near Taiwan; reduced the number of mainland Chinese tourists visiting Taiwan; demanded that other countries return Taiwan citizens accused of crimes to the PRC, rather than Taiwan; and, for the first time, tried a Taiwan activist on charges of attempted subversion of the PRC state.[60]

Perhaps of more significance, Taiwan was put on the front lines of threats from China's "sharp power," or malign authoritarian influence that tried to take advantage of the island's open democratic system to build support for China. Taiwan's Mainland Affairs Council said in July 2019 that the Chinese Communist Party was stepping up its united front work and efforts to infiltrate Taiwan, following Chinese president Xi Jinping's firm speech on reunification with Taiwan on January 1. Beijing's recent influence operations in Taiwan involved an aggressive political propaganda campaign in Taiwan through its penetration into Taiwan's information and political environments. In this information war, Chinese agents sought to influence Taiwanese political actors and society through distortion of information on social media and other platforms—all to ultimately benefit Chinese interests and objectives.[61]

Beijing long relied on the KMT and other like-minded political parties of the pan-blue to counter the policies and preferences of the DPP and the pan-green opposed to China's ambitions. Chinese officials were pleased with the strong KMT victory in the 2018 island-wide local elections that promised the removal of the DPP president and the DPP-controlled legislature in the January 2020 elections. During the 2018 and 2020 Taiwan election campaigns, Beijing intensified its efforts to add to its pan-blue influence by bypassing the central government in Taiwan and the ruling DPP. Instead, it relied increasingly on co-opted candidates, political parties, and various proxies in Taiwan to undermine democratic institutions, sow confusion within the public, and engineer electoral outcomes in its favor. In the view of some experts, this new approach was seen as an admission that previous strategies had failed and an acknowledgment that, as long as it stands, Taiwan's commitment to an identity as a democratic country unwilling to succumb to China's demands will prevent outcomes desired by Beijing.

Now facing four more years of DPP presidential and legislative rule, Beijing continued to apply the pressures of the recent past. The appeal of the KMT for China seemed reduced as the new KMT leadership appeared less than firm in support of the 1992 consensus. The coronavirus that emerged first in China underlined for many in Taiwan concrete reasons to remain separate from PRC control. Public opinion in Taiwan strongly opposed Beijing's use of its influence in the World Health Organization to prevent Taiwan participation in World Health Organization deliberation about the coronavirus, which was heavily impacting Taiwan as well as the PRC. [62]

## Trump Administration Support for Taiwan

Perhaps of more importance in Beijing's deliberations over strategy toward Taiwan was the recent strengthening of US support for Taiwan and the Tsai Ing-wen government. A major bright spot amid mediocre accomplishments of three years of Trump administration foreign policy was unprecedented improvement in US relations with Taiwan despite the risk of objection from China, a change in US policy warmly welcomed by Taiwan's leaders. [63]

Many incremental and some more substantial advances in US military, diplomatic, and economic support for Taiwan reached a high point in 2019 and continued into 2020. They represented a significant US counter to increased Chinese military, diplomatic, and economic pressures on Taiwan in the lead-up to and aftermath of Taiwan's January 2020 elections. The United States sought to reassure Taiwan and preserve the status quo that Beijing was attempting to change with intimidation and coercion. Thus far, the US steps didn't prompt a major backlash from China. Looking forward, key variables included President Trump's avowed unpredictability, possible election changes in the United States, and China's uncertain leadership calculus. This analysis judged that acute US rivalry with China was likely to advance, and so too should recent positive US relations with Taiwan.

## Recent US Advances despite China's Objections

*Military*

Military advances involved joint consultations, planning, exercises, exchanges of intelligence, and other matters out of public view. Public advances involved the sale of more than $11 billion in arms to Taiwan, including sixty-six F-16 jet fighters approved in 2019. Also, US warships were passing regularly through the Taiwan Strait. As noted earlier, when establishing ties with Beijing, the US publicly halted warship patrols in the Taiwan Strait. Some US warships secretly passed through the strait in later years. The Trump government began publicizing US warships passing through the strait (nine went through from mid-2018 to mid-2019). Meanwhile, the Defense Department's Indo-Pacific Strategy in June 2019, for the first time in an authoritative executive branch document in several decades, declared that Taiwan was a "country."

*Diplomatic*

The Department of State no longer acted as a gatekeeper more concerned with avoiding offending Beijing and thus restricting relations between Taiwan and other departments and Congress. Showing often unprecedented support for Taiwan, widely publicized visits by deputy assistant secretaries, carried out rarely in the past, were now common. Such high-profile meetings in Taiwan in 2019 dealt with Southeast Asia, China's advances in the Pacific Islands, and cooperation in the Indo-Pacific. Another unprecedented move saw the recall in September 2018 of US ambassadors from three Latin American countries after their government's switched diplomatic relations from Taiwan to Beijing.

Relatedly, National Security Adviser John Bolton held a publicized meeting with his Taiwan counterpart in May 2019. Past practice kept such meetings secret and at the level of deputy national security advisers. Another unprecedented move saw Tsai Ing-wen's running mate, vice president elect Lai Ching-te, visit the National Security Council while in Washington to attend the National Prayer Breakfast in February 2020. Since 2019, US ambassadors in the Pacific Island states were publicly helping Taiwan to sustain its official diplomatic relations among those small nations. Secretary Pompeo in October 2019 issued a statement urging Tuvalu to maintain diplomatic relations with Taiwan. Vice President Pence in September 2019 registered disapproval of the Solomon Islands breaking ties with Taiwan.

The American Institute in Taiwan, responsible to the State Department, offered unprecedented pledges of US support for Taiwan. The director said in June 2019 that Taiwan can "count on" US support to a "shared future" between the two, adding that "Taiwan will always have a home in the community of democracies."

*Economic*

Economic support came notably in June 2019 when visiting director of the US Overseas Private Investment Corporation (OPIC) promised assistance in helping Taiwan retain its diplomatic partners. Meanwhile, the scope and activism of the US-Taiwan Global Cooperation and Training Framework grew markedly in the past two years, impacting more foreign governments.

There were four driving forces supporting the advance of US relations with Taiwan during this period. First was Beijing's growing military, diplomatic, and economic pressure on Taiwan, which endeavored to change the status quo in cross-strait relations. The US pushback acted to counter Chinese pressures and sustain the status quo. Second, Taiwan's location and role in the Indo-Pacific region were deemed very important for US plans to counter adverse Chinese advances. Third, Taiwan's political democracy, free-market economy, and support for other such international norms were valued by US leaders who saw China's rising challenge to these norms as a major threat to US interests. Fourth, US relations with Taiwan imposed costs on Beijing.

There remained several factors that served to brake the forward movement of US support for Taiwan that Beijing opposed, but their importance was diminished in several cases. First, US government concern that advances with Taiwan will upset US relations with China was less now that the already acute US rivalry with China had intensified. Second, US government concern that US tensions with China over Taiwan would upset US allies and partners in the Asia-Pacific was also overtaken by the US-China rivalry. Third, US government suspicion that Taiwan leaders would use greater US support to move provocatively toward independence continued to be low during Tsai Ing-wen's presidency. The fourth factor braking forward US movement with Taiwan did not diminish. Beijing's rising military, political, and economic power remained the most important brake on advancing US support that might prompt strong PRC reactions.

## Outlook

Circumstances in 2020 presented China with major difficulties in dealing with Taiwan and the so-called Taiwan issue in US-China relations. The coronavirus had broad and uncertain implications, but it clearly worsened cross-strait relations and China's relations with the United States. Though Chinese military power and other levers of pressure seemed strong enough to preclude Taiwan from declaring independence or making other egregious moves to formally separate from China, the impasse over the 1992 consensus backed by broad disapproval in Taiwan of the one country, two system's formula favored by President Xi Jinping remained, with no obvious way out. The problem was compounded by the upsurge in US government support for Taiwan during the Trump administration. That support was influenced in part by the sharp decline in overall US-China relations over the past three years.

This analysis showing a likely outcome of the continued and intensifying US rivalry with China generally supported closer US ties with Taiwan. The Trump administration's improved ties with Taiwan departed from the practice of most US presidents since Nixon stressing improving relations with Beijing and curbing ties with Taiwan. Nevertheless, there were other such departures in the past. The biggest came after the Tiananmen crackdown, with strong American repudiation of China and an embrace of democratizing Taiwan. That six-year episode ended badly, with a major crisis in the Taiwan Strait in 1995–1996. However, there were occasions when the United States moved forward with arms sales and other sensitive support for Taiwan despite strenuous Chinese objections, and the result was minimal Chinese reactions—see, for example, China's moderate reaction to the US sale of 130 Chiang Ching-kuo fighters to Taiwan in the mid-1980s and its similar reaction to George W. Bush's initially very strong support for Taiwan in 2001.

Meanwhile, three key variables could change the recent pattern of improved US relations with Taiwan that would impact the problems Beijing faces in dealing with Taiwan. First, President Trump demonstrated little commitment to or concern regarding Taiwan. Thus, if seeking favor from Beijing, he could curb US support for Taiwan. Second is the result of the US election. Hillary Clinton's 2016 campaign pledged no change in the strict curbs on Taiwan in the Obama administration's China policy. Then vice president Joe Biden was a strong supporter of the Obama foreign policy. Many of Clinton's advisers in the 2016 campaign remain active in the Democratic Party and if returned to power may see less merit in moving forward in US relations with Taiwan than the leaders of the Trump administration. Third is uncertainty in Beijing. Xi Jinping adopted a defensive posture and a generally moderate approach in dealing with the broad US government pushback against China's challenges. Experts disagree on whether he will sustain this posture or be prone to more forceful actions against Taiwan and the United States, perhaps recalling the Taiwan Strait crisis of 1995–1996.

*Chapter Eight*

# Relations with Japan and Korea

Among China's neighbors in Asia, Chinese leaders gave highest priority to relations with the governments of northeastern Asia: Japan, North Korea, and South Korea. The reasons included the strategic location of these nations close to the economic centers of China's modernization; their economic, political, and military power and importance to China; and their close involvement with the United States. The record of Chinese foreign relations in this area in the post–Cold War period was very mixed.

Beijing's foreign practice generally followed the four stages of post–Cold War Chinese foreign policy behavior explained in chapter 1.

1. Japan was the most important developed country assisting China to break out of the isolation imposed by the Western-aligned nations after the Tiananmen crackdown of 1989. The early 1990s were the highest point of cooperative relations between the two countries since World War II. And Beijing reciprocated South Korea's strong interest in closer economic and diplomatic relations, while sustaining close ties with North Korea.

2. Japan was particularly alarmed by China's militant behavior in the Taiwan Strait crisis of 1995–1996 and strengthened security ties with the United States while assessing the intent of China's newly emphasized good-neighbor policy and its so-called new security concept in this period. Chinese president Jiang Zemin's visit to Japan in 1998 reflected wariness on both sides. Meanwhile, China played a secondary role in negotiations headed by the United States in resolving the 1994 crisis caused by North Korea's break from international agreements in seeking to develop nuclear weapons. China's relations with South Korea advanced steadily.

3. The period of China's avowed peaceful rise in the first decade of the twenty-first century saw continued steady improvement of Chinese relations with South Korea, while avoiding direct Chinese intervention into the sometimes acute differences between the progressive leaders of South Korea favoring détente with North Korea versus the harder line favored by the George W. Bush administration and the Japanese government. China's pragmatic and often accommodating policy toward the United States and allies and partners did not apply to Japan. Chinese nationalism stoked by Chinese government efforts emphasizing the evils imposed on China by Japan in the so-called century of humiliation impacted Chinese leaders and broad public opinion. Major anti-Japanese demonstrations broke out in Chinese cities in 2005. Japan's leaders took a tough position on these so-called history issues, with Prime Minister Junichiro Koizumi visiting annually the controversial Yasukuni Shrine memorializing Japanese war veterans, including the leaders convicted of major war crimes in China during the Pacific War. Chinese leaders eventually refused to deal with Koizumi.

4. The shift toward more assertive Chinese foreign behavior following China's ascendance after the global economic crisis was enhanced in Korea by China's decision to back North Korea even though it carried out provocative attacks in 2010 that killed South Korean forces and civilians, marking the transition from the rule of ailing Kim Jong Il (d. 2011) to his young and inexperienced son Kim Jong Un. US president Barack Obama complained in vain that China was engaging in willful blindness in refusing to allow the UN Security Council to take action on South Korea's complaints against North Korea. And Beijing strongly warned against a US–South Korean show of force in the Yellow Sea in response to North Korean provocations. As the conservative South Korean leader sided with the United States, Beijing's relations with Seoul declined markedly. Unfortunately for China, Beijing's support for North Korea was not reciprocated by the new leader in Pyongyang, who purged and killed scores of suspected opponents in the leadership, including his politically powerful uncle, said to have close ties with China, in 2013. Giving top priority to developing nuclear weapons and long-range ballistic missiles to deliver them, Kim Jong Un shunned Chinese advice favoring moderation and seriously alienated incoming leader Xi Jinping. The result was the most negative period in North Korea's relations with China that did not end until the Donald Trump administration in 2017 threatened war on the peninsula, forcing Kim to compromise and seek support from China, also anxious about dealing with American provocations.

Meanwhile, Beijing's assertiveness toward Japan resulted in the largest popular demonstrations against a foreign government in Chinese history. The demonstrations opposed Japan's purchase of disputed Senkaku (Diaoyu) Islands in 2012. Subsequent strident official statements and commentary repeatedly attacked and sought to demonize Japanese prime minister Shinzo Abe (2012–), who had Japanese forces stand against Chinese intrusions in the Japanese-controlled islands. Trade and investment dropped sharply. Japan did not buckle under Chinese pressure. It became China's main international opponent as it built defenses at home, maneuvered for advantage in Asia, and sought and received strong backing from an Obama government increasingly concerned with Chinese assertiveness and expansion. Xi Jinping eventually saw the wisdom in a less confrontational approach to Abe and agreed to meet him in 2014, beginning an erratic process of limited mutual accommodation amid continuing strong differences. Against this background and facing protracted serious trouble with the United States and President Trump's disruptive trade war, Xi in 2018 included Japan in efforts to ease neighboring tensions by focusing on the US danger. Abe successfully visited Beijing for a summit in 2018, and Xi's planned visit to Japan in spring 2020 was postponed because of the coronavirus plaguing the world.

## RELATIONS WITH JAPAN

China's relations with Japan were as erratic and crisis prone as China's relations with the United States in the post–Cold War period. As summarized above, relations reached a high point in the early 1990s as both Asian powers adjusted their bilateral relations amicably following the demise of the Soviet Union and its strategic influence in eastern Asia. But rivalry emerged and grew, along with deepening mutual suspicions between the two governments and peoples, to produce a tense and wary relationship up to the present.

### Sino-Japanese Rivalry

Signs of Sino-Japanese competition and rivalry that emerged in the 1990s and grew in importance in the twenty-first century included the following:[1]

- Competition for leadership in Asian regional organizations, including separate and seemingly competing proposals by China and Japan to establish free-trade arrangements with the ten Southeast Asian nations in the Association of Southeast Asian Nations (ASEAN) and the Sino-Japanese struggle for influence in the lead-up to the East Asia Summit of December 2005.
- Intensifying competition for control of energy and other resources and disputed territory in the East China Sea.

- Active Chinese international lobbying against high-priority Japanese efforts in 2005–2006 to gain a permanent seat on the UN Security Council.[2]
- Strong Japanese competition with China to gain improved access to Russian oil in the Far East.
- Greater Japanese support for Taiwan at a time of stronger US backing of Taiwan during the George W. Bush administration.[3]
- The first significant cutbacks in Japanese aid to China since the normalization of relations in the 1970s.
- Increased Japanese willingness to deploy military forces in Asia in support of US and UN initiatives.
- Stepped-up Japanese efforts to improve security, aid, and other relations with Australia, India, and other nations on China's southern and western flanks, including strong Japanese aid efforts for Pakistan, Afghanistan, and Central Asian countries.[4]
- Increased Japanese efforts to solidify relations with South Korea and the United States to form a closer Japan–South Korea–US alignment in reaction to China's refusal to condemn repeated North Korean aggression against South Korea in 2010 and related Chinese truculence over its territorial claims in the Yellow Sea.[5]

Underlying changes in Japan said to prompt greater Japanese-Chinese rivalry involved the following:

- A focus by strategic thinkers in the Japanese government and elsewhere in Japan on China's rising power as the major long-term security concern for Japan after the collapse of the Soviet Union and the end of the Cold War.
- An increasing view by the Japanese of China as a rival for regional influence, due to China's continued remarkable economic growth, rising political and military standing, and periodic assertiveness against Japan.
- A lessening of Japanese sensitivity and responsiveness to Chinese demands for special consideration on account of Japan's negative war record in China seventy years ago. These changes were due to the passage of time, the change in Japanese leadership generations, and Beijing's loss of moral standing in Japan due to its crackdown after the Tiananmen incident, its nuclear testing in the 1990s, and its intimidating military actions against Taiwan and in the East and South China Seas.[6]
- A strong sense of national pride and determination among Japanese leaders and the public to preserve Japanese interests in the face of perceived efforts by officials in the People's Republic of China (PRC) to use charges from the past and recent economic, political, and strategic issues to prompt Tokyo to give way to Chinese interests.

Meanwhile, changes in China leading to greater friction with Japan included the following:

- Chinese strategists' long-standing concerns about Japan's impressive military capabilities, which increased as a result of US-Japanese agreements from 1996 on and which to Chinese observers appeared to broaden Japan's strategic role in eastern Asia and provide US strategic support for Japanese politicians wishing to strike a military posture in the region less deferential to China than in the past.[7]
- Chinese concerns about stronger Japanese strategic support for the United States, seen in Japanese deployments of military forces to the Indian Ocean and Iraq during the George W. Bush administration and in the more recent Japanese emphasis on collective self-defense, allowing for greater scope of Japanese military actions in support of their American ally.
- Chinese government specialists' acknowledgment of changes in Japanese attitudes toward China and the judgment that Beijing appeared likely to meet even more opposition and gain less support from Japan. The Japanese decisions to cut aid to China seemed consistent with this trend.
- Chinese nationalism became a focal point of government-sponsored media and other publicity in recent years, especially following the Tiananmen incident and the collapse of communism in Europe and the Soviet Union at the end of the Cold War. Appealing to the sense of China as having been victimized by foreign aggressors in the past, the publicity focused heavily on Japan, by far the most important foreign aggressor in modern Chinese history. Government-sponsored publicity elicited widespread positive response in China and soured the overall atmosphere of China's relations with Japan.[8]

Crosscurrents of moderation running against the trend toward rivalry were often important. They saw the two powers avoid military conflict; but overall they were insufficient to halt the competitive drive:

- Both the Japanese and the Chinese governments remained domestically focused and continued to give high priority to the economic development of their countries, which seemed to require peaceful and cooperative relationships with Asian neighbors, notably with each other.
- China valued Japan for foreign investment and technology and as a market for Chinese goods; Japan was increasingly dependent on China as a market, source of imports, and offshore manufacturing base.
- Personnel exchanges between Japan and China grew markedly. Annual tourist flows, especially from China to Japan, came to number in the millions. Each year, thousands of Japanese and Chinese students visited or

studied in China and Japan. Government-sponsored exchange programs fostered interchange.
• Few if any governments active in Asian affairs benefited from or sought to promote greater Sino-Japanese friction.

In recent years, the Xi Jinping government's active foreign policy assertiveness, strident nationalism, and revanchist territorial claims focused strongly on an uncompromising Japan. This mix drove Sino-Japanese relations to their worst state since 1945.

## Post–Cold War Relations

In July 1990, Tokyo was the first of the G7 countries to announce a resumption of lending to China, ending those sanctions applied after the 1989 Tiananmen crackdown. A successful visit to China by the Japanese emperor in 1992 indicated just how far the two sides were willing to go in order to put the past behind them, at least for the time being. China became Japan's second-largest destination for foreign direct investment after the United States. Official dialogues and intergovernmental cooperation expanded, including cooperation in military and security matters. [9]

In 1995, several difficult political and security issues surfaced. China's nuclear testing program drew strong protests from Japan, which were followed by the freezing of a small part of Japan's large aid program to China. The fiftieth anniversary of the end of the Pacific War was used in China as an opportunity for extensive media examination of Japan's military past. [10]

In November 1995, the presidents of China and South Korea criticized Japan's alleged failure to address adequately its history of aggression. [11] Meanwhile, the Chinese military exercises designed to intimidate Taiwan in 1995 and 1996 alarmed many officials and opinion leaders in Japan and increased Japan's wariness of PRC ambitions in the region. [12]

Japanese leaders came to view the strategic situation in eastern Asia as more unsettled than during the Cold War, with a number of near-term flash points, notably North Korea and Taiwan, and longer-term uncertainties centered on China. [13] Japanese concerns regarding a possible North Korean attack on Japan and the possible negative implications of unification of the Korean Peninsula both involved China in indirect but important ways. More significant was Taiwan. An outbreak of hostilities in the Taiwan Strait involving US forces would draw Japan in under the US-Japan Defense Treaty and the US-Japan Defense Guidelines. The extent and role of Japanese involvement in a China-Taiwan-US military conflict would require difficult decisions of Japan as it weighed the need to support its ally against the costs such actions would entail for its future relationship with China. [14]

In China, concern focused on Japan's cooperation with the United States in strengthening the US-Japan alliance. Chinese officials in the 1990s and later often saw the United States as using the alliance with Japan to hold back or contain China's rising influence in eastern Asia. They disapproved of a new US-Japan dialogue over the situation in the Taiwan Strait; the emergence of a formal US-Japan-Australian strategic dialogue—establishing a broader web of US-led alliance relationships in Asia that excluded China; and Japanese military deployments in the Indian Ocean and other military measures to support the US-led wars in Afghanistan and Iraq, which raised concerns about the implications of strengthened US-Japan military cooperation in areas around China's periphery.[15] Subsequently, the strengthening of the Obama administration's support for Japan and other Asia-Pacific allies and associates, alarmed by assertive Chinese positions over maritime territorial disputes, was criticized in China as efforts to impede China's rise and "contain" China.[16]

Important history issues between the two powers focused on Japan's aggression against China in the seventy years prior to Japan's defeat in World War II, which received enormous attention in China.[17] It was the centerpiece of the Chinese government's strong promotion of nationalism, greatly enhanced after the Tiananmen crackdown, based on China's one-hundred-year struggle against foreign imperialists. Up to the present, Chinese government-supported media and other outlets repeatedly used accusations of Japanese militarism as a way to build nationalistic feeling in China, to put the Japanese government on the defensive, and to elicit concessions from the Japanese government in the form of aid, trading terms, and other benefits. For their part, Japanese officials sometimes exacerbated bilateral difficulties by denying the facts of history or equivocating on Japan's aggression against China up to the end of World War II. Repeated demands for apologies from China seemed particularly self-serving and undermined positive Japanese feelings toward the PRC regime, which had already lost considerable support in Japan because of its human rights record, weapons proliferation, and assertive nationalistic policies in the post–Cold War period. Japanese commonly judged that Beijing's attempts to discredit Japan were part of broader Chinese efforts to exert a dominant influence in Asia, placing Japan in a subservient position.[18]

Sino-Japanese tensions over territorial disputes involved islets in the East China Sea and claims to East China Sea resources, notably natural gas. Eight islets known as the Diaoyu Islands (in Chinese) or the Senkaku Islands (in Japanese) were uninhabited, but they occupied an important strategic location, and the region around them was considered highly prospective for gas and oil resources. The roots of the dispute went back to the nineteenth century. Japan had defeated China in a war and taken control of Taiwan in 1895. Following Japan's defeat in World War II, Taiwan was returned to China, but the uninhabited Senkaku (Diaoyu) Islands located north of Taiwan remained under US control. Japan's claim to the islets appeared strengthened when the United States returned them to Tokyo's control along with nearby Okinawa in 1971. Subsequently, the US government endeavored to keep from taking sides in the territorial dispute, though it often asserted that the US defense treaty with Japan would require the United States to help counter a Chinese attack on Japan, including in the Senkaku (Diaoyu) Islands.

In the 1970s, Tokyo and Beijing agreed to put the disputed islets issue aside as they normalized diplomatic relations and signed a peace treaty addressing issues stemming from World War II. Subsequently, periodic tensions involving fishing and other intrusions, surveillance by government ships and aircraft, and diplomatic protests alternated with periods of relaxed tensions. A spike in Chinese-Japanese friction coincided with assertive Chinese territorial claims, sometimes backed by military patrols, around its periphery in 2009–2010. Japan's arrest in September 2010 of a Chinese fishing boat captain whose ship was videotaped ramming Japanese coast guard vessels near the Senkaku (Diaoyu) Islands precipitated a standoff between the two governments that went on for two weeks, until Japan gave in to Chinese pressure and released the captain. Meanwhile, Japan sharply disputed China's actions, beginning in 2004, involving taking natural gas from East China Sea areas that Japan also claimed. [19]

Though economic interdependence tended to encourage pragmatic Sino-Japanese cooperation, economic relations between the two countries were troubled on several occasions. Alleged efforts by Japanese government-backed companies to dominate key sectors of China's market were an important focal point for anti-Japanese demonstrations in Chinese cities in the mid-1980s. [20] As China rose in economic power and prominence, Japan altered the level and scope of its aid program in China to focus on areas that offered less challenge to Japanese industry. Meanwhile, Japanese companies remained reluctant to share their most advanced technology with China, fearing that the technology would be used to compete with Japanese producers. As a demonstration of China's extensive range of hidden, disguised, or overlooked unconventional coercive elements that have been employed in its foreign policy tool kit in recent years and are highlighted in this volume, China's restrictions on so-called rare-earth exports to Japan, which were very important to Japanese manufacturers, came during a period of tense relations over territorial issues in 2010. The Chinese government's role in cutting off Japan was hidden, as such government action was contrary to WTO norms. But the restrictions were real, and the Chinese action alarmed Japanese leaders that the Chinese government would use growing Japanese economic dependence on China to compel Japanese subservience to China. [21]

Offsetting the above differences was the strong economic interdependence between China and Japan. Japan was China's top trading partner from

1993 to 2002. China became even more important for Japan as it surpassed the United States in 2008 to become the largest market for Japan's exports.[22] Bilateral trade was valued at $350 billion in 2019—$180 billion Chinese exports to Japan and $170 billion Chinese imports from Japan.[23] Regarding foreign investment in China, Japan was in the top ranks along with the United States. Japanese companies' investments were valued at $7.68 billion in China in 2010; sharp declines followed beginning in 2012, and in 2014 the value of Japanese investment in China was $4.33 billion. The outlook for Japanese investment in China was unclear. The US-China trade war led a number of Japanese firms to readjust their production chains away from China, but several firms increased their investments focused on manufacturing in China. Japan's aid was the most important in China in the 1990s, but it declined in importance after that.[24] Regarding exchanges, there were 115,000 Chinese students in Japan in 2018.[25] Japanese students visiting or studying in China numbered 14,230 in 2018.[26] Regarding tourism, there were more than 9 million Chinese visits to Japan in 2019.[27] In 2018 there were more than 2.5 million Japanese visits to China.[28]

## Growing Rivalry in the Twenty-First Century

The Sino-Japanese rivalry developed with starts and stops during the last two decades. Preoccupied with the Asian economic crisis of 1997–1998, neither government sought to exacerbate tensions over the array of issues that divided them. Despite serious differences, senior leadership meetings in Tokyo and Beijing proceeded, notably President Jiang Zemin's November 1998 visit to Japan.[29] While he emphasized Sino-Japanese economic and other compatible interests, Japanese prime minister Junichiro Koizumi (2001–2006) tested Chinese tolerance on the sensitive history issue with his repeated visits to the Yasukuni Shrine. After his third visit despite Chinese admonitions, Chinese officials made it known in 2003 that the Japanese prime minister would not be welcome in Beijing. By late 2005, senior Chinese leaders seemed unwilling to meet the Japanese prime minister under any circumstances because of his continued visits to the controversial war memorial.

Japan's impressive aid and relief efforts after the tsunami disaster in southern Asia in December 2004 allowed Japanese leaders to garner support for a permanent seat for Japan on the UN Security Council. The Chinese government opposed Japan's UN bid.[30] The violent anti-Japanese demonstrations in China during April 2005 came amid a variety of disputes involving visits to the Yasukuni Shrine, Japan's bid for a UN Security Council seat, publication of history books in Japan seen as whitewashing Japan's record in World War II, competitive drilling for gas resources in contested parts of the East China Sea, competition to win approval as the recipient of oil from a planned Russian pipeline, and repeated intrusions into Japanese-claimed waters by Chinese ships, including a secret intrusion of a Chinese nuclear-powered submarine that Japanese forces found and tracked in Japanese territorial waters near Okinawa. The impressive Chinese military buildup focused on Taiwan prompted Japanese countermeasures under the framework of the Japan-US alliance. Japan engaged in bilateral consultations with the United States over the Taiwan situation, worked in a trilateral forum with Australia and the United States that dealt with Taiwan and other Asian issues, was explicit in noting Japanese government concerns over the Taiwan situation, and backed the United States in seeking curbs on European and Israeli arms sales to China.[31] A large Chinese-Russian military exercise involving naval and air forces in the East China Sea in August 2005 was followed by Japan's detection in September of a flotilla of Chinese warships sailing near a Chinese gas rig that was exploiting resources in the East China Sea that were claimed by Japan.[32]

The weak Liberal Democratic Party (LDP) governments that followed Koizumi's departure from office in 2006 were welcomed by China. The Democratic Party of Japan (DPJ) administrations that followed in 2009 also received cordial receptions. Nonetheless, salient differences over fishing, territorial disputes, and trade in so-called rare earths important to Japanese manufacturing brought relations to another low point in late 2010 and to a nadir in 2012.[33]

DPJ leader Yukio Hatoyama campaigned with pledges to reexamine the planned realignment of US forces in Japan, especially those in the large US bases in Okinawa, agreed to by previous Japanese governments, and to pursue a more balanced foreign policy between the United States and Japan's neighbors, notably China. On entering office, he set forth to revise a 2006 Japan-US agreement to realign US troops in Okinawa, and he pressed his case publicly in initial official meetings with President Obama. The US government remained firm in support of the provisions stipulated in the 2006 agreement with Japan. The impasse between the two governments continued and ultimately led to Prime Minister Hatoyama's resignation in 2010.[34] Meanwhile, the Hatoyama government's calls for a more balanced Japanese foreign policy seemingly aligned Japan less closely with the United States and gave more attention to China, yet China was wary of the Japanese initiatives.[35] Sino-Japanese relations subsequently foundered over the increasingly contentious territorial disputes, which became acute when Japan arrested the Chinese fishing boat captain for ramming Japanese coast guard ships in 2010. Two years later, DPJ prime minister Yoshihiko Noda sought to limit the damage to Japan-China relations caused by Japanese right-wing politicians seeking to purchase some of the Senkaku (Diaoyu) Islands and use them to antagonize China. Noda decided in September 2012 to have the Japanese government purchase the islands instead, which led to the unprecedented anti-Japanese mass demonstrations in 120 Chinese cities, with associated burning and looting of Japanese properties. [36]

Japan became the number-one target of the new Chinese assertiveness in foreign affairs. China used coast guard forces, legal and administrative measures, trade pressures, diplomatic threats, and other means to force Japan to reverse its actions and negotiate with China over the disputed islands. The DPJ woes contributed to the landslide election victory of the Liberal Democratic Party under Shinzo Abe in late 2012. Abe was firm in the face of Chinese pressure; protracted tensions ensued. [37]

The Obama government welcomed Abe's ascendance. America shifted from a mediating role to a tougher stance critical of China's coercive behavior. [38] The US position overlapped closely with Abe's defensive but firm stance toward China. China stridently attacked Abe as he sought support against Chinese pressures by strengthening defense at home and seeking support in visits to all members of ASEAN as well as India, Australia, and others. For his part, President Obama, visiting Japan in April 2014, embraced close collaboration with Japan in Asia and underlined America's defense commitment to all areas under Japanese administrative control, including the Senkaku (Diaoyu) Islands. President Obama rebuked China for "flexing its muscles" to intimidate neighbors and gain control of disputed territory. [39]

Prime Minister Abe embraced the alliance with the United States and the Obama government rebalance policy initiatives. He increased Japan's defense budget for the first time in ten years, carried out defense reforms that enhanced Japanese military capabilities, and secured approval for the construction of the controversial new US Marine Corps base on Okinawa. He entered Japan into the US-led Trans-Pacific Partnership free-trade agreement negotiations and sought economic reforms favored by many in the United States.

Beijing now regularly deployed maritime law enforcement ships near the disputed Senkaku (Diaoyu) Islands and stepped up what China called "routine" patrols to assert jurisdiction in "China's territorial waters." China's patrols appeared to be an attempt to demonstrate that Beijing had a degree of administrative control over the islets and to underline that Japan must acknowledge that the territory is in dispute and begin negotiations with China on the dispute. Japan refused to acknowledge that the islands were in dispute. China and Japan did reach a four-point agreement announced at the time of the first Xi-Abe meeting in November 2014, but there was no mention in the document of the territorial dispute; and the Japanese government still did not recognize the dispute, nor did it begin talks with China about the dispute. [40] Beijing's November 2013 announcement that it would establish an air defense identification zone (ADIZ) over the East China Sea including the disputed Senkaku (Diaoyu) Islands was strongly condemned by Japan and the United States. Chinese expansion in the disputed South China Sea saw Japan align with the United States, Australia, India, and many of the countries of Southeast Asia against Chinese advances.

The failure of the Xi-Abe meeting in 2014 to substantially change the prevailing tension and rivalry between China and Japan meant that differences would continue. They included sensitive security and sovereignty questions involving competing claims in the East China Sea, China's expanding control over the South China Sea, and the respective buildups and forward deployments of Japanese and US forces facing China's large-scale military expansion along its maritime rim, as well as the long list of continuing disputes between Tokyo and Beijing that featured maneuvering for regional and international influence, historical arguments, and now prolonged negative public opinion. Taiwan under Ma Ying-jeou was less inclined than his DPP predecessor, Chen Shui-bian, to seek stronger support from Japan, but the election of DPP candidate Tsai Ing-wen in 2016 and her firm stance against Beijing's pressure on cross-strait issues foreshadowed closer Taipei-Tokyo ties. Regarding economic relations, the value of Japanese investment in China was cut in half from 2012 to 2015 and remained at that low level until a modest uptick in 2018. Chinese trade growth in 2015 and 2016 was nil, limiting Japanese trading opportunities.[41]

Prime Minister Abe was the first world leader to establish a strong personal rapport with president-elect Trump, which lasted up to the present. The results were good, but problems were evident. Regarding China, Japan cooperated closely with US defense and economic initiatives, competing sharply with China's regional ambitions. Abe was supportive of the Trump administration's more active military deployments in the South China Sea, sending the largest and most advanced Maritime Self-Defense ships to patrol the area in support of the US-led effort to curb China's changing of the regional status quo.[42]

Although the US president's signature punitive tariffs and export restrictions targeted China and prompted Beijing to ease tensions with Japan in response, the tariffs also had negative implications for Japanese businesses, notably those closely integrated with production chains in China. And the US president compelled Japan to negotiate a bilateral trade agreement, proposing punitive tariffs on Japanese car imports as a means to get Japan to agree to US terms. At that time, some analysts saw signs of the Abe government maneuvering to ease tensions and build common ground with China as well as reinforcing close relations with long-standing partners like Australia and India in order to secure Japanese interests jeopardized by the disruptive tactics of the unpredictable US president. But others judged that Japan's strategic vulnerability along with a wide range of other critical interests warranted close cooperation with US strategies in opposition to the severe dangers to Japan posed by North Korea and China. Overall, a better description of

Japan's approach at this time was hedging against China and keeping the United States engaged in Asia.[43]

Prime Minister Abe long sought to visit Beijing to manage the dangerous tensions with China. His meeting with Xi Jinping in November 2018 gave the appearance of better China-Japan relations. China was in a process of easing tensions with other powers as it faced the Trump government's punitive tariffs and the whole-of-government American pushback against challenges seen posed by China. Against this background, Beijing modified its negative commentary about Abe and Japanese policies in the interest of improving the atmosphere in China-Japan relations, although President Xi was very slow to confirm a date for the expected reciprocal visit. Nevertheless, differences over sensitive issues continued. Japanese air force scrambles against intruding Chinese planes, mainly over the Senkaku (Diaoyu) Islands, grew in 2018 compared to 2017. As of mid-2019, more than ten Japanese citizens had been detained in China on mainly espionage charges since 2015; seven were convicted. Japan continued to do its part in US-led efforts to challenge China in the South China Sea, deploying a joint Maritime Self-Defense–Coast Guard force for drills in the disputed waters.

A year-end assessment published at the outset of 2020 saw repeated references to the thaw in China-Japan relations wear thin as Xi Jinping delayed setting a date for his visit to Japan while the two governments vied for influence in Africa and the Pacific Islands as well as in Asia.[44] Xi eventually set a date for April, but the coronavirus forced postponement. Japanese financing and construction firms competed actively with China's efforts under the Belt and Road Initiative. Signs of Japanese interest in participating in the BRI came in tandem with Japanese efforts to cooperate with the United States, Australia, and India in countering the BRI. Japan led the effort to establish the eleven-member Comprehensive and Progressive Agreement for Trans-Pacific Partnership (CPTPP), which set high standards at odds with China's economic practices. The volatile economic situation caused by US-China trade war and other economic issues, as well as the massive economic impact of the coronavirus, raised more uncertainty about any sort of breakthrough in China-Japan relations.

## RELATIONS WITH THE KOREAN PENINSULA

Chinese policy and practice toward North and South Korea following the end of the Cold War showed China endeavoring to sustain a leading position in relations with both North and South Korea as it reacted to changing circumstances on the Korean Peninsula.[45] Chinese dealings with the North and South Korean governments often reflected the four stages in Chinese foreign policy and practice explained in chapter 1.

Thus, isolated from the West after the Tiananmen crackdown in 1989, Beijing in the following years sought to advance ties with other countries, including South Korea. Post-Mao China was already increasingly involved in closer relations with South Korea and its vibrant economy. Trade grew rapidly in the 1980s despite the absence of official relations between the two governments. As the Soviet Union steadily withdrew the expensive support it had been providing to North Korea and began reciprocating strong South Korean interest in improving relations with Moscow, Beijing did the same. The Soviet Union greatly irritated North Korea when it moved quickly to establish official diplomatic relations with South Korea in 1990. China endeavored to sustain good relations with North Korea while moving forward incrementally with South Korea, eventually establishing official diplomatic relations in 1992.[46]

South Korea was less impacted than Japan by Chinese aggressiveness against Taiwan and the United States during the Taiwan Strait crisis of 1995–1996, but it benefited from Beijing's ensuing good-neighbor policy and new security concept in the years after the Taiwan Strait crisis that were designed to reassure China's neighbors of China's benign intent. Trade and South Korean investment grew substantially. China won praise in Asia for not devaluing its currency during the Asian economic crisis of 1997–1998, a move that would have worsened already bad conditions in South Korea.[47]

Though China endeavored to continue mutually beneficial relations with North Korea, Beijing was placed on the defensive as developments involving North Korea's suspected nuclear weapons program led to a tense impasse with the United States, which was resolved temporarily in a compromise Agreed Framework agreement negotiated by US and North Korean officials in 1994. The heart of the Agreed Framework and the amending accords was a deal under which the United States would provide North Korea with a package of nuclear, energy, economic, and diplomatic benefits; in return, North Korea would halt the operations and infrastructure development of its nuclear program. Three years later, China agreed to participate in four-party talks on peace in the Korean Peninsula involving the two Koreas and the United States. Meanwhile, the sudden death in 1994 of long-standing North Korean leader Kim Il Sung, succeeded by his son Kim Jong Il, added to the volatility that challenged the stability on the peninsula sought by China. A serious famine ensued. China was the main source of food aid and oil to North Korea in this crisis period.[48]

Another surprise from North Korea was its remarkable turnabout in welcoming the progressive South Korean president Kim Dae Jung for an unprecedented summit meeting in North Korea in 2000. The announced meeting prompted China, the United States, and other governments involved in Korean affairs to seek high-level meetings with the heretofore reclusive Kim Jong Il. The North Korean leader had a summit with Chinese president Jiang

Zemin in China prior to his meeting with Kim Dae Jung. The extraordinary thaw in North Korea's relations with South Korea, China, and even the United States coincided with Beijing's new emphasis on China's "peaceful rise," which involved not only enhanced efforts at being a good neighbor but also strong efforts to reassure the United States of China's benign intent.[49]

Thus, in the first years of the twenty-first century, China's relations with South Korea entered a honeymoon period. Burgeoning economic and active diplomatic ties complemented the two governments' support for the asymmetrical accommodation of North Korea, the so-called sunshine policy— favored by South Korean president Kim Dae Jung and his successor Roh Moo Hyun (2003–2008). As the incoming George W. Bush government took a hard line on North Korea over its perceived violations of the Agreed Framework and covert development of nuclear weapons, Seoul and Beijing were together on the opposite side defending continued moderation and accommodation of North Korea. A careful review of the gains China made in improving relations with its Asian neighbors and elsewhere in this period showed South Korea as an area of considerable achievement. And since the Chinese advances with South Korea also coincided with the most serious friction in US–South Korean relations since the Korean War during the first term (2001–2005) of the George W. Bush administration, China's influence relative to the United States grew on the Korean Peninsula.[50]

The Bush administration's hard approach toward North Korea's nuclear weapons program reached a turning point in 2002. North Korea responded harshly to US accusations that North Korea was secretly developing a highly enriched uranium nuclear weapons program and to a US cutoff of oil to North Korea provided under the terms of the Agreed Framework. North Korea broke its promises in the Agreed Framework, withdrew from the Nuclear Nonproliferation Treaty, and proceeded with openly producing nuclear weapons.[51] In a subsequent mix of US pressure and negotiations that seemed to reflect continued strong differences within the Bush administration on how to deal with North Korea, US officials worked with China, and later with Japan, South Korea, and Russia, in multilateral talks, the six-party talks, seeking to curb and end North Korea's nuclear weapons program. Those talks went through ups and downs, mainly in reaction to North Korean moves, which in turn seemed at times to be in reaction to US steps that sometimes stressed a hard line to North Korea and sometimes a more flexible approach. North Korea stayed away from the six-party talks for much of 2004 and 2005. An agreement on principles governing a settlement of the North Korean nuclear issues was reached in the six-party talks in Beijing in September 2005. There was little progress after that.[52]

China's role as a convener and facilitator of the talks and an influential go-between for the United States and North Korea was greatly valued by US negotiators. North Korea at that time seemed to prefer to deal directly with the United States on this issue. While such bilateral interchange with North Korea presumably would have boosted US influence relative to that of China in peninsula affairs, the US government tended to see such US–North Korean contacts as counterproductive for American interests in securing a verifiable end of North Korea's nuclear weapons program. Thus, China's influence grew as it joined with the United States in the multilateral efforts to deal with the North Korean nuclear weapons issue on the one hand, while Beijing sustained its position as the foreign power having the closest relationship with the reclusive North Korean regime on the other.[53]

Against this background, China's relations with South Korea improved markedly.[54] China became South Korea's leading trade partner, the recipient in some years of the largest amount of South Korean foreign investment, and the most important foreign destination for South Korean tourists and students. South Korea's trade with China grew rapidly. Despite the global economic crisis of 2008–2009, the two countries met a goal of $200 billion in trade in 2010 according to Chinese figures. Chinese trade figures showed that about 30 percent of South Korean exports went to China and that China ran a $70 billion trade deficit with South Korea in 2010. South Korea became the third-largest source of foreign investment in China, and China became the largest destination of foreign investment from South Korea. And as noted earlier, for many years, China and South Korea remained close and often like-minded partners in dealing with issues posed by North Korea's nuclear weapons program and related provocations on the one hand, and in dealing with the Bush administration's hard-line policy toward North Korea on the other.[55]

As relations developed, however, China's economic importance for South Korea was seen by South Koreans more in both negative and positive ways. Periodic trade disputes came with growing concerns by South Korean manufacturers, political leaders, and public opinion about competition from fast-advancing Chinese enterprises. China's economic attractiveness to South Korean consumers declined markedly as a result of repeated episodes of Chinese exports of harmfully tainted consumer products to South Korean and other markets. Also, China was seen by South Korea to resort repeatedly to such non-WTO-compliant trade tactics as dumping products onto the South Korean market and threatening retaliation against South Korean imports if economic issues were not settled to China's satisfaction. South Korean leaders strove to break out of close dependence on economic ties with China through free-trade agreements and other arrangements with the United States, Japan, and the European Union that would ensure the inputs of foreign investment and technology needed for South Korea to stay ahead of Chinese competitors.[56]

Other differences between the two countries focused on competing Chinese and Korean claims regarding the scope and importance of the historical

Goguryeo kingdom, China's longer-term ambitions in North Korea, and Chinese treatment of North Korean refugees in China and of South Koreans endeavoring to assist them there. The disputes had a strong impact on nationalistic South Korean political leaders and public opinion. Public opinion polls showed a significant decline in South Korean views of China and its policies and practices since earlier in the decade.[57]

Regarding Chinese relations with North Korea, Chinese frustration followed North Korean nuclear weapons tests in 2006 and 2009 and other provocations.[58] The evidence of growing Chinese frustration with North Korea included the Chinese government allowing a public debate where relations with North Korea were often depicted as a liability for China, requiring serious readjustment in Chinese policy. On balance, the overall record of Chinese policy and practice demonstrated continuing caution. China endeavored to preserve important Chinese interests in stability on the Korean Peninsula through judicious moves that struck an appropriate balance among varied Chinese relations with concerned parties at home and abroad. China remained wary that North Korea, the United States, and others could shift course, forcing further Chinese adjustments in response.

Chinese leaders recognized that their cautious policies had failed to halt North Korea's nuclear weapons development; they probably judged that they would be living with a nuclear North Korea for some time to come, even as they emphasized continued diplomatic efforts to reverse North Korea's nuclear weapons development and create a nuclear-free peninsula. They appeared resigned to joining with US and other leaders in what was characterized as "failure management" as far as North Korean nuclear weapons development was concerned.[59] They endeavored to preserve stability and Chinese equities with concerned powers. As in the recent past, they avoided pressure or other risky initiatives on their own, waiting for the actions of others or changed circumstances that would increase the prospects of curbing North Korea's nuclear challenge and allow for stronger Chinese measures to deal with it.

China's often-repeated, overarching goal on the Korean Peninsula remained "stability." China's behavior in the face of various crises, initiated mainly by North Korea, seemed to underline this goal; by emphasizing stability, Chinese officials and commentators helped explain why China eschewed pressure on North Korea that could provoke a backlash or other developments adverse to stability on the peninsula. At the same time, China was also seen to have a longer-term interest in strengthening Chinese influence and reducing US and Japanese influence on the peninsula.[60] Chinese policy and practice at this time did not highlight this goal. However, China's strong objections for several months in 2010 to US and South Korean military exercises in the Yellow Sea raised questions about China's continued willingness to coexist with the US–South Korea alliance. The Chinese objections were much tougher than in the past, providing initial evidence of the more assertive Chinese approach to foreign affairs emerging in the second decade of the twenty-first century.

Later, the Chinese objective of challenging the US–South Korean alliance showed when China in 2015 began to publicly pressure South Korea not to allow the planned US deployment of the advanced THAAD (Terminal High Altitude Area Defense) missile in South Korea as a means to defend against North Korean ballistic missile attack. Beijing argued that the advanced American missile defense system had negative implications for Chinese security. Significantly for those following China's use of hidden, disguised, or denied unconventional levers of coercion to compel foreign countries to meet Chinese demands, the THAAD deployment resulted in an ostensibly unofficial boycott of South Korean companies involved with the deployment and a broader popular boycott that involved no direct official Chinese involvement, even as it was widely seen as orchestrated by Chinese authorities. As noted before, any such overt government use of boycotts in this manner was against WTO rules. As it happened, the costs of such non-WTO-compliant Chinese actions involved more than $20 billion in losses for South Korea.[61]

Beijing remained careful not to emphasize challenging US leadership in dealing with North Korea's nuclear proliferation and broader Korean affairs.[62] Its cautious and incremental efforts to strengthen its influence in the Korean Peninsula and thereby reduce US, Japanese, and other potentially adverse influence in this critically important bordering area were in line with China's overall approach in the period up to and during the Hu Jintao government (2002–2012) to advancing its interests in Asian and world affairs in the post–Cold War period. This pattern of Chinese post–Cold War interaction with neighboring states was to slowly but surely spread Chinese influence though diplomatic, economic, and security interaction that emphasized the positives and played down the negatives in the relationships between China and its neighbors. China also relied heavily on the steady growth of what senior Chinese foreign policy officials call China's "weight" to cause neighbors to improve their relations with China over time, eschew foreign connections and practices opposed by China, and thereby create a regional order more supportive of Chinese interests. Chinese officials suggested that China's weight included its salient and rapidly growing economic importance to Asian neighbors, its leadership in Asian multilateral groups and international diplomacy, and the rapidly expanding reach of advanced Chinese military forces.[63]

The Chinese government at this time was generally patient in pursuing regional influence. Domestic Chinese priorities required continued regional stability. While there remained active debate among commentators and officials in China over how assertive China should be in dealing with Asian and world affairs, the central leadership appeared to have stuck to a cautious approach that continued to avoid risks, costs, or commitments with potentially adverse consequences for the Chinese government's goals, which centered on sustaining their role in a supportive environment in China and abroad. [64]

In sum, it was important to look beyond China's ongoing concerns with stability on the Korean Peninsula. China's approach to North Korea was also driven by a broad, albeit slow-moving and low-risk, drive to establish an order in the Korean Peninsula more influenced by China and less influenced by foreign and other elements seen as adverse to Chinese interests. In this context, growing Chinese frustration with the twists and turns of North Korean behavior, especially Pyongyang's nuclear weapons development, did not result in a major change in China's reluctance to pressure North Korea to conform to international norms and eschew provocations and confrontation. China's focus was on preserving stability in an uncertain environment caused by internal pressures and the international provocations of North Korea, and sometimes by the erratic policies of the United States and South Korea. China continued to follow practices that gave priority to renewed negotiations in the six-party talks. It tried to use positive incentives rather than pressure to elicit North Korean willingness to avoid further provocations and to return to negotiations on eventual denuclearization.

## CHINA'S ASSERTIVENESS AND CRISES IN KOREA: FINDING THE RIGHT BALANCE IN DIFFICULT CIRCUMSTANCES

The above-noted sharp Chinese reactions to US–South Korean exercises in the Yellow Sea in 2010 and the later harsh pressure on South Korea over the THAAD deployment are emblematic of the growing assertiveness featured throughout Chinese foreign relations in the most recent decade. Chinese policy in Korea at this time was also heavily influenced by changes in leadership and policy, notably the crisis caused by the illness of Kim Jong Il and the rushed preparations for leadership succession to his inexperienced son Kim Jong Un, which was accompanied by North Korean military attacks on South Korean targets in 2010. Chinese policy was also influenced by Kim Jong Un's breaking with China in pushing strongly to develop nuclear weapons and long-range missiles potentially targeting the United States, and by the escalated threats and pressures by the incoming Donald Trump administration on North Korea and China to force a halt to developing such weapons.

China seemed to be making gains in 2009–2011 in solidifying its position as the most important and avid supporter of the North Korean leadership, as Pyongyang witnessed the most significant leadership transition in a generation amid poor domestic conditions and generally unfriendly international circumstances. [65] China also deepened economic relations with both North and South Korea. Though China–North Korean discussions remained secret, it appeared that bilateral relations registered significant improvement despite differences over North Korea's proliferation and military provocations.

The same was not the case for China's relations with South Korea. In 2010, those ties reached the lowest point since the establishment of China–South Korea diplomatic relations. China's refusal to criticize North Korean military attacks against South Korea left a lasting and widespread impression of where China's priorities lay when choosing between North and South Korea. Against this background and contrary to China's longer-term objective of diminishing US and Japanese influence on the Korean Peninsula, China faced strengthened US–South Korea and US-Japan alliance relationships and, for a time, closer strategic coordination between South Korea and Japan.[66]

China's top leader, Hu Jintao, was in the vanguard of Chinese representatives seeking to underline Chinese support for the leadership transition in North Korea. Hu hosted visiting North Korean leader Kim Jong Il during three trips to China, in May and August 2010 and May 2011. The visits presumably were related to the beginnings of a formal transition from Kim Jong Il to leaders, including Kim's son Kim Jong Un, who were elevated to top positions at the first Workers' Party of Korea party conference in forty-four years in September 2010. There followed a blizzard of speeches and publicity marking close China–North Korea relations, including important speeches by China's heir apparent, Vice President Xi Jinping, and a wide range of high-level party and security exchanges throughout the rest of the year and into 2011.[67]

The public displays of solidarity came along with some reports of differences between Beijing and Pyongyang over North Korea's proliferation activities and military attacks against South Korea. On balance, the Chinese leadership was clearly emphasizing the positive in its public posture toward Pyongyang. It backed up its support by thwarting South Korean–led efforts in the United Nations and elsewhere to press North Korea to bear consequences for the sinking in March 2010 of the South Korean warship *Cheonan*, which killed forty-three South Korean military personnel; the North Korean artillery barrage in November 2010 attacking South Korean soldiers and civilians on a coastal island, killing four and injuring others; and North Korea's nuclear weapons development and proliferation activities at home and abroad.

China also advanced various economic ties with North Korea. According to Chinese customs data, China–North Korea trade in the first half of 2010 amounted to $1.29 billion, a 16.8 percent annual increase. North Korea imported $940 million in goods from China and exported $350 million during the period. North Korea's imports from China rose markedly, with flour imports rising by 383 percent. North Korea's crude oil imports from China remained the same. Minerals and other natural resources continued to account for a large portion of North Korean exports to China. China also provided unspecified humanitarian assistance in 2010. China's trade and aid ties with North Korea raised concerns about the effects of those ties on UN and other international sanctions. Meanwhile, roads, railways, bridges, and other projects improving transportation between China and North Korea were under construction.[68]

Economic ties also grew between China and South Korea. The China–South Korea trade of $171 billion in 2010 was a 21 percent increase from $141 billion in 2009. South Korean investment in China in 2010 represented 21 percent of South Korea's total foreign direct investment (FDI). Meanwhile, the number of Chinese visitors to South Korea rose 48 percent in 2009, reaching 1.21 million. South Korean tourists were the largest group of foreign tourists visiting China in the first half of 2010, totaling 1.95 million; this marked an increase of 30 percent from the same period in 2008 and accounted for 15.5 percent of the total foreign tourists in China.[69]

Nevertheless, China's response to the *Cheonan* incident and other military provocations and proliferation activities placed the greatest strain on China–South Korean relations in a generation. They brought relations to a new low. They sparked significant debate in South Korea, highlighting the relative weakness of China–South Korea political and security ties and strategic coordination despite close trade and investment ties. These weak links contrasted sharply with Beijing's concurrent strengthening political ties with the current leadership in Pyongyang and increasing trade and economic exchanges at a time of stalled inter-Korean relations.[70]

Among other setbacks for China were the following:

- China's political and economic support of North Korea at a time of international condemnation of Pyongyang undermined perceptions of China's regional and international role as mediator of the six-party talks and as a responsible stakeholder in the international community. President Obama seemed to capture the sentiment of many world opinion leaders in criticizing China's "willful blindness" in the face of North Korea's provocations.[71]
- North Korea's provocations introduced a high level of frustration into China's relations with not only South Korea but also the United States, Japan, Australia, and a number of Western powers.
- North Korea's provocations pushed the North Korean issue to the top of the US policy agenda with China; China's failure to act to curb North Korea was accompanied by senior American leaders, including Secretary of Defense Robert Gates, warning bluntly in public that the North Korean nuclear program was now viewed as a direct threat to the United States. An implication was that if China did not act to rein in North Korea, the United States would have to take action on its own.[72]

- China's weak response to North Korea's provocations and its unanticipated assertions in 2010 that US–South Korea military exercises to counter North Korea were a threat to China helped solidify the already close US relationship with South Korea. The conservative South Korean president Lee Myung Bak (2008–2013) proved to be a close partner of President Obama, cooperating on matters relating to regional issues as well as global concerns. The two leaders also enhanced trilateral cooperation among the United States, South Korea, and Japan in order to deal effectively with North Korea in the absence of significant support from China.[73]

In sum, China faced a Korean Peninsula marked by growing tension and deepening involvement by the United States and Japan at odds with Chinese interests. China's credibility and broader international reputation were battered. In return, China had solidified relations with North Korea. Unfortunately for China, large questions soon emerged about North Korea's future trajectory and Chinese interests. Kim Jong Un consolidated his power by brutal means, in the process killing a variety of powerful subordinates. Kim's headlong pursuit of nuclear weapons and ballistic missiles upset normal relations with China as it opposed Chinese efforts to lead North Korea to denuclearization. North Korea's emphasis on self-reliance as its national development strategy contradicted Chinese efforts to promote Chinese-style reform and opening of the North. Kim Jong Un engaged in repeated provocations directed at South Korea, the United States, and the United Nations. Though talks were held and tentative agreements were reached with the new North Korean government and the United States on freezing nuclear weapons and ballistic missile development in return for food aid and other matters in February 2012, Kim Jong Un insisted on conducting a long-range missile launch in defiance of UN restrictions in April, thereby ending the deal. There followed repeated North Korean threats of nuclear attacks against the United States. Numerous missile tests in defiance of UN restrictions came along with a third nuclear weapons test in February 2013. Against this background, the abrupt execution of Kim's powerful uncle, Jang Sung Taek, known to have close ties with China, in December 2013 capped a series of gross affronts to Chinese interests.[74]

## Xi Jinping and the Korean Peninsula

The Xi Jinping government showed its displeasure by cutting back previous support and keeping the unpredictable North Korean government at arm's length. Beijing appeared to be marking time, awaiting changes in North Korea or elsewhere that would allow Chinese action in support of its interests without the major risk of North Korean backlash.

There was little of the nationalistic rhetoric featured in the Xi government touting China's strength and determination to achieve its objectives in this sensitive area of foreign affairs. Along with a big drop in China's overall foreign trade, China–North Korea bilateral trade dropped substantially in 2015. Trade in 2014 and 2013 were valued at $6.39 billion and $6.54 billion, respectively. Neighboring Chinese provinces reportedly continued investing in opportunities seen in North Korea's economy, making China the largest foreign investor in North Korea. Official data showed that China had not exported any crude oil to North Korea in 2014, a significant change from past practice that saw North Korea rely on oil exports from China. It was unclear how much food aid China was recently providing to the North Korean regime. As noted, China had been an important supplier in the past.[75]

Meanwhile, Xi Jinping improved relations with South Korea through friendly summit meetings and cordial diplomacy. China's Asian Infrastructure Investment Bank and various Silk Road investment plans elicited strong interest and support from South Korean officials and entrepreneurs. South Korea and China worked together in regional economic groups that excluded the United States, but South Korea also showed interest in the US-backed Trans-Pacific Partnership that was a centerpiece of the Obama government's rebalance policy in Asia and that excluded China.

As President Xi Jinping shifted toward a less supportive public policy in defense of North Korea's nuclear weapons and ballistic missile testing and other violations of UN sanctions and injunctions, Kim Jong Un, defying China, the United States, and other concerned powers, focused his regime on advancing Pyongyang's nuclear weapons capacity. North Korea conducted three nuclear tests between January 2016 and September 2017. The last test, its sixth, was its most powerful to date. Also in 2017, North Korea conducted multiple tests of missiles that demonstrated a capability of reaching the continental United States.[76]

Entering office in 2017, the Trump administration quickly adopted a policy of unprecedented military, economic, and diplomatic pressure on North Korea and on China and others to compel Pyongyang to halt its threatening nuclear weapons program. The danger of war seemed real to Chinese and other observers. Beijing took steps to more rigorously abide by UN sanctions. Its heretofore hidden and/or denied tool of statecraft—smuggling oil to North Korea—was now receiving greater international attention, including from a threatening American president. Seemingly bending to the US-led pressure, the Kim Jong Un government in early 2018 switched to a more forthcoming and moderate posture toward South Korea and later China and the United States. In the following months into 2019, the North Korean leader held four summit meetings with China, three with South Korea, two with the United States, and one with Russia. Highlights included Kim's two meetings with President Trump. The first, in Singapore in June 2018, greatly eased tensions on the Korean Peninsula, notably with North Korea's pledge to halt testing of ballistic missiles and nuclear weapons, but did little to resolve the disputes. The second, in Hanoi in February 2019, ended amicably but abruptly with North Korea's refusal to accept US demands, resulting in an impasse. Pyongyang soon began threatening renewal of weapons testing if the impasse continued.[77]

Xi Jinping moved to consolidate and normalize relations with Kim Jong Un and North Korea, holding three summits with Kim as the North Korean leaders prepared for and followed through on the results of the 2018 summit with President Trump. Xi further consolidated relations in a fourth summit with the North Korean leader, which set the stage for the second US–North Korean summit in Hanoi in 2019. Kim was obviously disappointed with the absence of any success in the Hanoi meeting, and he avoided stopping in Beijing to see Xi and Chinese leaders as his train passed through China on the way home. China seemed surprised by the failed US–North Korean summit. Nevertheless, developments since 2018 saw China emerge as a critically important player with a major role in all aspects of negotiations involving the crisis caused by North Korea's rapid development and repeated testing of nuclear weapons and the related development and testing of ballistic missiles capable of carrying a nuclear warhead as far as the continental United States.

Xi Jinping endeavored to consolidate ties with the Kim regime by traveling to North Korea in June 2019 for a cordial summit with Kim Jong Un. This marked his fifth such summit and the first time China's top leader had visited North Korea in fourteen years. High-level Chinese–North Korean government, party, and military contacts and exchanges resumed strongly. Bilateral trade grew by 15 percent in January–June 2019 compared to the same period in the previous year. North Korean exports to China grew by 14 percent, while imports from China increased by 15.5 percent, producing a $1.04 billion trade deficit in the first half of 2019. China's share of North Korea's trade was more than 90 percent in 2018 while trade between South Korea and North Korea was close to zero. Chinese reports to the UN Sanctions Committee said China's total supply of refined oil products to North Korea was 5,730 tons in January–May 2019, somewhat less than during the same period in 2018. Extensive illicit ship-to-ship transfers of oil to North Korea conducted in international waters involved many Chinese ships and were not reported to the United Nations. A UN panel of specialists looking into these illicit transfers saw that the amount sent by Chinese, Russian, and other suppliers in 2019 was likely to severely violate UN sanctions limiting the supply of oil to North Korea to less than five hundred thousand tons.[78]

China and Russia cooperated more extensively than in the past over recent issues in the Korean Peninsula. Russia's behavior toward the Korean Peninsula reflected China's ever-growing importance for Russian foreign policy. As Korea was vital for China's security and developments there were much more important for Beijing than Moscow, the government of Vladimir Putin tailored its approach to the region in ways that enhanced Russia's alignment and avoided serious friction with China. The result over the past three years was collaborative Russian-Chinese efforts pursuing interests at odds with the United States, Japan, and South Korea. Russia's relations with North Korea in recent years continued to improve, even as China's relations with Pyongyang declined. As China faced US threats of war in Korea in 2017, it applied greater economic pressure against North Korea. Russia avoided such pressure, smuggled oil to North Korea, and improved its political relations with Kim's regime. The prolonged deterioration of North Korean–Chinese relations (2013–2018) raised the possibility of Moscow advancing in influence in North Korea as China declined. But Russia instead took steps to advance policy coordination with China over North Korea and related issues. A Russia-China vice-ministerial dialogue on security in Northeast Asia, centered on Korean issues, began regularly scheduled meetings in 2015;[79] they involved representatives from both sides' defense and foreign ministries.[80]

More important was closer Russian-Chinese collaboration against American pressure in the Korean Peninsula in 2017. In March, China outlined a "suspension-for-suspension" plan that became known as the "double freeze" proposal. According to this plan, North Korea would suspend its nuclear and missile tests if the United States and South Korea would suspend their military exercises.[81] In May, Russia sought to capitalize on the new South Korean leader's interest in improving North-South Korean relations to propose new diplomatic efforts toward denuclearization. The steps reflected past Russian plans for a Korean settlement, including rejecting the use of force and unilateral sanctions, addressing the US military presence in Northeast Asia along with the North Korean weapons programs, and creating a new security architecture.[82] Moscow and Beijing announced their unified position on the North Korea crisis during the summit between Vladimir Putin and Xi Jinping in Moscow on July 4, 2017. The two leaders combined previous Chinese proposals of the "double freeze" (the halt of nuclear and missile programs by the North in exchange for suspension of massive US-ROK military drills) and "parallel advancement" (simultaneous talks on denuclearization and the creation of peace mechanisms on the peninsula) with the Russian-proposed stage-by-stage Korean settlement plan. It was the first time that China and Russia so clearly articulated their common position with respect to North Korea. Indeed, it marked the first joint position the two countries have taken on an international issue.[83] Moscow and Beijing now explicitly linked the resolution of the North Korea problem to America's willingness to make major strategic concessions in Northeast Asia. Aiming at the US alliances with South Korea and Japan, Russia and China insisted that "allied relations" between separate states should not inflict damage on the interests of "third parties" and expressed opposition to "any military presence of extra-regional forces in Northeast Asia." Such Russian-Chinese cooperation reemerged when the two powers proposed in late 2019 a draft UN resolution calling for a partial lifting of sanctions against North Korea.

South Korean president Moon Jae In and his government's ambitions to play a key role in facilitating outreach to North Korea and increased accommodation and cooperation on the Korean Peninsula suffered major setbacks with the impasse resulting from the second North Korean–US summit. Meanwhile, China maneuvered to become the key international mediator between North Korea and other powers. And, even though Beijing energized its relationship with North Korea, it moved slowly in improving relations with South Korea following the imposition of major costs on the South Korean economy as a result of China's resort to hidden state intervention in ostensibly unofficial action imposing heavy punitive economic restrictions on Korean companies. Even the usually robust South Korea–China economic relationship suffered, with trade flows in 2019 at the lowest level in ten years. South Korean investment in China did increase. Xi Jinping's reluctance to visit Seoul added to China's seeming relegation of South Korea to a position subordinate to North Korea as Beijing placed Xi as the main intermediary between North Korea and the rest of the world. [84]

China's cool treatment reinforced South Korean concern over the various hidden, denied, or heretofore unappreciated tools of Chinese statecraft challenging South Korean interests. Heading the list were the punitive trade costs imposed on South Korean companies as a result of the THAAD dispute. Beijing endeavored to disguise its violation of WTO norms by carrying out such measures through unofficial means. The coercive Chinese practices recalled the dumping and the truculence of China's posture during disputes over the garlic trade and kimchi sales in South Korea in the previous decade. The prominent role of the Chinese ambassador and a senior Chinese official dealing with North Korea, who were active in meeting with South Korean political leaders before the 2017 presidential election, was seen as inappropriate Chinese interference in South Korean elections. The Chinese embassy was seen as involved in mobilizing Chinese students to engage in sometimes violent pro-China demonstrations, most recently in violent clashes with South Korean university students showing support for the demonstrations in Hong Kong in 2019. China also influenced academic and media discourse on China by providing funding and access to China or denying access to those in disfavor. Those in South Korea and elsewhere who saw Confucius Institutes as agents of influence for China were concerned with the saturation of South Korea with twenty-three Confucius Institutes in twenty-two universities and thirteen Confucius Classrooms in thirteen middle and high schools. The wide array of institutes and organizations the Chinese authorities employed to control and steer foreign countries in directions China supports were very active in South Korea, influencing opinion leaders and media discourse. They involved a range of ostensibly unofficial so-called front organizations that were actually components of the Chinese government, party, and military, with connections to Chinese espionage.[85]

Meanwhile, it is estimated that one hundred thousand Chinese fishing boats are involved in illegal fishing in South Korean territorial waters annually. Chinese military aircraft repeatedly intrude into South Korean airspace, sometimes refusing to respond to South Korean jets scrambled to face them. The most egregious violation since the Cold War came on July 22, 2018, when a joint China-Russia air patrol entered both the southern and eastern portions of the Korean Air Defense Identification Zone (KADIZ). South Korean fighter jets scrambled and fired warning flares and shots in response to an accompanying Russian intelligence plane that entered South Korean–claimed airspace adjacent to the contested Dokdo/Takeshima Island. As the planes also violated Japanese territorial claims, such remarkable China-Russian cooperation signaled an expansion of the geographic scope of China-Russia military cooperation and an effort by Russia and China to exploit growing tensions between US allies Japan and South Korea.[86]

## Chapter Nine

# Relations with Southeast Asia, Australia, New Zealand, and the Pacific Islands

## SOUTHEAST ASIA

For much of the post–Cold War period, China's attentive diplomacy and growing trade, investment, infrastructure, and other economic linkages supported cooperative relations with its Southeast Asian neighbors. China joined and worked constructively with regional groups led by Association of Southeast Asian Nations (ASEAN) focused on promoting development and sustaining stability. China for many years reassured its Southeast Asian neighbors that China's remarkable military buildup, periodic violent displays of military force against Taiwan and the United States, and strong claims in the disputed South China Sea should not be seen as a threat. With China's greater assertiveness in foreign affairs beginning after the global economic crisis of 2008, China gave higher priority to pursuing control of disputed territory at its neighbors' expense. The drive was backed by rapid development of Chinese capabilities in military, coast guard, oil drilling, fisheries, and other aspects of state power and by increased Chinese nationalism and determination to defend Chinese claims.[1]

The balance between two Chinese goals changed. China continued to expand its influence through moderate diplomacy and mutually beneficial economic exchanges with Southeast Asian countries. But it was determined to have its way in countering other claimants' infringements on China's broad claim to most of the South China Sea.[2] The Chinese South China Sea drive and broader ambitions in Southeast Asia were reinforced by acute US-China rivalry for influence in Southeast Asia. And there was a marked in-

199

crease in applications of the multifaceted power of the Chinese Communist Party–state apparatus in international affairs, including the conventional and unconventional tools of Chinese statecraft assessed in other chapters dealing with other world areas. Overall, Beijing's foreign practice generally followed the four stages of post–Cold War Chinese foreign policy behavior explained in chapter 1.

## China–Southeast Asia Relations, 1989–1996

The first phase witnessed strong Chinese efforts to break out of the post-Tiananmen isolation and pressure imposed by the United States and Western-aligned countries by means of more active Chinese diplomacy. China resumed normal diplomatic relations with Indonesia and established diplomatic relations with Singapore. It accommodated international pressure leading to a peace settlement in Cambodia in 1991 and in the process shifted Chinese support from the reviled and discredited Khmer Rouge to its former adversary, Cambodian strongman Hun Sen. The withdrawal of Vietnamese forces from Cambodia and the peace agreement of 1991 led to normalization of China's relations with Vietnam.[3] Beijing leaders also solidified China's position as the main international backer of the military regime that grabbed power in Myanmar after aborted elections in 1988. China in this period engaged actively with ASEAN in order to improve political relations, build collaborative mechanisms, and curb the ability of the United States to pressure China over human rights and other sensitive issues.[4]

Chinese–Southeast Asian trade and other economic interchanges grew rapidly. By 1992, Sino-ASEAN trade was fifteen times the volume it was in 1975. It was valued at $20 billion in 1995. ASEAN was China's fifth-largest trading partner after Japan, Hong Kong, the United States, and the European Union (EU). In general, imports and exports in China-ASEAN trade were in balance.[5]

ASEAN-China investment also grew rapidly in the post–Cold War period, though it was mainly ASEAN investment in China and not the other way around. By mid-1994, Singapore became China's fifth-largest overseas investor, after Hong Kong, Taiwan, the United States, and Japan. By the end of 1996, there were 12,342 approved Southeast Asian investment projects in China, valued at $34 billion (of which $9.4 billion was already paid).[6] Chinese investment in ASEAN was much smaller in scale. It was less than $1 billion annually in the 1990s. The ASEAN-China Joint Committee on Economic and Trade Cooperation and the ASEAN-China Joint Committee on Scientific and Technological Cooperation were established in 1994.[7]

Each year beginning in 1991, the Chinese foreign minister attended, by invitation, the annual ASEAN foreign ministers' conference. In 1995, China asked to become a "full dialogue partner" of ASEAN at this annual meeting, and this was accepted in December 1997. On security issues, ASEAN invited China in 1994 to become a consultative partner in the regional security dialogue carried on by the ASEAN Regional Forum (ARF).[8]

Chinese leaders also joined others in the region in fostering Asia-only economic, political, and security groups that excluded or marginalized the United States. They strongly supported Malaysian prime minister Mahathir Mohamad's proposal to establish the East Asian Economic Caucus (EAEC). The proposed EAEC was viewed warily by the United States, which was to be excluded from membership in the group.[9]

China's imperative to protect and advance nationalistic sovereignty claims also rose. China passed a territorial law in 1992 strongly asserting claims to disputed territories. Chinese military and civilian security forces backed efforts by Chinese oil companies, fishing enterprises, and others to advance Chinese claims in the South China Sea against the expansion of such activities by Vietnam, the Philippines, Malaysia, and other claimants. A major incident in 1995 saw Chinese forces occupy Mischief Reef, located near and claimed by the Philippines. Leading states of ASEAN were alarmed, and the United States also voiced support for peaceful resolution of regional disputes. Meanwhile, the large-scale Chinese military exercises against Taiwan in 1995–1996 saw few of China's neighbors explicitly side with China or the United States. But many in Southeast Asia were seriously concerned with China's assertiveness and ambitions.[10]

## China–Southeast Asia Relations, 1996–2001

Trying to reduce growing regional fear of the "China threat," Chinese leaders at this time played down military actions and assertive commentary. They tried to reassure neighbors in Southeast Asia and other countries of China's peaceful intentions.[11] They propounded principles related to a "new security concept" that built on the moderate approach China had adopted in the 1950s, based on the so-called five principles of peaceful coexistence in international affairs. Chinese diplomacy was very active in bilateral relations, establishing various types of special partnerships and fostering good-neighbor policies. China also increased positive interaction with ASEAN, the ASEAN Regional Forum, and other Asian regional organizations. In the 1990s, top-level Chinese leaders like Jiang Zemin, Li Peng, and Zhu Rongji and the Chinese foreign and defense ministers traveled to ASEAN countries. When their Southeast Asian counterparts visited China, they received warm welcomes. In December 1997, President Jiang Zemin attended the informal ASEAN summit in Kuala Lumpur, and China and ASEAN issued their first joint statement. Earlier in 1997, ASEAN and China set up an umbrella panel, called the ASEAN-China Joint Cooperation Committee (JCC), to oversee ASEAN-China relations. The JCC was to identify projects to be undertaken by ASEAN and China and to coordinate four other parallel mechanisms dealing with political and economic issues. [12]

China preferred to deal with territorial issues bilaterally, as evidenced in the Sino-Philippines agreements reached in 1996 on a military code of conduct, military exchanges, and the establishment of some communications between military detachments in disputed areas in the South China Sea. China and the Philippines also reached agreement regarding joint maritime scientific research, fishing, control of piracy, and other endeavors. This convergence did not prevent continued friction, however. Indonesia succeeded in gaining China's participation in an annual multilateral workshop on "managing potential conflicts in the South China Sea." In the workshop, participants exchanged ideas on dealing with the disputed territories. Southeast Asian officials also discussed the territorial issues in ASEAN-China meetings of senior working-level officials. [13]

Chinese trade relations with Southeast Asia and other neighboring countries generally grew. The Chinese economy remained stable amid the Asian economic crisis of 1997–1998. China did not devalue its currency, it sustained economic growth, and it supported some international efforts to assist failing regional economies—developments that boosted China's stature in the region. [14]

At odds with China's reassurance of its neighbors, Beijing told neighboring states that its new security concept opposed US efforts to sustain and strengthen alliance relations or military relations in Asia, notably with Japan, South Korea, Australia, and some Southeast Asian nations. Beijing indicated that these states should follow China's approach and eschew closer alliance and military ties with the United States. [15]

## China–Southeast Asia Relations, 2001–2012

As discussed in chapter 6, the George W. Bush administration coincided with another shift in China's policy in Asia and elsewhere. The initially tough Bush administration approach to China involved supporting Taiwan, opposing China's military buildup and Chinese proliferation practices, strengthening US-Japan alliance relations, and developing ballistic missile defenses in Asia. These steps did not elicit strident criticism by Chinese officials or in official Chinese media, whereas in the recent past, even less serious US steps against Chinese interests were strongly denounced.

China eventually made clear that it was now broadening the scope of its ongoing efforts to reassure its neighbors that China was not a threat. The broadened efforts now included and focused on the United States. Chinese attacks on US alliances and Chinese advocacy of its new security concept were muted. In their place emerged a new and evolving Chinese emphasis reassuring Washington and all concerned governments that China's "rise" would be a peaceful one that represented many opportunities and no threat to concerned powers.[16]

The shift was accompanied by positive momentum in China's relations with Southeast Asia and ASEAN. China initiated in 2002 an ASEAN-China Free Trade Agreement (ACFTA) that other powers endeavored to duplicate in later years. It agreed that year in negotiations with ASEAN to the Declaration on the Conduct of the Parties in the South China Sea, which set guidelines on how territorial disputes should be managed. China was the first of ASEAN foreign partners to sign ASEAN's Treaty of Amity and Cooperation (TAC) in 2003. It played an active role in ASEAN-convened international groups. China's preference at the time was ASEAN Plus Three (China, Japan, and South Korea), which notably excluded the United States. China worked closely with Malaysia in creating the ASEAN-convened East Asia Summit in 2005. The plan was for China to host the 2006 meeting and for membership to be restricted to ASEAN Plus Three. The plan was thwarted because of opposition by Japan, Indonesia, Singapore, and others, fearing Chinese dominance in the group. ASEAN's chair remained the host of the East Asia Summit, and membership was opened to India, Australia, and New Zealand, with Russia and the United States joining later.[17]

The global economic crisis of 2008–2009 briefly curbed China-ASEAN trade, but the value of trade grew markedly in 2010, reaching $292.7 billion according to Chinese statistics, making China ASEAN's leading foreign trading partner and ASEAN China's fourth-largest trading partner. Investment by Southeast Asian countries into China was substantial, while Chinese investment in those countries remained comparatively much smaller. Investment patterns also showed China and ASEAN directly competing for investment funds from Western and advanced Asian countries, with China gaining a much greater share of foreign investment while ASEAN's share declined.[18]

A wide range of proposed and constructed highway, railroad, river, power generation, power grid, and pipeline connections integrated China ever more closely with those Southeast Asian countries that border China.[19] The new infrastructure opened heretofore inaccessible areas to greater economic development; they were welcomed by the Chinese and Southeast Asian governments and placed the economies of nearby Southeast Asian areas into ever closer relationships involving China. Hydroelectric dams and other projects prompted serious international criticism on grounds of environmental damage, population dislocation, and negative effects on downstream fishing and other interests.[20]

Meanwhile, in 2010, there were six thousand Chinese-language volunteers teaching fifty thousand Southeast Asian students in classes sponsored by, among others, thirty-five Confucius Institutes. By that time, almost eight hundred flights took place every week between major cities in China and Southeast Asian countries. Between January and October 2009, 4 million people from ASEAN countries visited China, and 3.7 million Chinese visited ASEAN countries. Chinese visitors represented more than 6 percent of foreign visitors to ASEAN countries.[21]

After the setback for China in seeking leadership in the East Asia Summit, China's attention to Southeast Asia and ASEAN appeared to decline for a few years. Chinese officials showed impatience with the slow pace of advancing relations with ASEAN and the region under the leadership of ASEAN governments preoccupied with other matters. China's proposed advances were postponed when Thailand had to cancel and reschedule the annual ASEAN summit and related meetings in late 2008 because of domestic political turmoil. The rescheduled meeting in Thailand in April 2009 was canceled and foreign delegates evacuated as hostile demonstrators invaded the meeting site. China now lagged behind the United States in appointing an ambassador to ASEAN. China also followed the US lead in setting up a representational office with the ASEAN headquarters in Jakarta.[22]

## Changes under Xi Jinping, 2012–Present

Beginning in 2009–2010, China adopted assertive practices regarding territorial claims with its Southeast Asian neighbors, but for a time they were mixed with strong reaffirmations of reassurance and peaceful intent. Under the leadership of Xi Jinping since 2012, Chinese intentions in the South China Sea and other territorial disputes became clearer. On the one hand, China's assertive and coercive use of security forces, island building, economic leverage, and diplomatic threats saw Beijing overcome regional resistance and US countermoves to build and arm island outposts that gave Chinese forces strong control of the disputed South China Sea. On the other hand, Xi's China married its tough policy on South China disputes with visionary publicity of China's massive global economic development plan, the Belt and Road Initiative (BRI). The plan attracted ASEAN states with generous funding for Chinese-built infrastructure projects, thereby reducing the opposition of most ASEAN members to China's power grab at the expense of ASEAN claimants in the South China Sea.

In 2012,[23]

- China employed its large and growing force of maritime and fishing security ships, targeted economic sanctions, and repeated diplomatic warnings to intimidate and coerce the Philippines to respect China's takeover of the disputed Scarborough Shoal.
- China deployed one of the world's largest (32,000-ton) fish processing ships and a fleet of thirty fishing boats supported by a supply ship to fish in disputed South China Sea areas.

- China created a new, multifaceted administrative structure backed by a new military garrison that covered wide swaths of disputed areas in the South China Sea. A state-controlled Chinese oil company offered nine new blocs in the South China Sea for foreign oil companies' development that were far from China but very close to Vietnam, with some of the areas already being developed by Vietnam.
- China ensured that the 2012 ASEAN chair, Cambodia, prevented South China Sea disputes from consideration at the annual ASEAN ministerial meeting. The result was a remarkable display of ASEAN disunity in the first failure of the annual ASEAN ministerial meeting to conclude with an agreed-upon communiqué in the forty-five-year history of the group.

At the same time, Chinese officials and official Chinese media commentaries emphasized the material benefits for regional countries in strengthening economic interaction with China, provided they avoided contesting China's claims in the South China Sea.

Subsequent developments showed increased Chinese determination to compel others to accommodate China on South China Sea issues. In 2014, China abruptly deployed a forty-story oil rig along with a protecting armada of over one hundred fishing, coast guard, and reportedly military vessels in the disputed Paracel Islands of the South China Sea. The results were confrontations at sea with Vietnamese coast guard and maritime militia and anti-China riots in Vietnam, destroying factories and killing some Chinese citizens. Concurrent disclosures showed large-scale dredging beginning the rapid creation and subsequent fortification of Chinese-controlled islands on previously submerged reefs in the disputed Spratly Islands for the purpose of surveillance and power projection far from the Chinese mainland.[24]

The regional reaction to the Sino-Vietnamese confrontation appeared to show unwillingness by most Southeast Asian countries to take a stand against China. The Philippines was very critical of Chinese actions, and Manila collaborated with Hanoi in seeking options. The United States came into the lead of international critics of Chinese coercion; Japan and Australia usually weighed in supporting the American stand. However, most Southeast Asian countries remained on the sidelines. Adding to uncertainty in the face of China's challenge was that the Obama government's rhetoric had yet to be supported with concrete actions as part of a clear strategy to get China to stop its coercive advances of territorial control at the expense of its neighbors.

Beijing seemed to judge that regional circumstances would require acceptance of China's new assertiveness. The Southeast Asian countries and ASEAN on their own seemed too weak and divided to resist; whatever will to resist there was would be undermined by China's growing economic sway over neighboring countries. It was later revealed that Beijing was also using various hidden, disguised, denied, or poorly recognized levers of statecraft to influence and control elites and the public in Southeast Asia and the adjoining Pacific countries.

Debate continued on whether China's new assertiveness and growing sway over Southeast Asia would be successful. China's economic influence over ASEAN continued to grow, but it remained far from dominant. According to ASEAN statistics, China, including Hong Kong, accounted for almost 18 percent of ASEAN's foreign trade in 2013; the figure was about 20 percent in 2018. And growing Chinese investment in ASEAN saw Chinese plus Hong Kong investment account for 10.5 percent of foreign investment to ASEAN in the 2011–2013 period. The figure was 13.2 percent in 2018.[25] As shown in chapter 3, China's economic importance for ASEAN had some limitations that made it less than likely that the regional governments would fall under China's sway for economic reasons. For example, ASEAN received more investment from the EU and Japan. ASEAN did proportionately less trade with China than did either Australia or South Korea, middle powers that repeatedly made clear to Beijing that their independence of action would not be compromised despite possible consequences for their economic relations with China. Meanwhile, as noted in chapter 3, it was probably incorrect to view the massive Chinese publicity in support of new Chinese lending to Southeast Asia and other countries along China's periphery as making China's neighbors bow to Chinese expansion in the East and South China Seas. Most notably, the propaganda failed to hide China's mixed record in Southeast Asian countries and other developing countries in following through with repeated multibillion-dollar foreign loans and investment pledges and other promises of economic support.

Further complicating purported Chinese dominance was the United States. The Obama government's multifaceted rebalance policy of broad engagement was widely welcomed in Southeast Asia and strongly supported by US allies Japan, Australia, and the Philippines. American leaders from President Obama on down took the lead internationally in warning China against coercive moves to change the regional status quo. In the end, President Obama's overall record was mediocre and often ineffective in countering a variety of challenges posed by more assertive Chinese behavior under the leadership of Xi Jinping.[26]

The Obama administration's defense secretary, Ashton Carter, and Pacific commander Admiral Harry Harris repeatedly spoke of China's "aggressive" actions and what Harris called Chinese "hegemony in East Asia." They and other defense officials pointed to US military plans and actions "to check" Chinese advances through deployments, regional collaboration, and assistance to China's neighbors. American officials also expected a Chinese defeat in a ruling in 2016 at the UN Law of the Sea (UNCLOS) arbitral tribunal at the Permanent Court of Arbitration in The Hague, undermining the broad and vague Chinese claims used to justify expansion in the South China Sea.

The above developments did not halt the opportunistic and incremental Chinese expansion in the South China Sea. From China's perspective, the benefits of Xi's challenges continued to outweigh the costs. Notably, President Xi was viewed in China as a powerful international leader, while President Obama appeared weak. China's probing expansion and intimidation efforts in the East China Sea ran up against firm and effective Japanese efforts supported strongly by the United States, and they were complicated for Beijing by China's inability to deal effectively with provocations from North Korea. The opportunities for expansion in the South China Sea were greater given the weaknesses of governments there. And the adverse judgment by the UNCLOS panel on July 12, 2016, in the case at The Hague was effectively dismissed by Beijing, with the United States under President Obama's cautious leadership seeking to calm the situation by offering few public objections to China's flaunting its egregious opposition to the legally binding ruling.

What these developments showed was that the Obama government's efforts to counter China in the South China Sea were significant. However, it was obvious to Beijing and anyone else paying attention that they were carefully measured to avoid serious disruption in the broader and multidimensional US-China relationship. The American government signaled that measured resolve was likely to continue to the end of the Obama government, and it did.

As discussed in chapter 6, President Trump in 2017 focused in Asia on North Korea's threatening nuclear weapons development and on building personal relations with senior leaders, notably Chinese president Xi Jinping, but in 2018 congressional and administration attention turned to China. As part of the administration's National Security Strategy and National Defense Strategy came stronger measures against Chinese challenges to US interest in the disputed South China Sea. The focus at first involved stepped-up US naval and air power shows of force, including much more frequent US freedom-of-navigation exercises carried out by US warships passing close to Chinese fortified islands in ways that directly challenged Beijing's territorial claims deemed illegal by the UNCLOS tribunal in 2016. As those efforts continued, there followed successful efforts to get allies Japan, Australia, Great Britain, France, and South Korea, as well as such important regional partners as India, to join in deployments in the disputed waters. The United States also joined with allies Japan and Australia in promoting investment mechanisms and related economic support that would compete with Beijing's Belt and Road Initiative. It also worked with a broad range of allies and partners in measures to thwart Chinese theft and acquisition of the high technology needed for Beijing's ambitions to dominate manufacturing in the economy of the future. Senior leaders repeatedly called out China for "bullying" its neighbors and for seeking regional dominance in a Chinese-led order where neighbors would be required to defer to Beijing's requirements.[27]

Coming in the wake of a very successful summit meeting during Xi Jinping's elaborate welcome for President Trump during the latter's trip to Asia in November 2017, the subsequent rapid succession of strongly antagonistic US official policy statements and punitive tariffs, export controls, and investment restrictions—all targeting China as America's number-one danger—came as a surprise. Chinese officials were on the defensive and cautious in response, seeking to avoid provoking the volatile president.[28]

Nevertheless, in Southeast Asia, Chinese leaders saw paths forward to continue advancing their interests at the expense of their neighbors in the South China Sea and to the detriment of its main international competitor, the United States. President Xi Jinping and Premier Li Keqiang during visits to annual leadership meetings in the region in fall 2018 highlighted Beijing's economic prominence, diplomatic resolve, and military power in hailing advancing Chinese influence. Xi's November visits to the Philippines, Brunei, and Papua New Guinea, including the annual Asia-Pacific Economic Cooperation (APEC) Leaders' Meeting in Port Moresby, and Li's November visit to Singapore and participation in the East Asia Summit, ASEAN Plus Three, and China-ASEAN meetings showed significant gains. Among those gains, China's power saw ASEAN pliant to Chinese preferences on South China Sea disputes, and Beijing showed new prominence as a rising power among the Pacific Island nations.[29]

In 2019, senior Chinese leaders devoted little attention to the South China Sea and China's relations with Southeast Asian countries. Infrequent comments depicted the slow progress that China preferred in negotiations on a code of conduct in the South China Sea and promoted steady advances in its Belt and Road Initiative, offering strong economic incentives for closer regional cooperation with China. ASEAN and Southeast Asian claimants adhered to Beijing's demands to avoid referring to the 2016 UNCLOS tribunal ruling against China's South China Sea claims and to handle disputes through negotiations without outside interference. Routine Chinese complaints about more frequent US freedom-of-navigation exercises and other US and allied military operations in the South China Sea came from lower-level ministry spokespersons.[30]

The annual heads of government regional meetings convened by ASEAN leaders in Bangkok, topped by the Fourteenth East Asian Summit on November 4, 2019, saw Beijing's leaders set the pace for slow-moving negotiations on a China-ASEAN code of conduct in the South China Sea. While publicly benign, in unpublicized moves Beijing used its impressive coast guard fleet and the massed maritime militia fishing fleets to harass ongoing oil and gas exploration efforts conducted by foreign firms for Vietnam and Malaysia. It also used the coast guard and maritime militia to safeguard Chinese interests in disputed territories held or claimed by the Philippines and Malaysia and to protect Chinese-claimed fishing rights in waters claimed by Indonesia. Xi Jinping told Philippines president Rodrigo Duterte, who strove to improve relations with China, that if the Philippines confronted China on territorial issues, it would be badly defeated. Senior Chinese leaders privately warned the Vietnamese in the same way. China seemed intent on purging foreign companies from oil and gas exploration in the South China Sea, leaving the other claimants little choice but to work together with China in developing needed resources. Indeed, China pressed the claimants to have the proposed code of conduct preclude coastal states from employing international oil firms to develop offshore resources and also the United States and other outside powers from conducting military operations in the South China Sea.[31]

## China's Unconventional Levers of Power and Influence

Chapters 1 and 4 discuss newly prominent, generally unconventional levers of power that China employs in its foreign policy statecraft. The discussion of these elements in chapter 1 focused on those employed in Asia and the Pacific. A closer look at the evidence in individual cases in Southeast Asia shows that Chinese confidence in its trajectory in Southeast Asia is based in part on its many often covert and even nefarious means of influencing regional governments to defer to China's wishes.

Corruption lies at the heart of Chinese influence among several Southeast Asian governments. A comprehensive study by the Asia Society of China's BRI being implemented in Southeast Asia recalled the extraordinary scale of corruption in the Razak government in Malaysia making deals with enormous payoffs in railway and other very expensive Chinese projects in the country. The study then advised that the Malaysian case was an exception only in that corrupt practices were exposed and publicized, concluding that "the pervasive use of bribery, cost padding, and kickbacks was also indicated in numerous other BRI projects in the region." It judged that there were no operational anticorruption mechanisms for monitoring, enforcement, and accountability in BRI projects, concluding that "no examples of penalties for corruption in Southeast Asian BRI projects could be identified in the course of our research."[32]

Transparency International's Corruption Perceptions Index for 2018 ranked Cambodia as the most corrupt nation in Southeast Asia, and it came in 161st out of the 180 ranked countries in terms of popular perceptions of corruption. An International Republican Institute (IRI) report showed how Chinese statecraft abetted such corrupt practices as a basis for Beijing's ever stronger relationship with Phnom Penh as China's most reliable client in

Southeast Asia. As a notable example, it cited Hun Sen awarding a Chinese company led by a former People's Liberation Army (PLA) officer a ninety-nine-year lease of territory more than half as large as New York's Manhattan Island along the South China Sea because the company funneled funding to support Hun Sen's three-thousand-strong private army. The IRI reported that the heads of Chinese firms seeking and implementing BRI-related agreements in Cambodia worked through the corrupt networks of Hun Sen's Cambodian People's Party pursuing nontransparent arrangements of benefit to Cambodian elites and Chinese firms. The deals remained unaccountable to those outside a small circle centered on Hun Sen.[33]

Meanwhile, Beijing found in Hun Sen an avid consumer of Chinese media and information control mechanisms and surveillance equipment. For his part, Hun Sen used these means to ensure that the Cambodian information environment remained friendly to Chinese interests and conducive to the continued extension of Chinese influence in Cambodia. China offered considerable technical support to the Cambodian information technology, telecommunications, education, and media sectors. This increased China's shaping of the Cambodian information environment, bolstering China's image in the country. The Chinese technical support also strengthened the Hun Sen regime's control over the population. Notably, China possessed the security and surveillance tools that the Hun Sen government sought to strengthen its hold on power. With concurrent greater Chinese control over Cambodian communications networks by the controversial Chinese firm Huawei, the direction of such surveillance deals added to deep Chinese penetration of Cambodian domestic operations of interest to China.[34]

As Beijing in the push to advance its BRI goals put aside conventional lending standards and engaged in what critics called predatory lending, Chinese negotiators backed by top-level government and party officials used China's strong leverage as Laos's most important neighbor and investor to create the funding and construction capacity to build the China–Laos railway project with a cost of $6 billion. China's role in the project was already so deep that official Chinese media sometimes characterized the railway as China owned. Indeed, about 60 percent, or US$3.5 billion, of the funding for the project was in the form of borrowing from the Export-Import Bank of China. A further 40 percent, amounting to $2.4 billion, was funded with equity in the form of a joint-venture company comprising three Chinese state-owned firms and one Laotian state-owned enterprise. The latter enterprise held a 30 percent stake. To fund this, the Laotian government committed $250 million from the national budget and took a second loan of $480 million from the Export-Import Bank of China.[35]

The railway was very important for China. Beijing needed this link to complete the long-sought high-speed railway from Kunming to Singapore. The feasibility for Laos was seriously questioned. One result for Laos was a mountain of debt with no sure means of repayment. Unfortunately, some estimates predicted that the railway would lose money for at least the first decade of operation instead of the annual 4.35 percent profit anticipated by the joint-venture company. Laos already made tax and land concessions to support the Kunming–Vientiane Railway project, significantly undercutting the benefits it will produce. Past experience suggested that further concessions may be necessary. In 2008, the Lao government had to cede land to a Chinese developer as compensation for back debts from a Chinese-built sports stadium in Vientiane.[36]

Laos was one of the Southeast Asian countries subject to another important unconventional source of international leverage not yet discussed, the use of the waters of the Mekong River. Laos and the other downriver states— Myanmar, Thailand, Cambodia, and Vietnam—depended on the river's water flows for hydroelectric power, fishing, and agriculture. Extensive Chinese dam building on the long upper Mekong River, known as the Lancang River in China, gave China control over how much water flows and how fast it flows to downriver countries. This control was particularly important during recurring periods of drought in recent years. Though different regional groupings discussed mutual use of the river, Beijing was careful to remain in control of the flow of the river's waters. Against the background of Beijing's frequent use of abrupt punishment such as cutoffs of trade to smaller countries that did not defer to Chinese demands on sensitive issues, the lower Mekong governments fully recognized that serious differences with China may prompt Beijing to use the river flow to punish smaller neighbors.[37]

## AUSTRALIA, NEW ZEALAND, AND THE PACIFIC ISLANDS

### Australia

Disputes over the South China Sea, stronger involvement of Australia and New Zealand in Asian regional bodies, and the expanded US role in the area under President Obama's rebalance policy and President Trump's Indo-Pacific strategy strengthened Chinese interest in relations with Australia, New Zealand, and the Pacific Island countries. As China's economic and political prominence grew, China's relations with Australia improved markedly for several years, based notably on an upswing in Australian raw material exports to China and a marked increase in Chinese exports to Australia. Official Chinese attention to Australia, as well as New Zealand and the Pacific Islands, was often extraordinary, with numerous high-level and other official visits. However, the sharp downturn in US relations with China during the Trump administration coincided with often lurid media disclosures and government testimony on usually disguised and hidden Chinese government efforts to penetrate and influence Australian government decision making through generous political payments, employment opportunities, manipulation of the Chinese Australian community, and covert espionage. Australia came to agree with the Trump administration on the dangers posed by China. Australia led international efforts in the Asia-Pacific, Europe, and elsewhere to guard against perceived Chinese security, economic, and political challenges. Though Australia and China endeavored to maintain close economic relations and the large number of Chinese students and tourists who studied and traveled in Australia, overall relations reached a low point in the post–Cold War period over the past three years. [38]

Australia established diplomatic relations with China in the early 1970s and became a major trading partner of the Chinese. China's rapid economic development required increasing imports of energy, iron ore, grain, and other resources, which Australia willingly provided; Chinese exports of manufactured goods to Australia also grew. A close ally of the United States, Australia generally adhered to a moderate policy and developed positive approaches in engagement with China. However, the newly installed conservative government of Prime Minister John Howard endorsed the US show of force during the 1996 Taiwan Strait crisis, a stance that reinforced a Chinese tendency to view Australian policy in the region as the same as that of the United States. Chinese efforts to improve relations with Australia were widely seen in Canberra as designed to weaken Australian cooperation with the United States against Chinese interests. [39]

Watching China's growing military capabilities warily, the Australian Labor Party government in 2007 opposed expanding the US-Japan-Australia strategic dialogue to include India—a step made in response to Chinese concerns. More recent governments since 2013 have been led by conservatives who gave high priority to close alliance ties with the United States. In the face of China's steady military buildup and more assertive policies along its rim in the past decade, Australia adopted military buildup plans and coordinated closely with the United States in countering perceived coercive practices by China in nearby seas and in support of the American strategic reengagement with the Asia-Pacific, including deployments of US forces to Australia. [40] For their part, Australian business representatives, politicians, and public opinion usually tended to be positive about China. [41]

China has become Australia's largest trading partner. In 2019, the annual trade was valued at $272.4 billion, with China (including Hong Kong) taking 35 percent of Australia's exports. Australia's 2019 trade surplus with China (including Hong Kong) was close to $50 billion. The foundation of the trade relations was China's purchase of Australian raw materials. [42] China (including Hong Kong) became a more important foreign investor in Australia but ranked much lower than the United States, the United Kingdom, and Japan. [43]

As relations over the past decade became troubled over security concerns regarding China's military buildup, disputes over Chinese efforts to buy stakes in Australian firms, Chinese human rights practices, and the highly publicized criminal investigation and conviction of an Australian business-man, both Vice President Xi Jinping and Vice Premier Li Keqiang visited Australia in efforts to mend fences in the period prior to taking the top leadership positions in 2012.[44] President Xi returned to Australia and the region in November 2014. In an unprecedented indication of top-level Chi-nese attention to Oceania, Xi spent ten days there, starting with his participa-tion in the November 15–16 G20 summit in Brisbane. After the summit, Xi spent several days each in Australia, New Zealand, and Fiji.[45]

This high point in summitry was eventually overshadowed by disclosures of secret Chinese efforts to influence and control Australian policy toward China. They involved four areas.[46]

First, Beijing endeavored to gain greater control of the ethnic Chinese diaspora in Australia. The diaspora amounted to 4.4 percent of the country's population and was supplemented by 184,000 Chinese students in Australia. There also were 1.4 million Chinese tourists visiting the country annually. Front organizations with links to the Chinese government and Communist Party rallied the Chinese diaspora in demonstrations in support of Chinese government objectives. Pro-Beijing interests took control of Chinese-lan-guage newspapers. Chinese media organizations also established well-funded television, radio, print, and social media operations to influence broader Aus-tralian audiences.

Second, selected Australian political leaders and other influential opinion leaders were encouraged, bribed, and sometimes coerced to support Chinese causes. Beijing-connected businesses funded politicians and political parties; leading politicians took on well-paid positions in Chinese corporations on retirement; media and academic leaders accepted first-class treatment in free trips to China, voicing on return support for controversial pro-Beijing poli-cies. Australian businesses with a big stake in China were leveraged to voice support for Chinese ambitions in the BRI, Huawei advancing in Australia, and other sensitive matters.

Third, Chinese agencies launched active cyber campaigns against govern-ment agencies, corporations, and influential community organizations and some prominent individuals. The purposes of the above wide range of uncon-ventional tools of statecraft ran the gamut from stealing commercial and government secrets to bullying and coercing opponents in Australia.

And the final element, which this writer experienced firsthand, involved penetration of high-level Australian intelligence and other government or-gans dealing with China for purposes of espionage.

These Chinese operations were revealed in a series of Australian govern-ment reports and testimonies, government leaks of classified information, and media reports in 2017. The Chinese Foreign Ministry and Chinese em-bassy in Australia vigorously denied the revelations, but the Malcolm Turnbull government took them seriously; it proposed and enacted counterespion-age laws, including the banning of foreign donations to candidates and political parties and other laws against foreign influence in Australian politics. In December, Prime Minister Turnbull named China as a country of concern behind the new legislation, prompting strong rebukes from Beijing. China imposed limits on high-level Australian visits to China. [47]

Meanwhile, a new concern emerged in 2018 for Australia, New Zealand, and other countries with a strong stake in Pacific Island security, notably the United States. Citing unnamed "senior security officials," the national security correspondents for two leading Australian newspapers disclosed on April 9 that China had approached the Vanuatu government about establishing a permanent military presence in the country, which the officials believed could culminate in a full military base. Vanuatu had become dependent on China as a major recipient of Chinese loans and other support. One project built by China, a large wharf ostensibly for cruise ships, was said to be suitable for naval vessels. The Vanuatu government vehemently denied the report, as did China, but the Australian government seemed alarmed and doubled down on efforts in close consultations with the United States to shore up allied efforts in the Pacific Islands in the face of Chinese advances. The Scott Morrison government also sided with the Trump administration on such controversial security matters involving China as the US determination to ban the Chinese company Huawei, viewed as a security threat by the United States, from building communications in countries allied with the United States or elsewhere, including the Pacific Islands. [48]

## New Zealand

China and New Zealand established diplomatic relations in 1972. New Zealand sought economic opportunities in China because of post-Mao economic reforms and supported China's entry into the World Trade Organization. In 2004 it was the first developed country to recognize China's market economy status. In 2008 New Zealand was the first developed country to sign a free-trade agreement with China. [49]

China surpassed Australia as New Zealand's most important trading partner in 2014 with bilateral trade valued at $18 billion. Two-way trade in goods and services with China was worth $33.4 billion in 2019, with exports worth $20.1 billion and imports $13.3 billion. The number of Chinese students in New Zealand was 36,000 in 2018. [50] The two countries also maintained active political and defense interchanges. Among differences, New Zealand joined Australia in sharply criticizing the competition between China and Taiwan in the Pacific Islands. And, like Australia, New Zealand warmly welcomed the Obama government's rebalance initiatives in the Asia-Pacific, which China viewed negatively. [51] Dealing effectively with China's rise added to reasons for New Zealand officials to seek to improve New Zealand's relations with the US government, which saw a breakthrough during the Obama administration that was sustained during the Trump administration as part of its Indo-Pacific strategy.[52] As the disclosures of Chinese influence operations in neighboring Australia came to light, there followed similar negative assessments of hidden Chinese party-state operations targeting the Chinese diaspora in New Zealand, utilizing prominent ethnic Chinese New Zealand politicians, and co-opting prominent government and opinion leaders. Notable was the prominence of a few ethnic Chinese New Zealanders with extensive ties in the PRC and strong records of supporting China's priorities in New Zealand through Chinese Communist Party united front organizations and other CCP-supported community groups in New Zealand. The purpose of the Chinese activism was to support Chinese government interests and weaken New Zealand alignment with Australia and the United States, including in the prime New Zealand area of strategic interest, the Pacific Islands.[53]

## The Pacific Islands

Chinese policy toward the Pacific Islands became reasonably clear in the 1990s. Chinese security interests seemed limited. China did build a satellite tracking station in 1997 in the equator-straddling country Kiribati, but China had to dismantle that operation a few years later when the island government switched sides and established diplomatic relations with Taiwan. China sought support among Pacific Island governments in the United Nations and other international bodies on issues of importance to China. This included Chinese efforts to block Japan's bid for a UN Security Council seat.[54]

On balance, however, the main driver of Chinese interest in the islands seemed to center, at least until very recently, on competition with Taiwan. In 2015, Taiwan was recognized officially by Kiribati, the Marshall Islands, Nauru, Palau, the Solomon Islands, and Tuvalu. Taiwan was also an unofficial "special dialogue" partner with the main regional organization, the South Pacific Forum, earlier called the Pacific Islands Forum. With the ending of the so-called diplomatic truce between China and Taiwan that prevailed during the accommodating policy toward China of Taiwan president Ma Ying-jeou (2008–2016), Beijing resumed strong efforts to woo the few remaining countries that officially recognized Taiwan. In 2019, the Solomon Islands and Kiribati switched from Taiwan to China.[55]

Both China and Taiwan engaged in corrupt practices bordering on bribery in their dealings with the Pacific Island governments in order to sustain diplomatic recognition in their mutual rivalry. Unlike Western donors, but similar to Chinese loans and other assistance offered up to now through the BRI and other means, the aid often came without principles of accountability, governance, transparency, or human rights as conditions for assistance.[56] Both governments also regularly hosted lavish and elaborate state visits for leaders of friendly island states, seeking to co-opt them into supporting Beijing or Taipei.[57]

Taiwanese-Chinese maneuvering and corrupt aid infuriated concerned officials and nongovernment elites in Australia and New Zealand. With the election in 2016 of the Tsai Ing-wen government and its less accommodating policy toward China, Beijing resumed strong efforts, including reported hidden payoffs and other methods, to woo venal officials in the few remaining countries that officially recognized Taiwan. As noted, the Solomon Islands and Kiribati switched sides from Taiwan to China in 2019.

Chinese economic interests in the region involved thousands of state and private Chinese companies that conducted business there, ranging from hotels to logging. China established a Pacific Trade Office in Beijing. In 2004, China joined the South Pacific Tourism Organization and granted "approved destination status" to several island countries.[58]

At the November 2013 Second China–Pacific Islands Countries Economic and Cooperation Forum in Guangzhou, China, Vice Premier Wang Yang announced a $1 billion increase in low-interest Chinese loans to be provided over the next four years to eight Pacific Island nations having official relations with China. Chinese media said that 150 Chinese companies invested about $1 billion dollars in the countries and the value of Chinese projects built there was $5.12 billion.[59]

An analysis by Australian specialists found that loans for projects came mainly from the Export-Import Bank of China and reflected the wishes of Pacific Island rulers. As in the case of a number of Chinese loans, the result was an unsustainable debt burden for several governments.[60]

President Xi Jinping's unprecedented trip to the region in November 2014 saw discussion of economic cooperation in meetings in Fiji with Pacific Island leaders who had official relations with China. China's media made clear that China's broadly defined Twenty-First Century Maritime Silk Road and its later global-oriented BRI included the Pacific Island countries.[61] In November 2018, President Xi held another summit meeting with the eight Pacific Island leaders whose governments had official relations with Beijing. The summit came in tandem with the Asia-Pacific Economic Cooperation (APEC) summit held in Papua New Guinea. At that time, Chinese media reported that China's trade value with Pacific Island countries in 2017 was $7.25 billion, and its accumulated investment was $3 billion. One hundred Chinese assistance projects completed in the islands involved power stations, roads, bridges, government buildings, and communications networks.[62]

US, Australian, and New Zealand officials and specialists criticized Beijing's predatory lending and hidden strategic objectives in advancing Chinese influence in the Pacific Islands.[63] Beijing created heavy debt dependency in the Cook Islands, Tonga, Fiji, and Vanuatu. Tonga's debt reached a point of being unserviceable with local resources. China funded the Melanesian Spearhead Group and the Pacific Islands Development Forum, rival groupings to the long-established Pacific Islands Forum. The latter group included Australia and New Zealand; the other two did not. China worked hard to woo Pacific Island elites through diplomacy, scholarships, financial assistance, showcase projects, and gifts. As in the case of Australia and New Zealand, Chinese companies working in the Pacific made campaign donations to politicians known to be friendly to China and offered them lucrative board memberships and other honors. For example, Tongan princess Pilolevu Tuita was a director on the board of the Tongan-Chinese-owned Pacific International Commercial Bank until it was closed down by the Tongan Reserve Bank for not submitting an audit report. The largest shareholder of the Pacific International Commercial Bank was Hu Jianhua, executive director of the Chinese People's Association for Friendship with Foreign Countries, a CCP united front organization. Princess Pilolevu, who had a prominent role in Tonga-China relations, was the honorary president of the Pacific-China Friendship Association, whose parent organization in China is the Chinese People's Association for Friendship with Foreign Countries. The Pacific-China Friendship Association linked Pacific business and political leaders with relevant Chinese organizations, administered China's thousands of scholarships in the Pacific, and ran cultural exchange and journalist training programs. The Pacific-China Friendship Association was also used to promote the BRI in Oceania.

Meanwhile, Chinese official television and other media secured a prominent position in persuading Pacific Islanders of China's beneficence amid a dwindling presence of other foreign or independent journalism. In the case of Chinese construction of a wharf in Vanuatu, the negotiations were hidden prior to media disclosure. Chinese negotiations to construct dual-use deepwater port facilities in Samoa were publicized, though the details of the arrangement were not yet disclosed.

## Antarctica

China began to play a more active role in Antarctica when Chinese scientists joined an Australian research expedition to the continent in 1979. In the 1980s, China set up its own scientific expedition bases and launched independent expeditions. China in the recent decade stepped up funding for upgrading existing Antarctic bases, establishing a new base, and increasing research involving Antarctica. In 2020 China had four Antarctic stations (Great Wall, Zhongshan, Taishan Summer Camp, and Kunlun/Dome A), with a fifth station being built on the Ross Ice Shelf, to be completed in 2022. China's capacity for travel to the region increased with the launch of China's second icebreaker in 2018. During his visit to Australia in 2014, President Xi Jinping signed an agreement with Australia on further Antarctica cooperation, visited the Australian Antarctica research operations in Hobart, spoke by video link with Chinese and Australian researchers working in the Antarctic, and visited the Chinese polar expedition research ship *Snow Dragon*, which was docked in Hobart. In a first for China, Beijing hosted the fortieth Antarctic Treaty Consultative Meeting in May 2017. During the meeting, it released the white paper, "China's Antarctic Activities." Though China's longer-term interests reportedly involve developing the resources of the region, as well as tourism, science, and shipping, China promised to abide by existing arrangements restricting development while doing more research in Antarctica and reaffirming strong support of the Antarctic Treaty System (ATS). Overall, China's involvement on the continent was more active than before but still modest. It seemed to reflect a stance that would ensure that China would not be left out should there be any possible opportunity in Antarctica in the future.[64]

## Chapter Ten

# Relations with Southern Asia and Central Asia

The end of the Cold War, the collapse of the Soviet Union, and improvement in Russia-China relations posed opportunities and challenges for China in countries to China's south and west. Maintaining close ties with Pakistan, China found India, previously aligned with Moscow against China, more open to improved relations. The new Central Asian republics were also open in a regional environment less controlled by Moscow.

Chinese relations with both areas generally followed the four stages of post–Cold War Chinese foreign policy behavior explained in chapter 1. The 1990s were a period of seeking new or renewed positive relationships, in contrast to China's isolation by Western-aligned countries after the Tiananmen crackdown. Countries in South and Central Asia were less alarmed by militant Chinese behavior in the Taiwan Strait Crisis and the South China Sea disputes of 1995–1996, while they benefited from China's emphasis on good-neighbor relations under the rubric of the new security concept stressing peaceful coexistence in the later 1990s. The advance of generally constructive Chinese relations with these regional states was interrupted in the case of India by the nuclear weapons tests of India and Pakistan in 1998 and the brief period of international pressure on both countries. But soon Beijing pragmatically joined the United States and other powers in continued improvement of relations with India while China remained close to Pakistan.

The US war against the Taliban regime in Afghanistan beginning in 2001 saw the United States become the most influential foreign power in Afghanistan, Pakistan, and India, with a few military bases in Central Asia. Consistent with its posture of "peaceful rise," China reacted moderately. It continued constructive involvement with regional countries. As Chinese leaders became more assertive in the most recent decade, China's profile grew with the ambitious Belt and Road Initiative (BRI). Fearing Chinese expansionist ambitions, India focused more than others on China's expanded military presence in the Indian Ocean and greater assertiveness along the disputed Sino-Indian border. Russian concerns were eased amid ever closer collaboration of Chinese-Russian leaders. Meanwhile, the US role in the region declined with the withdrawal of US and NATO forces from Afghanistan beginning in 2014, though closer US ties with India moved forward.[1]

## RELATIONS WITH SOUTHERN ASIA

Though an area of secondary priority in Chinese foreign relations, South Asia had increased prominence in the twenty-first century. The reasons included India's rise in power and ever closer relationship with the United States and China's need to secure trade transportation routes through the Indian Ocean.

After the Cold War, China improved relations with New Delhi, now devoid of a close strategic alignment with Moscow and more open to international economic and political exchange. The progress to some degree came at the expense of traditionally close Sino-Pakistani relations. China reportedly continued its support for Pakistan's nuclear weapons, ballistic missile, and other defense programs. The United States, not China, led international economic efforts to shore up Pakistan's crisis-prone economy during the war in Afghanistan.[2]

Indian nuclear weapons tests along with those of Pakistan in May 1998 posed the most serious challenge to China's policy in the region since the end of the Cold War. Beijing preserved close Chinese relations with Pakistan while working pragmatically with the United States in response to the crisis caused by the unexpected tests.[3] China showed evenhanded treatment of Indian-Pakistani differences during the so-called Kargil conflict of 1999 and similarly balanced treatment during flare-ups of India-Pakistan tensions in 2001–2002. It gave priority to avoiding war and limiting instability in southern Asia.[4]

Chinese officials adjusted to the sharp rise in US power and influence with war in Afghanistan beginning in 2001. On the positive side for China was US material and military aid and strong political support shoring up shaky Pakistani government finances. Growing US influence in India served to ease tensions with Pakistan and to avoid war in southern Asia.[5] On the other hand, some Chinese commentators saw alleged US ambition to encircle China militarily.[6] Chinese leaders played down these concerns, and in high-level visits and other diplomatic measures, Beijing publicly emphasized the positive and minimized the negative with all its South Asian neighbors, including India.[7]

Premier Li Peng visited India in 1990, and President Jiang Zemin traveled there in 1996.[8] The regular exchange of visits by top-level Chinese and Indian leaders in the following years were accompanied by many agreements, assertions of mutual determination to settle the border issue, and rapidly expanding economic cooperation and trade.[9]

As India and China improved relations, China continued to modify its long-standing support for Pakistan.[10] It was already evident that China was unwilling to take significant military action against India in the event of an Indo-Pakistani war. As noted above, China came to follow an increasingly evenhanded approach over the sensitive Indo-Pakistani dispute over Kashmir. By 2008 it was reported that Chinese president Hu Jintao offered to mediate between India and Pakistan on this matter. Terrorist attacks in Mumbai's financial district in November 2008 were linked to a Pakistani-based organization reportedly involved in resisting Indian control in Kashmir. China changed its past unwillingness to have the UN Security Council condemn the group and sided with a UN Security Council vote declaring the group to be a terrorist organization.[11] Continuing to benefit from Chinese military, economic, and political support, Pakistan chose to emphasize the positive. High points were repeated visits by the Pakistani prime minister to China, reports of transfers of jet fighters and other advanced Chinese military equipment to Pakistan, and advances in China's nuclear power cooperation with Pakistan.[12]

As Sino-Indian relations improved, both sides saw their interests best served by giving less attention than in the past to continued significant areas of disagreement.[13] The latter included the protracted dispute over the contested border, Chinese strategic ties with Pakistan and other South Asian countries seen in India as moves to constrain Indian influence, India's continued hosting of the Dalai Lama and his administration challenging China's control of Tibet, Chinese-Indian rivalry for leadership at the United Nations and among Asian multinational groups, and India's determination to develop a second-strike capacity to offset Chinese nuclear weapons advantage.

In general, Sino-Indian relations settled on a path of limited cooperation that endured for several years until more tensions over border issues and strategic rivalry arose with the coming to power of Chinese president Xi Jinping in 2013 and his more assertive foreign policy facing the strongly nationalist government of Prime Minister Narendra Modi, in power since 2014.[14]

Key elements of the rivalry that did not seem likely to be resolved quickly or easily included the following:[15]

- Pakistan remained India's most immediate strategic danger and also one of China's closest strategic partners. Beijing valued a stable and peaceful Pakistan that could assist in constraining India, protecting China's western

flank from Islamic extremists, and facilitating Chinese entrée to the Persian Gulf and the Islamic world.
- Predictions of progress in the protracted border negotiations waned amid clear signs of serious differences and deep-seated mutual suspicions.
- Competition for influence elsewhere in Asia intensified as both China and India rose in prominence. China was stronger in Southeast Asia and Central Asia, but India pushed its advantages in both subregions.[16]

Limited cooperation between China and India was also occurring on a number of issues.[17] During the 1990s, both looked for ways to promote a multipolar world order against the dominance of the US superpower. Subsequently, Indian, Chinese, and Russian foreign ministers met periodically in sessions that were portrayed at times as opposed to US international leadership. They added Brazil to form the so-called BRIC international grouping in 2009, and in 2011 they added South Africa to form the BRICS international grouping.[18] China and India at times seemed to stand together against Western demands that they take concrete measures to curb carbon emissions that cause climate change, and at times they joined coalitions opposed to plans in the World Trade Organization (WTO) for greater international trade liberalization.[19]

The two powers also expanded bilateral trade. Trade grew from $350 million in 1993 to nearly $7 billion in 2003 and reached $70 billion in 2014. Unfortunately for India, its trade deficit with China that year rose to $37.8 billion. China was India's largest trade partner since 2008. India remained relatively less important as a Chinese trading partner.[20]

## The Xi Jinping–Narendra Modi Period

India's long-fraught relations with China showed signs of increasing enmity in this period. China provided Pakistan with advanced weapons, nuclear technology, and foreign investment in conjunction with an increasing Chinese presence in the Indian Ocean region. India opposed the China-Pakistan Economic Corridor (CPEC) valued at $60 billion, which included planned projects in Indian-claimed Kashmir. It viewed warily China's broad-ranging Belt and Road Initiative involving construction of ports and installations in countries surrounding India. Some strategists in India judged that China had shifted from establishing a presence in South Asia and the Indian Ocean region to seeking preeminence there, as manifested in the BRI.[21]

At the same time, China remained India's largest trade partner. Trade amounted to more than $90 billion in both 2018 and 2019, but less than $20 billion each year was Indian exports to China. The value of trade in 2019 was less than in 2018.[22] Greater Chinese investment capital, technology, and management skills were welcomed by many in India. Prime Minister Modi regularly stated a desire to maintain nonadversarial relations with Beijing.[23] As discussed in chapters 8 and 9, India was sought after by Japan, some countries in Southeast Asia, and the United States as a possible counterweight to China. Both the US and Indian governments were concerned about China's illegal island building with military installations in the South China Sea. Indian border forces facing off with Chinese forces in Bhutan for several weeks in 2017 added to New Delhi's concerns over China. India's cooperation with the United States helped New Delhi to balance against the growing China danger, though Prime Minister Modi appeared less eager than the Trump government in pursuing security policy cooperation targeting China.[24]

China's rapid economic and military rise continued, impacting the strategic balance in Asia in favor of Beijing. India also faced Beijing's greater presence in South Asia. As India expanded its regional and global role, it repeatedly ran up against China. On the other hand, constructive Indian engagement with China also grew, but with keen Indian awareness of the need to prepare for contingencies in case China became more assertive. Following a low point during the 2017 border confrontation, bilateral relations improved with the April 2018 Wuhan summit between Modi and Xi. The two leaders met four times during 2018, pledging to enhance relations; top-level military exchanges also occurred. But escalating border tensions in June 2020 led to clashes (apparently devoid of firearms) by military units along the frontier, resulting in twenty Indian and an unknown number of Chinese dead.[25]

## Relations with Afghanistan and Pakistan

Looking out, two major uncertainties in Chinese relations with southern Asia were posed by the US-NATO withdrawal from Afghanistan and China's highly ambitious investment plans for Pakistan. The Afghanistan government of President Ashraf Ghani (2014–) sought China's assistance in dealing with the armed Taliban opposition and in investment in Afghanistan. In February 2015, China pledged and then followed through on offers to mediate stalled peace talks involving the Afghan government and the Taliban. In the end, the United States negotiated directly with the Taliban, reaching an agreement in 2020. Afghanistan presumably would benefit from China's strong stress on investment as part of its Silk Road economic initiatives, but advancing investment in Afghanistan faced serious challenges on account of pervasive insecurity.[26]

In 2014, the US-led coalition of military forces, the International Security Assistance Force (ISAF), proceeded rapidly with its withdrawal after more than a decade of intense military operations. In June 2013, Afghan National Security Forces (ANSF) took over responsibility for the security of the coun-

try. Armed opposition to the Afghan regime by Taliban insurgents intensified, seriously testing the strength of the ANSF and the central government.[27] Peace negotiations with the Taliban stalled. Overall economic conditions remained weak. The remaining American-led forces, around fourteen
thousand troops, transitioned to a smaller international mission consisting
primarily of training and advising the ANSF. US and allied military engagement in Afghanistan entered a final phase with a peace agreement that US
officials negotiated directly with Taliban interlocutors in 2020.[28] Deeply
rooted angst about the future was caused by continued weak and corrupt
Afghan governance and insurgent resiliency, with the Taliban controlling
half of the country.

Given the unstable and insecure internal situation, foreign relations
loomed large in determining developments in Afghanistan.[29] Regional powers played a more important role with the withdrawal of US-led NATO
forces. The neighboring country most important to Afghanistan's future was
Pakistan.[30] Afghan militants' safe haven in Pakistan remained one of the
most important threats to Afghan stability. Warning Pakistan, President
Trump said in August 2017 that "we can no longer be silent about Pakistan's
safe haven for terrorist organizations." Some argued that Pakistan viewed
Afghanistan as potentially providing it with strategic depth against India.
India endeavored to deny Pakistan such strategic depth in Afghanistan and to
deny Pakistan the ability to block India from trade and other connections to
Central Asia and beyond. India also sought to prevent militants in Afghani-
stan from attacking Indian targets in Afghanistan, India, and elsewhere.[31]

In this complicated and volatile situation, China, along with Russia and
Central Asian states, maintained an interest in Afghanistan's stability. Radical Islamic movements targeting these countries received safe haven in Afghanistan during the Taliban regime. China worried about Islamic extremists
entering China's restive Xinjiang Autonomous Region, and it deployed some
security forces inside Afghanistan along the short and remote Afghan-China
border. Beijing also worked with Pakistan, Russia, and others in efforts to
resolve the Afghan conflicts. Beijing was reluctant to pursue large proposed
economic projects because of the poor security situation in Afghanistan.
Also, restoring stability in Afghanistan would allow the country to be included in China's ambitious Belt and Road Initiative featuring infrastructure
and other projects along Central Asian trade routes. China seemed sympathetic with Pakistani efforts to block suspected Indian efforts to expand ties
with Afghanistan in order to weaken and encircle Pakistan.[32]

Meanwhile, China's relations with Pakistan were on an upswing. Pakistan
long viewed China as a counterweight against India, an alternative to the
United States, and a prime economic supporter. China remained Pakistan's
largest trading partner and largest supplier of military arms. Beijing generally
did not attempt to compete with the United States and other major donors to

Pakistan. Beijing preferred a posture of mutual benefit and "win-win" relations, which meant that China would not supply aid that was unlikely to be paid back unless there was some other significant benefit for China. Such arrangements seemed acceptable to both Pakistan and China as Beijing in 2013 began what was later called its Belt and Road Initiative. Against this background, Pakistan's government enabled a very favorable media image of China as opposed to the consistently negative image of the United States fostered by the government in the country's media. Thus, China enjoyed strong and broad approval in Pakistan.[33]

Pakistan figured prominently in the Chinese plan with what was known as the China-Pakistan Economic Corridor, featuring many proposed Chinese financed and built infrastructure projects in Pakistan. The cost of the planned projects was said to be $60 billion. Problems soon arose with several of the projects, notably because Pakistan's ability to pay seemed in doubt, especially with the latest of a series of IMF bailouts of Pakistan in 2019 and its impact on growth in the country. Some projects were withdrawn or put aside until an uncertain future time. Meanwhile, several major projects that went forward were in territories frequented by regional armed terrorists; they involved large numbers of Chinese workers sometimes targeted by the terrorists and often resented by local laborers. Pakistan had the added costs of providing thousands of soldiers to protect the vulnerable Chinese workers.[34]

Consistent with the practices of the unconventional, irregular, and hidden Chinese statecraft featured in other chapters of this volume dealing with other world areas, the Chinese projects in Pakistan were designed to facilitate Chinese international expansion and profit making; but as in the case of other world areas, the arrangements surrounding the projects were out of line with world norms and the broader common good, as they came at the expense of the best interests of the aid recipient country and the broader international order. Thus, for example, the terms of agreements governing most of the projects were hidden, with such nontransparency widely seen as leading to the broad corruption and rent seeking by various interest groups taking advantage of the incoming economic assistance.[35] Pakistan's poor record with corruption was underscored by the frustration of American official donors, as they had little to show by way of accomplishments carried out with more than $30 billion of US assistance to Pakistan since 2001.[36]

Among the Chinese projects that were being implemented in Pakistan was an effort to provide up to $15 billion to build electric power plants to ease the electric power shortage in Pakistan. Consistent with Chinese practices that tended to maximize China's benefit at the expense of the recipient country, the plants were reportedly subject to the corruption prevailing in a range of Chinese projects in Pakistan, and they were financially unsustainable, especially when also considering the various Chinese projects in Pakistan the power plants were designed to support. Also, the projects involved building power plants that Beijing was curbing inside China in order to meet pollution and climate change requirements. Instead, Beijing encouraged Chinese companies to export the plants for profit abroad, leading to results that added substantially to global pollutants and greenhouse gases. Finally, much has been said about China creating "debt traps" for countries with poor credit ratings like Pakistan by loading the country with debt and then requiring payment with infrastructure, land, or other equity in the country. In the case of the power plants in Pakistan, Chinese firms already controlled the plants, and China received assurance by the Pakistan government that the costs for building the plants would be met by Pakistani purchase of the power produced by the Pakistan-based Chinese-controlled power plants.[37]

Meanwhile, a key port developed by China at Gwadar had the potential for military use by China against India and for providing more secure lines of communication from the Middle East. China gaining rights for its first military base in Djibouti in 2017 occurred after the Djibouti government became heavily indebted to China over a Chinese-constructed railway, among other projects. Analysts outside of China judged that it was only a matter of time before Beijing used its economic leverage over Pakistan to gain military access to base facilities at Gwadar.[38]

## Other South Asian States

The other countries of South Asia tried to respond to China's growing presence by walking a careful line between New Delhi and Beijing. Moreover, the United States and the European Union (EU) also played significant roles influencing these South Asian states' foreign policy.

Bangladesh appeared generally successful in its continuing balancing act between Beijing and New Delhi. High-level visits between India and Bangladesh and the resolution of some long-standing issues institutionalized constructive bilateral relations. India provided a large line of credit for developing energy and infrastructure. China as well developed infrastructure in Bangladesh, a participant in China's BRI. China was well ahead of India in relations with the Bangladesh military. In 2018 Bangladesh was the second-largest importer of Chinese arms, after Pakistan. China also surpassed India as a source of imports, while the EU and the United States were the country's main export destinations.[39]

Nepal remained heavily dependent on India for many reasons, including its economic well-being; India was by far its largest trading partner. New Delhi also strongly impacted the country's security calculations. Nevertheless, Nepal's government at times sought to reduce Indian dominance with outreach toward China. Xi Jinping responded dramatically with a widely publicized visit to Nepal in October 2019. Xi was the first Chinese president to visit Nepal in twenty years. Xi's visit elevated ties between the two countries to a "strategic partnership of cooperation." Nepal was particularly interested in alternative land routes for exports and travel outside the country other than to India, and Xi foreshadowed as much in his statement that Nepal would no longer remain landlocked, anticipating that Nepal would be land-linked to China.[40]

Beijing in recent years built much more substantial relations with Sri Lanka and the Maldives. Developments in both countries reflected the use of corrupt practices, elite capture, unsustainable loans in nontransparent agreements, and other hidden and denied elements of Chinese foreign statecraft that expanded Chinese influence and control in other parts of the world, marking broadly used features accompanying China's expanding BRI. China's military and political support assisted the Sri Lankan government of President Mahinda Rajapaksa (2005–2015) in his ruthless pursuit of final victory in the long-running war with the separatist Tamil Tigers in 2009. This opened the way to closer strategic as well as economic and political cooperation. A major result was unsustainable large-scale Chinese financed and built development projects, featuring corruption and rent seeking by Sri Lankan leaders focused on political and personal gain. The loans proved to be impossible for Sri Lanka to support, resulting in China taking over control of a large port and airport in compensation. With a change in leadership in Sri Lanka in 2015, the incoming government endeavored to renegotiate terms to protect the country from the disadvantages of what was seen by foreigners and many in the country as a debt trap. But the costs of reneging on the loan payments and commitments of equity proved too much. By 2019, Mahinda Rajapaksa returned to power as prime minister with his brother as president, reassuring China that its past commitments to that country would pay dividends in the years ahead.[41]

A similar pattern prevailed during the strongman rule of Abdulla Yameen in the Maldives beginning in 2013. Working in close cooperation with China's Maritime Silk Road and later BRI, Yameen focused on infrastructure projects financed and built by China. The projects involved kickbacks and what later Maldives rulers called "willful corruption." The regime also enabled the Chinese Communist Party (CCP) to cultivate government officials who saw Chinese money as a means of personal enrichment. As in the case of Hun Sen's Cambodia and other strongman rulers developing self-serving ties with Chinese money providers, Yameen-ruled Maldives allowed Chinese state-owned enterprises to control information regarding the Maldives' infrastructure plans, leaving local media reliant on Chinese newspapers and contractors' websites for information. With a change of government in the Maldives in 2018, it remained unclear how the Maldives would deal with its debt trap situation. As in the case of Sri Lanka, it may find there is no viable way to reduce the debt to China other than to pay back with funds or equity. On the other hand, as noted in chapter 9, Myanmar and Malaysia were able to reduce the size of large Chinese infrastructure deals signed by corrupt governments, though ending the deals was deemed too costly even for reformers in Myanmar and Malaysia.[42]

## RELATIONS WITH CENTRAL ASIA

After the end of the Soviet Union, China expanded ties across Central Asia in order to stabilize its western frontier, gain access to the region's energy resources, and balance Western influence.[43] Improved ties with Central Asian states shielded China's Xinjiang region and its ethnically Turkic Uighur population from outside Muslim and pan-Turkic influence. For a time, US, Russian, and Chinese efforts to support antiterrorist initiatives in Central Asia beginning in 2001 reflected important common ground among the three powers.[44]

China's regional energy projects sought secure supplies and diverse sources. Beijing concluded agreements to develop Kazakhstan oil and gas fields and constructed oil and gas pipelines with Kazakhstan, Uzbekistan, Turkmenistan, and other countries. There were many signed agreements but slower progress toward completing the pipelines and filling them.[45] Among highlights, China signed an agreement with Turkmenistan in 2006 to export natural gas through a new pipeline reaching China through Uzbekistan and Kazakhstan. This pipeline was completed expeditiously and was supported by a separate natural gas pipeline linking Uzbekistan and Kazakhstan with China. The new efforts undercut what had been a situation of close control of the exporting of Central Asian natural gas by Russian pipeline administrators.[46]

The continuing civil war in Afghanistan had important implications for Central Asia. China generally urged all warring parties to stop fighting and to discuss their problems among themselves without any outside interference. The Chinese were also reported to suspect the Taliban faction in Afghanistan of being supportive of radicals in Xinjiang.[47] In the years prior to the US withdrawal of most of its forces in 2014, when the Obama government increased combat operations against a resurgent Taliban threat, China straddled the fence and avoided commitments. As noted in chapter 5, China endorsed the May 2, 2011, killing of Osama bin Laden by American forces.[48] Chinese commentary often viewed expanding NATO activities as US efforts to extend influence in the region, squeeze out Russia, and contain China.[49]

China's expanding influence in Central Asia generally prompted little overt opposition from Moscow, which heretofore had jealously guarded the region's resources. For its part, Beijing regarded a Central Asian power balance favoring Russia as advantageous to its own interests. China pursued its interests in Central Asia with care to avoid challenging Russia.[50]

The evolution of Chinese policy up to the strongman rule of Xi Jinping beginning in late 2012 reflected enduring Chinese interests included the following:

- Strategic position: China sought a stable and productive international environment around China's periphery while fostering a more widely accepted Chinese leadership role. Beijing also aimed to legitimate Chinese positions on major international issues, strengthen relations with Russia, and serve as a counter to US power and influence. China's diplomacy in Central Asia aimed to prevent the region from becoming a distraction from China's internal development and more important foreign policy goals.
- Security: China tried to curb outside support to separatist Uighurs in Xinjiang Province. It saw common ground with regional governments in working against terrorist and criminal elements.
- Borders: China sought to demarcate, demilitarize, and stabilize borders with Russia, Kazakhstan, Kyrgyzstan, and Tajikistan. Border stability was central to Chinese development plans and foreign policy priorities.
- Economics: China's main economic interest in the region was energy. China sought growing amounts of oil and gas abroad, and Central Asian countries, especially Kazakhstan and Turkmenistan, became major partners.[51]

Chinese-developed economic and transportation links strengthened China's regional approach.[52] This pattern was also seen in Chinese efforts to deepen channels of trade and communication involving rail, road, river, pipeline, electric transmission, and other links with various South and Southeast Asian countries bordering China. Following agreement with the Soviet Union in 1984 to build the first direct rail link between Xinjiang and Soviet Central Asia (what is now Kazakhstan), the two sides agreed to broaden their cooperation on this "Eurasian land bridge." China double-tracked some of its rail links leading to the cross-border line. It also built a line in the late 1990s into southwestern Xinjiang and used this line as the basis for plans to build a new rail link between Xinjiang and Kyrgyzstan. China also proposed building another rail link in northern Xinjiang, with a different crossing point into Kazakhstan. Highway links between Xinjiang and Central Asia improved markedly beginning in the 1990s, with five hard-surface roads linking China and Kazakhstan and a new road to Kyrgyzstan. The China–Kazakhstan pipelines, as well as the natural gas pipeline linking China with Turkmenistan, added to China's connections to the region.[53]

By 2014, China became the largest recipient of exports from Turkmenistan (68 percent of the country's exports), Uzbekistan (28 percent of exports), and Kazakhstan (22.7 percent of exports). It received 8 percent of

Tajikistan's exports and 5 percent of Kyrgyzstan's exports. Chinese exports of manufactured goods spread throughout Central Asia. China became the leading importer to Kyrgyzstan (51 percent of the country's imports), Tajikistan (40 percent of imports), Kazakhstan (30 percent of imports), and Uzbekistan (20 percent of imports). Chinese goods accounted for 13 percent of Turkmenistan's imports.[54]

### Regional Multilateral Cooperation: The Shanghai Cooperation Organization

China's interest in using multilateral organizations to pursue Chinese interests around its periphery in the post–Cold War period showed first in Central Asia. Building on a growing "strategic partnership" with Russia, China hosted in Shanghai in April 1996 the first meeting of representative leaders of what became known as the Shanghai Five. The Shanghai Five consisted of China, Russia, and the three other former Soviet republics that border China: Kazakhstan, Kyrgyzstan, and Tajikistan. The group focused at first on finalizing border settlements between China and the four former Soviet republics, demilitarizing their frontiers, and establishing confidence-building measures. These issues were dealt with in the 1996 Shanghai Five Agreement on Confidence Building in the Military Field along the Border Areas and the 1997 Agreement on Reducing Each Other's Military Forces along the Border Regions.[55] At their summit in July 2000, the Shanghai Five declared success in building a border belt of trust and transparency.[56] They also had begun collaborating against terrorism, arms smuggling, and a range of illegal transnational activities affecting their common interests. They agreed in 1999 to set up a joint antiterrorist center in Kyrgyzstan.

Uzbekistan joined the group in July 2001, establishing the Shanghai Cooperation Organization (SCO), with six members: Russia, China, Kazakhstan, Kyrgyzstan, Tajikistan, and Uzbekistan. The declaration of the creation of the SCO showed strong attention to regional security issues involving terrorism, drug trade, and other transnational crimes affecting the countries. Work in subsequent annual summit meetings of the group included efforts to establish a charter and small budget for the organization, to start the small antiterrorism center in Kyrgyzstan, and to set up an SCO secretariat headquartered in Beijing and paid for by China to foster cooperation on terrorism and other transnational issues.

Chinese leaders showed strong interest in broadening the scope of the SCO to include important economic development efforts, notably in building transportation infrastructure that would benefit western China.[57] At the SCO prime ministers' meeting in Tajikistan in September 2006, Prime Minister Wen Jiabao announced that China had set a goal of doubling the current level ($40 billion) of Chinese trade with SCO members in the next few years.[58]

Chinese leaders were compelled to deal with a sharp rise of US power and influence in Central Asia as a result of the US-led war against the Taliban rulers of Afghanistan soon after the terrorist attack on America in 2001. Logistical requirements of supporting large-scale US military operations in Afghanistan included bases of operations in Central Asia. The region for the first time was a top priority in America's strategy.[59] Reflecting the concurrent emphasis of China's peaceful rise in the first decade of the twenty-first century, Chinese officials remained low keyed about their concerns over the strong US military presence close to China. They advised that the SCO was not adverse to US interests, but they remained firm against proposals that would admit the United States or its allies to the group. They allowed Mongolia, Pakistan, Iran, and India to join as observers. India and Pakistan joined as members in 2017.[60]

Russia and China used the Shanghai Five summit meetings and other occasions to issue statements and make speeches against US domination and to call for a multipolar world, though such rhetoric dropped off for a time once Russia and then China moderated toward the Bush administration by mid-2001. Until mid-2001, Chinese officials and media were uniform in calling attention to the Shanghai Five as a model of the type of mutually respectful, consultative, and equal state relationships favored by China's new security concept, in contrast to the "power politics" and "hegemonism" practiced by the United States and its alliance relationships.[61]

Reflecting some revival of an anti-US emphasis, the SCO summit of July 2005 called on the United States and Western powers to set a deadline for the withdrawal of Western military forces from Central Asia. The SCO military exercise of August 2005 involving about ten thousand Chinese and Russian troops had little to do with traditional SCO concerns about border security and antiterrorism; they were focused instead on a show of force in waters east of China that appeared directed at Taiwan, Japan, and the United States. The expulsion of US forces in 2005 by SCO member Uzbekistan was welcomed by the group's leaders, Russia and China.[62]

Border settlements featured prominently in the early meetings of the Shanghai Five and the SCO. At the first Shanghai Five summit meeting on April 26, 1996, China proposed to address issues to stabilize the sometimes tense seven-thousand-kilometer border China shared with the former states of the Soviet Union. The Treaty of Deepening Military Trust in Border Regions signed at the summit called on the signatories to invite the others to observe military drills and inform about any military activities within one hundred kilometers of the border. It also forbade attacks on each other and restricted the scope and frequency of military maneuvers in border areas.[63] The next year, the Treaty on Reducing Military Forces in Border Regions was signed in Moscow. This agreement proposed to reduce the total number of military forces along the border to fewer than 130,400.[64] At a 1999 Shanghai Five summit in Bishkek, Kyrgyzstan, both the 1996 and the 1997 treaties were seen as successful, and the borders were said to be secure and stable.[65]

The 2000 Shanghai Five summit in Dushanbe, Tajikistan, moved beyond the previous emphasis on border security to stress a variety of regional issues of mutual concern. The gathered leaders discussed treaties to fight separatism, extremism, and terrorism—three "evils" stressed repeatedly by Chinese leaders. They also talked about dealing with drug trafficking and illegal immigration. In this context, the leaders agreed to hold regular meetings of officers from their justice, border control, customs, and public security departments.[66] They judged that developments and problems in the region had become more complicated and that the existing mechanisms under the Shanghai Five needed upgrading.[67]

At the summit in Shanghai in 2001, Uzbekistan was added to the group, prompting the declaration of the establishment of the Shanghai Cooperation Organization. The summit created a council of state coordinators to write a charter for the SCO and to establish regular meeting schedules.[68] The representatives of the six countries also signed the Shanghai Convention on Combating Terrorism, Separatism, and Extremism. The convention established a legal foundation for combating these problems.[69]

From that point on, SCO activities developed along several paths. In addition to the annual head of state meetings, regular meetings occurred at the levels of head of government, foreign minister, defense minister, and heads of law enforcement, energy, and trade departments. At the SCO summit in St. Petersburg in 2002, the group endorsed the SCO charter. It provided a legal basis of the principles, purpose, and tasks of the organization; the procedures for adopting new members; the legal effects of SCO decisions; and the means of cooperation with other multilateral organizations.[70]

In January 2004, the SCO opened two permanent bodies: a secretariat in Beijing and a regional antiterrorism structure based in Tashkent. Mongolia's foreign minister was present at the secretariat opening, and Iran, India, Pakistan, and Turkey expressed interest in joining.[71]

The smooth development of the SCO and China's interests in fostering regional cooperation and greater Chinese influence met serious challenge in 2008 because of Russia's invasion of Georgia and military support for and recognition of South Ossetia and Abkhazia, two small entities that broke away from Georgia with Russian support. On the one hand, China sought to sustain good relations with the newly assertive Russia and had little sympathy with Western-aligned Georgia and the proposed expansion of NATO to include Georgia. On the other hand, China was sensitive to its own secessionist problems in Tibet, Xinjiang, and Taiwan and was wary of close alignment with Russia's resort to military action that placed it in direct opposition to the United States and the West. A summit meeting of the SCO in Tajikistan a few weeks after the Russian invasion placed the spotlight on China and its Central Asian neighbors regarding their position on the Russian action. In the end, the SCO avoided strong support for Russia's action. Official Chinese commentary and expert opinion made clear that China remained focused on domestic concerns, sought to promote harmony in regional and world affairs, viewed the sharp decline in Russian relations with the United States and the rest of the West as a source of concern, and saw little benefit for China in taking sides in the disputes.[72]

## Chinese Security Interests

China's stronger support for multilateral security mechanisms in the SCO showed that Chinese officials recognized that internal security issues could not be met only with confidence building and other such measures among sovereign states. The dissolution of the Soviet Union; the civil wars in Tajikistan, Afghanistan, and Chechnya; and the rise of Islamic unrest in western China created a tense and unstable regional situation of great concern to Chinese leaders. Militant attacks in Xinjiang were related to the rise of Islamic extremism in Central Asia and the Taliban regime in Afghanistan. The Center for Strategic and International Studies reported in 2003 on more than two hundred militant attacks resulting in 162 deaths in Xinjiang over a decade after the end of the Cold War.[73]

Home to a large ethnic Turkish Muslim population of Uighurs who periodically resisted Chinese rule, Xinjiang remained central to Chinese concerns. Unrest and insurrection there was especially troubling for Beijing given Xinjiang's large size, vast resources, and vital strategic location. There were considerable Uighur populations in many Central Asian states, including 120,000 in Kazakhstan and 50,000 in Kyrgyzstan. Suppressing dissidents in Xinjiang affected China's relations with these neighboring governments. Nonetheless, rising militant activism directed against China and other SCO governments caused them to band together against the threat posed by militant Islam and the associated "three evils"—terrorism, separatism, and religious extremism.[74]

At the 2001 SCO summit in Shanghai, all members pledged a collective response in defense of a government attacked by militants.[75] This was followed by an agreement at the 2002 SCO foreign ministers' meeting that endorsed Chinese actions fighting the "East Turkistan terrorists," along with Russian suppression of terrorists in Chechnya.[76] At a subsequent SCO defense ministers' meeting in Moscow, the SCO representatives issued a communiqué on military cooperation and established a senior defense official commission and a joint expert group responsible for coordinating military exercises among SCO participants.[77]

In addition to cooperating against terrorists, the SCO participants agreed to cooperate more regarding general emergency situations. In October 2002, the Chinese and Kyrgyzstan militaries cooperated in a joint exercise in southern Kyrgyzstan, and in August 2003, five SCO members (not Uzbekistan) collaborated in a military exercise known as Coalition 2003.[78] Later notable exercises included the large exercise in 2005 mentioned earlier that seemed focused on the United States and its East Asian partners, the "Peace Mission 2007" joint antiterrorism exercise held in August that year, and the "Peace Mission 2010" involving five thousand troops for two weeks of exercises in southern Kazakhstan.[79]

The rise in Russian assertiveness in areas bordering Russia in 2008–2009 posed a new development affecting the Chinese calculus in Central Asia and more broadly. China appeared to follow a path of least resistance between conflicting Chinese goals, notably regarding the maintenance of good Chinese relations with the United States and the West on the one hand and good relations with Russia on the other. Russia's shift in 2010 to a more cooperative stance with the United States and NATO on arms control, security, and economic issues also seemed awkward for China as it stood in contrast with Chinese truculence toward the United States at that time over Taiwan arms sales, Tibet, US military surveillance near China, and economic issues. Of course, this phase passed with the sharp downturn in US-Russian relations over Ukraine and Crimea and Xi Jinping's prominent solidarity with Vladimir Putin in the face of Western sanctions.[80]

## Chinese Economic Interests

China also saw the SCO and broader regional cooperation as helpful in expanding Chinese economic growth and influence in the region. Chinese and Central Asian economies were complementary; Central Asian states had raw materials that China needed (notably oil and gas), while China had consumer goods sought by the people in these states. As Xinjiang's economic development was part of Beijing's strategy to calm unrest in the area, Chinese leaders paid special attention to Central Asian trade. China became the largest single country foreign trader of the Central Asian states, with forecasts of growing Chinese economic importance for these countries.

Russia endorsed closer trade relations with China. President Putin said at an SCO summit in Shanghai in 2001 that "cooperation in economics, trade and culture is far more important than military cooperation."[81] A statement from a meeting of SCO trade ministers in 2002 said that "the SCO is different from the 'Shanghai Five' because regional economic cooperation is its main task."[82] A 2003 meeting of SCO prime ministers issued the Outline for Multilateral Economic and Trade Cooperation of the SCO, furthering economic progress among the members.[83]

A key driver in China's economic interest in Central Asia was energy. With the rapid growth of China's economy, China became a net importer of oil. This greatly increased Chinese government interest in securing reliable supplies of foreign oil and natural gas. In this context, China's involvement in energy projects in Russia, Kazakhstan, Turkmenistan, Uzbekistan, and elsewhere was part of a broader Chinese effort to plan for the future. [84]

## China's Recent Strength in Central Asia

As discussed in chapter 3, the Xi Jinping government gave high priority to improving relations with China's neighbors to the north and west, revitalizing and expanding broadly defined Silk Roads marking Chinese economic and strategic interests. The Xi government pushed for greater economic interchange in the SCO. At the fourteenth SCO summit in Tajikistan in September 2014, Xi focused on a long list of Chinese priorities for the SCO to increase economic involvement. Among the sometimes bewildering array of Chinese billion-dollar initiatives involving the Silk Road plans, Xi promised a Chinese loan of $5 billion to support economic cooperation among SCO states and promised to increase by $1 billion China's contribution to the China-Eurasia Economic Cooperation Fund, which was launched in 2013, to $5 billion. [85]

As discussed in chapter 11 dealing with Chinese-Russian relations, China's professed neutrality regarding Russia's takeover of Crimea and continued aggression against Ukraine was accompanied by repeated summits with President Putin concerning consolidation of close economic relations and security ties. China stood against Western sanctions and other such interference. Progress with the SCO was not impeded as Beijing-Moscow ties strengthened across the board. [86]

Overall, Chinese foreign policy in Central Asia was effective in promoting border security, curbing transnational crime and terrorism, and supporting greater economic interaction. Active Chinese participation in the Shanghai Five and SCO marked clear advances in Chinese government willingness to engage vigorously with multilateral organizations and to put aside past Chinese suspicions that such international groups would invariably be influenced by forces hostile to Chinese interests. [87]

Nevertheless, the shortcomings and relative weakness of the SCO and of China's overall influence in Central Asia were also evident at various times. China and its Central Asian allies did little of consequence in dealing with the Taliban and the problems in Afghanistan. After September 11, 2001, the US-led Operation Enduring Freedom accomplished more in the area in five months than the Shanghai grouping had accomplished in five years. The SCO members remained wary of one another, and there were numerous obstacles to greater economic, political, and military cooperation. By contrast, at various times many of these governments, including Russia and China, were willing—and several were eager—to cooperate to varying degrees with the sharp increase in US military activity and presence in Central Asia after 2001.[88]

Economically, China's trade with the post-Soviet Central Asian republics expanded, while Russia's trade with them generally did not keep pace. Yet Russia was still an important trading partner. The Central Asian countries also turned their trade attention to Turkey and the European countries, which became important trading partners for the Central Asian states.[89] As Central Asia was rapidly transformed after September 11, 2001, from a peripheral area of US concern to a front line in the war on terrorism, China saw its increased influential position in Central Asia, built incrementally over the previous decade, diminished in comparative terms. The military, economic, technological, and political capabilities of the United States seemed to offer more to the Central Asian states than they could hope to obtain from China. China was put into a secondary role in Central Asia. However, its persistent drive to incrementally improve its stature and work with the SCO in the process was part of an apparent longer-term effort to sustain Chinese interests and relevance in regional political, economic, and security trends. The Chinese also took advantage of adverse developments affecting the US position in Central Asia, such as Uzbekistan's decision in 2005 to expel US forces from the country.[90]

Among important Chinese advances under the leadership of Xi Jinping, the start of the process that ultimately led to China's global economic program, the Belt and Road Initiative, began in Central Asia. During his first year in office, President Xi Jinping in 2013 made three stops in Central Asia along with participating in the G20 summit in St. Petersburg. A high point was his visit to Kazakhstan, where he gave a major speech focusing on PRC policy toward Central Asia at Nazarbayev University. He announced the "Silk Road economic belt," one part of what later came to be known as the Belt and Road Initiative. Xi also highlighted a ten-year program to fund scholarships for thirty thousand students from SCO countries and another to pay for ten thousand teachers and students from SCO member state Confucius Institutes to visit China. In Turkmenistan, Xi opened a new gas field at Galkynysh and committed to the construction of a new multibillion-dollar natural gas pipeline as part of the Central Asia–China Gas Pipeline, Line D, underlining China as the leading foreign consumer of Turkmenistan's gas. Xi also participated in his first annual SCO heads of state summit in Kyrgyzstan and signed deals there worth $3 billion, including funding for a gas pipeline from Turkmenistan to China and an oil refinery.[91]

China substantially increased its regional financing and trade activities, making it more important than Russia in these key economic areas. The value of Chinese trade in Central Asia in 2015 was $24.7 billion, surpassing the value of Russia's trade with Central Asia at $21 billion. By 2018, 21 percent of regional trade was with China and 18 percent was with Russia. The European Economic Area was the leading regional trade partner at 25 percent of regional trade. China outpaced Russia in total trade with all Central Asian countries except Kazakhstan. In Turkmenistan, China accounted for 44 percent of the country's total trade while Russia made up only 7 percent.[92]

China also provided billions of dollars to develop transport infrastructure, as part of the BRI, and manufacturing facilities. The infrastructure projects included a freight railway linking the Chinese port of Lianyungang with the Kazakh city of Almaty and plans for two rail corridors between southern China and Central Asia. China built a metallurgical plant in Tajikistan that opened in November 2017, and Chinese telecommunications companies Huawei and ZTE established assembly plants in Uzbekistan. Beijing also planned to develop the Kazakh city of Khorgas into a logistics and manufacturing hub. In comparison, the Russian-led Eurasian Economic Union proved to be much less important than China's BRI.[93]

Russia still remained the primary destination for Central Asian migrants working abroad, and remittances from the more than three million Central Asians who lived and worked in Russia made up a substantial part of the region's economies. It was said by some specialists that China's rise as a trade and financing partner in Central Asia did not necessarily conflict with Russia's interests and strategy in the region. Post-Soviet Russia was not a major investor in infrastructure in Central Asia, nor did it have the kind of capital that Beijing committed to such efforts. In addition, Russia needed Central Asia's raw materials much less than China did, and China, unlike Russia, had no need for the region's low-wage labor force.[94]

Such compatible elements in the two powers' economic priorities reinforced common interest in trying to stabilize Central Asia to protect against Islamic extremists and other militants. Beijing took care to support Russian leadership and to consult with Moscow as it pursued economic initiatives in Central Asia, including the BRI. In the event, Russia welcomed Chinese influence in the region, which helped stabilize Central Asia while enhancing Moscow's increasingly important relationship with Beijing.[95] China was Russia's ever-stronger leading partner in the Shanghai Cooperation Organization, but they appeared to compete in efforts to gain access to Central Asian energy resources and in other ways.[96]

Huawei was in the lead among Chinese information and communications technology firms with a growing presence in Central Asia. These networks were used to provide services and security in urban areas, but in restive areas of China they were used as a political tool, with facial recognition and other technologies collecting information about possible dissidents or other troublemakers challenging authoritarian rule. In 2019 Huawei signed a $1 billion deal with Uzbekistan to further its surveillance operations in the country. There were similar Chinese deals with Kazakhstan and Tajikistan. On the whole, Central Asian leaders anxious to enhance domestic control against oppositionists and others disrupting local order welcomed the enhanced technical capacity provided by Chinese firms. An added benefit for China was said to be the fact that the Chinese-provided surveillance and communication capacity allowed hidden access for interested Chinese authorities seeking intelligence and information for influencing the host countries.[97]

China's economic advance in Central Asia was not all smooth sailing. China was still awaiting the completion of the Central Asia–China Gas Pipeline, Line D. In 2018, China's existing three pipelines from Central Asia delivered 46.9 billion cubic meters (1.6 trillion cubic feet) of gas, providing nearly 40 percent of China's total gas imports, with the rest coming almost entirely as liquefied natural gas (LNG) delivered by sea. The capacity of the three pipelines was 55 billion cubic meters, justifying the planned Line D to add 25–30 billion cubic meters per year.[98]

Meanwhile, Chinese deals and the rising Chinese presence in Central Asian states faced wariness, periodic criticism, and demonstrations. Proposed Chinese purchases of agricultural land resulted in protest demonstrations in Kazakhstan and Tajikistan. The Chinese infrastructure and other projects were carried out by Chinese firms that favored the employment of Chinese workers. The distribution between China and Kazakhstan of the water from the Ili River that supplies Lake Balkhash and the Irtysh River remained in dispute. Demonstrations in Kyrgyzstan indicated anti-Chinese sentiment among the local population due to the growing presence of Chinese and the plight of the Muslim Kyrgyz in China.[99]

Chinese loans making up the vast majority of BRI assistance led the poorer Central Asian countries to fall into unsustainable debt. Indeed, at the end of 2018, Tajikistan's external debt represented 76 percent of GDP and Kyrgyzstan's 84 percent, with China a major holder in both cases. The debt situation had not reached the stage of other debt trap instances with Chinese firms taking control of equity in lieu of interest payments. But Tajikistan postponed the construction of the second unit of a Chinese-financed hydroelectric power plant, and Kyrgyzstan asked China to provide assistance—not a loan—for the continuation of a Chinese-financed road construction project.[100]

As shown in other chapters involving other parts of the world, China developed a reputation in the BRI of working cooperatively with and profiting from the corrupt practices of recipient countries' leaders. What this meant for the nontransparent Chinese deals with Central Asian regimes with well-earned reputations for corruption was that the deals were widely suspected to advance the private interests of the leaders and of China and thus not to serve the broad national interests of the recipient country.[101] One notable example was the sentencing in 2019 of a Kyrgyzstan former prime minister to fifteen years in prison because of corruption in a power plant deal with a Chinese firm.[102]

Other problems for China's relations with Central Asia included the ways that coercive Chinese measures in recent years, including internment and purported thought reform against Muslim Uighurs in the restive Xinjiang region adjoining Central Asia, impacted nearby countries. While regional governments saw their interests best served by avoiding criticism of harsh Chinese practices, the Chinese measures impacted Muslim Kazakhs and Kirgiz in China, along with many among hundreds of thousands of Uighurs in Central Asian countries who were resentful of Chinese practices. [103]

Meanwhile, an exception to the usually unobtrusive Chinese security involvement in Central Asia involved Tajikistan and Afghanistan's Wakhan Corridor. The deployment of People's Armed Police based in Tajikistan, as well as joint operations between Chinese security forces and Tajik and Afghan forces, remained focused on securing the Afghan border with Tajikistan and China. [104]

Looking out in 2020, China's approach to the Central Asian region seemed coherent, generally successful, and likely to continue along existing lines. Notably in contrast to Chinese approaches in eastern and southern Asia, there was less tension between China's national development emphasis on promoting peace and development abroad and Chinese national security, territorial, and national unification objectives that emphasized China's use of force against foreign threats in ways that alienated and alarmed some of China's neighbors and other concerned powers.

Also, governments that the Chinese leaders did not control and that strongly influenced Chinese foreign policy in other areas around China's rim did not play much of a role in China–Central Asian relations. For example, Taiwan was insignificant in Central Asia. Japan's role in Central Asia was also relatively small. The upswing in US military presence and influence in Central Asia after the terrorist attack on the United States proved to be temporary. The countries of the region were not included within the broad scope of the Obama government's rebalance policy to the Asia-Pacific region or the Trump administration's Indo-Pacific strategy. [105]

Meanwhile, the need for Chinese leaders to adopt tough policies on territorial and other nationalistic issues with Central Asian neighbors was less than in the case of Chinese relations with some neighbors to China's east and south. Part of the reason was that the Chinese government was successful in keeping Chinese media and other public attention focused away from territorial and nationalistic issues concerning China's Central Asian neighbors. In addition, China's territorial and nationalistic issues with its Central Asian neighbors seemed less salient to core Chinese interests in development and national power than such Chinese issues with some other neighbors. And the generally authoritarian Central Asian governments endeavored to deal constructively and pragmatically with China over territorial and other disputes, a contrast with the nationalistic posturing of some of China's eastern and southern neighbors.

A central question going forward focuses on Russia and its continuity in accommodating China's rise in an area of prime Russian concern. As seen in chapter 11, the close collaborative relations between the Russian and Chinese presidents appeared to override such potential obstacles, and those leaders were likely to continue to rule for some time to come.

## Mongolia

Mongolia considered itself separate from Central Asia; it nonetheless was often treated together with Central Asia in broad assessments of Chinese foreign relations. A long and often hostile history with China made Mongolia more wary of China than were the states in Central Asia. Without its Soviet ally, the Mongolian government moved toward free-market and democratic reforms; it watched carefully for signs of Chinese dominance while seeking reassurances from other powers, especially Russia and the United States. Beijing demonstrated little overt concern over Mongolia as the government carefully avoided standing against Chinese interests. [106]

In this decade, China dominated Mongolia's foreign trade. China received more than 90 percent of Mongolia's exports and was Mongolia's largest supplier. China was also the country's largest foreign investor. Mongolia relied on Russia for energy supplies, leaving it vulnerable to price increases; in the first eleven months of 2013, Mongolia purchased 76 percent of its gasoline and diesel fuel and a substantial amount of its electric power from Russia. [107]

Balancing Russia and China and attempting to ensure independence and sovereignty, Mongolia sought strong relations with "highly developed countries of the West and East," such as the United States, Japan, and Germany, as well as with India, South Korea, Thailand, Singapore, Turkey, Denmark, the Netherlands, Finland, Austria, Sweden, and Switzerland. The priority countries were Mongolia's so-called third neighbors, the United States, Japan, South Korea, Germany, and India. [108]

Mongolia supported the US role in Asian security, in particular in northeastern Asia. It also backed the United States in the war on terrorism and sent some troops in support of the US-led military action in Iraq. It welcomed Obama administration officials visiting the country as part of the rebalance policy. The cornerstone of the Mongolian-Chinese relationship was the 1994 Treaty of Friendship and Cooperation, which codified mutual respect for the independence and territorial integrity of both sides. [109]

The issue of Tibet was one of sometimes acute sensitivity in Mongolian-Chinese relations. Mongolia shared with Tibet its brand of Buddhism and in the 1990s and 2000s received visits from the Dalai Lama despite Chinese protests. Mongolians sympathized with the plight of Tibet, recognizing that but for the backing of the Soviet Union, they might have suffered a similar fate. Realistically, however, they knew that they could do little for Tibet. China repeatedly imposed serious economic sanctions on Mongolia as a result of visits by the Dalai Lama to Mongolia. In 2016, the Mongolian government said the Dalai Lama would no longer be allowed to visit the country. [110]

Over time, the realities of declining interest in Mongolia by the United States and other so-called third neighbors and the country's deepening economic dependence on China and continued strong reliance on Russia made it more difficult for Mongolia to maintain a posture independent of China and Russia. And as Russia and China aligned more closely in opposition to US interests, Mongolia's room for maneuver contracted. In particular, the Mongolian government in the past had eschewed pressures from China and Russia to join the Shanghai Cooperation Organization, which they led. Russia also pressed for Mongolia to join the Eurasia Economic Union, which it leads. But recently Ulan Bator reportedly saw little alternative to linking more closely with Beijing and Moscow, at the expense of its past professed preference for broader international independence. [111]

## Chapter Eleven

# Relations with Russia and Europe

Chinese relations with both Russia and Europe generally followed the four stages of post–Cold War Chinese foreign policy behavior explained in chapter 1. The 1990s featured China seeking new or renewed positive relationships, gradually reducing its isolation after the Tiananmen crackdown. The Russia-China relationship became a pathbreaker in growing Chinese partnerships with various countries under the rubric of Beijing's new security concept in which China in the late 1990s endeavored to have cooperative relations internationally but also strongly opposed US foreign policy "hegemonism" and the American-led alliance system. Russia and China together at this time harshly criticized a wide range of US foreign policies, but after the terrorist attack on America in 2001, Russia's Vladimir Putin switched to accommodate the United States. Beijing soon followed with its new foreign policy emphasis, which would last for most of the decade, on reassuring the United States and its allies that China was not a threat and its rise would be peaceful.

The Russia-China relationship reached a new stage of active collaboration in countering the United States with Putin's turn against the West and aggressive policies against Ukraine and the takeover of Crimea. Incoming Chinese leader Xi Jinping actively sought closer relations and became Russia's most important partner in challenging America and its interests.

China's shift toward assertiveness in Europe in this decade saw Beijing abandon previous efforts to foster European unity as part of the long-desired multipolar world. Experience in the previous decade showed repeated Chinese frustrations with Europe over its enduring alliance relationship with the United States and close accord with Washington on issues of values, governance, and economic practices that China opposed. In response, Beijing switched from failed efforts to encourage European unity against America

243

and strove to weaken and divide European unity, including that of the European Union (EU), on important economic and other issues. A divided Europe was easier for China to penetrate and manipulate as Beijing more actively applied a wide range of conventional and unconventional influence operations to expand its interests in tandem with Russia's more assertive approach to the West.[1]

## RELATIONS WITH RUSSIA

This section assesses major developments and trends in Russia-China relations leading to the extraordinary recent entente created by the dynamic presidents of the two countries, Vladimir Putin and Xi Jinping.[2]

China's relations with the Soviet Union moved in twenty years from formal alliance in 1950 to Soviet officers warning in 1969 that Soviet motorized troops numbering in the hundreds of thousands poised on the Chinese border were ready to invade China and destroy its nuclear weapons. China was so poorly prepared that the US secretary of state judged Soviet strike forces would reach and occupy Beijing in a short period of time. From that point forward, the USSR was China's number-one strategic concern, with the US downgraded and soon to be viewed as a useful counterweight and partner for China to deal with the massive Soviet threat. The Sino-American common front against what China called Soviet hegemonism endured until the end of the Cold War. Belatedly seeking to ease tensions with China, Soviet leader Leonid Brezhnev (d. 1982) and his immediate successors were incapable of meeting China's requirements for improved relations. Mikhail Gorbachev consolidated his power in the mid-1980s and made rapprochement with China a priority.

Gorbachev was prepared to make major changes in what China referred to as the "three obstacles" to improved Sino-Soviet relations: Soviet troops in Afghanistan, the buildup of Soviet forces along the border (including deployments in Mongolia), and the Soviet-backed Vietnamese military occupation of Cambodia.[3] Motivated by a desire to repair relations with China, ease the defense burden on the Soviet economy, and reciprocate China's reduction of its 4 million troops to 2.95 million from 1982 to 1986, the Soviet government announced in 1987 that a phased reduction of its troops (roughly sixty-five thousand) from Mongolia would be initiated with the aim of eliminating the deployment by 1992.[4] The Soviet formations in Mongolia had been kept at a higher level of readiness than others along the border, and the Chinese had long viewed them as a first-echelon strike force aimed at Beijing. In December 1988, Gorbachev announced at the United Nations that Soviet conventional forces would unilaterally be reduced by 500,000. Soviet spokesmen later clarified that, of the total, 120,000 would come from the troops arrayed against China and that remaining Far Eastern units would progressively be configured in a defensive mode. In late 1989, following Gorbachev's visit to Beijing in May, Chinese and Soviet officials began negotiations on reducing forces along the border, and during Prime Minister Li Peng's visit to Moscow in April 1990, an agreement was reached on governing principles regarding force reductions. By the time the Soviet Union collapsed in 1991, five rounds of talks on force reductions had been conducted.

The reduction of the conventional threat to China was complemented by the 1987 US-Soviet Intermediate-Range Nuclear Forces Treaty, under which Moscow dismantled all its medium- and intermediate-range nuclear missiles, including 180 mobile SS-20 missiles that were based in the Asian regions of the Soviet Union. Meanwhile, the Soviet Union agreed under the April 1988 Geneva Accords to withdraw its combat forces from Afghanistan by May 1989 and encouraged Vietnam to evacuate its troops from Cambodia by the end of 1989.

High-level political contacts helped alter the adversarial character of Sino-Soviet relations, the most important being the visits of Foreign Minister Eduard Shevardnadze and Gorbachev to Beijing in 1989 and of Li Peng and Chinese Communist Party general secretary Jiang Zemin to Moscow in 1990 and 1991. Talks on resolving the border dispute, derailed by the Soviet invasion of Afghanistan, resumed in 1987. A treaty delimiting the eastern sector of the border was signed in May 1991. These military and political transformations in Sino-Soviet relations were supplemented by a significant growth in trade—especially along the border—and agreements providing for thousands of Chinese workers to be employed in construction projects in Siberia and the Soviet Far East.[5]

## Relations with the Yeltsin Administration

The collapse of the Soviet Union in 1991 removed the Soviet military threat that had been the central focus of Beijing's strategic planning since the 1960s. The changes came at a time when Chinese leaders were beleaguered in the face of national and international resentment over their handling of the Tiananmen Square demonstrations of 1989. Representing one of the few surviving communist regimes in the post–Cold War world, Chinese officials were especially suspicious of Boris Yeltsin and his proposed democratic reforms, which were anathema to Chinese leaders determined to maintain the Communist Party's monopoly of political power. Nevertheless, more pragmatic consideration of the national interests of China and Russia saw Yeltsin and Chinese leaders continue the process of gradually improving relations begun in the 1980s.

Regarding political issues, the ideological grounds for polemics between Moscow and Beijing were basically removed in the Gorbachev years—party-to-party ties were reestablished during the 1989 Deng Xiaoping–Gorbachev summit. The end of Communist Party rule in Russia, coming against the background of the reforms that China had embarked on since 1978, rendered the old schismatic disputes about "revisionism," "social imperialism," and "hegemonism" irrelevant. Russia criticized Beijing's poor human rights record and its use of force to suppress the Tiananmen demonstrations, but they did not become major problems in government-to-government relations. Meanwhile, progress on resolving Russo-Chinese border disputes continued. The May 1991 eastern sector border agreement was followed by the signing of an agreement in September 1994 on the western sector of the border. As a result, except for some small areas, the entire Russo-Chinese border was delimited.[6]

In the 1990s, the presidents and premiers of China and Russia visited each other an average of once every two years. In addition, there were numerous meetings between foreign ministers, defense ministers, and economic officials from both countries.

Concerning military issues, in 1992 Yeltsin's government completed the withdrawal of troops from Mongolia initiated by Gorbachev in 1987. By May 1996, Russia reportedly had cut 150,000 troops from its Far Eastern deployment, and the Pacific Fleet had been reduced from its 1985 level by 50 percent.[7]

Efforts to reduce forces and institute confidence-building measures (CBMs) along the border became multilateral with the addition of the Soviet successor states Kazakhstan, Kyrgyzstan, and Tajikistan—all of which shared borders with China—to a joint Commonwealth of Independent States (CIS) delegation. Guidelines, including force reductions, warnings preceding military exercises, and the attendance at exercises of observers from the signatories, were incorporated into an agreement signed by the leaders of the four CIS states and China in Shanghai during Yeltsin's April 1996 visit. As discussed in chapter 10, this initiated the Shanghai Five, a precursor to the Shanghai Cooperation Organization (SCO), which was formed in June 2001 as the first multilateral organization involving Sino-Russian cooperation in Central Asia in the modern period.[8]

A joint declaration signed at the end of Yeltsin's visit to China in December 1992 pledged to eschew the use of force against each other, including the use of force in the domain of third countries, and to refuse to enter any "military and political alliances" directed against the other party or sign with third countries any treaties or agreements detrimental to the state sovereignty and security interests of the other party.[9] In July 1994, the Russian and Chinese defense ministers agreed on measures (such as preventing accidental missile launches, ending the electronic jamming of communications, and establishing signals to warn aircraft and ships in danger of violating the other side's border) to reduce the danger of inadvertent military escalation. In

September 1994, the two sides agreed to the principle of no first use for nuclear weapons and to retarget nuclear missiles away from each other's territory. [10]

China became the largest customer for Russian arms. Major purchases in the Yeltsin era included two hundred Su-27 fighter–ground attack aircraft, fifty T-72 tanks, one hundred S-300 surface-to-air missiles, ten Il-76 transport aircraft, several Kilo-class (diesel electric) submarines, and two Sovremenny-class destroyers. Moscow was also providing China with technology to improve the accuracy of its surface-to-surface and air-to-air missiles and training in Russia for personnel who would operate the weapons purchased. Several of the sales agreements were difficult to reach. The Su-27 transaction was in the works for years. The first twenty-four aircraft were delivered in 1992, but additional deliveries were held up by various disputes. Eventually, the way was cleared for the delivery of forty-eight Su-27s, and an agreement was reached (reportedly worth $2 billion) allowing China to manufacture this high-capability aircraft under license. [11]

For Russia, arms sales to China supplied much-needed hard currency and allowed for the purchase of consumer goods from China; provided orders for severely distressed Russian defense industries; and reduced the tendency of the United States, Japan, and others to take Russia for granted in the post–Cold War Far East. Russia's political disarray also facilitated these arms sales, as reduced central control from Moscow gave defense industries more independence to make such deals. For China, the Russian equipment was relatively cheap, compatible with the existing Chinese inventory, and came without political or other preconditions. Both Russian and Chinese leaders were sensitive to concerns in the United States and Japan and among Asian governments along China's periphery that the Russian transfers substantially added to China's power projection and altered the prevailing military balance in East Asia. In general, Russian and Chinese officials said that China had a long way to go before it could use the recently acquired Russian weapons effectively or project the augmented power in ways that would seriously upset the military balance in the region. [12]

Regarding economic and social interchange, trade between the two countries grew substantially from a low base. In 1985, Sino-Soviet trade was $300 million. Russian-Chinese trade reached $7 billion in 1995. China became Russia's second-largest trade partner after Germany. [13] Russia also signed contracts to build nuclear and hydroelectric power plants in China. Both countries planned extensive pipeline and other projects to carry Russian oil and natural gas to Chinese consumers. These agreements on expensive infrastructure projects were very slow in implementation. [14]

Problems came with an influx of Chinese into the Russian Far East, particularly an influx of those who remained in violation of visa regulations. The high population density and unemployment that prevailed on the Chinese side stimulated people to cross into the Russian Far East, which traditionally had suffered from severe labor shortages. The entire eastern third of Russia (east of Lake Baikal, a territory almost the size of the United States) had fewer than twenty million inhabitants, and its population was shrinking as people migrated toward Russia's European heartland. This was exacerbated by economic distress in the Russian Far East that was worse than in most other regions, including severe food and energy shortages and wage arrears. [15]

This era of Russia-China relations was characterized by frequent high-level visits featuring anti-US rhetoric by leaders of both countries. Joint Russo-Chinese statements supported a multipolar world, military cooperation increased, and Russia and China worked together politically and diplomatically to thwart US efforts at the UN Security Council and elsewhere to pressure countries like Serbia, Iraq, Iran, Libya, and others to conform to international norms supported by the United States. Internationally, Russia supported China's position on Taiwan, and China backed Russia's opposition to NATO enlargement. [16]

Russia badly needed the China market to export arms and industrial products. Food and inexpensive consumer goods from China played a vital role in helping to sustain the Russian Far East. Although China was economically far less dependent on Russia, Russia provided needed advanced weapons, nuclear reactor technology, and other industrial products. Both Russia and China used their improving bilateral relations for leverage against the West, particularly the United States. [17] China and Russia also shared other common interests: they saw the possible spread of radical Islam in Central Asia as a threat, they wanted to avoid crisis on the Korean Peninsula, and they wished to forestall the reemergence of Japan as a major military power. [18]

Nevertheless, despite much common ground, there were serious limits to cooperation. Russia's relative economic weakness and political instability in relation to China made many Russians nervous. Russia's population (roughly 150 million) was about half that of the former Soviet Union, and the already sparsely populated Russian Far East was losing people. Russia's economy had contracted significantly. Industrial production appeared in the late 1990s to be as low as 50 percent of the 1991 level. [19] With President Yeltsin's ailments and other problems, the political situation remained unstable. Moscow had difficulty controlling distant regions, such as eastern Siberia and the Far East. The deterioration of Russian military strength showed in the army's remarkably poor performance against armed insurgents in Chechnya. In contrast, from Moscow's perspective, China had a dynamic economy; huge and growing population; a stable, authoritarian political system; and a large and modernizing army. Some among the Russian policy elite were mindful of the history of Russia's seizure of vast territories in eastern Siberia and the Russian Far East from China in "unequal treaties" in the latter part of the nineteenth century and saw China's renaissance and burgeoning power as a challenge and potential threat.[20] Many in the Russian security community had serious reservations about the growing Russian arms sales to China.[21]

On the Chinese side, too, there were significant limitations and constraints on cooperation with Russia.[22] Radical swings in Soviet and Russian domestic politics and foreign policy since the mid-1980s inevitably made Russia appear somewhat unreliable in Chinese eyes. Russia's economic, political, and military weakness was duly noted by Chinese strategic planners. Russia was much less important economically to China than the United States and other developed countries. The markets, financing, and technology of the West and the developed countries of eastern Asia represented a key link in China's ongoing program of economic modernization, and economic modernization and the concrete benefits it gave to the broad masses of the Chinese people were key sources of political legitimacy for post-Mao leaders. At the turn of the twenty-first century, Chinese leaders seemed disinclined to allow closer military, political, or other ties with an economically anemic Russia to jeopardize China's vital links with the world's most important economies. When Chinese relations with the United States, Japan, and NATO were strained, Chinese officials fell back on relations with Moscow as a possible source of political leverage against the Western-aligned states. In general terms, Russian leaders tended to use their relationship with China in a similar way.

## Relations under Vladimir Putin and Hu Jintao

The course of Russian-Chinese relations in the early twenty-first century, under new leaders Vladimir Putin (2000) and Hu Jintao (2002), followed the same mixed pattern seen in the 1990s. Both sides placed priority on promoting an evolving "strategic partnership." Economic cooperation improved from a low base, and Russian oil exports to China increased bilateral trade levels. A strong arms sales and defense technology–sharing relationship provided critically important support for China's military buildup, though there was a widely publicized drop-off in such cooperation for a few years beginning in 2005. Political cooperation against US interests varied, with Russia's Putin and then Chinese leaders moving to moderate anti-US invective in the face of US resolve and power, especially at the start of the George W. Bush administration. When Putin later adopted a tougher stance against the United States and its allies at the end of the Bush administration, China offered only limited political support. China seemed similarly uninvolved when then prime minister Putin and Russian president Dmitry Medvedev responded positively to overtures from the Barack Obama government for advances regarding arms control, NATO, and economic issues.

Putin showed a notably positive response to the United States during his first meeting with George W. Bush in the spring of 2001. Cooperation between the United States and Russia was intensified following the September 11, 2001, terrorist attack on the United States. Russian support was essential in facilitating US-led military operations in Central Asia directed against the Taliban regime in Afghanistan. Russia saw its interests served by fostering closer economic and strategic cooperation with the United States and the West and by playing down past major differences.[23]

Maneuvering in the United Nations in the months prior to the war in Iraq in 2003 saw Russia join with France and others (including China to some degree) in standing against US military actions to topple Saddam Hussein without renewed UN approval. After the US-led coalition succeeded militarily in toppling Saddam Hussein and senior Bush administration officials made significant gestures to ease tensions with Moscow, Russia appeared prepared to resume a more cooperative stance toward the United States.[24]

Seeing Russia trim its opposition to the United States in 2001 caused China to lose some steam in its then strong anti-US rhetoric. China was critical of the American posture on missile defense and NATO expansion. Russia's actions added to China's imperatives to moderate its stance toward the United States by mid-2001, emphasizing repeated reassurances to the United States and its allies and partners that China's rise would be peaceful. The Chinese moderation set the stage for the most important improvement in US-China relations since the end of the Cold War.[25]

In this context, the improved Russian-Chinese relationship continued to grow; the two powers signed a Russian-Chinese friendship treaty in 2001 and numerous bilateral agreements. The growing ties appeared to have less negative implications for US interests in sustaining a leadership position and in promoting US objectives in Asia and elsewhere. Russian arms sales to and military cooperation with China continued the pattern of the past decade and increased for a few years as China stepped up the pace of military modernization focused on Taiwan. The higher trade figures were noted above. Political cooperation against US interests subsided from the intensified level of the late 1990s and early 2000s, which had at least partly resulted from various US actions (such as the intervention in Kosovo, posturing over Chechnya and Taiwan, US missile defense plans, and NATO expansion) that Moscow and Beijing perceived as contrary to their mutual interests.[26]

As discussed in chapter 10, there was an upsurge in public Russian-Chinese assertiveness against the United States in 2005 involving the US military presence in Central Asia and the US alliance with Japan.[27] Both Russia and China resisted US-backed efforts in 2005–2006 to pressure Iran to end its suspected nuclear weapons development.

On economic issues, Putin complained that China was purchasing Russian oil and other resources and not Russian manufactured goods. Chinese officials reportedly were irritated by Russian vacillation in determining the routing of an oil pipeline in Siberia. One route favored exports to Japan and another favored China, and Russia seemingly was using vacillation to extract concessions from Japan and China.[28] The Russian leadership's efforts to control the export of oil and gas from Central Asian republics clashed with Chinese efforts to build pipelines outside of Russian control and encourage exports of these commodities from Central Asian countries to China.[29] A marked decline in arms sales beginning around 2005 contrasted with the record of the previous ten years, when $25 billion worth of Russian air, naval, and ground military equipment was delivered to China. A major part of the problem was Russian complaints about China reverse engineering Russian arms; also involved was Russia's inability to fulfill some contracts.[30]

Russian-Chinese political cooperation against the United States remained limited.[31] China gave some political support to Russian complaints against the perceived Western encroachment on Russian security interests, but as discussed in chapter 10, when Russian military forces in August 2008 attacked Western-backed Georgia over territorial issues, Chinese leaders avoided taking sides. The weakness of any Russian-Chinese commitment against the United States and the West appeared again when Russia shifted for a time in 2010 to a more cooperative stance with the United States and NATO on arms control, security, and economic issues that stood in contrast with Chinese truculence toward the United States at that time over Taiwan arms sales, Tibet, US military surveillance near China, and economic issues.[32]

Taken together, the above developments led to a prevailing judgment that Russia-China cooperation represented an "axis of convenience" that complicated US efforts to manage relations with Russia and China but did not appear to change the overall orientation of Russian and Chinese policies, which continued to give primacy to relations with the United States over relations with one another.[33]

## Relations under Vladimir Putin and Xi Jinping

The partnership between Moscow and Beijing matured, broadened, and significantly strengthened over the past decade. The dispositions of President Vladimir Putin and President Xi Jinping supported forecasts of closer relations. The momentum was based on (1) common objectives and values, (2) perceived Russian and Chinese vulnerabilities in the face of US and Western pressures, and (3) perceived opportunities for the two powers to expand their influence at the expense of US and allied powers seen in decline. It no longer was an "axis of convenience" with limited impact on international affairs.[34] Ever-advancing signs of mutual Sino-Russian support against America caused some skeptics of China-Russia cooperation to reluctantly acknowledge the de facto alliance.[35]

Russia and China were now seen to pose increasingly serious challenges to the US-supported order in their respective priority spheres of concern—Russia in Europe and the Middle East and China in Asia along China's continental and maritime peripheries. Russia's challenges involved military and paramilitary actions in Europe and the Middle East, along with cyber and political warfare undermining elections in the United States and Europe, European unity, and NATO solidarity. China undermined US and allied resolve through covert and overt manipulation and influence operations employing economic incentives and propaganda. Chinese cyber attacks focused on massive theft of information and intellectual property to accelerate China's economic competitiveness to dominate world markets in key advanced technologies at the expense of leading US and other international companies. Coercion and intimidation of neighbors, backed by an impressive buildup of Chinese military and civilian security forces, expanded Beijing's regional control and influence.

Russia and China worked separately and together to complicate and curb US power and influence in Asian and world politics, economics, and security. They coordinated their moves and supported one another in their respective challenges to the United States and its allies and partners in Europe, the Middle East, and Asia. These joint efforts also involved diplomatic, security, and economic measures in multilateral forums and bilateral relations involving US opponents in Iran, Syria, North Korea, and Venezuela. The two powers also supported one another in the face of US and allied complaints about coercive Russian and Chinese expansion and other steps challenging regional order and global norms and institutions backed by the United States.

The two powers worked more closely together in response to the stronger pressures on China and Russia associated with the Donald Trump administration's national security and national defense strategies and the hardening of US government security, economic, and political leverage on both countries. President Trump remained an uncertainty in these relationships given his avowed unpredictability in foreign affairs; the president avoided using the strong rhetoric of administration policy documents when dealing with Chinese and Russian matters, and his determination to sustain close personal ties with both China's Xi Jinping and Russia's Vladimir Putin further complicated US relations with Beijing and Moscow.

After Russia annexed Crimea in 2014, it faced significant Western sanctions targeting energy investment and the provision of capital to state-owned enterprises. The sanctions and the wide-ranging disputes with the West over the crisis led Russia to reevaluate its relationship with China. The rising perception of threat from the West was accompanied in Moscow by a decreasing perception of the threat from China.[36] For Beijing, the Ukraine crisis distracted the Obama government from its rebalance policy in Asia, thereby providing China with opportunities to more assertively pursue its designs in the region. Notably, the crisis was seen to ease Chinese concerns about US reaction to the next stage of China's expansion in the South China Sea then underway with the start of massive Chinese island building in the disputed Spratly Islands.[37]

Presidents Xi and Putin met on at least twenty separate occasions between 2012 and 2017 and continued that pattern up to now. The two spent more time together than any other pair of recent world leaders. These interactions culminated in the signing of a joint statement on further deepening the two countries' comprehensive partnership of coordination in July 2017.[38] They witnessed increased military cooperation as well as greater Chinese investment in several major projects, including the Yamal liquefied natural gas project and the Power of Siberia gas pipeline project.[39] Increased Chinese and Russian cooperation was also visible in multilateral venues. The two countries repeatedly cast joint vetoes at the UN Security Council, and the UN was a major venue of Chinese and Russian political coordination.[40]

The year 2013 marked the start of Xi Jinping's signature Belt and Road Initiative (BRI), a massive infrastructure building operation that featured stronger economic, political, and other connectivity between China and, as discussed in chapter 10, the Central Asian states in particular. Those states had been part of the Soviet Union and were viewed by Moscow as part of its bordering sphere of influence. Predictably, Russia's initial reaction to this initiative was one of distrust in view of the risks of expanded Chinese influence undermining Russian prerogatives in its neighborhood. By March 2015, however, Russia overcame its suspicions, with Presidents Putin and Xi signing a declaration on "cooperation in coordinating the development of [the Russia-led Eurasian Economic Union] EEU and the Silk Road Economic Belt." Among the reasons for Russia's eventual acceptance of the BRI was China's implicit affirmation of Russia's status as the dominant power in Central Asia and Moscow's recognition that it could not make investments in Central Asia on the scale that China's plans promised.[41]

In Northeast Asia, China and Russia worked more closely in recent years in relations with South Korea and North Korea, repeatedly seeking to offset US pressures and undermine US influence. They notably adopted a joint position in strong opposition to the US deployment in 2017 of the THAAD anti–ballistic missile system in South Korea, and in 2017 they adopted a joint position in favor of step-by-step mutual accommodation leading to North Korean denuclearization, favored by Pyongyang and at odds with the much stronger US emphasis at that time on North Korean denuclearization. Both Russia and China played important roles in easing the strict economic sanctions against North Korea favored by the United States.[42]

As in the case of Russian accommodation of Chinese ambitions in Central Asia regarding Xi Jinping's Belt and Road Initiative, Russia willingly accommodated China's recent prominence in dealing with the Korean Peninsula. Developments in 2018 and 2019 saw China emerge as a critically important player with a major role in all aspects of negotiations involving the crisis caused by North Korea's rapid development and repeated testing of nuclear weapons and related development and its testing of ballistic missiles capable of carrying a nuclear warhead as far as the continental United States.

By contrast, Russia's role and influence declined in importance. The failed revival of the six-party talks, where Russia and Japan played a direct role along with North and South Korea, China, and the United States in dealing with the North Korean nuclear weapons crisis, and the current regional dynamic focused on only the four latter powers meant that Moscow and Tokyo were marginalized by recent developments. Such an outcome challenged the Russian government of President Vladimir Putin and its drive to play a prominent role as a leading world power on issues important to Russian interests. Nevertheless, the record showed Russia putting aside such concerns, repeatedly siding with China and playing second fiddle to Beijing in dealing with affairs on the Korean Peninsula. China, for its part, seemed comfortable with close cooperative relations with Russia as it dealt with Korean matters. Whatever differences the two might have had over Korean issues were difficult to discern amid their collaboration and cooperation.[43]

Russia also showed accommodation with Chinese interests in the South China Sea. Despite strong continuing Russian political relations with and arms sales to Vietnam, which contests Chinese South China Sea claims, Russian forces took part in joint naval exercises with China in the disputed waters in 2016, targeting the United States and its allies and partners. And Moscow strongly backed China in rejecting the 2016 UN Law of the Sea tribunal ruling against China's South China Sea claims that was supported by the United States and Vietnam.[44]

For its part, China reciprocated by accommodating Russian interests even at the risk of other Chinese interests. In particular, China's recent participation in exercises with Russian forces in the Baltic, Mediterranean, and Black Seas helped support Russian assertiveness in those areas even though China had strong interests in staying on good terms with the regional governments unnerved by Moscow's shows of force.[45] And China risked reputational costs by supporting Russia when the Putin government was rebuked in the West in March 2018 for employing a banned nerve agent in a failed attempt to kill a former Russian spy in England. Against the background of this controversy, the newly appointed Chinese defense minister visiting Moscow said in early April that he had come "to show Americans the close ties between the armed forces of China and Russia, especially in this situation. We've come to support you."[46]

Meanwhile, security and military strategy documents issued by each side in recent years targeted unilateral US military interventions and economic sanctions as they stressed a special relationship between the two states and outlined areas of expanded cooperation against such pressures. China's 2015 Defense White Paper cited Russia first in a list of military-to-military relations.[47] Similarly, Russia's 2015 National Security Strategy highlighted the relationship with China.[48] After relatively flat arms sales prior to 2014, Russia dramatically increased its sales to China after the 2014 sanctions. Russian affairs experts Alexander Gabuev and Vasily Kashin explained: "The sale of modern arms to China became part of the strategy to move closer to Beijing in response to the systemic crisis with the West."[49] Military exercise activity also increased considerably during this period, with the average number of combined or bilateral exercises now approaching three per year, along with a concurrent growth in the size of the individual exercises. Starting with Aerospace Security 2016 in May 2016, Russia and China began conducting joint missile defense exercises, pointing to possible cooperation in the air and missile defense domains.[50] As noted above and reflecting the increasing level of exercise collaboration established during this period, in September 2018, 3,200 PLA personnel actively participated for the first time in Vostok (East) 2018, indicating a new level of trust by the Russian military.

As far as the economic relationship was concerned, according to Alexander Gabuev, "after the Ukraine crisis began, the Russian government immediately started to assess the economic implications. In a series of study sessions [in Moscow] . . . experts . . . immediately spotted Russia's three weakest points: critical dependence on the European energy market, critical dependence on Western capital markets, and critical dependence on important technologies. . . . They concluded that if the West imposed sanctions, Russia would have no other choice than to be more and more accommodating to China—even if it turned Moscow into the junior partner in the relationship."[51] In sum, subsequent developments appeared to validate this forecast.

## RELATIONS WITH EUROPE

Relations with Europe were not of primary importance in Chinese foreign policy in the aftermath of the Cold War. Relations with the United States, Japan, and powers along China's periphery continued to receive top foreign policy attention. Burgeoning economic contacts, along with political and security concerns related to Chinese and some European governments' interest in creating a multipolar world and using cooperation in multilateral organizations to curb the US superpower, supported rapidly developing relations by the latter 1990s that continued into the new century.[52]

European leaders gradually eased the diplomatic isolation of China that came after the 1989 Tiananmen crackdown, and the rapidly growing Chinese economy became a focal point of interest for a wide array of visiting senior government officials from Europe. China's signature "strategic partnerships" with larger European and other world powers saw increasingly wider use in China's relations with smaller European governments and among large and small countries in other world areas. [53] The European Union (an entity of twenty-seven nations following the exit of the United Kingdom in 2020, as opposed to sixteen before 2004) became unusually active in the 1990s in building economic ties with China. [54]

In contrast, broader political and security cooperation remained hampered and constrained. China strongly opposed the expansion of NATO and the NATO-led intervention in Kosovo in the late 1990s. Consistent with its reassurance of the United States and its allies under the rubric of China's peaceful rise, China moderated its anti-US stance and opposition to NATO expansion by 2001 and hoped that improved China-Europe ties would prompt European countries to end the embargo on military sales to China that had been in place since the Tiananmen crackdown of 1989. However, strenuous US-led opposition to ending the arms embargo caused the Europeans to delay and vacillate, without the results China sought.

Against this background of continuing frustrations for China's ambitions in Europe into the twenty-first century, Chinese specialists over time came to see as unlikely Beijing's long-standing goal of working with a European "pole" to constrain America in the sought-after multipolar world. The European powers and the EU were seen as too weak, divided, and dependent on the United States to allow Europe to become an active great power in international relations. Moreover, the European powers, despite many differences with the United States, also seemed to share the same political values and strategic objectives as the United States in areas sensitive to the Chinese government. In particular, they supported China's movement toward democracy despite the strong determination of the Chinese government to maintain one-party rule, and they opposed Chinese threats to resort to force in dealing with the Taiwan issue. Even the positive development of European-Chinese economic relations was marred, from China's perspective, by numerous European efforts to curb rapidly growing Chinese exports to European markets, to join with the United States in complaining about alleged unfair Chinese trade practices, and to refuse strong Chinese efforts to gain recognition for China as a "market economy" under World Trade Organization (WTO) guidelines. [55]

Highlights of relations during the 1990s between China and the EU, then representing sixteen nations, included the EU's 1994 statement "Towards a New Asia Strategy," the EU's July 1995 statement "Long-Term Policy for Europe-China Relations," the EU-China summit of April 1998, and the

March 1998 EU document "The Establishment of Full Partnership with China." Even the Asian economic crisis of 1997–1998 failed to turn back European enthusiasm for investment in China's strongly growing economy.[56] China's trade with the EU states amounted to $43 billion in 1997 and increased by about 15 percent in 1998.[57]

Apart from European-Chinese economic relations, EU members placed emphasis on China's importance to broader European interests regarding such issues as the world trading system, the proliferation of weapons of mass destruction and related technology, and environmental concerns. Britain and Portugal had special concerns with China because of the reversion of their respective colonial possessions, Hong Kong and Macao, to Chinese control in 1997 and 1999.[58]

## Twenty-First Century Trends

There was debate among specialists fifteen years ago regarding the priority of relations with Europe in Chinese foreign policy and the overall importance of the relationship between Europe and China to international affairs in the twenty-first century. American Chinese affairs expert David Shambaugh highlighted in 2004 the development at that time of extensive economic and political contacts between China and Europe to argue that the relationship represented a centerpiece of Chinese foreign policy, creating an "emerging axis" independent of the United States that would be of major consequence in world affairs in the new century.[59] In contrast, French Chinese affairs expert Jean-Pierre Cabestan in 2006 tended to emphasize the limitations of Chinese-European cooperation, highlighting in particular the weaknesses and lack of coherence and unity in European approaches to China, major differences between the two sides, and much stronger US than Chinese influence in Europe, which served as a brake to significant European actions with China that would challenge the prevailing dynamics of European behavior or the interests of the United States in regional and world affairs.[60]

The record of European-Chinese relations since the end of the Cold War provided evidence for both perspectives. On balance, however, it demonstrated that growing Sino-European trade and other connections had to overcome substantial obstacles and diverging interests before consideration of a China-Europe partnership with major international consequences would appear warranted. By the latter part of the decade, initial optimists of Chinese-European convergence had changed their assessments, with David Shambaugh warning that relations had become more "complicated" and that for Europe the "China honeymoon was over."[61]

The EU in 2004 surpassed Japan and the United States to become China's largest trade partner, and China became the second-largest trade partner of the EU following the United States.[62] Trade grew impressively until the economic crisis of 2009. It rebounded and reached a value close to $500 billion in 2010. The value was $559 billion in 2013 and $615 billion in 2014. China-EU bilateral trade totaled $337.99 billion in the first half of 2019, growing 4.9 percent year-on-year.[63]

In 2010 the EU countries were the third-largest source of foreign investment in China. The total stock of European foreign direct investment (FDI) in China amounted to more than $70 billion. In 2013, the EU remained one of the top five foreign investors in China, but annual investment declined from €10 billion in 2012 to €8.2 billion in 2013. Chinese outbound flows to Europe grew quickly. In 2016, new Chinese investment in the EU was more than four times higher (reaching a record high of €35 billion) than the European FDI in China (€8 billion).[64] European countries were also the largest exporter of technologies to China, which allowed for upgrades to Chinese manufacturing and related capabilities. China and the EU also participated in a number of joint technology projects, including the world's largest cooperative science and technology research project, the EU-China Framework Agreement. Meanwhile, as discussed in chapter 3, many European countries joined as founding members of the China-initiated Asian Infrastructure Investment Bank (AIIB), and a number of European countries, including close US ally Italy, signed agreements with China and became part of its global Belt and Road Initiative.[65]

On the negative side was the large trade deficit Europe ran with China. It remained the source of Europe's largest trade deficit. The trend was exacerbated by the fact that China was the main beneficiary of the EU's Generalized System of Preferences program, which granted trade preferences to China. The deficit was €171 billion in 2008 and €185 billion in 2018.[66]

Significant European curbs were introduced beginning in 2005 against incoming Chinese textiles, shoes, televisions, and other products. Later curbs included restrictions on Chinese solar panels. European complaints against Chinese trade practices, intellectual property rights protection, and currency valuation policies grew.[67] The EU and many of its members, along with the United States, stood firm against strong Chinese pressure to be granted market economy status.[68] Barriers to trade in China for many years were estimated to cost EU businesses close to $30 billion in lost trade opportunities annually, and major losses came from counterfeiting and intellectual property rights violations in China. China remained the top nation prompting European trade barrier concerns in 2018.[69]

In the political realm, Chinese and European leaders held regular high-level meetings. But in 2008 the situation reached a low point following some dramatic events in China-Europe relations caused notably by Tibet, climate change, human rights, and other issues.[70] German chancellor Angela Merkel met the Dalai Lama in 2007 despite strenuous Chinese protests. The result was a notable cooling in Chinese relations with Germany. The Chinese government's suppression of violent Tibetan demonstrations in March 2008 coincided with the Olympic torch relay through Europe's capitals. Pro-Tibetan demonstrators disrupted the relay in London and Paris, and European leaders equivocated on whether they would attend the 2008 Beijing Olympic Games. The result further strained EU-China relations over the Tibet issue. When French president Nicolas Sarkozy indicated that he would meet the Dalai Lama and then did so in late 2008, Beijing abruptly postponed the planned EU-China annual summit scheduled to be held in France.

Premier Wen Jiabao traveled to Europe in early 2009 in an effort to shore up China-Europe relations, but he also continued Chinese efforts to isolate the French president. Meanwhile, there was widespread disapproval in Europe over what was seen as China's role as a major impediment to progress at the international conference on climate change in Copenhagen in December 2009. Also, China alienated many in Europe with its strident reaction and pressure on Norway and other European governments participating at the Nobel awards ceremonies in honor of a Chinese dissident receiving the 2010 Nobel Peace Prize.[71] French president Sarkozy tried to assuage China over the Tibet issue when he traveled to China in 2011 to further cement ties, but that visit was overshadowed by differences in China-Europe relations, in this case sharp Chinese complaints about NATO's use of military force against the regime of Libya's Muammar Gadhafi.[72]

At the nongovernment level, Europe welcomed the six million Chinese tourists visiting European sites each year,[73] but this seemed insufficient to offset European concerns about the economic disruption and perceived threat posed by massive Chinese imports. Moreover, there were broadening concerns about illegal Chinese immigration into Europe at a time of continued high levels of economic unemployment in many European countries. The number of Chinese students in Europe grew to nearly one hundred thousand in 2004 and rose to over three hundred thousand in later years, with more than one-third in the English-speaking United Kingdom.[74]

## Xi Jinping and China's Muscular and Manipulative Statecraft in Europe

Europe was slow to perceive the change in China's dealings with European countries to a more forceful and guileful approach. The recent Chinese dealings were multifaceted and were disguised in part by Beijing's professed goodwill and mutual benefit, seen notably in various BRI plans involving Europe. Over time, European leaders, often starting with their intelligence officers and moving to mainstream decision makers, think tanks, and investigative journalists, increasingly saw China as an ever more powerful and difficult competitor with ambitions for Europe and the international order adverse to prevailing European interests, norms, and values. Also seen were a variety of unspoken Chinese motives behind Chinese covert and overt influence operations that were seriously damaging to EU and NATO unity and to the interests of various governments seeking to avoid unwanted Chinese influence in their countries.

The urge to expose and strongly rebuff these Chinese pressures was held in check in several countries by an interest in benefiting from the investment and trade opportunities seen in China's BRI. Also, the European governments on the one hand were willing to work with the United States to restrict unwanted Chinese acquisition of high technology and to curb high-technology trade with China because China was viewed as seeking dominance of key industries in ways that undercut the West, and they were willing to cooperate with America, Japan, and others to thwart other Chinese trade, investment, and other economic practices adverse to Western interests. But, on the other hand, European governments were distracted by the Trump administration's heavy economic pressure on them as well as on China and its demands for more defense spending from NATO and other allied countries, with the result that Western cooperation and resolve against Chinese challenges was weakened.[75]

The discussion below highlights examples of a wide variety of overt and covert practices used by the Chinese government to influence and manipulate European countries to the advantage of China and its resistance to US and Western values, norms, and institutions, notably a strong NATO and European Union. There have been few comprehensive tallies of these recently disclosed Chinese modes of operation. The information on these modes of operation has come to light because of friction caused by Chinese behavior reaching the attention of the media and affected governments. As reviewed in other chapters, these modes of operation have been evident in other parts of the world, often under the cover of China's BRI. The publicity about these operations has been more prominent in Europe as well as in the United States, Australia, New Zealand, and other so-called Western-aligned countries. One reason for this is that these Western countries have been resisting and exposing the Chinese behavior through free media, government investigations, and independent think tank assessments.

The context and many aspects of recent Chinese statecraft in Europe were detailed in a rare public and comprehensive report by a European intelligence service. It came from the small and vulnerable state of Estonia in early 2020. Dealing with various threats, it naturally focused on Russia, Estonia's powerful neighbor. But the report also devoted a fifth of the document to dangers China posed to Estonia and the rest of Europe.[76]

It found that China was preparing the way for influence efforts in Europe with a large push to win support among the United Nations and in European gatherings for Xi Jinping's call for a "community of common destiny," a vision of the world order that received China's "highest priority" as it was submitted to the seventy-fourth session of the UN General Assembly in 2019. The Chinese vision portrayed a parallel world opposed to the current world order, with China assuming a leading role. The report corroborated the discussion in chapter 4 that the Chinese influence effort in the United Nations was extraordinary, with Beijing repeatedly attempting to instill its goals and narrative in the UN. Such efforts, along with China providing more training and education opportunities and with it beginning to mediate international conflicts, underlined Beijing's standing as a responsible superpower. The Estonian Foreign Intelligence Service judged that the underlying goal was to promote and ultimately impose China's worldview and standards, building a Beijing-led international environment that favored China.[77]

The report advised that in recent years and since 2018 in particular, European nations have experienced "unprecedented" levels of activity by Chinese missions, reflecting robust funding from the Chinese party-state apparatus. Chinese ambassadors and other diplomatic representatives spoke out more frequently on sensitive issues in the host country's media and even publicly made recommendations on what these countries' relations with China should be like. They often used provocative language, and if local media outlets refused to publish an opinion article, they bought newspaper advertising space for content marketing. Lobbying efforts orchestrated from Beijing involved diplomats but also Communist Party and other Chinese-backed front organizations, which focused on identifying countries most susceptible to China's agenda. Since the US government has rebuffed Chinese influence efforts in recent years, Europe became a higher priority, offering "much more fertile soil" for Chinese persuasion. One result was that targeted Europeans were encouraged to support the judgment that China was not a threat seeking to undermine Western unity against Chinese challenges. Building close personal relations with leading decision makers provided channels for influencing European government decisions along lines favored by Beijing. The report dealt with the common PRC practice described in other publications as "elite capture," winning over government elites and nongovernment opinion leaders with lucrative contracts or employment with Chinese firms or front organizations or with other favors. It went on to explain the outpouring of evidence of enhanced Chinese influence operations in Europe in recent years, with the judgment that the Chinese missions were more active where perceptions of China diverged most from China's self-image.

The report warned that the hidden objective of China's BRI in Europe and elsewhere was to build China's power as it controlled strategic trade channels and logistic nodes. Chinese loans and financing also served as a lever for steering other countries in directions favored by Beijing. On technology, Beijing was depicted as slowly but surely building dependencies on China through the provision of beneficial terms for Chinese communications and related high-technology equipment for European 5G, smart cities, and artificial intelligence applications. The Estonian authors warned other small states that they were an easier target than more powerful states for China to build dependencies and exert pressure later.

According to the Estonian report, the "key targets" of Chinese influence and espionage operations were politicians and public servants with influence and information on government decisions of Chinese concern, and business-people and specialists with information and access to business projects and scientific achievements useful to Chinese firms. It advised such individuals not to bring computers or other devices to China where the Chinese special services could gain access to proprietary data or personal information that could compromise the visitor.

The Chinese practices highlighted in the intelligence report showed up repeatedly in concurrent media, think tank, and government reports on the variety of methods used by Chinese government, party, and other authorities to make Europe more pliant for Chinese interests. A few examples follow.

*Italy joins the BRI: lobbying, elite "capture," and media control.* The lead-up to Italy's decision in 2019 to join the BRI—the first G7 government to do so—featured Chinese efforts to court Italian political and business elites and to influence and control Italian media coverage of China. [78] A prominent Italian front organization of the United Front Department of the Chinese Communist Party played an important and positive role in Italy's decision to join the BRI, according to a report on the meeting of a senior front organization leader with Chinese authorities in August 2019. China's powerful National Development and Reform Commission worked through the Italy branch of the Overseas Investment Union of China to lobby in favor of joining the BRI. Beijing had impressive accomplishments in courting Italian politicians with prominent positions in China-led initiatives. Former EU Commission president and Italian prime minister Romano Prodi was a member of the Belt and Road Forum advisory council, a group of retired international officials coordinated by the Chinese Foreign Ministry. Another former Italian premier, Massimo D'Alema, was on the board of directors of the Silk Road Cities Alliance (SRCA), a Beijing-based initiative whose mission involved "mobilizing, organizing and coordinating domestic and over-seas social resources" in the implementation of the BRI. Former Rome may-or Francesco Rutelli and former ambassador to China Alberto Bradanini also sat on the board of directors and the steering committee of the SRCA. Brada-nini was also president of a China studies think tank in Italy. Notably, D'Alema was conferred a "Silk Road Super Ambassador Award" for his contribution to the BRI.

As in many other countries in Europe and elsewhere, Chinese party-controlled media agencies expanded their cooperation with national news outlets in Italy in order to cultivate positive views of China and the BRI. In 2019, ANSA—Italy's leading newswire service—signed a cooperation agreement with Chinese party-state media company Xinhua for the cross-posting of Xinhua pieces on its platforms. Rai, Italy's national broadcaster, signed an agreement with the China Media Group (CMG)—the state media group that incorporates CCTV, China National Radio, and China Radio International (CRI). ClassEditori also signed an agreement with CMG for content exchange, coproduction, and publicizing documentaries produced by the Chinese propaganda agency. The above steps allowed the dissemination of China's views on domestic and international affairs via prominent European media, packaged as if it were independent news. As the Chinese vice consul general in Italy told a pro-China publishing house in 2018, "when it is Chinese media talking about BRI, the message comes across as propaganda, while when it is a Western media communicating [the message], perceptions change."[79]

*Montenegro's debt dependence and leveraging the 16+1 dialogue.* The government of Montenegro (population 631,000; GDP $4.7 billion in 2017) contracted with the Chinese state-owned enterprise China Road and Bridge Corporation (CRBC) to construct a controversial highway connecting Montenegro's port with landlocked Serbia. The first stage of construction began in 2015 and the second stage in 2020. The first stage cost about €1.3 billion, which was financed mainly by a loan from the Export-Import Bank of China. The small country's debt dependence on China became enormous, and as profits from the road remained uncertain, Montenegro's debt dependence on Beijing grew. The outcome met Chinese ambitions for its BRI to carry out lucrative infrastructure projects abroad. China also devoted special diplomatic attention in recent years to sixteen Central and Eastern European countries, including Montenegro, under the so-called 16+1 dialogue. The dialogue became 17+1 when Greece joined in 2019. That dialogue focused on China fostering and building closer ties with a group of European countries apart from existing leading groups such as the EU and NATO and encouraging the group members to adopt positions in support of China's interests, including the BRI. Four heads of state or government of the 16+1 group were among those participating in the Chinese Belt and Road summits of 2017 and 2019. Reflecting higher Chinese priority, in 2020 Xi Jinping reportedly planned to replace Prime Minister Li Keqiang as the main Chinese interlocutor with the 16+1. For their part, European Union officials were outspoken in criticizing the Chinese moves as designed to weaken European unity.

Why Montenegro would support this continuing and growing dependence on China rested with the usual nontransparent arrangements in Chinese deals under the BRI rubric. Montenegro's president, Milo Đukanović, has been either president or prime minister nearly uninterruptedly from 1991 and is notorious for corruption. He arranged for the deals with China to ensure that a third of the work must be done by local contractors. This arrangement reportedly allowed dispersing favors in the president's sophisticated and effective patronage network.[80]

*Sweden: extralegal practices and diplomatic bullying to compel deference.* The illegal practice of Chinese security services coercing Chinese abroad with foreign passports to return to China for alleged crimes clashed with the Swedish government's rights under international consular agreements. Gui Minhai, a Swedish citizen and passport holder, was a bookseller known for publishing books critical of Chinese leaders. In 2015, he disappeared from his home in Thailand and appeared later in Chinese custody in the PRC; this was part of a series of coerced efforts by Chinese authorities against booksellers active in Hong Kong promoting books on topics Beijing opposed. The Swedish government repeatedly demanded the right to meet with Gui in accordance with international consular agreements, but these were denied. The matter became more sordid when Gui was forced under duress to reacquire his Chinese nationality, thereby giving Beijing a reason to reject the Swedish demand under international consular agreements. The Swedish government maintained that "Swedish citizenship can only be renounced after an examination and a decision by the Swedish Migration Agency," so the impasse with China deepened. In late 2019, when a Swedish NGO awarded Gui a prize and a Swedish minister attended the award ceremony in Stockholm, the Chinese ambassador resorted to a series of outlandish charges and threatened to use a shotgun against Swedish opponents. The outbursts were roughly consistent with the "wolf warrior" or "tantrum" diplomacy China had used recently in other venues, as discussed in chapter 4. The ambassador's harsh comments and the concurrent cancellation of trade missions served as a warning to Swedish businesspeople with close ties to China, but the Swedish Foreign Ministry rebuked the ambassador. Swedish business leaders and others in Europe and elsewhere were well aware of China's frequently used tactic, in opposition to WTO rules and norms, of cutting off trade with uncooperative states in the event of a dispute on political, security, or other matters. The impasse was widely seen in Europe as a lesson on how a newly assertive China, now viewed by the European Commission as a "systematic rival" intent on having its way, would behave going forward. Given the continued interests in European economic ties with China, there was no united European response despite growing disapproval and unease over Chinese bullying.[81]

*Symbiosis with Serbian authoritarian rule.* Beijing's Belt and Road Initiative came at an opportune time for Serbian president Aleksandar Vučić (2012–). Increased Chinese financing and investment backed the strongman ruler and his political party. The timing of the deals and nontransparent Chinese funding supported Vučić and his party during their election campaigns. The deals also mandated the provision of material and labor from Serbia for Chinese-funded projects and enterprises, which were useful for

President Vučić and his party for patronage purposes. The Serbian regime also moved forward with contracts for Huawei to provide communications equipment and technology, as well as traffic and "safe city" surveillance systems, which facilitated control of the sometimes restive opposition and the broader public.[82]

Beijing seemed satisfied with the ongoing Serbian projects and enterprises supported and purchased by Chinese firms. The long-touted Chinese funded and built high-speed rail link to connect Belgrade, Serbia, with Budapest, Hungary, had made little progress since its announcement almost eight years earlier. But Serbia's growing debt dependency on China added to Chinese influence in Belgrade. Vučić repeatedly compared Chinese assistance, which Serbian media portrayed as gifts and not the loans they were in reality, favorably with the EU's stricter conditionality on assistance and possible Serbian membership in the European Union. Such publicity served Chinese purposes in weakening EU unity and opening the way for more Chinese influence and much less accountable and transparent economic involvement in Europe. Backed by Chinese funding, Vučić and his Serbian Progressive Party (SNS) increasingly controlled government agencies, the national security apparatus, and the media; the media was uniquely friendly to China. Serbian commentary was in the lead among European countries in expressing gratitude for Chinese provision of medical equipment to deal with the coronavirus outbreak of 2020. There was none of the skepticism and wariness of Chinese motives and alleged hypocrisy coming from the media outlets of other European countries.[83]

*Belgium: spies and a gateway for China.* The blurred line between Chinese influence operations and Chinese espionage was on display amid reportage of recent Chinese espionage cases in Europe. One in 2019 involved the director of a prominent Confucius Institute in Belgium, who was a leading academic specialist on European affairs from China's Renmin University. Media reports disclosed that the State Security Service of Belgium had charged that the professor acted as a recruiter for Chinese intelligence services and hired informants from the Chinese student and business communities in Belgium. Background media reports said the episode was the tip of an iceberg and that the number of spies in Brussels was as high as or higher than during the Cold War. An unpublished report by the EU's European External Action Service said that "about 250 Chinese spies" were working in Brussels, more than from Russia. The media also highlighted the Chinese range of usually disguised or hidden influence operations, from building close ties with foreign scientists, other academics, and businesspeople with access to the sensitive and high-technology information China sought, to mobilizing ethnic Chinese in the country to work for China's national goals, to enticing foreigners to spy for China for money. They averred that Brussels was a fruitful location for China's espionage, with loose surveillance and prime targets involving NATO, the EU, and high-technology enterprises and academic centers.[84]

As negative publicity grew concerning the wide variety of sometimes coercive and sometimes persuasive modes of operation of Chinese diplomats, other government and Communist Party officials, business operatives, and others working for Chinese interests, the view in Europe of China and its associated BRI, and the prevalence of communications firms like Huawei, moved in a negative direction. With intelligence services in several countries, some leaders in the European Union apparatus, and a variety of think tanks leading the way, China became increasingly viewed as a threat to the overall system of governance valued by Western democracies and to the unity and integrity of the kinds of established organizations instrumental in protecting Western values and interests, notably the EU and NATO. Xi Jinping's newly assertive China, in a headlong push to advance economic gains and international influence through the BRI and other channels, found Europe open, malleable, and relatively easy to divide and influence. It recognized that Europe still aligned with America but was much less resolved and more reluctant than Washington to counter various Chinese challenges.

Though the Trump administration set out coherent strategies to deal with these Chinese dangers, its implementation was erratic and ragged. The US president's approach to NATO allies and the European Union was often at odds with what was stated in his administration's national security and national defense strategies, both of which emphasized nurturing close and collaborative US relations with allies and like-minded partners. The overall result was more division in transatlantic relations, which enabled Chinese penetration of a more vulnerable Europe.

A case was being made in 2020 that China's so-called wolf warrior diplomacy headed the list of reasons for Europe to keep China at arm's length and build domestic strength in preparation for the struggle ahead, with the United States also countering Chinese challenges, sometimes in close consultation with European allies and partners and sometimes not.[85] But recent Chinese penetration of government and nongovernment elites in several European countries, along with the wide reliance of most of the region on Chinese markets and investments, raised major doubts as to how far and how fast the recent European shift against China would develop.[86]

## CANADA AND THE ARCTIC

A NATO member with strong ties to Europe and the United States, Canada in 1970 was among the first leading Western nations to establish diplomatic relations with China. It became a major trading partner with China. China's rapid economic development required more imports of energy, food, and other resources, which Canada willingly provided, while Chinese exports of manufactured goods to Canada grew enormously, leading to a large trade deficit for Canada.

Generally following a moderate course in dealing with China, Canada usually sought to avoid the acrimonious disputes and controversies that sometimes marked the erratic course of US-China relations in the recent period. An exception was the leadership of Prime Minister Stephen Harper (2005–2015), whose government for several years during the first decade of the twenty-first century highlighted political disputes with China, notably over human rights and Tibet, before calming those disputes in a more pragmatic pursuit of closer economic contacts. [87]

His successor, Justin Trudeau (2015–), actively engaged senior Chinese leaders in China and Canada, endeavoring to foster closer trade and economic ties while sustaining political values important to Canada and opposed by China. China was Canada's second-largest trading partner, with exports of CAN$23 billion and imports of CAN$75 billion in 2019. [88]

Overall relations took a nosedive when Canada complied with a US extradition request in December 2018 and detained the chief financial officer of Huawei in Vancouver and held her under house detention during a prolonged judicial process to determine whether to send her to the United States to face criminal charges. As seen in the new assertiveness of Chinese threats and actions on sensitive disputes involving many European countries as well as South Korea, Japan, Singapore, the Philippines, Australia, New Zealand, Palau, and of course Taiwan and others, China in response to the Canadian arrest employed harsh extralegal tools of retaliation. It notably detained and held two Canadians in China in disregard of accepted international procedures. It also employed thinly disguised interventions to halt or impede sales of Canadian products to China. The Canadian Parliament showed a negative turn against China in a major series of hearings highlighting the kinds of wariness toward Beijing and its ambitions seen concurrently in the United States, Australia, New Zealand, and European countries. Canadian public opinion turned sharply negative against China, registering a 22 percent increase in public disapproval of China, the largest in the world, in a major Pew International poll released in December 2019. [89]

China since 2008 has sought to become a permanent observer on the Arctic Council, an exclusive regional forum of eight member states (Canada, Denmark, Finland, Iceland, Norway, Russia, Sweden, and the United States) created in 1996 to promote collaboration and cooperation on Arctic issues. China became an observer in 2013. The five coastal states bordering the Arctic Ocean—Canada, Denmark, Norway, Russia, and the United States—signed a declaration in 2008 signaling that by virtue of their sovereignty, sovereignty rights, and jurisdiction in large areas of the Arctic Ocean, they are uniquely positioned to address the evolving contemporary issues of the

Arctic. The declaration represented an explicit statement that there was no need for a comprehensive Arctic Treaty on the lines of what exists in Antarctica. Chinese commentary took the position that the Arctic region possesses a "shared heritage of humankind," suggesting that China could oppose some of the Arctic states' sovereignty claims and assert claims of its own as the melting ice created easier access to resources in the area and eased barriers to more efficient sea transportation between China and European and North America ports.[90]

In January 2018, China published its first-ever official Arctic White Paper, which on the one hand underlined that the Chinese government respected the sovereign rights of the eight Arctic states in the region. On the other hand, it portrayed the Arctic as a globally shared space. In June 2017, the Arctic was incorporated into President Xi Jinping's flagship Belt and Road Initiative; China named the Arctic shipping lanes as the "Polar Silk Road." Chinese investors cooperated with Russian companies in facilitating Arctic shipping and energy development. Chinese mining and other interests in Greenland prompted increased US government involvement in the territory.[91]

## Chapter Twelve

# Relations with the Middle East, Africa, and Latin America

The remarkable resource-intensive growth of China's export-oriented economy in the twenty-first century was accompanied by an upsurge in the development of Chinese infrastructure and expanded urbanization and industrialization in China. As a result, there was a major increase in Chinese imports of oil, metals, timber, and other raw materials and agricultural products needed for Chinese economic development and industrial production. An authoritative Chinese commentator in 2010 said that China consumed more than four times the amount of oil to advance its GDP than the United States did, and more than eight times the amount of oil to advance its GDP than Japan. The voracious need for energy and other resources China did not have in adequate amounts in turn increased the importance of Chinese foreign relations with resource-rich countries throughout the world, notably in the Middle East, Africa, and Latin America.[1]

Those areas of the developing world received steady but generally low levels of Chinese government attention in the 1990s. The importance of the three regions to China grew in tandem with the growth of Chinese trade and other economic involvement requiring Chinese purchases of oil and other raw materials. Striving to balance Chinese imports and pursue economic opportunity, the Chinese government fostered programs that facilitated the widespread use of Chinese companies in construction projects and the rapid development of Chinese exports of manufactured goods to these regions. The impressive influx of Chinese merchants, construction laborers, and others saw close to one million Chinese working for 1,600 Chinese firms in Africa in 2010. As China grew to become the world's second-largest economy, largest trader, and largest holder of foreign exchange reserves, increased Chinese trade, investment, and foreign assistance activities in these areas received prominent attention in international media. The growth in China's economic profile included a large and growing share of foreign economic interactions in these regions. In contrast to sometimes sensational media reports, however, China did not dominate the economic interaction, as the Western-oriented developed countries led by the United States, countries of the European Union (EU), Japan, and international financial institutions overall played a far more important role than China as investors, aid providers, and markets for regional exports. A major exception came with an upsurge in Chinese state bank lending to developing countries, often surpassing that of the developed countries and the international financial institutions they supported.[2]

This increase in Chinese economic involvement was accompanied by political activism and some military support that backed improved Chinese relations with governments throughout the three regions. The imperatives of economic development underlined pragmatism in Chinese diplomacy. Throughout the first decade of the twenty-first century, when China reassured the United States and its allies and partners that China's rise would be peaceful, China sought to maintain good relations with all countries that eschewed formal contacts with Taiwan. It tried to avoid taking sides or alienating important actors in salient disputes such as the Middle East peace process and international efforts to curb Iran's suspected development of nuclear weapons. It adjusted in practical ways to changes affecting its energy and other interests, notably the breakaway of oil-rich southern Sudan as an independent country after a long armed struggle against the Chinese-backed regime in Khartoum. Though some Chinese initiatives sought to reduce the power and influence of the United States, Chinese officials generally gave secondary priority to undermining American authority.

The Xi Jinping government emphasis on China's Belt and Road Initiative (BRI) eventually included all of the Middle East, Africa, and Latin America–Caribbean within its scope. The Middle East was at the center of the BRI, whereas Africa and Latin America were along the edges. Chinese economic interaction with the former saw remarkable growth, whereas advances in Africa and Latin America endured despite periodic declines in trade, investment, and state bank funding. Meanwhile the international activism characteristic of the Xi Jinping era showed in steady advances in all three regions amid expanding Chinese-supported elite exchanges, training and education programs, and influence operations abroad. These gains came in parallel with Chinese firms obtaining contracts involving various countries' information and communications technologies, ports, and electric power generation, as well as the influence derived from these countries' debt and other dependence on China. In sum, as shown below and assessed in chapter 4, the Xi Jinping government was in a stronger position in these regions of the developing world as it challenged the United States and the liberal world order it supported, seeking not to supplant the United States but to weaken its ability to stand in the way of China's rise.

## RELATIONS WITH THE MIDDLE EAST

Chinese policy and behavior toward the Middle East in recent years followed a pattern seen in Chinese policy and behavior toward other regions of developing countries far from China—Africa and Latin America. On the one hand, there was an upswing of Chinese attention to the region, notably because of the growing Chinese need for oil and other energy sources and resources that are required to support China's remarkable economic growth. On the other hand, China's close relations with Iran and some other energy and resource exporters complicated China's efforts to stay on good terms with the United States and developed countries important in Chinese foreign policy.[3] Iran continued to be seen as a major deviant from world norms regarding nuclear weapons proliferation, terrorism, human rights, and other sensitive issues that were supported by the United States, the EU, and other powers of importance to China.

In the period when Beijing emphasized China's peaceful rise at the start of the twenty-first century, the Chinese government was more reluctant than in the 1990s to take strong public positions against the United States and its allies in dealing with Iran, as well as Iraq and other issues of controversy, as it gave higher priority to managing differences and advancing common ground with Washington.[4] Under the activist foreign policy of Xi Jinping, China became more deeply involved in the regional economy and exerted more influence that worked to weaken American interests without taking sides on the many contested regional issues or directly challenging continued US security leadership in the Middle East.

Following the Tiananmen crackdown and the end of the Cold War, Chinese leaders were concerned with a wide range of more pressing domestic and international priorities. The priority of the Middle East was low. Beijing had a role as an interested party in the Middle East peace process and in international disputes with Iraq. China rhetorically opposed US strategic dominance in the Persian Gulf and elsewhere in the region, but the criticism did not upset Beijing's more important effort to stabilize US-China relations. China kept on good terms with all sides in the often contentious politics of the region, including notably establishing official relations with Israel in 1992. In this way, China could serve its economic interests of ensuring diverse supplies of oil and access to regional markets for economic benefit and arms transfers.[5]

Because of China's isolation from Western and other governments as a result of the Tiananmen incident of 1989, President Yang Shangkun, Premier

Li Peng, and Foreign Minister Qian Qichen traveled widely in the area, as well as other Third World locales, to demonstrate that the Chinese government could not be effectively isolated. Beijing's multibillion-dollar arms sales to both sides during the Iran-Iraq War of the 1980s was followed by the establishment of diplomatic relations with Saudi Arabia in 1990 supported by a multibillion-dollar sale of older Chinese intermediate-range ballistic missiles.[6] In addition to Chinese–Middle Eastern trade valued at $3 billion a year by the early 1990s, Beijing earned on average more than a half billion dollars annually from labor contracts involving construction projects in the region since the late 1970s.[7]

The Persian Gulf War in 1990–1991 added to regional economic difficulties, which included Western sanctions, crimped regional economic development, and curbed opportunities for Chinese economic interchange and arms sales. Meanwhile, the US-led victory in the Persian Gulf War came at China's political expense. Beijing's efforts to keep on good terms with all sides were swept away as US-backed power moved to dominate the region. It was at this juncture that Chinese officials moved forward in relations with many Arab governments and with Iran, partly as a move to counter US dominance and pressure.[8]

At this time and continuing up to the present, the Middle East was seen as important to China because of its relationship to Islamic separatists and other radicals in China's unstable western areas, especially Xinjiang. Chinese crackdowns in Xinjiang met with public and private disapproval from some Middle Eastern governments.

As China became a net importer of oil in 1993, Beijing worked harder to diversify its international supplies. China's oil import bill was about $5 billion in 1997, with half coming from the Middle East. The Chinese also sought to develop trade in military items and technologies with countries that were on poor terms with the United States (for example, Iran). And China purchased military equipment from Israel in order to modernize its military, despite the Western arms embargo against China.[9]

Chinese officials continued to lean toward the Arab and Palestinian positions on Middle East peace issues but duly acknowledged the legitimacy of Israeli concerns. China disapproved of US- or Western-backed pressure against so-called rogue states like Iraq, Iran, Libya, and Syria, though Chinese policy usually followed the international consensus in the United Nations when it dealt with Iraq's recalcitrance or other issues.[10]

The improvement in US-Chinese relations after 1996, and especially the summit meetings of 1997 and 1998, had an indirect impact on Chinese policy in the Middle East. Chinese leaders during the summit meetings with the United States promised to stop cooperation with Iran on nuclear development, to halt sales of antiship cruise missiles to Iran, and to halt support for Iran's ballistic missile development. Beijing also strove to work in support of

US-led efforts to revitalize the stalled Middle East peace process, notably through the visit of vice premier and foreign minister Qian Qichen to front-line states in December 1997 and his subsequent interchanges with US officials on Middle East peace issues.[11]

Nevertheless, Beijing still saw its interests as well served by staking out tough public anti-US stances on sensitive regional questions.[12] China repeatedly joined Russia and others in trying to moderate US-backed pressure on Iraq over weapons inspection issues, urging diplomatic negotiations over the use of force and reiterating calls for the eventual easing of sanctions.[13] During Qian Qichen's visit to the frontline states, the envoy boosted China's pro-Arab profile on the peace process and took the opportunity to register Beijing's growing impatience with US-backed international sanctions against Libya and Iraq. Visiting Israel, Qian said China understood Israel's security concerns and strongly opposed terrorism. At other stops, however, Qian blamed the Israeli government for the impasse in the peace process.[14]

## Twenty-First Century Policy Contradictions and Dilemmas

Chinese policy and behavior in the Middle East in the twenty-first century featured a series of decision points involving often contradictory imperatives. These imperatives posed sometimes serious dilemmas for Chinese leaders and seemed to require pragmatic and careful cost-benefit assessments by Chinese officials. One-sided decisions ran the risk of serious negative consequences for Chinese interests. In general, the Chinese leaders adopted positions that were well balanced, had the broadest international appeal, and did the least damage to China's often conflicting interests in the Middle East. At the same time, the kind of mixed-up overall message seen in China's actions in the Middle East in the 1990s continued into the new century.[15]

Heading the list of complications and conflicting imperatives in Chinese policy toward the Middle East was Chinese leaders' need to strengthen their relations with oil and gas exporters, including targets of US-backed international pressure (like Iran) and countries that periodically wished to show greater independence from the United States (like oil-rich Saudi Arabia). Building better Chinese relations with these two energy giants was further complicated by their deep mutual suspicion and conflicting interests.

Chinese domestic economic growth and political stability depended on stable energy supplies. The main sources of Chinese energy demand involved industrial activities, infrastructure development, and transportation growth. The large increase in the number of cars in China strengthened the need for imported oil. Despite China's efforts to diversify its sources of oil imports, the Middle East accounted for more than half of China's overall imports, with Saudi Arabia and Iran being the biggest or among the biggest suppliers in the region.[16] China's stronger drive for international energy resources included a variety of high-level Chinese visits and energy-related agreements with Iran, as well as even more interactions and agreements with the major energy power in the region, Saudi Arabia. Saudi Arabia was the largest supplier of oil to China for many years until it was surpassed by Russia with its recent pipelines in China, accounting for about 15 percent of Chinese imports. In 1999, President Jiang Zemin visited Saudi Arabia and opened the Saudi oil and gas market to China. Saudi Arabian enterprises followed by reaching agreements to expand and modernize oil refineries in China.[17] Top-level visits took place in 2006 and 2009.[18] By 2013, Sino–Saudi Arabian trade amounted to more than $73 billion a year. China was the largest importer of Saudi oil. Chinese trade with the Middle East at this time was well over $200 billion a year.[19]

Meanwhile, even though China was well aware that Saudi Arabia and Iran had a number of serious differences and were often on opposite sides regarding Middle Eastern problems, China pursued its long-standing ties with Tehran given China's ever-growing energy needs. In October 2004, the Chinese government agreed with Iran to buy large quantities of Iranian natural gas over a twenty-five-year period. China later agreed to develop an oil field in western Iran, and in 2009 a deal worth more than $3 billion was reportedly reached involving Chinese development of a natural gas field in Iran. Chinese firms were also deeply involved in developing the Tehran subway, electricity, dam, and other industries and infrastructure. These steps reinforced Chinese reluctance to see sanctions or other pressures imposed on Tehran by the United States and Western powers concerned with Iran's nuclear development program, though China also continued to avoid standing alone against such international opposition.[20] Top-level Chinese leaders visited Iran less frequently than Saudi Arabia, but they met cordially with the controversial Iranian president in China and at international meetings elsewhere. Iranian officials said in 2011 that direct Chinese trade with Iran was valued at $29 billion, and indirect trade through countries neighboring Iran brought the total to $38 billion in 2010. They added that Iran was then China's third-largest supplier of crude oil, providing China with roughly 12 percent of its total annual oil consumption.[21] Active collaboration between Iranian and Chinese energy firms indicated that China would continue to rely on imports from the country. In 2014 China imported 9 percent of its foreign oil from Iran.[22]

In contrast with China's treatment of Iran was Chinese leaders toning down their anti-US posturing seen in the 1990s in order to strengthen Chinese policy of moderation toward the United States. The interest here was to avoid conflict and convince the United States and its partners of China's determination to conform to international norms as it sought greater economic development, international influence, and power. China also did not wish to appear to challenge the long-standing US relationship with Saudi Arabia for fear of seriously antagonizing the United States. Furthermore, Chinese strategists saw their access to the energy resources of the Persian Gulf as heavily influenced by the strong US military presence in the Gulf and the broader Middle East. Manifestations of Chinese moderation included China's reluctance to stand against the US-led military assault against Saddam Hussein in 2003. Regarding the later controversy over Iran's nuclear program, the Chinese government acted as though it did not want to choose between its important energy and other ties with Iran and its concern to nurture the continued cooperation of the United States, the EU, and others who strongly pressed Iran over a variety of issues, notably its suspected efforts to develop nuclear weapons. Chinese officials at times endeavored to slow and delay actions in the United Nations that would result in condemnation of or sanctions against Iran, and at times they worked closely with Russia in fending off pressure from the United States and the EU powers for more decisive UN action. However, China tried to avoid standing alone against Western pressure, and it bent to such pressure in allowing the issue to be brought before the UN Security Council despite earlier pledges to resist such a step. In June 2010, China voted for a UN Security Council resolution approving new sanctions against Iran on account of its suspected nuclear weapons development.[23]

Chinese relations with Israel posed another set of contradictions and complications for Chinese foreign policy in the Middle East. China benefited greatly from economic and military transfers from Israel; the latter were especially valuable to China because of the continued Western arms embargo against China. China resented US pressure to curb Israeli military transfers to China.[24] Beijing accepted Israel's right to exist and eschewed past support for radical elements aiming at Israel's destruction—steps that significantly improved China's relations with the United States and other concerned Western powers. At the same time, China supported the Palestinian Authority (PA) in its opposition to various Israeli pressures and maneuvers seen as designed to weaken the PA and to reduce its legitimate territorial claims. It was sharply critical of Israel's December 2008 invasion of Gaza and the resulting humanitarian crisis. The victory of the radical Hamas movement in PA legislative elections in the middle of the decade and growing Hamas control over the Palestinian government posed a serious complication. China was low keyed in accepting Hamas in the face of strong US and Israeli opposition to international support for what they deemed a terrorist organization. The Chinese Foreign Ministry spokesperson welcomed the April 2011 agreement between Hamas and its Fatah rival, paving the way to the formation of an interim government to prepare for elections determining the future administration of the Palestinian Authority.[25]

A more serious set of complications was raised by the war in July–August 2006 between Israel and Hezbollah forces based in southern Lebanon. Chinese commentary moved from a more or less evenhanded position to one that sided against Israel and to a degree the United States. China did not want to seriously alienate any major party or make major commitments or take risks in the volatile situation; this was illustrated by the bland and noncommittal remarks of its Foreign Ministry "special envoy" sent to tour the region and by much of the Chinese media's commentary. The United States, the European powers, Israel, Iran, and Syria loomed much more important in the conflict and in the efforts to resolve it. As one veteran scholar of China–Middle East relations concluded, China's behavior during the crisis showed that Beijing continued to talk much and do little regarding serious regional issues.[26] China did respond to UN and European requests for peacekeeping forces and agreed to provide one thousand personnel for the UN peacekeeping operation in Lebanon. According to Chinese diplomats, the Chinese personnel were used in support functions.[27]

An additional set of contradictions was posed by China's ongoing efforts to suppress dissent and splitist activities by Muslim adherents in Xinjiang. It was deemed essential that these elements be suppressed to preserve order and stability in China. At the same time, the tough Chinese measures negatively affected China's image among the Islamic governments in the Middle East. Finally, Chinese antiterrorist efforts at home and abroad, notably in the Shanghai Cooperation Organization (SCO), were seen as vital to Chinese national security and regional stability and as an important foundation for greater Chinese cooperation with the United States and other Western powers. At the same time, China's interests in Iran required Chinese leaders to allow the president of Iran to participate in the elaborate fifth-anniversary summit of the SCO in Shanghai and later meetings of the group, despite strong accusations from Israel, the United States, and Western powers that Tehran supported terrorist activities against Israel, in Iraq, and elsewhere. Finally, Chinese fence straddling showed in avoiding a veto of UNSC Resolution 1973 against the Gadhafi regime in 2011 while complaining at the highest levels about the violence in Libya resulting from NATO forces employing military coercion in the country under the auspices of the UNSC resolution.[28]

## The Middle East in Xi Jinping's Foreign Policy

For a few years, President Xi Jinping wrestled with these contradictory imperatives. During that time, Xi and his colleagues were unable to get beyond China's traditional low profile in the Middle East. However, the continued strong growth in Chinese trade, investments, and other economic interests in the region, involving Chinese dependence on oil imports and Chinese exports of manufactured goods, meshed with President Xi's ambitious Belt and Road

Initiative, thereby giving pride of place to the Middle East as a region of growing strategic importance to China.

Though Xi took the reins of power in late 2012 and quickly established a reputation as one of the world's most traveled heads of state, neither President Xi nor Prime Minister Li Keqiang visited the region through 2015. The main reasons had to do with the pervasive violence in the region and the resulting danger to the safety of Chinese leaders.

Caution and practicality determined China's reaction to the upsurge of mass demonstrations against authoritarian regimes throughout North Africa and nearby Asia in 2011. The Chinese government focused domestically, tightening already extensive Chinese internal controls to guard against possible spillover effects that might challenge continued one-party rule in China. In the region, Chinese officials adjusted pragmatically to the new administrations taking form in Tunisia and Egypt. The armed conflict in Libya cost Chinese enterprises invested there dearly; the Chinese government was effective in facilitating the evacuation of more than thirty thousand Chinese nationals from the country. China seemed to depart from its past practice in abstaining rather than blocking UNSC Resolution 1973 in March 2011 authorizing all measures, including military action, against the Libyan government of Muammar Gadhafi, then engaging in armed resistance against populist forces struggling for his ouster. An examination of the costs of blocking the measure showed that they outweighed the benefits China would have derived from vetoing the measure.[29]

However, Beijing came to regret this decision and began to oppose NATO military action against Gadhafi. It joined Russia in blocking UN action in opposition to the Bashar al-Assad government in the Syrian civil war. Still supporting the Assad government in Syria, China avoided full endorsement of US calls for strong action against the radical Islamic State in Iraq and Syria. Regional turmoil spread with the fall of the government of Yemen to militants in early 2015. Saudi Arabia intervened with bombing raids against the militants. Xi Jinping had been planning a visit to Saudi Arabia and Egypt along with Pakistan and Indonesia in March 2015. He changed plans in the wake of the Saudi bombings, scrapped both the Saudi Arabia and Egypt visits, and confined the trip to Pakistan and Indonesia. The Xi trip predictably underlined China's Silk Road economic initiatives that included the states in the Middle East, but security dangers combined with the various contradictions facing Chinese policy inclined Chinese leaders at the time to avoid a potentially dangerous and counterproductive higher profile in the volatile Middle East.[30]

Against this background, President Xi Jinping's first visit to the Middle East in January 2016 avoided controversy; he focused on energy and economics and avoided security and political issues. Showing careful balance, Xi stopped initially in Saudi Arabia, where the two countries signed a com-

prehensive strategic partnership, and he then visited Iran and did the same
thing. Nevertheless, by this time it was becoming clear that China's importance in the Middle East was expanding rapidly, reaching a point at the end
of the decade where China was the biggest trade partner and external investor
for many countries in the region. Other important benchmarks included the
following: In 2019 China had $65 billion in investment agreements with
Saudi Arabia, it was building a $10.7 billion Sino-Oman industrial city in
Duqm (Oman), it was a large and growing player in the Israeli high-tech
sector, and in 2017 its trade volume with Iran exceeded $30 billion. Chinese
tourism in Egypt was growing fast since a comprehensive strategic partnership was signed between the two countries in 2014, and Beijing was taking
the lead in building a new capital and enlarging the Suez Canal.[31]

In 2015 China officially became the biggest global importer of crude oil,
with almost half of its supply coming from the Middle East. The Middle East
was also a key supplier of China's liquefied natural gas. Chinese trade with
the Middle East continued to advance rapidly. From the vantage point of
2018, the trade value that year grew to more than four times the value in
2004. China became the region's largest trade partner. China still endeavored
to diversify its foreign sources of oil. Forty-five countries supplied crude oil
to China, but close to half (44.1 percent) of Chinese imported crude originat-
ed from nine Middle Eastern nations, and six Persian Gulf states were among
the top fifteen crude oil suppliers to Beijing. This energy relationship was set
to continue. The International Energy Agency (IEA) expected Beijing to
double its oil imports from the region by 2035.[32]

The value of China–Middle East trade consistently surpassed Chinese
trade with Africa by a significant margin, and it remained robust despite the
decline in oil and other raw material prices a few years ago that resulted in a
large decline in the value of China trade with Africa beginning in 2014. The
value of China–Middle East trade in 2018 was about $285 billion, whereas
Chinese trade with Africa that year was $185 billion. The China–Middle East
trade value increased to $294.4 billion by 2019. Beijing's investments in the
Middle Eastern states from 2013 to 2019 were valued at $93.3 billion, with
more than half in the energy sector.[33]

China's imperative to construct large-scale infrastructure projects under
the BRI meshed well with Middle Eastern countries under pressure to create
more diverse economies involving massive infrastructure and construction
projects. The value of Middle East contracts awarded to China in 2018 was
$40 billion. One source said there were seventy thousand Chinese contract
workers in the Middle East that year, though the reported number of Chinese
people, mainly workers, in the region numbered as high as six hundred
thousand.[34] Meanwhile, Chinese companies were operating ports and industrial parks seen as central to the cooperation and connectedness fostered by
the BRI. The projects created economic links from China to the Persian Gulf,

the Arabian Sea, the Red Sea, and the Mediterranean Sea. Examples included such industrial parks as the Khalifa Port Free Trade Zone (KPFTZ) in Abu Dhabi, UAE; the Duqm Special Economic Zone Authority (SEZAD) in Oman; the Jazan City for Primary and Downstream Industries (JCPDI) in Saudi Arabia; and the TEDA-Suez zone in Ain Sokhna, Egypt. And they included such ports as the Khalifa Industrial Zone Abu Dhabi (KIZAD); SEZAD in Oman; the People's Liberation Army Support Base in Djibouti; and Port Said in Egypt. Taken together, these sites offered China a chain of strategically situated hubs in the Persian Gulf, the Arabian Sea, the Red Sea, and the Mediterranean Sea.[35]

The higher diplomatic profile China gave to the region showed up in China's partnerships with the region. As of 2019, China had signed comprehensive strategic partnerships with five states and strategic partnerships with eight others. Saudi Arabia, the United Arab Emirates (UAE), Iran, Egypt, and Algeria were comprehensive strategic partnerships. With the exception of Egypt, all of these partnership agreements came in the past decade.[36] China also employed two multilateral groups dealing with regional matters. The China-Gulf Cooperation Council (GCC) Strategic Dialogue began in Beijing in 2010 and involved the council members; and the China–Arab States Cooperation Forum (CASCF) established in 2004 involved China and the states of the twenty-two-member Arab League. China's recent policy in the region was guided by China's Arab Policy Paper, released in 2016 to coincide with President Xi's trip to the Middle East.[37]

The Arab Policy Paper referred to China's BRI plans in the Middle East and introduced the "1+2+3" cooperation pattern, under which China and Arab countries would upgrade energy cooperation, infrastructure construction, and trade and investment and seek to develop together in nuclear energy, space satellites, and new energy. At a CASCF ministerial meeting in Beijing in 2018, China pledged more than $23 billion in loans, aid, and investments.[38]

Among non-Arab states in the Middle East, Iran remained the most important. Bilateral trade was over $30 billion in 2017, and Chinese investments in Iran between 2005 and 2018 totaled more than $27 billion. Iran supplied 11 percent of Chinese oil imports between 2011 and 2016. There were important BRI connectivity projects between the two countries.[39] Among other benefits China derived from Iran were that it added to reasons for the United States to divert strategic attention from China to the Middle East, and it weakened and sometimes fractured the US-led Western alliance that China opposed. Closer China-Iran relations also prompted Saudi Arabia to work harder to improve relations with Beijing through advantageous trade and investment. Politically isolated Iran made it much easier for Chinese companies to carry out advantageous trade, investment, and construction projects there. Iran had little economic leverage over China; it needed what

China provided, whereas China's trade and overall economic dependence on Iran was small.[40]

A significant advance in China's willingness to depart from its traditional low profile on security matters in the Middle East came in 2019. Against the backdrop of high tensions between the United States and Iran over suspected Iranian attacks on oil tankers and Iran's detention of an oil tanker in the Persian Gulf, China joined Russia and Iran in a naval exercise in the Indian Ocean. Beijing in 2015 joined naval exercises with Russia in the Mediterranean Sea near Syria and in the Black Sea.[41]

Turkey had a significant role in China's proposed BRI connections, providing an overland route to the Aegean Sea and Chinese company Cosco's Piraeus Port in Greece. Trade between China and Turkey was $10 billion in 2006 and $26 billion in 2017; Turkey received $15 billion in Chinese foreign direct investment (FDI) between 2005 and 2018. Differences had arisen in the past when Turkey officials occasionally voiced support for Muslim Uighurs in Xinjiang who were being subjected to extraordinary Chinese government coercion and control, including an episode in 2019 when Turkey became the first Muslim-majority state to publicly criticize China for its mass internment of Uighurs in Xinjiang.[42]

In Israel, Chinese close involvement with the country's high-technology sector and the involvement of China's Shanghai International Port Group in a twenty-five-year contract to operate the Haifa port, which also supports the BRI, raised major issues regarding Israel's defense relationship with the United States. At the same time, Israel's troubled relations with many of its neighbors complicated the relationship for China. At bottom, the China-Israel relationship appeared challenged on both sides, suggesting limited growth possibilities.[43]

Looking out, China seemed likely to slowly but surely advance its economic connections and related influence. China's example of economic growth under authoritarian rule appealed to the many authoritarian rulers in the region who were even more wary of political liberalism following the chaotic results of the Arab uprisings of 2011. Under these circumstances, there were few of the episodes seen in other world regions of Middle Eastern governments countering perceived challenges posed by Chinese government involvement in their domestic affairs. The symbiosis between the region's regimes and Chinese rulers remained strong, precluding significant challenge to China's advancing influence. Against this background, the recent worldwide political activism of Chinese embassies and other Chinese government, party, and related front organizations building closer Chinese ties with indigenous elites, media, political parties, think tanks, universities, and other influential elements saw the Middle East as relatively unencumbered with significant obstacles for China's advancement.

Meanwhile, as elsewhere in the world, China's strong support for Huawei and other Chinese companies building communications connections was not only focused on economic benefit and market share. The Chinese strategy to promote economic ties represented an effort to embed Chinese technology in infrastructure, which was increasingly successful, meaning that the recipient states became ever more dependent on China for support in maintaining and upgrading the expensive and sophisticated infrastructure. More broadly, Chinese state-owned enterprises, construction firms, and technology flows all created an engagement turning into dependency.[44] Meanwhile, the ever stronger Chinese relationship with Russia facilitated more Chinese involvement in regional security matters on the side of those seeking to weaken the United States and to complicate and undermine its interests. Beijing remained reluctant to take sides in the region's many disputes or to undertake responsibility for regional order. It still appeared to leave the latter task mainly in the hands of US power, which China worked to weaken and to make more malleable to Chinese ambitions over the longer haul.

## RELATIONS WITH AFRICA

The history of Chinese relations with Africa is full of often visionary and sometimes quixotic efforts to throw off outside influence and foster rapid development and social progress. Chinese aid efforts waxed and waned according to the urgency of changing Chinese priorities. At times during the Cold War, Beijing was an important supplier of basic military equipment and training to a number of liberation groups and newly emerged governments.[45] China relied heavily on backing from African countries in order to gain entry for China and to remove Taiwan from the United Nations in 1971. Large-scale demonstration projects also characterized Chinese policy in Africa at this time, notably the Tan–Zam Railway, which linked Zambia's copper fields and the Tanzanian coast.

Post-Mao Chinese leaders curbed expensive overseas projects and sharply cut foreign aid to $100 million annually for the entire world. China successfully competed with African countries for support from the World Bank and other international financial institutions. China-Africa trade levels remained low, valued at $2.2 billion in 1988.[46] Meanwhile, long-standing Chinese efforts to offer university and other training for African students were clouded by several publicized incidents showing apparent Chinese social bias against Africans in the late 1980s.[47]

Chinese incentives to improve relations with African countries increased after the Tiananmen incident of 1989.[48] Officials anxiously sought African and other Third World support to offset Beijing's isolation and to reduce international pressure against China. Foreign Minister Qian Qichen visited eleven African countries one month after Tiananmen. African states, which seemed to be marginalized as major Western and Asian investors turned their attention elsewhere in the post–Cold War period, generally welcomed China's renewed emphasis on strengthening ties.[49] Chinese motives centered on competing with Taiwan for international recognition, building solidarity with members of the Third World bloc in the United Nations and other world organizations, facilitating some advantageous trade in oil and other commodities, and portraying China as a power with growing international stature and influence.

President Yang Shangkun visited three African countries in 1992, Vice Premier Zhu Rongji visited seven countries in 1995, President Jiang Zemin visited six countries in 1996, Premier Li Peng visited seven countries in 1997, and Vice President Hu Jintao visited four countries in 1999.[50] The Chinese military was also active in Africa in exchanges, training, and a variety of small-arms sales.[51] Consistent with China's opposition to the United States and its alliance structures seen in China's emphasized new security concept in the latter 1990s, People's Republic of China (PRC) leaders typically characterized PRC–Third World solidarity as essential for promoting China's multipolar worldview, defending PRC positions in international forums such as the United Nations, and standing firm against US global dominance.

China's strong economic growth in the 1990s saw Chinese firms pursue oil deals, notably with Nigeria, Sudan, and Angola; mineral extraction rights with the Democratic Republic of the Congo and Zambia; exports of textiles, consumer goods, machinery, and other manufactured goods to multiple countries; and notably a multimillion-dollar trade-investment package deal with South Africa.[52] Chinese involvement in the construction of infrastructure projects throughout Africa financed by international and Chinese sources became common. There were arms sales to several African states, and Beijing registered considerable success in whittling away Taiwan's diplomatic relations on the continent, with Nelson Mandela's South Africa establishing formal diplomatic relations on January 1, 1998.

## Twenty-First Century Chinese Advances in Africa

The new century saw an upsurge in Chinese trade, investment financing, and high-level official interaction with African countries that stood in contrast with the often stagnant and contentious relations African countries had with developed countries and international financial institutions. A marked increase in Chinese purchases of oil and other raw materials from Africa, a concurrent effort to foster Chinese exports to African markets, and an increase in Chinese financed and built construction projects throughout Africa were new and important drivers of Chinese interest in the continent. Politically, China continued to compete with Taiwan and to nurture solidarity with African countries in the United Nations and other world organizations in order to promote China's international stature. Consistent with its emphasis at this time on reassuring the United States and its partners of China's intentions as it rose in prominence and power, China tended to avoid antagonism with the United States and other powers as it endeavored to pursue a path of "peaceful development."[53]

In general, the advance of Chinese relations in Africa faced fewer complications than concurrent Chinese advances among developing countries in the Middle East or Latin America. In the latter two areas, the security, political, and economic roles of the United States, European countries, and other foreign powers generally were significantly more important than China's newly rising prominence. In the case of Africa and especially sub-Saharan Africa, however, China's involvement reached high prominence in a setting where other powers appeared less vigorously involved. Assessments of China's status in Africa varied.[54] Available data up to 2015 did not show Chinese dominance, nor did China seem to reach a status of Africa's leading foreign power. China's trade had grown impressively but had slowed recently, Chinese investment remained low, and China's noncommercial interests in Africa seemed limited. The *Economist* in January 2015 assessed the situation and saw China as "one among many" large outside powers that continued to have a major impact on African development over the years.[55] That said, China up to that time clearly played a leading role in regional affairs, along with the United States and European countries and the international organizations they supported. And China had now established itself as the leader in state bank–financed infrastructure projects in Africa. Western powers and others sometimes criticized aspects of Chinese involvement in Africa, but they also moved to consult and work more closely with China in dealing with regional issues. Meanwhile, though the Chinese government usually sustained good relations with African government leaders, it found that China's increasing impact on Africa resulted in sometimes mixed reactions below the national government level, with some strong negative responses on the part of constituencies adversely affected by Chinese interaction with their countries.[56]

A landmark in China's efforts to formulate a comprehensive outreach to Africa came in October 2000 when China's leaders and the leaders of forty-five African countries met in Beijing to form the China-Africa Cooperation Forum (CACF). They agreed that the CACF would meet every three years to further mutual economic development and cooperation. The Chinese government endeavored to enhance cooperation by using the first CACF meeting to pledge forgiveness of $1.2 billion in African debt covering thirty-two nations and to expand Chinese foreign aid to Africa. At the second ministerial CACF conference held in Addis Ababa, Ethiopia, in December 2003, China promised to cooperate with Africa in priority sectors identified in the African governments' New Partnership for Africa's Development. These African priorities included infrastructure development, prevention and treatment of diseases such as HIV/AIDS, human resources development, and agricultural development. China also agreed to begin negotiations on reducing tariffs to zero for some exports to China from the least-developed African countries. Prime Minister Wen Jiabao was reported by Chinese and international media to have pledged at the CACF meeting in Ethiopia in 2003 that China would gradually increase aid to Africa, provide training for ten thousand Africans over three years, and increase Chinese tourism to Africa.[57]

Continued high-level attention to Africa included the release in January 2006 of the Chinese government's first official white paper on African policy, which was highlighted in President Hu Jintao's visit to Morocco, Kenya, and Nigeria in April 2006. Prime Minister Wen Jiabao visited seven African countries in mid-2006. Chinese trade with Africa reached $40 billion in 2005, up rapidly from $10 billion in 2000.[58]

China hosted the CACF summit in November 2006. At the summit, China pledged $5 billion in preferential loans and credits and to double aid to Africa by 2009. It announced support for health and education efforts in Africa and said that trade would expand from the 2005 level of $40 billion to reach $100 billion by 2010. The Council on Foreign Relations reported in 2006 that there were nine hundred Chinese doctors serving in Africa at that time.[59] Meanwhile, Chinese companies at the CACF meeting signed fourteen commercial contracts and agreements valued at $1.9 billion.[60]

Chinese investment in Africa also grew from a low base. Though some media accounts grossly exaggerated the size and scope of such investments, the level remained about 5 percent of foreign investment in Africa.[61] A Chinese government official told the *China Daily* in April 2011 that Chinese investment in Africa, then "about $1 billion" a year, was "dwarfed by the West" in contributions to overall annual foreign investment in Africa amounting to $80–$90 billion.[62]

The main exceptions to this prevailing pattern of modest Chinese investment and even more modest Chinese aid outlays in Africa involved deeper Chinese involvement with financing infrastructure and development in some of the main oil- and resource-producing African states, such as Sudan, Angola, and Congo. Reflecting its ever-growing need to secure international sources of oil and other resources, by 2005 China came to account for 31 percent of the global growth in oil demand and imported 28 percent of its oil from Africa. These circumstances drove substantial Chinese financing for often Chinese construction of infrastructure and other means to extract oil and other raw materials needed for China's development.[63]

Other salient data underlining the importance of Africa in Chinese foreign relations prior to the ascendance of Xi Jinping to leadership in 2012 included the following:

- *Leadership attention and contacts.* President Hu Jintao visited four African countries in February 2009, marking his fourth visit to Africa since becoming president in 2003. Premier Wen Jiabao led China's delegation to the fourth China-Africa Cooperation Forum (CACF), held in Egypt in November 2009. He pledged to double the $5 billion low-cost loan for African development promised at the 2006 CACF, and he detailed a wide range of debt relief, environmental, education, training, and other Chinese offers and opportunities for African countries. China had diplomatic relations and embassies in all but a small handful of African states (four still recognized Taiwan), maintained extensive party ties with African political parties, and developed growing relations with regional and subregional organizations like the African Development Bank.
- *Economic relations.* China's trade with Africa grew by 30 percent a year in the previous decade, reaching $106.8 billion in 2008. The trade was spread among various countries, with Angola and South Africa being the most important trading partners. Chinese success in selling manufactured and other goods to Africa generally balanced China's large-scale imports of African commodities. In 2009 China became Africa's largest trading partner. China's cumulative investment at the end of 2010 was said by official Chinese media to be worth $9.3 billion. Chinese aid included forgiveness of debts to China by poorer African countries valued at almost $3 billion. There were several billion dollars of financing provided by a special Sino-African development fund, as well as financing, including loans from official Chinese banks backed by commodities and other collateral, in support of large-scale infrastructure projects in Angola, Sudan, Congo, and other resource-rich countries. China's provision of such financing engendered serious controversy among Western countries and some African constituencies concerned with China's provisions to support corrupt or otherwise unsavory regimes.
- *Social, cultural, and other interchange.* The more than one million Chinese in Africa included professionals in Chinese commercial and government institutions, Chinese laborers working on projects throughout the continent, and Chinese traders and small-business people focused on selling Chinese commodities to African consumers. The Chinese government followed past practice in pursuing active cultural exchange programs with African countries and sending Chinese medical personnel to Africa. Chinese-funded Confucius Institutes, whose mission is to spread Chinese language and culture abroad, were established in a dozen locations in Africa.

• *Military relations*. China sustained an active program of military exchanges throughout Africa. Chinese arms sales generally remained at a low level, though Chinese arms sales to controversial governments like Sudan and Zimbabwe received critical attention in international media. Chinese military and other security forces were active participants in UN-backed peacekeeping efforts in several African countries. Since 2009, China maintained warships along the Horn of Africa to work with international security efforts to counter pirate attacks against international shipping off the coast of Somalia.[64]

## Africa in Xi Jinping's Foreign Policy

Xi Jinping's assertiveness in Chinese foreign policy was less in evidence in Africa than in relations with the United States, Russia, China's neighbors in Asia, and much of Europe. China sustained its position as Africa's largest trading partner, with about 15 percent of Africa's trade. However, the value of trade dropped more than 30 percent in 2016. Chinese media lauded the annual trade levels of 2018 and 2019 of a bit over $200 billion, forgetting the headlines in official Chinese media in 2015 noting a trade value of close to $300 billion that year and a forecast of $400 billion by 2020.[65] China's OECD-equivalent aid to Africa averaged about $2.5 billion, and its foreign direct investment to Africa was about $3 billion annually. China accounted for about 5 percent of Africa's global FDI stock.[66]

Africa was belatedly added to China's Belt and Road Initiative. China remained the largest bilateral provider of funds for African infrastructure projects, claiming a 40 percent share. Some large projects were successfully completed (the $4.5 billion Addis Ababa–Djibouti Railway); others were underway but delayed and much more costly than forecast (Kenya's 80 percent Chinese-financed railway from Mombasa to Nairobi went four times over budget); and some were seriously stalled (the $11 billion megaport and economic zone at Bagamoyo, Tanzania).[67]

The centerpiece of Chinese high-level engagement with African countries remained the Forum on China-Africa Cooperation (FOCAC). Meeting every three years, the forum continued to highlight China's regional engagement strategies; launched educational and cultural initiatives; and promoted large bilateral trade, investment, and aid initiatives. Beijing stressed close relations and commitment to each African nation during the Chinese president's meetings with each visiting African head of state. Along with FOCAC, China collaborated closely with the African Union, with China in 2015 accrediting its first full-time ambassador to the AU. Only the United States had done so before.[68]

The most recent FOCAC, held in Beijing in 2018, was attended by more Africa heads of state and government than attended the UN General Assembly that year. The meeting nonetheless reflected a slowing in China's previously rigorous growth in involvement with Africa. China's pledges of financing at FOCAC sessions routinely went well beyond the previous forum. They were $5 billion in 2006, $10 billion in 2009, $20 billion in 2012, and $60 billion in 2015. In 2018 the pledge registered no increase at $60 billion. Moreover, the amount of concessionality and preferentiality of the Chinese financing decreased. Meanwhile, China highlighted investment in Africa at the 2018 FOCAC, but actual Chinese investment in Africa in the previous year was less than 20 percent of Chinese investment in Latin America. Chinese cumulative investment stock in Latin America was more than $200 billion by the end of 2017, while Chinese investment in Africa was half that amount.[69]

Other notable features of Chinese engagement with Africa included the pattern seen in other parts of the world of sometimes thinly disguised but nonetheless active efforts of Chinese Communist Party (CCP) organs and front organizations in building Chinese influence abroad. In Africa, overt cooperation between the CCP and African ruling parties involved frequent exchanges of delegations. The CCP provided cadre training and occasionally material support for African parties. Its relationship with the ruling parties in South Africa and Ethiopia was particularly strong.[70]

Beijing also launched media expansion in Africa in January 2009 with a $6.6 billion investment. Xinhua opened additional news bureaus throughout the continent, and by 2012 the English-language *China Daily* launched an African edition, and state-run China Central Television, later known as the China Global Television Network, opened a broadcast studio—its first outside China—in Kenya. Under the auspices of FOCAC, China also increased the number of scholarships and job training programs that brought Africans to China. At the 2012 FOCAC meeting, President Hu Jintao promised that the Chinese government would increase the number of scholarships to eighteen thousand in the next three years. China also greatly expanded the number of "people-to-people" exchanges involving academics, students, government officials, think tank analysts, journalists, and others. The China-Africa Joint Research and Exchange Program first met in 2010. The China-Africa Think Tank Forum first met in October 2011. Confucius Institutes also supported China's public diplomacy in a majority of African states.[71]

Another element of strong Chinese influence in Africa was the notable development that, as of 2019, 70 percent of Africa's 4G networks were built by the Chinese telecommunications giant Huawei. The firm also constructed compact cell towers wherever it built networks. Thus, Robert Rotberg concluded that nearly all of the nations of the continent relied on Chinese-made technology and were seemingly content with this fact.[72]

On security matters, China was the top supplier of weapons to sub-Saharan Africa, accounting for 27 percent of the region's imports between 2013 and 2017, a 55 percent increase compared to 2008–2012. Beijing also built defense institutional capabilities, with China's State Administration for Science, Technology, and Industry for National Defense (SASTIND) having bilateral agreements with forty-five African countries. China expanded its participation in peacekeeping operations on the continent, including those in Mali, Liberia, Congo, Sudan, and South Sudan. China established its first military base abroad in Djibouti in 2017.[73]

Overall, many African countries acknowledged and appreciated China's role in critical areas, notably infrastructure development and peacekeeping operations. Few governments turned down promising opportunities under the rubric of China's BRI. Occasional outbursts of negative racist treatment of the African diaspora in China failed to upset state relations. Periodically, a change in leadership in an African country led to negative reevaluation concerning Chinese-funded projects, resulting sometimes in abandoning or cutting back on the overly ambitious projects of the previous government. Some governments and a large number of civil society organizations in Africa became wary of potential downsides of dependency and security arrangements that compromised national independence because of onerous debt. Among concerned powers, the United States led efforts to counter debt dependence on China on the part of African and other developing states. Djibouti was seen as debt dependent because of the expensive Chinese-funded railroad joining the country with Ethiopia; for this and other reasons, Djibouti was viewed as more susceptible to Chinese requests to establish a military base there.[74]

Apart from using debt dependence to pursue arrangements in line with China's ambitions and not necessarily those of the African states was the pervasive corruption associated with the nontransparent deals carried out under the BRI in Africa and elsewhere. As explained in diplomatic language in a recent US government publication, "Chinese companies in Africa cultivated relationships with local politicians and elites through personal ties, favors, and personal benefits. The practice allowed Chinese state-backed industrialists and entrepreneurs to make inroads in the largely under-regulated African political and business environment where personal ties often trump regulations and accountability."[75]

This pattern of corrupt practices was especially the case in the many authoritarian-ruled governments in Africa and elsewhere, where leaders faced no formal accountability for their actions. For instance, Zambia's president Edgar Lungu (2015–) used Chinese-financed infrastructure to strengthen his move toward greater authoritarian control. The opaque deals featured Zambia paying much more for the actual work being done, allowing the regime and Chinese involved to pocket the difference for their personal use. The Lungu government also contracted for a Chinese firm to revamp and basically control Zambia's national broadcasting service. This was in part to ensure that the service would not criticize China or the Lungu government.[76]

President Adama Barrow of the small state of The Gambia engaged in corrupt practices with a Chinese company, winning favors by funneling funds through his wife, and with numerous Chinese infrastructure projects having unaccountable funding channels that placed The Gambia in a position where its debt burden reached 130 percent of its GDP in 2017. Not dissimilar with what Zambia did to its national broadcast service, the Gambia government of President Barrow contracted with Huawei to reconstruct its National Broadband Network. The United States and Western-aligned governments saw such exposure to Huawei and comparable Chinese firms as opening the state's communications network to Chinese penetration and influence operations.[77]

Unfortunately for those in Africa seeking to preserve national integrity and protect against unwanted foreign penetration, authoritarian leaders like those in Zambia and The Gambia often viewed Chinese-controlled communications and related surveillance systems as helping them to keep track of dissidents and to suppress them if necessary. Indeed, the *Wall Street Journal* in 2019 released a feature story of how employees of Huawei, the dominant communications and security systems provider in both Zambia and Uganda, worked for several days assisting security officers in both states to track the whereabouts and penetrate the communications of leading dissidents in the two countries.[78]

## RELATIONS WITH LATIN AMERICA

Throughout much of the post–Cold War period, China followed a low-key and pragmatic effort to build better relations with Latin American–Caribbean (LAC)[79] countries. Beijing was well aware of China's limited standing in the region. The region remained dominated by US power and influence and also had considerable economic and political relations with European powers, Japan, South Korea, and others. Radical movements in the region in the past looked to Moscow rather than Beijing for support and guidance. Throughout the 1990s and into the next decade, China seemed content to maintain an active diplomatic presence; to engage in a wide variety of government-sponsored political, economic, and military contacts; and to see China's economic relations with the region grow to a point where China–Latin America trade, while only a small fraction of Chinese overall trade, surpassed Chinese trade with Africa by the late 1990s.[80]

Post-Mao leaders pursued pragmatic approaches in order to build conventional political, economic, and military relations with the established Latin American governments. As in other parts of the developing world, Chinese leaders eschewed the tendency of Maoist leaders to take sides on Latin American issues, especially those having symbolic value in the East-West and Sino-Soviet competition for global influence. Instead, they sought to align China with whatever consensus was emerging among Latin American states over sensitive issues.

A year-end assessment in December 1997 emphasized the economic incentives driving China's policy toward Latin America at that time. It said the region's overall growth had reached a seventeen-year high of 5 percent, and it highlighted Latin America's new openness to trade, investments, and other economic interchange with various world economic centers. China's trade with the region had more than doubled since 1990, growing from $3 billion in that year to $8 billion in 1998.[81] A steady stream of generally second-level Chinese leaders traveled to Latin America and welcomed Latin American dignitaries visiting China.[82] There were some exchanges between military leaders. China gave high priority to countering Taiwan's influence in the region. Criticism of US dominance in Latin America was a staple of Chinese propaganda, but it dropped off beginning in mid-2001, foreshadowing the emphasis on China's "peaceful rise."

At the start of the twenty-first century, the priority that Chinese leaders gave to the region was relatively low, similar to Chinese attention to the Middle East and Africa. Chinese activities reflected multifaceted political and economic interests focused on competition with Taiwan and a search for advantageous trade opportunities. Beijing also nurtured relations with Latin American countries to ensure their support in the United Nations and other world bodies.[83]

As China became increasingly interested in obtaining oil and other needed resources in the twenty-first century, Chinese interest in Latin America rose markedly, as did Chinese interest in the Middle East and Africa, for similar reasons. This increased China's public profile in Latin American affairs, and some in the region sought to cultivate ties with China in opposition to the United States. Chinese leaders for their part welcomed positive attention from the region but remained reluctant to take any leadership role that would involve major commitments or compromise their efforts to sustain businesslike relations with the United States. They also found that closer economic relations with Latin American countries came with significant complaints and resentments that complicated Chinese relations with several countries in the region.

Economically, two-way trade flows increased more than 500 percent, from $8 billion in 1999 to $40 billion in 2004, and kept growing. Much of the activity centered on Chinese efforts to secure access to natural resources. As a result, the large increases in trade focused on a few Latin American countries that provided the raw materials China was seeking, notably copper, nickel, iron ore, petroleum, grains, wood, frozen fish, fish meal, sugar, leather, and chemical substances. Increased trade also saw a large upsurge in Chinese manufactured goods exported throughout Latin American markets. From 1990 to 2003, Latin American exports to China grew 21.1 percent annually, while imports from China increased by 30 percent annually. The pattern continued in later years. [84]

These developments meant that the relative importance of China as a trading partner for Latin America increased markedly. The downturn in US and other Western economies during the economic recession beginning in 2008 and numerous large Chinese investments and multibillion-dollar lines of credit to secure energy and other resources in Latin America saw China emerge as the top trading partner of Brazil and a leading trader in several other Latin American countries. However, in 2011, total China–Latin America trade flows remained one-fourth of the trade that occurred between Latin American countries and the United States. [85]

Reports of large amounts of Chinese investment in Latin America, including a reported $100 billion in investment projected up to 2015, were featured during President Hu Jintao's widely publicized visit to Latin America in late 2004. [86] At first, actual investments were slow in coming. Later multibillion-dollar projects represented a significant shift in Chinese investment trends, which emerged as China's economy and its foreign exchange holdings grew. The turn of the decade registered a significant increase in Chinese investment. Between 2000 and 2017, Chinese firms invested in 328 transactions worth a total of $109.1 billion. By value, Brazil (China's largest regional trading partner) accounted for $48 billion (44 percent) of Chinese FDI, followed by Peru at $18.3 billion (16.7 percent) and Argentina at $11.9 billion (10.1 percent). The largest number of Chinese FDI transactions went to Brazil with 107 (32.6 percent), Mexico with 68 (20.7 percent), and Peru with 31 (10.1 percent). China became the region's fourth-largest foreign investor. [87] China's investments were directed toward projects that facilitated the procurement of natural resources (for example, roads and port facilities), and they were concentrated in a few countries where the resource base is significant (Brazil, Argentina, Chile, Peru, Venezuela, and Ecuador). As Chinese investment abroad grew, it became more widely known that figures showing cumulative Chinese investment in Latin America could be exaggerated, as a large proportion of this "investment" went to such tax havens as the British Virgin Islands and the Cayman Islands, [88] and these tax havens were also the source of most of the Latin American investment going to China. [89]

As in the case of Chinese financing of infrastructure efforts in African and other developing countries, China engaged in similar financing efforts to build roads, railroads, refineries, ports, and other facilities in Latin America. Little of this would be considered foreign assistance by Western standards, and Chinese foreign assistance to Latin America was thought to be very low. From 2005 to the turn of the decade, the China Development Bank and the

Export-Import Bank of China provided $150.4 billion in financing to Latin American governments and their state-owned enterprises (SOEs), exceeding the combined lending from the World Bank, the Inter-American Development Bank, and the CAF-Development Bank of Latin America. The China Development Bank accounted for nearly $120 billion of this lending, and the Export-Import Bank of China comprised the remaining $30.4 billion. In 2009 and 2010, the China Development Bank extended multibillion-dollar lines of credit to energy companies and government entities, notably in Brazil, Ecuador, and Venezuela. The loans were secured by revenue earned from the sale of oil at market prices to Chinese national oil companies. The loans were distinguished by their large size and long terms. They were attractive at that time because many companies were postponing major investments in oil development as a result of cash flow problems, and other financial institutions were unwilling to lend such large amounts of capital for such long terms.[90]

The positive effects of China becoming Latin America's largest creditor nation amid growing Chinese economic ties with Latin America were reduced by a variety of complications and negative features of the economic ties. The loans-for-oil deals were often unsustainable and became major problems in Chinese relations with Venezuela and Ecuador in recent years. As in other developing countries, Chinese-funded projects were usually carried out by Chinese firms, which sometimes employed Chinese labor. The overall situation led to local resentment over the perceived absence of local employment and development opportunities as China concentrated on access and cost-effective removal of raw materials in ways reminiscent of past foreign entrepreneurs.[91]

Meanwhile, countries in Latin America that were not major exporters of resources tended to focus on the fact that they could not compete with incoming Chinese manufactured goods and that those goods also took their important markets in the United States and elsewhere. Countries that exported products similar to those of China (notably Mexico, but also many Central American and Caribbean countries) experienced intense competition with China.[92] Additionally, important constituents in the resource-exporting countries also reacted negatively to incoming Chinese manufactured imports and overall Chinese competition for world markets. Brazil's Industrial Federation of São Paulo condemned a move by the Brazilian government to declare China a market economy as a "political decision" that left "Brazilian industry in a vulnerable position" and would bring "prejudicial consequences to various industrial sectors." Similarly, reports that Brasilia and Beijing were soon to begin negotiations for a free-trade agreement (FTA) were quelled when Brazilian business leaders feared that local businesses would not be able to compete with Chinese companies.[93]

Politically, the Taiwan factor continued to drive China's political relations in Latin America. Almost half of the governments that officially recognized Taiwan were in Latin America and the Caribbean. Other than Paraguay, all were in Central America and the Caribbean. These countries were a major focus of Taiwan's foreign policy, and Taiwan maintained their loyalty with generous economic aid packages. In 2003, for example, Taiwan was the single largest aid donor to Haiti, Grenada, St. Kitts and Nevis, St. Vincent and the Grenadines, and Dominica.[94] In return, this bloc annually cosponsored resolutions in the UN General Assembly calling on the body to consider membership for Taiwan. Given the "dollar diplomacy" of Beijing and Taipei as they competed for international recognition, small countries often switched recognition when given a good offer from one side or the other.[95] As noted in chapter 7, the coming to power in 2008 of the moderate Ma Ying-jeou administration in Taiwan resulted in an understanding with Beijing that halted the competitive pursuit of diplomatic recognition.[96]

Latin America, including Central America and the Caribbean, also remained significant to China because of the number of votes the region represented in international bodies, especially the United Nations. China also sought allies among Latin American countries as it quietly pursued admittance to a number of regional organizations. It established ties with the Organization of American States, the Association for Latin American Integration, the Caribbean Development Bank, and the Inter-American Development Bank.

China's relations with Latin American countries also had a South-South dimension that supported Chinese efforts to work over the long term against US dominance and to create a multipolar world. China's support for Brazil's bid to become a permanent member of the UN Security Council, cooperation agreements in the areas of science and technology, and solidarity in pushing for a favorable international trade regime were part of Beijing's South–South agenda that long existed in Chinese foreign policy. Chinese leaders also participated actively and often cooperatively with Brazilian leaders in various international groups dealing with global development and governance. Notably, China collaborated closely with Brazil, India, and Russia in a new international grouping known as the BRIC. As noted, the group was joined by South Africa in 2011, becoming BRICS.[97]

China's political relationship with Latin America's leftist leaders was more complicated. China was cautious in its political relations with Venezuela, despite Beijing's strong interest in Venezuela's oil. Chinese officials at this time were reluctant to posture against the United States in Latin America.[98] Regarding Cuba, China sustained a long-term relationship. From the end of the Cold War and the termination of Soviet aid to Cuba, Sino-Cuban relations increased. China's top leaders visited the island, including Hu Jintao in 1997, 2004, and 2008.[99] Following Hu's stop during his 2004 Latin

American tour, China announced that it would extend Cuba interest-free loans, donate $12 million for hospitals and school uniforms, and strengthen ties in the areas of biotechnology, oil exploration, mining, tourism, and telecommunications. There also were repeated reports of deepening China-Cuba military and intelligence cooperation. They centered on reported Chinese arms sales and Chinese acquisition of former Soviet-operated signals intelligence outposts in Cuba.[100] Whatever was taking place was not seen as posing a threat to the United States, according to US officials.[101]

Another cluster of allegations against China focused on supposed Chinese maneuvers to control the Panama Canal. The concern stemmed from the fact that Hong Kong–based Hutchinson Whampoa Limited, a company that had links to China, owned the port facilities in Cristobel and Balboa, on both ends of the canal, and had received an offer to develop a former US facility at Rodman's Point. Some judged that the company was a cover for the Chinese government and that it engaged in surveillance and might resort to sabotage in the event of a Sino-US war over Taiwan.[102] No action was taken on this concern.

## Latin America in Xi Jinping's Foreign Policy

Xi Jinping traveled to Latin America on several occasions, most recently to attend the G20 meeting in Argentina in 2019. The government's goals for the region focusing on economic relations and political influence were set forth in Xi's address to leaders of the Community of Latin American and Caribbean States (CELAC). This thirty-three-country bloc formed in 2011 did not include the United States or Canada. It gathered in Beijing for the first time for a two-day forum in January 2015. There Xi announced that Chinese investment in Latin America over the next ten years would be valued at $250 billion and China's trade with the region in the time period would reach $500 billion.[103] At the forum, China and the CELAC countries agreed to a five-year cooperation plan covering politics, security, trade, investment, finance, infrastructure, energy, resources, industry, agriculture, science, and people-to-people exchanges.[104]

Coincident with Xi's visit to the region in November 2016, the Chinese government released its second policy paper on the Latin America–Caribbean region that outlined major objectives and vehicles for engagement with the region. This document largely reiterated the economic and trade priorities first outlined in China's 2008 policy paper. It stated that China sought to strengthen cooperation on the basis of "equality and mutual benefit" in several key areas, including exchanges and dialogues, trade and investment, agriculture, energy, infrastructure, manufacturing, and technological innovation. The paper stated that China would "actively carry out military exchanges and cooperation with Latin American and Caribbean countries" but also emphasized that China "does not target or exclude any third party." The policy paper also endeavored to strengthen diplomatic, political, and security cooperation through China's direct engagement with CELAC as an alternative to the US-led Organization of American States. At a second China-CELAC ministerial meeting held in January 2018, both sides agreed to an updated cooperation plan extending through 2021. In 2017, Xi also invited Latin American countries to participate in his signature Belt and Road Initiative, which focused on infrastructure development in various regions around the world.[105]

For their part, regional leaders and officials frequently visited China. Bilateral partnership agreements with the PRC were signed with several countries in the region, including "strategic partnerships" with Argentina, Brazil, Chile, Costa Rica, Ecuador, Mexico, Peru, Uruguay, and Venezuela. Recently sixteen Latin American and Caribbean countries participated in the BRI. Only one Latin American head of state, Chile's president, attended China's second Belt and Road Forum in 2019.[106]

Economic trends showed an enduring relationship. As noted above, China was the region's top creditor, second-largest trading partner, and fourth-largest investor. While overall second to the United States in the region, China was the number-one trading partner for Brazil, Chile, and Peru. In 2016, China accounted for nearly 9 percent of regional exports and 18 percent of regional imports. Latin American–Caribbean exports to China focused on agriculture, mining, and oil extraction, with these three sectors accounting for 70 percent of LAC exports to China, 70 percent of Chinese state financing to the region, and 52 percent of Chinese foreign direct investment to the region by value. The predominance of soybeans, copper, iron ore, and oil in exports deepened LAC's dependence on commodities for economic growth. In addition, increasing imports of low-cost Chinese-manufactured goods were directly competing with LAC's manufacturers.[107] Regional trade with China hit record levels in 2019; the region exported $141.5 billion in goods to China and imported $161.7 billion in Chinese goods. Since both exports and imports rose at about the same rate, the resulting merchandise trade deficit held steady from 2018. Regional exports were mainly soybeans, copper, petroleum, and iron. Countries that exported these commodities ran trade surpluses with China; other LAC countries saw growing trade deficits. The China-US trade war created an upsurge in Chinese imports of soybeans from South American suppliers to replace the soybeans previously supplied by US exporters.[108]

From 2005 to 2015, Chinese state policy banks provided more than $150 billion in loans to the region, exceeding the combined lending from the World Bank, the Inter-American Development Bank, and the CAF-Development Bank of Latin America. This financing weakened the influence of the United States and the international financial institutions it supported. Chinese financing also increased the seemingly unsustainable indebtedness of countries such as Venezuela and Ecuador. As in other parts of the world, China leveraged a country's financial and economic dependence to support Chinese foreign policy objectives and gain control of strategic assets. Chinese firms participated in nearly one hundred regional infrastructure projects. As seen throughout China's BRI, some projects enhanced regional integration and spurred economic growth, others were not completed or were never started, and others proved not to be cost effective, thereby saddling some regional governments with massive debt burdens and threatening their long-term economic growth.[109]

In a departure from large-scale official Chinese lending in the recent past, regional development finance from the China Development Bank and the Export-Import Bank of China fell to $1.1 billion in 2019, its lowest level in more than a decade. Ecuador, Brazil, and Venezuela ceased borrowing. As noted, both Ecuador and Venezuela faced large debt burdens, leading to hard choices for Chinese creditors seeking payback for their loans. There was an uptick in 2019 in announced Chinese investment for new (greenfield) projects, with $12 billion in new announcements. As in the past, infrastructure involving ports and hydroelectric dams were at the center of Chinese investment interests.[110]

Corruption was a prevailing feature of China's deep involvement with the Venezuelan government of Hugo Chavez (1999–2013) and Nicolás Maduro (2013–), widely viewed as prone to fraudulent practices. China's large loans-for-oil deals resulted in China, with roughly $67 billion loaned since 2007, becoming a main source of Venezuela's external financing, as well as an important partner of its oil-based economy.[111] From 2007 to 2017, Beijing provided more than $60 billion in financing to Venezuela, representing more than 40 percent of total Chinese lending in Latin America. These loans involved mining research and exploration, housing projects, communication satellites, and a railway company. Maduro signed many more bilateral agreements with China during a Beijing visit in 2018. Additionally, reflecting the symbiosis seen in Chinese interactions with other authoritarian regimes seeking to control and suppress dissent, China provided the Maduro government with technological assistance for surveillance and social control through the "homeland card." The card was inspired by China's national identity card program and was used by the Venezuelans to provide surveillance, including tracking voting and social media use, as well as to allocate food and medicine to citizens.[112]

Corrupt practices were on display in Chinese dealings with Ecuador president Rafael Correa (2007–2017) and his government. The regime turned away from the country's traditional sources of financing requiring transparency and accountability. The government leaders relied heavily on China; they concluded sometimes massive infrastructure and other deals for the personal benefit of the ruling elite that caused significant economic and social harm for the country. Heading the list was the Coca Coda Sinclair hydroelectric facility. A Chinese contractor was the required bidder. Chinese loans of $1.7 billion for the project were at a 7 percent interest rate. The Chinese construction of the project led to major flaws, which meant the dam did not produce the anticipated electricity and was not commercially viable. Corrupt practices throughout were apparent in that almost every top Ecuadorian official involved in the dam's construction was convicted on bribery charges. The project represented about 9 percent of Ecuador's $19 billion repayments to China until 2024, involving 80 percent of the county's oil exports.[113]

Despite the above shortcomings, Chinese involvement in major infrastructure projects in Latin American countries led to commitments by the recipient country that seemed expensive to reverse, assuring China of influence in these countries for some time to come. The same Chinese company involved with the Coca Coda Sinclair dam was involved in thirteen of the twenty-eight hydropower projects Chinese firms were carrying out in the region. Chinese firms were also involved in fifteen port construction projects and a few notable power transmission deals. Regarding information and communications technology (ICT) projects, Huawei worked with most of Latin America's telecommunications providers, winning contracts to support and build telecommunications networks in more than twenty countries. Along with the involvement of ZTE and related Chinese firms in regional countries, Huawei's strong influence in the region caused major concern among American policy makers about "placing the region's communications backbone on Chinese networks."[114]

As elsewhere throughout the world, Latin America featured well-funded Chinese efforts to influence and control discourse about China, seeking to portray the Chinese government as a reliable partner and to encourage support for Chinese policies and objectives. In 2018, Latin American and Caribbean countries hosted thirty-nine Confucius Institutes and eleven Confucius Classrooms serving more than fifty thousand students and involving more than eight million people in its cultural activities. Additionally, a China-CELAC Cooperation Plan saw China promise to provide six thousand governmental scholarships, six thousand training opportunities, and four hundred opportunities for on-the-job master's degree programs for CELAC citizens in China between 2015 and 2019, and another six thousand government scholarships between 2019 and 2021. The Chinese government brought a planned one thousand LAC political leaders to China between 2015 and 2020 and another two hundred CELAC politicians by 2021. Chinese media training for regional professionals largely underscored Chinese information management and propaganda techniques, eschewing editorial independence and investigatory journalism.[115]

China's overall military and security activities in Latin America remained limited. As in the past, China maintained high levels of personnel exchanges and engaged in military exercises with Chile, Brazil, Venezuela, and Cuba. Exchanges of officers for training in each other's professional military institutions involved all states that recognized China. The majority of China's military sales in the region were to some of the members of the ALBA alliance (the Bolivarian Alliance for the Americas), a regional pact to counter US regional hegemony. Major recipients were Venezuela, Bolivia, and Ecuador. In 2015 Argentina's government announced its intention to purchase almost $1 billion in Chinese weapons systems, but the deal stalled with a change in government. [116]

As discussed in chapter 7, the rise to power in Taiwan in 2016 of DPP president Tsai Ing-wen, who was unwilling to endorse Beijing's view of Taiwan under its one-China principle, resulted in Beijing resuming strong competition seeking to persuade some of the remaining countries officially recognizing Taiwan to switch to China. In 2017 and 2018, Panama, the Dominican Republic, and El Salvador switched recognition to China. [117]

Looking out, China seemed poised to advance its economic connections and related influence in the Latin American–Caribbean region. China's example of economic growth under authoritarian rule appealed to rulers with authoritarian and sometimes corrupt ambitions in the region. For them and many others, China represented a source of funding and markets during a period of declining interest in Latin America by the United States and Europe. [118] China was viewed positively in most Latin American states. [119] Against this background, the recent worldwide political activism in Chinese embassies and other Chinese government, party, and related front organizations in building closer ties with indigenous elites, media, political parties, think tanks, universities, and other influential elements were relatively unencumbered in pursuing China's advancement. Chinese financing and deep participation in communications networks, hydroelectric projects, and port construction created sinews of influence that would be expensive and difficult to replace.

Limitations on China's advance in the region came from China's uncertain interest and capacity as well as conditions in Latin America. Chinese investors often viewed the region's distance from Asia as an obstacle. The region's regulatory environments and bidding processes remained complex and taxing. Chinese companies' failure to practice due diligence in pursuing nontransparent deals led to unforeseen conflicts, project delays, and cost overruns. Corruption negatively impacted Chinese projects in several countries. Many promised agreements failed to materialize. China has expressed interest in about 150 transport infrastructure projects in Latin America and the Caribbean since 2002, but only half have entered some phase of construction. Recent restrictions on Chinese capital outflows were forecast to tighten on account of the COVID-19 pandemic and related economic decline. Regional antipathy toward China as the source of COVID-19 grew in 2020. And Latin America remained on the edge of the scope of China's BRI; Chinese companies and banks were inclined to pursue opportunities closer to home, where costs were lower and networks were well established. [120]

*Chapter Thirteen*

# Assessing China's Rise amid Acute Rivalry with America

As promised in chapter 1, this concluding chapter addresses the question of how to gauge China's foreign ascendance amid acute rivalry with America. It does so by first examining China's ambitions in Asia and the world and by assessing its conventional strengths and weaknesses and the strengths and weaknesses of its main rival in Asia and the world, the United States. It finds that any power shift from the United States to China in leading the Asia-Pacific remains in the future. China's recent aggressive overreach elicited a powerful American response that will hobble China's path forward in the days ahead. The chapter also considers China's various unconventional sources of power and influence that previously were poorly understood but now figure more prominently in this and other assessments of China's international influence. This author's judgment is that the impact of these unconventional tools of Chinese statecraft does not fundamentally change the balance of power between the United States and China. However, they do require close attention and corrective countermeasures by the United States and other concerned powers going forward and thus are listed in an appendix at the end of the chapter for the reader's consideration.

## XI JINPING'S FOREIGN POLICY VISION

Xi Jinping and supporting publicists built on gains in China's rising influence in Asian and world affairs to craft a vision called the China Dream. Though supported by Chinese elite and popular opinion, the image of a powerful and benign China moving smoothly to international leadership proved weak in the face of realities constraining China.[1] Xi Jinping's China

dream of "national rejuvenation" sought a unified and powerful China as
Asia's leader and a great power. As noted earlier, Xi broke with the more
restrained policies of previous leaders following Deng Xiaoping's instructions in foreign affairs. Xi was bolder and no longer emphasized reassurance
of the United States, Asian neighbors, and others.

 Xi's new foreign policy approach involved major challenges for America
and its interests in the prevailing international order:

- Growing military, paramilitary, economic, and other state power coerced
  neighbors to give way to China's broad territorial claims and other interests, thereby challenging the United States and its defense of regional
  stability and the status quo.
- Often hidden efforts by Chinese spies and other party, government, and
  military agents fostered influence and favorable elite and public opinion in
  a wide range of developed and developing countries. Beijing sought support for Chinese foreign policies at odds with those backed by the United
  States.
- The Belt and Road Initiative (BRI) and other institutions that undermined
  US leadership or excluded the United States used China's large foreign
  exchange reserves and massive excess industrial capacity to launch various self-serving international economic development programs.
- China's military buildup was aimed at American forces in the Asia-Pacific
  region, and China built forces for use beyond China's rim while fostering
  debt and other dependencies among smaller, strategically located states,
  thus allowing for positive responses from them to host Chinese military
  forces overseas.
- An ever stronger entente with Russia in pursuit, through coercive and
  other means, of revisionist ambitions undermining US interests in respective spheres of influence.
- Continuing gross violations of World Trade Organization (WTO) norms
  and practices through cyber theft of economic assets, widespread intellectual property rights (IPR) violations, unfair market access restrictions on
  US and other developed countries' companies, state-directed industrial
  policies leading to targeted acquisition of US and other high technology,
  large-scale overcapacity disadvantaging US and other foreign producers,
  and currency practices disadvantaging US and other foreign traders. Made
  in China 2025, a massive effort benefiting from the above economic practices, sought dominance in high-technology industries to protect China
  from feared US technological leadership.
- Intensified internal repression and tightened political control, all with serious adverse consequences for US interests and those of other developed
  countries.

President Barack Obama was slow and ineffective in responding to Xi Jinping's advances. American critics, who rose in influence after President Obama left office, saw Xi Jinping duplicitously playing a double game, pretending to seek cooperation while relentlessly undermining America.[2] US opinion was negative about the Chinese government but sought to avoid confrontation. Though China was not deemed a high priority by most candidates, a tougher US approach toward China was endorsed by both leading candidates and most others in the 2016 US presidential election campaign.[3]

International factors facilitating Xi's foreign advances in fulfilling the China Dream were an irresolute American government; a decline in the ability and willingness of US allies and partners to counter China's affronts; weaknesses in Asia, notably Southeast Asia, allowing Chinese expansion of control into the disputed South China Sea; and Russia, facing strong sanctions in the West and thus becoming ever more dependent on China.[4] Against this background, Xi and Chinese officials and publicists fostered an image of China as a generous and benign power, contributing more to the United Nations and other international organizations favored by Beijing and fostering growth through the BRI and other China-favored mechanisms. They even reinterpreted Chinese history to support an ahistorical assertion common in Beijing today that China never was aggressive in its long history and would not be so today.

## IMAGE MEETS REALITIES: CONSTRAINTS ON CHINA'S RISE

Constraints on Chinese influence in regional and world affairs started at home. Chinese leaders faced an ongoing and major challenge in trying to sustain one-party rule in the world's largest society, one that is both dynamic and economically vibrant. To sustain one-party rule required massive expenditures and widespread leadership attention to internal security and control and strong continued economic growth that advanced the material benefits of the Chinese people and ensured general public support and legitimacy for the communist government. As shown below, these domestic concerns were multifaceted, expensive to deal with, and very hard to resolve; they represented the main focus of China's large government and Communist Party apparatus.[5]

Moreover, the prime importance of economic growth and continued one-party rule required stability at home and abroad, especially in nearby Asia where conflict and confrontation would have a serious negative impact on Chinese economic growth. Unfortunately for uniform adherence to these policy priorities, the Chinese leaders had other seemingly contradictory priorities. They involved protecting Chinese security and advancing Chinese control of sovereign claims. These other top concerns were evident in the long and costly buildup of military forces to deal with a Taiwan contingency involving the United States and more recent use of various means of state power to advance territorial control in nearby disputed seas. Of course, these priorities seemed to contradict the priority of stability in Asia for the sake of needed economic development. This made for a muddled Chinese approach to its nearby neighbors and other concerned powers, notably the United States. China's portrayal as benevolent and focused on mutual benefit was mixed with strong determination to have its way at others' expense on sensitive sovereignty disputes and related security issues.

Meanwhile, looking beyond nearby Asia, there was less clarity among specialists in China and abroad as to where Chinese international ambitions for regional and global leadership fit in the current priorities of China's leaders. However, there was little doubt that domestic concerns got overall priority.[6] As discussed in chapter 1, significant domestic concerns involved problems in leadership legitimacy, corruption, widening income gaps and social division, widespread social turmoil and mass demonstrations,[7] a highly resource-intensive economy and related enormous environmental damage, an aging population, and an economic model at the point of diminishing returns with no clear path to effective reform.

Domestic preoccupations, reinforced by extraordinary measures to deal with the COVID-19 pandemic, meant China's continued reluctance to undertake the costs and risks of international leadership because it had so many important requirements at home. One result was that China continued to rely on the US-led world order where it benefited China, while moving incrementally to displace US leadership.

As far as international constraints were concerned, the so-called trade war with the United States brought home to Chinese leaders how strongly China depended on the United States economically. The United States exerted much greater influence than China on international technology, financial, and trade flows that China depended on. The economic face-off with America caused major harm to Chinese economic development—the linchpin of regime legitimacy in China.[8] China also depended on the United States for secure passage of its growing imports of oil and gas from the Persian Gulf. Moreover, neither side could deal effectively with North Korea without the other. Additional areas of interdependence involved climate change, antiterrorism, nuclear nonproliferation, and cyber security.

The respite in the trade war provided by the so-called phase one trade agreement in January 2020 was quickly overshadowed by strident acrimony and acute rivalry prompted by the COVID-19 pandemic. Notably, China launched a world propaganda campaign that covered up responsibility for initially mishandling the virus and causing a global plague. China was portrayed as effectively curbing the virus at home and generously offering medical supplies abroad. Some prominent Americans argued for closer US government cooperation with China to deal with the crisis, but President Trump, Democratic presidential candidates, bipartisan congressional majorities, mainstream media, and public opinion all viewed China more negatively. US hardening deepened as it became clear that in the initial stages of the outbreak China cornered the world market in the medical equipment and supplies needed to fight the virus. The result was that many states, ill stocked to deal with the outbreak, including the United States, found no available supplies because of Chinese hoarding, profiteering, and targeted international donations to burnish China's world image.[9]

The broad negative US view of China also prompted forecasts that Republican political strategists would continue through the election year to blame China and thereby distract attention from the Trump administration's ineffective handling of the crisis. President Trump shifted sharply against China, alleging that Beijing was working against his reelection. One source of acrimony was the Trump administration mustering evidence to show that Chinese malfeasance in a highly sensitive research laboratory in Wuhan was the likely cause of the epidemic, calling for an international investigation into the matter, and charging that Beijing should be held liable for the massive international costs.[10]

Regarding China's ascendance in its top foreign policy priority area, nearby Asia, Beijing's record remained mediocre. As noted in chapter 1, an inventory of China's relationships with other leading regional powers, notably Japan and India, and important middle powers like South Korea and Australia, showed serious reversals over the past two decades. Similarly serious downturns occurred in areas keenly sensitive to Chinese interests, Taiwan, Hong Kong, and North Korea. Notably, Beijing's passivity in the face of protracted anti-China mass demonstrations in Hong Kong in 2019 and its failure to influence Taiwan's elections in 2020 projected a constrained rather than decisive Chinese leadership. These setbacks offset widely touted gains China made in the South China Sea and among some Southeast Asian and other neighboring countries. Beijing's strong intervention in 2020, forcing implementation of a national security law and coercive law enforcement measures, seemed to overwhelm opposition in Hong Kong but deepened already strong disapproval of the Chinese government among Democratic governments and some other foreign countries.[11] This mixed record had persisted for thirty years as China tried with mediocre results to expand its influence in nearby Asia after the Cold War. Unfortunately for China, negative legacies of past violent and coercive policies and practices prompted regional wariness of contemporary Chinese intentions. Chinese foreign policy in post–Cold War Asia also showed conflicting objectives involving peaceful development of mutual interest on the one hand and steely determination to gain control of disputed territories and resources at neighbors' expense on the other. There were repeated switches, at times stressing reassu-

rance and peaceful development and at other times stressing determination
and intimidation in pursuing sensitive issues of sovereignty and security.

Looking out, whether China's importance as a powerful military force
and prime trader and investor with nearby Asia will override security, sovereignty, and other differences is hard to predict and is unlikely to be resolved
anytime soon. Uncertainty over US resolve to sustain regional leadership
remained an important determinant in China's quest for Asian primacy,
though, as shown below, recent US government hardening toward China
clearly complicated and constrained China's rise going forward.

Regarding Chinese foreign policy concerns in the broad-ranging Belt and
Road Initiative begun in 2013, Beijing advanced and modified the strong
"going out" policies of Chinese investment and financing abroad seen in the
previous decade.[12] That past effort focused on attaining access to oil and
other raw materials needed for China's resource-hungry economy. Recent
Chinese economic reforms sought to reduce such intense resource use. The
recent push for Chinese foreign investment and financing was to enable
construction abroad of Chinese-supplied infrastructure provided by the enormous excess capacity of Chinese companies for such construction and supply
now that major infrastructure development inside China had been curtailed
under recent economic reforms. Locating some of China's heavily resource-
intensive and polluting industries abroad eased China's serious pollution
problems and enhanced its ability to meet commitments to international climate change agreements. Economically, the recent outward push of Chinese
investment also helped connect the poorer regions of central and western
China to international markets and thereby advanced their development, the
BRI provided investment opportunities promising better returns for China's
$3 trillion foreign exchange reserves invested in low-yield foreign securities,
and the investment push broadened the international use of China's currency.
Strategically, the BRI improved Chinese access to key international land and
sea corridors, reduced China's vulnerability posed by actual or possible US
military control of transit choke points for Chinese shipping, and advanced
overall Chinese relations with important countries. Several countries became
"debt dependent" on Chinese financing; many more became dependent on
sophisticated Chinese supplied and maintained information and communications technology (ICT) products, hydroelectric dams, advanced port facilities, and other infrastructure very difficult and expensive to replace.

The BRI was also the centerpiece of exaggerated Chinese image building
that portrayed China as a confident and generous global economic leader.
The realities seen in summing up the results of China's decade-long "going
out" strategy and the trends in recent Chinese economic behavior showed not
only substantial growth in Chinese economic activism, influence, and power
but also pervasive constraints and strong negative international reactions.

In particular, trade significantly declined in importance as an element of Chinese influence abroad. After China joined the WTO in 2001, Beijing relied on its burgeoning trade with Asian and international markets as the primary source of Chinese international economic influence. For several years China's trade grew at double the rate of China's economic growth of around 10 percent. In contrast, while the Chinese economy continued to grow at a rate of around 7 percent in 2015 and 2016, the growth of Chinese trade collapsed—growth was zero in those two years. The value of trade began to rise again in 2017, but a return to the days of previous high annual growth seemed unlikely, and that even before the onset of the major negative impacts of the US-China trade war and the COVID-19 pandemic. [13]

There also were substantial constraints in Chinese investments and loans. "Going out" policies begun twenty years before were accompanied by massive publicity for Chinese multibillion-dollar agreements to invest in various developing countries and to promote infrastructure constructed by Chinese companies with loans from Chinese banks. The recent BRI and related initiatives were also accompanied by such positive publicity. In contrast, foreign expert assessments were more sober. China's actual investment in developing countries remained limited. Its more important position as the leading world provider of financing for infrastructure resulted in only a few instances, often very controversial, where China represented the dominant international economic power (e.g., Venezuela, Cambodia, Djibouti). More commonly, Beijing was seen as a growing source of influence but still as only "one among several" foreign sources of economic influence and support. [14]

As discussed in earlier chapters detailing developments in different parts of the world, serious shortcomings emerged in China's role as a provider of infrastructure financing to developing countries. The past record of China announcing massive deals and delivering much less continued. The reasons hinged on the difficulty in carrying out large projects in poorly governed countries that were bad credit risks. Other factors included changes in governments and much greater opposition to Chinese practices by the United States and some other developed countries. The US government as well as think tanks and the media in the United States and other developed countries were in the lead recently in exposing how the Chinese government used loans and economic dependency to infiltrate and influence decision making in vulnerable developing countries to benefit Chinese expansion abroad. Special attention was devoted to China seeking ports in the Indo-Pacific region for its forces, the expansion of Chinese telecommunications to dominant positions in these countries, and backing for Chinese expansion in the South China Sea and its egregious crackdown against dissent in the Xinjiang region of China. [15]

# THE US POSITION IN ASIA

Until the past decade, a comparison of Chinese policies and practices with those of the United States in the Asia-Pacific region and the rest of the world underlined how far China had to go to supersede American leadership. However, after many years of US accommodation of China's rise through constructive engagement and downplaying differences came the erratic and unpredictable foreign policy behavior of the current US president, adding to regional and international uncertainty about American leadership. Extraordinary domestic distractions, notably the congressional impeachment of the president in 2019 and the pandemic of 2020, compounded the difficulties of leaders throughout the world in predicting American resolve to stay the course in Asian and world affairs. Going forward, would the United States persist in its past leadership role in competition with China in the Asia-Pacific region? Other possibilities ranged from retrenchment to conflict. In particular, retrenchment meant that existing constraints on China in Asia would weaken substantially and China would have a freer hand in advancing toward regional dominance.

Nevertheless, realities of US power and practice demonstrated enduring strengths. And the past three years saw a sharp US policy shift away from past drift in order to confront rising China, now widely viewed as America's number-one opponent. The new American toughness was led by the administration and bipartisan congressional leaders. It was reinforced by an ever-growing outpouring of government and nongovernment assessments disclosing in detail China's heretofore often hidden measures to expand at American expense while publicly avowing cooperation. Beijing was now widely viewed as duplicitous, making meaningful agreements and accommodation more difficult going forward. Media and public opinion became significantly more negative, and sharp criticism of China came from the leading Democratic presidential candidates. [16]

China's leaders did not anticipate the recent American shift and the array of troubles it posed for China's economy, international influence, security, and sovereignty. Facing an aroused America, Xi Jinping's strategy in pursuit of the China Dream came under revision, the latest episode in China being compelled by circumstances to shift strategy in order to accommodate changing conditions and rising constraints.

The basic determinants of US strength and influence in the Asia-Pacific region involved five factors, starting with security. [17] In most of Asia, governments were viable and made the decisions that determined their direction in foreign affairs. Popular, elite, media, and other opinions might influence government officials in their policy toward the United States and other countries, but in the end officials made decisions on the basis of their own calculus. In general, officials saw their governments' legitimacy and success rest-ing on nation building and economic development, which required a stable and secure international environment. Unfortunately, Asia was not particularly stable, and most regional governments were privately wary of, and tended not to trust, each other. As a result, they looked to the United States to provide the security they needed to pursue goals of development and nation building in an appropriate environment. They recognized that the US security role was very expensive and involved great risk, including large-scale casualties if necessary, for the sake of preserving Asian security. They also recognized that neither rising China, nor any other Asian power or coalition of powers, was able or willing to undertake even a small part of these risks, costs, and responsibilities.

Second, the nation-building priority of most Asian governments depended greatly on export-oriented growth. As noted above, much of Chinese and Asian trade depended heavily on exports to developed countries, notably the United States. America ran a massive trade deficit with China and a total annual trade deficit with Asia valued at more than US$500 billion. Asian government officials recognized that China, which consistently ran an overall trade surplus, and other trading partners in Asia were unwilling and unable to bear even a fraction of the cost of such large trade deficits, which nonetheless were very important for Asian governments.

Third, despite the negative popular view in Asia of the George W. Bush administration's policies in Iraq and the broader war on terror, the administration was generally effective in its interactions with Asia's powers—notably China, Japan, and India. The Obama administration built on these strengths. The Obama government's broad rebalancing with regional governments and multilateral organizations had a scope ranging from India to the Pacific Island states to Korea and Japan. Its emphasis on consultation with and inclusion of international stakeholders before coming to policy decisions on issues of importance to Asia and the Pacific was also broadly welcomed and stood in contrast with the previously perceived unilateralism of the Bush administration. Meanwhile, the US Indo-Pacific Command and other US military commands and security and intelligence organizations were at the edge of wide-ranging and growing US efforts to build and strengthen webs of military and related intelligence and security relationships throughout the region.

Fourth, the United States for decades, reaching back to past centuries, engaged the Asia-Pacific region through business, religious, educational, media, and other interchange. Such active nongovernment interaction put the United States in a unique position and reinforced overall American influence. Meanwhile, more than fifty years of generally color-blind US immigration policy, since the ending of discriminatory American restrictions on Asian immigration in 1965, resulted in the influx of millions of Asia-Pacific migrants who called America home and who interacted with their countries of origin in ways that underpinned and reflected well on the US position in the region.

Fifth, part of the reason for the success of US efforts to build webs of security-related and other relationships with Asia-Pacific countries had to do with active contingency planning by many Asia-Pacific governments. As power relations changed in the region, notably on account of China's rise, regional governments generally sought to work positively and pragmatically with rising China on the one hand, but they sought the reassurance of close security, intelligence, and other ties with the United States on the other hand in case rising China shifted to greater assertiveness or dominance.

Against the background of recent Chinese demands, coercion, and intimidation, the Asia-Pacific governments' interest in closer ties with the United States meshed well with the Obama administration's engagement with regional governments and multilateral organizations. The US concern with maintaining stability while fostering economic growth overlapped constructively with the priorities of the majority of regional governments as they pursued their respective nation-building agendas.

Under President Trump, the positive role of the Indo-Pacific Command, legal immigration, and nongovernment American engagement in Asia continued. The president's rhetoric and actions raised questions about support for alliances, but they were offset to some degree with high-level US reassurance and the actions of US national security policy makers. America's role as economic partner was in doubt with the scrapping of the Trans-Pacific Partnership (TPP) and the disruptive trade war with China, but the US market continued to absorb massive flows of regional imports. Nevertheless, media focus rightfully highlighted President Trump's disruptive relations with the region as he ended the rebalance and the US commitment to the TPP, causing a decline in confidence in the United States. Employing unpredictable unilateral actions, he cast doubt on past US commitment to positive regional relations. He also junked related policy transparency, carefully measured responses, and avoidance of dramatic action, linkage, or spillover among competing interests. Those features of US foreign policy had been stressed by the Obama and earlier administrations and were welcomed by Asia-Pacific allies and partners. Trump's presidency showed episodic engagement featuring special attention to North Korea and China. As noted, a strong focus on China as an opponent grew, resulting in the bipartisan toughening toward China, which only strengthened in the lead-up to the 2020 US presidential elections.

In sum, China remained encumbered in nearby regions of Asia, but US influence in the region was in decline. If the US decline continued, China would advance, foreshadowing a major power shift in Asia. Much depended on the effectiveness of American leadership going forward.

A major feature of this volume is the repeated attention going beyond the past practice of examining evidence of conventional Chinese behavior and levers of power and influence in foreign affairs to assess newly prominent, unconventional aspects of Chinese actions and levers of influence that have heretofore been disguised, hidden, denied, or otherwise neglected or unappreciated by foreign specialists assessing Chinese foreign relations. The treatment in this volume notes the importance of these latter means of Chinese foreign policy practice (see the appendix below for a list of the unconventional elements of influence in Chinese foreign policy). Many of these tools clearly advanced Chinese power and influence, but many led to negative outcomes for Chinese interests. Among the most negative outcomes for Chinese interests were the reactions of the United States and some of its allies and partners. In particular, many of the hidden, denied, or otherwise neglected and unappreciated elements of Chinese foreign policy practice showed American policy makers that engagement with China, an ostensibly positive policy toward building constructive relations, was repeatedly being manipulated and exploited by the Chinese party-state in often nefarious ways to undermine the power and influence of the United States in world affairs. And adding to the duplicity and mendacity seen coming from senior Chinese officials on these matters were platitudes of China's benign intent under such rubrics as seeking a "new type of great-power relationship" with the United States and a "community of common destiny" abroad.

China remained prepared to counter any US charges of duplicity with a long list of complaints against American duplicity in its engagement with China. Some of these complaints have merit. For example, to China's chagrin, the United States did not withdraw from Taiwan in the way implied in the Nixon and Carter administrations. However, the point of the discussion here is to assess how well the unconventional tools of Chinese foreign policy tradecraft served China's rise in relation to US power and influence. The answer, in this author's judgment, is that the strong American reaction to China's unconventional practices and the duplicity and mendacity of Chinese officials about these matters substantially added to the harsh US hardening against a broad range of challenges seen posed by China. Against that background, while China widely used unconventional practices to advance its influence and power abroad in recent years, the overall impact of these practices did not redound to China's overall benefit in its competition with the United States in Asian and world affairs.

# APPENDIX: CHINA'S UNCONVENTIONAL ACTIONS AND LEVERS OF INFLUENCE IN FOREIGN AFFAIRS

Since few studies have provided comprehensive treatment of China's unconventional practices in foreign affairs, detailed below is a list to use as a reference for those with an interest in these practices, with some assessment of their impact on China's rise in rivalry with America.

To start, perhaps the most impactful Chinese practices advancing Chinese influence and undermining American interests came within the scope of China's three-decades-long effort using state-directed development policies that plundered foreign intellectual property rights and undermined international competitors. Beijing did so with hidden and overt state-directed economic coercion, egregious government subsidies and other interventions, and import protection and export promotion using highly protected and state-supported products to drive out foreign competition in key industries. The profits went into efforts to achieve dominance in major world industries and build military power to secure China's primacy in Asia and world leadership. They allowed companies like Huawei to attempt to dominate international communications enterprises. The profits also supported China's massive state-directed efforts to lead the high-technology industries that will define economic and eventually military leadership in world affairs. The fact that the United States faced major challenges in countering the adverse implications of China's Belt and Road Initiative and the penetration of Huawei and other ICT firms abroad rested to a considerable degree on the above practices.

Related to this was the impact of Chinese trade, investment, financing, and infrastructure on a wide range of foreign countries. On the one hand, Chinese officials held out offers of trade, investment, funding, and other economic benefits to encourage countries to align more closely with China on issues of importance to the Chinese government. This represented a common and conventional practice in international affairs. On the other hand, Beijing also steadily used these economic relations to develop strong dependency on China. A graphic example was the so-called debt trap for a number of states, brought about by excessive and unsustainable borrowing from Chinese state banks, which did not abide by responsible lending guidelines of developed countries and the international lending and financial institutions they supported. Often the excessive debt was sought by short-sighted, selfish, and corrupt foreign leaders; their successors found that easing the debt burden was impossible without China's close cooperation, as the costs of canceling overly ambitious Chinese-financed infrastructure projects often precluded this action. Such debt dependency on China made these states more accommodating regarding Chinese demands for repayment in equity (e.g., land, ports, and airfields) or Chinese requests for access to military facilities or other favors.

Meanwhile many countries relied heavily on exports to China. They included those selling advanced equipment and manufactured goods and components and those selling oil, gas, iron ore, agricultural products, and other raw materials. Many states depended on Chinese imports and the inflow of Chinese tourists and students to their countries. And many of China's neighbors invested heavily in China. In all such cases, Beijing repeatedly put aside or manipulated WTO norms to use such dependence as leverage to compel the country to meet China's demands on other foreign policy issues. This coercion was applied or threatened by the Chinese government directly or through party channels mobilizing boycotts, demonstrations, and other pressures in China against foreign targets. The many foreign countries subject to these kinds of threats in recent years included Argentina, Australia, Canada, France, Germany, Great Britain, Japan, New Zealand, Norway, the Philippines, South Korea, Taiwan, and the United States. The chapters of this volume also testify to Chinese demands that specific businesses adhere to Chinese requirements over their handling of Taiwan, Hong Kong, and other issues sensitive to China.

As shown in chapters dealing with various authoritarian or corrupt governments, China used practices, unencumbered by WTO, World Bank, IMF, or other international finance institution guidelines, in carrying out nontransparent deals with various states. The agreements served the interests of China in enabling profitable Chinese infrastructure development and deepening Chinese influence while serving the power and personal wants of the authoritarian or corrupt foreign leaders. This symbiosis of Chinese–foreign government interests represented a strong asset in China's growing international influence. Added to this bond was China's provision of communications and surveillance systems that assisted the foreign leaders in tracking and suppressing opponents. Close cooperation in building mutual ties also allowed Chinese construction of communications systems and robust interchange with media outlets in various states. Those outlets pursued news coverage and information that was positive concerning the government and China. Another source of Chinese influence came as such communications and surveillance systems, along with Chinese-provided hydroelectric dams and port operations, caused recipient countries to rely ever more heavily on Chinese firms for maintenance and made the Chinese ties difficult and expensive to replace with another provider. Communications and surveillance systems were also seen as serving the purposes of Chinese intelligence collection and opinion manipulation in the country in ways favorable to China.

Other unconventional coercive methods used to intimidate neighboring states involved usually unpublicized Chinese deployment of maritime militia and coast guard vessels to deter and "bully" governments challenging China's expansive claims in the South and East China Seas. In tandem with such deployments, China recently privately warned Vietnam and the Philippines that countering China on these matters would lead to their decisive military defeat. Repeated shows of force by Chinese naval and air forces in the South and East China Seas and around Taiwan were used for similar purposes of deterring these governments from countering China's demands for deference. Beijing bombers last year teamed up with Russian bombers to probe and challenge the airspace of South Korea and Japan, thereby serving notice of China-Russia cooperation against the claims of these US allies.

The well-funded influence operations abroad of Chinese party and state agents and the front organizations they supported had significant success in mobilizing the Chinese diaspora in various countries, in achieving success in so-called elite capture (winning over foreign dignitaries to work in support of Chinese objectives), and in gaining influence with and control over media and journalism in a number of states. They were backed by diplomats abroad prepared to resort to outrageous invective and threats in demanding deference to China's objectives. Behind these influence operations rested strong efforts to penetrate high-technology centers for desired information through the Chinese government's Thousand Talents Program and other means, including common IPR theft. Also active were Chinese agents recruiting foreign individuals to serve the purposes of Chinese espionage.

China's disregard for international law in pursuit of expansion showed egregiously in its rejection of the July 2016 ruling of an UNCLOS tribunal finding against China's expansive South China Sea claims. China also practiced illegal abduction and prolonged detention of Chinese nationals resident abroad holding foreign citizenship, ignoring the provisions of international conventions. Beijing also used arrests and detentions of foreigners in China as leverage against foreign governments.

Though China denied malign intent, China and Russia worked ever more cooperatively to reduce US influence in their respective spheres of influence, China in Asia and Russia in Europe and the Middle East. With similar denials, China also worked steadily to reduce the unity of ASEAN and of the European Union. It appealed to some members of these groupings at the expense of the unity of the group, which otherwise would impede Chinese ambitions in Southeast Asia and Europe.

Other levers of Chinese influence depended on circumstances. Chinese dams control the flow of water in the Mekong River, strongly impacting countries downriver—Myanmar, Laos, Thailand, Cambodia, and Vietnam—and influencing their postures toward China. Beijing's strong ties with armed separatist groups inside Myanmar provided a major source of leverage in that country.

# Notes

## 1. CONTINUITY AND CHANGE IN CONTEMPORARY CHINESE FOREIGN POLICY

1. White House, *National Security Strategy of the United States*, December 2017, https://www.whitehouse.gov/wp-content/uploads/2017/12/NSS-Final-12-18-2017-0905.pdf; US Department of Defense, *Summary of the National Defense Strategy of the United States*, January 2018, https://www.defense.gov/Portals/1/Documents/pubs/2018-National-Defense-Strategy-Summary.pdf; Anthony Capaccio, "US Faces 'Unprecedented Threat' on China Tech Takeover," *Bloomberg*, June 22, 2018, https://www.bloomberg.com/news/articles/2018-06-22/china-s-thousand-talents-called-key-in-seizing-u-s-expertise.

2. Capaccio, "US Faces 'Unprecedented Threat'"; "Bipartisan Groups of Senators Urge Administration to Safeguard Critical Military and Dual-Use Technology from China," US Senate release, May 22, 2018, https://www.cornyn.senate.gov/content/news/bipartisan-group-senators-urge-administration-safeguard-critical-military-and-dual-use; transcript of speech of Senator Mark Warner at Brookings Institution, Washington, DC, May 9, 2019, https://www.brookings.edu/wp-content/uploads/2019/05/fp_20190509_global_china_transcript.pdf.

3. For an overview of developments in Trump administration policy toward China in 2017–2018, see Robert Sutter, "Trump, America and the World—2017 and Beyond," H-Diplo/ISSF Policy Series, January 19, 2019, https://networks.h-net.org/node/28443/discussions/3569933/issf-policy-series-sutter-trump%E2%80%99s-china-policy-bi-partisan.

4. US Congress, House Armed Services Committee, *Reform and Rebuild: The Next Steps—National Defense Authorization Act FY-2019*, July 2018, https://republicans-armedservices.house.gov/sites/republicans.armedservices.house.gov/files/wysiwyg_uploaded/FY19%20NDAA%20Conference%20Summary%20.pdf; Vivian Salama, "Trump Signs Defense Bill to Boost Military, Target China," *Wall Street Journal*, August 13, 2018, https://www.wsj.com/articles/trump-signs-defense-bill-to-boost-military-target-china-1534196930; Robert Sutter, "The 115th Congress Aligns with the Trump Administration in Targeting China," *Pac-Net* 62 (Honolulu, HI: Pacific Forum CSIS, August 30, 2018), https://csis-prod.s3.amazonaws.com/s3fs-public/publication/180830_PacNet_62.pdf?t5zMcyxJDl_Jf7EjtQ3ooYNd2i0jq52i.

5. Christopher Johnson, "Xi Jinping Unveils His Foreign Policy Vision," *Thoughts from the Chairman* (Washington, DC: Center for Strategic and International Studies, December 2014); Yun Sun, "China's Peaceful Rise: Peace through Strength?," *PacNet* 25 (Honolulu, HI: Pacific Forum CSIS, March 31, 2014); Yong Deng, "China: The Post-Responsible Power," *Washington Quarterly* 37, no. 4 (Winter 2015): 117–32; Center for a New American Security,

*More Willing and Able: Charting China's International Security Activism* (Washington, DC: Center for a New American Security, 2015); Christopher Johnson, *Decoding China's Emerging "Great Power" Strategy in Asia* (Washington, DC: Center for Strategic and International Studies, June 2014).

6. See, for example, Avery Goldstein, *Rising to the Challenge: China's Grand Strategy and International Security* (Stanford, CA: Stanford University Press, 2005); Bates Gill, *Rising Star: China's New Security Diplomacy* (Washington, DC: Brookings Institution, 2007).

7. See, among others, Aaron Friedberg, *The Contest for Supremacy* (New York: Norton, 2011); Denny Roy, *Return of the Dragon: Rising China and Regional Security* (New York: Columbia University Press, 2013); Ashley Tellis, *Balancing without Containment* (Washington, DC: Carnegie Endowment for International Peace Report, January 22, 2014); Michael Pillsbury, *The Hundred-Year Marathon* (New York: Holt, 2015).

8. Denny Roy, *China's Foreign Relations* (Lanham, MD: Rowman & Littlefield, 1998), 36–39; Samuel Kim, "China's International Organizational Behavior," in *Chinese Foreign Policy: Theory and Practice*, ed. Thomas Robinson and David Shambaugh (New York: Oxford University Press, 1994), 401–5; Harry Harding, "China's Changing Role in the Contemporary World," in *China's Foreign Relations in the 1980s*, ed. Harry Harding (New Haven, CT: Yale University Press, 1985), 177–79.

9. Kim, "China's International Organizational Behavior," 402.

10. Robert Sutter, *Foreign Relations of the PRC: The Legacies and Constraints of China's International Politics since 1949*, 2nd ed. (Lanham, MD: Rowman & Littlefield, 2019), 11.

11. Ezra Vogel, *Deng Xiaoping and the Transformation of China* (Cambridge, MA: Harvard University Press, 2011), 266–92.

12. Robert Sutter, *Historical Dictionary of Chinese Foreign Policy* (Lanham, MD: Scarecrow Press, 2011), 117–18, 194; Andrew Small, "First Movement: China and the Belt and Road Initiative," *Asia Policy*, no. 24 (July 2017): 80–87.

13. For background, see, among others, A. Doak Barnett, *China and the Major Powers in East Asia* (Washington, DC: Brookings Institution, 1977); Michael Yahuda, *China's Role in World Affairs* (New York: St. Martin's, 1978); Allen Whiting, *The Chinese Calculus of Deterrence: India and Indochina* (Ann Arbor: University of Michigan Press, 1975); Robert Ross and Jiang Changbin, eds., *Reexamining the Cold War* (Cambridge, MA: Harvard University Press, 2001); Michael H. Hunt, *The Genesis of Chinese Communist Foreign Policy* (New York: Columbia University Press, 1996); Harold Hinton, *China's Turbulent Quest* (New York: Macmillan, 1972); Peter Van Ness, *Revolution and Chinese Foreign Policy* (Berkeley: University of California Press, 1970); Melvin Gurtov and Byong-Moo Hwang, *China under Threat* (Baltimore, MD: Johns Hopkins University Press, 1981); John Garver, *Foreign Relations of the People's Republic of China* (Englewood Cliffs, NJ: Prentice Hall, 1993); Lowell Dittmer, *Sino-Soviet Normalization and Its International Implications, 1945–1990* (Seattle: University of Washington Press, 1992); Yong Deng, *China's Struggle for Status: The Realignment of International Relations* (New York: Cambridge University Press, 2008); M. Taylor Fravel, *Strong Borders, Secure Nation: Cooperation and Conflict in China's Territorial Disputes* (Princeton, NJ: Princeton University Press, 2008); Bobo Lo, *Axis of Convenience: Moscow, Beijing, and the New Geopolitics* (Washington, DC: Brookings Institution, 2008); Lorenz M. Luthi, *The Sino-Soviet Split: Cold War in the Communist World* (Princeton, NJ: Princeton University Press, 2008); Andrew Nathan and Andrew Scobell, *China's Search for Security* (New York: Columbia University Press, 2012); James Reilly, *China's Economic Statecraft: Turning Wealth into Power* (Sydney: Lowy Institute, November 2012); David Shambaugh, *China Goes Global: Partial Power* (New York: Oxford University Press, 2013); David Shinn and Joshua Eisenman, *China and Africa* (Philadelphia: University of Pennsylvania Press, 2012); Thomas Christensen, *The China Challenge: Shaping the Choices of a Rising Power* (New York: Norton, 2015); Rosemary Foot and Andrew Walter, *China, the United States and the Global Order* (New York: Cambridge University Press, 2011); David Michael Lampton, *Following the Leader: Ruling China from Deng Xiaoping to Xi Jinping* (Berkeley: University of California Press, 2014); Evelyn Goh, *The Struggle for Order: Hegemony, Hierarchy and Transition in Post–Cold War East Asia* (Oxford: Oxford University Press, 2013); John Garver, *China's Quest: The History of the Foreign Relations of the People's Republic of China* (New York:

Oxford University Press, 2016); Robert Bickers, *Out of China: How the Chinese Ended the Era of Western Domination* (Cambridge, MA: Harvard University Press, 2017); M. Taylor Fravel, *Active Defense: China's Military Strategy since 1949* (Princeton, NJ: Princeton University Press, 2019); David Shambaugh, ed., *China and the World* (New York: Oxford University Press, 2020); Hu Sheng, *Imperialism and Chinese Politics* (Beijing: Foreign Language Press, 1985); Jiang Changbin and Robert S. Ross, eds., *Cong Duizhi zouxiang Huanhe: Lengzhan Shiqi Zhong Mei Guanxi zai Tantao* [From confrontation toward détente: A reexamination of US-China relations during the Cold War] (Beijing: Shijie Zhishi Chubanshe, 2000); Pei Jian-zhang, *Yanjiu Zhou Enlai: Waijiao sixiang yu shijian* [Researching Zhou Enlai: Diplomatic thought and practice] (Beijing: Shijie Zhishi Chubanshe, 1989); Wang Taiping et al., *Zhonghua renmin gongheguo waijiao shi, 1957–1969* [A diplomatic history of the People's Republic of China, 1957–1969] (Beijing: Shijie Zhishi, 1998); Gong Li, *Kuayue: 1969–1979 nian Zhong Mei guanxi de yanbian* [Across the chasm: The evolution of China-US Relations, 1969–1979] (Henan: Henan People's Press, 1992); Lin Qing, *Zhou Enlai zaixiang shengya* [The career of Prime Minister Zhou Enlai] (Hong Kong: Changcheng Wenhua Chubanshe, 1991); Wang Shuzhong, ed., *Mei-Su zhengba zhanlue wenti* [The question of contention for hegemony between the United States and the Soviet Union] (Beijing: Guofang Daxue Chubanshe, 1988); Wang Yu-san, ed., *Foreign Policy of the Republic of China* (New York: Praeger, 1990); Xie Yixian, *Zhongguo Waijiao Shi: 1949–1979* [China's diplomatic history: 1949–1979] (Henan: Henan Renmin Chubanshe, 1988); Men Honghua, *China's Grand Strategy: A Framework Analysis* (Beijing: Beijing Daxue Chubanshe, 2005); Yan Xuetong, *Zhongguo guojia liyi fenxi* [The analysis of China's national interest] (Tianjin: Tianjin Renmin Chubanshe, 1996).

14. See Sutter, *Foreign Relations of the PRC*, 13–16.

15. Foot and Walter, *China, the United States, and the Global Order*.

16. Wayne Morrison, *China's Economic Rise*, Congressional Research Service Report RL33534 (Washington, DC: Library of Congress, 2019).

17. Elizabeth Economy, *The Third Revolution: Xi Jinping and the New Chinese State* (New York: Council on Foreign Relations, 2018); Peter Gries, *China's New Nationalism* (Berkeley: University of California Press, 2004); Suisheng Zhao, *A Nation-State by Construction: Dynamics of Modern Chinese Nationalism* (Stanford, CA: Stanford University Press, 2004).

18. Phillip Saunders, Arthur Ding, Andrew Scobell, Andrew N. D. Yang, and Joel Wuthnow, *Chairman Xi Remakes the PLA* (Washington, DC: National Defense University Press, 2019).

19. Zhao, *A Nation-State by Construction*; Gries, *China's New Nationalism*; Anne-Marie Brady, *Marketing Dictatorship: Propaganda and Thought Work in Contemporary China* (Lanham, MD: Rowman & Littlefield, 2008), 151–74; John Garver, *Foreign Relations of the People's Republic of China* (Englewood Cliffs, NJ: Prentice Hall, 1993), 1–28.

20. John Deutch, "Is Innovation China's New Great Leap Forward?," *Issues in Science and Technology*, Summer 2018, 37–47.

21. Aaron Friedberg, *Beyond Air-Sea Battle: The Debate over US Military Strategy in Asia*, Adelphi Paper 444 (London: International Institute for Strategic Studies, 2014).

22. Denny Roy, "US Strategy toward China: Three Key Questions for Policy-Makers," *PacNet* 30 (Honolulu, HI: Pacific Forum CSIS, May 28, 2019), https://www.pacforum.org/sites/default/files/20190528_PacNet_30.pdf.

23. In addition to a few source notes providing additional supporting information, this assessment is based on Sutter, *Foreign Relations of the PRC*, 297–311. For differing views on China and the United States in Asia, see Dennis Blair, "A Strong Foundation but Weak Blueprint for National Security," in *Strategic Asia 2015–16: Foundations of National Power in the Asia-Pacific*, ed. Michael Wills, Ashley J. Tellis, and Alison Szalwinski (Seattle, WA: National Bureau of Asian Research, 2016), 224–58; "Roundtable: Contending Visions of the Regional Order in East Asia," *Asia Policy* 13, no. 2 (April 2018): 2–68; Hugh White, "Without America: Australia in the New Asia," video, https://www.quarterlyessay.com.au/essay/2017/11/without-america; Ashley Tellis, "China's Not So Long March toward Preeminence," in *Strategic Asia 2019: China's Expanding Strategic Ambitions*, ed. Ashley Tellis, Alison Szalwinski, and Michael Wills (Seattle, WA: National Bureau of Asian Research, 2019), 2–48.

24. Reviewed in Robert Sutter and Chin-Hao Huang, "Beijing Leads Regional Agenda, Rejects US Challenges," *Comparative Connections* 21, no. 3 (January 2020): 65–66.

## 2. LEADERSHIP PRIORITIES, DECISION MAKING, AND WORLDVIEWS

1. For sources regarding the discussion below of recent activism and assertiveness in Xi Jinping's foreign policy, see Yang Jiechi, "Advancing China's Major-Country Diplomacy under the Guidance of Xi Jinping Thought on Foreign Affairs," *Qiushi Journal* 11, no. 4, issue 41 (October–December 2019), http://english.qstheory.cn/2020-01/13/c_1125443556.htm; Elizabeth Economy, *The Third Revolution: Xi Jinping and the New Chinese State* (New York: Council on Foreign Relations, 2018), 121–51, 186–230; Suisheng Zhao, "China's Foreign Policy Making Process: Players and Institutions," in *China and the World*, ed. David Shambaugh (New York: Oxford University Press, 2020), 85–112; Alastair Iain Johnston, "China in a World of Orders," *International Security* 44, no. 2 (Fall 2019): 9–60; Ashley J. Tellis, Alison Szalwinski, and Michael Wills, eds., *Strategic Asia 2019: China's Expanding Strategic Ambitions* (Seattle, WA: National Bureau of Asian Research, 2019); Melanie Hart and Blaine Johnson, *Mapping China's Global Governance Ambitions: Democracies Still Have Leverage to Shape Beijing's Reform Agenda* (Washington, DC: Center for American Progress, February 28, 2019); Nadege Rolland, *China's Vision for a New World Order* (Seattle, WA: National Bureau of Asian Research, 2020); Liza Tobin, "Xi's Vision for Transforming Global Governance: A Strategic Challenge for Washington and Its Allies," in *China's Global Influence*, ed. Scott McDonald and Michael Burgoyne (Honolulu, HI: Asia-Pacific Center for Security Studies, 2020), 38–56.

2. Robert Sutter, *Shaping China's Future in World Affairs* (Boulder, CO: Westview, 1996), 32–33.

3. Harry Harding, *A Fragile Relationship: The U.S. and China since 1972* (Washington, DC: Brookings Institution, 1992), 235–39; Ashley J. Tellis and Travis Tanner, eds., *Strategic Asia 2012–13: China's Military Challenge* (Seattle, WA: National Bureau of Asian Research, 2012).

4. Joseph Fewsmith, *China since Tiananmen* (New York: Cambridge University Press, 2001), 21–43, 75–158.

5. Robert Suettinger, *Beyond Tiananmen: The Politics of U.S.-China Relations, 1989–2000* (Washington, DC: Brookings Institution, 2003), 194–99.

6. Sutter, *Shaping China's Future in World Affairs*, 33–34.

7. Andrew Nathan and Robert Ross, *The Great Wall and Empty Fortress* (New York: Norton, 1997), 158–77.

8. Sutter, *Shaping China's Future in World Affairs*, 33–34.

9. Shirley Kan, *China as a Security Concern in Asia*, Congressional Research Service Report 95-465 (Washington, DC: Library of Congress, December 22, 1994).

10. David Michael Lampton, ed., *The Making of Chinese Foreign and Security Policy in the Era of Reform, 1978–2000* (Stanford, CA: Stanford University Press, 2001), 34–36.

11. Evan Medeiros and M. Taylor Fravel, "China's New Diplomacy," *Foreign Affairs* 82, no. 6 (November–December 2003): 22–35; Zhang Yunling and Tang Shiping, "More Self-Confident China Will Be a Responsible Power," *Straits Times*, October 2, 2002, 8; Denny Roy, "Rising China and U.S. Interests: Inevitable vs. Contingent Hazards," *Orbis* 47, no. 1 (2003): 125–37.

12. Sutter, *Shaping China's Future in World Affairs*, 35.

13. Chinese Academy of Social Sciences, *Trends of Future Sino-U.S. Relations and Policy Proposals* (Beijing: Institute for International Studies of the Academy of Social Sciences, September 1994).

14. David Michael Lampton, *Same Bed, Different Dreams: Managing U.S.-China Relations* (Berkeley: University of California Press, 2001), 59–60.

15. Fewsmith, *China since Tiananmen*, 159–89.

16. H. Lyman Miller and Liu Xiaohong, "The Foreign Policy Outlook of China's 'Third Generation' Elite," in *The Making of Chinese Foreign and Security Policy in the Era of Reform, 1978–2000*, ed. David Michael Lampton (Stanford, CA: Stanford University Press, 2001), 123–50; Ye Zicheng, *Xin Zhongguo waijiao sixiang: Cong Maozedong dao Dengxiaoping* (Beijing: Beijing Daxue Chubanshe, 2001).

17. Robert Sutter, *Chinese Policy Priorities and Their Implications for the United States* (Lanham, MD: Rowman & Littlefield, 2000), 18.

18. Barry Naughton, "China's Economy: Buffeted from within and Without," *Current History*, September 1998, 273–78.

19. Joseph Fewsmith, "China in 1998," *Asian Survey* 39, no. 1 (January–February 1999): 99–113.

20. Jean-Pierre Cabestan, "The Tenth National People's Congress and After," *China Perspectives* 47 (May–June 2003): 4–20.

21. Thomas Christensen, "China," in *Strategic Asia 2001–02: Power and Purpose*, ed. Richard Ellings and Aaron Friedberg (Seattle, WA: National Bureau of Asian Research, 2001), 27–70, and "China," in *Strategic Asia 2002–03: Asian Aftershocks*, ed. Richard J. Ellings, Aaron L. Friedberg, and Michael Wills (Seattle, WA: National Bureau of Asian Research, 2001), 51–94.

22. David Michael Lampton, *The Three Faces of Chinese Power: Might, Money, and Minds* (Berkeley: University of California Press, 2008).

23. Ashley Tellis, "The Return of US-China Strategic Competition," in *Strategic Asia 2020: US-China Competition for Global Influence*, ed. Ashley Tellis, Alison Szalwinski, and Michael Wills (Seattle, WA: National Bureau of Asian Research, 2020), 3–44.

24. Cheng Li, *China's Emerging Middle Class* (Washington, DC: Brookings Institution, 2010).

25. Susan Shirk, "Power Shift in China—Part III," *YaleGlobal Online*, April 20, 2012, https://yaleglobal.yale.edu/content/power-shift-china-part-iii.

26. Zhao, "China's Foreign Policy Making Process"; Economy, *The Third Revolution*.

27. Cheng Li, *China's Leaders: The New Generation* (Lanham, MD: Rowman & Littlefield, 2001); Cheng Li, "Power Shift in China—Part I," *YaleGlobal Online*, April 16, 2012, https://yaleglobal.yale.edu/content/power-shift-china-part-i; David Michael Lampton, *Following the Leader: Ruling China from Deng Xiaoping to Xi Jinping* (Berkeley: University of California Press, 2014), 47–77.

28. Alice L. Miller, "Institutionalization and the Changing Dynamics of Chinese Leadership Politics," in *China's Changing Political Landscape: Prospects for Democracy*, ed. Cheng Li (Washington, DC: Brookings Institution, 2008), 61–79.

29. Jing Huang, "Institutionalization of Political Succession in China," in Li, *China's Changing Political Landscape*, 80–98; Lampton, *Following the Leader*, 68–77.

30. Dennis Blasko, *The Chinese Army Today: Tradition and Transformation in the 21st Century* (London: Routledge, 2012).

31. Economy, *The Third Revolution*; Zhao, "China's Foreign Policy Making Process."

32. C. Fred Bergsten et al., *China's Rise* (Washington, DC: Peterson Institute for International Economics and Center for Strategic and International Studies, 2008), 105–30; Wayne Morrison, *China's Economic Conditions*, Congressional Research Service Report RL33534 (Washington, DC: Library of Congress, 2014).

33. Wayne Morrison, *China's Economic Conditions*, Congressional Research Service Report RL33534 (Washington, DC: Library of Congress, June 24, 2011).

34. Arthur Kroeber, *China's Economy: What Everyone Needs to Know* (New York: Oxford University Press, 2016), 155–62.

35. Kroeber, *China's Economy*; Wayne Morrison, *China's Economic Rise*, Congressional Research Service Report RL33534 (Washington, DC: Library of Congress, 2019); Nicholas Lardy, *The State Strikes Back* (Washington, DC: Peterson Institute for International Economics, 2019).

36. Tony Saich, *Governance and Politics of China* (New York: Palgrave, 2004), 135, 233–67; Bruce Dickson, "Updating the China Model," *Washington Quarterly* 34, no. 4 (Fall

2011): 39–58; Sebastian Heilmann, ed., *China's Political System* (Lanham, MD: Rowman & Littlefield, 2017), 193–241.

37. Bergsten et al., *China's Rise*, 75–90.

38. Wayne Morrison, *China's Economic Conditions*, Congressional Research Service Report RL33534 (Washington, DC: Library of Congress, November 20, 2008), 17–18.

39. Min Ye, "Fragmentation and Mobilization: Domestic Politics of the Belt and Road in China," *Journal of Contemporary China*, February 26, 2019, https://www.tandfonline.com/doi/abs/10.1080/10670564.2019.1580428?af=R&journalCode=cjcc20; Lee Jones and Jinghan Zeng, "Understanding China's 'Belt and Road Initiative,' beyond 'Grand Strategy' to a State Transforming Analysis," *Third World Quarterly*, February 20, 2019, https://www.tandfonline.com/doi/abs/10.1080/01436597.2018.1559046.

40. Minxin Pei, *China's Trapped Transition: The Limits of Development Autocracy* (Cambridge, MA: Harvard University Press, 2006), 83–84, 189, 200–204; Thomas Lum, *Human Rights in China and U.S. Policy*, Congressional Research Service Report RL34729 (Washington, DC: Library of Congress, July 18, 2011), 28–29; Thomas Lum, *Human Rights in China and U.S. Policy*, Congressional Research Service Report RL44897 (Washington, DC: Library of Congress, July 17, 2017).

41. Josh Chin, "China Spends More on Domestic Security as Xi's Powers Grow," *Wall Street Journal*, March 6, 2018, https://www.wsj.com/articles/china-spends-more-on-domestic-security-as-xis-powers-grow-1520358522; "Life Inside China's Total Surveillance State," video, *Wall Street Journal*, March 6, 2018, https://www.wsj.com/articles/china-spends-more-on-domestic-security-as-xis-powers-grow-1520358522.

42. Lum, *Human Rights in China and U.S. Policy* (2017); Martin King Whyte, "China's Dormant and Active Volcanoes," *China Journal*, January 2016, 9–37.

43. On Chinese leaders' goals, especially as they relate to world affairs, see the discussion in subsequent chapters and in the selected bibliography in this book.

44. See sources in note 1.

45. Richard Ellings and Robert Sutter, eds., *Axis of Authoritarians* (Seattle, WA: National Bureau of Asian Research, 2018).

46. Avery Goldstein, *Rising to the Challenge: China's Grand Strategy and International Security* (Stanford, CA: Stanford University Press, 2005); Yong Deng, "Hegemon on the Offensive: Chinese Perspectives on U.S. Global Strategy," *Political Science Quarterly* 116, no. 3 (Fall 2001): 343–65; Qian Qichen, "The International Situation and Sino-U.S. Relations since the 11 September Incident," *Waijiao xueyuan xuebao* (Beijing) 3 (September 25, 2002): 1–6.

47. Linda Jakobson and Dean Knox, "New Foreign Policy Actors in China," SIPRI Policy Paper 26 (Stockholm: Stockholm International Peace Research Institute, September 2010); David Shambaugh, "Coping with a Conflicted China," *Washington Quarterly* 34, no. 1 (Winter 2011): 7–27.

48. David Shambaugh, "China's Military Views the World," *International Security* 24, no. 3 (Winter 1999–2000): 52–79; Alan Tonelson, *A Necessary Evil? Current Chinese Views of America's Military Role in East Asia* (Washington, DC: Henry Stimson Center, May 2003).

49. Reviewed in Robert Sutter, *The United States and Asia: Regional Dynamics and Twenty-First-Century Relations*, 2nd ed. (Lanham, MD: Rowman & Littlefield, 2020), 77–142.

50. Lampton, *Making of Chinese Foreign and Security Policy*; Medeiros and Fravel, "China's New Diplomacy," 22–35; People's Republic of China State Council Information Office, "China's Peaceful Development Road," *People's Daily Online*, December 22, 2005, https://www.chinadaily.com.cn/english/doc/2005-12/22/content_505678.htm; Jakobson and Knox, "New Foreign Policy Actors in China"; Yun Sun, *Chinese National Security Decision-Making: Process and Challenges* (Washington, DC: Brookings Institution, May 2013); Zhao, "China's Foreign Policy Making Process."

51. Lampton, *Same Bed, Different Dreams*, 59–61; Robert Sutter, *China's Rise in Asia: Promises and Perils* (Lanham, MD: Rowman & Littlefield, 2005), 29.

52. John Keefe, *Anatomy of the EP-3 Incident* (Alexandria, VA: Center for Naval Analysis, 2002); Michael Swaine and Zhang Tuosheng, eds., *Managing Sino-American Crises: Case Studies and Analysis* (Washington, DC: Carnegie Endowment, 2006).

53. James Przystup, "Japan-China Relations: No End to History," *Comparative Connections* 7, no. 2 (July 2005): 119–32.

54. Chinese practices are reviewed in the following chapters dealing with Japan and Korea, Southeast Asia, and South Asia. Triannual reports on Chinese behavior are provided in sections of the e-journal *Comparative Connections*, http://cc.pacforum.org.

55. Consultations with US government officials, Washington, DC, 1999–2001; Swaine and Zhang, *Managing Sino-American Crises*.

56. "Friend or Foe? A Special Report on China's Place in the World," *The Economist*, December 4, 2010, 3–16; Christopher Johnson, "Xi Jinping Unveils His Foreign Policy Vision," *Thoughts from the Chairman* (Washington, DC: Center for Strategic and International Studies, December 2014); Yun Sun, "China's Peaceful Rise: Peace through Strength?," *PacNet* 25 (Honolulu, HI: Pacific Forum CSIS, March 31, 2014).

57. Consultations with US government officials, Washington, DC, November 1999.

58. Interviews and consultations with Chinese officials and foreign policy specialists, Beijing and Shanghai, May–June 2006, Beijing, June 2010.

59. Scott Snyder, "China-Korea Relations: China's Post–Kim Jong Il Debate," Council on Foreign Relations, May 14, 2012, http://www.cfr.org/north-korea/china-korea-relations-chinas-post-kim-jong-il-debate/p28282.

60. Yi Qinfu, "What Will China's National Security Commission Actually Do?," *Foreign Policy*, May 8, 2014, http://foreignpolicy.com/2014/05/08/what-will-chinas-national-security-commission-actually-do; Zhao, "China's Foreign Policy Making Process," 94.

61. Zhao, "China's Foreign Policy Making Process," 92–95.

62. Zhao, "China's Foreign Policy Making Process," 96–98.

63. Peter Mattis and Matthew Brazil, *Chinese Communist Espionage* (Annapolis, MD: Naval Institute Press, 2019).

64. Johnson, "Xi Jinping Unveils"; Brad Glosserman and Denny Roy, "Asia's Next China Worry," *National Interest*, July 23, 2014, https://nationalinterest.org/blog/the-buzz/asias-next-china-worry-xi-jinpings-growing-power-10939.

65. Carola McGiffert, ed., *Chinese Images of the United States* (Washington, DC: CSIS, 2006), 9–22.

66. Lampton, *Making of Chinese Foreign and Security Policy*; Medeiros and Fravel, "China's New Diplomacy," 22–35.

67. "Priorities Set for Handling Foreign Affairs," *China Daily*, August 24, 2006, 1.

68. Foreign specialists debate how revisionist China has become in foreign affairs. For a moderate perspective, see Johnston, "China in a World of Orders," 9–60.

69. Consultations with Chinese specialists in Beijing, March 2019, and several consultations in Washington, DC, during 2018–2020.

70. Suisheng Zhao, *A Nation-State by Construction: Dynamics of Modern Chinese Nationalism* (Stanford, CA: Stanford University Press, 2004); Peter Gries, *China's New Nationalism* (Berkeley: University of California Press, 2004); Anne-Marie Brady, *Marketing Dictatorship: Propaganda and Thought Work in Contemporary China* (Lanham, MD: Rowman & Littlefield, 2008), 151–74.

71. See assessment by John Garver, *Foreign Relations of the People's Republic of China* (Englewood Cliffs, NJ: Prentice Hall, 1993), 1–28.

72. Yan Xuetong, "The Instability of China-US Relations," *Chinese Journal of International Politics* 3, no. 3 (2010): 1–30; Suisheng Zhao, "China's Pragmatic Nationalism: Is It Manageable?," *Washington Quarterly* 29, no. 1 (Winter 2005–2006): 131–44.

73. Among foreign studies on this subject, see David Kang, *China's Rising: Peace, Power, and Order in East Asia* (New York: Columbia University Press, 2007).

74. Denny Roy, *China's Foreign Relations* (Lanham, MD: Rowman & Littlefield, 1998), 36–39; Samuel Kim, "China's International Organizational Behavior," in *Chinese Foreign Policy: Theory and Practice*, ed. Thomas Robinson and David Shambaugh (New York: Oxford University Press, 1994), 401–5; Harry Harding, "China's Changing Role in the Contemporary World," in *China's Foreign Relations in the 1980s*, ed. Harry Harding (New Haven, CT: Yale University Press, 1985), 177–79.

## 3. CHINA'S ROLE IN THE WORLD ECONOMY

1. On China's recent economic rise, see Nicholas Lardy, *The State Strikes Back: The End of Economic Reform in China* (Washington, DC: Peterson Institute for International Economics, 2018); Barry Naughton, "China's Global Economic Interactions," in *China and the World*, ed. David Shambaugh (New York: Oxford University Press, 2020), 113–36; Arthur Kroeber, *China's Economy: What Everyone Needs to Know* (New York: Oxford University Press, 2016); Wayne Morrison, *China's Economic Rise*, Congressional Research Service Report RL33534 (Washington, DC: Library of Congress, June 25, 2019); on China's covert use of economic leverage in foreign affairs, see Daniel Russel and Blake Berger, *Navigating the Belt and Road Initiative* (New York: Asia Society Policy Institute, June 2019); Melanie Hart and Blaine Johnson, *Mapping China's Global Governance Ambitions: Democracies Still Have Leverage to Shape Beijing's Reform Agenda* (Washington, DC: Center for American Progress, February 28, 2019); Melanie Hart and Kelly Magsamen, *Limit, Leverage and Compete: A New Strategy on China* (Washington, DC: Center for American Progress, April 2019); Matt Schrader, *Friends and Enemies: A Framework for Understanding Chinese Political Influence in Democratic Countries* (Washington, DC: German Marshall Fund, April 22, 2020); David Shullman, ed., *Chinese Malign Influence and the Corrosion of Democracy* (Washington, DC: International Republican Institute, 2019); Daniel Kliman, Rush Doshi, Kristine Lee, and Zack Cooper, *Grading China's Belt and Road* (Washington, DC: Center for New American Security, April 2019); Ashley Tellis, Alison Szalwinski, and Michael Wills, eds., *Strategic Asia 2020: US-China Competition for Global Influence* (Seattle, WA: National Bureau of Asian Research, 2020); Nadege Rolland, *China's Vision for a New World Order* (Seattle, WA: National Bureau of Asian Research, January 2020); Scott McDonald and Michael Burgoyne, eds., *China's Global Influence* (Honolulu, HI: Asia-Pacific Center for Security Studies, 2020); Thomas Mahnken, Ross Babbage, and Toshi Yoshihara, *Countering Comprehensive Coercion* (Washington, DC: Center for Strategic and Budgetary Assessments, 2018); Ross Babbage, *Winning without Fighting: Chinese and Russian Political Warfare Campaigns* (Washington, DC: Center for Strategic and Budgetary Assessments, 2018).

2. Hart and Johnson, *Mapping China's Global Governance Ambitions*; Tellis et al., *Strategic Asia 2020: US-China Competition*; Rolland, *China's Vision for a New World Order*; Liza Tobin, "Xi's Vision for Transforming Global Governance: A Strategic Challenge for Washington and Its Allies," in McDonald and Burgoyne, *China's Global Influence*, 38–56.

3. White House, *National Security Strategy of the United States*, December 2017, https://www.whitehouse.gov/wp-content/uploads/2017/12/NSS-Final-12-18-2017-0905.pdf; US Department of Defense, *Summary of the National Defense Strategy of the United States*, January 2018, https://www.defense.gov/Portals/1/Documents/pubs/2018-National-Defense-Strategy-Summary.pdf; Anthony Capaccio, "US Faces 'Unprecedented Threat' on China Tech Takeover," *Bloomberg*, June 22, 2018, https://www.bloomberg.com/news/articles/2018-06-22/china-s-thousand-talents-called-key-in-seizing-u-s-expertise; Transcript of speech by Senator Mark Warner at Brookings Institution, Washington, DC, May 9, 2019, https://www.brookings.edu/wp-content/uploads/2019/05/fp_20190509_global_china_transcript.pdf; Robert Sutter, "Trump, America and the World—2017 and Beyond," H-Diplo/ISSF Policy Series, January 19, 2019, https://networks.h-net.org/node/28443/discussions/3569933/issf-policy-series-sutter-trump%E2%80%99s-china-policy-bi-partisan.

4. Russel and Berger, *Navigating the Belt and Road Initiative*; Hart and Johnson, *Mapping China's Global Governance Ambitions*; Schrader, *Friends and Enemies*; Shullman, *Chinese Malign Influence*; Kliman et al., *Grading China's Belt and Road*; Tellis et al., *Strategic Asia 2020: US-China Competition*.

5. The importance of China's economic influence in defining China's international power has varied over the years. See Arvind Subramanian, "The Inevitable Superpower: Why China's Rise Is a Sure Thing," *Foreign Affairs* 90, no. 5 (September–October 2011): 66–78; Carl Dahlman, *The World under Pressure: How China and India Are Influencing the Global Economy and Environment* (Stanford, CA: Stanford University Press, 2011); Thomas Christensen, *The China Challenge: Shaping the Choices of a Rising Power* (New York: Norton, 2015);

Aaron Friedberg, "Competing with China," *Survival* 60, no. 3 (June 2018): 7–64; Jennifer Lind, "Life in China's Asia: What Regional Hegemony Would Look Like," *Foreign Affairs* 97, no. 2 (March–April 2018): 71–82; David Shambaugh, "China and the World: Future Challenges," in *China and the World*, ed. David Shambaugh (New York: Oxford University Press, 2020), 343–65; Kishore Mahbubani, "Kishore Mahbubani on the Dawn of the Asian Century," *The Economist*, April 20, 2020, https://www.economist.com/by-invitation/2020/04/20/kishore-mahbubani-on-the-dawn-of-the-asian-century.

    6. Robert Sutter, *Foreign Relations of the PRC* (Lanham, MD: Rowman & Littlefield, 2013), 150–51.

    7. Robert Lighthizer, "The Era of Offshoring U.S. Jobs Is Over," *New York Times*, May 12, 2020, A27.

    8. See review in Lardy, *The State Strikes Back.*

    9. Wayne Morrison, *China's Economic Rise*, Congressional Research Service Report RL33534 (Washington, DC: Library of Congress, October 9, 2014), summary page.

    10. "Catching the Eagle," *The Economist*, August 22, 2014, http://www.economist.com/blogs/graphicdetail/2014/08/chinese-and-american-gdp-forecasts.

    11. Frank Tang, "Coronavirus: China Seen Pursuing Lower 2020 Economic Growth," *South China Morning Post*, April 21, 2020, https://www.scmp.com/economy/china-economy/article/3080882/coronavirus-china-seen-pursuing-lower-2020-economic-growth.

    12. Morrison, *China's Economic Rise* (2019), 5.

    13. "China's Outward Investment Tops $161 Billion in 2016," Reuters, December 26, 2016, http://www.reuters.com/article/us-china-economy-investment-idUSKBN14F07R.

    14. Zhong Nan, "China's Foreign Trade Volume Falls 6.4% in Q1," *China Daily*, April 14, 2020, https://global.chinadaily.com.cn/a/202004/14/WS5e952001a3105d50a3d16086.html.

    15. Wayne Morrison, *China's Economic Rise*, Congressional Research Service Report RL33534 (Washington, DC: Library of Congress, September 15, 2017), 13.

    16. "China's Processing Trade Still a Pillar of Foreign Trade," *China Daily*, August 20, 2019, https://www.ciie.org/zbh/en/news/exhibition/News/20190820/17949.html.

    17. Miaojie Yu and Wei Tian, "China's Processing Trade," *East Asia Forum*, October 27, 2012, http://www.eastasiaforum.org/2012/10/27/chinas-processing-trade.

    18. Pu Zhendong, "Singapore Supports Strengthened Free-Trade Agreement with Beijing," *China Daily*, August 30, 2013, http://usa.chinadaily.com.cn/epaper/2013-08/30/content_16932418.htm.

    19. Morrison, *China's Economic Rise* (2019), 16.

    20. "Foreign Investment in China Hits Record in 2010," *Agence France-Presse*, January 18, 2011; Ding Qingfen, "ODI Set to Overtake FDI 'within Three Years,'" *China Daily*, May 6, 2011, 1; Xin Zhiming, "Trade Surplus Reaches New Peak," *China Daily*, September 11, 2008, 13; Diao Ying, "Firms Urged to Diversify Export Markets," *China Daily*, December 24, 2008, 1.

    21. Morrison, *China's Economic Rise* (2019), 17.

    22. Thomas Lum, *Comparing Global Influence: China's and U.S. Diplomacy, Foreign Aid, Trade, and Investment in the Developing World*, Congressional Research Service Report RL34620 (Washington, DC: Library of Congress, August 15, 2008), 59–60.

    23. Xiao Geng, *China's Round-Tripping FDI: Scale, Causes and Implications*, working paper (Hong Kong: University of Hong Kong, July 2004); Randall Morck, Bernard Yeung, and Minyuan Zhao, *Perspectives on China's Outward Foreign Direct Investment*, working paper (Washington, DC: International Monetary Fund, August 2007).

    24. Carol Lancaster, *The Chinese Aid System* (Washington, DC: Center for Global Development, June 2007); Bao Chang and Ding Qingfen, "No Hidden Strings Tied to Aid," *China Daily*, April 27, 2011, 3.

    25. Lum, *Comparing Global Influence*, 33–34.

    26. Deborah Brautigam, *The Dragon's Gift: The Real Story of China in Africa* (New York: Oxford University Press, 2009), 168–69; Deborah Brautigam, *Africa and China: Issues and Insights—A Summary of a Conference* (Washington, DC: Georgetown University, November 7, 2008), https://asianstudies.georgetown.edu.

27. "Full Text: China's Foreign Aid," *Xinhua*, July 10, 2014, http://news.xinhuanet.com/english/china/2014-07/10/c_133474011.htm.

28. Denghua Zhang, *China's Second White Paper on Foreign Aid*, Australian National University INBRIEF 2014/26, accessed June 5, 2015, http://ips.cap.anu.edu.au/sites/default/files/IB-2014-26-Zhang-ONLINE.pdf.

29. Michael Field, "Uproar in Tonga: China's 'Gift' Troubles New Prime Minister," *Nikkei Asian Review*, March 28, 2015.

30. Yun Sun, "One Year On, the Role of the Chinese International Development Administration Remains Cloudy," Brookings Institution, April 30, 2019, https://www.brookings.edu/blog/africa-in-focus/2019/04/30/one-year-on-the-role-of-the-china-international-development-cooperation-administration-remains-cloudy.

31. Naohiro Kitano, *Estimating China's Foreign Aid: 2017–2018, Preliminary Figures*, JICA Research Institute Tokyo, September 27, 2019, https://www.jica.go.jp/jica-ri/publication/other/l75nbg000018z3zd-att/20190926_01.pdf.

32. "China's Financial Diplomacy: Rich but Rash," *The Economist*, January 31, 2015, http://www.economist.com/news/finance-and-economics/21641259-challenge-world-bank-and-imf-china-will-have-imitate-them-rich.

33. Thomas Lum, *U.S.-Funded Assistance Programs in China*, Congressional Research Service Report RS22663 (Washington, DC: Library of Congress, January 28, 2008), 3; "Trump Calls on World Bank to Stop Lending Money to China," Reuters, December 7, 2019, https://www.cnbc.com/2019/12/07/trump-calls-for-world-bank-to-stop-lending-money-to-china.html; Asian Development Bank and the People's Republic of China, *Fact Sheet*, 2018, https://www.adb.org/sites/default/files/publication/27789/prc-2018.pdf.

34. Fu Jing and Hu Haiyan, "China, UN Jointly Unveil Five-Year Aid Framework," *China Daily*, April 2, 2010; Gillian Wong, "China Rises and Rises, Yet Still Gets Foreign Aid," Associated Press, September 27, 2010.

35. UN Development Program, *National Human Development Report: Special Edition*, December 19, 2019, https://www.cn.undp.org/content/china/en/home/library/human_development/national-human-development-report-special-edition.html.

36. Joanna Lewis, "China's Strategic Priorities in International Climate Change Negotiations," *Washington Quarterly* 31, no. 1 (Winter 2007–2008): 165.

37. National Development and Reform Commission, *China's Policies and Actions for Addressing Climate Change—The Progress Report 2009*, November 2009, 47.

38. Antoine Dechezlepretre et al., "Technology Transfer by CDM Projects," *Energy Policy* 37, no. 2 (2009): 1.

39. Keith Bradsher, "China Leading Global Race to Make Clean Energy," *New York Times*, January 31, 2010, https://www.nytimes.com/2010/01/31/business/energy-environment/31renew.html.

40. World Bank, "Global Environmental Facility (GEF) Projects in China," July 2009; World Bank, "World Bank, GEF-Backed Energy Efficiency Program Expands in China," January 2008; Asian Development Bank, *Asian Development Bank and People's Republic of China: Fact Sheet*, December 2008, 3.

41. Morrison, *China's Economic Rise* (2017), 15; Morrison, *China's Economic Rise* (2019), 16–17.

42. Kevin Gallagher, "China's Role as the World's Development Bank Cannot Be Ignored," NPR, October 11, 2018, https://www.npr.org/2018/10/11/646421776/opinion-chinas-role-as-the-world-s-development-bank-cannot-be-ignored.

43. Reviewed in "Ambitious Economic Initiatives amid Boundary Disputes," *Comparative Connections* 17, no. 1 (May 2015): 57–61.

44. Among assessments of the BRI and its predecessors, see Naughton, "China's Global Economic Interactions"; Matt Geraci, "An Update on American Perspectives on the Belt and Road Initiative," ICAS Issue Primers, Washington, DC, January 23, 2020; *The Belt and Road Initiative: Views from Washington, Moscow and Beijing* (Washington, DC: Carnegie-Tsinghua Center for Global Policy, April 8, 2019); "How Will the Belt and Road Initiative Advance China's Interests?," CSIS ChinaPower Project, Washington, DC, September 2018; Mingjiang Li, "The Belt and Road Initiative: Geo-economics and Indo-Pacific Security Competition,"

*International Affairs* 96, no. 1 (2020): 169–87; Nadege Rolland, ed., *Securing the Belt and Road Initiative*, NBR Special Report No. 80 (Seattle, WA: National Bureau of Asian Research, September 3, 2019).

45. The plan is available at "Initiative Offers Road Map for Peace, Prosperity," *China Daily*, March 30, 2015, http://europe.chinadaily.com.cn/china/2015-3/30/content_19950708.htm.

46. "Ambitious Economic Initiatives amid Boundary Disputes"; Min Ye, "Fragmentation and Mobilization: Domestic Politics of the Belt and Road in China," *Journal of Contemporary China*, February 26, 2019, https://www.tandfonline.com/doi/abs/10.1080/10670564.2019.1580428?af=R&journalCode=cjcc20; Lee Jones and Jinghan Zeng, "Understanding China's 'Belt and Road Initiative,' beyond 'Grand Strategy' to a State Transforming Analysis," *Third World Quarterly*, February 20, 2019, 1415–39.

47. Huang Yiping, "Pragmatism Can Lead to Silk Roads Success," *China Daily*, February 25, 2015.

48. Matina Stevis, "China Launches $2 Billion African Development Fund," *Wall Street Journal*, May 22, 2014, http://www.wsj.com/articles/SB10001424052702303749904579577881407374244.

49. Toh Han Shih, "Chinese Investors Warned about African Mining Risks," *South China Morning Post*, December 16, 2013, http://www.scmp.com/business/commodities/article/1381796/chinese-investors-warned-about-african-mining-risks.

50. Linda Yulisman, "Indonesia: Indonesia to Push China to Realize Investment," *Jakarta Post*, April 4, 2015, http://www.thejakartapost.com/news/2015/04/04/indonesia-push-china-realize-investment.html; Dinna Wisnu, "Indonesia: Jokowi's Visits to Japan and China: What's in It for Us?," *Jakarta Post*, April 7, 2015, http://www.thejakartapost.com/news/2015/04/07/jokowi-s-visits-japan-and-china-what-s-it-us.html.

51. Top ten sources of foreign direct inflows in ASEAN (table 27), accessed June 6, 2015, http://www.asean.org/images/2015/January/foreign_direct_investment_statistic/Table%2027.pdf; "China in Africa: One among Many," *The Economist*, January 17, 2015, http://www.economist.com/news/middle-east-and-africa/21639554-china-has-become-big-africa-now-backlash-one-among-many; *2013 China-Latin America Bulletin*, 12, accessed June 5, 2015, http://www.bu.edu/pardee/files/2014/01/Economic-Bulletin-2013.pdf.

52. "Ambitious Economic Initiatives amid Boundary Disputes," 59–60.

53. "Ambitious Economic Initiatives amid Boundary Disputes," 60–61.

54. Ministry of Foreign Affairs, "Wang Yi Attends the Symposium on the International Situation and China's Foreign Relations in 2019," December 13, 2019, https://www.fmprc.gov.cn/mfa_eng/zxxx_662805/t1724299.shtml.

55. Nadege Rolland, *China's Eurasian Century?* (Seattle, WA: National Bureau of Asian Research, 2017); Russel and Berger, *Navigating the Belt and Road Initiative*; Hart and Johnson, *Mapping China's Global Governance Ambitions*; Schrader, *Friends and Enemies*; Shullman, ed., *Chinese Malign Influence*; Kliman et al., *Grading China's Belt and Road*; Tellis et al., *Strategic Asia 2020: US-China Competition*; Rolland, *China's Vision for a New World Order*; McDonald and Burgoyne, *China's Global Influence*; Mahnken et al., *Countering Comprehensive Coercion*; Babbage, *Winning without Fighting*.

56. In addition to the above sources, see Andrew Foxall and John Hemmings, *The Art of Deceit: How China and Russia Use Sharp Power to Subvert the West* (London: Henry Jackson Society, 2019); Samantha Hoffman, *Engineering Global Consent: The Chinese Communist Party's Data-Driven Power Expansion* (Canberra: APSI Policy Brief, 2019).

57. See, in addition, Hart and Magsamen, *Limit, Leverage and Compete*; Tobin, "Xi's Vision for Transforming Global Governance."

58. Ye, "Fragmentation and Mobilization"; Jones and Zeng, "Understanding China's 'Belt and Road Initiative.'"

59. Bonnie Glaser, "US-China Relations," *Comparative Connections* 22, no. 1 (January–April 2020).

60. Satoru Mori, "US Technological Competition with China: The Military, Industrial and Digital Network Dimensions," *Asia-Pacific Review* 26, no. 1 (2019): 77–120.

61. The developments in this and later paragraphs are assessed in Sutter, "Trump, America and the World—2017 and Beyond."

62. This paragraph and following paragraphs are based on Mori, "US Technological Competition with China"; Elsa Kania, "Technology and Innovation in China's Strategy and Global Influence," in McDonald and Burgoyne, *China's Global Influence*, 229–46; Graham Allison, "Is China Beating America to AI Supremacy?," *National Interest*, December 22, 2019, https://nationalinterest.org/feature/china-beating-america-ai-supremacy-106861. A useful framework for understanding recent American debate on this issue is in Kenneth Boutin, *Economic Security and Sino-American Relations* (Northamton, MA: Edward Elgar, 2019).

63. See, among others, Elsa Kania, "The China Challenge in 5G," in *Securing Our 5G Future* (Washington, DC: Center for New American Security, November 2019), 7–11.

64. Kania, *Securing Our 5G Future*, 11–23.

65. Victor Shih, "US-China Relations in 2019," testimony before the US-China Economic and Security Review Commission, September 4, 2019, https://www.uscc.gov/sites/default/files/Panel%20I%20Shih_Written%20Testimony.pdf.

66. See treatment of these difficulties in Morrison, *China's Economic Rise* (2019), 25–34.

67. Aaron Friedberg, "'Going Out': China's Pursuit of Natural Resources and Implications for the PRC's Grand Strategy," *NBR Analysis* 17, no. 3 (September 2006): 1–35; David Brewster, *China's New Network of Indian Ocean Bases*, Lowy Institute, January 30, 2018, https://www.lowyinstitute.org/the-interpreter/chinas-new-network-indian-ocean-bases.

68. Robert Sutter, *Chinese Policy Priorities and Their Implications for the United States* (Lanham, MD: Rowman & Littlefield, 2000), 188.

69. Elizabeth Economy, "China's Environmental Challenge," *Current History* 105, no. 692 (September 2005): 278–79; Sutter, *Chinese Policy Priorities and Their Implications for the United States*, 189.

70. Elizabeth Economy, "China: A Rise That's Not So 'Win-Win,'" *International Herald Tribune*, November 15, 2005.

71. Te Kan, "Past Successes and New Goal," *China Daily*, December 26, 2005–January 1, 2006, supplement, 9.

72. Joanna Lewis, "The State of U.S.-China Relations on Climate Change," *China Environmental Series* 11 (2010–2011): 7–39.

73. Hua Jianmin, "Strengthen Cooperation for Clean Development," Chinese Foreign Ministry statement, January 12, 2006, accessed January 30, 2006, http://www.fmprc.gov.cn/eng.

74. Kenneth Lieberthal and David Sandalow, *Overcoming Obstacles to U.S.-China Cooperation on Climate Change*, John L. Thornton China Center Monograph Series 1 (Washington, DC: Brookings Institution, January 2009).

75. Lewis, "The State of U.S.-China Relations on Climate Change."

76. Joel Kirkland, "Global Emissions Predicted to Grow through 2035," *Scientific American*, May 26, 2010, http://www.scientificamerican.com/article/global-emissions-predicted-to-grow.

77. Carolyn Beeler, "Is China Really Stepping Up as the World's New Climate Leader?," *PRI*, November 9, 2017, https://www.usatoday.com/story/news/world/2017/11/09/china-really-stepping-up-worlds-new-climate-leader/847270001.

78. Elizabeth Economy, "Why China Is No Climate Leader," *Politico*, June 12, 2017, https://www.politico.com/magazine/story/2017/06/12/wh; y-china-is-no-climate-leader-215249; Susan Lawrence et al., *US-China Relations*, Congressional Research Service Report R45898 (Washington, DC: Library of Congress, September 3, 2019), 39.

# 4. CHINA, MULTILATERALISM, AND INTERNATIONAL GOVERNANCE

1. Jing-dong Yuan, "China's Role in Establishing and Building the Shanghai Cooperation Organization (SCO)," *Journal of Contemporary China* 19, no. 67 (November 2010): 855–70; Wu Xinbo, "Chinese Perspectives on Building an East Asian Community in the Twenty-First Century," in *Asia's New Multilateralism*, ed. Michael Green and Bates Gill (New York: Co-

lumbia University Press, 2009), 55–77; Robert Sutter, *Historical Dictionary of Chinese Foreign Policy* (Lanham, MD: Scarecrow Press, 2011), citations for "G20" and "BRIC"; Katherine Morton, "China's Global Governance Interactions," in *China and the World*, ed. David Shambaugh (New York: Oxford University Press, 2020), 156–80; Michael Mazarr, Timothy Heath, and Astrid Stuth Cevallos, *China and the International Order* (Santa Monica, CA: RAND Corporation, 2018); Andrew Scobell et al., *At the Dawn of the Belt and Road: China in the Developing World* (Santa Monica, CA: RAND Corporation, 2018).

2. Jianwei Wang, "China's Multilateral Diplomacy in the New Millennium," in *China Rising: Power and Motivation in Chinese Foreign Policy*, ed. Yong Deng and Fei-Ling Wang (Lanham, MD: Rowman & Littlefield, 2005), 159–66; Chen Zheng, "China's Domestic Debate on Global Governance," *The Diplomat*, November 23, 2016, https://thediplomat.com/2016/11/chinas-domestic-debate-on-global-governance; Morton, "China's Global Governance Interactions."

3. David Zweig and Bi Jianhai, "China's Global Hunt for Energy," *Foreign Affairs* 84, no. 5 (September–October 2005): 25–38.

4. Remarks by a Chinese official during a workshop the author attended in Beijing, March 29, 2015.

5. Catherine Wong, "ASEAN Split on Joint Response to South China Sea Row," *South China Morning Post*, July 25, 2016, https://www.scmp.com/news/china/diplomacy-defence/article/1994235/asean-split-joint-response-south-china-sea-row.

6. Jianwei Wang, "China's Multilateral Diplomacy in the New Millennium," 166–77; Ellen Frost, *Rival Regionalisms and the Regional Order*, National Bureau of Asian Research Special Report 48, December 2014, http://www.nbr.org/publications/specialreport/pdf/free/021115/SR48.pdf; Ashley Tellis, Alison Szalwinski, and Michael Wills, eds., *Strategic Asia 2020: US-China Competition for Global Influence* (Seattle, WA: National Bureau of Asian Research, 2020).

7. Ming Wan, "Democracy and Human Rights in Chinese Foreign Policy," in Deng and Wang, *China Rising*, 279–304; Andrew Nathan, "Self-Interest Shapes China's Policies toward the International Order," *East Asia Forum*, December 19, 2017, https://www.eastasiaforum.org/2017/12/19/self-interest-shapes-chinas-policies-toward-the-international-order.

8. Evan Medeiros, *Reluctant Restraint: The Evolution of China's Nonproliferation Policies and Practices, 1980–2004* (Stanford, CA: Stanford University Press, 2007); National Bureau of Asian Research, *China-Russia Entente and the Korean Peninsula*, NBR Special Report No. 79, March 2019.

9. This framework of analysis benefited from conference presentations by Bates Gill; see Bates Gill, *Rising Star: China's New Security Diplomacy* (Washington, DC: Brookings Institution, 2007).

10. Samuel Kim, "China and the United Nations," in *China Joins the World: Progress and Prospects*, ed. Elizabeth Economy and Michael Oksenberg (New York: Council on Foreign Relations, 1999), 46–47.

11. Alastair Iain Johnston and Paul Evans, "China's Engagement," in *Engaging China: The Management of an Emerging Power*, ed. Alastair Iain Johnston and Robert Ross (New York: Routledge, 1999), 235–72.

12. Bates Gill, "Two Steps Forward, One Step Back: The Dynamics of Chinese Nonproliferation and Arms Control Policy-Making in an Era of Reform," in *The Making of Chinese Foreign and Security Policy in the Era of Reform, 1978–2000*, ed. David Michael Lampton (Stanford, CA: Stanford University Press, 2001), 257–88; Johnston and Evans, "China's Engagement," 253.

13. Yong Deng and Thomas Moore, "China Views Globalization: Toward a New Great-Power Politics?," *Washington Quarterly* 27, no. 3 (Summer 2004): 117–36; Allen Carlson, "More Than Just Saying No: China's Evolving Approach to Sovereignty and Intervention," in *New Directions in the Study of China's Foreign Policy*, ed. Alastair Iain Johnston and Robert S. Ross (Stanford, CA: Stanford University Press, 2006), 217–41.

14. Margaret Pearson, "China in Geneva: Lessons from China's Early Years in the World Trade Organization," in Johnston and Ross, *New Directions in the Study of China's Foreign Policy*, 242–75.

15. Samuel Kim, "Chinese Foreign Policy Faces Globalization Challenges," in Johnston and Ross, *New Directions in the Study of China's Foreign Policy*, 276–308.

16. Michael Swaine, *Chinese Views of Global Governance since 2008–2009: Not Much New* (Washington, DC: Carnegie Endowment, 2016).

17. Suisheng Zhao, "A Revisionist Stakeholder: China and the Post–World War II World Order," *Journal of Contemporary China* 27, no. 113 (2018): 643–58.

18. Mazarr et al., *China and the International Order.*

19. Alastair Iain Johnston, "China in a World of Orders," *International Security* 44, no. 2 (Fall 2019): 9–60.

20. Daniel Russel and Blake Berger, *Navigating the Belt and Road Initiative* (New York: Asia Society Policy Institute, June 2019); Melanie Hart and Blaine Johnson, *Mapping China's Global Governance Ambitions* (Washington, DC: Center for American Progress, February 28, 2019); Melanie Hart and Kelly Magsamen, *Limit, Leverage and Compete: A New Strategy on China* (Washington, DC: Center for American Progress, April 2019); Matt Schrader, *Friends and Enemies: A Framework for Understanding Chinese Political Influence in Democratic Countries* (Washington, DC: German Marshall Fund, April 22, 2020); David Shullman, ed., *Chinese Malign Influence and the Corrosion of Democracy* (Washington, DC: International Republican Institute, 2019); Daniel Kliman, Rush Doshi, Kristine Lee, and Zack Cooper, *Grading China's Belt and Road* (Washington, DC: Center for New American Security, April 2019); Tellis et al., *Strategic Asia 2020: US-China Competition*; Nadege Rolland, *China's Vision for a New World Order* (Seattle, WA: National Bureau of Asian Research, January 2020); Larry Diamond and Orville Schell, coordinators, *Chinese Influence and American Interests* (Stanford, CA: Hoover Institution Press, 2018); Scott McDonald and Michael Burgoyne, eds., *China's Global Influence* (Honolulu, HI: Asia-Pacific Center for Security Studies, 2020); Thomas Mahnken, Ross Babbage, and Toshi Yoshihara, *Countering Comprehensive Coercion* (Washington, DC: Center for Strategic and Budgetary Assessments, 2018); Ross Babbage, *Winning without Fighting: Chinese and Russian Political Warfare Campaigns* (Washington, DC: Center for Strategic and Budgetary Assessments, 2018); Matt Geraci, "An Update on American Perspectives on the Belt and Road Initiative," ICAS Issue Primers, Washington, DC, January 23, 2020; Nadege Rolland, ed., *Securing the Belt and Road Initiative* (Seattle, WA: National Bureau of Asian Research, September 3, 2019); Andrew Foxall and John Hemmings, *The Art of Deceit* (London: Henry Jackson Society, 2019); Samantha Hoffman, *Engineering Global Consent* (Canberra: APSI Policy Brief, 2019); Peter Harrell, Elizabeth Rosenberg, and Edoardo Saravalle, *China's Use of Coercive Economic Measures* (Washington, DC: Center of New American Security, June 11, 2018).

21. Liza Tobin, "Xi's Vision for Transforming Global Governance: A Strategic Challenge for Washington and Its Allies," in McDonald and Burgoyne, *China's Global Influence*, 38–56; Fu Ying, "China's Vision for the World: A Community of Shared Future," *The Diplomat*, June 22, 2017, https://thediplomat.com/2017/06/chinas-vision-for-the-world-a-community-of-shared-future; PRC State Council Information Office, *China and the World in the New Era*, November 2019, http://english.www.gov.cn/archive/whitepaper/201909/27/content_WS5d8d80f9c6d0bcf8c4c142ef.html.

22. Liu Xuan, "Expert Hails China's Contribution to International Order and UN System," *China Daily*, August 13, 2019, 11; Karl Wilson, "China Tops World in Diplomatic Posts," *China Daily*, November 27, 2019, https://www.chinadailyhk.com/articles/157/45/10/1574828103413.html; "World Embraces Xi's Vision for Development," *China Daily*, March 5, 2019, 4.

23. "FM Wang Yi Speech at 56th Munich Security Conference," *China Daily*, February 16, 2020, https://www.chinadaily.com.cn/a/202002/16/WS5e490ce7a310128217277dc8.html; Ministry of Foreign Affairs, "Wang Yi Attends the Symposium on the International Situation and China's Foreign Relations in 2019," December 13, 2019, https://www.fmprc.gov.cn/mfa_eng/zxxx_662805/t1724299.shtml.

24. "Is China Challenging the United States for Global Leadership?," *The Economist*, April 1, 2017, https://www.economist.com/china/2017/04/01/is-china-challenging-the-united-states-for-global-leadership.

25. "World Embraces Xi's Vision for Development."

26. Elizabeth Economy, "Yes, Virginia, China Is Exporting Its Model," Council on Foreign Relations blog post, December 11, 2019, https://www.cfr.org/blog/yes-virginia-china-exporting-its-model.

27. Barry Naughton, "China's Global Economic Interactions," in *China and the World*, ed. David Shambaugh (New York: Oxford University Press, 2020), 125.

28. Georg Struver, "China's Partnership Diplomacy: International Alignment Based on Interests or Ideology," *Chinese Journal of International Politics* 10, no. 1 (Spring 2017): 31–65.

29. For background, see discussion of these elements in Avery Goldstein, *Rising to the Challenge: China's Grand Strategy and International Security* (Stanford, CA: Stanford University Press, 2005); Gill, *Rising Star*.

30. Tobin, "Xi's Vision for Transforming Global Governance," 42–45.

31. The following four paragraphs are based on Shengsong Yue, "Towards a Global Partnership Network: Implications, Evolution and Prospects of China's Partnership Diplomacy," *Copenhagen Journal of Asian Affairs* 36, no. 2 (2018): 5–27.

32. Harrell et al., *China's Use of Coercive Economic Measures*.

33. "China Cuts Australian Beef Imports as Coronavirus Tensions Escalate," *Los Angeles Times*, May 12, 2020, https://www.latimes.com/world-nation/story/2020-05-12/china-cuts-australian-beef-imports-coronavirus-tension.

34. Fumi Matsumoto and Kensaku Ihara, "Fear of China's Election Meddling Triggers Reforms across Pacific," *Nikkei Asian Review*, December 7, 2019, https://asia.nikkei.com/Politics/International-relations/Fear-of-China-s-election-meddling-triggers-reforms-across-Pacific.

35. "China Committed to Globalization," *China Daily*, January 23, 2020, http://www.chinadaily.com.cn/a/202001/23/WS5e2901eca310128217272f52.html.

36. Hart and Magsamen, *Limit, Leverage and Compete: A New Strategy on China*, 17–19.

37. Wayne Morrison, *China's Economic Rise*, Congressional Research Service Report RL33534 (Washington, DC: Library of Congress, June 25, 2019), 36–37; Wayne Morrison, *US-China Trade Issues*, Congressional Research Service Report IF10030 (Washington, DC: Library of Congress, June 23, 2019); David Lynch, "Trump's Raise the Stakes Strategy Raises Anxiety," *Washington Post*, July 21, 2018, A14.

38. Benjamin Haas, "Marriott Apologizes to China over Tibet and Taiwan Error," *The Guardian*, January 12, 2018, https://www.theguardian.com/world/2018/jan/12/marriott-apologises-to-china-over-tibet-and-taiwan-error.

39. Ashifa Kassan and Tom Phillips, "Chinese Minister Vents Anger," *The Guardian*, July 2, 2016, https://www.theguardian.com/law/2016/jun/02/chinese-foreign-minister-canada-angry-human-rights-question.

40. Rosie Perper, "China and the NBA Are Coming to Blows over a pro-Hong Kong Tweet," *BusinessInsider*, October 22, 2019, https://www.businessinsider.com/nba-china-feud-timeline-daryl-morey-tweet-hong-kong-protests-2019-10.

41. Yanan Wang, "Xi Says China 'Will Never Seek Hegemony,'" Associated Press, December 18, 2018, https://www.theglobeandmail.com/business/international-business/asia-pacific-business/article-chinas-xi-pledges-unswerving-reforms-but-on-own-terms.

42. Jacob Mardell, "The Community of Common Destiny in Xi Jinping's New Era," *The Diplomat*, October 25, 2017, https://thediplomat.com/2017/10/the-community-of-common-destiny-in-xi-jinpings-new-era.

43. "China-Southeast Asia Relations," *Comparative Connections* 21, no. 3 (January 2020): 61–62.

44. "China-Southeast Asia Relations," *Comparative Connections* 20, no. 3 (January 2020): 55.

45. Economy, "Yes, Virginia, China Is Exporting Its Model"; "In Virus-Hit America, World Health Organization in Firing Line," *Japan Times*, April 9, 2020, https://www.japantimes.co.jp/news/2020/04/09/world/world-health-organization-america/#.XsA_42hKiM8.

46. Tobin, "Xi's Vision for Transforming Global Governance: A Strategic Challenge for Washington and Its Allies," 54–56.

47. "China's Zhou Says IMF Members Frustrated with Quota Reform Delay," *Xinhua*, April 18, 2015, http://news.xinhuanet.com/english/2015-04/18/c_134160977.htm.

48. Samuel Kim, "China and the United Nations," in *China Joins the World: Progress and Prospects*, ed. Elizabeth Economy and Michael Oksenberg (New York: Council on Foreign Relations, 1999), 46–47.

49. These insights from such specialists as Rosemary Foot, Bates Gill, and David Shambaugh came at an international meeting cosponsored by George Washington University and Centre Asie Ifri (Paris), January 2002; see, notably, Rosemary Foot, *Rights beyond Borders: The Global Community and the Struggle over Human Rights in China* (New York: Oxford University Press, 2000), and Rosemary Foot and Andrew Walter, *China, the United States and the Global Order* (New York: Cambridge University Press, 2010).

50. Joseph Logan and Patrick Worsnip, "Anger after Russia, China Block UN Action on Syria," Reuters, February 5, 2012, http://www.reuters.com/article/2012/02/05/us-syria-idUSTRE80S08620120205.

51. Kim, "China and the United Nations," 42–89, and "Chinese Foreign Policy Faces Globalization Challenges," 276–308.

52. Carlson, "More Than Just Saying No," 217–41.

53. Jianwei Wang, "China's Multilateral Diplomacy in the New Millennium," 164–66; Jianwei Wang, "Managing Conflict: Chinese Perspectives on Multilateral Diplomacy and Collective Security," in *In the Eyes of the Dragon: China Views the World*, ed. Yong Deng and Fei-Ling Wang (Lanham, MD: Rowman & Littlefield, 1999), 75–81; "Beijing May Open Door to WHO for Taiwan," *South China Morning Post*, December 19, 2008.

54. Yu-jie Chen and Jerome Cohen, "Why Does WHO Exclude Taiwan?," Council on Foreign Relations, April 9, 2020, https://www.cfr.org/in-brief/why-does-who-exclude-taiwan.

55. "Financing Peacekeeping," United Nations Peacekeeping, accessed June 8, 2015, http://www.un.org/en/peacekeeping/operations/financing.shtml.

56. "Bearing More Responsibilities: China Increases Its Share of International Responsibilities," China Institute of International Studies, January 16, 2013, http://www.ciis.org.cn/english/2013-01/16/content_5674643.htm.

57. "China, Japan and the Future of UN Peacekeeping," *The Diplomat*, July 21, 2017, https://thediplomat.com/2017/07/china-japan-and-the-future-of-un-peacekeeping.

58. "President Xi Jinping's Pledges at UN Show That China Can Meet Its Global Responsibilities," editorial, *South China Morning Post*, October 1, 2015, https://www.scmp.com/comment/insight-opinion/article/1863079/president-xi-jinpings-pledges-un-show-china-can-meet-its.

59. He Yin, "China Takes the Lead in UN Peacekeeping," *China Daily*, September 26, 2019, https://www.chinadaily.com.cn/a/201909/26/WS5d8bfa01a310cf3e3556d7f3.html.

60. Laurel Wamsley, "U.N. Warns of Budget Crisis," NPR, October 10, 2019, https://www.npr.org/2019/10/10/769095931/u-n-warns-of-budget-crisis-if-nations-dont-pay-1-3-billion-in-dues-they-owe.

61. Marc Santora, Somini Sengupta, and Benjamin Wiser, "Former UN President and Chinese Billionaire Accused in Graft Scheme," *New York Times*, October 6, 2015, https://www.nytimes.com/2015/10/07/nyregion/john-ashe-top-united-nations-official-is-accused-in-bribery-scheme.html.

62. Kristine Lee and Alexander Sullivan, *People's Republic of the United Nations* (Washington, DC: Center for New America Security, May 2019).

63. Colum Lynch, "China Bids to Lead World Agency Protecting Intellectual Property," *Foreign Policy*, November 26, 2019, https://foreignpolicy.com/2019/11/26/china-bids-lead-world-intellectual-property-organization-wipo.

64. He Yin, "China Takes the Lead."

65. Robert Sutter, *China's Rise in Asia: Promises and Perils* (Lanham, MD: Rowman & Littlefield, 2005), 177–208, 249–64; Jianwei Wang, "China's Multilateral Diplomacy in the New Millennium," 166–86.

66. Zhou Gang, "Status Quo and Prospects of China-ASEAN Relations," *Foreign Affairs Journal* (Beijing) 80 (June 2006): 14–21.

67. The rebalance policy, China's reaction, and consequences for Asia are reviewed in Robert Sutter, *The United States and Asia*, 2nd ed. (Lanham, MD: Rowman and Littlefield, 2020), 62–72.

68. Wang Haiyun, "Prospect for Sino-Russian Relations in 2006," *Foreign Affairs Journal* (Beijing) 79 (March 2006): 50–54.

69. Robert Sutter, *China-Russia Relations: Strategic Implications and US Policy*, National Bureau of Asian Research, NBR Special Report No. 73, September 2018; Rajeswari Pillai Rajagopalan, "Growing Russia-China-India Tensions," *The Diplomat*, March 17, 2020, https://thediplomat.com/2020/03/growing-russia-india-china-tensions-splits-in-the-ric-strategic-triangle.

# 5. CHINESE NATIONAL SECURITY POLICIES

1. People's Republic of China State Council Information Office, "China's Peaceful Development Road," *People's Daily Online*, December 22, 2005, accessed July 7, 2006; "Full Text of Chinese President Hu Jintao's Speech at Opening Session of Boao Forum," *China Daily*, April 15, 2011.

2. Interview, Chinese Foreign Ministry, Beijing, May 30, 2006.

3. I benefited notably from comprehensive briefings on China's national security policy given by leaders of the PLA's Academy of Military Science in Beijing in June 2008 and June 2011 and briefings by senior representatives of the academy at a public meeting at Georgetown University, Washington, DC, in October 2008.

4. People's Republic of China State Council Information Office, *China's National Defense in 2004* (Beijing: People's Republic of China State Council Information Office, December 27, 2004); *China's National Defense in 2006* (Beijing: People's Republic of China State Council Information Office, December 29, 2006); *China's National Defense in 2008* (Beijing: People's Republic of China State Council Information Office, January 2009); *China's National Defense in 2010* (Beijing: People's Republic of China State Council Information Office, March 2011); "Document: China's Military Strategy," *USNI News*, May 26, 2015, http://news.usni.org/2015/05/26/document-chinas-military-strategy; "Full Text: China's National Defense in the New Era, *Xinhua*, July 24, 2019, http://www.xinhuanet.com/english/2019-07/24/c_138253389.htm.

5. Paul Godwin, "China as a Major Asian Power: The Implications of Its Military Modernization (A View from the United States)," in *China, the United States, and Southeast Asia: Contending Perspectives on Politics, Security, and Economics*, ed. Evelyn Goh and Sheldon Simon (New York: Routledge, 2008), 145–66.

6. Chu Shulong and Lin Xinzhu, "It Is Not the Objective of Chinese Military Power to Catch Up and Overtake the United States," *Huanqiu Shibao* (Beijing), June 26, 2008, 11.

7. US Department of Defense, *Annual Report on the Military Power of the People's Republic of China, 2008* (Washington, DC: US Department of Defense, March 2008); *Annual Report on the Military Power of the People's Republic of China, 2009* (Washington, DC: US Department of Defense, March 2009); and *Military and Security Developments Involving the People's Republic of China, 2010* (Washington, DC: US Department of Defense, August 2010).

8. People's Republic of China State Council Information Office, *China's National Defense in 2010*, 4.

9. People's Republic of China State Council Information Office, *China's National Defense in 2010*, 4; Martin Indyk, Kenneth Lieberthal, and Michael O'Hanlon, *Bending History: Barack Obama's Foreign Policy* (Washington, DC: Brookings Institution, 2012), 61–62.

10. "China's National Defense in the New Era"; Anthony Cordesman, *China's New Defense White Paper* (Washington, DC: Center for Strategic and International Studies, July 24, 2019), https://csis-prod.s3.amazonaws.com/s3fs-public/publication/190724_China_2019_Defense.pdf.

11. David Shambaugh, "Coping with a Conflicted China," *Washington Quarterly* 34, no. 1 (Winter 2011): 7–27; M. Taylor Fravel, "China's Search for Military Power," *Washington*

*Quarterly* 33, no. 3 (Summer 2008): 125–41; briefings by Major General Luo Yuan and Senior Colonel Fan Gaoyue of the Academy of Military Science, Georgetown University, Washington, DC, October 2, 2008; People's Republic of China State Council Information Office, *China's National Defense in 2010*, 4.

12. Dennis Blasko, "Steady as She Goes: China's New Defense White Paper," War on the Rocks, August 12, 2019, https://warontherocks.com/2019/08/steady-as-she-goes-chinas-new-defense-white-paper.

13. Hu Xiao, "Japan and U.S. Told, Hands Off Taiwan," *China Daily*, March 7, 2005, 1; Academy of Military Science briefings, June 2008, October 2008; People's Republic of China State Council Information Office, *China's National Defense in 2004*; "Chinese FM Refutes Fallacies on the South China Sea Issue," *China Daily*, July 25, 2010, 1; Robert Sutter, "The US and Taiwan Embrace Despite China's Objections, but Will It Last?," *PacNet* 58 (Honolulu, HI: Pacific Forum CSIS, November 12, 2019), https://www.pacforum.org/sites/default/files/20191112_PacNet_58_0.pdf.

14. Gordon Chang, "Hillary Clinton Changes America's China Policy," *Forbes*, July 28, 2010, https://www.forbes.com/2010/07/28/china-beijing-asia-hillary-clinton-opinions-columnists-gordon-g-chang.html#1cd05ca550c7.

15. "China-Southeast Asia Relations," *Comparative Connections* 9, no. 3 (October 2007): 75, http://cc.pacforum.org/2007/10/myanmar-challenges-chinas-successes.

16. "China-Southeast Asia Relations," *Comparative Connections* 10, no. 4 (January 2009), http://cc.pacforum.org/2009/01/economic-concerns-begin-hit-home; "US Fears China-Backed Resort in Cambodia Could House Military," *South China Morning Post*, July 19, 2019, https://www.scmp.com/news/asia/southeast-asia/article/3019387/us-fears-china-backed-resort-cambodia-could-house-military.

17. Evan Medeiros, "Strategic Hedging and the Future of Asia-Pacific Stability," *Washington Quarterly* 29, no. 1 (Winter 2005–2006): 145–67; Elisabeth Bumiller, "U.S. Will Counter Chinese Arms Buildup," *New York Times*, January 8, 2011, https://www.nytimes.com/2011/01/09/world/asia/09military.html.

18. "BRI Will Help China to Add to Its International Military Bases, Says Pentagon," *Straits Times*, May 3, 2019, https://www.straitstimes.com/world/united-states/bri-will-help-china-add-to-its-international-military-bases-says-pentagon.

19. Richard Bush and Michael O'Hanlon, *A War like No Other: The Truth about China's Challenge to America* (Hoboken, NJ: Wiley, 2007); Elsa Kania and Peter Wood, "Major Themes in China's 2019 Defense White Paper," *Jamestown Foundation China Brief* 19, no. 14 (July 31, 2019), https://jamestown.org/program/major-themes-in-chinas-2019-national-defense-white-paper.

20. Dan Blumenthal, "Fear and Loathing in Asia," *Journal of International Security Affairs* (Spring 2006): 81–88; US Department of Defense, *Military and Security Developments Involving the People's Republic of China, 2010*; US Defense Intelligence Agency, *China Military Power* (Washington, DC: US Defense Intelligence Agency, 2019), https://www.dia.mil/Portals/27/Documents/News/Military%20Power%20Publications/China_Military_Power_FINAL_5MB_20190103.pdf.

21. Godwin, "China as a Major Asian Power"; US Department of Defense, *Military and Security Developments Involving the People's Republic of China, 2010*; Andrew Erickson and David Yang, "On the Verge of a Game-Changer," *Proceedings* 135, no. 5 (May 2009): 26–32; US Defense Intelligence Agency, *China Military Power*; Ashley Tellis, "Overview," in *Strategic Asia 2019: China's Expanding Strategic Ambitions*, ed. Ashley Tellis, Alison Szalwinski, and Michael Wills (Seattle, WA: National Bureau of Asian Research, 2019), 34–40.

22. Ashley J. Tellis and Travis Tanner, eds., *Strategic Asia 2012–13: China's Military Challenge* (Seattle, WA: National Bureau of Asian Research, 2012).

23. Michael Swaine, "China's Regional Military Posture," in *Power Shift: China and Asia's New Dynamics*, ed. David Shambaugh (Berkeley: University of California Press, 2005), 266; David Michael Lampton, *The Three Faces of Chinese Power: Might, Money, and Minds* (Berkeley: University of California Press, 2008), 40–42; Eric Heginbotham et al., *China's Evolving Nuclear Deterrent* (Santa Monica, CA: RAND Corporation, 2017).

24. David Shambaugh, "China's Military Modernization: Making Steady and Surprising Progress," in *Strategic Asia 2005–06: Military Modernization in an Era of Uncertainty*, ed. Ashley Tellis and Michael Wills (Seattle, WA: National Bureau of Asian Research, 2005), 67–104; Ashley Tellis, "China's Military Modernization and Asian Security," in *Strategic Asia 2012–13: China's Military Challenge*, ed. Ashley J. Tellis and Travis Tanner (Seattle, WA: National Bureau of Asian Research, 2012), 3–26; Tellis, "Overview."

25. The discussion here and in the following several paragraphs was adapted from Swaine, "China's Regional Military Posture," 268–72. The discussion was updated with reference to annual Department of Defense reports to Congress on the Chinese military. See US Department of Defense, *Military and Security Developments Involving the People's Republic of China, 2019* (Washington, DC: Office of the Secretary of Defense, 2019).

26. The section below benefited from the comprehensive treatment of recent PLA developments and reforms in Phillip Saunders et al., eds., *Chairman Xi Remakes the PLA* (Washington, DC: National Defense University Press, 2019); see also US Defense Intelligence Agency, *China Military Power*; US Department of Defense, *Military and Security Developments Involving the People's Republic of China, 2019*; Tellis, "Overview."

27. Satoru Mori, "US Technological Competition with China: The Military, Industrial and Digital Network Dimensions," *Asia-Pacific Review* 26, no. 1 (2019): 77–120; Graham Allison, "Is China Beating America to AI Supremacy?," *National Interest*, December 22, 2019, https://nationalinterest.org/feature/china-beating-america-ai-supremacy-106861; Julian Baird Gewitz, "China's Long March to Technology Supremacy, *Foreign Affairs*, August 27, 2019, https://www.foreignaffairs.com/articles/china/2019-08-27/chinas-long-march-technological-supremacy; Elsa Kania, "Technology and Innovation in China's Strategy and Global Influence," in *China's Global Influence*, ed. Scott McDonald and Michael Burgoyne (Honolulu, HI: Asia-Pacific Center for Security Studies, 2020), 229–46.

28. John Garver, *Foreign Relations of the People's Republic of China* (Englewood Cliffs, NJ: Prentice Hall, 1993), 249–64; Thomas Christensen, "Windows and War: Trend Analysis and Beijing's Use of Force," in *New Directions in the Study of China's Foreign Policy*, ed. Alastair Iain Johnston and Robert S. Ross (Stanford, CA: Stanford University Press, 2006), 50–85. Robert Sutter, *Foreign Relations of the PRC* (Lanham, MD: Rowman & Littlefield, 2013), 10–14.

29. Robert Suettinger, *Beyond Tiananmen: The Politics of U.S.-China Relations, 1989–2000* (Washington, DC: Brookings Institution, 2003), 200–263.

30. Saunders et al., *Chairman Xi Remakes the PLA*, 1–44.

31. Michael Chase, Jeffrey Engstrom, Tai Ming Cheung, Kristen Gunness, Scott Harold, Susan Puska, and Samuel Berkowitz, *China's Incomplete Military Transformation* (Santa Monica, CA: RAND Corporation, 2015); Saunders et al., *Chairman Xi Remakes the PLA*, 203–519.

32. Aaron Friedberg, *Beyond Air-Sea Battle: The Debate over U.S. Military Strategy in Asia* (New York: Routledge, 2014), 91–93.

33. Michael Swaine, "Chinese Views of Weapons of Mass Destruction," in US National Intelligence Council, *China and Weapons of Mass Destruction: Implications for the United States*, Conference Report (Washington, DC: US National Intelligence Council, November 5, 1999), 165–82; Bates Gill, "China and Nuclear Arms Control," *SIPRI Insights* 4 (April 2010); M. Taylor Fravel and Evan Medeiros, "China's Search for Assured Retaliation," *International Security* 35, no. 2 (Fall 2010): 48–87; Heginbotham et al., *China's Evolving Nuclear Deterrent.*

34. Evan Medeiros, *Reluctant Restraint: The Evolution of China's Nonproliferation Policies and Practices, 1980–2004* (Stanford, CA: Stanford University Press, 2007).

35. For background, see Shirley Kan, *China and Proliferation of Weapons of Mass Destruction and Missiles: Policy Issues*, Congressional Research Service Report RL31555 (Washington, DC: Library of Congress, January 5, 2015). See also Saunders et al., *Chairman Xi Remakes the PLA*, 393–518. For Chinese views, see the periodic defense white papers referenced previously.

36. Bates Gill and James Mulvenon, "The Chinese Strategic Rocket Forces: Transition to Credible Deterrence," in US National Intelligence Council, *China and Weapons of Mass Destruction*, 11–58; Shambaugh, "China's Military Modernization," 89–94; David Logan, "Mak-

ing Sense of China's Missile Forces," in Saunders et al., *Chairman Xi Remakes the PLA*, 293–436.

37. William S. Murray, "Revisiting Taiwan's Defense Strategy," *Naval War College Review* 61, no. 3 (Summer 2008): 13–38; Ronald O'Rourke, *China's Naval Modernization*, Congressional Research Service Report RL33153 (Washington, DC: Library of Congress, April 24, 2020).

38. Eric Croddy, "Chinese Chemical and Biological Warfare (CBW) Capabilities," in US National Intelligence Council, *China and Weapons of Mass Destruction*, 59–110; Kan, *China and Proliferation*, 16–18.

39. Medeiros, *Reluctant Restraint*; Kan, *China and Proliferation*.

40. See, among others, Bill Gertz, "U.S. Hits China with Sanctions over Arms Sales," *Washington Times*, January 25, 2002, and "CIA Sees Rise in Terrorist Weapons," *Washington Times*, January 31, 2002. See also Kan, *China and Proliferation*, summary page; "China Demands US Immediately Withdraw North Korea Sanctions," *Washington Post*, August 23, 2017, https://www.washingtonpost.com/world/china-bristles-at-us-imposed-sanctions-on-north-korea-trade/2017/08/23/32bfba3c-87ba-11e7-9ce7-9e175d8953fa_story.html.

41. Evan Medeiros, "The Changing Character of China's WMD Proliferation Activities," in US National Intelligence Council, *China and Weapons of Mass Destruction*, 135–38; Kan, *China and Proliferation*.

42. Bates Gill, "Two Steps Forward, One Step Back: The Dynamics of Chinese Nonproliferation and Arms Control Policy-Making in an Era of Reform," in *The Making of Chinese Foreign and Security Policy in the Era of Reform*, ed. David Michael Lampton (Stanford, CA: Stanford University Press, 2001), 257–88; Garver, *Foreign Relations of the People's Republic of China*, 249–64.

43. Kan, *China and Proliferation*, 2–3.

44. Medeiros, "The Changing Character of China's WMD Proliferation Activities"; Kan, *China and Proliferation*.

45. Kan, *China and Proliferation*, 2–3, 7–18, 18–49; Kinling Lo, "China Backs Iran Nuclear Deal as US Walks Away, *South China Morning Post*, May 9, 2018, https://www.scmp.com/news/china/diplomacy-defence/article/2145406/china-backs-iran-nuclear-deal-united-states-walks-away.

46. Pranay Vaddi, *Leaving the INF Treaty Won't Help Trump Counter China* (Washington, DC: Carnegie Endowment for International Peace, January 31, 2019), https://carnegieendowment.org/2019/01/31/leaving-inf-treaty-won-t-help-trump-counter-china-pub-78262; Tom O'Connor, "China 'Will Never' Join Arms Control Deal with U.S. and Russia, Says Donald Trump Has Not Even Followed Past Agreements," *Newsweek*, May 20, 2019, https://www.newsweek.com/china-arms-deal-us-russia-1431025.

47. Robert Sutter, *China's Rise in Asia: Promises and Perils* (Lanham, MD: Rowman & Littlefield, 2005), 77–94; Andrew Small, "China's Caution on Afghanistan-Pakistan," *Washington Quarterly* 33, no. 3 (July 2010): 81–97; "China Says Bin Laden's Death a Milestone for Anti-terrorism," *China Daily*, May 3, 2011, http://www.chinadaily.com.cn.

48. Zhao Huasheng, "Chinese View of Post 2014 Afghanistan," *Asia Policy* 17 (January 2014), http://www.nbr.org/publications/element.aspx?id=725.

49. Nadege Rolland, ed., *Securing the Belt and Road Initiative*, NBR Special Report No. 80 (Seattle, WA: National Bureau of Asian Research, September 3, 2019), 72, https://www.nbr.org/wp-content/uploads/pdfs/publications/sr80_securing_the_belt_and_road_sep2019.pdf.

50. Garver, *Foreign Relations of the People's Republic of China*, 168–73.

51. Bates Gill and Melissa Murphy, "China's Evolving Approach to Counterterrorism," *Harvard Asia Quarterly*, Winter–Spring 2005, 21–22.

52. Andrew Scobell, "Terrorism and Chinese Foreign Policy," in *China Rising: Power and Motivation in Chinese Foreign Policy*, ed. Yong Deng and Fei-Ling Wang (Lanham, MD: Rowman & Littlefield, 2005), 315.

53. Sutter, *China's Rise in Asia*, 256–59; Bates Gill, *Rising Star: China's New Security Diplomacy* (Washington, DC: Brookings Institution, 2007), 37–47.

54. Gill and Murphy, "China's Evolving Approach to Counterterrorism," 25–28; Scobell, "Terrorism and Chinese Foreign Policy," 311–18; "China Thanks Nations for Support for Olympic Security," *China Daily*, September 11, 2008.

55. Murray Scott Tanner, *China's Response to Terrorism* (Washington, DC: Center for Naval Analysis, June 2016), https://www.cna.org/CNA_files/PDF/IRM-2016-U-013542-Final.pdf.

56. Daniel Byman and Israa Saber, *Is China Ready for Global Terrorism?* (Washington, DC: Brookings Institution, September 2019), https://www.brookings.edu/wp-content/uploads/2019/09/FP_20190930_china_counterterrorism_byman_saber-1.pdf.

57. Kenneth Allen and Eric McVadon, *China's Foreign Military Relations*, Report 32 (Washington, DC: Henry Stimson Center, October 1999); Kristen Gunness, *China's Military Diplomacy in an Era of Change* (Alexandria, VA: CNA Corporation, 2006); Gill, *Rising Star*; People's Republic of China State Council Information Office, *China's National Defense in 2010*.

58. Richard Weitz, *The Expanding China-Russia Defense Partnership* (Washington, DC: Hudson Institute, May 2019).

59. Shirley Kan, *U.S.-China Military Contacts: Issues for Congress*, Congressional Research Service Report RL32496 (Washington, DC: Library of Congress, June 10, 2014); US Department of Defense, *Military and Security Developments Involving the People's Republic of China, 2019*, 107–13, 118–20.

60. David Shambaugh, "China-Europe Relations Get Complicated," *Brookings Northeast Asia Commentary* 9 (May 2007); US Department of Defense–Israeli Ministry of Defense joint press statement, News Release No. 846-05 (Washington, DC: US Department of Defense, August 16, 2005).

61. Richard Grimmett, *Conventional Arms Transfers to Developing Nations*, Congressional Research Service Report RL34187 (Washington, DC: Library of Congress, September 26, 2007); "China Becomes the World's Third Largest Arms Exporter," *BBC News*, March 15, 2015, http://sinosphere.blogs.nytimes.com/2015/03/16/china-becomes-worlds-third-largest-arms-exporter/?_r=0; "How Dominant Is China in the Global Arms Market?," *Chinapower CSIS*, 2019, https://chinapower.csis.org/china-global-arms-trade.

62. Robert Sutter, *Chinese Policy Priorities and Their Implications for the United States* (Lanham, MD: Rowman & Littlefield, 2000), 192–93.

63. "China's Military Diplomacy Forging New Ties," *Xinhua*, October 28, 2002, replayed by FBIS Document ID: CPP20021028000111.

64. "China's Military Diplomacy in 2004," *People's Daily Online*, January 5, 2005, accessed January 6, 2005; People's Republic of China State Council Information Office, *China's National Defense in 2010*; Zhao Shengnan, "Military Outreach Gets New Emphasis," *China Daily*, February 2, 2015, http://www.chinadaily.com.cn/cndy/2015-02/02/content_19462377.htm; Weitz, *The Expanding China-Russia Defense Partnership*.

65. International Crisis Group, *China's Growing Role in UN Peacekeeping*, Asia Report 166 (Brussels: International Crisis Group, April 17, 2009); Gill, *Rising Star*, 200–202; People's Republic of China State Council Information Office, *China's National Defense in 2010*; Lucy Best, "What Motivates Chinese Peacekeeping," Council on Foreign Relations, January 7, 2020, https://www.cfr.org/blog/what-motivates-chinese-peacekeeping.

66. Allen Carlson, "More Than Just Saying No: China's Evolving Approach to Sovereignty and Intervention," in *New Directions in the Study of China's Foreign Policy*, ed. Alastair Iain Johnston and Robert S. Ross (Stanford, CA: Stanford University Press, 2006), 217–41.

67. Huang Jingjing, "Keeping Peace in the Sahara," *Global Times*, November 12, 2014, http://backup.globaltimes.cn/DesktopModules/DnnForge%20-%20NewsArticles/Print.aspx?tabid=99&tabmoduleid=94&articleId=891479&moduleId=405&PortalID=0; "China Peacekeepers in South Sudan to Focus on Protecting Civilians," *Voice of America*, January 15, 2015, http://www.voanews.com/content/south-sudan-china-peacekeepers-unmiss/2599640.html.

68. "China Supports in UN Peacekeeping Operations," *China Daily*, March 31, 2011; International Crisis Group, *China's Growing Role in UN Peacekeeping*; "Nation to Chip in More for UN Kitty," *China Daily*, December 31, 2009, 2; He Yin, "China Takes the Lead in UN

Peacekeeping," *China Daily*, September 26, 2019, https://www.chinadaily.com.cn/a/201909/26/WS5d8bfa01a310cf3e3556d7f3.html.

69. Joseph Logan and Patrick Worsnip, "Anger after Russia, China Block UN Action on Syria," Reuters, February 5, 2012, http://www.reuters.com/article/2012/02/05/us-syria-idUSTRE80S08620120205.

# 6. RELATIONS WITH THE UNITED STATES

1. Robert Zoellick, "Whither China: From Membership to Responsibility," speech, September 21, 2005, http://2001-2009.state.gov/s/d/former/zoellick/rem/53682.htm; Elizabeth Economy and Adam Segal, "The G-2 Mirage," *Foreign Affairs*, May–June 2009, http://www.foreignaffairs.com/articles/64996/elizabeth-c-economy-and-adam-segal/the-g-2-mirage.

2. The findings of this chapter are treated in greater depth in Robert Sutter, *U.S.-Chinese Relations* (Lanham, MD: Rowman & Littlefield, 2013). For other perspectives, see, among others, David Shambaugh, ed., *Tangled Titans* (Lanham, MD: Rowman & Littlefield, 2012).

3. Michael Schaller, *The United States and China: Into the Twenty-First Century* (New York: Oxford University Press, 2002), 204–5.

4. Robert Sutter, *U.S. Policy toward China* (Lanham, MD: Rowman & Littlefield, 1998), 26–44.

5. James Mann, *About Face* (New York: Knopf, 1999), 274–78. Authoritative assessments of US-China relations in the 1990s include David Michael Lampton, *Same Bed, Different Dreams* (Berkeley: University of California Press, 2001), and Robert Suettinger, *Beyond Tiananmen* (Washington, DC: Brookings Institution, 2003).

6. For this and the next two paragraphs, see Robert Sutter, *Historical Dictionary of United States–China Relations* (Lanham, MD: Scarecrow Press, 2006), lxix–lxx.

7. Assessments of US-China relations in this period include Jeffrey Bader, *Obama and China's Rise* (Washington, DC: Brookings Institution, 2012); Martin Indyk, Kenneth Lieberthal, and Michael O'Hanlon, *Bending History: Barack Obama's Foreign Policy* (Washington, DC: Brookings Institution, 2012), 24–69; Aaron Friedberg, *A Contest for Supremacy* (New York: Norton, 2011); Kenneth Lieberthal and Wang Jisi, *Addressing U.S.-China Strategic Distrust* (Washington, DC: Brookings Institution, March 2012); Andrew Nathan and Andrew Scobell, *China's Search for Security* (New York: Columbia University Press, 2012); Denny Roy, *Return of the Dragon: Rising China and Regional Security* (New York: Columbia University Press, 2013); Nina Hachigian, ed., *Debating China* (New York: Oxford University Press, 2014); and Thomas Christensen, *The China Challenge* (New York: Norton, 2015). See also Sutter, *U.S.-Chinese Relations* and Shambaugh, *Tangled Titans*.

8. On Bush's reliance on China to deal with North Korea, see "Bush, Kerry Square Off in 1st Debate," *Japan Today*, October 1, 2004, accessed March 21, 2008, http://www.japantoday.com/jp/news/313422/all.

9. Condoleezza Rice, remarks at Sophia University, Tokyo, Japan, March 19, 2005, accessed March 21, 2008, http://www.state.gov/secretary/rm/2005/43655.htm; Evan Medeiros, "Strategic Hedging and the Future of Asia-Pacific Stability," *Washington Quarterly* 29, no. 1 (Winter 2005–2006): 15–28.

10. Rosemary Foot, "Chinese Strategies in a U.S.-Hegemonic Global Order: Accommodating and Hedging," *International Affairs* 82, no. 1 (2006): 77–94; Wang Jisi, "China's Search for Stability with America," *Foreign Affairs* 84, no. 5 (September–October 2005): 39–48; Yong Deng and Thomas Moore, "China Views Globalization: Toward a New Great-Power Politics?," *Washington Quarterly* 27, no. 3 (Summer 2004): 117–36.

11. Sutter, *U.S.-Chinese Relations*, 129–30.

12. For an overview of the Obama government's approach to China, see notably Bader, *Obama and China's Rise*.

13. Indyk et al., *Bending History*, 24–69.

14. Bonnie Glaser and Brittany Billingsley, "Friction and Cooperation Co-exist Uneasily," *Comparative Connections* 13, no. 2 (September 2011): 27–40; Minxin Pei, "China's Bumpy

Ride Ahead," *The Diplomat*, February 16, 2011; Robert Sutter, *Positive Equilibrium in U.S.-China Relations: Durable or Not?* (Baltimore: University of Maryland School of Law, 2010).

15. Bader, *Obama and China's Rise*, 69–129; "Interview of Hillary Clinton with Greg Sheridan of the *Australian*," November 8, 2010, https://2009-2017.state.gov/secretary/20092013clinton/rm/2010/11/150671.htm.

16. See assessments of prominent Chinese specialists in Hachigian, *Debating China*, and Wu Xinbo, "Chinese Visions of the Future of U.S.-China Relations," in *Tangled Titans: The United States and China*, ed. David Shambaugh (Lanham, MD: Rowman & Littlefield, 2012), 371–88.

17. Christopher Johnson, "Xi Jinping Unveils His Foreign Policy Vision," *Thoughts from the Chairman* (Washington, DC: Center for Strategic and International Studies, December 2014); Yun Sun, "China's Peaceful Rise: Peace through Strength?," *PacNet* 25 (Honolulu, HI: Pacific Forum CSIS, March 31, 2014); Yong Deng, "China: The Post-Responsible Power," *Washington Quarterly* 37, no. 4 (Winter 2015): 117–32.

18. Mark E. Manyin, Stephen Daggett, Ben Dolven, Susan V. Lawrence, Michael F. Martin, Ronald O'Rourke, and Bruce Vaughn, *Pivot to the Pacific? The Obama Administration's "Rebalancing" toward Asia*, Congressional Research Service Report 42448 (Washington, DC: Library of Congress, March 28, 2012); Philip Saunders, *The Rebalance to Asia: U.S.-China Relations and Regional Security* (Washington, DC: National Defense University, Institute for National Security Studies, 2012); Richard Ellings, testimony before the House Committee on Foreign Affairs Subcommittee on Asia and the Pacific, Washington, DC, Hearing on the Obama Administration's Pivot to Asia, December 6, 2016, accessed June 6, 2016, https://www.nbr.org/publication/step-or-stumble-the-obama-administrations-pivot-to-asia; Choi Kang and Lee Jayhyon, eds., "What Asia Wants from the US: Voices from the Region," Asan Report (Seoul: Asan Institute, September 2018), http://en.asaninst.org/contents/what-asia-wants-from-the-us—mainly about the US rebalance; Robert Sutter, Michael Brown, and Timothy Adamson, *Balancing Acts: The U.S. Rebalance and Asia-Pacific Stability* (Washington, DC: George Washington University, Elliott School of International Affairs, 2013); Timothy Adamson, Michael Brown, and Robert Sutter, *Rebooting the U.S. Rebalance to Asia* (Washington, DC: George Washington University, Elliott School of International Affairs, 2014). For a book-length compendium on the rebalance, see Hugo Meijer, ed., *Origins and Evolution of the U.S. Rebalance toward Asia: Diplomatic, Military and Economic Dimensions* (London: Palgrave Macmillan, 2015). For an authoritative account of a key US official, see Kurt Campbell, *The Pivot* (New York: Hachette, 2016).

For an overview of US relations with allies and partners in Asia, see Ashley Tellis, Abraham Denmark, and Greg Chaffin, eds., *Strategic Asia 2014–15: U.S. Alliances and Partnerships at the Center of Global Power* (Seattle, WA: National Bureau of Asian Research, 2014). For an in-depth assessment foreseeing gradual American decline in Asia, see Xenia Dormandy, with Rory Kinane, *Asia-Pacific Security: A Changing Role for the United States* (London: Chatham House, Royal Institute of International Affairs, April 2014).

19. This concept dropped from use in 2015 as it was incorporated into the Defense Department's Joint Concept for Access and Maneuver in the Global Commons, https://news.usni.org/2015/01/20/pentagon-drops-air-sea-battle-name-concept-lives.

20. Roy, *Return of the Dragon*; Yun Sun, "China's New Calculations in the South China Sea," *Asia-Pacific Bulletin*, no. 267 (June 10, 2014).

21. "Beyond the US-China Summit," *Foreign Policy Research Institute*, February 4, 2011.

22. Bonnie Glaser and Brittany Billingsley, "Strains Increase and Leadership Transitions," *Comparative Connections* 14, no. 3 (January 2012): 29–40; Manyin et al., *Pivot to the Pacific?*

23. Daljit Singh, "US-China Dialogue Process: Prospects and Implications," *East Asia Forum*, November 2, 2012, http://www.eastasisforum.org.

24. Richard Bush, *Uncharted Strait* (Washington, DC: Brookings Institution, 2013), 213–50.

25. Aries Poon, Jenny Hsu, and Fanny Liu, "Taiwan Election Results Likely to Complicate Relations with China," *Wall Street Journal*, December 1, 2014, http://www.wsj.com/articles/taiwan-election-results-set-to-complicate-relations-with-china-1417366150.

26. Bonnie Glaser and Brittany Billingsley, "Xi Visit Steadies Ties; Dissident Creates Tension," *Comparative Connections* 14, no. 1 (May 2012): 29–30; Bonnie Glaser and Brittany Billingsley, "Creating a New Type of Great Power Relations," *Comparative Connections* 14, no. 2 (September 2012): 29.

27. Donilon's speech and US officials' media briefing on the president's Asia trip were released on November 15, 2012, at http://www.whitehouse.gov/the-press-office.

28. Orville Schell and Susan Shirk, *US Policy toward China* (New York: Asia Society, 2017).

29. Candidate Trump notably called for Japan and South Korea to pay more for America's defense; and if they didn't, he advocated US withdrawal. He allowed that the powers then might seek to develop nuclear weapons, which he viewed as an unfortunate but unavoidable consequence. On North Korea, Mr. Trump called for direct talks between US and North Korean leaders. The coverage of the US election in this chapter builds on the findings in Robert Sutter and Satu Limaye, *America's 2016 Election Debate on Asia Policy and Asian Reactions* (Honolulu, HI: East-West Center, 2016).

30. Jeffrey M. Jones, "Americans See China's Economic Power as Diminished Threat," Gallup, February 26, 2015, http://www.gallup.com/poll/181733/americans-china-economic-power-diminished-threat.aspx; Lydia Saad, "Americans See China as Top Economy Now, but U.S. in Future," Gallup, February 22, 2016, http://www.gallup.com/poll/189347/americans-china-top-economy-future.aspx.

31. Maggie Haberman, "Donald Trump Says He Favors Big Tariffs on Chinese Exports," *New York Times*, January 7, 2016, http://www.nytimes.com/politics/first-draft/2016/01/07/donald-trump-says-he-favors-big-tariffs-on-chinese-exports; Donald Trump, "'America First' Foreign Policy Speech," Washington, DC, April 27, 2016.

32. Sutter and Limaye, *America's 2016 Election Debate*, 21.

33. Robert Sutter, "The United States and Asia in 2017," *Asian Survey* 58, no. 1 (2018): 10–20.

34. Bonnie Glaser and Collin Norkiewicz, "North Korea and Trade Dominate the Agenda," *Comparative Connections* 19, no. 2 (September 2017): 21–34.

35. Bonnie Glaser and Kelly Flaherty, "Hurtling toward a Trade War," *Comparative Connections* 20, no. 1 (May 2018): 19–22; these various events are reviewed in Robert Sutter, "Trump, America and the World—2017 and Beyond," H-Diplo/ISSF Policy Series, January 19, 2019, https://networks.h-net.org/node/28443/discussions/3569933/issf-policy-series-sutter-trump%E2%80%99s-china-policy-bi-partisan.

36. White House, *National Security Strategy of the United States*, December 2017, https://www.whitehouse.gov/wp-content/uploads/2017/12/NSS-Final-12-18-2017-0905.pdf; US Department of Defense, *Summary of the National Defense Strategy of the United States*, January 2018, https://www.defense.gov/Portals/1/Documents/pubs/2018-National-Defense-Strategy-Summary.pdf.

37. David Lynch, "Trump's Raise the Stakes Strategy," *Washington Post*, July 21, 2018, A14; for an overview of developments, see Robert Sutter, "Pushback: America's New China Strategy," *The Diplomat*, November 2, 2018, https://thediplomat.com/2018/11/pushback-americas-new-china-strategy.

38. Chicago Council on Global Affairs, "China Not Yet Seen as a Threat by the American Public," October 19, 2018.

39. The discussion of congressional actions in the remainder of this section is taken from Robert Sutter, "Congress and Trump Administration China Policy," *Journal of Contemporary China* 28, no. 118 (2019): 519–37, https://www.tandfonline.com/doi/full/10.1080/10670564.2018.1557944.

40. Reviewed in Sutter, "Trump, America and the World—2017 and Beyond."

41. US Congress, House Armed Services Committee, *Reform and Rebuild: The Next Steps—National Defense Authorization Act FY-2019*, July 2018, https://republicans-armedservices.house.gov/sites/republicans.armedservices.house.gov/files/wysiwyg_uploaded/FY19%20NDAA%20Conference%20Summary%20.pdf.

42. "Bipartisan Group of Senators Urge Administration to Safeguard Critical Military and Dual-Use Technology from China," United States Senate Release, May 22, 2018, https://www.

cornyn.senate.gov/content/news/bipartisan-group-senators-urge-administration-safeguard-critical-military-and-dual-use; "Senators Urge Trump Administration to Counter Chinese Meddling in Democracies," *Daily Beast*, June 12, 2018, http://commentators.com/senators-urge-trump-administration-to-counter-chinese-meddling-in-democracies; Siobhan Hughes and Josh Zumbrun, "Senators Signal Concerns over China's Global Investments," *Wall Street Journal*, August 5, 2018, https://www.wsj.com/articles/senators-signal-concerns-over-chinas-global-investments-1533517099.

43. Bill Gertz, "Congress to Crack Down on Chinese Influence in US," *Washington Free Beacon*, June 4, 2018, http://freebeacon.com/national-security/congress-crack-chinese-influence-u-s; "Bipartisan Group of Senators"; "Senators Urge Trump"; Hughes and Zumbrun, "Senators Signal Concerns."

44. Burgess Everett, "Republicans Gobsmacked by Trump's Tariffs," *Politico*, May 31, 2018, https://www.politico.com/story/2018/05/31/trump-tariffs-canada-mexico-republican-response-615479.

45. Shannon Tiezzi, "Brace Yourselves: The US-China Trade War Is about to Begin," *The Diplomat*, June 5, 2018, https://thediplomat.com/2018/06/brace-yourselves-the-us-china-trade-war-is-about-to-begin; Lara Seligman, "Congress Caves to Trump in Fight over China's ZTE," *Foreign Policy*, July 26, 2018.

46. Glaser and Flaherty, "Hurtling toward a Trade War," 23.

47. Jackson Diehl, "Taiwan Seems to Be Benefiting from Trump's Presidency," *Washington Post*, April 29, 2018, https://www.washingtonpost.com/opinions/global-opinions/taiwan-seems-to-be-benefiting-from-trumps-presidency-so-why-is-no-one-celebrating/2018/04/29/f5d38166-4966-11e8-827e-190efaf1f1ee_story.html; Zhenhua Lu, "To Avoid Beijing's Ire, Trump Won't Send High-Level Officials to Opening of De-Facto Embassy in Taiwan," *South China Morning Post*, June 5, 2018, https://www.politico.com/story/2018/06/05/trump-china-taiwan-embassy-598150.

48. US Congress, House Armed Services Committee, *Reform and Rebuild: The Next Steps*; Vivian Salama, "Trump Signs Defense Bill to Boost Military, Target China," *Wall Street Journal*, August 13, 2018, https://www.wsj.com/articles/trump-signs-defense-bill-to-boost-military-target-china-1534196930.

49. See Sutter, "Pushback: America's New China Strategy"; see also Robert Sutter, "United States and Asia 2018," *Asian Survey* 59, no. 1 (2019): 10–20.

50. US Special Trade Representative, *Update Concerning China's Acts, Policies and Practices*, November 20, 2018, https://ustr.gov/sites/default/files/enforcement/301Investigations/301%20Report%20Update.pdf; "China Releases White Paper on Facts and Its Position on Trade Friction with US," *Xinhua*, September 24, 2018, http://www.xinhuanet.com/english/2018-09/24/c_137490176.htm.

51. These developments are reviewed in Sutter, "Trump, America and the World—2017 and Beyond."

52. For coverage of developments in late 2018, see Bonnie Glaser, "US-China Relations," *Comparative Connections* 20, no. 3 (2019): 21–30; see also Sutter, "Trump, America and the World—2017 and Beyond."

53. Sutter, "The United States and Asia in 2017."

54. Robert Sutter, "Washington's 'Whole of Government' Pushback against Chinese Challenges—Implications and Outlook," *PacNet* 26 (Honolulu, HI: Pacific Forum CSIS, April 23, 2019), https://www.pacforum.org/sites/default/files/20190423_PacNet_26.pdf.

55. Justin McCarthy, "Americans' Favorable Views of China Take a 12-Point Hit," Gallup News, March 11, 2019, https://news.gallup.com/poll/247559/americans-favorable-views-china-point-hit.aspx.

56. Reviewed in Sutter, "Washington's 'Whole of Government' Pushback"; see also Ben Schreckinger, "CPAC's New Boogeyman: China," *Politico*, February 28, 2019, https://www.politico.com/story/2019/02/28/cpac-conservatives-china-1194212.

57. Bonnie Glaser, "The Diplomatic Relationship," in Shambaugh, *Tangled Titans*, 172–76.

58. Shannon Tiezzi, "Is a Thaw Coming in US-China Relations?," *The Diplomat*, November 7, 2018, https://thediplomat.com/2018/11/is-a-thaw-coming-in-us-china-relations.

59. Robert Sutter, "Has U.S. Government Angst over the China Danger Diminished?," East-West Center Washington, *Asia-Pacific Bulletin*, no. 497 (January 22, 2020), https://www.eastwestcenter.org/publications/has-us-government-angst-over-the-china-danger-diminished; Bonnie Glaser and Kelly Flaherty, "US-China Relations Hit New Lows amid Pandemic," *Comparative Connections* 22, no. 1 (May 2020): 28–39; "Episode 135: How Might a Democratic President Deal with China?," Carnegie-Tsinghua Center for Global Policy, *China in the World* podcast transcript, June 25, 2019, https://carnegieendowment.org/files/Episode_-_How_Might_a_Democratic_President_Deal_with_China_1.pdf; Craig Kafura, "Americans Favor US-China Trade, Split over Tariffs," Chicago Council on Global Affairs, September 3, 2019, https://www.thechicagocouncil.org/publication/lcc/americans-favor-us-china-trade-split-over-tariffs; Ryan Hass, "Why Has China Become Such a Big Political Issue?," Brookings Institution, November 15, 2019, https://www.brookings.edu/policy2020/votervital/why-has-china-become-such-a-big-political-issue; Richard Fontaine, "Great-Power Competition Is Washington's Top Priority—but Not the Public's," *Foreign Affairs*, September 9, 2019, https://www.foreignaffairs.com/articles/china/2019-09-09/great-power-competition-washingtons-top-priority-not-publics; Kathrin Hille, "US 'Surgical' Attack on Huawei Will Reshape Tech Supply Chain," *Financial Times*, May 18, 2020, https://www.ft.com/content/c614afc5-86f8-42b1-9b6c-90bffbd1be8b; Democratic candidates' remarks taken from East-West Center Washington, "2020 US Presidential Candidates on the Indo-Pacific," accessed August 5, 2020, https://eastwestcentercharts.gistapp.com/2020-presidential-candidates-and-the-indo-pacific.

60. "Attorney General William Barr Delivers the Keynote Address to the Department of Justice's China Initiative Conference," Department of Justice, February 6, 2020, https://www.justice.gov/opa/speech/attorney-general-william-p-barr-delivers-keynote-address-department-justices-china.

61. Ren Qi, "Anti-China Stance at Munich Security Conference Criticized," *China Daily*, February 18, 2020, https://www.chinadaily.com.cn/a/202002/18/WS5e4b47b5a310128217278510.html.

62. Josh Rogin, "Covid-19 Sparks Unity on US China Policy," *Washington Post*, May 22, 2020, A23.

63. Kat Devlin, Laura Silver, and Christine Huang, "U.S. Views of China Increasingly Negative amid Coronavirus Outbreak," Pew Research Center, April 21, 2020, https://www.pewresearch.org/global/2020/04/21/u-s-views-of-china-increasingly-negative-amid-coronavirus-outbreak; Marc Caputo, "Anti-China Sentiment Is on the Rise," *Politico*, May 20, 2020, https://www.politico.com/news/2020/05/20/anti-china-sentiment-coronavirus-poll-269373.

64. Jonathan Martin and Maggie Haberman, "GOP Aiming to Make China the Scapegoat," *New York Times*, April 19, 2020, A1; David Lynch, "President Ties Trade Angst to China's Virus Response," *Washington Post*, May 16, 2020, A1; Emily Rauhala, Teo Armus, and Gerry Shih, "With Ultimatum, Trump Deepens Crisis with World Health Organization," *Washington Post*, May 20, 2020, A29; Morgan Phillips, "Trump on China Trade Deal," Fox News, May 19, 2020, https://www.foxnews.com/politics/trump-china-trade-deal-i-feel-differently. Daniel Lynch and Emily Rauhala, "Trump Lashes Out at China, Orders Action on Hong Kong," *Washington Post*, May 30, 2020, A1.

# 7. RELATIONS WITH TAIWAN

1. Authoritative Chinese statements regarding Taiwan include the PRC State Council Taiwan Affairs Office and Information Office, *The Taiwan Question and the Reunification of China*, September 1, 1993, http://www.gwytb.gov.cn, and *The One-China Principle and the Taiwan Issue*, February 21, 2000, http://www.gwytb.gov.cn; the 2005 Chinese Anti-Secession Law, text carried by *BBC News*, March 14, 2005, http://news.bbc.co.uk/2/hi/asia-pacific/4347555.stm; and "Join Hands to Promote Peaceful Development of Cross-Strait Relations," speech by Hu Jintao, *Xinhua*, December 31, 2008.

2. Susan Shirk, *China: Fragile Superpower* (New York: Oxford University Press, 2007), 181–211.

3. *Taiwan: Issues for Congress*, Congressional Research Service Report R44946 (Washington, DC: Library of Congress, October 30, 2017), 38–39.

4. Robert Sutter, "The US and Taiwan Embrace despite China's Objections, but Will It Last?," *PacNet* 58 (Honolulu, HI: Pacific Forum CSIS, November 12, 2019).

5. For Chinese perspectives, see, among others, Deng Xiaoping, "An Idea for the Peaceful Reunification of the Chinese Mainland and Taiwan," remarks delivered June 26, 1983, in *Selected Works of Deng Xiaoping*, vol. 3, *1982–1992* (Beijing: Foreign Languages Press, 1994), 40–41; "One Country—Two Systems," remarks delivered June 22–23, 1984, in *Selected Works of Deng Xiaoping*, vol. 3, *1982–1992*, 70–71; and "Shemma wenti dou keyi taolun: Qian Qichen fuzongli jieshou 'huashengdun youbao' jizhe pan wen caifang," *Shijie Zhishi* 3 (February 2001): 14. For Taiwanese perspectives, see, among others, Lee Teng-hui, *Creating the Future: Towards a New Era for the Chinese People* (Taipei: Government Information Office, 1992); Zou Jingwen, *Li Denghui zhizheng gaobai shilu* (Taipei: INK, 2001); and Su Chi, *Taiwan's Relations with Mainland China: A Tail Wagging Two Dogs* (New York: Routledge, 2008).

6. For Chinese perspectives, see, among others, Deng Xiaoping, "An Idea for the Peaceful Reunification of the Chinese Mainland and Taiwan"; for Taiwanese perspectives, see, among others, Lee Teng-hui, *Creating the Future: Towards a New Era for the Chinese People*, and Chi, *Taiwan's Relations with Mainland China: A Tail Wagging Two Dogs*.

7. Charles Freeman, "Preventing War in the Taiwan Strait," *Foreign Affairs* 77, no. 4 (July–August 1998): 6–11; Steven Goldstein, *Taiwan Faces the Twenty-first Century* (New York: Foreign Policy Association, 1997).

8. Nancy Bernkopf Tucker, "China-Taiwan: U.S. Debates and Policy Choices," *Survival* 40, no. 4 (Winter 1998–1999): 150–67.

9. John Garver, *Face-Off* (Seattle: University of Washington Press, 1997).

10. Robert Sutter, *Taiwan: Recent Developments and U.S. Policy Choices*, Congressional Research Service Issue Brief 98034 (Washington, DC: Library of Congress, December 29, 1999).

11. *Taiwan–Mainland China Talks: Competing Approaches and Implications for U.S. Policy*, Congressional Research Service Report 98-887 (Washington, DC: Library of Congress, November 22, 1998).

12. Sutter, *Taiwan: Recent Developments and US Policy Choices.*

13. Denny Roy, *Taiwan: A Political History* (Ithaca, NY: Cornell University Press, 2003), 235.

14. David G. Brown, "Of Economics and Elections," *Comparative Connections* 3, no. 3 (October 2001); Bruce Gilley and Maureen Pao, "Defenses Weaken," *Far Eastern Economic Review*, October 4, 2001; Yu-Shan Wu, "Taiwan in 2000," *Asian Survey* 41, no. 1 (January–February 2001): 40–48.

15. David G. Brown, "Strains over Cross-Strait Relations," *Comparative Connections* 5, no. 4 (January 2004); T. J. Cheng, "China-Taiwan Economic Linkage," in *Dangerous Strait: The U.S.-Taiwan-China Crisis*, ed. Nancy Bernkopf Tucker (New York: Columbia University Press, 2005), 93–130.

16. Nancy Bernkopf Tucker, *Strait Talk: United States–Taiwan Relations and the Crisis with China* (Cambridge, MA: Harvard University Press, 2009); Philip Yang, "Cross-Strait Relations under the First Chen Administration," in *Presidential Politics in Taiwan: The Administration of Chen Shui-bian*, ed. Steven Goldstein and Julian Chang (Norwalk, CT: Eastbridge, 2008), 211–72.

17. David G. Brown, "China-Taiwan Relations: Campaign Fallout," *Comparative Connections* 6, no. 4 (January 2005); Shi Yinhong, "Beijing's Lack of Sufficient Deterrence to Taiwan Leaves a Major Danger," *Ta Kung Pao* (Hong Kong), June 23, 2004.

18. China's Anti-Secession Law of March 2005 was among the PRC pronouncements that displayed firmness against Taiwan's moves toward independence mixed with signs of flexibility on cross-strait issues. Interviews with Chinese officials and specialists and US government officials and specialists, Washington, DC, March–June 2005.

19. Consultations with thirty Taiwanese government officials and specialists in Taiwan in May–June 2004, with twenty such officials and specialists visiting the United States in 2004–2005, and twenty such officials and specialists in Taipei in May–June 2005.

20. Brown, "China-Taiwan Relations"; interviews with Chinese government officials and specialists, Washington, DC, January–March 2004.

21. International Crisis Group, "China-Taiwan: Uneasy Détente," *Asia Briefing* 42 (Brussels: International Crisis Group, September 21, 2005).

22. Michael Swaine, "Managing Relations with the United States," in Goldstein and Chang, *Presidential Politics in Taiwan*, 197–98.

23. Steven Goldstein, "Postscript: Chen Shui-bian and the Political Transition in Taiwan," in Goldstein and Chang, *Presidential Politics in Taiwan*, 296–98.

24. Goldstein, "Postscript," 299–304.

25. David Brown, "Taiwan Voters Set a New Course," *Comparative Connections* 10, no. 1 (April 2008): 75.

26. For a comprehensive assessment of cross-strait relations under the Ma government, see Richard Bush, *Uncharted Strait* (Washington, DC: Brookings Institution, 2013); see also Dennis Hickey, "Beijing's Evolving Policy toward Taipei: Engagement or Entrapment," *Issues and Studies* 45, no. 1 (March 2009): 31–70; Alan Romberg, "Cross-Strait Relations: 'Ascend the Heights and Take a Long-Term Perspective,'" *China Leadership Monitor* 27 (Winter 2009); interviews and consultations with international affairs officials, including repeated meetings with senior officers up to minister level, Taipei (May, July, August, and December 2008; April 2009).

27. David Brown, "Economic Cooperation Framework Agreement Signed," *Comparative Connections* 12, no. 2 (July 2010): 77–79.

28. David Brown, "Looking Ahead to 2012," *Comparative Connections* 12, no. 4 (January 2011).

29. Donald Zagoria, *Trip to Seoul, Taipei, Beijing, Shanghai, and Tokyo—May 8–25, 2010* (New York: National Committee on American Foreign Policy, 2010), 2–6.

30. Interviews and consultations with international affairs officials, including repeated meetings with senior officers up to minister level, Taipei (May, July, August, and December 2008; April 2009).

31. Shirley Kan, *Taiwan: Major U.S. Arms Sales since 1990*, Congressional Research Service Report RL30957 (Washington, DC: Library of Congress, August 29, 2014); Kathrin Hille and Demetri Sevastopulo, "U.S. and China Set to Resume Military Talks," *Financial Times*, June 21, 2009.

32. Interviews and consultations, Taiwan, December 2008, April 2009; David Shear, "Cross-Strait Relations in a New Era of Negotiation," remarks at the Carnegie Endowment for International Peace, Washington, DC, July 7, 2010, http://www.state.gov.

33. Bonnie Glaser, "The Honeymoon Ends," *Comparative Connections* 12, no. 1 (April 2010): 23–27.

34. Kan, *Taiwan: Major U.S. Arms Sales*.

35. Shirley Kan and Wayne Morrison, *U.S.-Taiwan Relationship: Overview of Policy Issues*, Congressional Research Service Report R41952 (Washington, DC: Library of Congress, April 22, 2014), 26.

36. Jason Pan, "Reliance on China Makes Taiwan Vulnerable: Clinton," *Taipei Times*, June 25, 2014, 1.

37. Kan and Morrison, *U.S.-Taiwan Relationship*, 40–41.

38. Kan and Morrison, *U.S.-Taiwan Relationship*, 41–42.

39. Wei-chin Lee, *The Mutual Non-denial Principle, China's Interests, and Taiwan's Expansion of International Participation* (Baltimore: University of Maryland Carey School of Law, 2014).

40. David Brunnstrom, "Taiwan Presidential Hopeful Seeks to Ease U.S. Concerns on China," Reuters, June 3, 2015, http://www.reuters.com/article/2015/06/03/us-taiwan-china-usa-idUSKBN0OJ30H20150603.

41. Taken from Robert Sutter, "More American Attention to Taiwan amid Heightened Competition with China," *American Journal of Chinese Studies* 22, no. 1 (April 2015): 1–16.

42. Sutter, "More American Attention to Taiwan," 6.

43. Kan and Morrison, *U.S.-Taiwan Relationship*, 14.

44. "Upsetting China," *The Economist*, April 27, 2001, http://www.economist.com/node/594078.

45. William Lowther, "U.S. Senator Not Convinced on F-16 Bid," *Taipei Times*, September 23, 2010.

46. "Senator Questions Arms Sales to Taiwan," Reuters, June 16, 2010.

47. Kerry Dumbaugh, "Underlying Strains in Taiwan-U.S. Political Relations," Congressional Research Service Report RL33684 (Washington, DC: Library of Congress, April 20, 2007); Robert Sutter, "Taiwan's Future: Narrowing Straits," *NBR Analysis*, May 2001, 19–22.

48. "A Way Ahead with China: Steering the Right Course with the Middle Kingdom," recommendations from the Miller Center for Public Affairs Roundtable, Miller Center for Public Affairs, University of Virginia, March 2011; Charles Glaser, "Will China's Rise Lead to War?," *Foreign Affairs* 90, no. 2 (March–April 2011): 80–91; Michael Swaine, *America's Challenge* (Washington, DC: Carnegie Endowment for International Peace, 2011); Bill Owens, "America Must Start Treating China as a Friend," *Financial Times*, November 17, 2009.

49. Daniel Russel, "Evaluating U.S. Policy on Taiwan on the 35th Anniversary of the Taiwan Relations Act," testimony before the Senate Committee on Foreign Affairs Subcommittee on East Asian and Pacific Affairs, April 3, 2014; Joseph Yeh, "Taiwan Lauded for Response to Beijing ADIZ Move: AIT," *China Post*, December 14, 2013.

50. Josh Hicks, "Obama Foreign Policy Sparks Bi-Partisan Criticism," *Washington Post*, August 31, 2014; "Inviting an Asian Crimea," *Wall Street Journal*, April 6, 2014; William Lowther, "US Senator Rubio Seeks Answers on the 'Six Assurances,'" *Taipei Times*, April 5, 2014, 1; William Lowther, "US Academic Warns over Pace, Extent of Cross Strait Moves," *Taipei Times*, June 20, 2014, 3.

51. Dean Cheng, "Taiwan's Maritime Security," *Heritage Foundation Backgrounder*, March 19, 2014, http://www.heritage.org/research/reports/2014/03/taiwans-maritime-security-a-critical-american-interest; William Lowther, "US Study Urges 'Offshore Control' Strategy for China," *Taipei Times*, January 12, 2014, 3; Wendell Minnick, "US Might Tap into Taiwan Early Warning Radar," *Defense News*, May 8, 2014.

52. The options noted below are discussed in Robert Sutter, "Dealing with America's China Problem in Asia—Target China's Vulnerabilities," *PacNet* 58 (Honolulu, HI: Pacific Forum CSIS, July 21, 2014).

53. The author thanks the Taiwan Economic and Cultural Representative Office (TECRO) in Washington, DC, for their assistance in filling out the full scope of these interchanges.

54. Kan and Morrison, *U.S.-Taiwan Relationship*, 15–16, 26–28.

55. William Lowther, "US Report Supports TPP Membership," *Taipei Times*, April 19, 2014, 1.

56. Jim Wolf, "Senior U.S. Senator Faults Taiwan over Arms 'Complacency,'" Reuters, February 11, 2013.

57. William Lowther, "Taiwan Slipping Off US Agenda: Panel," *Taipei Times*, April 13, 2013, 3.

58. Dan Blumenthal, "5 Faulty Assumptions about Taiwan," *Foreign Policy*, February 12, 2014.

59. John Mearsheimer, "Say Goodbye to Taiwan," *National Interest*, February 25, 2014.

60. Syaru Shirley Lin, "How Taiwan's High Income Trap Shapes Its Options in US-China Competition," in *Strategic Asia 2020: US-China Competition for Global Influence*, ed. Ashley Tellis, Alison Szalwinski, and Michael Wills (Seattle, WA: National Bureau of Asian Research, 2020), 133–62; Richard Bush, "From Persuasion to Coercion: Beijing's Approach to Taiwan and Taiwan's Response," Brookings Institution, November 2019, https://www.brookings.edu/research/from-persuasion-to-coercion-beijings-approach-to-taiwan-and-taiwans-response; Michael Chase, "A Rising China's Challenges to Taiwan," in *Strategic Asia 2019: China's Expanding Strategic Ambitions*, ed. Ashley Tellis, Alison Szalwinski, and Michael Wills (Seattle, WA: National Bureau of Asian Research, 2019), 111–42; Lauren Dickey, "Taiwan Policymaking in Xi Jinping's 'New Era,'" *China Brief*, November 10, 2017, https://jamestown.org/program/taiwan-policymaking-xi-jinpings-new-era.

61. Rush Doshi, "China Steps Up Its Information War against Taiwan," *Foreign Affairs*, January 9, 2020, https://www.foreignaffairs.com/articles/china/2020-01-09/china-steps-its-information-war-taiwan.

62. David Brown and Kyle Churchman, "Coronavirus Embitters Cross-Strait Relations," *Comparative Connections* 22, no. 1 (May 2020): 73–82.

63. The paragraphs below are taken from Sutter, "The US and Taiwan Embrace despite China's Objections."

# 8. RELATIONS WITH JAPAN AND KOREA

1. Michael Green, "Managing Chinese Power: The View from Japan," in *Engaging China*, ed. Alastair Iain Johnston and Robert Ross (New York: Routledge, 1999), 152–75; Benjamin Self, "China and Japan: A Façade of Friendship," *Washington Quarterly* 26, no. 1 (Winter 2002–2003): 77–88; Kent E. Calder, "China and Japan's Simmering Rivalry," *Foreign Affairs* 85, no. 2 (2006): 129–40; Richard Bush, *The Perils of Proximity: China-Japan Security Relations* (Washington, DC: Brookings Institution, 2010); Richard McGregor, *Asia's Reckoning: China, Japan, and the Fate of US Power in the Pacific Century* (New York: Viking, 2017); June Teufel Dreyer, *The Middle Kingdom and the Empire of the Rising Sun* (New York: Oxford University Press, 2016); Michael Yahuda, *Sino-Japanese Relations after the Cold War* (New York: Routledge, 2013); Sheila Smith, *Intimate Rivals* (New York: Columbia University Press, 2015).

2. According to Japanese officials interviewed in Japan in May 2006, the Chinese international lobbying ranged widely and included governments in Africa and the Pacific Islands, among others (interviews, Japan, May 2006).

3. Dan Blumenthal, "The Revival of the U.S.-Japanese Alliance," American Enterprise Institute's *Asian Outlook*, February–March 2005.

4. S. Frederick Starr, "A Strong Japanese Initiative in Central Asia," *Central Asia–Caucasus Institute Analyst*, October 20, 2004; *U.S.-Japan-India Report* (Washington, DC: Center for Strategic and International Studies, August 16, 2007).

5. David Kang and Ji-Young Lee, "The New Cold War in Asia?," *Comparative Connections* 12, no. 4 (January 2011).

6. Yoshihisa Komori, "Rethinking Japan-China Relations: Beyond the History Issue," paper presented at a scholarly conference at the Sigur Center for Asian Affairs, George Washington University, Washington, DC, December 5, 2001.

7. Wu Xinbo, "The End of the Silver Lining: A Chinese View of the U.S.-Japanese Alliance," *Washington Quarterly* 29, no. 1 (Winter 2005–2006): 119–30.

8. Green, "Managing Chinese Power"; Self, "China and Japan"; Susan Shirk, *China: Fragile Superpower* (New York: Oxford University Press, 2007), 140–80; Denny Roy, *Stirring Samurai, Disapproving Dragon* (Honolulu, HI: Asia-Pacific Center for Security Studies, September 2003). See also "Noted Scholar Discusses 'New Thinking' in Sino-Japanese Relations," *Renmin Wang* (Beijing), January 1, 2004; Liu Xiaobiao, "Where Are Sino-Japanese Relations Heading?," *Renmin Wang* (Beijing), August 13, 2003; and Shi Yinhong, "On Crisis Formation, Control in Sino-Japanese Relations," *Wen Hui Po* (Hong Kong), June 1, 2005, cited in Robert Sutter, *China's Rise in Asia: Promises and Perils* (Lanham, MD: Rowman & Littlefield, 2005), 151.

9. Robert Sutter, *Chinese Policy Priorities and Their Implications for the United States* (Lanham, MD: Rowman & Littlefield, 2000), 82.

10. *Japan-China Relations: Status, Outlook, and Implications for the United States*, Congressional Research Service Report 96-864F (Washington, DC: Library of Congress, October 30, 1996).

11. "The New Korea," *Asiaweek*, December 1, 1995, http://www.asia.com/asiaweek/95/1201/ed.html.

12. Sutter, *Chinese Policy Priorities and Their Implications for the United States*, 83.

13. Richard Samuels, *Securing Japan: Tokyo's Grand Strategy and the Future of East Asia* (Ithaca, NY: Cornell University Press, 2007).

14. Robert Sutter, "China and Japan: Trouble Ahead?," *Washington Quarterly* 25, no. 4 (Autumn 2002): 39.

15. Chen Zhijiang, "Japan Accelerates Construction of Missile Defense System," *Guangming Ribao* (Beijing), June 23, 2003, 1.

16. Wu Xinbo, "The End of the Silver Lining"; Ralph Cossa and Brad Glosserman, "More of the Same, Times Three," *Comparative Connections* 12, no. 4 (January 2011).

17. Shirk, *China*, 164–76.

18. Self, "China and Japan"; Sutter, "China and Japan."

19. James Przystup, "Japan-China Relations," *Comparative Connections* 12, no. 3 (October 2010), 105–8.

20. Shirk, *China*, 160–61.

21. "China Cuts Rare Earth Export Quotas," *Los Angeles Times*, December 28, 2010.

22. James Przystup, "Abe Opens New Fronts," *Comparative Connections* 17, no. 1 (May 2015): 109.

23. "Japan Imports by Country," Trading Economics, accessed May 20, 2020, https://tradingeconomics.com/japan/imports-by-country.

24. Przystup, "Abe Opens New Fronts," 108–9; "Japan Imports by Country"; "Japanese Investment in China," *Konaxis*, accessed May 5, 2011, http://www.konaxis.com; Feng Zhaokui, "Japan's Role in China's Economic Reforms," *China Daily*, October 20, 2008.

25. "Foreign Student Numbers Don't Tell the Whole Tale," *Japan Times*, April 12, 2019, https://www.japantimes.co.jp/opinion/2019/04/12/commentary/japan-commentary/foreign-student-numbers-dont-tell-whole-tale/#.Xnpj04hKiM8.

26. Ministry of Education of the PRC, *Statistical Report on International Students in China for 2018*, April 17, 2019, http://en.moe.gov.cn/documents/reports/201904/t20190418_378692.html.

27. "Chinese Visitors Spend 1.8 Trillion Yen in Japan in 2019," Nippon.com, February 12, 2020, https://www.nippon.com/en/japan-data/h00646/chinese-visitors-spend-%C2%A51-8-trillion-in-japan-in-2019.html.

28. "Is China Attracting Foreign Visitors?," Chinapower CSIS [no date], https://chinapower.csis.org/tourism.

29. Shirk, *China*, 166–74.

30. Shirk, *China*, 171–76.

31. Thomas Christensen, "Have Old Problems Trumped New Thinking? China's Relations with Taiwan, Japan, and North Korea," *China Leadership Monitor* 14 (June 2005).

32. James Przystup, "Japan-China: Summer Calm," *Comparative Connections* 7, no. 3 (October 2005).

33. Przystup, "Japan-China Relations" (October 2010).

34. Jeffrey Bader, *Obama and China's Rise* (Washington, DC: Brookings Institution, 2012), 42–43; David Allen, "Japan to Revisit Base Plan, SOFA," *Stars and Stripes*, September 11, 2009, http://www.stripes.com/news/japan-to-revisit-base-plan-sofa-1.94627.

35. John Hemmings, "Understanding Hatoyama's East Asia Community Idea," *East Asia Forum*, January 22, 2010, http://www.eastasiaforum.org/2010/01/22/understanding-hatoyamas-east-asian-community-idea.

36. James Przystup, "Japan-China Relations," *Comparative Connections* 14, no. 3 (January 2013): 109–11.

37. Kosuke Takahashi, "Shinzo Abe's Nationalist Strategy," *The Diplomat*, February 13, 2014, http://thediplomat.com/2014/02/shinzo-abes-nationalist-strategy.

38. Mark Valencia, "Asian Threats, Provocations Giving Rise to Whiffs of War," *Japan Times*, June 9, 2014, http://www.japantimes.co.jp/opinion/2014/06/09/commentary/world-commentary/asian-threats-provocations-giving-rise-whiffs-war/#.U6VP6JRdXxA.

39. White House Office of the Press Secretary, *Fact Sheet: U.S.-Japan Global and Regional Cooperation*, April 25, 2014; Matt Spetalnick and Nathan Layne, "Obama Accuses China of Flexing Muscles in Disputes with Neighbors," Reuters, April 28, 2015, http://www.reuters.com/article/2015/04/29/us-usa-japan-idUSKBN0NJ09520150429.

40. Shannon Tiezzi, "A China-Japan Breakthrough," *The Diplomat*, November 7, 2014, http://thediplomat.com/2014/11/a-china-japan-breakthrough-a-primer-on-their-4-point-consensus; Michael Green, "Xi Meets Abe: Skillful Diplomacy but Tensions Remain," *CSIS Asia Maritime Transparency Initiative*, November 11, 2014, http://amti.csis.org/xi-meets-abe-skillful-diplomacy-but-tensions-remain.

41. June Dreyer, "Sino-Japanese Relations: In a Holding Pattern," *Comparative Connections* 22, no. 1 (May 2020): 109–18; see also earlier reports in this series.

42. Robert Sutter, *The United States and Asia* (Lanham, MD: Rowman & Littlefield, 2020), 201–3.

43. Sheila Smith and Charles McClean, "Stability in Tokyo, Disruption in Washington," *Comparative Connections* 20, no. 3 (2019): 13–20; Céline Pajon, "Japan's Indo-Pacific Strategy: Shaping a Hybrid Regional Order," War on the Rocks, December 18, 2019, https://warontherocks.com/2019/12/japans-indo-pacific-strategy-shaping-a-hybrid-regional-order.

44. June Dreyer, "Sino-Japanese Relations: Speaking Softly but Planning for the Worst," *Comparative Connections* 21, no. 3 (January 2020): 109–15; Dreyer, "Sino-Japanese Relations: In a Holding Pattern."

45. International Crisis Group, *North Korea's Nuclear Test: The Fallout*, Asia Briefing 56 (Brussels: International Crisis Group, November 13, 2006); Scott Snyder, *China's Rise and the Two Koreas* (Boulder, CO: Lynne Rienner, 2009); Samuel Kim, *The Two Koreas and the Great Powers* (New York: Cambridge University Press, 2006), 42–101; David Shambaugh, "China and the Korean Peninsula," *Washington Quarterly* 26, no. 2 (Spring 2003): 43–56; Denny Roy, "China and the Korean Peninsula: Beijing's Pyongyang Problem and Seoul Hope," *Asia-Pacific Security Studies* 3, no. 1 (January 2004); Jae Ho Chung, "From a Special Relationship to a Normal Partnership?," *Pacific Affairs* 76, no. 3 (Winter 2003–2004): 549–68; You Ji, "Understanding China's North Korea Policy," *Jamestown Foundation China Brief*, March 3, 2004; Ming Liu, "China and the North Korean Crisis," *Pacific Affairs* 76, no. 3 (Fall 2003): 347–73; Andrew Scobell, "China and North Korea," *Current History* 101, no. 656 (September 2002): 278–79; Fu Mengzi, "China and Peace Building on the Korean Peninsula," *Xiandai guoji guanxi* (Beijing) 17 (July 2007): 27–40.

46. Samuel Kim, "The Changing Role of China on the Korean Peninsula," *International Journal of Korean Studies* 8, no. 1 (2004): 79–112; Kim, *The Two Koreas and the Great Powers*.

47. Snyder, *China's Rise and the Two Koreas*; Kim, *The Two Koreas and the Great Powers*.

48. Sutter, *United States and Asia*, 146–48.

49. Robert Sutter, *Foreign Relations of the PRC* (Lanham, MD: Rowman & Littlefield, 2019), 220–21.

50. Kim, "The Changing Role of China on the Korean Peninsula"; Jae Ho Chung, "China's 'Soft' Clash with South Korea," *Asian Survey* 49, no. 3 (2009): 468–83.

51. Charles L. Pritchard, *Failed Diplomacy* (Washington, DC: Brookings Institution, 2007), 25–44.

52. Sutter, *United States and Asia*, 150–51.

53. Kim, "The Changing Role of China on the Korean Peninsula"; Sutter, *United States and Asia*, 151.

54. Chung, "China's 'Soft' Clash with South Korea," 468–83.

55. Scott Snyder, "Post Olympic Hangover: New Backdrop for Relations," *Comparative Connections* 10, no. 3 (October 2008): 101–7.

56. Scott Snyder, "DPRK Provocations Test China's Regional Role," *Comparative Connections* 12, no. 4 (January 2011).

57. Scott Snyder, "Lee Myung-bak and the Future of Sino-South Korean Relations," *Jamestown Foundation, China Brief* 8, no. 4 (February 14, 2008): 5–8.

58. Bonnie Glaser, "China's Policy in the Wake of the Second DPRK Nuclear Test," *China Security* 5, no. 2 (2009): 1–11.

59. Christopher Twomey, "Chinese Foreign Policy toward North Korea," *Journal of Contemporary China* 17, no. 56 (2008): 422.

60. Roy, "China and the Korean Peninsula"; Fei-Ling Wang, *Tacit Acceptance and Watchful Eyes: Beijing's Views about the U.S.-ROK Alliance* (Carlisle, PA: US Army War College, 1997).

61. Jeremy Page, Jay Solomon, and Julian Barnes, "China Warns U.S. as Korea Tensions Rise," *Wall Street Journal*, November 26, 2010; Scott Snyder, "South Korea's Diplomatic Triangle," *Comparative Connections* 17, no. 1 (January 2015): 94–95.

62. This paragraph and the next two rely on Robert Sutter, *Chinese Foreign Relations: Power and Policy since the Cold War* (Lanham, MD: Rowman & Littlefield, 2010), 203–8.

63. Interviews with senior officials in charge of Chinese foreign relations, Beijing, May 30, 2006.

64. Wang Jisi, "China's Search for a Grand Strategy," *Foreign Affairs* 90, no. 2 (March–April 2011): 68–80.

65. Snyder, "DPRK Provocations Test China's Regional Role."

66. Snyder, "DPRK Provocations Test China's Regional Role"; Scott Snyder and See-won Byun, "Consolidating Ties with New DPRK Leadership," *Comparative Connections* 12, no. 3 (October 2010).

67. Snyder, "DPRK Provocations Test China's Regional Role," 91.

68. Snyder, "DPRK Provocations Test China's Regional Role," 94.

69. Snyder and Byun, "Consolidating Ties with New DPRK Leadership."

70. Ralph Cossa and Brad Glosserman, "U.S. Profile Rises, China's Image Falls, North Korea Changes," *Comparative Connections* 12, no. 3 (October 2010): 1–5; Snyder and Byun, "Consolidating Ties with New DPRK Leadership."

71. Mark Landler, "Obama Urges China to Check North Koreans," *New York Times*, December 6, 2010.

72. Elisabeth Bumiller and David Sanger, "Gates Warns of North Korea Missile Threat to U.S.," *New York Times*, January 11, 2011.

73. Cossa and Glosserman, "U.S. Profile Rises," 3–5.

74. Scott Snyder, "Crying Uncle No More: Stark Choices for Relations," *Comparative Connections* 15, no. 3 (January 2014): 89–91.

75. Snyder, "South Korea's Diplomatic Triangle," 93–94; Scott Snyder, "The China–North Korea Relationship," *Council on Foreign Relations Backgrounder*, August 22, 2014, http://www.cfr.org/china/china-north-korea-relationship/p11097.

76. Elise Hu, "North Korea Claims Successful Hydrogen Bomb Test," NPR, September 3, 2017, https://www.npr.org/sections/thetwo-way/2017/09/03/523913820/north-korea-possibly-conducts-sixth-nuclear-test-south-korea-says.

77. Sutter, *United States and Asia*, 154–61; Sue Mi Terry, "Assessment of the Trump-Kim Hanoi Summit," CSIS, February 28, 2019, https://www.csis.org/analysis/assessment-trump-kim-hanoi-summit.

78. Scott Snyder, "A New Chapter," *Comparative Connections* 21, no. 2 (September 2019): 87–91.

79. "On the First Meeting of Russia-China Dialogue on Security in Northeast Asia," Ministry of Foreign Affairs of the Russian Federation, April 25, 2015, http://www.mid.ru/foreign_policy/news/-/asset_publisher/cKNonkJE02Bw/content/id/1207275.

80. Press release on the eighth round of Russian-Chinese Dialogue on Security in Northeast Asia, Ministry of Foreign Affairs of the Russian Federation, October 10, 2017, http://www.mid.ru/foreign_policy/news/-/asset_publisher/cKNonkJE02Bw/content/id/2895093.

81. Ministry of Foreign Affairs of the People's Republic of China, "Foreign Minister Wang Yi Meets the Press," March 8, 2017, http://www.fmprc.gov.cn/mfa_eng/zxxx_662805/t1444204.shtml.

82. "Nuclear Weapons and Russian–North Korean Relations," Foreign Policy Research Institute, 2017, https://www.fpri.org/wp-content/uploads/2017/11/NuclearWeaponsRussiaDPRKDec2017.pdf.

83. Ministry of Foreign Affairs of the Russian Federation, "Joint Statement by the Russian and Chinese Foreign Ministries on the Korean Peninsula's Problems," July 4, 2017, http://www.mid.ru/en/web/guest/maps/kr/-/asset_publisher/PR7UbfssNImL/content/id/2807662.

84. Snyder, "A New Chapter."

85. Choi Kang, *Chinese Interference in Internal Affairs of Democratic Countries: South Korea* (Seoul: Asan Institute, April 24, 2018).

86. Kang, *Chinese Interference in Internal Affairs of Democratic Countries*; "South Korean Warplanes Fire Warning Shot at Russian Military Plane," *New York Times*, July 23, 2018, https://www.nytimes.com/2019/07/23/world/asia/south-korean-warning-shots-russia-planes.html.

# 9. RELATIONS WITH SOUTHEAST ASIA, AUSTRALIA, NEW ZEALAND, AND THE PACIFIC ISLANDS

1. Donald Weatherbee, *International Relations in Southeast Asia* (Lanham, MD: Rowman & Littlefield, 2014); M. Taylor Fravel, "China's Strategy in the South China Sea," *Contemporary Southeast Asia* 33, no. 3 (2011): 292–319.

2. International Crisis Group, *Stirring Up the South China Sea I*, Asia Report 223 (Brussels: International Crisis Group, April 23, 2012).

3. Sophie Richardson, *China, Cambodia, and the Five Principles of Peaceful Coexistence* (New York: Columbia University Press, 2010); International Crisis Group, *China's Myanmar Strategy*, Asia Briefing 112 (Brussels: International Crisis Group, September 21, 2010).

4. "China Reassures Neighbors, Deepens Engagement," *Comparative Connections* 13, no. 1 (May 2011); Brantly Womack, "China and Southeast Asia: Asymmetry, Leadership, and Normalcy," *Pacific Affairs* 76, no. 3 (Winter 2003–2004): 529–48; Alice Ba, *(Re)Negotiating East and Southeast Asia* (Stanford, CA: Stanford University Press, 2009); John Wong and Sarah Chan, "China-ASEAN Free Trade Agreement," *Asian Survey* 43, no. 3 (May–June 2003): 507–26; Evelyn Goh and Sheldon Simon, eds., *China, the United States, and Southeast Asia* (London: Routledge, 2007); Stanley Foundation, *China and Southeast Asia*, Stanley Foundation Policy Bulletin (Muscatine, IA: Stanley Foundation, October 2003); Rosemary Foot, "China and the ASEAN Regional Forum," *Asian Survey* 38, no. 5 (May 1998): 425–40.

5. *China–Southeast Asia Relations: Trends, Issues, and Implications for the United States*, Congressional Research Service Report 97-553F (Washington, DC: Library of Congress, May 20, 1997), 3–6.

6. Robert Sutter, *Chinese Policy Priorities and Their Implications for the United States* (Lanham, MD: Rowman & Littlefield, 2000), 129; *China–Southeast Asia Relations*, 115; Robert Sutter, "Small Advances, Trouble with Vietnam," *Comparative Connections* 10, no. 3 (October 2008): 67.

7. Wong and Chan, "China-ASEAN Free Trade Agreement," 519; Sutter, *Chinese Policy Priorities and Their Implications for the United States*, 129; *China–Southeast Asia Relations*, 115; Robert Sutter and Chin-Hao Huang, "Economic Concerns Begin to Hit Home," *Comparative Connections* 10, no. 4 (January 2009): 68.

8. Sutter, *Chinese Policy Priorities and Their Implications for the United States*, 129; *China–Southeast Asia Relations*, 116; "PRC Expands Cooperation with ASEAN," *Xinhua*, January 4, 1998, carried by FBIS, cited in Sutter, *Chinese Policy Priorities and Their Implications for the United States*, 129.

9. Robert Sutter, *China's Rise in Asia: Promises and Perils* (Lanham, MD: Rowman & Littlefield, 2005), 190.

10. Lyall Breckon, "China Caps a Year of Gains," *Comparative Connections* 4, no. 4 (January 2003); for background, see Ian Storey, *Southeast Asia and the Rise of China* (New York: Routledge, 2013).

11. Bates Gill, *Rising Star: China's New Security Diplomacy* (Washington, DC: Brookings Institution, 2007).

12. Sutter, *Chinese Policy Priorities and Their Implications for the United States*, 129; *China–Southeast Asia Relations*, 116.

13. ASEAN, *Declaration on the Conduct of Parties in the South China Sea*, November 2002, accessed December 2002, http://www.aseansec.org/13163.htm; Breckon, "China Caps a Year of Gains."

14. Ming Wan, *The Political Economy of East Asia* (Washington, DC: CQ Press, 2008), 171–94.

15. Gill, *Rising Star.*

16. Bonnie Glaser and Evan Medeiros, "The Changing Ecology of Foreign Policy Making in China: The Ascension and Demise of the Theory of 'Peaceful Rise,'" *China Quarterly* 190 (June 2007): 291–310.

17. Robert Sutter, *The United States in Asia* (Lanham, MD: Rowman & Littlefield, 2009), 110–12; Robert Sutter and Chin-Hao Huang, "U.S. Intervention Complicates China's Advances," *Comparative Connections* 12, no. 3 (October 2010): 65.

18. Thomas Lum, *Comparing Global Influence: China's and U.S. Diplomacy, Foreign Aid, Trade, and Investment in the Developing World*, Congressional Research Service Report RL34620 (Washington, DC: Library of Congress, August 15, 2008), 51, 53; "China Reassures Neighbors, Deepens Engagement"; Catherin Dalpino and Juo-yu Lin, "China and Southeast Asia," in *Brookings Northeast Asia Survey, 2002–2003*, ed. Richard Bush and Catherin Dalpino (Washington, DC: Brookings Institution, 2003), 83.

19. "China Reassures Neighbors, Deepens Engagement."

20. Elizabeth Economy, "Asia's Water Security Crisis: China, India, and the United States," in *Strategic Asia 2008–09: Challenges and Choices*, ed. Ashley Tellis, Mercy Kuo, and Andrew Marble (Seattle, WA: National Bureau of Asian Research, 2008), 380–82; "China Reassures Neighbors, Deepens Engagement."

21. "Trade Agreement Registers China's Prominence," *Comparative Connections* 12, no. 1 (April 2010): 58–59.

22. "Cyclone, Earthquake Put Spotlight on China," *Comparative Connections* 10, no. 2 (July 2008): 76–77; "From Bad to Worse," *Comparative Connections* 10, no. 4 (January 2009): 5–6.

23. The following 2012 events are explained in greater detail in "China Muscles Opponents on South China Sea," *Comparative Connections* 14, no. 2 (September 2012).

24. The 2014 events are explained in greater detail in "China Advances, More Opposition in South China Sea," *Comparative Connections* 16, no. 2 (September 2014).

25. ASEAN, "Top Ten ASEAN Trade Partner Countries/Regions, 2013," accessed June 19, 2015, http://www.asean.org/images/2015/January/external_trade_statistic/table20_asof04Dec14.pdf; ASEAN, "Top Ten Sources of Foreign Direct Investment Inflows in ASEAN," accessed June 19, 2015, http://www.asean.org/images/resources/Statistics/2014/ForeignDirectInvestment/Aug/Table%2027.pdf; ASEAN, *ASEAN Key Figures 2019*, ASEAN Statistics 2091, 36, 45, https://www.aseanstats.org/wp-content/uploads/2019/11/ASEAN_Key_Figures_2019.pdf.

26. For the following three paragraphs, see Robert Sutter, *US-China Relations* (Lanham, MD: Rowman & Littlefield, 2018), 158–59.

27. Robert Sutter, *The United States and Asia*, 2nd ed. (Lanham, MD: Rowman & Littlefield, 2020), 212.

28. Evan Medeiros, "China Reacts: Assessing Beijing's Response to Trump's New China Strategy," *China Leadership Monitor*, March 1, 2019, https://www.prcleader.org/medeiros.

29. "Xi Jinping, Li Keqiang Advance China's Influence, Counter US Pushback," *Comparative Connections* 20, no. 3 (January 2019): 53–55.

30. "Beijing Confident amid US, Regional Challenges," *Comparative Connections* 21, no. 1 (May 2019): 55.

31. "Beijing Leads Regional Agenda, Rejects US Challenges," *Comparative Connections* 21, no. 3 (January 2020): 59–62.

32. Daniel Russel and Blake Berger, *Navigating the Belt and Road Initiative* (New York: Asia Society Policy Institute, June 2019), 16–17, https://asiasociety.org/sites/default/files/2019-06/Navigating%20the%20Belt%20and%20Road%20Initiative_2.pdf.

33. David Shullman, ed., *Chinese Malign Influence and the Corrosion of Democracy* (Washington, DC: International Republican Institute, 2019), 11–16.

34. Shullman, *Chinese Malign Influence*, 11–16; John Ciorciari, "A Chinese Model for Patron-Client Relations? The Sino-Cambodia Partnership," *International Relations of the Asia-Pacific* 15, no. 2 (2014): 8–21.

35. Nick Freeman, "Can Laos Profit from China Rail Link despite Being US$1.5 Billion in Debt?," *South China Morning Post*, December 10, 2019, https://www.scmp.com/week-asia/opinion/article/3041394/can-laos-profit-china-rail-link-despite-being-us15-billion-debt.

36. Russel and Berger, *Navigating the Belt and Road Initiative*, 14.

37. "From Low Priority to High Tensions," *Comparative Connections* 22, no. 1 (May 2020): 67–69.

38. Sutter, *The United States and Asia*, 233–34.

39. Interviews with twenty Australian officials, Canberra, June 2004; twenty-five Australian officials, Canberra, June 2006; and twenty Australian officials, Canberra, August 2010.

40. Bates Gill, "The U.S.-Australia Alliance: A Deepening Partnership in Emerging Asia," in *Strategic Asia 2014–15: U.S. Alliances and Partnerships at the Center of Global Power*, ed. Ashley Tellis, Abraham Denmark, and Greg Chaffin (Seattle, WA: National Bureau of Asian Research, 2014), 87–118.

41. Graeme Dobell, "Australia-US/East Asia," *Comparative Connections* 19, no 2 (September 2017), 125–34.

42. Daniel Workman, "Australia's Top Trading Partners," World's Top Exports, May 3, 2020, http://www.worldstopexports.com/australias-top-import-partners.

43. Australian Government Department of Foreign Affairs and Trade, *Trade and Investment at a Glance 2019*, https://www.dfat.gov.au/about-us/publications/trade-investment/trade-at-a-glance/trade-investment-at-a-glance-2019/Pages/default#foreign-investment.

44. "ASEAN and Asian Regional Diplomacy," *Comparative Connections* 11, no. 4 (January 2010); "China Reassures Neighbors, Wary of U.S. Intentions," *Comparative Connections* 12, no. 4 (January 2011).

45. "Beijing Sets Positive Agenda, Plays Down Disputes," *Comparative Connections* 16, no. 3 (January 2015).

46. Adapted from Ross Babbage, "China's Political Warfare Operations in Australia," in *Winning without Fighting: Chinese and Russian Political Warfare Campaigns*, vol. 2, *Case Studies* (Washington, DC: Center of Strategic and Budgetary Assessments, 2019), 49–56; see also, Larry Diamond and Orville Schell, coordinators, *Chinese Influence & American Interests* (Stanford, CA: Hoover Institution Press, 2018), 146–51.

47. "Xi Jinping, Li Keqiang Ease Regional Tensions, Consolidate Gains," *Comparative Connections* 19, no. 3 (January 2018): 58.

48. "Xi Jinping Stresses Cooperation and Power," *Comparative Connections* 20, no. 1 (May 2018): 57.

49. Robert Sutter, *Historical Dictionary of Chinese Foreign Policy* (Lanham, MD: Scarecrow Press, 2011), 179–80.

50. Government of New Zealand, "China Top Trade Partner for 2019," March 2, 2020, https://www.stats.govt.nz/news/china-top-trade-partner-for-2019; "International Students in New Zealand," *Education Counts*, https://www.educationcounts.govt.nz/statistics/international-education/international-students-in-new-zealand.

51. Mark Manyin, coord., *Pivot to the Pacific? The Obama Administration's "Rebalancing" toward Asia*, Congressional Research Service Report R42448 (Washington, DC: Library of Congress, March 28, 2012), 2–6; Rebecca Howard, "China, New Zealand Trade Exceeds Hopes," *Wall Street Journal*, June 27, 2014, http://blogs.wsj.com/economics/2014/06/27/china-new-zealand-trade-exceeds-hopes.

52. Sutter, *The United States and Asia*, 234–35.

53. Anne-Marie Brady, "China's Political Warfare Operations in New Zealand," in *Winning without Fighting: Chinese and Russian Political Warfare Campaigns*, vol. 2, *Case Studies*, by Ross Babbage (Washington, DC: Center of Strategic and Budgetary Assessments, 2019), 37–47.

54. John Henderson and Benjamin Reilly, "Dragon in Paradise," *National Interest*, Summer 2003, 93–94; Tamara Shie, "Rising Chinese Influence in the South Pacific," *Asian Survey* 47, no. 2 (March–April 2007): 307–26.

55. Sutter, *Historical Dictionary of Chinese Foreign Policy*, 193–94; ROC Foreign Ministry, "Embassies and Missions," accessed December 22, 2019, http://www.mofa.gov.tw/en/default.html.

56. Henderson and Reilly, "Dragon in Paradise," 93–94; "China Has Become a 'Major Donor' in the Pacific Islands Region," interview with Lowy Institute analyst Philippa Brant, *DW*, March 3, 2015, http://www.dw.de/china-has-become-a-major-donor-in-the-pacific-islands-region/a-18290737.

57. Australian Parliamentary Library Research Service, *Directions in China's Foreign Relations*, December 5, 2005, 51–54; "President Ma Praises ROC-Palau Ties," *Taiwan Today*, October 14, 2013, http://www.taiwantoday.tw/ct.asp?xItem=210435&CtNode=436.

58. Australian Parliamentary Library Research Service, *Directions in China's Foreign Relations*, 51–54.

59. "Beijing Shifts to the Positive, Plays Down Disputes," *Comparative Connections* 15, no. 3 (January 2014): 57, http://cc.pacforum.org/2014/01/beijing-shifts-positive-downplays-disputes.

60. Matthew Dornan, Denghua Zhang, and Philippa Brant, "More Chinese Loans to Pacific Islands but No Debt Forgiveness," *East Asia Forum*, November 20, 2013, http://www.eastasiaforum.org/2013/11/20/more-chinese-loans-to-pacific-islands-but-no-debt-forgiveness.

61. "Beijing Shifts to the Positive, Plays Down Disputes"; "Ambitious Economic Initiatives amid Boundary Disputes," *Comparative Connections* 17, no. 1 (May 2015).

62. "Xi Jinping, Li Keqiang Advance China's Influence, Counter US Pushback."

63. The following three paragraphs are drawn from Anne-Marie Brady, "China's Activities in the Island States of the South Pacific," in *Winning without Fighting: Chinese and Russian Political Warfare Campaigns*, vol. 2, *Case Studies*, by Ross Babbage (Washington, DC: Center of Strategic and Budgetary Assessments, 2019), 27–36.

64. Anne-Marie Brady, "China's Rise in Antarctica," *Asian Survey* 50, no. 4 (2010): 759–85; "Xi Jinping Visits Chinese and Australian Antarctic Scientific Researchers and Inspects Chinese Research Vessel 'Snow Dragon,'" Ministry of Foreign Affairs of People's Republic of China, November 18, 2014, http://www.fmprc.gov.cn/mfa_eng/topics_665678/xjpzxcxesgjtldrdjcfhdadlyxxlfjjxgsfwbttpyjjdgldrhw/t1212943.shtml; Nengye Liu, "What Are China's Intentions in Antarctica?," *The Diplomat*, June 14, 2019, https://thediplomat.com/2019/06/what-are-chinas-intentions-in-antarctica.

# 10. RELATIONS WITH SOUTHERN ASIA AND CENTRAL ASIA

1. See, among others, Andrew Scobell et al., *At the Dawn of the Belt and Road: China in the Developing World* (Santa Monica, CA: RAND Corporation, 2018), 89–146; Marlene Laurelle, ed., *China's Belt and Road Initiative and Its Impact on Central Asia* (Washington, DC: George Washington University, 2018); Nadege Rolland, *China's Eurasian Century?* (Seattle, WA: National Bureau of Asian Research, 2017); Andrew Small, *The China-Pakistan Axis* (New York: Oxford University Press, 2015); Jonathan Holslag, *China and India* (New York: Columbia University Press, 2009); Kanti Pajpai, ed., *China-India Relations* (New York: Routledge, 2017).

Chinese perspectives on these issues include Cheng Ruisheng, "China-India Diplomatic Relations: Six Decades' Experience and Inspiration," *Foreign Affairs Journal* (Beijing) 96 (Summer 2010): 59–70; Wang Shida, "The Way to a Secure and Stable Afghanistan," *Contemporary International Relations* (Beijing) 20, no. 6 (November–December 2010): 123–31; Feng Yujun, "Strategic Orientation and Prospects of the Shanghai Cooperation Organization," *Contemporary International Relations* (Beijing), special issue (September 2010): 121–28; Li Li, "India's Engagement with East Asia and the China Factor," *Contemporary International Relations* (Beijing) 20, no. 5 (September–October 2010): 97–109; Ye Hailin, "China and South Asian Relations in a New Perspective," in *Making New Partnership: A Rising China and Its Neighbors*, ed. Zhang Yunling (Beijing: Social Sciences Academic Press, 2008), 217–43; Ma

Jiali, "Is Competitive Partnership between China and India Viable?," in Zhang Yunling, *Making New Partnership*, 177–89.

2. John Garver, *Protracted Contest: Sino-Indian Rivalry in the Twentieth Century* (Seattle: University of Washington Press, 2001); Francine Frankel and Harry Harding, eds., *The India-China Relationship: What the United States Needs to Know* (New York: Columbia University Press, 2004); Jing-dong Yuan, "The Dragon and the Elephant: Chinese-Indian Relations in the 21st Century," *Washington Quarterly* 30, no. 3 (Summer 2007): 131–44; Jean-François Huchet, "Emergence of a Pragmatic India-China Relationship: Between Geostrategic Rivalry and Economic Competition," *China Perspectives* 3 (2008): 50–67; Holslag, *China and India*; Shalendra Sharma, *China and India in the Age of Globalization* (New York: Cambridge University Press, 2009); Andrew Small, *The China-Pakistan Axis: Asia's New Geopolitics* (New York: Oxford University Press, 2015).

3. *South Asian Crisis: China's Assessments and Goals*, Congressional Research Service Memorandum (Washington, DC: Library of Congress, June 6, 1998).

4. Devin Hagerty, "China and Pakistan: Strains in the Relationship," *Current History*, September 2002, 289.

5. John Garver, "China's Influence in Central and South Asia: Is It Increasing?," in *Power Shift: China and Asia's New Dynamics*, ed. David Shambaugh (Berkeley: University of California Press, 2005), 213–18.

6. Wu Yixue, "U.S. Dreams of Asian NATO," *China Daily*, July 18, 2003, 4.

7. Abu Taher Salahuddin Ahmed, "India-China Relations in the 1990s," *Journal of Contemporary Asia* 26, no. 1 (1996): 100–115; Robert Sutter, *China's Rise in Asia: Promises and Perils* (Lanham, MD: Rowman & Littlefield, 2005), 231–48.

8. Denny Roy, *China's Foreign Relations* (Lanham, MD: Rowman & Littlefield, 1998), 170–74.

9. "Indian Prime Minister Ends China Visit," *China Daily*, January 15, 2008, 1; Fu Xiaoqiang, "Wen's Visit Benefits South Asia," *China Daily*, December 23, 2010, 8.

10. Robert Sutter, *Chinese Policy Priorities and Their Implications for the United States* (Lanham, MD: Rowman & Littlefield, 2000), 135.

11. Tarique Niazi, "Sino-Pakistani Relations Reach New Level after Zadari's Visit," *China Brief* 8, no. 24 (December 19, 2008): 7–9; Christopher Griffin, "Hu Loves Whom? China Juggles Its Priorities on the Subcontinent," *China Brief* 6, no. 25 (December 19, 2006): 1–3.

12. Stephanie Ho, "China to Sell Outdated Nuclear Reactors to Pakistan," VOANews.com, March 24, 2011; Li Xiaokun and Ai Yang, "Wen Delivers on Flood Aid as Visit to Pakistan Begins," *China Daily*, December 18–19, 2010, 1; L. C. Russell Hsiao, "China and Pakistan Enhance Strategic Partnership," *China Brief* 8, no. 19 (October 7, 2008).

13. J. Mohan Malik, "Chinese-Indian Relations in the Post-Soviet Era," *China Quarterly* 142 (June 1995): 317–55; Garver, *Protracted Contest*; Sutter, *China's Rise in Asia*, 233; Holslag, *China and India*; C. Raja Mohan, "Sino-Indian Relations: Growing yet Fragile," *RSIS Commentaries* 174 (December 20, 2010); "India and China Eye Each Other Warily," IISS, *Strategic Comments* 9, no. 27 (December 2010).

14. Robert Sutter, *The United States and East Asia: Dynamics and Implications* (Lanham, MD: Rowman & Littlefield, 2003), 116; Robert Sutter, *The United States and Asia* (Lanham, MD: Rowman & Littlefield, 2015), 233–68.

15. Yuan, "The Dragon and the Elephant"; Huchet, "Emergence of a Pragmatic India-China Relationship."

16. Sutter, *China's Rise in Asia*, 240; "India and China Eye Each Other Warily."

17. Sutter, *The United States and East Asia*, 117; Yuan, "The Dragon and the Elephant"; Huchet, "Emergence of a Pragmatic India-China Relationship."

18. Preetam Sohani, "The New Superpower Coalition: Indian, Chinese, and Russian Foreign Ministers to Meet in Russia," *India Daily*, May 30, 2005, accessed February 10, 2009; "BRICS Group," *New York Times*, April 20, 2011.

19. Huchet, "Emergence of a Pragmatic India-China Relationship," 66.

20. "Chinese President Makes Five-Point Proposal for Sino-Indian Economic Cooperation," *China Daily*, November 23, 2006, 1; Li Xiaokun and Li Xiang, "Trade Target Set at $100b," *China Daily*, December 17, 2010, 1; Han Hua, "China, India Vital to Asia's Growth Story,"

*China Daily*, May 15, 2015, http://www.chinadaily.com.cn/opinion/2015-05/15/content_20722050.htm; Sutter, *China's Rise in Asia*, 239–46; "India and China Eye Each Other Warily."

21. Sumit Ganguly, "India and China: On a Collision Course?," *Pacific Affairs* 91, no. 2 (June 2018): 231–44.

22. "India-China Trade Dips by Nearly \$3 Billion in 2019," Livemint.com, January 14, 2020, https://www.livemint.com/news/india/india-china-trade-dips-by-nearly-3-billion-in-2019-11579011500398.html.

23. "India-East Asia Relations," *Comparative Connections* 21, no. 3 (January 2020): 146–47.

24. Cara Abercrombie, "Realizing the Potential: Mature Defense Cooperation and the US-India Strategic Partnership," *Asia Policy* 14, no. 1 (January 2019): 119–44; Ananth Krishnan, "For Modi 2.0, India's US-China Balancing Act Just Got Trickier," *South China Morning Post*, May 25, 2019, https://www.scmp.com/week-asia/geopolitics/article/3011748/modi-20-indias-us-china-balancing-act-just-got-trickier; Richard Fontaine, "US-India Relations: The Trump Administration's Foreign Policy Bright Spot," War on the Rocks, January 24, 2019, https://warontherocks.com/2019/01/u-s-india-relations-the-trump-administrations-foreign-policy-bright-spot.

25. "India-East Asia Relations," *Comparative Connections* 20, no. 3 (January 2019): 125–28; Steven Lee Myers, "China's Saber Rattles Neighbors, but Signal Is for US," *New York Times*, June 26, 2020, A14.

26. Marina Golovnina, "China Offers to Mediate in Stalled Afghan Taliban Peace Talks," Reuters, February 12, 2015, http://www.reuters.com/article/2015/02/12/us-pakistan-china-idUSKBN0LG1UP20150212; Sutter, *The United States and Asia*, 233–68.

27. Stephen Biddle, "Afghan Legacy: Emerging Lessons of an Ongoing War," *Washington Quarterly* 37, no. 2 (Summer 2014): 73–86.

28. C. Raja Mohan, "An Afghan Trifecta," *Carnegie India*, January 29, 2019, https://carnegieindia.org/2019/01/29/afghan-trifecta-pub-78224; Clayton Thomas, *Afghanistan: Background and US Policy in Brief*, Congressional Research Service Report R45122 (Washington, DC: Library of Congress, May 1, 2020).

29. Michael Wills, "Afghanistan beyond 2014," *Asia Policy* 17 (January 2014): 2–6.

30. Larry P. Goodson, "The New Great Game: Pakistan's Approach to Afghanistan after 2014," *Asia Policy*, no. 17 (January 2014): 33–40.

31. Robert Sutter, *The United States and Asia*, 2nd ed. (Lanham, MD: Rowman & Littlefield, 2020): 280–81.

32. Sutter, *United States and Asia*, 2nd ed., 281–82.

33. David Shullman, ed., *Chinese Malign Influence and the Corrosion of Democracy* (Washington, DC: International Republican Institute, 2019), 17–20.

34. John Gill, "China and South Asia," in *China's Global Influence*, ed. Scott McDonald and Michael Burgoyne (Honolulu, HI: Asia-Pacific Center for Security Studies, 2020), 77–79.

35. Shullman, *Chinese Malign Influence*, 18.

36. Susan Epstein and K. Alan Kronstadt, *Pakistan: US Foreign Assistance*, Congressional Research Service Report R41856 (Washington, DC: Library of Congress, July 1, 2013), 35, https://fas.org/sgp/crs/row/R41856.pdf.

37. Daniel Kliman et al., *Grading China's Belt and Road* (Washington, DC: Center for New American Security, April 2019), 15.

38. Krzysztof Iwanek, "No, Pakistan's Gwadar Port Is Not a Chinese Naval Base (Just Yet)," *The Diplomat*, November 19, 2019, https://thediplomat.com/2019/11/no-pakistans-gwadar-port-is-not-a-chinese-naval-base-just-yet.

39. Ishrat Hossain, "Bangladesh Balances between Big Brothers, China and India," *East Asia Forum*, June 6, 2018, https://www.eastasiaforum.org/2018/06/06/bangladesh-balances-between-big-brothers-china-and-india.

40. Shi Jiangtao, "Xi Jinping's Visit to India and Nepal," *South China Morning Post*, October 15, 2019, https://www.scmp.com/news/china/diplomacy/article/3032900/xi-jinpings-trip-india-and-nepal-seen-much-needed-win-china.

41. Sudha Ramachandran, "Sri Lanka's Rajapaksas Are Back in Power," *The Diplomat*, November 18, 2019, https://thediplomat.com/2019/11/sri-lankas-rajapaksas-are-back-in-power; Shullman, *China's Malign Influence*, 21–25; Gill, "China and South Asia," 75–76.

42. Shullman, *China's Malign Influence*, 59–64.

43. See, among others, Scobell et al., *At the Dawn of the Belt and Road*, 89–114; Laurelle, *China's Belt and Road Initiative and Its Impact on Central Asia*; Rolland, *China's Eurasian Century?* For background, see Bates Gill and Matthew Oresman, *China's New Journey to the West* (Washington, DC: Center for Strategic and International Studies, August 2003); Garver, "China's Influence in Central and South Asia"; Kathleen Collins and William Wohlforth, "Defying 'Great Game' Expectation," in *Strategic Asia 2003–04: Fragility and Crisis*, ed. Richard Ellings and Aaron Friedberg (Seattle, WA: National Bureau of Asian Research, 2003), 291–320; Tang Shiping, "Economic Integration in Central Asia," *Asian Survey* 40, no. 2 (March–April 2000): 360–76; Venera Galyamova, "Central Asian Countries and China: Managing the Transition," in Zhang Yunling, *Making New Partnership*, 282–323; Yitzhak Shichor, "China's Central Asian Strategy and the Xinjiang Connection," *China and Eurasia Forum Quarterly* 6, no. 2 (2008): 55–73; Chin-Hao Huang, "China and the Shanghai Cooperation Organization: Post-summit Analysis and Implications for the United States," *China and Eurasia Forum Quarterly* 4, no. 3 (August 2006): 15–21; Niklas Swanstrom, "China and Central Asia: A New Great Game or Traditional Vassal Relations?," *Journal of Contemporary China* 14, no. 45 (November 2005): 109–28; Jen-kun Fu, "Reassessing the 'New Great Game' between India and China in Central Asia," *China and Eurasia Forum Quarterly* 8, no. 1 (2010); Raffaello Pantucci, "China and Central Asia in 2013," *China Brief* 13, no. 2 (January 18, 2013), http://www.jamestown.org/programs/chinabrief/single/?tx_ttnews%5Btt_news%5D=40332& cHash=734a6e4544f563fb65d87ffdce73a63f#.VYgoI_lViko; Jean-Pierre Cabestan, "The Shanghai Cooperation Organization, Central Asia, and the Great Powers, an Introduction," *Asian Survey* 53, no. 3 (2013): 423–35; Marlene Laurelle and Sebastien Peyrouse, eds., *The Chinese Question in Central Asia: Domestic Order, Social Change, and the Chinese Factor* (New York: Columbia University Press, 2012); Wang Jisi, *"Marching Westwards": The Rebalancing of China's Geostrategy*, International and Strategic Studies Report 73 (Beijing: Peking University, October 7, 2012); Zhao Huasheng, "China's View of and Expectations from the Shanghai Cooperation Organization," *Asian Survey* 53, no. 3 (2013): 436–60.

44. Gill and Oresman, *China's New Journey to the West*, viii–ix.

45. Zhou Yan, "A Lifeline from Central Asia," *China Daily*, February 17, 2011; Sebastien Peyrouse, "Sino-Kazakh Relations: A Nascent Strategic Partnership," *China Brief* 8, no. 21 (November 7, 2008): 11–15.

46. Peyrouse, "Sino-Kazakh Relations," 12; Kevin Sheives, "China and Central Asia's New Energy Relationship: Keeping Things in Perspective," *China-Eurasia Forum Quarterly*, April 2005, 18; Stephen Blank, "The Strategic Implications of the Turkmenistan-China Pipeline Project," *China Brief* 10, no. 3 (February 4, 2010): 10–12.

47. "Year Ender on Peace in Afghanistan," *Xinhua*, December 8, 1997, carried by FBIS, cited in Sutter, *Chinese Policy Priorities and Their Implications for the United States*, 148.

48. Andrew Small, "China's Caution on Afghanistan-Pakistan," *Washington Quarterly* 33, no. 3 (July 2010): 81–97; "China Says Bin Laden's Death a Milestone for Anti-terrorism," *China Daily*, May 3, 2011.

49. Guang Wan, "The U.S. New Central Asian Strategy," *Xiandai guoji guanxi* (Beijing) 11 (November 27, 1997): 13–16.

50. Sutter, *Chinese Policy Priorities and Their Implications for the United States*, 143.

51. Adapted from Gill and Oresman, *China's New Journey to the West*, viii–ix.

52. Garver, "China's Influence in Central and South Asia," 206–9; John Garver, "Development of China's Overland Transportation Links with Central, Southwest, and South Asia," *China Quarterly* 185 (March 2006): 1–22.

53. Wan Zhihong, "China Agrees on New Gas Line," *China Daily*, June 14, 2010, 6.

54. Central Intelligence Agency, *World Factbook*, accessed June 22, 2015, https://www.cia.gov/library/publications/the-world-factbook/fields/2061.html.

55. "China: Reproducing Silk Road Story," *China Daily*, June 5, 2001.

56. Gill and Oresman, *China's New Journey to the West*, 7.

57. Gill and Oresman, *China's New Journey to the West*, 6–10; Jianwei Wang, "China's Multilateral Diplomacy in the New Millennium," in *China Rising: Power and Motivation in Chinese Foreign Policy*, ed. Yong Deng and Fei-Ling Wang (Lanham, MD: Rowman & Littlefield, 2005), 177–87.

58. Qin Jize, "Wen: SCO Trade Is Set to Double," *China Daily*, September 16–17, 2006, 1.

59. James Nichol, *Central Asia*, Congressional Research Service Report RL33458 (Washington, DC: Library of Congress, March 21, 2014), 8–9.

60. *Chief Zhang Says SCO Will "Absolutely Never Become Euro-Asian Military Alliance,"* Report CPP20060116001017 (Washington, DC: Foreign Broadcast Information Service, January 16, 2006).

61. Gill and Oresman, *China's New Journey to the West*, 10–12.

62. Yu Bin, "China-Russia Relations: A New World Order according to Moscow and Beijing," *Comparative Connections* 7, no. 3 (October 2005): 143–47.

63. "China: Reproducing the Silk Road Story."

64. "China: Reproducing the Silk Road Story."

65. Jyotsna Bashki, "Sino-Russian Strategic Partnership in Central Asia: Implications for India," *Strategic Analysis* 25, no. 2 (May 2001): 4.

66. "China: Reproducing the Silk Road Story."

67. *"People's Daily* Editorial Hails SCO Founding," *Xinhua*, June 15, 2001.

68. "China: Regional Co-op Boosted," *China Daily*, June 15, 2001.

69. *"People's Daily* Editorial Hails SCO Founding."

70. "SCO Charter Adopted," *China Daily*, June 8, 2002.

71. Yu Bin, "Party Time," *Comparative Connections* 5, no. 2 (July 2003).

72. Joseph Ferguson, "Disappointment in Dushanbe," *PacNet* 47 (Honolulu, HI: Pacific Forum CSIS, September 9, 2008); Zhu Feng, *Russia-Georgia Military Conflict: Testing China's Responsibility*, CSIS Freeman Report, November 2008, 1–3.

73. Gill and Oresman, *China's New Journey to the West*, 17.

74. James Millward, *Eurasian Crossroads: A History of Xinjiang* (New York: Columbia University Press, 2007); Gill and Oresman, *China's New Journey to the West*, 18; Yu Bin, "Coping with the Post-Kosovo Fallout," *Comparative Connections* 1, no. 1 (July 1999).

75. Stephen Blank, "Central Asia's Strategic Revolution," *NBR Analysis* 14, no. 4 (November 2003): 51–77.

76. "SCO Officials Vow to Pursue Peace," *China Daily*, January 8, 2002.

77. "SCO Defense Ministers Sign Communiqué on Military Cooperation," *Xinhua*, May 15, 2002.

78. "Shanghai Five Fight Terrorism," *China Daily*, August 12, 2003.

79. "Hijacked Airline Tests SCO's Anti-terror Skills," *Xinhua*, August 7, 2003; "China's Top Legislature Approves Treaty on SCO Joint Military Exercises," *Xinhua*, December 27, 2008; Richard Weitz, "China's Growing Clout in the SCO," *China Brief* 10, no. 20 (October 8, 2010): 8–11.

80. Stephen Blank, "Recent Trends in Russo-Chinese Military Relations," *China Brief* 9, no. 2 (January 22, 2009): 6–8; Edward Wong, "China Quietly Extends Its Footprints into Central Asia," *New York Times*, January 2, 2011.

81. Yu Bin, "Treaties Scrapped, Treaties Signed," *Comparative Connections* 3, no. 2 (July 2001).

82. "Roundup: Economic Cooperation to Add New Light to SCO," *Xinhua*, May 28, 2002.

83. Yu Bin, "The Russian-Chinese Oil Politik," *Comparative Connections* 5, no. 4 (October 2003).

84. Bernard D. Cole, *Oil for the Lamps of China: Beijing's 21st-Century Search for Energy* (Honolulu, HI: University Press of the Pacific), viii, 70; Sheives, "China and Central Asia's New Energy Relationship," 18.

85. Yu Bin, "Russia's Pride and China's Power," 124–25.

86. Yu Bin, "Russia's Pride and China's Power," 124–25.

87. "SCO Charter Adopted."

88. Matthew Oresman, "The SCO: A New Hope or a Graveyard of Acronyms?," *PacNet* 21 (Honolulu, HI: Pacific Forum CSIS, May 22, 2003).

89. Garver, "China's Influence in Central and South Asia," 213; European Commission, *Trade Issues: Central Asia*, accessed February 12, 2009, http://www.csis.org/media/csis/pubs/pac0819.pdf; Central Intelligence Agency, *World Factbook*, Export Partners, accessed June 23, 2015, https://www.cia.gov/library/publications/the-world-factbook/fields/2050.html.

90. Yu Bin, "China-Russia Relations."

91. Scobell et al., *At the Dawn of the Belt and Road*, 98.

92. Research Gate, "Central Asia's Total Trade with China and Russia," https://www.researchgate.net/figure/Central-Asias-total-trade-with-China-and-Russia-billion-Note-Total-trade-is-a-sum_fig4_320659496; "Central Asia's Economic Evolution from Russia to China," Stratfor, April 5, 2018, https://worldview.stratfor.com/article/central-asia-china-russia-trade-kyrgyzstan-kazakhstan-turkmenistan-tajikistan-uzbekistan.

93. "Central Asia's Economic Evolution from Russia to China."

94. "Central Asia's Economic Evolution from Russia to China."

95. Rolland, *China's Eurasian Century?*

96. Robert Sutter, *Chinese Foreign Relations* (Lanham, MD: Rowman & Littlefield, 2012), 250–65.

97. Yao Tsz Yan, "Smart Cities or Surveillance: Huawei in Central Asia," *The Diplomat*, August 7, 2019, https://thediplomat.com/2019/08/smart-cities-or-surveillance-huawei-in-central-asia.

98. "China's Gas Supplies Shadowed by Stalled Pipeline," Radio Free Asia, June 24, 2019, https://www.rfa.org/english/commentaries/energy_watch/chinas-gas-supplies-shadowed-by-stalled-pipeline-06242019101235.html.

99. Scott McDonald and Michael Burgoyne, *China's Global Influence* (Honolulu, HI: Asia-Pacific Center for Security Studies, 2020), 90–93; Fatima Kukeyeva et al., "Is Ili/Irtysh Rivers a 'Casualty' of Kazakhstan-China Relations?," *Academy of Strategic Management Journal* 17, no. 3 (2018), https://www.abacademies.org/articles/is-iliirtysh-rivers-a-casualty-of-kazakhstanchina-relations-7304.html; Sebastien Peyrouse, "Understanding Sinophobia in Central Asia," *The Diplomat*, May 1, 2020, https://thediplomat.com/2020/04/understanding-sinophobia-in-central-asia.

100. "Central Asia's Economic Evolution from Russia to China."

101. "The Perfect Storm of Corruption in Central Asia," Radio Free Europe/Radio Liberty, June 4, 2016, https://www.rferl.org/a/corruption-central-asia/27779246.html; "Central Asia's Economic Evolution from Russia to China."

102. Catherine Putz, "Former Kyrgyz Prime Minister Faces 20 Years on Corruption Charge," *The Diplomat*, January 7, 2019, access May 23, 2020, https://thediplomat.com/2019/01/former-kyrgyz-prime-minister-faces-20-years-on-corruption-charges.

103. Mansur Mirovalev, "Why Are Central Asian Countries So Quiet on Uighur Persecution?," Al Jazeera, February 24, 2020, https://www.aljazeera.com/indepth/features/central-asian-countries-quiet-uighur-persecution-200224184747697.html.

104. Nadege Rolland, ed., *Securing the Belt and Road Initiative*, NBR Special Report No. 80 (Seattle, WA: National Bureau of Asian Research, September 3, 2019), 72.

105. Sutter, *The United States and Asia*, 2nd ed., 292.

106. Sutter, *The United States and Asia*, 2nd ed., 300–308. For background, see Justin Li, "Chinese Investment in Mongolia," *East Asia Forum*, February 2, 2011; "China, Mongolia Finalize 4,677-km Border," *China Daily*, December 1, 2005.

107. Central Intelligence Agency, *World Factbook*, "Mongolia Economy," https://www.cia.gov/library/publications/the-world-factbook/geos/mg.html.

108. Discussed in Susan Lawrence, *Mongolia: Issues for Congress*, Congressional Research Service Report R41867 (Washington, DC: Library of Congress, June 14, 2011), 5–10.

109. Yuriy Humber and Michael Kohn, "Few Roads Leading to China Tell Tale of Mongolian Fears," *Bloomberg*, July 4, 2013, http://www.bloomberg.com/news/articles/2013-07-04/few-roads-leading-to-china-tell-a-tale-of-mongolia-s-trad.

110. "China Says Hopes Mongolia Learned Lesson after Dalai Lama Visit," Reuters, January 24, 2017, https://www.reuters.com/article/us-china-mongolia-dalailama-idUSKBN158197.

111. Sergey Radchenko, "As China and Russia Draw Closer, Mongolia Feels the Squeeze," *Asan Forum*, October 11, 2018, http://www.theasanforum.org/as-china-and-russia-draw-closer-mongolia-feels-the-squeeze/#a2.

## 11. RELATIONS WITH RUSSIA AND EUROPE

1. For Chinese sources providing background on recent Chinese relations with Russia and Europe, see Chen Dongxiao, "Opportunities and Challenges in China's Relations with Major Powers," *Foreign Affairs Journal* (Beijing) 97 (August 2010): 55–68; Ji Zhiye, "Strategic Prospects for Russia," *Contemporary International Relations* (Beijing) 20, no. 5 (September–October 2010): 1–16; Xing Guangcheng, "Work for Mutual Trust and Mutual Benefit in Deepening Sino-Russian Relations," *Foreign Affairs Journal* (Beijing) 80 (June 2006): 8–13; Li Shaoxian, "China-Russia Bond," *Xiandai guoji guanxi* (Beijing) 17 (January 2007): 5–21; Liu Mingli, "Reflection on EU-China Relations," *Contemporary International Relations* (Beijing) 20, no. 3 (May–June 2010): 115–22; Xia Liping, "Sino-EU Security Relations," *Contemporary International Relations* (Beijing) 20, no. 1 (January–February 2010): 102–8; Mei Zhaorong, "Sino-European Relations in Retrospect and Prospect," *Foreign Affairs Journal* (Beijing) 79 (March 2006): 17–27; Shen Qiang, "Properly Handle Problems Arising from Development of the Sino-EU Relations," *Foreign Affairs Journal* (Beijing) 90 (Winter 2008): 92–103; Feng Zhongping, "China-EU Relationship," *Xiandai guoji guanxi* (Beijing) 17 (January 2007): 47–55; Tang Xizhong et al., "Zhong E Guanxi," in *The Bilateral and Multilateral Relations between China and Her Neighbor Countries* (Beijing: Zhongguo Shehui Kexue Chubanshe, 2003), 186–99; and Zhou Hong, "Lun Zhong ou Huoban guanxi zhong de bu dui Cheng Xing yu Dui Cheng Xing," in *World Politics—Views from China* (Beijing: Xin Shijie Chubanshe, 2007), 298–315.

2. For background on development of Russia-China relations prior to the recent entente, see Jeannne Wilson, *Strategic Partners: Russian-Chinese Relations in the Post-Soviet Era* (Armonk, NY: Sharpe, 2004); Yu Bin, "China and Russia: Normalizing Their Strategic Partnership," in *Power Shift: China and Asia's New Dynamics*, ed. David Shambaugh (Berkeley: University of California Press, 2005), 228–46; Robert Sutter, *China's Rise in Asia: Promises and Perils* (Lanham, MD: Rowman & Littlefield, 2005), 107–22; Peter Ferdinand, "Sunset, Sunrise: China and Russia Construct a New Relationship," *International Affairs* 83, no. 5 (2007): 841–67; Bobo Lo, *Axis of Convenience: Moscow, Beijing, and the New Geopolitics* (Washington, DC: Brookings Institution, 2008).

3. Rajan Menon, "The Strategic Convergence between Russia and China," *Survival* 39, no. 2 (Summer 1997): 101–25.

4. James Clay Moltz, "Regional Tension in the Russo-Chinese Rapprochement," *Asian Survey* 35, no. 6 (June 1995): 511–27.

5. Stephen Uhalley, "Sino-Soviet Relations: Continued Improvement amidst Tumultuous Change," *Journal of East Asian Affairs* 6, no. 1 (Winter–Spring 1992): 171–92.

6. Robert Sutter, *Chinese Policy Priorities and Their Implications for the United States* (Lanham, MD: Rowman & Littlefield, 2000), 65.

7. Menon, "The Strategic Convergence between Russia and China"; Stephen Blank, *Dynamics of Russian Weapons Sales to China* (Carlisle, PA: US Army War College, Strategic Studies Institute, March 4, 1997).

8. Bates Gill and Matthew Oresman, *China's New Journey to the West* (Washington, DC: Center for Strategic and International Studies, August 2003), 5–6.

9. Moltz, "Regional Tension in the Russo-Chinese Rapprochement," 518.

10. Sutter, *Chinese Policy Priorities and Their Implications for the United States*, 66.

11. Blank, *Dynamics of Russian Weapons Sales to China*; *China's Rising Military Power*, Congressional Research Service Report 96-647F (Washington, DC: Library of Congress, July 31, 1998).

12. Sutter, *Chinese Policy Priorities and Their Implications for the United States*, 67.

13. Menon, "The Strategic Convergence between Russia and China."

14. Sutter, *Chinese Policy Priorities and Their Implications for the United States*, 67.

15. Sutter, *Chinese Policy Priorities and Their Implications for the United States*, 68.

16. Peter Rodman, "A New Russian-Chinese Alliance?," *Los Angeles Times*, March 25, 1996, accessed March 25, 1996; Alexander Nemets and Thomas Torda, *The Russian Chinese Alliance* (West Palm Beach, FL: Newsmax.com, 2002).

17. Sutter, *Chinese Policy Priorities and Their Implications for the United States*, 68.

18. Gilbert Rozman, "Russian Foreign Policy in Northeast Asia," in *The International Relations of Northeast Asia*, ed. Samuel Kim (Lanham, MD: Rowman & Littlefield, 2004), 201–11.

19. Stuart Goldman, *Russian-Chinese Cooperation: Prospects and Implications*, Congressional Research Service Report 97-185F (Washington, DC: Library of Congress, January 27, 1997), 13.

20. Rozman, "Russian Foreign Policy in Northeast Asia."

21. Rouben Azizian, "Russia's China Debate," in *Asia's China Debate* (Honolulu, HI: Asia-Pacific Center for Security Studies, December 2003), 6–7.

22. Sutter, *Chinese Policy Priorities and Their Implications for the United States*, 74–75.

23. William Wohlforth, "Russia," in *Strategic Asia 2002–03: Asian Aftershocks*, ed. Richard Ellings and Aaron Friedberg (Seattle, WA: National Bureau of Asian Research, 2002), 183–222.

24. Wohlforth, "Russia," 165–80; Joseph Ferguson, "Energizing the Relationship," *Comparative Connections* 5, no. 3 (October 2003).

25. Ching Cheong, "U.S.-Russia Summit Worries China," *Straits Times*, May 31, 2002; Willy Wo-Lap Lam, "Moscow Tilts West, Beijing Worries," *China Brief* 12, no. 12 (June 6, 2002): 1–3; Yu Bin, "A 'Nice' Treaty in a Precarious World," *Comparative Connections* 3, no. 3 (October 2001).

26. Robert Sutter, *The United States and East Asia: Dynamics and Implications* (Lanham, MD: Rowman & Littlefield, 2003), 114; Azizian, "Russia's China Debate"; Rozman, "Russian Foreign Policy in Northeast Asia"; Sutter, *China's Rise in Asia*, 121.

27. Yu Bin, "The New World Order according to Moscow and Beijing," *Comparative Connections* 7, no. 3 (October 2005).

28. Yu Bin, "China's Year of Russia and the Gathering Nuclear Storm," *Comparative Connections* 8, no. 1 (April 2006): 145–51.

29. Michael Richardson, "China and Russia Spread Their Influence over Central Asia," *Canberra Times*, August 2, 2007.

30. Yu Bin, "China-Russia: Embracing a Storm and Each Other?," *Comparative Connections* 10, no. 3 (October 2008): 135; Stephen Blank, "Recent Trends in Russo-Chinese Military Relations," *China Brief* 9, no. 2 (January 22, 2009): 6–8.

31. Sutter, *The United States and East Asia*, 115; Azizian, "Russia's China Debate"; Yu Bin, "Reset under Medvedev: Zapad-Plitik and Vostok 2010," *Comparative Connections* 11, no. 2 (2010); Rozman, "Russian Foreign Policy in Northeast Asia."

32. Yu Bin, "Reset under Medvedev"; Yu Bin, "Guns and Games of August: Tales of Two Strategic Partners," *Comparative Connections* 10, no. 3 (October 2008): 131–38.

33. Yu Bin, "Pragmatism Dominates Russia-China Relations," *PacNet* 11 (Honolulu, HI: Pacific Forum CSIS, March 20, 2006); Lo, *Axis of Convenience.*

34. Lo, *Axis of Convenience.* This section is taken from Robert Sutter, *China-Russia Relations: Strategic Implications and US Policy Options*, NBR Special Report No. 73 (Seattle, WA: National Bureau of Asian Research, September 2018). Other major studies involving China-Russia relations and US interests include Julianne Smith, *A Transatlantic Strategy for Russia* (Washington, DC: Carnegie Endowment for International Peace, 2016); Angela Stent, *Russia, China and the West after Crimea* (Washington, DC: TransAtlantic Academy, 2016); Kathleen Hicks and Lisa Sawyer Samp, *Recalibrating US Strategy toward Russia* (Washington, DC: Center for Strategic and International Studies, March 2017); Eugene Rumer, Henry Sokolsky, and Andrew Weiss, *Guiding Principles of a Sustainable U.S. Policy toward Russia, Ukraine, and Eurasia: Key Judgments from a Joint Task Force* (Washington, DC: Carnegie Endowment for International Peace, February 2017); Julianne Smith and Adam Twardowski, *The Future of US-Russian Relations* (Washington, DC: Center for New American Security, January 2017); Robert Blackwill and Ashley Tellis, *Council Special Report: Revising U.S. Grand Strategy*

*toward China* (Washington, DC: Council on Foreign Relations, April 2015); Orville Schell and Susan Shirk, chairs, *US Policy toward China: Recommendations for a New Administration* (New York: Asia Society, 2017); Bobo Lo, *A Wary Embrace: A Lowy Institute Paper* (Sidney, Australia: Penguin Special Studies, 2017); Simon Saradzhyan and Ali Wyne, *China-Russia Relations: Same Bed, Different Dreams? Why Converging Interests Are Unlikely to Lead to a Full-Fledged Alliance* (Cambridge, MA: Harvard University Belfer Center for Science and International Affairs, June 2018); Graham Allison and Dmitri Simes, "China-Russia: New Best Friends?," *National Interest*, January–February 2019.

35. Yu Bin, "China-Russia Relations: Crouching Army, Hidden Alliance," *Comparative Connections* 20, no. 3 (January 2019): 113.

36. Alexander Gabuev, *Friends with Benefits: Russian-Chinese Relations after the Ukraine Crisis* (Moscow: Carnegie Endowment for International Peace, 2016).

37. Howard French, "China's Dangerous Game," *The Atlantic*, November 2014, https://www.theatlantic.com/magazine/archive/2014/11/chinas-dangerous-game/380789.

38. "China, Russia to Further Deepen Partnership amid New International Situation," *China Daily*, July 5, 2017, 1.

39. Jane Perlez, "China and Russia Reach 30-Year Gas Deal," *New York Times*, May 21, 2014.

40. Alexander Gabuev, "Why Russia and China Are Strengthening Security Ties," Carnegie Moscow Center, September 24, 2018, https://carnegie.ru/2018/09/24/why-russia-and-china-are-strengthening-security-ties-pub-77333.

41. Andrew Scobell et al., *At the Dawn of Belt and Road: China in the Developing World* (Santa Monica, CA: RAND Corporation, 2018), 259–60.

42. See, among others, Artyom Lukin, "A Russian Perspective: Russia's Gambit in the Korean Nuclear Crisis," *Asan Forum* 7, no. 1 (January–February 2019), http://www.theasanforum.org/a-russian-perspective.

43. This assessment benefited from Artyom Lukin's judgments on Russia-China-Korean relations in a presentation at an invitation-only workshop on China, Russia, and the Korean Peninsula at the Asan Foundation in Seoul, Korea, in May 2018 and in his article in Jaewoo Choo, Youngjun Kim, Artyom Lukin, and Elizabeth Wishnick, *The China-Russia Entente and the Korean Peninsula*, NBR Special Report No. 78 (Seattle, WA: National Bureau of Asian Research, March 2019).

44. Alexander Korolev, "Russia in the South China Sea," *Foreign Policy Analysis*, February 2018, https://www.researchgate.net/publication/323201523_Russia_in_the_South_China_Sea_Balancing_and_Hedging1.

45. Vasily Kashin, "Why Russian and Chinese Warships Joined Forces in the Baltic Sea This Week," *Moscow Times*, July 28, 2017, https://www.themoscowtimes.com/2017/07/28/why-russian-and-chinese-warships-met-in-the-baltic-sea-a58525.

46. "Chinese Defense Minister Says China Will 'Support' Russia against America," *National Interest*, April 4, 2018, https://nationalinterest.org/blog/the-buzz/chinese-defense-minister-says-china-will-%E2%80%98support%E2%80%99-russia-25216.

47. State Council Information Office of the People's Republic of China, "White Paper on China's Military Strategy, Beijing," May 2015, section 6.

48. National Security Strategy of the Russian Federation, Moscow, December 2015, section 93.

49. Alexander Gabuev and Vasily Kashin, *Vooruzhennaya druzhba—kak Rossiya i Kitay torguyut oruzhiem* [Friendship in arms: How Russia and China trade in weapons] (Moscow: Moscow Carnegie Center, November 2, 2017), 13.

50. "China and Russia Close Ranks against US Missile-Defense System," *South China Morning Post*, October 12, 2016, https://www.scmp.com/news/china/diplomacy-defence/article/2027171/china-and-russia-close-ranks-against-us-missile-defence.

51. Alexander Gabuev, "Eurasian Silk Road Union: Toward a Russia-China Consensus?," *The Diplomat*, June 5, 2015.

52. Michael Yahuda, "China and Europe: The Significance of a Secondary Relationship," in *Chinese Foreign Policy: Theory and Practice*, ed. Thomas W. Robinson and David Shambaugh (New York: Oxford University Press, 1994), 266–82; David Shambaugh, "The New Strategic

Triangle: U.S. and European Reactions to China's Rise," *Washington Quarterly* 29, no. 3 (Summer 2005): 7–25; Lanxin Xiang, "China's Eurasian Experiment," *Survival* 46, no. 2 (Summer 2004): 109–22; Hou Yousheng, "Oumeny yu Meiguo dai hua zhanlue bijiao," *Xiandai guoji guanxi* (Beijing) 8 (August 2006): 1–6; Hou Zhengdo, "Guanyu Zhong Ou zhanlue guanxi jige xiangfa," *Guoji Wenti Yanjiu* (Beijing) 2 (April 2005): 22–25. Publications resulting from dialogues among European, Chinese, and other specialists examining the status and outlook of China-Europe relations include Bates Gill and Melissa Murphy, *China-Europe Relations: Implications and Policy Responses for the United States* (Washington, DC: Center for Strategic and International Studies, May 2008); David Shambaugh and Gudrun Wacker, eds., *American and European Relations with China* (Berlin: Stiftung Wissenschaft und Politik, 2008); David Shambaugh, Eberhard Sandschneider, and Zhou Hong, eds., *China-Europe Relations: Perceptions, Policies, and Prospects* (London: Routledge, 2007); Jing Men and Guiseppe Balducci, eds., *Prospects and Challenges for EU-China Relations in the Twenty-First Century* (Brussels: PIE–Peter Lang, 2010); European Commission, "Joint Statement: Deepening the EU-China Comprehensive Strategic Partnership for Mutual Benefit," press release, March 31, 2014; "Full Text of China's Policy Paper on the EU," *Xinhua*, April 2, 2014, cited in Sutter, *Chinese Policy Priorities and Their Implications for the United States*, 172; Theresa Fallon, "China's Pivot to Europe," *America Foreign Policy Interests* 36 (2014): 175–82.

53. "Ambassador: China-Portugal Strategic Partnership Will Be More Fruitful," *Xinhua*, February 7, 2009, accessed February 20, 2009.

54. Jean-Pierre Cabestan, "A European Role in Cross-Strait Relations?," paper presented for the Fifth Northeast Asian Forum titled "The Taiwan Strait and Northeast Asian Security," Stiftung Wissenschaft und Politik, Berlin, December 15–17, 2005, 2.

55. Jean-Pierre Cabestan, "European Union–China Relations and the United States," paper prepared for the fifty-eighth annual meeting of the Association for Asian Studies, San Francisco, April 6–9, 2006; Jean-Pierre Cabestan, "European Union–China Relations and the United States," *Asian Perspective* 30, no. 4 (Winter 2006): 11–38; Francois Godement, *A Global China Policy* (Paris: European Council on Foreign Relations Policy Brief, 2010).

56. Sutter, *Chinese Policy Priorities and Their Implications for the United States*, 150, 173.

57. "China Posts First EU Trade Surplus in Five Years," Reuters, February 4, 1998 (internet version); "PRC-EU Trade Growth in 1999," *Xinhua*, January 22, 1999. Both sources are cited in Sutter, *Chinese Policy Priorities and Their Implications for the United States*, 172.

58. "Towards a New Asia Strategy," Commission of the European Communities, Brussels, July 13, 1994; *A Long-Term Policy for China-Europe Relations*, Commission of the European Communities, Brussels, July 5, 1995; "Regarding the Asia-Europe Meeting (ASEM) to Be Held in Bangkok on 1–2 March 1996," communication to the Council and Parliament, Commission of the European Communities, Brussels, 1996; "Building Comprehensive Partnership with China," Commission of the European Communities, Brussels, June 29, 1998; "Text of China-EU Summit Statement," *Xinhua*, April 2, 1998, cited in Sutter, *Chinese Policy Priorities and Their Implications for the United States*, 173.

59. David Shambaugh, "China and Europe: The Emerging Axis," *Current History* 103, no. 674 (September 2004): 243–48.

60. Cabestan, "European Union–China Relations and the United States," 11–38.

61. David Shambaugh, "China-Europe Relations Get Complicated," *Brookings Institution Northeast Asia Commentary*, May 2007; David Shambaugh, "The 'China Honeymoon' Is Over," *International Herald Tribune*, November 26, 2007, accessed November 26, 2007.

62. Hou Na, "Fifth China-EU Strategic Dialogue Calls for Closer Ties," CCTV, May 6, 2015, accessed June 24, 2015, http://english.cntv.cn/2015/05/06/VIDE1430891651506439.shtml.

63. Stanley Crossick, Fraser Cameron, and Alex Berkofy, *EU-China Relations: Toward a Strategic Partnership*, working paper (Brussels: European Policy Centre, July 2005), 26; "Senior Chinese Official Calls for Enhanced Trade, Economic Cooperation with EU," *Xinhua*, December 29, 2010; "Full Text of China's Policy Paper on the EU"; "Fifth China-EU Strategic Dialogue Calls for Closer Ties"; Zhong Nan, "EU-China Investment Vital for Trade Growth," *China Daily*, July 24, 2019, http://www.chinadaily.com.cn/a/201907/24/WS5d37af19a310d83056400a7b.html.

64. Valbona Zeneli, "Mapping China's Investments in Europe," *The Diplomat*, March 14, 2019, https://thediplomat.com/2019/03/mapping-chinas-investments-in-europe.

65. "Senior Chinese Official Calls for Enhanced Trade, Economic Cooperation with EU"; Crossick et al., *EU-China Relations*, 26–27; Xu Xuanping, "Li's Visit Pushes China-EU Ties toward New Stage," *China Daily*, January 6, 2011, 8; European Union, "EU-China Trade," November, 3, 2015, http://eeas.europa.eu/delegations/china/press_corner/all_news/news/2015/20150311_en.htm; Zeneli, "Mapping China's Investments."

66. Cabestan, "European Union–China Relations and the United States," 11–38, 18–19; Crossick et al., *EU-China Relations*, 26–27; "Senior Chinese Official Calls for Enhanced Trade, Economic Cooperation with EU"; European Commission, *Trade—China*, accessed June 24, 2015. Recent trade figures are from *Eurostat*, accessed May 23, 2020, https://ec.europa.eu/eurostat/web/products-eurostat-news/-/EDN-20190409-1.

67. "EU Policy Paper Stresses Closer China Relations," *China Daily*, October 25, 2006, 1; Jonathan Stearns, "Three China Solar Panel Firms Lose EU Tariff Exemptions," *Bloomberg*, June 15, 2015, http://www.bloomberg.com/news/articles/2015-06-05/three-china-solar-panel-groups-lose-eu-tariff-exemptions.

68. Cabestan, "European Union–China Relations and the United States," 11–38, 19–20.

69. *EU-China Trade in Facts and Figures*, Europa MEMO/09/40, January 30, 2009; "China, US Pushed Trade Barriers to Record High in 2018: EU," Reuters, June 17, 2019, https://www.reuters.com/article/us-eu-trade-protectionism/china-u-s-pushed-trade-barriers-to-record-high-in-2018-eu-idUSKCN1TI1S9.

70. Francois Godement, "China's Apparent Cost-Free Slight to Europe," *PacNet* 65 (Honolulu, HI: Pacific Forum CSIS, December 9, 2008); "Wen Ends EU Tour with Optimism," *China Daily*, February 2, 2009, 1.

71. Tania Branihan and Jonathan Watts, "Chinese PM Rebuts Criticism over Copenhagen Role," *The Guardian*, March 14, 2010; Goeff Dyer and Andrew Ward, "Europe Defies China's Nobel Threat," *Financial Times*, November 5, 2010.

72. "China's Attitude on Libya: Give Peace a Chance," *People's Daily*, March 31, 2011, http://en.people.cn/90001/90776/90883/7335771.html.

73. Travel China, Guide, *China Outbound Tourism 2014*, accessed June 24, 2015, http://www.travelchinaguide.com/tourism/2014statistics/outbound.htm; "Three Million Chinese Tourists Visit Europe in First Half of 2019," *People's Daily*, August 22, 2019, 2020, http://en.people.cn/n3/2019/0822/c90000-9608224.html.

74. Riazat Butt, "A Class Act—UK Universities Attract More Chinese Students," *China Daily*, April 13, 2015, http://europe.chinadaily.com.cn/business/2015-04/13/content_20419388.htm; Richard Adams, "Third of non-EU Students in UK Come from China," *The Guardian*, January 16, 2020, https://www.theguardian.com/education/2020/jan/16/third-of-non-eu-university-students-in-uk-come-from-china.

75. See, among others, Erik Brattberg and Philippe Le Corre, *The EU and China in 2020: More Competition Ahead* (Washington, DC: Carnegie Endowment, February 19, 2020); Mario Esteban and Miguel Otero-Iglesias, *Europe in the Face of US-China Rivalry* (Madrid, Spain: European Think-Tank Network on China, January 2020).

76. Estonian Foreign Intelligence Agency, *International Security and Estonia, 2020*, 3, 70–78, https://www.valisluureamet.ee/pdf/raport-2020-en.pdf.

77. *International Security and Estonia, 2020*, 3.

78. Andrew Foxall and John Hemmings, *The Art of Deceit: How Russia and China Use Sharp Power to Subvert the West* (London: Henry Jackson Society, 2019), 14–20, https://henryjacksonsociety.org/wp-content/uploads/2019/12/HJS-Sharp-Power-Report-FINAL.pdf.

79. Foxall and Hemmings, *The Art of Deceit*, 17.

80. Austin Doehler, "Montenegro Moves on to Next Phase of Highway Project and Further into China's Debt-Trap," *National Interest*, March 25, 2020, https://nationalinterest.org/feature/montenegro-moves-next-phase-highway-project-and-further-china%E2%80%99s-debt-trap-137242; Laura Zhou, "Chinese President Xi Jinping to Take Over as Host of 17+1 Summit," *South China Morning Post*, January 2, 2020, https://www.scmp.com/news/china/diplomacy/article/3044359/chinese-president-xi-jinping-take-over-host-171-summit.

81. Charlie Duxbury, "Sweden's Lonely Boxing Match with Beijing," *Politico*, February 12, 2020, https://www.politico.eu/article/sweden-china-diplomatic-spat; Jerome A. Cohen, "Why Has China Claimed the Detained Bookseller Gui Minhai," *Jerry's Blog*, http://www.jeromecohen.net/jerrys-blog/gui-minhai-and-chinese-nationality; "How Sweden Copes with Chinese Bullying," *The Economist*, February 20, 2020, https://www.economist.com/europe/2020/02/20/how-sweden-copes-with-chinese-bullying.

82. David Shullman, ed., *Chinese Malign Influence and the Corrosion of Democracy* (Washington, DC: International Republican Institute, 2019), 25–28.

83. Shullman, *Chinese Malign Influence*, 25–28; "Chinese Donation Diplomacy Raises Tensions," *New York Times*, April 14, 2020, https://www.nytimes.com/2020/04/14/us/politics/coronavirus-china-trump-donation.html.

84. "Chinese Professor Accused of Spying by Belgium," *South China Morning Post*, October 30, 2019, https://www.scmp.com/news/china/diplomacy/article/3035627/chinese-professor-accused-spying-belgium-barred-entering; Alan Crawford and Peter Martin, "How Belgium Became Europe's Den of Spies and Gateway for China," *Bloomberg*, November 28, 2019, https://www.bloomberg.com/news/articles/2019-11-28/how-belgium-became-europe-s-den-of-spies-and-a-gateway-for-china.

85. Brattberg and Le Corre, *The EU and China in 2020*.

86. Esteban and Otero-Iglesias, *Europe in the Face of US-China Rivalry*.

87. Robert Sutter, *Historical Dictionary of Chinese Foreign Policy* (Lanham, MD: Scarecrow Press, 2011), 60.

88. China Institute, *China-Canada Trade: 2019*, 2, https://www.ualberta.ca/china-institute/media-library/media-gallery/research/analysis-briefs/trade-report2019.

89. Mike Blanchfield, "The Chill Is Real," *CTV News*, February 7, 2020, https://www.ctvnews.ca/politics/the-chill-is-real-ambassador-on-canada-china-relationship-1.4799020; "Attitudes toward China," Pew Research Center, December 5, 2019, https://www.pewresearch.org/global/2019/12/05/attitudes-toward-china-2019.

90. Francois Perreault, "Can China Become a Major Arctic Player?," *RSIS Commentaries*, 073/2012, April 24, 2012, accessed July 8, 2012, http://www.rsis.edu.sg/publications/Perspective/RSIS0732012.pdf.

91. Sanna Kopra, "China and Its Arctic Trajectories," Arctic Institute, March 17, 2020, https://www.thearcticinstitute.org/china-arctic-trajectories-the-arctic-institute-china-series-2020/?cn-reloaded=1; Blake Hounshell, "Pompeo Aims to Counter China's Ambitions in the Arctic," *Politico*, May 6, 2019, https://www.politico.com/story/2019/05/06/pompeo-arctic-china-russia-1302649.

# 12. RELATIONS WITH THE MIDDLE EAST, AFRICA, AND LATIN AMERICA

1. A Chinese government specialist wrote in an editorial in 2010 that China "consumed 0.82 ton of standard oil for every $1,000 increase in GDP value," while "in the U.S. and Japan, the figure was 0.20 ton and 0.10 ton respectively." Feng Zhaokui, "China Still a Developing Nation," *China Daily*, May 6, 2010, 12. Among Chinese perspectives on relations with the Middle East, Africa, and Latin America over the years are Li Shaoxian and Wei Liang, "New Complexities in the Middle East since 9.11," *Contemporary International Relations* (Beijing) 20, special issue (September 2010): 22–32; Li Shaoxian and Tang Zhichao, "China and the Middle East," *Xiandai guoji guanxi* (Beijing) 17 (January 2007): 22–31; Tang Jizan, "The Middle East Situation Is Full of Variables," *Foreign Affairs Journal* (Beijing) 79 (March 2006): 63–72; "White Paper on China-Africa Economic Cooperation and Trade Cooperation," *China Daily*, December 24, 2010, 9; Zeng Qiang, "FOCAC: A Powerful Engine for the Continued Development of Friendship between China and Africa," *Contemporary International Relations* (Beijing) 20, no. 6 (November–December 2010): 45–59; Xu Weizhong, "Beijing Summit Promotes Sino-African Relations," *Xiandai guoji guanxi* (Beijing) 17 (January 2007): 72–79;

"Full Text of China's Africa Policy," *People's Daily*, January 12, 2006, accessed January 12, 2006; He Wenping, "The Balancing Act of China's Africa Policy," *China Security* 3, no. 3 (Summer 2007): 23–41; Wu Hongying, "Latin America: Key Trends and Challenges," *Contemporary International Relations* (Beijing) 20, special issue (September 2010): 33–42; and Wu Hongying, "A New Era of Sino-Latin American Relations," *Xiandai guoji guanxi* (Beijing) 17 (January 2007): 64–71.

2. For background reviews, see Phillip C. Saunders, *China's Global Activism: Strategy, Drivers, and Tools*, Occasional Paper 4 (Washington, DC: National Defense University, Institute for National Strategic Studies, June 2006), 2; Thomas Lum, coord., *Comparing Global Influence: China's and U.S. Diplomacy, Foreign Aid, Trade, and Investment in the Developing World*, Congressional Research Service Report RL34620 (Washington, DC: Library of Congress, August 15, 2008); Lowell Dittmer and George T. Yu, eds., *China, the Developing World, and the New Global Dynamic* (Boulder, CO: Lynne Rienner, 2010); "China in Africa: One among Many," *The Economist*, January 17, 2015, http://www.economist.com/news/middle-east-and-africa/21639554-china-has-become-big-africa-now-backlash-one-among-many; *2013 China–Latin America Bulletin*, accessed June 5, 2015, http://www.bu.edu/pardee/files/2014/01/Economic-Bulletin-2013.pdf; Wenzhen Tan, "About Half of Chinese Loans to Developing Countries Are Hidden," CNBC, July 12, 2019, https://www.cnbc.com/2019/07/12/chinas-lending-to-other-countries-jumps-causing-hidden-debt.html. A more contemporary review is Andrew Scobell et al., *At the Dawn of the Belt and Road* (Santa Monica, CA: RAND Corporation, 2018).

3. John Garver, *China and Iran: Ancient Partners in a Post-imperial World* (Seattle: University of Washington Press, 2006).

4. Jon B. Alterman and John Garver, *The Vital Triangle: China, the United States, and the Middle East* (Washington, DC: Center for Strategic and International Studies, 2008); John Garver, "Is China Playing a Dual Game in Iran?," *Washington Quarterly* 34, no. 1 (Winter 2011): 75–88.

5. Lillian Harris, *China Considers the Middle East* (London: Tauris, 1993); Guang Pan, "China's Success in the Middle East," *Middle East Quarterly*, December 1997, 35–40; Lillian Harris, "Myth and Reality in China's Relations with the Middle East," in *Chinese Foreign Policy: Theory and Practice*, ed. Thomas W. Robinson and David Shambaugh (New York: Oxford University Press, 1994), 322–47; Alexander Lennon, "Trading Guns, Not Butter," *China Business Review*, March–April 1994, 47–49.

6. Robert Sutter, *Chinese Policy Priorities and Their Implications for the United States* (Lanham, MD: Rowman & Littlefield, 2000), 156.

7. Han Xiaoxing, "China–Middle East Links," *China Business Review*, March–April 1994, 44–46.

8. Lennon, "Trading Guns, Not Butter"; Guang Pan, "China's Success in the Middle East."

9. Guang Pan, "China's Success in the Middle East"; Harris, *China Considers the Middle East*; Wenran Jiang, "China's Growing Energy Relations with the Middle East," *China Brief* 7, no. 14 (July 11, 2007): 12–15; Xia Liping, "Sino-Israeli Contacts as Seen from Declassified Foreign Ministry Files," *Dangdai Zhongguoshi Yenjiu* [Contemporary China History Studies] 12, no. 3 (May 2005): 76–82; Sutter, *Chinese Policy Priorities and Their Implications for the United States*, 157.

10. Huai Chengbo, "Why Do Arab Nations Widen the Gap with the United States?," *Liaowang* 11 (March 16, 1998): 42; Yitzhak Shichor, "China and the Role of the United Nations in the Middle East: Revised Policy," *Asian Survey* 31, no. 3 (March 1991): 255–69.

11. Evan Medeiros, *Reluctant Restraint: The Evolution of China's Nonproliferation Policies and Practices, 1980–2004* (Stanford, CA: Stanford University Press, 2007), 58–65, 81–82; "U.S. Lists Accords with China at Summit," Reuters, June 27, 1998; "Qian Qichen Speaks to Chinese Reporters, Concludes Trip," *Xinhua*, December 26, 1997, carried by Foreign Broadcast Information Service (internet version).

12. Sutter, *Chinese Policy Priorities and Their Implications for the United States*, 158.

13. Tang Jian, Wang Yadong, and Hou Jia, "Qian Qichen's Tour of the Middle East Is a Complete Success," *Xinhua*, December 26, 1997.

14. Sutter, *Chinese Policy Priorities and Their Implications for the United States*, 160.

15. Chas W. Freeman Jr., "The Middle East and China," remarks to a conference of the U.S Institute of Peace, Georgetown University, Washington, DC, February 17, 2015; Alterman and Garver, *The Vital Triangle*; Garver, "Is China Playing a Dual Game in Iran?,"; Mao Yufeng, "China's Interests and Strategy in the Middle East," in *China and the Developing World: Beijing's Strategy for the Twenty-First Century*, ed. Joshua Eisenman, Eric Heginbotham, and Derek Mitchell (Armonk, NY: Sharpe, 2007), 113–32; Yitzhak Shichor, "China's Middle East Strategy," in *China, the Developing World, and the New Global Dynamic*, ed. Lowell Dittmer and George Yu (Boulder, CO: Lynne Rienner, 2010), 157–76; Daniel Blumenthal, "Providing Arms," *Middle East Quarterly* (Spring 2005): 11–19; Jing-dong Yuan, "China and the Iranian Nuclear Crisis," *China Brief* 6, no. 3 (February 1, 2006): 6–8; Yitzhak Shichor, "China's Kurdish Policy," *China Brief* 6, no. 1 (January 3, 2006): 3–6.

16. Flynt Leverett and Jeffrey Bader, "Managing China-U.S. Energy Competition in the Middle East," *Washington Quarterly* 29, no. 1 (Winter 2005–2006): 187–201.

17. John Calabrese, "Saudi Arabia and China Extend Ties beyond Oil," *China Brief* 5, no. 12 (May 24, 2005): 1–4.

18. "The Great Well of China," *The Economist*, June 20, 2015, http://www.economist.com/news/middle-east-and-africa/21654655-oil-bringing-china-and-arab-world-closer-economically-politics-will; Fatah Al-Rahman Youssef, "Saudi Arabia, China Sign Nuclear and Renewable Energy Agreement," *Asuarq Al-Awsat*, August 11, 2014, http://www.aawsat.net/2014/08/article55335276/saudi-arabia-china-sign-nuclear-and-renewable-energy-agreement; "Saudi Arabia Ties Get a Boost," *China Daily*, February 12, 2009, 1; Calabrese, "Saudi Arabia and China Extend Ties beyond Oil"; Australian Parliamentary Library Research Service, *Directions in China's Foreign Relations: Implications for East Asia and Australia*, Parliamentary Library Research Brief 9:2005–2006 (Canberra: Australian Parliamentary Library Research Service, December 5, 2005), 16–20.

19. "China-Saudi Trade Reached Record High in 2010," Chinese embassy in Saudi Arabia, February 9, 2011, http://sa2.mofcom.gov.cn/article/chinanews/201102/20110207391731.shtml; "The Great Well of China."

20. Borzou Daragahi, "Iran Signs $3.2 Billion Natural Gas Deal with China," *Los Angeles Times*, March 14, 2009, accessed March 18, 2009; Garver, "Is China Playing a Dual Game in Iran?"

21. "Iran-China Trade Volume Reaches $38 Billion," Press TV, February 13, 2011, accessed May 18, 2011, http://www.presstv.ir/detail/165011.html.

22. Michael Richardson, "Middle East Balancing Act Is Becoming Harder for China," *International Herald Tribune*, July 28, 2008; "The Great Well of China."

23. Bonnie Glaser, "Pomp, Blunders, and Substance: Hu's Visit to the U.S.," *Comparative Connections* 8, no. 2 (July 2006): 35–36, 40; Bonnie Glaser, "Cooperation Faces Challenges," *Comparative Connections* 12, no. 2 (July 2010): 38–39.

24. Blumenthal, "Providing Arms," 6.

25. Chris Zambelis, "China's Palestine Policy," *China Brief* 9, no. 5 (March 4, 2009): 9–12; "China Welcomes Hamas-Fatah Unity Deal," *China Daily*, April 29, 2011.

26. Yitzhak Shichor, "Silent Partner: China and the Lebanon Crisis," *China Brief* 6, no. 17 (August 16, 2006): 2–4.

27. Consultations with Chinese diplomats, Washington, DC, December 18, 2006.

28. Yu Bin, "SCO Five Years On: Progress and Growing Pains," *Comparative Connections* 8, no. 2 (July 2006): 140; "Hu Slams Use of Force, Seeks Libyan Ceasefire," *China Daily*, March 31, 2011.

29. "Smooth Evacuation," *People's Daily Online*, March 6, 2011; Yun Sun, "China's Acquiescence on UNSCR 1973: No Big Deal," *PacNet* 20 (Honolulu, HI: Pacific Forum CSIS, March 31, 2011).

30. Mu Chunshan, "Revealed: How the Yemen Crisis Wrecked Xi Jinping's Middle East Travel Plans," *The Diplomat*, April 22, 2015, http://thediplomat.com/2015/04/revealed-how-the-yemen-crisis-wrecked-xi-jinpings-middle-east-travel-plans.

31. Gawdat Bahgat, "Chinese Relations with the Middle East and North Africa," in *China's Global Influence*, ed. Scott McDonald and Michael Burgoyne (Honolulu, HI: Asia-Pacific Center for Security Studies, 2020), 100; see also, Andrew Small, *China's Role in the Middle*

*East* (Washington, DC: German Marshall Fund, January 25, 2016), http://www.gmfus.org/commentary/china%E2%80%99s-role-middle-east.

32. Mordechai Chaziza, "China's New Silk Road Strategy and the Middle East," Begin-Sadat Center for Strategic Studies, March 8, 2020, https://besacenter.org/perspectives-papers/china-silk-road-middle-east.

33. ChinaMed Data, "Middle East," https://www.chinamed.it/chinamed-data/middle-east; Bahgat, "Chinese Relations with the Middle East."

34. ChinaMed Data, "Middle East"; Chaziza, "China's New Silk Road Strategy"; Jon Alterman, "Chinese and Russian Influence in the Middle East," testimony before the House Subcommittee on the Middle East, May 9, 2019, https://docs.house.gov/meetings/FA/FA13/20190509/109455/HHRG-116-FA13-Wstate-AltermanJ-20190509.pdf.

35. Jonathan Fulton, *China's Changing Role in the Middle East* (Washington, DC: Atlantic Council, June 2019), 7, https://www.atlanticcouncil.org/wp-content/uploads/2019/06/Chinas_Changing_Role_in_the_Middle_East.pdf.

36. Fulton, *China's Changing Role*, 3.

37. Fulton, *China's Changing Role*, 4.

38. Fulton, *China's Changing Role*, 6.

39. Fulton, *China's Changing Role*, 8; "Iran-China Trade Up by 31%," Tasmin News Agency, July 26, 2017, https://www.tasnimnews.com/en/news/2017/07/26/1474872/iran-china-bilateral-trade-up-by-31-report.

40. Alterman, testimony.

41. Ben Westcott and Hamdi Alkhshali, "China, Russia and Iran Hold Joint Naval Drills in Gulf of Oman," CNN, December 27, 2019, https://www.cnn.com/2019/12/27/asia/china-russia-iran-military-drills-intl-hnk/index.html.

42. Fulton, *China's Changing Role*, 8.

43. Yoman Evron, "The Challenge of Implementing the Belt and Road Initiative in the Middle East," *China Quarterly*, no. 237 (March 2019): 202–10.

44. Alterman, testimony.

45. Philip Snow, *The Star Raft: China's Encounter with Africa* (Ithaca, NY: Cornell University Press, 1988); Alaba Ogunsanwo, *China's Policy in Africa, 1958–1971* (New York: Cambridge University Press, 1979); Christopher Alden, Daniel Large, and Ricardo de Oliveria, *China Returns to Africa: A Superpower and a Continent Embrace* (New York: Columbia University Press, 2008); Ian Taylor, *China's New Role in Africa* (Boulder, CO: Lynne Rienner, 2008).

46. Sutter, *Chinese Policy Priorities and Their Implications for the United States*, 163–64.

47. Sutter, *Chinese Policy Priorities and Their Implications for the United States*, 164.

48. Philip Snow, "China and Africa: Consensus and Camouflage," in *Chinese Foreign Policy: Theory and Practice*, ed. Thomas W. Robinson and David Shambaugh (New York: Oxford University Press, 1994), 318–21.

49. Sutter, *Chinese Policy Priorities and Their Implications for the United States*, 164.

50. These visits were covered extensively in *China Daily* and other official Chinese media.

51. Xiong Guangkai, "China's Defense Policy and Sino-African Relations—Speech at Zimbabwean Defense Staff College on June 2, 1997," *International Strategic Studies* (Beijing) 3 (July 1997): 1–5.

52. "Sudanese Minister on Growing Trends with China," *Xinhua*, February 24, 1998; "Jiang Zemin–Democratic Congo President Hold Talks," *Xinhua*, December 18, 1997; "Official Comments on Sino-African Trade Cooperation," *Xinhua*, January 14, 1998; "China to Set Up Investment Promotion Center in Zambia," *Xinhua*, April 3, 1998; *Conventional Arms Transfers to Developing Countries, 1990–1997*, Congressional Research Service Report 98-647 (Washington, DC: Library of Congress, July 31, 1998).

53. Deborah Brautigam, *The Dragon's Gift: The Real Story of China in Africa* (New York: Oxford University Press, 2009); George Yu, "China's Africa Policy," in *China, the Developing World, and the New Global Dynamic*, ed. Lowell Dittmer and George Yu (Boulder, CO: Lynne Rienner, 2010), 129–56; Alden et al., *China Returns to Africa*; Taylor, *China's New Role in Africa*; Robert I. Rotberg, ed., *China into Africa: Trade, Aid, and Influence* (Washington, DC: Brookings Institution, 2008); David Shinn and Joshua Eisenman, *Responding to China in*

*Africa* (Washington, DC: American Foreign Policy Council, July 2008); Council on Foreign Relations, *More than Humanitarianism: A Strategic U.S. Approach toward Africa*, Independent Task Force Report 56 (New York: Council on Foreign Relations, January 2006); "Full Text of China's Africa Policy"; *China and Sub-Saharan Africa*, Congressional Research Service Report RL33055 (Washington, DC: Library of Congress, August 29, 2005).

54. Brautigam, *Dragon's Gift*; David Shinn and Joshua Eisenman, *China and Africa: A Century of Engagement* (Philadelphia: University of Pennsylvania Press, 2012); Howard French, *China's Second Continent* (New York: Random House, 2014).

55. "China in Africa: One among Many."

56. *Africa and China: Issues and Insights—Conference Report* (Washington, DC: Georgetown University, School of Foreign Service, Asian Studies Department, November 7, 2008); Shinn and Eisenman, *China and Africa*; "China in Africa: One among Many."

57. Chin-Hao Huang, *China's Rising Stakes in Africa*, Asian Studies Research Paper (Washington, DC: Georgetown University, April 2006), 7.

58. *China's African Policy* (Beijing: State Council Information Office, January 2006), http://english.people.com.cn/200601/12/print20060112_234894.html; Yan Yang, "China-Africa Trade Prospects Look Promising: President Hu Jintao Promotes Nation on Tour of the Continent," *China Daily*, April 26, 2006, 9; "Support for Africa 'Not a Temporary Measure,'" *China Daily*, July 3, 2006, 3; Wenran Jiang, "China's Booming Energy Relations with Africa," *China Brief* 6, no. 13 (June 21, 2006): 3–5.

59. Lum, *Comparing Global Influence*, 33; Claire Provost, "China Publishes First Report on Foreign Aid Policy," *The Guardian*, April 28, 2011; Council on Foreign Relations, *More than Humanitarianism*, 42.

60. Sun Shangwu, "Bright, Prosperous Relations," *China Daily*, November 6, 2006, 1.

61. See the discussion of this problem in Saunders, *China's Global Activism*, 13–14.

62. Ding Qingfen, "Countries 'Seek More Investment for Development,'" *China Daily*, April 27, 2011, 1.

63. Council on Foreign Relations, *More than Humanitarianism*, 42.

64. Ding, "Countries 'Seek More Investment for Development'"; Zeng Qiang, "FOCAC"; "White Paper on China-Africa Economic Cooperation and Trade Cooperation," *China Daily*, December 23, 2010; David Smith, "China Poised to Pour $10bn into Zimbabwe's Ailing Economy," *The Guardian*, February 1, 2011; He Wenping, "Equal Platform, Mutual Benefit," *China Daily*, July 17, 2010, 5; "China-Africa Trade Hits Record High," *China Daily*, December 24, 2010, 3.

65. "China-Africa Trade Approaches $300 Billion in 2015," *China Daily*, November 10, 2015, https://www.chinadaily.com.cn/business/2015-11/10/content_22417707.htm.

66. David Shinn, "China's Just Another Great Power in Africa," *East Asia Forum*, May 17, 2018, https://www.eastasiaforum.org/2018/05/17/chinas-just-another-great-power-in-africa.

67. Wade Shepherd, "What China Is Really up to in Africa," *Forbes*, October 3, 2019, https://www.forbes.com/sites/wadeshepard/2019/10/03/what-china-is-really-up-to-in-africa/#2e532c495930.

68. Phillip Carter, Raymond Gilpin, and Paul Nantulya, "China in Africa," in *China's Global Influence*, ed. Scott McDonald and Michael Burgoyne (Honolulu, HI: Asia-Pacific Center for Security Studies, 2020), 114.

69. Yun Sun, "China's 2018 Financial Commitments to Africa: Adjustment and Recalibration," Brookings Institution, September 5, 2018, https://www.brookings.edu/blog/africa-in-focus/2018/09/05/chinas-2018-financial-commitments-to-africa-adjustment-and-recalibration.

70. Shinn, "China's Just Another Great Power."

71. Scobell et al., *At the Dawn of the Belt and Road*, 185.

72. Robert Rotberg, "Strengthening Network Reception in Africa," *China-US Focus*, April 4, 2019, https://www.chinausfocus.com/society-culture/strengthening-network-reception-in-africa.

73. Scobell et al., *At the Dawn of the Belt and Road*, 116.

74. Carter et al., "China in Africa," 112–13.

75. Carter et al., "China in Africa," 110.

76. David Shullman, ed., *Chinese Malign Influence and the Corrosion of Democracy* (Washington, DC: International Republican Institute, 2019), 36.

77. Shullman, *Chinese Malign Influence*, 47–49.

78. Joe Parkinson, Nicholas Bariyo, and Josh Chin, "Huawei Technicians Helped African Governments Spy on Political Opponents," *Wall Street Journal*, August 15, 2019, https://www.wsj.com/articles/huawei-technicians-helped-african-governments-spy-on-political-opponents-11565793017.

79. For purposes of convenience, this book will often use the term *Latin America* to include all Western Hemisphere countries south of the United States, even though the more precise term is *Latin America–Caribbean*.

80. Cecil Johnson, *Communist China and Latin America* (New York: Columbia University Press, 1970); Samuel Kim, *The Third World in Chinese World Policy* (Princeton, NJ: Princeton University Press, 1989); Frank O. Mora, "Sino–Latin American Relations: Sources and Consequences," *Journal of Interamerican Studies and World Affairs* 41, no. 2 (Summer 1999): 91–116; Chein-hsun Wang, "Peking's Latin American Policy in the 1980s," *Issues and Studies* 27, no. 5 (May 1991): 103–18.

81. "China to Boost Trade with Latin America," *Xinhua*, January 10, 1999.

82. "NPC's Tian Visits Brazil," *Xinhua*, May 8, 1998; "CPC Senior Official Meets Guatemalan Party Leader," *Xinhua*, February 27, 1998; "NPC Delegation to Visit Latin America," *Xinhua*, April 30, 1998.

83. Jorge Dominguez, *China's Relations with Latin America: Shared Gains, Asymmetrical Hopes*, working paper (Washington, DC: Inter-American Dialogue, June 2006); R. Evan Ellis, *U.S. National Security Implications of Chinese Involvement in Latin America* (Carlisle, PA: US Army War College Strategic Studies Institute, June 2005); R. Evan Ellis, *China in Latin America* (Boulder, CO: Lynne Rienner, 2009); Kerry Dumbaugh and Mark Sullivan, *China's Growing Interest in Latin America*, Congressional Research Service Report RS22119 (Washington, DC: Library of Congress, April 20, 2005); Riordan Roett and Guadalupe Paz, eds., *China's Expansion into the Western Hemisphere* (Washington, DC: Brookings Institution, 2007); Robert Delvin et al., *The Emergence of China: Challenges and Opportunities for Latin America and the Caribbean* (Cambridge, MA: Harvard University Press, 2006).

84. *Asia and Latin America and the Caribbean: Economic Links, Cooperation, and Development Strategies*, discussion paper for annual meeting of governors (Washington, DC: Inter-American Development Bank, March 21, 2005).

85. *Asia and Latin America and the Caribbean*; John Paul Rathbone, "China Is Now Region's Biggest Partner," *Financial Times*, April 26, 2011, http://www.ft.com.

86. Dumbaugh and Sullivan, *China's Growing Interest in Latin America*.

87. Katherine Koleski and Alec Blivas, *China's Engagement with Latin America and the Caribbean* (Washington, DC: US-China Economic and Security Review Commission, October 17, 2018), 13, 28, https://www.uscc.gov/sites/default/files/Research/China%27s%20Engagement%20with%20Latin%20America%20and%20the%20Caribbean_.pdf; Wang Xiaotian and Chen Ma, "RMB Fund Planned to Aid Latin America," *China Daily*, April 29, 2011, 13; Brian Winter and Brian Ellsworth, "Brazil and China: A Young Marriage on the Rocks," Reuters, February 3, 2011; "Brazil Leads Surge in LatAm Foreign Investment," *UV10*, May 18, 2011, accessed May 18, 2011, http://www.uv10.com/brazil-leads-surge-in-latam-foreign-investment_800548463.

88. Dumbaugh and Sullivan, *China's Growing Interest in Latin America*.

89. David Shambaugh, "China's New Foray into Latin America," *YaleGlobal Online*, November 17, 2008, accessed November 18, 2008, https://yaleglobal.yale.edu/content/chinas-new-foray-latin-america.

90. Thomas Lum, *China's Foreign Aid Activities in Africa, Latin America, and Southeast Asia*, Congressional Research Service Report R40361 (Washington, DC: Library of Congress, February 25, 2009), 15; Erica Downs, *Inside China, Inc: China Development Bank's Cross-Border Energy Deals*, John Thornton China Center Monograph Series 3 (Washington, DC: Brookings Institution, March 2011), 1.

91. "Magic or Realism: China and Latin America," *The Economist*, December 29, 2004, accessed January 10, 2005; Stuart Grudgings, "Analysis: Surge in Chinese Investment Reshapes Brazil Ties," Reuters, August 10, 2010.

92. Inter-American Development Bank, in Delvin et al., *The Emergence of China*, 85, 111; Robert Sutter, *Historical Dictionary of Chinese Foreign Policy* (Lanham, MD: Scarecrow Press, 2011) (for Mexico).

93. Larry Rohter, "China Widens Economic Role in Latin America," *New York Times*, November 20, 2004, accessed November 20, 2004; Winter and Ellsworth, "Brazil and China."

94. "Taiwan Is Largest Aid Donor in Many Caribbean Nations," *Caribbean News*, December 9, 2003, accessed December 10, 2003.

95. "Any Port in a Storm," *The Economist*, December 29, 2004.

96. "Ma Reaffirms 'Modus Vivendi' Diplomatic Approach," *China Post*, March 15, 2011.

97. Sutter, *Historical Dictionary of Chinese Foreign Policy*, entries for "BRIC" and "BASIC."

98. William Ratliff, "Pragmatism over Ideology: China's Relations with Venezuela," *China Brief* 6, no. 6 (March 15, 2006): 3–5; "Venezuela's Crude Oil Exports to U.S. Average 1 Million BPD," *El Universal*, April 4, 2011.

99. Guillermo R. Delamer et al., "Chinese Interest in Latin America," in *Latin American Security Challenges: A Collaborative Inquiry from North and South*, ed. Paul D. Taylor, Newport Paper 21 (Newport, RI: Naval War College, 2004), 94; Shambaugh, "China's New Foray into Latin America."

100. Stephen Johnson, *Balancing China's Growing Influence in Latin America*, Heritage Foundation Backgrounder 1888 (Washington, DC: Heritage Foundation, October 24, 2005), 4.

101. "Testimony of Rogelio Pardo-Maurer, Assistant Secretary of Defense for Latin America, before the House Committee on International Affairs, Subcommittee on Western Hemisphere Affairs," April 6, 2005, accessed May 7, 2005.

102. Johnson, *Balancing China's Growing Influence in Latin America*, 5.

103. Megha Rajagopalan, "China's Xi Woos Latin America with $250 Billion Investments," Reuters, January 7, 2015, https://www.reuters.com/article/us-china-latam/chinas-xi-woos-latin-america-with-250-billion-investments-idUSKBN0KH06Q20150108.

104. *China's Engagement with Latin America and the Caribbean*, Congressional Research Service Report IF1890 (Washington, DC: Library of Congress, April 18, 2019), 1, https://fas.org/sgp/crs/row/IF10982.pdf.

105. Congressional Research Service, *China's Engagement with Latin America and the Caribbean*, 1–2; Koleski and Blivas, *China's Engagement with Latin America and the Caribbean*, 15–16.

106. Congressional Research Service, *China's Engagement with Latin America and the Caribbean*, 1; "Second Belt and Road Forum Top-Level Attendees," *The Diplomat*, April 27, 2019, https://thediplomat.com/2019/04/second-belt-and-road-forum-top-level-attendees.

107. Koleski and Blivas, *China's Engagement with Latin America and the Caribbean*, 3.

108. Rebecca Ray and Pedro Henrique Batista Babosa, *China–Latin American Economic Bulletin, 2020 edition* (Boston, MA: Boston University Global Development Policy Center, 2020), 1, https://www.bu.edu/gdp/files/2020/03/GCI-Bulletin_2020.pdf.

109. Koleski and Blivas, *China's Engagement with Latin America and the Caribbean*, 3.

110. Ray and Babosa, *China–Latin American Economic Bulletin, 2020*, 1.

111. Christina Guevara, *China's Support for the Maduro Regime: Enduring or Fleeting* (Washington, DC: Atlantic Council, January 13, 2020), https://www.atlanticcouncil.org/blogs/new-atlanticist/chinas-support-for-the-maduro-regime-enduring-or-fleeting.

112. Koleski and Blivas, *China's Engagement with Latin America and the Caribbean*, 23–24.

113. Koleski and Blivas, *China's Engagement with Latin America and the Caribbean*, 27; Shullman, *Chinese Malign Influence*, 31–32.

114. Koleski and Blivas, *China's Engagement with Latin America and the Caribbean*, 14–15.

115. Koleski and Blivas, *China's Engagement with Latin America and the Caribbean*, 16.

116. Koleski and Blivas, *China's Engagement with Latin America and the Caribbean*, 20–21.

117. Congressional Research Service, *China's Engagement with Latin America and the Caribbean*, 1.

118. *Chinese Strategic Intentions*, Strategic Multilayer Assessment White Paper (Washington, DC: US Department of Defense, December 2019), 127, https://nsiteam.com/social/wp-content/uploads/2019/10/SMA-Chinese-Strategic-Intentions-White-Paper-FINAL-01-Nov-2.pdf.

119. Laura Silver et al., "People around the Globe Are Divided in Opinions of China," Pew Research Center, December 5, 2019, https://www.pewresearch.org/fact-tank/2019/12/05/people-around-the-globe-are-divided-in-their-opinions-of-china.

120. Margaret Myers, "The Reasons for China's Cooling Interest in Latin America," *Americas Quarterly*, April 23, 2019, https://www.americasquarterly.org/content/how-beijing-sees-it; Igor Patrick, "Latin America Used to Be Positive to China; COVID-19 Might Change That," *The Diplomat*, April 10, 2020, https://thediplomat.com/2020/04/latin-america-used-to-be-positive-toward-china-covid-19-might-change-that.

# 13. ASSESSING CHINA'S RISE AMID ACUTE RIVALRY WITH AMERICA

1. Over the past twenty years, this writer has assessed the strengths and weaknesses of China's rise in Asian and world affairs in various publications. Those detailed assessments duly consider differing perspectives on China's strengths and weaknesses and those of the United States and other concerned powers. For those interested in the evolution of these assessments and various sources used, see Robert Sutter, *The United States and Asia* (Lanham, MD: Rowman & Littlefield, 2020), 327–34; Robert Sutter, *Foreign Relations of the PRC* (Lanham, MD: Rowman & Littlefield, 2019), 297–301; Robert Sutter, *US-China Relations: Perilous Past, Uncertain Present* (Lanham, MD: Rowman & Littlefield, 2017), 272–82; and the earlier editions of this book. The assessment in this chapter builds on those previous assessments.

2. Robert Sutter, "Obama's Cautious and Calibrated Approach to an Assertive China," *YaleGlobal Online*, April 19, 2016, http://yaleglobal.yale.edu/content/obamas-cautious-and-calibrated-approach-assertive-china.

3. Robert Sutter and Satu Limaye, *America's 2016 Election Debate on Asia Policy & Asian Reactions* (Honolulu, HI: East-West Center, 2016).

4. Robert Sutter, *Russia-China Relations: Assessing Common Ground and Strategic Fault Lines* (Seattle, WA: National Bureau of Asian Research, July 2017), http://nbr.org/publications/element.aspx?id=950.

5. See, among others, Elizabeth Economy, *The Third Revolution: Xi Jinping and the New Chinese State* (New York: Council on Foreign Relations, 2018); Sebastian Heilmann, ed., *China's Political System* (Lanham, MD: Rowman & Littlefield, 2017); David Shambaugh, *China's Future* (Cambridge, UK: Polity Press, 2016); Bruce Dickson, *The Dictator's Dilemma: The Chinese Communist Party's Strategy for Survival* (New York: Oxford University Press, 2016); Arthur Kroeber, *China's Economy: What Everyone Needs to Know* (New York: Oxford University Press, 2016); Elizabeth Perry, "Growing Pains: Challenges for a Rising China," *Daedalus* 143, no. 2 (Spring 2014): 5–13; Martin King Whyte, "China's Dormant and Active Volcanoes," *China Journal* (January 2016): 9–37; Deborah Davis, "Demographic Challenges for a Rising China," *Daedalus* 143, no. 2 (Spring 2014): 26–38; Cheng Li, "The End of the CCP's Resilient Authoritarianism? A Tripartite Assessment of Shifting Power in China," *China Quarterly* 211 (September 2012): 595–623; Minxin Pei, *China's Crony Capitalism: The Dynamics of Regime Decay* (Cambridge, MA: Harvard University Press, 2016); Daniel Lynch, *China's Futures: PRC Elites Debate Economics, Politics, and Foreign Policy* (Stanford, CA: Stanford University Press, 2015); William Callahan, *China: The Pessioptimist Nation* (Oxford, UK: Oxford University Press, 2010).

6. See Shambaugh, *China's Future*.

7. Ben Blanchard and John Ruwitch, "China Hikes Defense Budget, to Spend More in Internal Security," Reuters, March 5, 2013, http://www.reuters.com/article/2013/03/05/us-china-parliament-defence-idUSBRE92403620130305.

8. Victor Shih, "US-China Relations in 2019: A Year in Review," testimony before the US-China Economic and Security Review Commission, September 4, 2019, https://www.uscc.gov/Hearings/us-china-relations-2019-year-review.

9. *COVID-19: China Medical Supply Chains and Broader Trade Issues*, Congressional Research Service Report R46304 (Washington, DC: Library of Congress, April 6, 2020).

10. Josh Rogin, "The Coronavirus Is Turning Americans in Both Parties against China," *Washington Post*, April 8, 2020, https://www.washingtonpost.com/opinions/2020/04/08/coronavirus-crisis-is-turning-americans-both-parties-against-china; Paul Heer, "Why the Coronavirus Is a Hinge for the Future of US-China Relations," *National Interest*, April 7, 2020, https://nationalinterest.org/feature/why-coronavirus-hinge-future-us-china-relations-141792?page=0%2C1; Henry Olsen, "Get Ready for an Election All about China," *Washington Post*, May 5, 2020, A23; *COVID-19 and China: A Chronology of Events*, Congressional Research Service Report R46354 (Washington, DC: Library of Congress, May 13, 2020).

11. Vivian Wong and Alexandra Stevenson, "In Hong Kong, Arrests and Fear Mark First Day of New Security Law," *New York Times*, July 1, 2020, https://www.nytimes.com/2020/07/01/world/asia/hong-kong-security-law-china.html.

12. For background and sources, see discussion in chapter 3 and chapters 9–12 covering regional relations. Notable summations include David Shinn, "China Just Another Great Power in Africa," *EASTASIAFORUM*, May 17, 2018, https://www.eastasiaforum.org/2018/05/17/chinas-just-another-great-power-in-africa, and Margaret Myers, "The Reasons for China's Cooling Interest in Latin America," *Americas Quarterly*, April 23, 2019, https://www.americasquarterly.org/content/how-beijing-sees-it.

13. Shih, "US-China Relations."

14. Shinn, "China Just Another Great Power in Africa"; Myers, "The Reasons for China's Cooling Interest in Latin America."

15. Ashley Tellis, Alison Szalwinski, and Michael Wills, eds., *Strategic Asia 2020: U.S.-China Competition for Global Influence* (Seattle, WA: National Bureau of Asian Research, 2020).

16. Robert Sutter, "Has US Government Angst over the China Danger Diminished?," *Asia-Pacific Bulletin*, January 22, 2020, https://www.eastwestcenter.org/publications/has-us-government-angst-over-the-china-danger-diminished; Rogin, "The Coronavirus Is Turning Americans in Both Parties against China"; Paul Heer, "Stop the Coronavirus Blame Game," *National Interest*, May 15, 2020, https://www.realclearworld.com/2020/05/15/stop_the_coronavirus_blame_game_491681.html.

17. See sources in note 1.

# Selected Bibliography

Acharya, Amitav. "Power Shift or Paradigm Shift? China's Rise and Asia's Emerging Security Order." *International Studies Quarterly* 58, no. 1 (March 2014): 158–73.

Alden, Christopher, Daniel Large, and Ricardo de Oliveria. *China Returns to Africa: A Superpower and a Continent Embrace.* New York: Columbia University Press, 2008.

Alterman, Jon B. *The Other Side of the World: China, the US and the Struggle for Middle East Security.* Washington, DC: Center for Strategic and International Studies, 2017.

Alterman, Jon B., and John Garver. *The Vital Triangle: China, the United States, and the Middle East.* Washington, DC: Center for Strategic and International Studies, 2008.

Andrews-Speed, Philip. *The Governance of Energy in China: Transition to a Low-Carbon Economy.* New York: Palgrave Macmillan, 2012.

Auslin, Michael. *The End of the Asian Century: War, Stagnation, and the Risks to the World's Most Dynamic Region.* New Haven, CT: Yale University Press, 2017.

Austin, Greg. *Cybersecurity in China: The Next Wave.* New York: Springer, 2018.

Ba Zhongtan et al. *Zhongguo Guojia anquan zhanlue wenti yanjiu.* Beijing: Zhongguo Junshi Kexue Chubanshe, 2003.

Babbage, Ross. *Winning without Fighting: Chinese and Russian Political Warfare Campaigns.* Washington, DC: Center for Strategic and Budgetary Assessments, 2018.

Bader, Jeffrey. *Obama and China's Rise: An Insider's Account of America's Asia Strategy.* Washington, DC: Brookings Institution, 2012.

Beckley, Michael. "China's Century? Why America's Edge Will Endure." *International Security* 36, no. 3 (Winter 2011–2012): 41–78.

Bhattasali, Deepak, Shantong Li, and Will Martin. *China and the WTO: Accession, Policy Reform, and Poverty Reduction Strategies.* Washington, DC: World Bank, 2004.

Blackwill, Robert, and Ashley Tellis. *Council Special Report: Revising US Grand Strategy toward China.* Washington, DC: Council on Foreign Relations, April 2015.

Blasko, Dennis. *The Chinese Army Today: Tradition and Transformation in the 21st Century.* London: Routledge, 2012.

Bolt, Paul, and Sharyl Cross. *China, Russia and Twenty-First Century Global Geopolitics.* New York: Oxford University Press, 2018.

Brady, Anne-Marie. *China as a Polar Great Power.* Cambridge: Cambridge University Press, 2017.

Brautigam, Deborah. *The Dragon's Gift: The Real Story of China in Africa.* New York: Oxford University Press, 2009.

Brazinsky, Gregg. *Winning the Third World: Sino-American Rivalry during the Cold War.* Chapel Hill: University of North Carolina Press, 2017.

Brophy, David. *Uyghur Nation: Reform and Revolution on the Russia-China Frontier.* Cambridge, MA: Harvard University Press, 2016.

Brown, Kerry. *China and the EU in Context: Insights for Business and Investors.* London: Palgrave Macmillan, 2014.

Bush, Richard. *Hong Kong in the Shadow of China: Living with the Leviathan.* Washington, DC: Brookings Institution, 2016.

———. *The Perils of Proximity: China-Japan Security Relations.* Washington, DC: Brookings Institution, 2010.

———. *Uncharted Strait: The Future of China-Taiwan Relations.* Washington, DC: Brookings Institution, 2013.

———. *Untying the Knot: Making Peace in the Taiwan Strait.* Washington, DC: Brookings Institution, 2005.

Bush, Richard, and Michael O'Hanlon. *A War like No Other: The Truth about China's Challenge to America.* Hoboken, NJ: Wiley, 2007.

Cabestan, Jean-Pierre. "European Union–China Relations and the United States." *Asian Perspective* 30, no. 4 (Winter 2006): 11–38.

———. "The Shanghai Cooperation Organization, Central Asia, and the Great Powers, an Introduction." *Asian Survey* 53, no. 3 (2013): 423–35.

Campbell, Kurt. *The Pivot: The Future of American Statecraft in Asia.* New York: Hachette, 2016.

Carlson, Allen. "More Than Just Saying No: China's Evolving Approach to Sovereignty and Intervention." In *New Directions in the Study of China's Foreign Policy*, edited by Alastair Iain Johnston and Robert S. Ross, 217–41. Stanford, CA: Stanford University Press, 2006.

Center for a New American Security. *More Willing and Able: Charting China's International Security Activism.* Washington, DC: Center for a New American Security, 2015.

Cha, Victor. *The Impossible State: North Korea Past and Future.* New York: HarperCollins, 2012.

Chen Zhimin and Xueying Zhang. "Chinese Conceptions of the World Order in the Turbulent Trump Era." *Pacific Review* 33 (2020): 438–68.

Cheng Ruisheng. "China-India Diplomatic Relations: Six Decades' Experience and Inspiration." *Foreign Affairs Journal* (Beijing) 96 (Summer 2010): 59–70.

Cheung, Joseph Y. S. "Sino-ASEAN Relations in the Early 21st Century." *Contemporary Southeast Asia* 23, no. 3 (December 2001): 420–52.

Cheung, Tai Ming, and Thomas Mahnken. *The Gathering Pacific Storm: Emerging US-China Strategic Competition in Defense Technology and Industrial Development.* Amherst, NY: Cambria Press, 2018.

Chi, Su. *Taiwan's Relations with Mainland China: A Tail Wagging Two Dogs.* New York: Routledge, 2008.

Christensen, Thomas. *The China Challenge: Shaping the Choices of a Rising Power.* New York: Norton, 2015.

———. "Fostering Stability or Creating a Monster? The Rise of China and US Policy toward East Asia." *International Security* 31, no. 1 (Summer 2006): 81–126.

———. "Windows and War: Trends Analysis and Beijing's Use of Force." In *New Directions in the Study of China's Foreign Policy*, edited by Alastair Iain Johnston and Robert S. Ross, 50–85. Stanford, CA: Stanford University Press, 2006.

Chu Shulong. "Quanmian jianshe xiaokang shehui shiqi de Zhongguo waijiao zhan-lue." *Shijie Jingji yu Zhengzhi* 8 (August 2003).

Chu, Yun-han, Larry Diamond, and Kharis Templeman. *Taiwan's Democracy Challenged: The Chen Shui-bian Years.* Boulder, CO: Lynne Rienner, 2016.

Chung, Jae Ho, ed. *Assessing China's Power.* New York: Palgrave Macmillan, 2015.

———. *Between Ally and Partner: Korea-China Relations and the United States.* New York: Columbia University Press, 2007.

———. "From a Special Relationship to a Normal Partnership?" *Pacific Affairs* 76, no. 3 (Winter 2003): 549–68.

Cliff, Roger. *China's Military Power: Assessing Current and Future Capabilities.* New York: Cambridge University Press, 2015.

Cohen, Warren I. *America's Response to China: A History of Sino-American Relations*. New York: Columbia University Press, 2010.

———. "China's Rise in Historical Perspective." *Journal of Strategic Studies* 30, nos. 4–5 (August–October 2007): 683–704.

Cole, Bernard. *The Great Wall at Sea: China's Navy in the Twenty-First Century*. Annapolis, MD: Naval Institute, 2010.

Cole, J. Michael. *Convergence or Conflict in the Taiwan Strait*. New York: Routledge, 2017.

Cui Liru. "A Multipolar World in the Globalization Era." *Contemporary International Relations* (Beijing) 20, special issue (September 2010): 1–11.

Dahlman, Carl. *The World under Pressure: How China and India Are Influencing the Global Economy and Environment*. Stanford, CA: Stanford University Press, 2011.

Dai Bingguo. "Stick to the Path of Peaceful Development." *Beijing Review* 51 (December 23, 2010).

Deng Hao. "China's Relations with Central Asian Countries: Retrospect and Prospect." *Guoji Wenti Yanjiu* (Beijing), May 13, 2002, 8–12.

Deng, Yong. *China's Struggle for Status: The Realignment of International Relations*. New York: Cambridge University Press, 2008.

———. "The Chinese Conception of National Interests in International Relations." *China Quarterly* 154 (June 1998): 308–29.

———. "Hegemon on the Offensive: Chinese Perspectives on U.S. Global Strategy." *Political Science Quarterly* 116, no. 3 (Fall 2001): 343–65.

Deng, Yong, and Fei-Ling Wang, eds. *China Rising: Power and Motivation in Chinese Foreign Policy*. Lanham, MD: Rowman & Littlefield, 2005.

Deng, Yong, and Thomas Moore. "China Views Globalization: Toward a New Great-Power Politics?" *Washington Quarterly* 27, no. 3 (Summer 2004): 117–36.

Diamond, Larry, and Orville Schell, coordinators. *Chinese Influence and American Interests: Promoting Constructive Vigilance*. Stanford, CA: Hoover Institution Press, 2018.

Dickson, Bruce. *The Dictator's Dilemma: The Chinese Communist Party's Strategy for Survival*. New York: Oxford University Press, 2016.

Dittmer, Lowell. *China's Asia: Triangular Dynamics since the Cold War*. Lanham, MD: Rowman & Littlefield, 2018.

———. *Sino-Soviet Normalization and Its International Implications, 1945–1990*. Seattle: University of Washington Press, 1992.

———, ed. *Taiwan and China: Fitful Embrace*. Oakland: University of California Press, 2017.

Dittmer, Lowell, and George T. Yu, eds. *China, the Developing World, and the New Global Dynamic*. Boulder, CO: Lynne Rienner, 2010.

Downs, Erica. *Brookings Foreign Policy Studies Energy Security Series: China*. Washington, DC: Brookings Institution, 2006.

———. *Inside China, Inc: China Development Bank's Cross-Border Energy Deals*. John Thornton China Center Monograph Series 3. Washington, DC: Brookings Institution, March 2011.

Dreyer, June Teufel. *Middle Kingdom and Empire of the Rising Sun: Sino-Japanese Relations, Past and Present*. New York: Oxford University Press, 2016.

Easton, Ian. *The Chinese Invasion Threat: Taiwan's Defense and American Strategy in Asia*. Washington, DC: Project 2049 Institute, 2017.

Economy, Elizabeth. *The Third Revolution: Xi Jinping and the New Chinese State*. New York: Council on Foreign Relations, 2018.

Economy, Elizabeth, and Michael Levy. *By All Means Necessary: How China's Resource Quest Is Changing the World*. New York: Oxford University Press, 2014.

Eisenman, Joshua, and Eric Heginbotham. *China Steps Out: China's Major Power Engagement with the Developing World*. New York: Routledge, 2018.

Eisenman, Joshua, Eric Heginbotham, and Derek Mitchell, eds. *China and the Developing World: Beijing's Strategy for the Twenty-First Century*. Armonk, NY: Sharpe, 2007.

Ellis, R. Evan. *China in Latin America: The Whats and Wherefores*. Boulder, CO: Lynne Rienner, 2009.

Fang Ning, Wang Xiaodong, and Qiao Liang. *Quanqihua yinying xia de Zhongguo zhilu.* Beijing: Chinese Academy of Social Sciences, 1999.

Feng Huiyun and Kai He. "The Study of Chinese Scholars in Foreign Policy Analysis: An Emerging Research Program." *Pacific Review* 33 (2020): 362–85.

Feng Zhongping. "China-EU Relationship." *Xiandai guoji guanxi* (Beijing) 17 (January 2007): 47–55.

———. "EU's China Policy Analyzed." *Contemporary International Relations* (Beijing) 8, no. 4 (April 1998): 1–6.

Fewsmith, Joseph. *China since Tiananmen: From Deng Xiaoping to Hu Jintao.* New York: Cambridge University Press, 2008.

Fewsmith, Joseph, and Stanley Rosen. "The Domestic Context of Chinese Foreign Policy: Does 'Public Opinion' Matter?" In *The Making of Chinese Foreign and Security Policy in the Era of Reform*, edited by David Michael Lampton, 179–86. Stanford, CA: Stanford University Press, 2001.

Finkelstein, David. *China Reconsiders Its National Security: The Great Peace and Development Debate of 1999.* Alexandria, VA: CNA, December 2000.

Foot, Rosemary. "China and the ASEAN Regional Forum." *Asian Survey* 38, no. 5 (1998): 425–40.

———. "Chinese Strategies in a U.S.-Hegemonic Global Order: Accommodating and Hedging." *International Affairs* 82, no. 1 (2006): 77–94.

———. *The Practice of Power: U.S. Relations with China since 1949.* New York: Oxford University Press, 1997.

Foot, Rosemary, and Andrew Walter. *China, the United States and the Global Order.* New York: Cambridge University Press, 2011.

Foxall, Andrew, and John Hemmings. *The Art of Deceit: How China and Russia Use Sharp Power to Subvert the West.* London: Henry Jackson Society, 2019.

Fravel, M. Taylor. *Active Defense: China's Military Strategy since 1949.* Princeton, NJ: Princeton University Press, 2019.

———. "China's Strategy in the South China Sea." *Contemporary Southeast Asia* 33, no. 3 (2011): 292–319.

———. *Strong Borders, Secure Nation: Cooperation and Conflict in China's Territorial Disputes.* Princeton, NJ: Princeton University Press, 2008.

Fravel, M. Taylor, and Evan Medeiros. "China's Search for Assured Retaliation." *International Security* 35, no. 2 (Fall 2010): 48–87.

French, Howard. *China's Second Continent: How a Million Migrants Are Building a New Empire in Africa.* New York: Random House, 2014.

Friedberg, Aaron. *Beyond Air-Sea Battle: The Debate over US Military Strategy in Asia.* New York: Routledge, 2014.

———. "Competing with China." *Survival* 60, no. 3 (June 2018): 7–64.

———. *A Contest for Supremacy: China, America, and the Struggle for Mastery in Asia.* New York: Norton, 2011.

———. "The Future of U.S.-China Relations: Is Conflict Inevitable?" *International Security* 30, no. 2 (2005): 7–45.

———. "'Going Out': China's Pursuit of Natural Resources and Implications for the PRC's Grand Strategy." *NBR Analysis* 17, no. 3 (September 2006): 1–40.

Fu Mengzi. "China and Peace Building on the Korean Peninsula." *Xiandai guoji guanxi* (Beijing) 17 (July 2007): 27–40.

———. "Sino-US Relations." *Xiandai guoji guanxi* (Beijing) 17 (January 2007): 32–46.

Fu Ying. "China's Vision for the World: A Community of Shared Future." *The Diplomat*, June 22, 2017.

Gao Zugui. "An Analysis of Sino-U.S. Strategic Relations on the 'Western Front.'" *Xiandai guoji guanxi* (Beijing) 12 (December 20, 2004).

Garnett, Sherman, ed. *Rapprochement or Rivalry? Russia-China Relations in a Changing Asia.* Washington, DC: Carnegie Endowment for International Peace, 2000.

Garver, John. *China and Iran: Ancient Partners in a Post-imperial World.* Seattle: University of Washington Press, 2006.

———. *China's Quest: The History of the Foreign Relations of the People's Republic of China.* New York: Oxford University Press, 2016.

———. *Face-Off: China, the United States, and Taiwan's Democratization.* Seattle: University of Washington Press, 1997.

———. *Protracted Contest: Sino-Indian Rivalry in the 20th Century.* Seattle: University of Washington Press, 2001.

Gill, Bates. *Rising Star: China's New Security Diplomacy.* Washington, DC: Brookings Institution, 2007.

———. "Two Steps Forward, One Step Back: The Dynamics of Chinese Nonproliferation and Arms Control Policy-Making in an Era of Reform." In *The Making of Chinese Foreign and Security Policy in the Era of Reform,* edited by David Michael Lampton, 257–88. Stanford, CA: Stanford University Press, 2001.

Gill, Bates, and Melissa Murphy. "China's Evolving Approach to Counterterrorism." *Harvard Asia Quarterly*(Winter–Spring 2005): 21–32.

Gill, Bates, and Matthew Oresman. *China's New Journey to the West: China's Emergence in Central Asia and Implications for U.S. Interests.* Washington, DC: Center for Strategic and International Studies, August 2003.

Glaser, Charles. "Will China's Rise Lead to War?" *Foreign Affairs* 90, no. 2 (March–April 2011): 80–91.

Godwin, Paul. "China as a Major Asian Power: The Implications of Its Military Modernization (A View from the United States)." In *China, the United States, and Southeast Asia: Contending Perspectives on Politics, Security, and Economics,* edited by Evelyn Goh and Sheldon Simon, 145–66. New York: Routledge, 2008.

Goh, Evelyn. *Meeting the China Challenge: The United States in Southeast Asian Regional Security Strategies.* Policy Studies 21. Washington, DC: East-West Center, 2006.

———. "The Modes of China's Influence: Cases from Southeast Asia." *Asian Survey* 54, no. 5 (2014): 825–48.

———, ed. *Rising China's Influence in Developing Asia.* New York: Oxford University Press, 2016.

———. "Southeast Asia: Strategic Diversification in the 'Asian Century.'" In *Strategic Asia 2008–09: Challenges and Choices,* edited by Ashley Tellis, Mercy Kuo, and Andrew Marble, 261–96. Seattle, WA: National Bureau of Asian Research, 2008.

———. *The Struggle for Order: Hegemony, Hierarchy and Transition in Post–Cold War East Asia.* Oxford: Oxford University Press, 2013.

Goldstein, Avery. *Rising to the Challenge: China's Grand Strategy and International Security.* Stanford, CA: Stanford University Press, 2005.

Goldstein, Lyle. *Meeting China Halfway: How to Defuse the Emerging US-China Rivalry.* Washington, DC: Georgetown University Press, 2015.

Goldstein, Steven. *China and Taiwan.* Cambridge, UK: Polity Press, 2015.

———. *Taiwan Faces the Twenty-First Century: Continuing the "Miracle."* New York: Foreign Policy Association, 1997.

Goldstein, Steven, and Julian Chang, eds. *Presidential Politics in Taiwan: The Administration of Chen Shui-bian.* Norwalk, CT: Eastbridge, 2008.

Gong Li. "Deng Xiaoping dui Mei zhengce sixing yu Zhong-Mei guanxi." *Guoji Wenti Yanjiu* 6 (2004): 13–17.

———. *Kuayue: 1969–1979 nian Zhong Mei guanxi de yanbian* [Across the chasm: The evolution of China-US relations, 1969–1979]. Henan: Henan People's Press, 1992.

———. "The Official Perspective: What Chinese Government Officials Think of America." In *Chinese Images of the United States,* edited by Carola McGiffert, 25–32. Washington, DC: CSIS, 2006.

Green, Michael. *Japan's Reluctant Realism: Foreign Policy Challenges in an Era of Uncertain Power.* New York: Palgrave, 2003.

Green, Michael, and Benjamin Self. "Japan's Changing China Policy: From Commercial Liberalism to Reluctant Realism." *Survival* 38, no. 2 (Summer 1996): 34–58.

Gries, Peter. *China's New Nationalism: Pride, Politics, and Diplomacy.* Berkeley: University of California Press, 2004.

*Guoji Zhanlue yu Anquan Xingshi Pinggu 2001–2002.* Beijing: Shishi Chubanshe, 2002.

*Guoji Zhanlue yu Anquan Xingshi Pinggu 2003–2004.* Beijing: Shishi Chubanshe, 2004.

*Guoji Zhanlue yu Anquan Xingshi Pinggu 2004–2005.* Beijing: Shishi Chubanshe, 2005.

Hachigian, Nina, ed. *Debating China: The U.S. China Relationship in Ten Conversations.* New York: Oxford University Press, 2014.

Halper, Stefan. *The Beijing Consensus: Legitimizing Authoritarianism in Our Time.* New York: Basic Books, 2010.

Hamilton, Clive. *Silent Invasion: China's Influence in Australia.* Richmond, Australia: Hardie Grant Books, 2018.

Harding, Harry. *China's Foreign Relations in the 1980s.* New Haven, CT: Yale University Press, 1985.

———. *China's Second Revolution: Reform after Mao.* Washington, DC: Brookings Institution, 1987.

———. *A Fragile Relationship: The U.S. and China since 1972.* Washington, DC: Brookings Institution, 1992.

Harris, Lillian Craig, and Robert Worden, eds. *China and the Third World: Champion or Challenger?* Dover, MA: Auburn House, 1986.

Hart, Melanie, and Blaine Johnson. *Mapping China's Global Governance Ambitions: Democracies Still Have Leverage to Shape Beijing's Reform Agenda.* Washington, DC: Center for American Progress, February 28, 2019.

Hart, Melanie, and Kelly Magsamen. *Limit, Leverage and Compete: A New Strategy on China.* Washington, DC: Center for American Progress, April 2019.

He Zhipeng. "International Law Debates in China." *Pacific Review* 33 (2020): 550–73.

Heginbotham, Eric, and George Gilboy. *Chinese and Indian Strategic Behavior: Growing Power and Alarm.* New York: Cambridge University Press, 2012.

Heginbotham, Eric, et al. *China's Evolving Nuclear Deterrent: Major Drivers and Issues for the United States.* Santa Monica, CA: RAND Corporation, 2017.

Heilmann, Sebastian, ed. *China's Political System.* Lanham, MD: Rowman & Littlefield, 2017.

Henderson, John, and Benjamin Reilly. "Dragon in Paradise." *National Interest*, Summer 2003, 93–102.

Herberg, Mikkal, and Kenneth Lieberthal. "China's Search for Energy Security: Implications for U.S. Policy." *NBR Analysis* 17, no. 1 (April 2006): 1–54.

Hoffman, Samantha. *Engineering Global Consent: The Chinese Communist Party's Data-Driven Power Expansion.* Canberra: APSI Policy Brief, 2019.

Holslag, Jonathan. *China and India: Prospects for Peace.* New York: Columbia University Press, 2009.

Horesh, Niv, ed. *Toward Well-Oiled Relations: China's Presence in the Middle East.* New York: Palgrave Macmillan, 2016.

Hou Zhengdo. "Guanyu Zhong Ou zhanlue guanxi jige xiangfa." *Guoji Wenti Yanjiu* (Beijing) 2 (April 2005).

Hu Angang. *Daguo zhanlue liyi yu shiming.* Liaoning: Liaoning Renmin Chubanshe, 2000.

Hu Angang and Meng Honghua, eds. *Jiedu Meiguo dazhanlue.* Hangzhou: Zhejiang Renmin Chubanshe, 2003.

———. "Zhongmeiriieying youxing zhanlue ziyuan bijiao." *Zhanlue yu Guanli* 2 (2002): 26–41.

Hu Guocheng. "Chinese Images of the United States: A Historical Review." In *Chinese Images of the United States*, edited by Carola McGiffert, 3–8. Washington, DC: CSIS, 2006.

Huang Meibo and Jianme Hu. "Foreign Aid Study: Chinese Schools and Chinese Points." *Pacific Review* 33 (2020): 520–49.

Huang Renwei. *Zhongguo jueji de shijian he kongjian.* Shanghai: Shanghai Academy of Social Sciences, 2002.

Huchet, Jean-François. "Emergence of a Pragmatic India-China Relationship: Between Geostrategic Rivalry and Economic Competition." *China Perspectives* 3 (2008): 50–67.

Hung, Ho-fung. *The China Boom: Why China Will Not Rule the World.* New York: Columbia University Press, 2015.

Hunt, Michael H. *The Genesis of Chinese Communist Foreign Policy*. New York: Columbia University Press, 1996.

Institute for International and Strategic Studies. *China's Grand Strategy: A Kinder, Gentler Turn*. London: Institute for International and Strategic Studies, November 2004.

Institute of Strategic Studies, CCP Central Party School. *Zhongguo heping jueji xindaolu*. Beijing: Zhonggong Zhongyang Dangxiao Chubanshe, 2004.

International Crisis Group. *China and North Korea: Comrades Forever?* Asia Report 112. Brussels: International Crisis Group, February 1, 2006.

———. *China-Taiwan: Uneasy Détente*. Asia Briefing 42. Brussels: International Crisis Group, September 21, 2005.

———. *China's Growing Role in UN Peacekeeping*. Asia Report 166. Brussels: International Crisis Group, April 17, 2009.

———. *China's Myanmar Strategy*. Asia Briefing 112. Brussels: International Crisis Group, September 21, 2010.

———. *China's Thirst for Oil*. Asia Report 153–59. Brussels: International Crisis Group, June 2008.

———. *North Korea's Nuclear Test: The Fallout*. Asia Briefing 56. Brussels: International Crisis Group, November 13, 2006.

Jakobson, Linda, and Dean Knox. "New Foreign Policy Actors in China." SIPRI Policy Paper 26. Stockholm: Stockholm International Peace Research Institute, September 2010.

Jenner, C. J., and Tran Truong Thuy. *The South China Sea: A Crucible of Regional Cooperation or Conflict-Making Sovereignty Claims?* New York: Cambridge University Press, 2016.

Ji Zhiye. "Strategic Prospects for Russia." *Contemporary International Relations* (Beijing) 20, no. 5 (September–October 2010): 1–16.

Jia Qingguo. "Peaceful Development: China's Policy of Reassurance." *Australian Journal of International Affairs* 59, no. 4 (December 2005): 493–507.

Johnson, Christopher. *Decoding China's Emerging "Great Power" Strategy in Asia*. Washington, DC: Center for Strategic and International Studies, June 2014.

Johnston, Alastair Iain. "China in a World of Orders." *International Security* 44, no. 2 (Fall 2019): 9–60.

———. "How New and Assertive Is China's New Assertiveness?" *International Security* 37, no. 4 (Spring 2013): 7–48.

———. "Is China a Status Quo Power?" *International Security* 27, no. 4 (Spring 2003): 5–56.

———. *Social States: China in International Institutions, 1980–2000*. Princeton, NJ: Princeton University Press, 2008.

Johnston, Alastair Iain, and Paul Evans. "China's Engagement." In *Engaging China: The Management of an Emerging Power*, edited by Alastair Iain Johnston and Robert Ross, 235–72. New York: Routledge, 1999.

Johnston, Alastair Iain, and Robert S. Ross, eds. *New Directions in the Study of China's Foreign Policy*. Stanford, CA: Stanford University Press, 2006.

Kang, David. *China Rising: Peace, Power, and Order in East Asia*. New York: Columbia University Press, 2007.

———. "Getting Asia Wrong: The Need for New Analytical Frameworks." *International Security* 27, no. 4 (2003): 57–85.

Keller, William, and Thomas Rawski, eds. *China's Rise and the Balance of Influence in Asia*. Pittsburgh, PA: University of Pittsburgh Press, 2007.

Kim, Samuel, ed. *China and the World: New Directions in Chinese Foreign Relations*. Boulder, CO: Westview, 1989.

———. *China, the United Nations and World Order*. Princeton, NJ: Princeton University Press, 1979.

———. "Chinese Foreign Policy Faces Globalization Challenges." In *New Directions in the Study of China's Foreign Policy*, edited by Alastair Iain Johnston and Robert S. Ross, 276–308. Stanford, CA: Stanford University Press, 2006.

———. *The Third World in Chinese World Policy*. Princeton, NJ: Princeton University Press, 1989.

————. *The Two Koreas and the Great Powers*. New York: Cambridge University Press, 2006.

Kissinger, Henry. *On China*. New York: Penguin, 2011.

Kitano, Naohiro, and Yukinori Harada. *Estimating China's Foreign Aid, 2001–2013*. Tokyo: JICA Research Institute, June 2014.

Kleine-Ahlbrandt, Stephanie, and Andrew Small. "China's New Dictatorship Diplomacy." *Foreign Affairs* 87, no. 1 (January–February 2008): 38–56.

Kliman, Daniel, Rush Doshi, Kristine Lee, and Zack Cooper. *Grading China's Belt and Road*. Washington, DC: Center for New American Security, April 2019.

Kroeber, Arthur. *China's Economy: What Everyone Needs to Know*. New York: Oxford University Press, 2016.

Kurlantzick, Joshua. *Charm Offensive: How China's Soft Power Is Transforming the World*. New Haven, CT: Yale University Press, 2007.

Lampton, David Michael. *Following the Leader: Ruling China from Deng Xiaoping to Xi Jinping*. Berkeley: University of California Press, 2014.

————, ed. *The Making of Chinese Foreign and Security Policy in the Era of Reform, 1978–2000*. Stanford, CA: Stanford University Press, 2001.

————. *Power Constrained: Sources of Mutual Strategic Suspicion in US-China Relations*. NBR Analysis, June 2010, 5–25.

————. *Same Bed, Different Dreams: Managing U.S.-China Relations*. Berkeley: University of California Press, 2001.

————. *The Three Faces of Chinese Power: Might, Money, and Minds*. Berkeley: University of California Press, 2008.

Lanteigne, Marc. *Chinese Foreign Policy: An Introduction*. New York: Routledge 2020.

Lardy, Nicholas. *The State Strikes Back: The End of Economic Reform in China*. Washington, DC: Peterson Institute for International Economics, 2019.

Laurelle, Marlene, and Sebastien Peyrouse, eds. *The Chinese Question in Central Asia: Domestic Order, Social Change, and the Chinese Factor*. New York: Columbia University Press, 2012.

Lee, David Tawei. *The Making of the Taiwan Relations Act: Twenty Years in Retrospect*. New York: Oxford University Press, 2000.

Lee Teng-hui. *Creating the Future: Towards a New Era for the Chinese People* (a compilation of speeches and remarks by President Lee Teng-hui). Taipei: Government Information Office, 1992.

Lewis, Joanna. "China's Strategic Priorities in International Climate Change Negotiations." *Washington Quarterly* 31, no. 1 (Winter 2007–2008): 155–74.

————. *Green Innovation in China: China's Wind Power Industry and the Global Transition to a Low-Carbon Economy*. New York: Columbia University Press, 2013.

————. "The State of U.S.-China Relations on Climate Change." *China Environmental Series* 11 (2010–2011): 7–39.

Li, Cheng. *Chinese Politics in the Xi Jinping Era*. Washington, DC: Brookings Institution, 2016.

————, ed. *China's Changing Political Landscape: Prospects for Democracy*. Washington, DC: Brookings Institution, 2008.

Li Li. "India's Engagement with East Asia and the China Factor." *Contemporary International Relations* (Beijing) 20, no. 5 (September–October 2010): 97–109.

Li Shaoxian. "China-Russia Bond." *Xiandai guoji guanxi* (Beijing) 17 (January 2007): 5–21.

Li Shaoxian and Tang Zhichao. "China and the Middle East." *Xiandai guoji guanxi* (Beijing) 17 (January 2007): 22–31.

Li Shaoxian and Wei Liang. "New Complexities in the Middle East since 9.11." *Contemporary International Relations* (Beijing) 20, special issue (September 2010): 22–32.

Li Shengming and Wang Yizhou, eds. *Nian quanqiu zhengzhi yu anquan baogao*. Beijing: Shehui Kexue Wenxian, 2003.

Lieberthal, Kenneth, and Mikkal Herberg. "China's Search for Energy Security: Implications for U.S. Policy." *NBR Analysis* 17, no. 1 (April 2006): 1–54.

Lieberthal, Kenneth, and David Sandalow. *Overcoming Obstacles to U.S.-China Cooperation on Climate Change*. John L. Thornton China Center Monograph Series 1. Washington, DC: Brookings Institution, January 2009.

Lieberthal, Kenneth, and Wang Jisi. *Addressing U.S.-China Strategic Distrust*. Washington, DC: Brookings Institution, March 2012.

Lin, Syara Shirley. *Taiwan's China Dilemma*. Stanford, CA: Stanford University Press, 2016.

Liu Baolai. "Broad Prospects for China-Arab Relations." *Foreign Affairs Journal* (Beijing) 79 (March 2006): 38–44.

Liu Hongsong. "Chinese Perception of Chinese Engagement in Multilateralism and Global Engagement." *Pacific Review* 33 (2020): 469–96.

Liu Jianfei. *Meiguo yu fangong zhuyi: Lun Meiguo dui shehui zhuyi guojia de yishixingtai wijiao*. Beijing: Chinese Social Science Press, 2001.

Liu Ming. "China and the North Korean Crisis." *Pacific Affairs* 76, no. 3 (Fall 2003): 347–73.

Liu Tainchun. *Riben hui hua zhengce yu zhongri guanxi*. Beijing: Renmin Chubanshe, 2004.

Lo, Bobo. *Axis of Convenience: Moscow, Beijing, and the New Geopolitics*. Washington, DC: Brookings Institution, 2008.

Lo, Shui-hing. *The Politics of Cross-Border Crime in Greater China*. New York: Routledge, 2009.

Lou Yaoliang. *Diyuan zhengzhi yu Zhongguo guofang zhanlue*. Tianjin: Tianjin Press, 2002.

Lu Fanghua. "An Analysis of U.S. Involvement in the South China Sea." *Contemporary International Relations* (Beijing) 20, no. 6 (November–December 2010): 132–41.

Lu Gang and Guo Xuetang. *Zhongguo weixie shui: Jiedu "Zhong weixie lun."* Shanghai: Xueling Chubanshe, 2004.

Lu Ning. *The Dynamics of Foreign Policy Decision Making in China*. Boulder, CO: Westview, 1997.

Lukin, Alexander. *China and Russia: The New Rapprochement*. Cambridge, UK: Polity, 2018.

Luthi, Lorenz M. *The Sino-Soviet Spilt: Cold War in the Communist World*. Princeton, NJ: Princeton University Press, 2008.

Lynch, Daniel. *China's Futures: PRC Elites Debate Economics, Politics, and Foreign Policy*. Stanford, CA: Stanford University Press, 2015.

Ma Jiali. "Emerging Sino-Indian Relations." *Xiandai guoji guanxi* (Beijing) 17 (May 2007): 71–80.

Ma Licheng. "Duiri guanxi xinsiwei." *Zhanlue yu Guanli* 6 (2002): 41–47.

MacFarquhar, Roderick, and John K. Fairbank, eds. *The Cambridge History of China*. Vol. 15, *The People's Republic, Part 2: Revolutions within the Chinese Revolution, 1966–1982*. Cambridge: Cambridge University Press, 1991.

MacFarquhar, Roderick, and Michael Schoenhals. *Mao's Last Revolution*. Cambridge, MA: Harvard University Press, 2006.

Mahnken, Thomas, Ross Babbage, and Toshi Yoshihara. *Countering Comprehensive Coercion*. Washington, DC: Center for Strategic and Budgetary Assessments, 2018.

Malik, J. Mohan. "The China Factor in the India-Pakistan Conflict." *Parameters*, Spring 2003, 35–50.

———. "Chinese-Indian Relations in the Post-Soviet Era." *China Quarterly* 142 (June 1995): 317–55.

Mann, Jim. *About Face: A History of America's Curious Relationship with China, from Nixon to Clinton*. New York: Knopf, 1999.

Marks, Robert. *China: An Environmental History*. Lanham, MD: Rowman & Littlefield, 2017.

Mazarr, Michael, Timothy Heath, and Astrid Stuth Cevallos. *China and the International Order*. Santa Monica, CA: RAND Corporation, 2018.

McDonald, Scott, and Michael Burgoyne, eds. *China's Global Influence*. Honolulu, HI: Asia-Pacific Center for Security Studies, 2020.

McGiffert, Carola, ed. *Chinese Images of the United States*. Washington, DC: CSIS, 2006.

Medeiros, Evan. "Is Beijing Ready for Global Leadership?" *Current History* 108, no. 719 (September 2009): 250–56.

———, ed. *Pacific Currents: The Responses of U.S. Allies and Security Partners in East Asia to China's Rise*. Santa Monica, CA: RAND Corporation, 2008.

———. *Reluctant Restraint: The Evolution of China's Nonproliferation Policies and Practices, 1980–2004*. Stanford, CA: Stanford University Press, 2007.

———. "Strategic Hedging and the Future of Asia-Pacific Stability." *Washington Quarterly* 29, no. 1 (Winter 2005–2006): 145–67.

Medeiros, Evan, and M. Taylor Fravel. "China's New Diplomacy." *Foreign Affairs* 82, no. 6 (November–December 2003): 22–35.

Mei Zhaorong. "Sino-European Relations in Retrospect and Prospect." *Foreign Affairs Journal* (Beijing) 79 (March 2006): 17–27.

Meijer, Hugo. *Trading with the Enemy: The Making of US Export Control Policy toward the People's Republic of China.* New York: Oxford University Press, 2016.

Men Honghua. *China's Grand Strategy: A Framework Analysis*. Beijing: Beijing Daxue Chubanshe, 2005.

Menon, Rajan. "The Strategic Convergence between Russia and China." *Survival* 39, no. 2 (Summer 1997): 101–25.

Miller, Alice Lyman, and Richard Wich. *Becoming Asia*. Stanford, CA: Stanford University Press, 2011.

Miller, H. Lyman, and Liu Xiaohong. "The Foreign Policy Outlook of China's 'Third Generation' Elite." In *The Making of Chinese Foreign and Security Policy in the Era of Reform, 1978–2000*, edited by David Michael Lampton, 123–50. Stanford, CA: Stanford University Press, 2001.

Miller, Tom. *China's Asian Dream: Empire Building along the New Silk Road.* London: Zed Books, 2017.

Millward, James. *Eurasian Crossroads: A History of Xinjiang.* New York: Columbia University Press, 2007.

Minzner, Carl. *End of an Era: How China's Authoritarian Revival Is Undermining Its Rise.* New York: Oxford University Press, 2018.

Mitter, Rana. *A Bitter Revolution: China's Struggle with the Modern World*. New York: Oxford University Press, 2004.

Mochizuki, Mike. "Terms of Engagement: The U.S.-Japan Alliance and the Rise of China." In *The U.S.-Japan Relationship in the New Asia-Pacific*, edited by Ellis Krauss and T. J. Pempel, 87–115. Stanford, CA: Stanford University Press, 2004.

Moltz, James Clay. "Regional Tension in the Russo-Chinese Rapprochement." *Asian Survey* 35, no. 6 (June 1995): 511–27.

Moore, Thomas. "Chinese Foreign Policy in an Age of Globalization." In *China Rising: Power and Motivation in Chinese Foreign Policy*, edited by Yong Deng and Fei-Ling Wang, 121–58. Lanham, MD: Rowman & Littlefield, 2005.

Morck, Randall, Bernard Yeung, and Minyuan Zhao. *Perspectives on China's Outward Foreign Direct Investment*. Working paper. Washington, DC: International Monetary Fund, August 2007.

Morrison, Wayne. *China's Economic Conditions*. Congressional Research Service Report RL33534. Washington, DC: Library of Congress, June 26, 2012.

———. *China's Economic Rise*. Congressional Research Service Report RL33534. Washington, DC: Library of Congress, June 25, 2019.

———. *China-U.S. Trade Issues*. Congressional Research Service Report RL33536. Washington, DC: Library of Congress, July 30, 2018.

Murray, William S. "Revisiting Taiwan's Defense Strategy." *Naval War College Review* 61, no. 3 (Summer 2008): 13–38.

Nathan, Andrew, and Robert Ross. *The Great Wall and Empty Fortress*. New York: Norton, 1997.

Nathan, Andrew, and Andrew Scobell. *China's Search for Security*. New York: Columbia University Press, 2012.

Naughton, Barry. *The Chinese Economy*. Cambridge, MA: MIT Press, 2018.

Niu Haibin. "China's International Responsibility Examined." *Xiandai guoji guanxi* (Beijing) 17 (July 2007): 81–93.

Niu Jun. *From Yan'an to the World: The Origin and Development of Chinese Communist Foreign Policy*. Edited and translated by Steven I. Levine. Norwalk, CT: Eastbridge, 2005.

Norris, William. *Chinese Economic Statecraft.* Ithaca, NY: Cornell University Press, 2016.

Nyiri, Pal. *Reporting for China: How Chinese Correspondents Work with the World.* Seattle: University of Washington Press, 2017.

O'Rourke, Ronald. *China's Naval Modernization.* Congressional Research Service Report RL33153. Washington, DC: Library of Congress, May 21, 2020.

Pang Guang. "An Analysis of the Prospects of 'Shanghai Five.'" In *Thinking of the New Century,* edited by Ling Rong. Beijing: Central Party School Press, 2002.

———. "China's Asian Strategy: Flexible Multilateralism." *World Economy and Politics* (Beijing) 10 (2001).

———, ed. *Quanqiuhua, fanquangiuhua yu Zhongguo: Lijie quanqiuhua de fuzhanxin yu duoyangxin.* Shanghai: Renmin, 2002.

———. "SCO under New Circumstances: Challenge, Opportunity and Prospect for Development." *Journal of International Studies* (Beijing) 5 (2002): 40–52.

Paulson, Henry. "The Right Way to Engage China: Strengthening U.S.-Chinese Ties." *Foreign Affairs,* September–October 2008.

Pearson, Margaret. "China in Geneva: Lessons from China's Early Years in the World Trade Organization." In *New Directions in the Study of China's Foreign Policy,* edited by Alastair Iain Johnston and Robert S. Ross, 242–75. Stanford, CA: Stanford University Press, 2006.

Pei, Minxin. *China's Crony Capitalism: The Dynamics of Regime Decay.* Cambridge, MA: Harvard University Press, 2016.

———. *China's Trapped Transition: The Limits of Development Autocracy.* Cambridge, MA: Harvard University Press, 2006.

People's Republic of China Ministry of Foreign Affairs. "China's Africa Policy." *People's Daily,* January 12, 2006.

———. *China's Arab Policy Paper.* January 13, 2016.

———. *China's EU Policy Paper.* Beijing: Ministry of Foreign Affairs, October 13, 2003.

People's Republic of China Ministry of Foreign Affairs, Department of Policy Planning. *China's Foreign Relations 2010.* Beijing: World Affairs Press, 2010.

People's Republic of China State Council Information Office. *China and the World in the New Era.* November 2019. http://english.www.gov.cn/archive/whitepaper/201909/27/content_WS5d8d80f9c6d0bcf8c4c142ef.html.

———. *China's Foreign Aid.* April 21, 2011.

———. *China's Foreign Aid.* July 10, 2014.

———. *China's National Defense in 2002.* Beijing: People's Republic of China State Council Information Office, December 9, 2002.

———. *China's National Defense in 2004.* Beijing: People's Republic of China State Council Information Office, December 27, 2004.

———. *China's National Defense in 2006.* Beijing: People's Republic of China State Council Information Office, December 29, 2006.

———. *China's National Defense in 2008.* Beijing: People's Republic of China State Council Information Office, January 2009.

———. *China's National Defense in 2010.* Beijing: People's Republic of China State Council Information Office, March 2011.

———. *China's National Defense in the New Era.* Beijing: People's Republic of China State Council Information Office, July 24, 2019.

———. "China's Peaceful Development Road." *People's Daily,* December 22, 2005.

People's Republic of China State Council, Taiwan Affairs Office and Information Office. *The One-China Principle and the Taiwan Issue.* February 12, 2000. http://www.gwytb.gov.cn.

———. *The Taiwan Question and the Reunification of China.* September 1, 1993. http://www.gwytb.gov.cn.

Percival, Bronson. *The Dragon Looks South: China and Southeast Asia in the New Century.* Westport, CT: Praeger, 2007.

Pillsbury, Michael. *The Hundred-Year Marathon.* New York: Holt, 2015.

Plesner, Jonas Parello, and Mathieu Duchatel. *China's Strong Arm: Protecting Citizens and Assets Abroad.* London: International Institute for Strategic Studies, 2015.

Pollack, Jonathan. *No Exit: North Korea, Nuclear Weapons, and International Security.* New York: Routledge, 2011.

———. "The Transformation of the Asian Security Order: Assessing China's Impact." In *Power Shift: China and Asia's New Dynamics,* edited by David Shambaugh, 329–46. Berkeley: University of California Press, 2005.

Qian Qichen. "Adjustment of the United States National Security Strategy and International Relations in the Early New Century." *Foreign Affairs Journal* (Beijing) 71 (March 2004): 1–7.

———. "Xinshiji de guoji guanxi." *Xuexi Shibao,* October 18, 2004.

Ranganathan, C. V. "India and China: 'Learning to Learn.'" In *Prime Minister Vajpayee's China Visit June 2003,* 45–54. Occasional Studies 1. New Delhi: Institute of Chinese Studies, October 2003.

Reardon-Anderson, James, ed. *The Red Star and the Crescent: China and the Middle East.* New York: Oxford University Press, 2018.

Reilly, James. *China's Economic Statecraft: Turning Wealth into Power.* Sydney: Lowy Institute, November 2012.

Ren Xiao. "Grown from within: Building a Chinese School of International Relations." *Pacific Review* 33 (2020): 386–412.

Ren Xiao and Liu Ming. *Chinese Perspectives on International Relations in the Xi Jinping Era.* Seattle, WA: National Bureau of Asian Research, June 2020.

Richardson, Sophie. *China, Cambodia, and the Five Principles of Peaceful Coexistence.* New York: Columbia University Press, 2010.

Rigger, Shelley. *Taiwan's Rising Rationalism: Generations, Politics, and "Taiwanese Nationalism."* Washington, DC: East-West Center, 2006.

———. *Why Taiwan Matters.* Lanham, MD: Rowman & Littlefield, 2011.

Robinson, Thomas W., and David Shambaugh, eds. *Chinese Foreign Policy: Theory and Practice.* New York: Oxford University Press, 1994.

Rolland, Nadege. *China's Eurasian Century?* Seattle, WA: National Bureau of Asian Research, 2017.

———. *China's Vision for a New World Order.* Seattle, WA: National Bureau of Asian Research, January 2020.

———, ed. *Securing the Belt and Road Initiative.* NBR Special Report No. 80. Seattle, WA: National Bureau of Asian Research, September 3, 2019.

Rose, Caroline. *Sino-Japanese Relations: Facing the Past, Looking to the Future.* New York: RoutledgeCurzon, 2005.

Rosen, Daniel, and Thilo Hanemann. *An American Open Door: Maximizing the Benefits of Chinese Foreign Direct Investment.* New York: Asia Society, 2011.

Ross, Robert S., ed. *After the Cold War.* Armonk, NY: Sharpe, 1998.

———. *The Indochina Tangle.* New York: Columbia University Press, 1988.

———. *Negotiating Cooperation: The United States and China, 1969–1989.* Stanford, CA: Stanford University Press, 1995.

———. "Taiwan's Fading Independence Movement." *Foreign Affairs* 85, no. 2 (March–April 2006): 141–48.

Ross, Robert, and Jo Inge Bekkevold, eds. *China in the Era of Xi Jinping.* Washington, DC: Georgetown University Press, 2016.

Ross, Robert, and Zhu Feng, eds. *China's Ascent: Power, Security and the Implications for International Politics.* Ithaca, NY: Cornell University Press, 2009.

Roy, Denny. *China's Foreign Relations.* Lanham, MD: Rowman & Littlefield, 1998.

———. *Return of the Dragon: Rising China and Regional Security.* New York: Columbia University Press, 2013.

———. "Rising China and U.S. Interests: Inevitable vs. Contingent Hazards." *Orbis* 47, no. 1 (2003): 125–37.

———. *Taiwan: A Political History.* Ithaca, NY: Cornell University Press, 2003.

Rozman, Gilbert. *Chinese Strategic Thought toward Asia.* New York: Palgrave Macmillan, 2010.

Russel, Daniel, and Blake Berger. *Navigating the Belt and Road Initiative.* New York: Asia Society Policy Institute, June 2019.

Sa Benwang. "Some Observations on Building a Harmonious World." *Foreign Affairs Journal* (Beijing) 80 (June 2006): 37–42.

Saich, Tony. *Governance and Politics of China.* New York: Palgrave, 2004.

Samuels, Richard. *Securing Japan: Tokyo's Grand Strategy and the Future of East Asia.* Ithaca, NY: Cornell University Press, 2007.

Sandalow, David. *Guide to Chinese Climate Policy 2019.* New York: Columbia University Center on Global Energy Policy, September 13, 2019.

Saunders, Phillip. "China's America Watchers: Changing Attitudes toward the United States." *China Quarterly* (March 2000): 41–65.

———. *China's Global Activism: Strategy, Drivers, and Tools.* Occasional Paper 4. Washington, DC: National Defense University, Institute for National Strategic Studies, June 2006.

Saunders, Phillip, and Andrew Scobell, eds. *PLA Influence on China's National Security Policymaking.* Stanford, CA: Stanford University Press, 2015.

Saunders, Phillip, et al. *Chairman Xi Remakes the PLA.* Washington, DC: National Defense University Press, 2019.

Schell, Orville, and Susan Shirk, chairs. *Course Correction: Toward an Effective and Sustainable China Policy.* New York: Asia Society, 2019.

———. *US Policy toward China: Recommendations for a New Administration.* New York: Asia Society, 2017.

Schrader, Matt. *Friends and Enemies: A Framework for Understanding Chinese Political Influence in Democratic Countries.* Washington, DC: German Marshall Fund, April 22, 2020.

Scobell, Andrew. "Terrorism and Chinese Foreign Policy." In *China Rising: Power and Motivation in Chinese Foreign Policy*, edited by Yong Deng and Fei-Ling Wang, 305–24. Lanham, MD: Rowman & Littlefield, 2005.

Scobell, Andrew, et al. *At the Dawn of the Belt and Road: China in the Developing World.* Santa Monica, CA: RAND Corporation, 2018.

Self, Benjamin. "China and Japan: A Façade of Friendship." *Washington Quarterly* 26, no. 1 (Winter 2002–2003): 77–88.

Shambaugh, David. *Beautiful Imperialist: China Perceives America, 1972–1990.* Princeton, NJ: Princeton University Press, 1991.

———. "China and Europe: The Emerging Axis." *Current History* 103, no. 674 (September 2004): 243–48.

———, ed. *China and the World.* New York: Oxford University Press, 2020.

———. *China Goes Global: Partial Power.* New York: Oxford University Press, 2013.

———. *China's Communist Party: Atrophy and Adaptation.* Washington, DC: Woodrow Wilson Center, 2008.

———. "Coping with a Conflicted China." *Washington Quarterly* 34, no. 1 (Winter 2011): 7–27.

———. *Modernizing China's Military: Progress, Problems, Prospects.* Berkeley: University of California Press, 2002.

———, ed. *Power Shift: China and Asia's New Dynamics.* Berkeley: University of California Press, 2005.

———, ed. *Tangled Titans: The United States and China.* Lanham, MD: Rowman & Littlefield, 2012.

Sheives, Kevin. "China Turns West: Beijing's Contemporary Strategy toward Central Asia." *Pacific Affairs* 79, no. 2 (Summer 2006): 205–24.

Sheng Lijun. *China's Influence in Southeast Asia.* Trends in Southeast Asia Series 4. Singapore: Institute of Southeast Asian Studies, 2006.

Shi Yinhong. "Zhongri jiejin yu 'waijiao geming.'" *Zhanlue yu Guanli* (Beijing) 2 (2003): 71–75.

Shie, Tamara. "Rising Chinese Influence in the South Pacific." *Asian Survey* 47, no. 2 (March–April 2007): 307–26.

Shinn, David, and Joshua Eisenman. *China and Africa: A Century of Engagement.* Philadelphia: University of Pennsylvania Press, 2012.

Shirk, Susan. *China: Fragile Superpower.* New York: Oxford University Press, 2007.

Shullman, David, ed. *Chinese Malign Influence and the Corrosion of Democracy.* Washington, DC: International Republican Institute, 2019.

Small, Andrew. *The China-Pakistan Axis: Asia's New Geopolitics.* New York: Oxford University Press, 2015.

Smith, Warren. *Tibet's Last Stand? The Tibetan Uprising of 2008 and China's Response.* Lanham, MD: Rowman & Littlefield, 2009.

Snyder, Scott. *China's Rise and the Two Koreas: Politics, Economics, Security.* Boulder, CO: Lynne Rienner, 2009.

———. *South Korea at the Crossroads: Autonomy and Alliance in an Era of Power Rivals.* New York: Columbia University Press, 2018.

Stahle, Stefan. "China's Shifting Attitude towards United Nations Peacekeeping Operations." *China Quarterly* 195 (September 2008): 631–55.

Storey, Ian James. "Living with the Colossus: How Southeast Asian Countries Cope with China." *Parameters,* Winter 1999–2000, 111–25.

———. *Southeast Asia and the Rise of China: The Search for Security.* London: Routledge, 2011.

———. *The United States and ASEAN-China Relations: All Quiet on the Southeastern Asian Front.* Carlisle, PA: Strategic Studies Institute, U.S. Army War College, 2007.

Su Ge. *Meiguo: Dui hua zhengce yu Taiwan wenti* [America: China Policy and the Taiwan Issue]. Beijing: Shijie Zhishi Chubanshe, 1998.

Suettinger, Robert. *Beyond Tiananmen: The Politics of U.S.-China Relations, 1989–2000.* Washington, DC: Brookings Institution, 2003.

Sun, Yun. *Chinese National Security Decision-Making: Process and Challenges.* Washington, DC: Brookings Institution, May 2013.

Sutter, Robert. "Assessing China's Rise and U.S. Leadership in Asia—Growing Maturity and Balance." *Journal of Contemporary China* 19, no. 65 (June 2010): 591–604.

———. *China's Rise: Implications for U.S. Leadership in Asia.* Washington, DC: East-West Center, 2006.

———. *China's Rise in Asia: Promises and Perils.* Lanham, MD: Rowman & Littlefield, 2005.

———. *Chinese Foreign Relations: Power and Policy since the Cold War.* Lanham, MD: Rowman & Littlefield, 2016.

———. *Foreign Relations of the PRC: The Legacies and Constraints of China's International Politics since 1949,* 2nd ed. Lanham, MD: Rowman & Littlefield, 2019.

———. *The United States and Asia: Regional Dynamics and Twenty-First-Century Relations,* 2nd ed. Lanham, MD: Rowman & Littlefield, 2020.

———. *U.S.-Chinese Relations: Perilous Past, Uncertain Present.* 3rd ed., Lanham, MD: Rowman & Littlefield, 2018.

Swaine, Michael. *America's Challenge: Engaging a Rising China in the Twenty-First Century.* Washington, DC: Carnegie Endowment for International Peace, 2011.

———. "China's Regional Military Posture." In *Power Shift: China and Asia's New Dynamics,* edited by David Shambaugh, 266–88. Berkeley: University of California Press, 2005.

———. *Creating a Stable Asia.* Washington, DC: Carnegie Endowment, 2016.

Swaine, Michael, and Ashley Tellis. *Interpreting China's Grand Strategy, Past, Present and Future.* Santa Monica, CA: RAND Corporation, September 2001.

Swaine, Michael, Tousheng Zhang, and Danielle F. S. Cohen. *Managing Sino-American Crises: Case Studies and Analysis.* Washington, DC: Carnegie Endowment, 2006.

Swanstrom, Niklas. "China and Central Asia: A New Great Game or Traditional Vassal Relations?" *Journal of Contemporary China* 14, no. 45 (November 2005): 569–84.

Tan, Andrew T. H., ed. *Handbook of US-China Relations.* Cheltenham: Edward Elgar, 2016.

Tang Shiping and Zhang Yunling. "Zhongguo de diqu zhanlue." *Shijie Jingli Yu Zhengzhi* 6 (2004): 8–13.

Tang, Wenfang. *Populist Authoritarianism: Chinese Political Culture and Regime Sustainability.* New York: Oxford University Press, 2016.

Taylor, Ian. *China's New Role in Africa.* Boulder, CO: Lynne Rienner, 2008.

Taylor, Jay. *The Generalissimo.* Cambridge, MA: Harvard University Press, 2009.

———. *The Generalissimo's Son: Chiang Ching-kuo and the Revolutions in China and Taiwan.* Cambridge, MA: Harvard University Press, 2000.

Tellis, Ashley. *Balancing without Containment.* Washington, DC: Carnegie Endowment for International Peace Report, January 22, 2014.

Tellis, Ashley, Alison Szalwinski, and Michael Wills, eds. *Strategic Asia 2020: US-China Competition for Global Influence.* Seattle, WA: National Bureau of Asian Research, 2020.

Tian Peiliang. "China and Africa in New Period." *Foreign Affairs Journal* (Beijing) 70 (December 2003): 36–42.

———. "Nationalism: China and Japan." *Foreign Affairs Journal* (Beijing) 63 (March 2002): 63–83.

Tain Zengpei, ed. *Gaige kaifang yilai de Zhongguo waijiao* [Chinese diplomacy since reform and opening]. Beijing: Shijie Zhishi Chubanshe, 1993.

Tiang Zhongqing. "East Asia Cooperation and China's Strategic Interest." *Dangdai Yatai* (Beijing) 5 (2003).

Tucker, Nancy Bernkopf. "China-Taiwan: U.S. Debates and Policy Choices." *Survival* 40, no. 4 (Winter 1998–1999): 150–67.

———, ed. *Dangerous Strait: The U.S.-Taiwan-China Crisis.* New York: Columbia University Press, 2005.

———. *Strait Talk: United States–Taiwan Relations and the Crisis with China.* Cambridge, MA: Harvard University Press, 2009.

———. *Taiwan, Hong Kong, and the United States, 1945–1992: Uncertain Friendships.* New York: Twayne, 1994.

United States–China Economic and Security Review Commission. *Report to Congress 2019.*

US Department of Defense. *Military and Security Developments Involving the People's Republic of China, 2019.* http://www.defense.gov/pubs/pdfs/2012_CMPR_Final.pdf.

US National Intelligence Council. *China and Weapons of Mass Destruction: Implications for the United States.* Conference Report. Washington, DC: U.S. National Intelligence Council, November 5, 1999.

———. *China's Future: Implications for U.S. Interests.* Conference Report CR99-02. Washington, DC: US National Intelligence Council, September 1999.

US Senate, Committee on Foreign Relations. *China's Foreign Policy and "Soft Power" in South America, Asia, and Africa.* Washington, DC: US Government Printing Office, 2008.

Wachman, Alan. *Why Taiwan: Geostrategic Rationales for China's Territorial Integrity.* Stanford, CA: Stanford University Press, 2007.

Wan, Ming. *Sino-Japanese Relations: Interaction, Logic, and Transformation.* Stanford, CA: Stanford University Press, 2006.

Wang Dong and Weizhan Meng. "China Debating the Regional Order." *Pacific Review* 33 (2020): 497–519.

Wang, Fei-Ling. "Beijing's Incentive Structure: The Pursuit of Preservation, Prosperity, and Power." In *China Rising: Power and Motivation in Chinese Foreign Policy,* edited by Yong Deng and Fei-Ling Wang, 19–50. Lanham, MD: Rowman & Littlefield, 2005.

———. *The China Order: Centralia, World Empire and the Nature of Chinese Power.* Albany: State University of New York Press, 2017.

Wang Gungwu. *China and Southeast Asia: Myths, Threat, and Culture.* EAI Occasional Paper 13. Singapore: National University of Singapore, 1999.

———. "The Fourth Rise of China: Cultural Implications." *China: An International Journal* 2, no. 2 (September 2004): 311–22.

Wang Jianwei. "China's Multilateral Diplomacy in the New Millennium." In *China Rising: Power and Motivation in Chinese Foreign Policy,* edited by Yong Deng and Fei-Ling Wang, 177–87. Lanham, MD: Rowman & Littlefield, 2005.

Wang Jisi. "China's Search for a Grand Strategy." *Foreign Affairs* 90, no. 2 (March–April 2011): 68–79.

————. "China's Search for Stability with America." *Foreign Affairs* 84, no. 5 (September–October 2005): 39–48.

————. *"Marching Westwards": The Rebalancing of China's Geostrategy.* International and Strategic Studies Report 73 (Beijing: Peking University, October 7, 2012).

————. "Xinxingshi de Zhuyao Tedian he Zhongguo Waijiao." *Xiabdai Guoji Guanxi* (Beijing) 4 (April 2003): 1–3.

Wang Shida. "The Way to a Secure and Stable Afghanistan." *Contemporary International Relations* (Beijing) 20, no. 6 (November–December 2010): 123–31.

Wang Shuzhong, ed. *Mei-Su zhengba zhanlue wenti* [The question of contention for hegemony between the United States and the Soviet Union]. Beijing: Guofang Daxue Chubanshe, 1988.

Wang, T. Y. "Taiwan's Foreign Relations under Lee Teng-hui's Rule, 1988–2000." In *Sayonara to the Lee Teng-Hui Era*, edited by Wei-chin Lee and T. Y. Wang, 250–60. Lanham, MD: University Press of America, 2003.

Wang Xiaolong. "The Asia-Pacific Economic Cooperation and the Regional Political and Security Issues." *Dangdai Yatai* (Beijing) 4 (2003).

Wang Yizhou. *Quanqiu zhengzhi he Zhongguo waijiao.* Beijing: Shijie Zhishi Chubanshe, 2004.

Weatherbee, Donald. *International Relations in Southeast Asia: The Struggle for Autonomy.* 3rd ed. Lanham, MD: Rowman & Littlefield, 2014.

————. "Strategic Dimensions of Economic Interdependence in Southeast Asia." In *Strategic Asia 2006–07: Trade, Interdependence and Security*, edited by Ashley Tellis and Michael Wills, 271–302. Seattle, WA: National Bureau of Asian Research, 2006.

Wei Ling. "Striving for Achievement in a New Era: China Debates Its Global Role." *Pacific Review* 33 (2020): 413–37.

Weiss, Jessica. *Powerful Patriots: Nationalist Protests in China's Foreign Relations.* New York: Oxford University Press, 2014.

White, Hugh. *The China Choice.* Collingwood: Australia Black, 2012.

Whiting, Allen S. *China Crosses the Yalu: The Decision to Enter the Korean War.* New York: Macmillan, 1960.

————. *The Chinese Calculus of Deterrence: India and Indochina.* Ann Arbor: University of Michigan Press, 1975.

Wilson, Jeanne. *Strategic Partners: Russian-Chinese Relations in the Post-Soviet Era.* Armonk, NY: Sharpe, 2004.

Wishnick, Elizabeth. "Russia and China: Brothers Again?" *Asian Survey* 41, no. 5 (September–October 2001): 797–821.

Womack, Brantly. "China and Southeast Asia: Asymmetry, Leadership, and Normalcy." *Pacific Affairs* 76, no. 3 (Winter 2003–2004): 529–48.

————. *China and Vietnam: The Politics of Asymmetry.* New York: Cambridge University Press, 2006.

Wong, John, and Sarah Chan. "China-ASEAN Free Trade Agreement." *Asian Survey* 43, no. 3 (May–June 2003): 507–26.

Wu Hongying. "Latin America: Key Trends and Challenges." *Contemporary International Relations* (Beijing) 20, special issue (September 2010): 33–42.

————. "A New Era of Sino-Latin American Relations." *Xiandai guoji guanxi* (Beijing) 17 (January 2007): 64–71.

Wu Xinbo. "Chinese Perspectives on Building an East Asian Community in the Twenty-First Century." In *Asia's New Multilateralism*, edited by Michael Green and Bates Gill, 55–77. New York: Columbia University Press, 2009.

————. "The End of the Silver Lining: A Chinese View of the U.S.-Japanese Alliance." *Washington Quarterly* 29, no. 1 (Winter 2005–2006): 119–30.

————. "Four Contradictions Constraining China's Foreign Policy Behavior." *Journal of Contemporary China* 10, no. 27 (May 2001): 293–302.

Xing Guangcheng. "Work for Mutual Trust and Mutual Benefit in Deepening Sino-Russian Relations." *Foreign Affairs Journal* (Beijing) 80 (June 2006): 8–13.

Xiong Guangkai. "Dongqian quanqiu fankongxing shi jiqi qiying zhanwang." *Guoji Zhanlue Yanjiu* (Beijing) 2 (2003).

———. "A Review of International Strategic Situation and Its Prospects." *Guoji Zhanlüe Yanjiu* [*International Strategic Studies*, English version] 71, no. 1 (January 2004): 3.

Xu Weizhong. "Beijing Summit Promotes Sino-African Relations." *Xiandai guoji guanxi* (Beijing) 17 (January 2007): 72–79.

Yahuda, Michael. *The International Politics of the Asia-Pacific*. 4th ed. London: Routledge, 2019.

———. *Sino-Japanese Relations after the Cold War*. New York: Routledge, 2013.

Yan Xuetong. "The Instability of China-US Relations." *Chinese Journal of International Politics* 3, no. 3 (2010): 1–30.

———. "The Rise of China and Its Power Status." *Chinese Journal of International Politics* 1 (2006): 5–33.

Yan Xuetong et al. *Ancient Chinese Thought, Modern Chinese Power*. Princeton, NJ: Princeton University Press, 2011.

Yang Jianmian. *Da mo he*. Tianjin: Renmin Chubanshe, 2007.

Yang Wenchang. "Sino-U.S. Relations in Retrospect and Prospect." *Foreign Affairs Journal* (Beijing) 80 (June 2006): 1–7.

Ye Zicheng. *Xin Zhongguo waijiao sixiang: Cong Maozedong dao Dengxiaoping*. Beijing: Beijing Daxue Chubanshe, 2001.

———. "Zhongguo Shixing daguo waijiaozhanlue shizai bixing." *Shijie Jingli yu Zhengzhi* 1 (2000): 5–10.

Yee, Herbert, and Ian Storey. *The China Threat: Perceptions, Myths, and Reality*. London: Routledge, 2002.

Yu Bin. "China and Russia: Normalizing Their Strategic Partnership." In *Power Shift: China and Asia's New Dynamics*, edited by David Shambaugh, 228–46. Berkeley: University of California Press, 2005.

Yuan, Jing-dong. "China's Role in Establishing and Building the Shanghai Cooperation Organization (SCO)." *Journal of Contemporary China* 19, no. 67 (November 2010): 855–70.

———. "The Dragon and the Elephant: Chinese-Indian Relations in the 21st Century." *Washington Quarterly* 30, no. 3 (Summer 2007): 131–44.

Yuan Peng. "A Harmonious World and China's New Diplomacy." *Xiadai guoji guanxi* (Beijing) 17 (May 2007): 1–26.

———. "9.11 Shijian yu Zhongmei Guanxi." *Xiandai guoji guanxi* (Beijing), November 11, 2001, 19–23, 63.

Zeng Qiang. "FOCAC: A Powerful Engine for the Continued Development of Friendship between China and Africa." *Contemporary International Relations* (Beijing) 20, no. 6 (November–December 2010): 45–59.

Zhang Biwu. "Chinese Perceptions of American Power, 1991–2004." *Asian Survey* 45, no. 5 (September–October 2005): 667–86.

Zhang Wenmu. "Quanqiuhua jincheng zhong de Zhongguo guojia liye." *Zhanlue yu Guanli* 1 (2002): 52–64.

Zhang Yunling. "East Asian Cooperation and the Construction of China-ASEAN Free Trade Area." *Dangdai Yatai* (Beijing) 1 (2002): 20–32.

———, ed. *Huoban haishi duishou: Tiao zheng Zhong de Mei Ri E Guanxi*. Beijing: Social Science Departments Press, 2000.

———, ed. *Making New Partnership: A Rising China and Its Neighbors*. Beijing: Social Sciences Academic Press, 2008.

———. "New Thinking Needed to Promote East Asian Cooperation." *Foreign Affairs Journal* (Beijing) 96 (September 2010): 17–23.

———, ed. *Weilai 10–15 Nian Zhongguo zai yatai diqu mianlin de guoji huanjing*. Beijing: Zhongguo Shehui Kexue Chubanshe, 2003.

Zhang Yunling and Tang Shiping. "China's Regional Strategy." In *Power Shift: China and Asia's New Dynamics*, edited by David Shambaugh, 48–70. Berkeley: University of California Press, 2005.

Zhao, Huasheng. "China's View of and Expectations from the Shanghai Cooperation Organization." *Asian Survey* 53, no. 3 (2013): 436–60.

Zhao, Suisheng, ed. *China in Africa*. New York: Routledge, 2015.

———. "Chinese Nationalism and Its International Orientations." *Political Science Quarterly* 115, no. 1 (Spring 2000): 1–33.

———. *A Nation-State by Construction: Dynamics of Modern Chinese Nationalism*. Stanford, CA: Stanford University Press, 2004.

Zheng Bijian. "China's 'Peaceful Rise' to Great-Power Status." *Foreign Affairs* 84, no. 5 (2005): 18–24.

Zheng Ruixiang. "New Development of Relations between China and South Asian Countries." *Foreign Affairs Journal* (Beijing) 76 (June 2005): 40–46.

Zhou Gang. "Status Quo and Prospects of China-ASEAN Relations." *Foreign Affairs Journal* (Beijing) 80 (June 2006): 14–21.

Zhou Yuhao. *Liyi youguan*. Beijing: Zhongguo Chuanmei Daxue Chubanshe, 2007.

Zhu Feng. "Zai lishi gui yi zhong bawo Zhong Mei guanxi." *Huanqiu Shibao Guoji Luntan*, February 28, 2002.

Zhu Tingchang et al., eds. *Zhongguo zhoubian anquan huanjin yu anquan zhanlue*. Beijing: Shishi Chubanshe, 2002.

Zhu, Zhiqun. *A Critical Decade: China's Foreign Policy (2008–2018)*. Singapore: World Scientific, 2020.

Zou Jingwen. *Li Denghui zhizheng gaobai shilu*. Taipei: INK, 2001.

# Index

# ASIA IN WORLD POLITICS
## Series Editor: Samuel S. Kim

# About the Author

**Robert G. Sutter** has been professor of practice of international affairs at the Elliott School of International Affairs (ESIA) at George Washington University since 2011. From 2012 to 2019, he also directed the ESIA Bachelor of Arts in International Affairs program, involving two thousand students.

A PhD graduate in history and East Asian languages from Harvard University, Sutter taught full time at Georgetown University (2001–2011) and part time during the previous thirty years at Georgetown, George Washington, and Johns Hopkins Universities and the University of Virginia. He has published twenty-two books, more than two hundred articles, and several hundred government reports dealing with the United States, China, and contemporary Asian and Pacific affairs. His most recent book is *The United States and Asia: Regional Dynamics and Twenty-First-Century Relations*, 2nd ed. (Rowman & Littlefield, 2020). The second edition of his *Foreign Relations of the PRC: The Legacies and Constraints of China's International Politics since 1949* (Rowman & Littlefield) was published in 2019, and the third edition of his *US-China Relations: Perilous Past, Uncertain Present* (Rowman & Littlefield) was published in 2018. Also in 2018 he published (with Richard Ellings) *Axis of Authoritarians: Implications of China-Russia Cooperation* (National Bureau of Asian Research 2018).

Sutter's government career (1968–2001) involved work on Asian and Pacific affairs and US foreign policy. He was for many years the senior specialist and director of the Foreign Affairs and National Defense Division of the Congressional Research Service. He was also the national intelligence officer for East Asia and the Pacific at the US government's National Intelligence Council, the China Division director at the Department of State's Bureau of Intelligence and Research, and a professional staff member of the Senate Foreign Relations Committee.

Lightning Source UK Ltd.
Milton Keynes UK
UKHW011309080622
404125UK00008B/118